Environmental Health

SOURCEBOOK

Fourth Edition

Health Reference Series

Fourth Edition

Environmental Health
SOURCEBOOK

*Basic Consumer Health Information about the Environment
and Its Effects on Human Health, Including Facts about Air,
Water, and Soil Contamination, Hazardous Chemicals,
Foodborne Chemicals and Illnesses, Natural Disasters
Household Hazards such as Mold, Radon, and Carbon
Monoxide, Consumer Hazards from Toxic Products and
Imported Goods, and Disorders Linked to Environmental
Causes, Including Chemical Sensitivity, Cancer, Allergies,
and Asthma.*

*Along with Information about Technologically Altered
Foods, Radiation Exposure, a Glossary of Related Terms,
and Resources for Additional Help and Information.*

OMNIGRAPHICS
155 W. Congress, Suite 200 Detroit, MI 48226

Bibliographic Note

Because this page cannot legibly accommodate all the copyright notices, the Bibliographic Note portion of the Preface constitutes an extension of the copyright notice.

* * *

Omnigraphics, Inc.

Editorial Services provided by Omnigraphics, Inc.,
a division of Relevant Information, Inc.

Keith Jones, *Managing Editor*

* * *

Copyright © 2016 Relevant Information, Inc.

ISBN 978-0-7808-1351-9
E-ISBN 978-0-7808-1398-4

Table of Contents

Part II: Health Concerns and Their Environmental Triggers

Part III: Outdoor Environmental Hazards

Part IV: Household and Indoor Environmental Hazards

Part V: Foodborne Hazards

Part VI: Consumer Products and Medical Hazards

Part VII: Additional Help and Information

Preface

About This Book

The environment has always contained hazards to health, but modern and man-made factors compound the risks. Humans are now exposed to pollution in the air, water, and the soil. Contaminants are increasingly found throughout the food chain, in homes and schools, and in manufactured goods. Furthermore, in today's global economy, health hazards can even come from far away through tainted fish, imported toys, and technologically altered foods. Although some environmental hazards lead to immediate illness, often the risks are not identified until medical researchers link long-term exposures to chronic disease.

Environmental Health Sourcebook, Fourth Edition, offers updated information about the effects of the environment on human health. It discusses specific populations—including pregnant women and their fetuses, children, the elderly, and minorities—in which the effects of environmental exposures are especially harmful and, in some cases, can have a lasting impact that extends to future generations. Airborne, waterborne, foodborne, and chemical hazards are discussed, and facts about cancer, respiratory problems, infertility, autism, and other diseases with suspected environmental triggers are presented. A section on consumer products and medical hazards examines health risks associated with some common household items. The book concludes with a glossary and a directory of resources for additional information.

How to Use This Book

This book is divided into parts and chapters. Parts focus on broad areas of interest. Chapters are devoted to single topics within a part.

Part I: Understanding the Health Effects of Environmental Hazards provides information and risk assessment tools to help readers determine what health threats may be present in the world around them. It offers suggestions for reducing possible exposure to dangers, and discusses issues of special concern to children, women, the elderly, and minority populations.

Part II: Health Concerns and Their Environmental Triggers provides readers with in-depth details on individual diseases with suspected environmental causes, including cancer, respiratory problems, and viral infections. It details the effects of the environment on fertility and pregnancy, and explains how fetal and childhood exposures to some hazards can lead to diseases and conditions such as autism, later in life.

Part III: Outdoor Environmental Hazards explores hazards, both natural and man-made, that are found in the outdoor environment. Readers will learn about air, water and soil pollution, ocean contamination and how it affects the environment and human health, as well as how chemicals and pesticides have spread through the food chain and how they can be avoided. It also explores hazards—such as noise and light pollution, particle pollution, smog, and acid rain, climate change and extreme heat conditions—caused by the modern urban environment.

Part IV: Household and Indoor Environmental Hazards discusses the hazards people face in the environment where they spend up to 90% of their time—inside their homes, offices, and schools. These risks include indoor air contaminants, such as carbon monoxide, mold, asbestos, and lead, as well as unsafe indoor activities, such as smoking or inappropriately using chemicals and pesticides. In addition, it discusses the risks of radiation exposure from cell phones, microwaves, and electromagnetic fields.

Part V: Foodborne Hazards includes facts about food safety regulations, potentially problematic food additives, and chemical contaminants in the food supply. It provides tips for avoiding the most common foodborne illnesses and for safely preparing food at home. Because most Americans rely on the industrial food chain for the majority of their food, it also discusses safety concerns related to food technologies, including genetic engineering, the use of antibiotics and hormones.

Part VI: Consumer Products and Medical Hazards tells readers about the health risks they face from consumer products, including everyday objects such as insect repellants, hand soap, and plastics. It discusses the safety of imported goods, now found in virtually every home, and it describes concerns about the use of untested chemicals and additives in personal care products.

Part VII: Additional Resources includes a glossary of important terms, and a directory of organizations providing information and advocacy on environmental health topics.

Bibliographic Note

This volume contains documents and excerpts from publications issued by the following U.S. government agencies: Agency for Toxic Substances & Disease Registry (ATSDR); Centers for Disease Control and Prevention (CDC); Environmental Health Perspectives (EHP); Environmental Protection Agency (EPA); Food and Drug Administration (FDA); National Cancer Institute (NCI); National Heart, Lung, and Blood Institute (NHLBI); National Institute of Diabetes and Digestive and Kidney Diseases (NIDDK); National Institute of Environmental Health Sciences (NIEHS); The National Institute for Occupational Safety and Health (NIOSH); National Oceanic and Atmospheric Administration (NOAA); and U. S. Department of Human Health and Services (DHHS).

About the Health Reference Series

The *Health Reference Series* is designed to provide basic medical information for patients, families, caregivers, and the general public. Each volume takes a particular topic and provides comprehensive coverage. This is especially important for people who may be dealing with a newly diagnosed disease or a chronic disorder in themselves or in a family member. People looking for preventive guidance, information about disease warning signs, medical statistics, and risk factors for health problems will also find answers to their questions in the *Health Reference Series*. The *Series*, however, is not intended to serve as a tool for diagnosing illness, in prescribing treatments, or as a substitute for the physician/patient relationship. All people concerned about medical symptoms or the possibility of disease are encouraged to seek professional care from an appropriate health care provider.

A Note about Spelling and Style

Health Reference Series editors use *Stedman's Medical Dictionary* as an authority for questions related to the spelling of medical terms and the *Chicago Manual of Style* for questions related to grammatical structures, punctuation, and other editorial concerns. Consistent adherence is not always possible, however, because the individual volumes within the *Series* include many documents from a wide variety of different producers, and the editor's primary goal is to present material from each source as accurately as is possible. This sometimes means that information in different chapters or sections may follow other guidelines and alternate spelling authorities.

Our Advisory Board

We would like to thank the following board members for providing guidance to the development of this Series:

- Dr. Lynda Baker, Associate Professor of Library and Information Science, Wayne State University, Detroit, MI

- Nancy Bulgarelli, William Beaumont Hospital Library, Royal Oak, MI

- Karen Imarisio, Bloomfield Township Public Library, Bloomfield Township, MI

- Karen Morgan, Mardigian Library, University of Michigan-Dearborn, Dearborn, MI

- Rosemary Orlando, St. Clair Shores Public Library, St. Clair Shores, MI

Health Reference Series Update Policy

The inaugural book in the *Health Reference Series* was the first edition of Cancer Sourcebook published in 1989. Since then, the *Series* has been enthusiastically received by librarians and in the medical community. In order to maintain the standard of providing high-quality health information for the layperson the editorial staff at Omnigraphics felt it was necessary to implement a policy of updating volumes when warranted.

Medical researchers have been making tremendous strides, and it is the purpose of the *Health Reference Series* to stay current with the most recent advances. Each decision to update a volume is made on an individual basis. Some of the considerations include how much new information is available and the feedback we receive from people who use the books. If there is a topic you would like to see added to the update list, or an area of medical concern you feel has not been adequately addressed, please write to:

Managing Editor
Health Reference Series
Omnigraphics, Inc.
155 W. Congress, Suite 200
Detroit, MI 48226

Part One

Understanding the Health Effects of Environmental Hazards

Chapter 1

Environmental Health–Overview

Overview

Humans interact with the environment constantly. These inter-actions affect quality of life, years of healthy life lived, and health disparities. The World Health Organization (WHO) defines environ-ment, as it relates to health, as "all the physical, chemical, and bio-logical factors external to a person, and all the related behaviors."[1] Environmental health consists of preventing or controlling disease, injury, and disability related to the interactions between people and their environment.

The Healthy People 2020 Environmental Health objectives focus on 6 themes, each of which highlights an element of environmental health:

1. Outdoor air quality

2. Surface and ground water quality

3. Toxic substances and hazardous wastes

4. Homes and communities

Text in this chapter is excerpted from "Environmental Health," Healthypeople. gov managed by the U.S. Department of Human and Health Services (DHHS), July 1, 2015.

5. Infrastructure and surveillance

6. Global environmental health

Creating health-promoting environments is complex and relies on continuing research to understand more fully the effects of exposure to environmental hazards on people's health.

Why Is Environmental Health Important?

Maintaining a healthy environment is central to increasing quality of life and years of healthy life. Globally, nearly 25 percent of all deaths and the total disease burden can be attributed to environmental factors.[1] Environmental factors are diverse and far reaching. They include:

- Exposure to hazardous substances in the air, water, soil, and food

- Natural and technological disasters

- Physical hazards

- Nutritional deficiencies

- The built environment

Poor environmental quality has its greatest impact on people whose health status is already at risk. Therefore, environmental health must address the societal and environmental factors that increase the likelihood of exposure and disease.

Understanding Environmental Health

The 6 themes of the environmental health topic area draw attention to elements of the environment and their linkages to health.

Outdoor Air Quality

Poor air quality is linked to premature death, cancer, and long-term damage to respiratory and cardiovascular systems. Progress has been made to reduce unhealthy air emissions, but, in 2008, approximately 127 million people lived in U.S. counties that exceeded national air quality standards.[2] Decreasing air pollution is an important step in creating a healthy environment.

Surface and Ground Water

Surface and ground water quality applies to both drinking water and recreational waters. Contamination by infectious agents or chemicals can cause mild to severe illness. Protecting water sources and minimizing exposure to contaminated water sources are important parts of environmental health.

Toxic Substances and Hazardous Wastes

The health effects of toxic substances and hazardous wastes are not yet fully understood. Research to better understand how these exposures may impact health is ongoing. Meanwhile, efforts to reduce exposures continue. Reducing exposure to toxic substances and hazardous wastes is fundamental to environmental health.

Homes and Communities

People spend most of their time at home, work, or school. Some of these environments may expose people to:

- Indoor air pollution
- Inadequate heating and sanitation
- Structural problems
- Electrical and fire hazards
- Lead-based paint hazards

These hazards can impact health and safety. Maintaining healthy homes and communities is essential to environmental health.

Infrastructure and Surveillance

Prevention of exposure to environmental hazards relies on many partners, including State and local health departments. Personnel, surveillance systems, and education are important resources for investigating and responding to disease, monitoring for hazards, and educating the public. Additional methods and greater capacity to measure and respond to environmental hazards are needed.

Global Environmental Health

Water quality is an important global challenge. Diseases can be reduced by improving water quality and sanitation and increasing access to adequate water and sanitation facilities.

Emerging Issues in Environmental Health

Environmental health is a dynamic and evolving field. While not all complex environmental issues can be predicted, some known emerging issues in the field include:

Climate Change

Climate change is projected to impact sea level, patterns of infectious disease, air quality, and the severity of natural disasters such as floods, droughts, and storms.[3, 4]

Disaster Preparedness

Preparedness for the environmental impact of natural disasters as well as disasters of human origin includes planning for human health needs and the impact on public infrastructure, such as water and roadways.[5]

Nanotechnology

The potential impact of nanotechnology is significant and offers possible improvements to:

- Disease prevention, detection, and treatment
- Electronics
- Clean energy
- Manufacturing
- Environmental risk assessment

However, nanotechnology may also present unintended health risks or changes to the environment.

The Built Environment

Features of the built environment appear to impact human health-influencing behaviors, physical activity patterns, social networks, and access to resources.[6]

Exposure to Unknown Hazards

Finally, every year, hundreds of new chemicals are introduced to the U.S. market. It is presumed that some of these chemicals may present new, unexpected challenges to human health, and, therefore, their safety should be evaluated prior to release.

These cross-cutting issues are not yet understood well enough to inform the development of systems for measuring and tracking their impact. Further exploration is warranted. The environmental health landscape will continue to evolve and may present opportunities for additional research, analysis, and monitoring.

Blood Lead Levels

The number of children with elevated blood lead levels in the U.S. is steadily decreasing. As a result, determining stable national prevalence estimates and changes in estimated prevalence over time using NHANES is increasingly difficult. Eliminating elevated blood lead levels in children remains a goal of utmost importance to public health. The sample sizes available with the currently structured NHANES are too small to produce statistically reliable estimates and preclude the ability to have a viable target for *Healthy People 2020*. Efforts must and will continue to reduce blood lead levels and to monitor the prevalence of children with elevated blood lead levels.

References

[1] World Health Organization (WHO). Preventing disease through healthy environments. Geneva, Switzerland: WHO; 2006.

[2] US Environmental Protection Agency (EPA), Office of Air Quality Planning and Standards. Our Nation's air: Status and trends through 2008. Washington: EPA; 2010.

[3] Patz J, Campbell-Lendrum D, Holloway T, et al. Impact of regional climate change on human health. Nature. 2005 Nov. 17; 438(7066): 310-7.

[4] Kinney PL. Climate change, air quality, and human health. Am J Prev Med. 2008 Nov.; 35(5):459-67.

[5] Noji E, Lee CY. Disaster preparedness. In: Frumpkin H. Environmental health, from global to local, 1st edition. San Francisco: Jossey-Bass; 2005.

[6] Srinivasan S, O'Fallon LR, Dearry A. Creating healthy communities, healthy homes, healthy people: Initiating a research agenda on the built environment and public health. Am J Public Health. 2003 Sep.; 93(9):1446-50.

Chapter 2

Toxic Substances

Chapter Contents

Section 2.1

Toxic Substances and Types

Text in this section begins with excerpts from "What is a Toxic Substance?" United States Environmental Protection Agency (EPA), May 9, 2012. Text in this section beginning with "Aluminum" is excerpted from "Most Viewed Toxic Substance," Agency for Toxic Substances & Disease Registry (ATSDR), June 29, 2015.

What Is a Toxic Substance?

A toxic substance means any chemical or mixture that may be harmful to the environment and to human health if inhaled, swallowed, or absorbed through the skin. Did you know that some toxic substances are found in nature? There are naturally occurring toxins (poisonous substances coming from living organisms) found in certain plants like poinsettias and even some wild mushrooms and berries. However, the toxic substances contained in most everyday household products are synthetic which means they are man-made. The opposite of toxics substances are called non-toxic substances. Non-toxic substances are safe to use, and do not harm humans and the environment.

Many of the products you find in your home may have toxic substances. These products include:

- drain cleaners
- oven cleaners
- laundry detergents
- floor or furniture polish
- paints and
- pesticides

While these products are useful at home, some of the chemicals in these products can irritate your skin, eyes, nose and throat, or can even poison you.

Aluminum

Aluminum is the most abundant metal in the earth's crust. It is always found combined with other elements such as oxygen, silicon, and fluorine. Aluminum as the metal is obtained from aluminum-containing minerals. Small amounts of aluminum can be found dissolved in water. Aluminum metal is light in weight and silvery-white in appearance. Aluminum is used for beverage cans, pots and pans, airplanes, siding and roofing, and foil. Aluminum is often mixed with small amounts of other metals to form aluminum alloys, which are stronger and harder. Aluminum compounds have many different uses, for example, as alums in water-treatment and alumina in abrasives and furnace linings. They are also found in consumer products such as antacids, astringents, buffered aspirin, food additives, and antiperspirants.

Ammonia

Ammonia occurs naturally and is produced by human activity. It is an important source of nitrogen which is needed by plants and animals. Bacteria found in the intestines can produce ammonia.

Ammonia is a colorless gas with a very distinct odor. This odor is familiar to many people because ammonia is used in smelling salts, many household and industrial cleaners, and window-cleaning products.

Ammonia gas can be dissolved in water. This kind of ammonia is called liquid ammonia or aqueous ammonia. Once exposed to open air, liquid ammonia quickly turns into a gas.

Ammonia is applied directly into soil on farm fields, and is used to make fertilizers for farm crops, lawns, and plants. Many household and industrial cleaners contain ammonia.

Arsenic

Arsenic is a naturally occurring element widely distributed in the earth's crust. In the environment, arsenic is combined with oxygen, chlorine, and sulfur to form inorganic arsenic compounds. Arsenic in animals and plants combines with carbon and hydrogen to form organic arsenic compounds. Inorganic arsenic compounds are mainly used to preserve wood. Copper chromated arsenic (CCA) is used to make "pressure-treated" lumber. CCA is no longer used in the U.S. for residential uses; it is still used in industrial applications. Organic arsenic compounds are used as pesticides, primarily on cotton plants.

Asbestos

Asbestos is the name given to a group of six different fibrous minerals (amosite, chrysotile, crocidolite, and the fibrous varieties of tremolite, actinolite, and anthophyllite) that occur naturally in the environment. Asbestos minerals have separable long fibers that are strong and flexible enough to be spun and woven and are heat resistant. Because of these characteristics, asbestos has been used for a wide range of manufactured goods, mostly in building materials (roofing shingles, ceiling and floor tiles, paper products, and asbestos cement products), friction products (automobile clutch, brake, and transmission parts), heat-resistant fabrics, packaging, gaskets, and coatings. Some vermiculite or talc products may contain asbestos.

Benzene

Benzene is a colorless liquid with a sweet odor. It evaporates into the air very quickly and dissolves slightly in water. It is highly flammable and is formed from both natural processes and human activities.

Benzene is widely used in the United States; it ranks in the top 20 chemicals for production volume. Some industries use benzene to make other chemicals which are used to make plastics, resins, and nylon and synthetic fibers. Benzene is also used to make some types of rubbers, lubricants, dyes, detergents, drugs, and pesticides. Natural sources of benzene include volcanoes and forest fires. Benzene is also a natural part of crude oil, gasoline, and cigarette smoke.

Cadmium

Cadmium is a natural element in the earth's crust. It is usually found as a mineral combined with other elements such as oxygen (cadmium oxide), chlorine (cadmium chloride), or sulfur (cadmium sulfate, cadmium sulfide).

All soils and rocks, including coal and mineral fertilizers, contain some cadmium. Most cadmium used in the United States is extracted during the production of other metals like zinc, lead, and copper. Cadmium does not corrode easily and has many uses, including batteries, pigments, metal coatings, and plastics.

Chromium

Chromium is a naturally occurring element found in rocks, animals, plants, soil, and in volcanic dust and gases. Chromium is present in the environment in several different forms. The most common forms are chromium (0), chromium (III), and chromium (VI). No taste or odor is associated with chromium compounds. Chromium (III) occurs naturally in the environment and is an essential nutrient. Chromium (VI) and chromium (0) are generally produced by industrial processes. The metal chromium, which is the chromium (0) form, is used for making steel. Chromium (VI) and chromium (III) are used for chrome plating, dyes and pigments, leather tanning, and wood preserving.

DDT, DDE, DDD

DDT (dichlorodiphenyltrichloroethane) is a pesticide once widely used to control insects in agriculture and insects that carry diseases such as malaria. DDT is a white, crystalline solid with no odor or taste. Its use in the U.S. was banned in 1972 because of damage to wildlife, but is still used in some countries. DDE (dichlorodiphenyldichloroethylene) and DDD (dichlorodiphenyldichloroethane) are chemicals similar to DDT that contaminate commercial DDT preparations. DDE has no commercial use. DDD was also used to kill pests, but its use has also been banned. One form of DDD has been used medically to treat cancer of the adrenal gland.

Formaldehyde

At room temperature, formaldehyde is a colorless, flammable gas that has a distinct, pungent smell. It is also known as methanal, methylene oxide, oxymethyline, methylaldehyde, and oxomethane. Formaldehyde is naturally produced in small amounts in our bodies. It is used in the production of fertilizer, paper, plywood, and urea-formaldehyde resins. It is also used as a preservative in some foods and in many products used around the house, such as antiseptics, medicines, and cosmetics.

Lead

Lead is a naturally occurring bluish-gray metal found in small amounts in the earth's crust. Lead can be found in all parts of our environment. Much of it comes from human activities including burning fossil fuels, mining, and manufacturing. Lead has many different uses. It is used in the production of batteries, ammunition, metal products (solder and pipes), and devices to shield X-rays. Because of health concerns, lead from gasoline, paints and ceramic products, caulking, and pipe solder has been dramatically reduced in recent years.

Mercury

Mercury combines with other elements, such as chlorine, sulfur, or oxygen, to form inorganic mercury compounds or "salts," which are usually white powders or crystals. Mercury also combines with carbon to make organic mercury compounds. The most common one, methylmercury, is produced mainly by microscopic organisms in the water and soil. More mercury in the environment can increase the amounts of methylmercury that these small organisms make.

Metallic Mercury is a dense liquid that vaporizes easily at room temperature. Metallic mercury is not easily absorbed into unbroken skin. However, it vaporizes, even at room temperature. The higher the temperature, the more vapors are released. Mercury vapors are colorless and odorless, though they can be seen with the aid of an ultraviolet light.

Metallic mercury is used to produce chlorine gas and caustic soda, and is also used in thermometers, dental fillings, and batteries. Mercury salts are sometimes used in skin lightening creams and as antiseptic creams and ointments.

Polychlorinated Biphenyls (PCBs)

Polychlorinated biphenyls are mixtures of up to 209 individual chlorinated compounds (known as congeners). There are no known natural sources of PCBs. PCBs are either oily liquids or solids that are colorless to light yellow. Some PCBs can exist as a vapor in air. PCBs have no known smell or taste. Many commercial PCB mixtures are known in the U.S. by the trade name Aroclor. PCBs have been used as coolants and lubricants in transformers, capacitors, and other electrical equipment because they don't burn easily and are good insulators.

The manufacture of PCBs was stopped in the U.S. in 1977 because of evidence they build up in the environment and can cause harmful health effects. Products made before 1977 that may contain PCBs include old fluorescent lighting fixtures and electrical devices containing PCB capacitors, and old microscope and hydraulic oils.

Polycyclic Aromatic Hydrocarbons (PAHs)

Polycyclic aromatic hydrocarbons (PAHs) are a group of over 100 different chemicals that are formed during the incomplete burning of coal, oil and gas, garbage, or other organic substances like tobacco or charbroiled meat. PAHs are usually found as a mixture containing two or more of these compounds, such as soot.

Some PAHs are manufactured. These pure PAHs usually exist as colorless, white, or pale yellow-green solids. PAHs are found in coal tar, crude oil, creosote, and roofing tar, but a few are used in medicines or to make dyes, plastics, and pesticides.

Toluene

Toluene is a clear, colorless liquid with a distinctive smell. Toluene occurs naturally in crude oil and in the tolu tree. It is also produced in the process of making gasoline and other fuels from crude oil and making coke from coal. Toluene is used in making paints, paint thinners, fingernail polish, lacquers, adhesives, and rubber and in some printing and leather tanning processes.

Trichloroethylene (TCE)

Trichloroethylene (TCE) is a nonflammable, colorless liquid with a somewhat sweet odor and a sweet, burning taste. It is used mainly as a solvent to remove grease from metal parts, but it is also an ingredient in adhesives, paint removers, typewriter correction fluids, and spot removers. Trichloroethylene is not thought to occur naturally in the environment. However, it has been found in underground water sources and many surface waters as a result of the manufacture, use, and disposal of the chemical.

Section 2.2

Effects of Hazardous Substances

Text in this section is excerpted from "Health and Ecological Hazards Caused by Hazardous Substances," United States Environmental Protection Agency (EPA), April 21, 2015.

Health and Ecological Hazards Caused by Hazardous Substances

Emergency response efforts must consider the health and ecological hazards of a hazardous substance release. These hazards impact emergency responders and effected communities. In some cases, hazardous substances may irritate the skin or eyes, make it difficult to breathe, cause headaches and nausea, or result in other types of illness. Some hazardous substances can cause far more severe health effects, including:

- behavioral abnormalities,

- cancer,

- genetic mutations,

- physiological malfunctions (e.g., reproductive impairment, kidney failure, etc.),

- physical deformations, and

- birth defects.

Impacts on the environment can be just as devastating: killing organisms in a lake or river, destroying animals and plants in a contaminated area, causing major reproductive complications in animals, or otherwise limit the ability of an ecosystem to survive. Certain hazardous substances also have the potential to explode or cause a fire, threatening both animals and human populations.

Some hazardous substances produce toxic effects in humans or the environment after a single, episodic release. These toxic effects are referred to as the acute toxicity. Other hazardous substances produce toxic effects in humans or the environment after prolonged exposure to the substance, which is called chronic toxicity.

EPA uses the acute and chronic toxicity of hazardous substances to guide different aspects of the emergency response. The toxicity of a hazardous substance are also used to establish its Superfund reportable quantities (RQs). If the substance is released into the environment with an amount equal to or greater than the RQ, the release must be reported to the federal government. This helps EPA respond to the release to protect human health and the environment from the adverse effects of that hazardous substance.

Section 2.3

Natural Disasters and Environmental Hazards

Text in this section is excerpted from "Natural Disasters &
Environmental Hazards," Centers for Disease Control and
Prevention (CDC), August 1, 2013.

Environmental Hazards

Air

Air pollution has decreased in many parts of the world, but it is
worsening in certain industrializing countries. Polluted air can be
difficult or impossible to avoid, but the risk to healthy short-term
travelers is most likely low. People with preexisting heart and lung
disease, children, and older adults are at higher risk.

Travelers should be familiar with the air quality at their destination. The AirNow website (http://airnow.gov/) provides information
about the effects of particulate matter and ozone, as well as links to
international air quality sites. Historical data on outdoor air pollution in urban areas is available from the World Health Organization
at http://gamapserver.who.int/gho/interactive_charts/phe/oap_expo-
sure/atlas.html.

Travelers should also limit exposure to indoor air pollution and
carbon monoxide. Possible sources of indoor air pollutants include environmental tobacco smoke and cooking or combustion sources (such as
kerosene, coal, wood, or animal dung). Major sources of indoor carbon
monoxide include gas ranges and ovens, unvented gas or kerosene
space heaters, and coal- or wood-burning stoves.

Travelers to countries where air pollution may be a problem should
consider the following:

- For people with preexisting conditions such as asthma,
  chronic obstructive pulmonary disease, and heart disease,
  limit strenuous or prolonged outdoor activity, particularly in
  cities.

- For long-term travelers and expatriates, consider investing in an indoor air filtration system.

- Avoid indoor areas with high levels of indoor air pollutants such as tobacco smoke.

- As much as possible, look for lodging with working smoke and carbon monoxide detectors.

Travelers to areas where air pollution is reported to be high might inquire about the advisability of wearing face masks. Centers for Disease Control and Prevention (CDC) has no recommendations regarding the use of face masks for travelers. One small study in Beijing showed that wearing a dust respirator appeared to mitigate the effects of air pollution on blood pressure and heart rate. However, it should be noted that the respirators used in the study had better filtration than the surgical masks commonly worn in some countries. The decision to wear a mask should be left to the traveler's discretion.

Mold Contamination

Extensive water damage after hurricanes or floods can lead to mold contamination in buildings. Travelers may visit flooded areas overseas as part of emergency, medical, or humanitarian missions. Mold is a more serious health hazard for people who are immunocompromised or have respiratory problems. To prevent exposure that could result in adverse health effects from disturbed mold, people should adhere to the following recommendations:

- Avoid areas where mold contamination is obvious.

- If the traveler will be working in a moldy environment (such as on a medical or humanitarian mission), use personal protective equipment (PPE), such as gloves, goggles, and a fit-tested N-95 respirator or higher. These travelers should take sufficient PPE with them, as these may be scarce in the countries visited.

- Keep hands, skin, and eyes clean and free from mold-contaminated dust.

- Review the CDC guidance, Mold Prevention Strategies and Possible Health Effects in the Aftermath of Hurricanes and Major Floods, which provides recommendations for dealing with mold in these settings.

Radiation

Natural background radiation levels can vary substantially from region to region, but these variations are not a health concern. Travelers should be aware of regions known to have been contaminated with radioactive materials, such as the areas surrounding the Chernobyl nuclear power plant in Ukraine and the Fukushima Daiichi nuclear power plant in Japan.

The Chernobyl plant is located 100 km (62 miles) northwest of Kiev. The 1986 accident contaminated regions in 3 republics—Ukraine, Belarus, and Russia—but the highest radioactive ground contamination is within 30 km (19 miles) of Chernobyl.

The Fukushima Daiichi plant is located 240 km (150 miles) north of Tokyo. After the accident in 2011, the area within a 20-km (32-mile) radius of the plant was evacuated, and Japanese authorities also advised evacuation from locations farther away to the northwest of the plant. As Japanese authorities continue to clean the affected areas and monitor the situation, access requirements and travel advisories change. The Department of State recommends against all unnecessary travel to areas designated by the Japanese government. For up-to-date information or any travel advisories, see the Department of State's information for Japan.

In most countries, areas of known radioactive contamination are fenced or marked with signs. Any traveler seeking long-term (more than a few months) residence near a known or suspected contaminated area should consult with staff of the nearest US embassy and inquire about any advisories regarding drinking water quality or purchase of meat, fruit, and vegetables from local farmers. Radiation emergencies are rare events. In case of such an emergency, however, travelers should follow instructions provided by local authorities. If such information is not forthcoming, US travelers should seek advice from the nearest US embassy or consulate.

Natural disasters (such as floods) may also displace industrial or clinical radioactive sources. In all circumstances, travelers should exercise caution when they encounter unknown objects or equipment, especially if they bear the basic radiation tri-foil symbol or other radiation signs. Travelers who encounter a questionable object should notify local authorities.

Chapter 3

Health Risk Assessment: Determining Whether Environmental Substances Pose a Risk to Human Health

Introduction

A human health risk assessment is the process to estimate the nature and probability of adverse health effects in humans who may be exposed to chemicals in contaminated environmental media, now or in the future.

To explain this better, a human health risk assessment addresses questions such as:

- What types of health problems may be caused by environmental stressors such as chemicals and radiation?

- What is the chance that people will experience health problems when exposed to different levels of environmental stressors?

- Is there a level below which some chemicals don't pose a human health risk?

- What environmental stressors are people exposed to and at what levels and for how long?

Text in this chapter is excerpted from "Human Health Risk Assessment," United States Environmental Protection Agency (EPA), July 31, 2012.

- Are some people more likely to be susceptible to environmental stressors because of factors such as age, genetics, pre-existing health conditions, ethnic practices, gender, etc.?

- Are some people more likely to be exposed to environmental stressors because of factors such as where they work, where they play, what they like to eat, etc.?

The answers to these types of questions help decision makers, whether they are parents or public officials, understand the possible human health risks from environmental media.

How does EPA conduct a Human Health Risk Assessment?

Human health risk assessment includes 4 basic steps, and is generally conducted following various EPA guidance documents.

- **Planning – Planning and Scoping process.**

  EPA begins the process of a human health risk assessment with planning and research.

- **Step 1 – Hazard Identification.**

  Examines whether a stressor has the potential to cause harm to humans and/or ecological systems, and if so, under what circumstances.

- **Step 2 – Dose-Response Assessment.**

  Examines the numerical relationship between exposure and effects.

- **Step 3 – Exposure Assessment.**

  Examines what is known about the frequency, timing, and levels of contact with a stressor.

- **Step 4 – Risk Characterization.**

  Examines how well the data support conclusions about the nature and extent of the risk from exposure to environmental stressors.

Planning a Human Health Risk Assessment

Planning – There is a need to make judgments early when planning major risk assessments regarding the purpose, scope,

and technical approaches that will be used. **To simplify our discussion of planning the following structure focuses on human health risk assessment.**

Risk assessors will typically ask the following questions when planning a human health risk assessment:

Who/What/Where is at risk?

- Individual
- General population
- Lifestages such as children, teenagers, pregnant/nursing women
- Population subgroups – highly susceptible (for example, due to asthma, genetics, etc.) and/or highly exposed (for example, based on geographic area, gender, racial or ethnic group, or economic status)

What is the environmental hazard of concern?

- Chemicals (single or multiple/cumulative risk)
- Radiation
- Physical (dust, heat)
- Microbiological or biological
- Nutritional (for example, diet, fitness, or metabolic state)
- Socio-Economic (for example, access to health care)

Where do these environmental hazards come from?

- Point sources (for example, smoke or water discharge from a factory; contamination from a Superfund site)
- Non-point sources (for example, automobile exhaust; agricultural runoff)
- Natural sources

How does exposure occur?

- Pathways (recognizing that one or more may be involved)
  - Air
  - Surface water

23

- Groundwater
- Soil
- Solid waste
- Food
- Non-food consumer products, pharmaceuticals
- Routes (and related human activities that lead to exposure)
  - Ingestion (both food and water)
  - Contact with skin
  - Inhalation
  - Non-dietary ingestion (for example, "hand-to-mouth" behavior)

What does the body do with the environmental hazard and how is this impacted by factors such as age, race, sex, genetics, etc.?

- Absorption—does the body take up the environmental hazard
- Distribution—does the environmental hazard travel throughout the body or does it stay in one place?
- Metabolism—does the body breakdown the environmental hazard?
- Excretion—how does the body get rid of it?

What are the health effects?

- Example of some health effects include cancer, heart disease, liver disease and nerve disease.

How long does it take for an environmental hazard to cause a toxic effect? Does it matter when in a lifetime exposure occurs?

- How long?
  - Acute – right away or within a few hours to a day
  - Subchronic – weeks or months (for humans generally less than 10% of their lifespan)
  - Chronic – a significant part of a lifetime or a lifetime (for humans at least seven years)
  - Intermittent

- Timing

  1. Is there a critical time during a lifetime when a chemical is most toxic (e.g., fetal development, childhood, during aging)?

Step 1 – Hazard Identification

To identify the types of adverse health effects that can be caused by exposure to some agent in question, and to characterize the quality and weight of evidence supporting this identification.

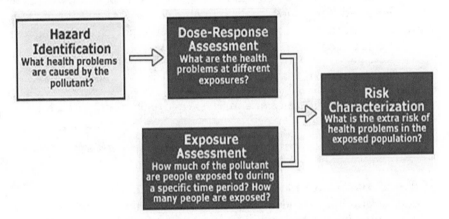

Figure 3.1. The 4-Step Risk Assessment Process – Hazard Identification

Hazard Identification is the process of determining whether exposure to a stressor can cause an increase in the incidence of specific adverse health effects (e.g., cancer, birth defects) and whether the adverse health effect is likely to occur in humans. In the case of chemical stressors, the process examines the available scientific data for a given chemical (or group of chemicals) and develops a weight of evidence to characterize the link between the negative effects and the chemical agent.

Exposure to a stressor may generate many different adverse effects in a human: diseases, formation of tumors, reproductive defects, death, or other effects.

Sources of Data

Statistically controlled clinical studies on humans provide the best evidence linking a stressor, often a chemical, to a resulting effect.

However, such studies are frequently not available since there are significant ethical concerns associated with human testing of environmental hazards.

Epidemiological studies involve a statistical evaluation of human populations to examine whether there is an association between exposure to a stressor and a human health effect. The advantage of these studies is that they involve humans while their weakness results from generally not having accurate exposure information and the difficulty of teasing out the effects of multiple stressors.

When data from human studies are unavailable, data from animal studies (rats, mice, rabbits, monkeys, dogs, etc) are relied on to draw inference about the potential hazard to humans. Animal studies can be designed, controlled, and conducted to address specific gaps in knowledge, but there are uncertainties associated with extrapolating results from animal subjects to humans.

Key Components of Hazard Identification

A wide variety of studies and analysis are used to support a hazard identification analysis.

- **Toxicokinetics** considers how the body absorbs, distributes, metabolizes, and eliminates specific chemicals.

- **Toxicodynamics** focus on the effects that chemicals have on the human body. Models based on these studies can describe mechanisms by which a chemical may impact human health, thus providing insights into the possible effects of a chemical.

When assessing a chemical for potential carcinogenic behavior, current EPA practice is to focus on analysis of a **mode of action**. Mode of action is a sequence of key events and processes, starting with interaction of an agent and a cell, proceeding through operational and anatomical changes, and resulting in cancer formation. A given agent may work by more than one mode of action, both at different tumor sites as well as at the same site. Analysis of mode of action is based on physical, chemical, and biological information that helps to explain key events in an agent's influence on tumor development.

A key component of hazard characterization involves evaluating the weight of evidence regarding a chemical's potential to cause adverse human health effects. The weight of evidence narrative may include some standard 'descriptors' that signify certain qualitative threshold levels of evidence or confidence have been met, such as 'Carcinogenic to humans' or 'Suggestive evidence of carcinogenic potential'.

Step 2 – Dose-Response Assessment

To document the relationship between dose and toxic effect.

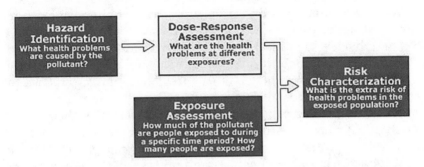

Figure 3.2. *The 4-Step Risk Assessment Process—Dose-Response Assessment*

A dose-response relationship describes how the likelihood and severity of adverse health effects (the responses) are related to the amount and condition of exposure to an agent (the dose provided). Although this webpage refers to the "dose-response" relationship, the same principles generally apply for studies where the exposure is to a concentration of the agent (e.g., airborne concentrations applied in inhalation exposure studies), and the resulting information is referred to as the "concentration-response" relationship. The term "exposure-response" relationship may be used to describe either a dose-response or a concentration-response, or other specific exposure conditions.

Typically, as the dose increases, the measured response also increases. At low doses there may be no response. At some level of dose the responses begin to occur in a small fraction of the study population or at a low probability rate. Both the dose at which response begin to appear and the rate at which it increases given increasing dose can be variable between different pollutants, individuals, exposure routes, etc.

The shape of the dose-response relationship depends on the agent, the kind of response (tumor, incidence of disease, death, etc.), and the experimental subject (human, animal) in question. For example, there may be one relationship for a response such as 'weight loss' and a different relationship for another response such as 'death'. Since it is impractical to study all possible relationships for all possible responses, toxicity research typically focuses on testing for a limited number of adverse effects. Upon considering all available studies, the response (adverse effect), or a measure of response that leads to an adverse effect (known as a 'precursor' to the effect), that occurs at the lowest dose is selected as the critical effect for risk assessment. The underlying assumption is that if the critical effect is prevented from occurring, then no other effects of concern will occur.

As with hazard identification, there is frequently a lack of dose-response data available for human subjects. When data are available, they often cover only a portion of the possible range of the dose-response relationship, in which case some extrapolation must be done in order to extrapolate to dose levels that are lower than the range of data obtained from scientific studies. Also, as with hazard identification, animal studies are frequently done to augment the available data. Studies using animal subjects permit the use of study design to control the number and composition (age, gender, species) of test subjects, the levels of dose tested, and the measurement of specific responses. Use of a designed study typically leads to more meaningful statistical conclusions than does an uncontrolled observational study were additional confounding factors must also be considered for their impact on the conclusions. However, dose-response relationships observed from animal studies are often at much higher doses that would be anticipated for humans, so must be extrapolated to lower doses, and animal studies must also be extrapolated from that animal species to humans in order to predict the relationship for humans. These extrapolations, among others, introduce uncertainty into the dose-response analysis.

Dose-response assessment is a two-step process. The first step is an assessment of all data that are available or can be gathered through experiments, in order to document the dose-response relationship(s) over the range of observed doses (i.e., the doses that are reported in the data collected). However, frequently this range of observation may not include sufficient data to identify a dose where the adverse effect is not observed (i.e., the dose that is low enough to prevent the effect) in the human population. The second step consists of extrapolation to estimate the risk (probably of adverse effect) beyond the lower range of available observed data in order to make inferences about the critical region where the dose level begins to cause the adverse effect in the human population.

Basic Dose-Response Calculations and Concepts

As a component of the first step of the process discussed above, the scientific information is evaluated for a better biological understanding

28

of how each type of toxicity or response (adverse effect) occurs; the understanding of how the toxicity is caused is called the "mode of action" (which is defined as a sequence of key events and processes, starting with interaction of an agent with a cell, proceeding through operational and anatomical changes, and resulting in the effect, for example, cancer formation). Based on this mode of action, the Agency determines the nature of the extrapolation used in the second step of the process discussed above, either through non-linear or linear dose-response assessment.

Non-linear dose-response assessment

Non-linear dose response assessment has its origins in the threshold hypothesis, which holds that a range of exposures from zero to some finite value can be tolerated by the organism with essentially no chance of expression of the toxic effect, and the threshold of toxicity is where the effects (or their precursors) begin to occur. It is often prudent to focus on the most sensitive members of the population; therefore, regulatory efforts are generally made to keep exposures below the population threshold, which is defined as the lowest of the thresholds of the individuals within a population. If the "mode of action" information (discussed above) suggests that the toxicity has a threshold, which is defined as the dose below which no deleterious effect is expected to occur, then type of assessment is referred to by the Agency as a "non-linear" dose-response assessment. The term "nonlinear" is used here in a narrower sense than its usual meaning in the field of mathematics; a nonlinear assessment uses a dose-response relationship whose slope is zero (i.e., no response) at (and perhaps above) a dose of zero.

A No-Observed-Adverse-Effect Level (NOAEL) is the highest exposure level at which no statistically or biologically significant increases are seen in the frequency or severity of adverse effect between the exposed population and its appropriate control population. In an experiment with several NOAELs, the regulatory focus is normally on the highest one, leading to the common usage of the term NOAEL as the highest experimentally determined dose without a statistically or biologically significant adverse effect. In cases in which a NOAEL has not been demonstrated experimentally, the term "lowest-observed-adverse-effect level (LOAEL)" is used, which is the lowest dose tested.

Mathematical modeling, which can incorporate more that one effect level (i.e., evaluates more data than a single NOAEL or LOAEL), is sometimes used to develop an alternative to a NOAEL known as a Benchmark Dose (BMD) or Benchmark Dose Lower-confidence Limit (BMDL). In developing the BMDL, a predetermined change in the response rate of an adverse effect (called the benchmark response or BMR; generally in the range of 1 to 10% depending on the power of a toxicity study) is selected, and the BMDL is a statistical lower confidence limit on the dose that produces the selected response. When the non-linear approach is applied, the LOAEL, NOAEL, or BMDL is used as the point of departure for extrapolation to lower doses.

The reference dose (RfD) is an oral or dermal dose derived from the NOAEL, LOAEL or BMDL by application of generally order-of-magnitude uncertainty factors (UFs). These uncertainty factors take into account the variability and uncertainty that are reflected in possible differences between test animals and humans (generally 10-fold or 10x) and variability within the human population (generally another 10x); the UFs are multiplied together: 10 x 10 = 100x. If a LOAEL is used, another uncertainty factor, generally 10x, is also used. In the absence of key toxicity data (duration or key effects), an extra uncertainty factor(s) may also be employed. Sometimes a partial UF is applied instead of the default value of 10x, and this value can be less than or greater than the default. Often the partial value is ½ log unit (the square root of 10) or 3.16 (rounded to 3-fold in risk assessment). Note, that when two UFs derived from ½ log units are multiplied together (3 x 3) the result is a 10 (equal to the full UF from which the two partial factors were derived).

Thus, the RfD is determined by use of the following equation:

RfD = NOAEL (or LOAEL or BMDL) / UFs

In general, the RfD is defined as an estimate (with uncertainty spanning perhaps an order of magnitude) of a daily oral exposure to the human population (including sensitive groups, such as asthmatics, or life stages, such as children or the elderly) that is likely to be without an appreciable risk of deleterious effects during a lifetime. The RfD is generally expressed in units of milligrams per kilogram of bodyweight per day: mg/kg/day.

A similar term, know as reference concentration (RfC), is used to assess inhalation risks, where concentration refers to levels in the air (generally expressed in the units of milligrams agent per cubic meter of air: mg/m^3).

Linear dose-response assessment

If the "mode of action" information (discussed above) suggests that the toxicity does not have a threshold, then this type of assessment is referred to by the Agency as a "linear" dose-response assessment. In the case of carcinogens, if "mode of action" information is insufficient, then linear extrapolation is typically used as the default approach for dose-response assessment. In this type of assessment, there is theoretically no level of exposure for such a chemical that does not pose a small, but finite, probability of generating a carcinogenic response. The extrapolation phase of this type of assessment does not use UFs; rather, a straight line is drawn from the point of departure for the observed data (typically the BMDL) to the origin (where there is zero dose and zero response). The slope of this straight line, called the slope factor or cancer slope factor, is use to estimate risk at exposure levels that fall along the line. When linear dose-response is used to assess cancer risk, EPA calculates excess lifetime cancer risk (i.e., probability that an individual will contract cancer over a lifetime) resulting from exposure to a contaminant by considering the degree to which individuals were exposed, as compared to the slope factor. Thus,

Cancer Risk = Exposure x Slope Factor

Total cancer risk is calculated by adding the individual cancer risks for each pollutant in each pathway of concern (i.e., inhalation, ingestion, and dermal absorption), then summing the risk for all pathways.

A similar term, know as inhalation unit risk (IUR), is used to assess inhalation risks, where the exposure-response relationship refers to concentrations in the air.

Step 3 – Exposure Assessment

To calculate a numerical estimate of exposure or dose.

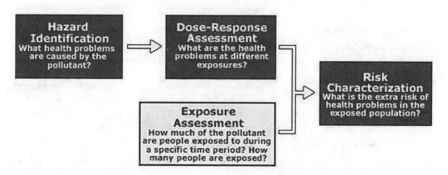

Figure 3.3. The 4-Step Risk Assessment Process – Exposure Assessment

31

EPA defines exposure as 'contact between an agent and the visible exterior of a person (e.g. skin and openings into the body)'. Exposure assessment is the process of measuring or estimating the magnitude, frequency, and duration of human exposure to an agent in the environment, or estimating future exposures for an agent that has not yet been released. An exposure assessment includes some discussion of the size, nature, and types of human populations exposed to the agent, as well as discussion of the uncertainties in the above information. Exposure can be measured directly, but more commonly is estimated indirectly through consideration of measured concentrations in the environment, consideration of models of chemical transport and fate in the environment, and estimates of human intake over time.

Different Kinds of Doses. Exposure assessment considers both the exposure pathway (the course an agent takes from its source to the person(s) being contacted) as well as the exposure route (means of entry of the agent into the body). The exposure route is generally further described as intake (taken in through a body opening, e.g. as eating, drinking, or inhaling) or uptake (absorption through tissues, e.g. through the skin or eye). The applied dose is the amount of agent at the absorption barrier that is available for absorption. The potential dose is the amount of agent that is ingested, inhaled, or applied to the skin. The applied dose may be less than the potential dose if the agent is only partly bioavailable. The internal dose or absorbed dose is the amount of an agent that has been absorbed and is available for interaction with biologically significant receptors within the human body. Finally, the delivered dose is the amount of agent available for interaction with any specific organ or cell.

Range of Exposure. For any specific agent or site, there is a range of exposures actually experienced by individuals. Some individuals may have a high degree of contact for an extended period (e.g. factory workers exposed to an agent on the job). Other individuals may have a lower degree of contact for a shorter period (e.g. individuals using a recreational site downwind of the factory). EPA policy for exposure assessment requires consideration of a range of possible exposure levels. Two common scenarios for possible exposure are "Central Tendency" and "High End." "Central Tendency" exposure is an estimate of the average experienced by the affected population, based on the amount of agent present in the environment and the frequency and duration of exposure. "High End" exposure is the highest dose estimated to be experienced by some individuals, commonly stated as approximately equal to the 90th percentile exposure category for individuals.

Quantifying Exposure. There are three basic approaches for quantifying exposure. Each approach is based on different data, and has different strengths and weaknesses; using the approaches in combination can greatly strengthen the credibility of an exposure risk assessment.

- **Point of Contact Measurement** – The exposure can be measured at the point of contact (the outer boundary of the body) while it is taking place, measuring both exposure concentration and time of contact, then integrating them.

- **Scenario Evaluation** – The exposure can be estimated by separately evaluating the exposure concentration and the time of contact, then combining this information.

- **Reconstruction** – the exposure can be estimated from dose, which in turn can be reconstructed through internal indicators (biomarkers, body burden, excretion levels, etc) after the exposure has taken place (reconstruction).

Step 4 – Risk Characterization

To summarize and integrate information from the proceeding steps of the risk assessment to synthesize an overall conclusion about risk.

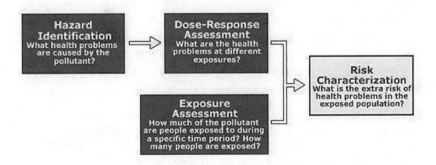

Figure 3.4. The 4-Step Risk Assessment Process – Risk Characterization

A risk characterization conveys the risk assessor's judgment as to the nature and presence or absence of risks, along with information about how the risk was assessed, where assumptions and uncertainties still exist, and where policy choices will need to be made. Risk characterization takes place in both human health risk assessments and ecological risk assessments.

In practice, each component of the risk assessment (e.g. hazard assessment, dose-response assessment, exposure assessment) has an individual risk characterization written to carry forward the key findings, assumptions, limitations, and uncertainties. The set of these individual risk characterizations provide the information basis to write an integrative risk characterization analysis.

The final, overall risk characterization thus consists of the individual risk characterizations plus an integrative analysis. The overall risk characterization informs the risk manager and others about the rationale behind EPA's approach to conducting the risk assessment - why EPA did what it did to assess the risk.

Principles of Conducting Risk Characterizations

A good risk characterization will restate the scope of the assessment, express results clearly, articulate major assumptions and uncertainties, identify reasonable alternative interpretations, and separate scientific conclusions from policy judgments. EPA's Risk Characterization Policy calls for conducting risk characterizations in a manner that is consistent with the following principles:

- **Transparency** – The characterization should fully and explicitly disclose the risk assessment methods, default assumptions, logic, rationale, extrapolations, uncertainties, and overall strength of each step in the assessment.

- **Clarity** – The products from the risk assessment should be readily understood by readers inside and outside of the risk assessment process. Documents should be concise, free of jargon, and should use understandable tables, graphs, and equations as needed.

- **Consistent** – The risk assessment should be conducted and presented in a manner which is consistent with EPA policy, and consistent with other risk characterizations of similar scope prepared across programs within the EPA.

- **Reasonable** – The risk assessment should be based on sound judgment, with methods and assumptions consistent with the current state-of-the-science and conveyed in a manner that is complete and balanced, informative.

These four principles—Transparency, Clarity, Consistency, and Reasonableness—are referred to collectively as TCCR. In order to achieve TCCR in a risk characterization, the same principles need to have been applied in all of the prior steps in the risk assessment which lead up to the risk characterization.

Why does EPA evaluate whether children may be at greater health risks than adults?

Almost 500 years ago Paracelsus (1493–1541) wrote: *"Dosis facit venenum"* or "the dose makes the poison." The relationship between dose and response (health effect) is still one of the most fundamental concepts of toxicology—or is it? For pollutants that act as developmental toxicants, the same dose that may pose little or no risk to an adult can cause drastic effects in a developing fetus or a child. Methyl mercury is but one example of a chemical that is much more toxic early in life. Scientists have become increasingly aware that children may be more vulnerable to environmental exposures than adults because:

- their bodily systems are developing;

- they eat more, drink more, and breathe more in proportion to their body size; and

- their behavior, such as crawling and hand-to-mouth activity, can expose them more to chemicals and microorganisms.

In light of what is now known about the greater susceptibility early in life to some stressors, Executive Order 13045—Protection of Children from Environmental Health Risks and Safety Risks—was issued in 1997. This Executive Order directs that all federal agencies, including EPA, shall make it a high priority to identify and assess environmental health risks and safety risks that may disproportionately affect children; and shall ensure that their policies, programs, activities, and standards address disproportionate risks to children that result from environmental health risks or safety risks.

Chapter 4

Environmental Hazards for Children

Children's Health

Overview

- Children are often more likely to be at risk from environmental hazards than adults because of:

  - Unique activity patterns and behavior.

  - Physiological differences.

  - Windows of susceptibility during early lifestages including fetal development and puberty.

- Children are also dependent upon adults to ensure that their environment is safe.

Unique Activity Patterns + Behavior

- Children crawl and play close to the ground making them more likely to come into contact with dirt and dust, which can include toxicants.

- Children often put their hands, toys, and other items into their mouths.

Text in this chapter is excerpted from "Protecting Children's Environmental Health," United States Environmental Protection Agency (EPA), June 30, 2015.

Physiology

- Children eat, breathe, and drink more relative to their body mass than adults do.

- Children's natural defenses are less developed.

  - More permeable blood-brain barrier.

  - Less effective filtration in nasal passages.

  - Highly permeable skin.

  - Lower levels of circulation of plasma proteins.

  - Digestive system, metabolic pathways, renal clearances, and vital organs are still developing.

Windows of Susceptibility

- The timing of exposure to chemicals or other insults is critical in determining the consequences to children's health.

- Because of the differing windows of susceptibility, the same dose of a chemical during different periods of development can have very different consequences.

- For example, fetal loss or birth defects are most likely to occur as a result of exposures to chemicals during the embryonic period, when organs are beginning to differentiate.

- Even after the basic structure of an organ has been established, disruption of processes such as growth and cell migration can have lifelong consequences on the function of key organ systems.

- Due to the complexity and speed of development during the prenatal period, organ system development is particularly susceptible to adverse effects resulting from environmental exposures.

What You Can Do to Protect Children from Environmental Risks

Listed below are tips to help protect children from environmental risks.

- Pesticides
- Chemical Poisoning

- Breathe Easier
- Lead Poisoning
- Carbon Monoxide Poisoning
- Contaminated Fish
- Radon
- Too Much Sun
- Mecury
- Healthier Communities

Keep pesticides and other toxic chemicals away from children

- Store food and trash in closed containers to keep pests from coming into your home.
- Use baits and traps when you can; place baits and traps where kids can't get them.
- Read product labels and follow directions.
- Store pesticides and toxic chemicals where kids can't reach them – never put them in other containers that kids can mistake for food or drink.
- Keep children, toys, and pets away when pesticides are applied; don't let them play in fields, orchards, and gardens after pesticides have been used for at least the time recommended on the pesticide label.
- Wash fruits and vegetables under running water before eating - peel them before eating, when possible.

Protect children from chemical poisoning

If a child has swallowed or inhaled a toxic product such as a household cleaner or pesticide, or gotten it in their eye or on their skin:

- Call 911 if the child is unconscious, having trouble breathing, or having convulsions.
- Check the label for directions on how to give first aid.
- Call the Poison Control Center at 800-222-1222 for help with first aid information.

Help children breathe easier

- Don't smoke and don't let others smoke in your home or car.

- Keep your home as clean as possible. Dust, mold, certain household pests, secondhand smoke, and pet dander can trigger asthma attacks and allergies.

- Limit outdoor activity on ozone alert days when air pollution is especially harmful.

- Walk, use bicycles, join or form carpools, and take public transportation.

- Limit motor vehicle idling.

- Avoid open burning.

Protect children from lead poisoning

- Get kids tested for lead by their doctor or health care provider.

- Test your home for lead paint hazards if it was built before 1978.

- Wash children's hands before they eat; wash bottles, pacifiers, and toys often.

- Wash floors and window sills to protect kids from dust and peeling paint contaminated with lead - especially in older homes.

- Run cold water until it becomes as cold as it can get. Use only cold water for drinking, cooking, and making baby formula.

Protect children from carbon monoxide (CO) poisoning

- Have fuel-burning appliances, furnace flues, and chimneys checked once a year.

- Never use gas ovens or burners for heat; never use barbecues or grills indoors or in the garage.

- Never sleep in rooms with unvented gas or kerosene space heaters.

- Don't run cars or lawnmowers in the garage.

- Install in sleeping areas a CO alarm that meets UL, IAS, or Canadian standards.

Protect children from contaminated fish and polluted water

- Be alert for local fish advisories and beach closings. Contact your local health department.

- Take used motor oil to a recycling center; properly dispose of toxic household chemicals.

- Learn what's in your drinking water – call your local public water supplier for annual drinking water quality reports; for private drinking water wells, have them tested annually by a certified laboratory. Call 1-800-426-4791 for help.

Safeguard children from high levels of radon

- Test your home for radon with a home test kit.

- Fix your home if your radon level is 4 pCi/L or higher. For help, call your state radon office or 1-800-SOS-RADON.

Protect children from too much sun

- Wear hats, sunglasses, and protective clothing.

- Use sunscreen with SPF 15+ on kids over six months; keep infants out of direct sunlight.

- Limit time in the mid-day sun – the sun is most intense between 10 and 4.

Keep children and mercury apart

- Eat a balanced diet but avoid fish with high levels of mercury.

- Replace mercury thermometers with digital thermometers.

- Don't let kids handle or play with mercury.

- Never heat or burn mercury.

- Contact your state or local health or environment department if mercury is spilled—never vacuum a spill.

Promote healthier communities

- Walk, use bicycles, join or form carpools, and take public transportation to reduce air pollution, including greenhouse gases .

- Spearhead a clean school bus campaign in your community. Clean School Bus USA emphasizes three ways to reduce public school bus emissions:

  1. Anti-idling strategies: Unnecessary idling pollutes the air, wastes fuel, and causes excess engine wear. It also wastes

money and results in the wear and tear of the vehicle's engine.

2. Engine retrofit and clean fuels: Retrofitted engines run cleaner because they have been fitted with devices designed to reduce pollution and/or use cleaner fuel.

3. Bus replacement: Older buses are not equipped with today's pollution control or safety features. Pre-1990 buses have been estimated to emit as much as six times more pollution as new buses that were built starting in 2004 and as much as 60 times more pollution as buses that meet the 2007 standards.

Develop safe routes so that children can walk to and from school, limiting vehicle use and increasing physical activity. Conduct walkability audits in your community to understand where you can and cannot walk. Children can help for a fun and educational activity.

- Encourage your school to use EPA's *Healthy School Environments Assessment Tool* (HealthySEAT). This software helps school districts evaluate and manage key environmental, safety, and health issues. HealthySEAT can be customized and used by district-level staff to conduct voluntary self assessments of their schools and other facilities and to track and manage information on environmental conditions school by school.

- Promote green building. Green building considerations include:

  - Careful site selection to minimize impacts on the surrounding environment and increase alternative transportation options.

  - Energy and water conservation to help ensure efficient use of natural resources and lower utility bills.

  - Responsible stormwater management to help limit disruption of natural watershed functions and reduce the environmental impacts of stormwater runoff.

  - Improved indoor air quality through the use of low volatile organic compound products and careful ventilation practices during construction and renovation.

- Use Indoor Air Quality Design Tools to create healthy school environments. Indoor air quality (IAQ) is a critically important aspect of creating and maintaining school facilities. *IAQ Design*

Tools for Schools provides detailed guidance and links to other resources to help design new schools and repair, renovate and maintain existing facilities. IAQ Design Tools for Schools is Web-based guidance to assist school districts, architects, and facility planners design and construct the next generation of schools.

- Support local smart growth activities. Smart growth is development that serves the economy, the community, and the environment. EPA helps states and communities realize the economic, community, and environmental benefits of smart growth by:

  - Providing information, model programs, and analytical tools to inform communities about growth and development.

  - Working to remove federal barriers that may hinder smarter community growth.

  - Creating new resources and incentives for states and communities pursuing smart growth.

- Protect children's environmental health. Children may be more vulnerable to environmental exposures than adults because:

  - Their bodily systems are still developing

  - They eat more, drink more, and breathe more in proportion to their body size

  - Their behavior can expose them more to chemicals and organisms

Protecting Children's Health During and After Natural Disasters

Floods

Children's Health in the Aftermath of Floods

Children are different from adults. They may be more vulnerable to chemicals and organisms they are exposed to in the environment because:

- Children's nervous, immune response, digestive and other bodily systems are still developing and are more easily harmed;

- Children eat more food, drink more fluids, and breathe more air than adults in proportion to their body size—so it is important to take extra care to ensure the safety of their food, drink and air;

- They way children behave—such as crawling and placing objects in their mouths—can increase their risk of exposure to chemicals and organisms in the environment.

Potential hazards to children's health after floods:

- Mold

- Carbon Monoxide

- Contaminated Water

Mold

After homes have been flooded, moisture can remain in drywall, wood furniture, cloth, carpet, and other household items and surfaces and can lead to mold growth. Exposure to mold can cause hay-fever-like reactions (such as stuffy nose, red, watery or itchy eyes, sneezing) to asthma attacks. It is important to dry water-damaged areas and items within 24–48 hours to prevent mold growth. Buildings wet for more than 48 hours will generally contain visible and extensive mold growth.

Some children are more susceptible than others to mold, especially those with allergies, asthma and other respiratory conditions. To protect your child from mold exposure, you can clean smooth, hard surfaces such as metal and plastics with soap and water and dry thoroughly. Flood water damaged items made of more absorbent materials cannot be cleaned and should be discarded. These items include paper, cloth, wood, upholstery, carpets, padding, curtains, clothes, stuffed animals, etc.

If there is a large amount of mold, you may want to hire professional help to cleanup the mold. If you decide to do the cleanup yourself, please remember:

- Clean and dry hard surfaces such as showers, tubs, and kitchen countertops.

- If something is moldy, and can't be cleaned and dried, throw it away.

- Use a detergent or use a cleaner that kills germs.

- Do not mix cleaning products together or add bleach to other chemicals.

- Wear an N-95 respirator, goggles, gloves so that you don't touch mold with your bare hands, long pants, a long-sleeved shirt, and boots or work shoes.

Homes or apartments that have sustained heavy water damage will be extremely difficult to clean and will require extensive repair or complete remodeling. We strongly advise that children not stay in these buildings.

Carbon Monoxide

NEVER use portable generators indoors! Place generators outside and as far away from buildings as possible. Do not put portable generators on balconies or near doors, vents, or windows and do not use them near where you or your children are sleeping. Due to loss of electricity, gasoline- or diesel-powered generators may be used in the aftermath of floods. These devices release carbon monoxide, a colorless, odorless and deadly gas. Simply opening doors and windows or using fans will not prevent carbon monoxide buildup in the home or in partially enclosed areas such as a garage. In 2001 and 2002, an average of nearly 1,000 people died from non-fire-related carbon monoxide poisoning, and 64% of nonfatal carbon monoxide exposures occurred in the home.

If your children or anyone else in your family starts to feel sick, dizzy or weak or experiences a headache, chest pain or confusion, get to fresh air immediately and seek medical care as soon as possible. Your child's skin under the fingernails may also turn cherry-red if he/she has been exposed to high levels of carbon monoxide. Fetuses and infants are especially vulnerable to the life-threatening effects of carbon monoxide.

Install a carbon monoxide detector that is Nationally Recognized Testing Laboratory (NRTL) approved (such as UL). These are generally available at local hardware stores. Carbon Monoxide is lighter than air, so detectors should be placed closer to the ceiling. Detectors should be placed close enough to sleeping areas to be heard by sleeping household members.

Contaminated Water

While all people need safe drinking water, it is especially important for children because they are more vulnerable to harm from contaminated water. If a water source may be contaminated with flood waters, children, pregnant women and nursing mothers should drink only bottled water, which should also be used to mix baby formula and for cooking. We also recommend you sponge bathe your children with warm bottled water until you are certain your tap water is safe to drink.

Your child may or may not show symptoms or become ill from swallowing small amounts of contaminated water. Symptoms can vary by contaminant. If your child drinks water contaminated with disease-causing organisms, he/she may come down with symptoms similar to the "stomach flu." These include stomach ache, nausea, vomiting, and diarrhea, and may cause dehydration.

Some contaminants, such as pesticides and gasoline, may cause the water to smell and taste strange, and others such as lead and disease-causing organisms may not be detectable. Drinking water contaminated with chemicals such as lead or gasoline may not cause immediate symptoms or cause your child to become ill but could still potentially harm your child's developing brain or immune system.

Because you cannot be sure if the water is safe until private wells are professionally tested or city water is certified as safe by local officials, we urge parents to take every precaution to make sure their child's drinking water is safe.

If you have a flooded well, do NOT turn on the pump, and do NOT flush the well with water. Contact your local or state health department or agriculture extension agent for specific advice on disinfecting your well.

Your public water system or local health agency will inform you if you need to boil water prior to using it for drinking and cooking.

Tap water that has been brought to a rolling boil for at least 1 minute will kill disease-causing organisms. Boiling will not remove many potentially harmful chemicals, and may actually increase concentrations of heavy metals (including lead), which can be harmful to a child's developing immune system. Chemically treating tap water with either chlorine or iodine will kill many disease-causing organisms, but will not remove harmful chemicals or heavy metals.

Household Items Contaminated by Floodwaters

Drinking Water Containers: Clean thoroughly with soap and water, then rinse. For gallon-sized containers, add approximately 1 teaspoon of bleach to a gallon of water to make a bleach solution. Cover the container and agitate the bleach solution thoroughly, allowing it to contact all inside surfaces. Cover and let stand for 30 minutes, then rinse with potable water.

Kitchenware and Utensils: In general, metal and glazed ceramic that are thoroughly washed and dried can be sanitized and kept. Follow local public health guidance on effective and safe sanitation procedures. Wood items must be thrown away, as these items can absorb contaminants or grow mold from the exposure to flood water and they cannot be properly sanitized.

Children's Toys and Baby items: Throw away ALL soft or absorbent toys because it is impossible to clean them and they could harm your child. Throw away ALL baby bottles, nipples, and pacifiers that have come in contact with flood waters or debris.

Other Flood Topics

Teenagers: Teens are still growing and developing, especially their reproductive, nervous and immune systems. Teens are less likely to understand dangers and may underestimate the dangers of certain situations, or they may be reluctant to voice their concerns about potential dangers. Whenever possible, teens should not participate in post-flood clean-up that would expose them to contaminated water, mold and hazardous chemicals. Older teens may help adults with minor clean-ups if they wear protective gear including goggles, heavy work gloves, long pants, shirts, socks, boots and a properly fitting N-95 respirator.

Older Adults and People Living with Chronic Diseases: Flooding often leads to the development of micro-organisms and the release of dangerous chemicals in the air and water. Older adults and people living with chronic diseases are especially vulnerable to these contaminants.

Bleach: Household bleach contains chlorine, a very corrosive chemical which can be harmful if swallowed or inhaled. It is one of the most common cleaners accidentally swallowed by children. Children—especially those with asthma—should not be in the room while using these products. Call Poison Control at 800-222-1212 immediately in case of poisoning.

Formerly Flooded or Debris-filled Areas: Children in these areas may be at risk of exposure to dirt and debris that may have been contaminated with hazardous chemicals like lead, asbestos, oil and gasoline. Children can be exposed by direct contact through their skin, by breathing in dust particles or fumes, or by putting their hands in their mouths.

Mosquitoes and Disease-Causing Pests: Flood water may increase the number of mosquitoes and other disease-causing pests. To protect your child, ensure that they use insect repellents containing up to 30% Deet, Picardin, or Oil of Lemon Eucalyptus. The American Academy of Pediatrics recommends that Deet not be used on infants less than 2 months of age and that Oil of Lemon Eucalyptus not be used on children under 3 years of age. Other ways to protect children include staying indoors while the sun is down, wearing light colored, long sleeved shirts and pants, covering baby carriages and playpens with mosquito netting, and clear standing water or empty flower pots, etc of water.

Extreme Heat

Extreme Heat: Effects on Children and Pregnant Women

Heat-related illnesses are common, yet preventable on hot days. Children and pregnant women need to take extra precautions to avoid overheating on days of extreme heat. Dehydration, heat stroke, and other heat illnesses may affect a child or pregnant woman more severely than the average adult.

Why are children more susceptible to extreme heat?

- Physical characteristics – Children have a smaller body mass to surface area ratio than adults, making them more vulnerable to heat-related morbidity and mortality. Children are more likely to become dehydrated than adults because they can lose more fluid quickly.

- Behaviors – Children play outside more than adults, and they may be at greater risk of heat stroke and exhaustion because they may lack the judgment to limit exertion during hot weather and to rehydrate themselves after long periods of time in the heat. There are also regular reports of infants dying when left in unattended vehicles, which suggests a low awareness of the dangers of heat events.

How do I know if my child is dehydrated?

- Decreased physical activity
- Lack of tears when crying
- Dry mouth
- Irritability and fussiness

What should I do if my child has become dehydrated?

- Have the child or infant drink fluid replacement products
- Allow for rehydration to take a few hours, over which children should stay in a cool, shaded area and sip fluids periodically
- Call your doctor if symptoms do not improve or if they worsen

How do I know if my child has suffered a heat stroke?

Heat stroke, a condition in which the body becomes overheated in a relatively short span of time, can be life-threatening and requires immediate medical attention.

- Skin is flushed, red and dry

- Little or no sweating

- Deep breathing

- Dizziness, headache, and/or fatigue

- Less urine is produced, of a dark yellowish color

- Loss of consciousness

What should I do if my child has suffered a heat stroke?

- Immediately remove child from heat and place in a cool environment

- Place child in bath of cool water and massage skin to increase circulation (do not use water colder than 60%F – may restrict blood vessels)

- Take child to hospital or doctor as soon as possible

How can children be protected from the effects of extreme heat?

- Hydration – Make sure children are drinking plenty of fluids while playing outside, especially if they are participating in sports or rigorous physical activity. Fluids should be drunk before, during and after periods of time in extreme heat.

- Staying indoors – Ideally, children should avoid spending time outdoors during periods of extreme heat. Playing outside in the morning or evenings can protect children from dehydration or heat exhaustion. Never leave a child in a parked car, even if the windows are open.

- Light clothing – Children should be dressed in light, loose-fitting clothes on extremely hot days. Breathable fabrics such as cotton are ideal because sweat can evaporate and cool down the child's body.

How do I care for my infant during hot weather?

- Check your baby's diaper for concentrated urine, which can be a sign of dehydration.

- If your infant is sweating, he or she is too warm. Remove him or her from the sun immediately and find a place for the baby to cool down.

- Avoid using a fan on or near your baby; it dehydrates them faster.

- A hat traps an infant's body heat and should only be worn in the sun to avoid sunburn.

- Never leave an infant in a parked car, even if the windows are open.

Why are pregnant woman especially at risk during periods of extreme heat?

An increase in the core body temperature of a pregnant woman may affect the fetus, especially during the first trimester.

How can pregnant women protect themselves from the effects of extreme heat?

- Wear light loose fitting clothing

- Stay hydrated by drinking six to eight glasses of water a day

- Avoid caffeine, salt, and alcohol

- Balance fluids by drinking beverages with sodium and other electrolytes

- Limit midday excursions when temperatures are at their highest

- Call doctor or go to emergency room if woman feels dizzy, short of breath, or lightheaded

Volcanic Ash

Wildfires

Wildfires expose children to a number of environmental hazards, e.g., fire, smoke, psychological conditions, and the byproducts of combustion. After a wildfire, children may be exposed to a different set of environmental hazards involving not only their homes, but also nearby structures, land, and recovery activities.

Children's Health and Volcanic Ash

Volcanic ash consists of tiny pieces of rock and glass that is spread over large areas by wind. During volcanic ash fall, people should take measures to avoid unnecessary exposure to airborne ash and gases.

Short-term exposure to ash usually does not cause significant health problems for the general public, but special precautions should be taken to protect susceptible people such as infants and children. Most volcanic gases such as carbon dioxide and hydrogen sulfide blow away quickly. Sulfur dioxide is an irritant volcanic gas that can cause the airways to narrow, especially in people with asthma. Precaution should be taken to ensure that children living close to the volcano or in low-lying areas (where gases may accumulate) are protected from respiratory and eye irritation.

While children face the same health problems from volcanic ash particles suspended in the air as adults (namely respiratory and irritation of the nose, throat, and eyes), they may be more vulnerable to exposure due to their smaller physical size, developing respiratory systems, and decreased ability to avoid unnecessary exposure. Small volcanic ash particles—those less than 10 micrometers in diameter—pose the greatest health concern because they can pass through the nose and throat and get deep into the lungs. This size range includes fine particles, with diameters less than 2.5 micrometers, and coarse particles, which range in size from 2.5 to 10 micrometers in diameter. Particles larger than 10 micrometers do not usually reach the lungs, but they can irritate your eyes, nose, and throat. The volcanic ash may exacerbate the symptoms of children suffering from existing respiratory illnesses such as asthma, cystic fibrosis, or tuberculosis.

Precautions for Children if Ash is Present

- **Always pay attention to warnings and obey instructions from local authorities.**

  - Check the Air Quality Index forecast for your area.

  - Stay alert to news reports about volcanic ash warnings.

- **Keep children indoors.**

  - Children should avoid running or strenuous activity during ash fall. Exertion leads to heavier breathing which can draw ash particles deeper into the lungs.

  - Parents may want to plan indoor games and activities that minimize activity when ash is present.

  - If your family must be outdoors when there is ash in the air, they should wear a disposable mask. If no disposable masks are available, make-shift masks can be made by moistening fabric such as handkerchiefs to help to block out large ash particles.

- Volcanic ash can irritate the skin; long-sleeved shirts and long pants should be worn if children must go outdoors.

- **Children should not play in areas where ash is deep or piled-up, especially if they are likely to roll or lie in the ash piles.**

- **Children should wear glasses instead of contact lens to avoid eye irritation.**

  - Create a "clean room" where children sleep and play to help to minimize exposure to ash in indoor air.

  - Keep windows and doors closed. Close any vents or air ducts (such as chimneys) that may allow ash to enter the house.

  - Run central air conditioners on the "recirculate" option (instead of "outdoor air intake"). Clean the air filter to allow good air flow indoors.

  - Avoid vacuuming as it will stir up ash and dust into the air.

  - Do not smoke or burn anything (tobacco, candles, incense) inside the home. This will create more indoor pollutants.

  - If it is too warm or difficult to breathe inside with the windows closed, seek shelter elsewhere.

- **A portable room air filter may be effective to remove particles from the air.**

  - Choosing to buy an air cleaner is ideally a decision that should be made *before* a smoke/ash emergency occurs. Going outside to locate an appropriate device during an emergency may be hazardous, and the devices may be in short supply.

  - An air cleaner with a HEPA filter, an electrostatic precipitator (ESP), or an ionizing air cleaner may be effective at removing air particles provided it is sized to filter two or three times the room air volume per hour.

  - Avoid ozone generators, personal air purifiers, "pure-air" generators and "super oxygen" purifiers as these devices emit ozone gas into the air at levels that can irritate airways and exacerbate existing respiratory conditions. These devices are also not effective at removing particles from the air.

Children's Environmental Health Facts

Asthma

- Asthma is a common chronic disease among children in the United States.

- In 2006, 9.9 million children under 18 years of age were reported to have ever been diagnosed with asthma; 6.8 million children had an asthmatic episode in the last 12 months.

- The hospitalization rate for asthma remained at 27 per 10,000 children from 2002–2004.

- Asthma is the third ranking cause of non-injury related hospitalization among children less than 15 years of age.

- Although asthma deaths among children are rare, 195 children under 18 years of age died from asthma in 2003.

Disparities of Asthma

- Asthma disproportionately affects children from lower-income families and children from various racial and ethnic groups.

- African-American children have a 500% higher mortality rate from asthma as compared with Caucasian children.

- In 2005, 13% of African-American children were reported to have asthma as compared with 9% of Hispanic children and 8% of non-Hispanic white children.

- Larger disparities exist within the Hispanic population such that 20% of Puerto Rican children were reported to have asthma as compared with 7% of Mexican children.

- While national level surveys suggest Asian and Pacific Islander children do not have high rates of asthma, small scale surveys however show a high prevalence of asthma among subgroups of Asian and Pacific Islander children.

  - Filipino children have an asthma prevalence of 23.8%

  - Pacific Islander children have an asthma prevalence of 21%

Economic Impact of Asthma

- In 2002, children 5–17 years old missed 14.7 million school days due to asthma.

- The direct and indirect costs of asthma to the U.S. economy were $19.7 billion in 2007.

- Approximately $14.7 billion dollars are directly associated with the medical care costs of asthma

- Approximately $5 billion are associated with lost productivity

- Asthmatic patients and their families pay a higher portion of their medical care costs than patients with other diseases due to heavy reliance on prescription medication combined with lower insurance coverage for prescription drugs.

Lead Exposure

- Currently, no level of lead in blood has been identified as safe for children. The U.S. Centers for Disease Control and Prevention (CDC) recommend public health actions be initiated for children with a reference level of 5 micrograms of lead per deciliter of blood.

- Today, elevated blood lead levels in children are due mostly to ingestion of contaminated dust, paint and soil.

- Other sources of lead exposure include ceramics, drinking water pipes and plumbing fixtures, consumer products, batteries, gasoline, solder, ammunition, imported toys, and cosmetics.

- In 2010, an estimated 535,000 children had a blood lead level of 5 μg/dL. The number of children affected by lead poisoning has decreased significantly from 4.7 million in 1978.

- The decline in blood lead levels is due to the phasing out of lead in gasoline between 1973 and 1995 and the reduction in the number of homes with lead-based paint from 64 million in 1990 to 38 million in 2000. About 24 million homes still have significant lead-based paint hazards.

- Lead exposure in young children can result in lowered intelligence, reading and learning disabilities, impaired hearing, reduced attention span, hyperactivity, delayed puberty, and reduced postnatal growth.

Disparities in Lead Exposure

- Blood lead levels are higher for children ages 1–5 years old from lower-income families and for certain racial and ethnic groups.

- The median blood lead level in Black non-Hispanic children ages 1–5 years old is higher than the level in White non-Hispanic children, Mexican-American children, and children of "All Other Races/Ethnicities."

- The median blood lead level for children living in families with incomes below poverty level is higher than for children living in families at or above poverty level.

Economic Impact of Lead Exposure

- The cost of reduced cognitive ability is measured by IQ scores and valued in terms of forgone earnings and is estimated to be about $9,600 per IQ point lost.

- The cost of not eliminating lead exposure to children between 2000–2010 is expected to be about $22 billion in forgone earnings.

Childhood Cancer

- In 2007, an estimated 10,400 new cancer cases were expected to occur among children aged 0–14 years old. An estimated 1,545 deaths from cancer were expected to occur among children in 2007.

- Leukemia is the most common cancer in children under 15, accounting for 30 percent of all childhood cancers, followed by brain and other nervous system cancers.

- Cancer is the second leading cause of death among children ages 1–14 years of age, with unintentional injuries being the leading cause.

- The causes of childhood cancer are poorly understood, though different forms of cancer have different causes. A number of studies suggest that environmental contaminants, including radiation, secondhand smoke, pesticides and solvents, may play a role in the development of childhood cancers.

Disparities in Childhood Cancer

- Hispanic children were reported to have a higher incidence of acute lymphocytic Leukemia (ALL) than non-Hispanic white children.

- Although national studies indicate that Asian Pacific Islander American (APIA) children overall do not have higher rates of Cancer compared to non-Hispanic whites, a smaller scale study conducted in California showed APIA children are at increased risk of developing acute non lymphocytic Leukemia (ANLL) compared with non-Hispanic white infants.

Economic Impact of Childhood Cancer

- The total cost per case of childhood cancer was estimated to be about $623,000.

Developmental Disabilities

- In 2001–2004, about 7 children out of every 1,000 children were reported to be diagnosed with mental retardation.

- Between 3–8 percent of the babies born each year will be affected by developmental disorders such as attention-deficit/ hyperactivity disorder or mental retardation. In 2003–2004, an estimated 300,000 U.S. children aged 4–17 years were reported to have Autism.

Disparities in Developmental Disabilities

- Mental retardation is more common for children from lower income families and for certain racial and ethnic groups.

Economic Impact of Developmental Disabilities

- During the 2001–2002 school year, an estimated 6.5 million children were enrolled in special education programs. This is almost 75% increase from 1976–1977.

- The economic costs associated with autism are approximately $35 billion dollars per year.

- Expenditures can range from 1.6 times (for students with specific learning disabilities) to 3.1 times (for students with multiple disabilities) higher than expenditures for a regular education student.

Chapter 5

Environment and Women's Health

The environment

What do you mean by "the environment"?

The environment is everything around you, indoors or outdoors. The air you breathe, water you drink, the ground you walk on, and food you eat are all part of your environment. It's important that you know what things in the environment can affect your health and what you can do to help protect yourself and your family.

How can the environment affect women's health?

Chemicals and other substances in the environment can cause serious health problems in women, such as cancer, lung disease, or reproductive system problems. They can also make health conditions worse. Scientists are studying the ways toxins in the environment may play a role in conditions such as breast cancer, endometriosis, and menopause.

Text in this chapter is excerpted from "Environment and Women's Health," Office on Women's Health, U.S. Department of Health and Human Services (DHHS), July 16, 2012.

How can the environment affect children's health?

Many types of environmental exposures are more harmful for children than for adults. There are many reasons for this:

- Relative to their body weight, children eat, breathe, and drink more than adults do. So children take in higher concentrations of any toxins in their food, water, or air.

- As organs develop, they are more likely to be damaged by exposure to toxins.

- The ways that toxins are removed from the body are not fully developed in children.

- Children spend more time outdoors, where they may be exposed to outdoor air pollution and ultraviolet radiation.

- Children do more intense physical activity, causing them to breathe air pollutants more deeply into their lungs.

- Young children tend to put their hands, dirt, or objects into their mouths.

How can the environment affect women who are pregnant or nursing?

Exposure to some toxic substances—including lead, mercury, arsenic, cadmium, pesticides, solvents, and household chemicals—can increase the risk of miscarriage, preterm birth, and other pregnancy complications. These and other environmental toxins can also harm the developing bodies of fetuses and infants. Women who are pregnant or nursing or who plan to become pregnant should take special care to avoid exposure to certain chemicals discussed here.

How can the environment affect older women?

Pollutants in the environment can contribute to some illnesses that are more common in older adults. Indoor and outdoor air pollution can aggravate the symptoms of cardiovascular and lung diseases, including high blood pressure, chronic obstructive pulmonary disease, and asthma. These conditions are more common in women over the age of 50 than in men over 50.

Older adults may be more susceptible to the health effects of toxic chemicals. People who are exposed to pollutants over the course of a lifetime may have health problems when they are older.

For instance, long-term exposure to pesticides may cause cancer or dementia.

Lead is a toxic metal that may be stored in bones. In postmenopausal women who were exposed to lead early in life, bone loss can release lead into the bloodstream. This may cause kidney damage, increase the risk of high blood pressure, and decrease cognitive functions.

Outdoor air pollution

What is outdoor air pollution and how can I be exposed to it?

There are many sources of pollution outdoors, such as:

- Emissions from cars and trucks

- Power plants that burn fossil fuels

- Factories and forest fires

What are the health effects of outdoor air pollution?

Outdoor air pollution can cause your eyes and nose to burn, your throat to itch, and even breathing problems. Exposure to air pollutants at high levels over a long period of time may lead to cancer, birth defects, brain and nerve damage, and long-term injury to the lungs and breathing passages.

Air pollution affects everyone. Children are especially susceptible to the effects of air pollution because their lungs are developing. They also spend more time active outdoors. People with lung and heart diseases are also more sensitive to outdoor air pollution.

The U.S. Environmental Protection Agency (EPA) sets limits on certain air pollutants throughout the United States. Ground-level ozone and particle pollution are two of the most common pollutants and pose the greatest threat to human health in the United States.

What can I do to reduce exposure to outdoor air pollution?

To find out about the level of outdoor air pollution in your community, you can check the daily Air Quality Index (AQI). The AQI is a measure of five pollutants: ozone (OH-zohn), particle pollution, sulfur dioxide (SUHL-fur deye-OKS-eyed), nitrogen oxide (NEYE-troh-jen OKS-eyed), and carbon monoxide (kar-bun moh-NOKS-eyed). Many newspaper, radio, and television weather forecasts also include the AQI.

When the levels of air pollution are high, you can protect yourself and your family by limiting outdoor physical activity. This is because physical activity can cause you to take faster, deeper breaths, inhaling more pollutants into your lungs.

What is ground-level ozone and how can I be exposed to it?

Ozone is a gas that is naturally found in earth's upper atmosphere, where it forms the ozone layer. The ozone layer blocks some of the sun's harmful ultraviolet (UV) rays.

Ground-level ozone is ozone in the lower atmosphere, close to the Earth's surface. This is one of the main components of smog. Ground-level ozone is formed when sunlight and heat cause chemical reactions between nitrogen oxides and volatile organic compounds (VOCs). VOCs are pollutants released by motor vehicles, factories and power plants, and chemicals such as paints and cleaners. Ground-level ozone is a pollutant that can harm the environment, crops, and human health.

What are the health effects from exposure to ground-level ozone?

High levels of ground-level ozone can make it difficult to breath deeply, cause coughing and throat irritation, and even damage the lining of your lungs. People with chronic lung conditions such as asthma, emphysema, and bronchitis may be more sensitive to the effects of ozone. Ozone can also have a greater impact on the health of children and adults who are physically active outdoors when ozone levels are high.

What is particle pollution and how can I be exposed to it?

Particle pollution are tiny solid particles and liquid droplets in the air. This is also called particle matter or PM. These particles come from dust, fires, motor vehicles, power plants, and factories. Many types of particle pollution are too small to be seen with the naked eye. Particle pollution causes haze.

What are the health effects from exposure to particle pollution?

Exposure to particle pollution can irritate your eyes, nose, and throat. Inhaling these particles can cause coughing and wheezing, even if you are healthy. Long-term exposures to particle pollution can reduce lung function and lead to chronic bronchitis. High levels of particle pollution may aggravate symptoms of lung and heart diseases.

What is "acid rain"?

"Acid rain" is a term used to describe rain, snow, fog, dry gases, and particles containing acids. Sulfur dioxide and nitrogen oxides released by power plants, cars and trucks, and other sources are the primary cause of acid rain. Acid rain harms plants, animals, fish, and building surfaces.

What are the health effects from acid rain?

Acid rain does not directly affect human health. But the main components of acid rain—sulfur dioxide and nitrogen oxides—do. These gases contribute to particulate pollution, which can affect the heart and lungs. High levels of sulfur dioxide can aggravate lung and heart diseases. Nitrogen oxides increase levels of ground-level ozone, react with other chemicals to form toxins, and contribute to global warming.

What is global warming?

Global warming is an increase in the Earth's average temperature. This increase can cause a variety of changes in local climates around the world, such as changes in rainfall patterns and a rise in sea level. It also triggers a wide range of changes in plants, wildlife, and human life.

"Greenhouse gases," including carbon dioxide and methane, trap the heat of the Earth. In the last 200 years, human activities—like burning fossil fuels—have increased the levels of greenhouse gases in the atmosphere. This has caused average temperatures to rise. Temperatures are expected to continue to rise in the future.

What are the health effects of global warming?

Scientists predict that global warming may affect human health in many ways:

- Extremely high summer temperatures may lead to more heat-related deaths.

- Warmer climates can increase the spread of some infectious diseases.

- Climate change may lead to more extreme weather events, such as hurricanes and floods.

- Higher temperatures can increase concentrations of ozone and particulate pollution.

What can I do to reduce outdoor air pollution and global warming?

Motor vehicles and power plants that burn fossil fuels are major sources of air pollution. They also release greenhouse gases that lead to climate change. But there are many steps you can take to use less energy and reduce air pollution and greenhouse gases. Many of these steps can also save you money.

- Replace incandescent (in-kand-ESS-ent) light bulbs with compact fluorescent (flor-ESS-ent) bulbs.
- Turn off lights and appliances when they're not in use.
- Reuse and recycle to conserve raw materials and energy.
- Buy ENERGY STAR appliances.
- Choose a vehicle with good fuel economy and low emissions.
- Drive less. Carpool, walk, bike, or use public transportation if you can.

Indoor air pollution

What is indoor air pollution and how can I be exposed to it?

Most people spend about 90 percent of their time indoors. Therefore, indoor air pollution is as great a concern as outdoor air pollution.

Sources of indoor air pollution include:

- Gases from burning oil, gas, coal, or wood for heating and cooking
- Smoke from tobacco products
- Building materials, such as asbestos insulation and products made from pressed wood
- Outdoor pollutants, such as radon, that can accumulate indoors
- Chemicals used for cleaning, pest control, and painting
- Personal care products such as hair spray and nail polish remover
- Biological contaminants, such as bacteria, molds and mildew, and pet dander

If your home does not have enough ventilation, pollutants may build up to unhealthy levels.

What are the health effects of exposure to indoor air pollution?

Indoor air pollution can cause immediate effects. It can irritate your eyes, nose and throat; cause headaches; and make you feel dizzy or tired. These symptoms may be mistaken for symptoms of a cold or flu, but if the symptoms disappear when you are away from home, they may signal an indoor air problem.

Indoor air pollution can also cause more serious health problems, such as heart and lung diseases and cancer. These problems may develop many years after you were exposed to the pollution or after years of repeated exposures.

Some people are more sensitive to indoor air pollution than others are. As with outdoor air pollution, children, the elderly, and people with heart or lung conditions are more likely to be affected.

How can I improve the indoor air quality in my home?

The best way to reduce indoor air pollution is to get rid of potential sources of pollution. You can also improve the ventilation in your home by running exhaust and attic fans and opening doors and windows. This is especially important when you are using products, like paints and cleaners, that may increase levels of indoor air pollution for a short time. Air cleaners may also help remove indoor air pollutants. The effectiveness of air cleaners varies.

What are combustion products and how can I be exposed to them?

Stoves, heaters, fireplaces, and chimneys need to be vented correctly. If not, they can release dangerous amounts of carbon monoxide, nitrogen dioxide, and particle pollution into your home. Fuel-burning appliances may also release formaldehyde (form-AL-duh-hyd).

What are the health effects of exposure to combustion products?

Carbon monoxide and nitrogen dioxide are colorless, odorless gases. Carbon monoxide can cause headaches, dizziness, nausea, or fatigue. Breathing air with high levels of carbon monoxide may cause you to lose consciousness and may be deadly. Nitrogen dioxide can irritate your eyes, nose, and throat, and make it difficult to breathe. Eventually, it may contribute to lung infections and diseases.

What can I do to reduce exposure to combustion products?

You can minimize the emissions from fuel-burning stoves and heaters.

- If you use unvented space heaters, follow the manufacturer's directions and open a window or door to increase ventilation.
- Use exhaust fans, vented to the outdoors, over gas stoves and ranges.
- In your woodstove, use wood that is aged and dried and is not treated with chemicals.
- Have a trained contractor inspect, clean, and tune-up furnaces, flues, chimneys, and gas appliances every year. Repair any leaks as soon as you can. Change filters at least once every month during periods of use.

Do not operate cars, trucks, lawn mowers, snow blowers, and other machines with gasoline-powered engines in enclosed spaces. These engines release carbon monoxide.

Installing a carbon monoxide detector can also help protect you and your family from this dangerous gas.

What is secondhand tobacco smoke and how can I be exposed to it?

The smoke from burning tobacco products and the smoke exhaled by smokers are called secondhand smoke. These products include cigarettes, cigars, and pipes.

What are the health effects of exposure to secondhand tobacco smoke?

Nonsmokers who are exposed to secondhand smoke have an increased risk of lung cancer. Children of parents who smoke are more likely to suffer from pneumonia, bronchitis, ear infections, asthma, and sudden infant death syndrome (SIDS).

What can I do to reduce exposure to secondhand tobacco smoke?

To help protect yourself and your family from the harmful effects of secondhand smoke:

- Don't smoke in your home or car or allow others to do so.
- Ask smokers to smoke outside. Ventilation (opening windows, running exhaust fans, etc.) cannot completely protect nonsmokers and children from exposure to secondhand smoke.

- Don't smoke, or allow others to smoke, around children, especially infants and toddlers.

What is radon and how can I be exposed to it?

Uranium (yoor-AYN-ee-um) is a natural radioactive substance found in many types of rocks and soil. As uranium decays, it releases radon (ray-don). Radon is a colorless, odorless, and tasteless radioactive gas. Small amounts of radon are present in outdoor air. High levels of radon can accumulate in enclosed spaces. Because radon comes out of the ground, it is more likely to accumulate in basements and the lower floors of buildings.

It is estimated that one out of every 15 homes in the United States may have high radon levels. Radon can enter any type of home through small gaps and cracks in walls and floors. In some areas, radon may also be present in groundwater.

What are the health effects of exposure to radon?

Exposure to high levels of radon can cause lung cancer.

How can I tell if my home has a radon problem?

You can test the air in your home for radon. Hardware stores and other retailers sell many types of inexpensive radon test kits that allow you to test your home yourself. You can also hire a qualified radon testing professional. The EPA recommends that all homes should be tested below the third floor.

Two types of radon tests are available: short-term tests and long-term tests. Short-term tests provide results in less than 90 days. However, because radon levels may vary throughout the year, long-term tests, lasting more than 90 days, will give you a better idea of the average radon levels in your home year-round.

If a short-term test finds radon levels of 4 picoCuries per liter (pCi/l) of air or higher, you should conduct a second test. You should fix your home to reduce radon levels if the second test is:

- A long-term test, showing radon levels of 4 pCi/l or higher

  or

- A short-term test, and the average of the first and second tests was 4 pCi/l or higher

What can I do to reduce exposure to radon?

A qualified radon contractor can fix your home to reduce radon levels. Costs can range from $800 to $2,500. If radon levels are high in your indoor air and you have a private well, you should also have your water tested and treated if need be.

Your state radon office can provide information about radon in the ground and water in your area. They can also refer you to qualified radon testers and radon contractors.

What is asbestos and how can I be exposed to it?

Asbestos (ass-BESS-tohs) is a fiber that has been used in insulation and fireproofing materials. The EPA has banned many asbestos products. Many companies have also cut down on their use of asbestos. Today, asbestos is most often found in:

- Older homes (in building, pipe, and insulation materials)
- Textured paints
- Floor tiles

Asbestos fibers are released into the air when asbestos-containing materials are disturbed. The most dangerous asbestos fibers are too small to see.

What are the health effects from exposure to asbestos?

After asbestos fibers are inhaled, they can remain in the lungs. Asbestos can cause:

- Lung cancer
- Lung scarring (asbestosis)
- Cancer of the chest and stomach lining (mesothelioma)

These health problems may develop many years after exposure.

What can I do to reduce exposure to asbestos?

Asbestos should only be removed by trained professionals. Do not attempt to remove asbestos-containing materials yourself. If asbestos-containing materials are in good condition, it may be safest to leave them alone.

If you think your house may contain asbestos that has been disturbed, contact a trained contractor. A professional may recommend removing the materials or sealing them off to keep fibers out of the air. Call the EPA's Toxic Substances Control Act Hotline at 202-554-1404 to find out if your state has a program to train and certify contractors who specialize in removing asbestos.

What are volatile organic compounds (VOCs), and how can I be exposed to them?

Volatile organic compounds (VOCs) are emitted as gases from certain solids or liquids. VOCs include a variety of chemicals. Many types of household products contain VOCs, including paints, paint strippers, adhesives, cleaners, pesticides, building materials, and office equipment.

What are the health effects from exposure to VOCs?

VOCs may cause eyes, nose, and throat irritation; dizziness and nausea; and memory loss. Some VOCs are more toxic than others. Some of these chemicals can damage the liver, kidneys, or central nervous system or cause cancer. The health effects may depend on the amount and length of exposure.

Some common VOCs that can affect your health are listed below.

- Formaldehyde is a strong-smelling, colorless gas found in some building materials and household products. It can irritate your eyes and respiratory tract, cause nausea, and trigger allergic reactions or asthma attacks. Formaldehyde has also been shown to cause cancer in animals and may cause cancer in humans. Pressed-wood products—commonly used in paneling, shelving, furniture, and cabinets—are major sources of formaldehyde in homes. When these products are new, they release more formaldehyde into the air. Heat and humidity also increase emissions. Smoke from unvented, fuel-burning appliances and tobacco products may also contain formaldehyde.

- Methylene chloride (meth-ih-LEEN KLOR-eyed), found in paint and adhesive removers and aerosol spray paints, is known to cause cancer in animals. Exposure can also cause symptoms similar to carbon monoxide poisoning.

- Benzene (BEN-zeen) is found in secondhand smoke, stored fuels, paint supplies, and car emissions. It is a known carcinogen.

- Perchloroethylene (known as "perc"), used in dry cleaning, has been shown to cause cancer in animals and is likely to be a human carcinogen. It also causes reproductive effects and neurological damage and can harm a developing fetus.

What can I do to reduce exposure to VOCs?

- When using cleaners, painting supplies, and other household chemicals, read the warnings on the label and follow the directions carefully.
- Use products outside or in well-ventilated areas.
- Gases may leak from products stored in closed containers. Store chemicals in well-ventilated areas, out of the reach of children.
- Dispose of old or unneeded products. Some chemicals can contaminate the environment. So it is important to dispose of chemicals properly. Follow the instructions on the label. Contact local government agencies, waste services, or community organizations to find out if there are programs to collect hazardous household chemicals in your area.
- Properly vent garages and fuel-burning appliances so that combustion products do not contaminate indoor air.
- Check the formaldehyde content of pressed-wood products before you buy them. You can also reduce formaldehyde in the air by increasing ventilation, keeping your house cool, and using a dehumidifier.
- Use a dry cleaner that uses alternative cleaners, or make sure your drycleaner properly dries your clothes before returning them. The clothes should not have a strong chemical odor.

What are biological pollutants and how can I be exposed to them?

Biological pollutants include viruses, bacteria, animal dander, cockroach and rodent droppings, dust mites, mold, and mildew.

What are the health effects from exposure to biological pollutants?

These pollutants are small enough to be inhaled and may trigger allergies, asthma, or flu-like symptoms.

What can I do to reduce exposure to biological pollutants?

Many biological pollutants grow well in warm, moist areas. You can reduce moisture in your home by using ventilation fans and dehumidifiers to keep indoor humidity between 30 and 50 percent. Regularly empty and clean evaporation trays in dehumidifiers, refrigerators, and air conditioners. If carpets or building materials become water damaged, they should be thoroughly cleaned and dried or removed to get rid of mold.

You can also reduce biological pollutants by regularly cleaning to remove dust, pet dander, and other allergens.

Workplace environment

How does the environment at work affect my health?

Some occupations and industries involve the use or production of chemicals or substances that may be toxic or hazardous to unprotected workers. Some workers may also carry dangerous substances home on their hands or clothes. To find information about health hazards in the workplace and what you can do to protect yourself from dangerous exposures, visit the Occupational Safety and Health Administration's (OSHA) website or call 800-321-6742.

What is "sick building" syndrome?

"Sick building syndrome" describes a situation in which people spending time in a building experience a range of symptoms that they believe are related to that building. Poor indoor air quality may be the cause of these symptoms. But other factors such as lighting, noise, poorly designed workstations, and psychological and social factors may contribute to sick building syndrome.

Common indoor air pollutants can affect air quality in the workplace, including biological contaminants such as mold and mildew and VOCs from cleaners, adhesives, office machines, furniture, or building materials.

Many office buildings built since the 1970s were designed to maximize energy efficiency by allowing very little outdoor air into the building through windows or ventilation systems. Poor ventilation and heat and air conditioning systems can lead to the buildup of Indoor air pollution.

Symptoms of sick building syndrome may include irritation of the eyes, nose, or throat; dizziness; nausea; headaches; or fatigue. In some cases, the symptoms may appear when you enter the building and go away after you leave. In other cases, the symptoms may continue after exposure.

If you think Indoor air pollution could be causing your health problems, report your concerns. Talk to the employee health nurse or safety officer on your job site. Also, talk with your doctor. The National Institute for Occupational Safety and Health (NIOSH) can give you information on how to have your office tested. Call 800-35-NIOSH. You can also contact the Occupational Safety and Health Administration (OSHA) at 800-321-OSHA (6742).

UV radiation

What is UV radiation?

Sunlight contains ultraviolet (UV) rays, a type of radiation.

What are the health effects of exposure to UV radiation?

Too much exposure to UV radiation can damage your skin and may lead to skin cancer. Sunburns during childhood may increase your chances of developing the most severe form of skin cancer, melanoma, later in life. Overexposure to UV rays can also cause cataracts and weaken your immune system.

How does the ozone layer protect us from UV radiation?

The ozone layer is a naturally occurring concentration of ozone molecules in the upper atmosphere. Unlike ground-level ozone, ozone in the upper atmosphere is not a pollutant and does not damage human health. The ozone layer protects us from harmful UV rays.

The use of synthetic ozone depleting substances (ODS) has reduced ozone levels in the upper atmosphere. These are chemicals that were once used in refrigeration, fire extinguishers, and aerosols. Because the ozone layer is thinner than it used to be, more UV rays reach the Earth's surface, leading to higher rates of skin cancer.

The United States and other countries are working to phase out the use of ODS. Thanks to these efforts, the ozone layer has not become thinner since 1998 and has started to recover. Because ODS can remain in the atmosphere for 50–100 years, scientist predict that ozone will not return to pre-1980 levels until the second half of the 21st century.

Car and home air conditioners and refrigerators may contain ODS. You can help protect the ozone layer by making sure these systems are in good repair and do not leak. Have them serviced by an EPA-certified technician who can recover and recycle the refrigerant. When purchasing new appliances, make sure the refrigerants are not ODS.

What can I do to reduce exposure to UV radiation?

You can prevent overexposure to UV radiation.

- UV radiation levels are highest in the middle of the day. Limit your time outdoors between 10 a.m. and 4 p.m.

- A half hour before spending time outdoors, apply a sunscreen with a sun protection factor (SPF) of at least 15. Follow the package directions and reapply as needed. Even waterproof or water-resistant sunscreens should be reapplied after swimming or sweating.

- Protect your face and neck by wearing a wide-brimmed hat.

- Shield your skin from UV rays by wearing tightly woven, loose-fitting clothing.

- Protect your eyes by wearing sunglasses that block 100 percent of UV rays.

- Avoid sunlamps and tanning beds.

The UV index is a forecast of UV levels in your area. The higher the number, the greater your risk of overexposure to UV radiation. You should take extra precautions to protect yourself and your family when UV levels are very high.

Water contamination

What is water contamination and how can I be exposed to it?

Tap water, well water, and even bottled water may contain small amounts of contaminants such as:

- Bacteria and parasites

- Minerals and metals, such as lead (see section on lead below)

- Sources of radiation, such as radon

- Pesticides

- VOCs

- Disinfectants (cleaning products) and disinfectant byproducts

What are the health effects from exposure to water contamination?

As long as levels of these contaminants are low enough to meet EPA standards, your water is safe to drink. People with weakened immune systems from HIV/AIDS, chemotherapy, or organ transplants may be more sensitive to microbes. Microbes are small organisms such as parasites. Infants and children are also more vulnerable to microbes and other types of water contamination.

What can I do to reduce exposure to water contamination?

The EPA regulates contaminants in public water systems to make sure water is safe to drink. If you get your water from a public system, your water supplier is required to send you an annual report about the quality of your water.

If there is a problem with your drinking water, your water supplier is required to notify you by mail or through newspaper, radio, and television announcements. The supplier should tell you what steps to take to ensure your water is safe to drink.

The EPA does not regulate well water. If you get your water from a private well, you should have your water tested at least once a year.

If you are concerned about your water quality, talk to your doctor about whether you should take additional steps, such as:

- Boiling your water for one minute to kill any microbes
- Filtering your tap water
- Drinking bottled water that has been treated by distillation, reverse osmosis (os-MOHS-iss), UV light, or filtration with an absolute one-micron filter

Should I drink bottled water instead of tap water?

Bottled water is required to meet the same standards as tap water. Both bottled water and tap water are safe to drink if they meet these standards. Bottled water is not necessarily safer than tap water, unless it has been specially treated to remove more contaminants.

If you have a weakened immune system and wish to drink bottled water instead of boiling or filtering your tap water, read bottled water labels or contact bottlers to find out how the water was treated. Look for water that has been treated in one of the following ways:

- Distillation
- Reverse osmosis

- UV light
- Micron filtration with a filter in which the holes are one micron or smaller (absolute one-micron filter)

What are the health effects of fluoride in water?

Many public water systems add fluoride to water to help prevent cavities. According to the Centers for Disease Control and Prevention, water with 0.7–1.2 milligrams/liter (mg/L) of fluoride is safe and effective.

Water may also contain natural fluoride. Some water sources contain more natural fluoride than others. Studies have shown that water with more than 2 mg/L of fluoride may pose health risks, including enamel fluorosis in children under the age of 8. This is staining and pitting of tooth enamel. Studies have also shown an increased risk of bone fractures in people who drink high-fluoride water all their lives.

Contact your water supplier to find out how much fluoride is in your water. Most bottled waters do not contain added fluoride.

Lead

What is lead and how can I be exposed to it?

In the past, lead was commonly used in products such as gasoline and paint. By the 1980s, the use of lead in consumer products was limited or banned in the United States. Today, some common sources of lead are:

- Lead-based paint in houses built before 1978
- Soil and household dust, especially if it is contaminated by chips or dust from lead-based paints
- Water from pipes that contain lead or lead solder

Although the use of lead-based paints in toys was banned in the United States in 1978, other countries may still use paints that contain lead. Paint on imported toys and toys manufactured in the United States before 1978 may pose a risk to children. Lead is also used in some plastic toys. The U.S. Consumer Product Safety Commission issues recalls for toys that may expose children to lead. Visit Consumer Products Safety Commission website or call 800-638-2772 to find information about toys that have been recalled.

73

What are the health effects from exposure to lead?

Lead is a toxic metal that can cause health effects in both adults and children. Infants and children under 6 years old are at the greatest risk of health problems due to lead poisoning. In children, lead can harm the brain and nervous system, causing learning problems and lowered intelligence quotients (IQs). Lead can also harm a developing fetus, so it is important for pregnant women to avoid lead exposure.

Adults exposed to lead may experience health effects such as reproductive problems, high blood pressure, artherosclerosis (ah-thuh-roh-skluh-ROH-suhss), muscle and joint pain, problems with memory or concentration, and decreased cognitive function. Lead is stored in the body in bone. Osteoporosis (oss-tee-oh-puh-RO-sis) causes bones to break down, releasing lead into the blood. After menopause, women are more likely to lose bone mass, increasing the risk of lead exposure. Women who were exposed to high levels of lead earlier in their lives are especially at risk.

Lead is dangerous when it is inhaled or ingested. When lead-based paint is disturbed or removed, it may release fine dust that is dangerous if inhaled. Small children have a high risk of lead exposure because they put so many things in their mouths. Children's lead levels are often highest at age 2.

How can I find out if my children or I have been exposed to lead?

Talk to your doctor about testing you or your children for lead. Children with blood lead levels higher than 10 micrograms per deciliter (μg/dL) are considered to have excess lead exposure. However, studies have shown that lower blood lead levels can affect children's IQs and learning abilities. No level of lead is considered safe for children.

How is lead poisoning treated?

There are medicines that can reduce high levels of lead in the blood. But treatments cannot reverse damage caused by lead poisoning. This is why it is important to prevent exposure to lead.

What can I do to reduce exposure to lead?

You can have your home tested for lead. This is especially important if your home was built before 1978 and if the paint is flaking, chipping, or cracking. If lead-based paint is in good condition, it may not be hazardous. If you plan to remove lead paint or perform other renovations, hire a contractor specially trained to deal with lead paint. You should leave the house until renovations are completed and the house is cleaned to remove any lead dust. The National Lead Information Center at 800-424-LEAD (5323) can provide information about professionals in your area who are trained in lead testing and removal.

Lead may be present in the water service lines or plumbing of older homes. Contact your local health department to find out if you should be concerned about lead in your drinking water. Boiling water will not remove lead. However, you can take steps to reduce the amount of lead in your drinking water.

- Never use hot water from the faucet to make baby formula or for cooking.
- Run cold water for at least a minute before using it.
- Use a water filter certified by NSF International to remove lead.

You can take other steps to prevent you or your children from being exposed to lead:

- Keep areas where children play as dust-free and clean as you can.
- Mop floors and wipe window ledges and frames weekly.
- Wash children's hands and things children put in their mouths—bottles, pacifiers, and toys—often.
- Prevent children from eating dirt or paint chips and from chewing on painted surfaces such as windowsills.
- Serve meals high in iron and calcium; these nutrients block the absorption of lead.

Mercury

What is mercury and how can I be exposed to it?

Mercury (MERK-yoor-ee) is a toxic metal found in many types of rock, including coal. When coal is burned, mercury is released into the air. Coal-fired power plants are a major source of mercury emissions in the United States. This mercury makes its way into lakes, rivers, and oceans, where microorganisms convert it into methylmercury (meth-ihl MERK-yoor-ee). Microorganisms are very small and can only be seen with a microscope. Fish eat these microorganisms, and the methylmercury becomes concentrated in the bodies of fish and shellfish. Eating fish and shellfish is the main way humans are exposed to this toxin.

What are the health effects from exposure to mercury?

Children, infants, and unborn babies are most sensitive to mercury. High levels can damage the developing nervous system. In both children and adults, high levels of mercury may affect the brain, heart, kidneys, lungs, and immune system.

Is it safe to eat fish?

Fish and shellfish contain protein, omega-3 fatty acids, and other nutrients that have important health benefits. However, small amounts of mercury are found in most types of fish and shellfish. Different kinds of fish contain different amounts, depending on how long they live and what they eat. Choosing fish low in mercury can help you limit your mercury exposure. This is especially important for pregnant women and young children.

What can I do to reduce exposure to mercury?

You can limit the amount of mercury consumed from fish. The EPA and the U.S. Food and Drug Administration (FDA) recommend that women who may become pregnant, women who are pregnant or nursing, and young children follow these guidelines:

- Don't eat shark, swordfish, king mackerel, or tilefish. These fish are high in mercury.

- Limit your consumption of fish low in mercury to 12 ounces—or about 2 meals—each week. Fish that are low in mercury include shrimp, canned light tuna, salmon, pollock, and catfish.

- Limit your consumption of albacore (white) tuna to 6 ounces or 1 meal each week. Albacore tuna contains higher levels of mercury than canned light tuna.

- Before eating fish caught in your area, check local fish safety advisories. If you can't find information about the safety of local fish, eat no more than 6 ounces a week and do not eat any other fish that week.

Pesticides

What are pesticides and how can I be exposed to them?

Pesticides (PESS-tih-syds) are chemicals used to kill pests such as insects, rodents, weeds, mold, and bacteria. Yet these chemicals can also cause health problems in people.

What are the health effects from exposure to pesticides?

Health effects will depend on the type of pesticide, the amount of exposure, and the frequency of exposure. These health effects may include birth defects, nerve damage, and cancer. Health problems might not appear until many years after exposure.

Pesticides pose greater health risks for children than adults because children's organs are still developing, they eat more food relative to their body weight, and they are more likely to put contaminated objects in their mouths.

What can I do to reduce exposure to pesticides?

First, the EPA limits the amount of pesticides that may be used to grow food and may remain on food sold to consumers.

You can also take steps to limit your exposure to pesticides from food.

- Reduce the pesticides on your fruits and vegetables by washing and scrubbing them under running water, peeling off the skin, and trimming outer leaves.

- In meat, pesticide chemicals may be stored in fat. Trimming the fat can reduce your exposure.

- You can choose organic foods, which are grown without the use of synthetic pesticides. You can find more information about organic foods at the National Organic Program website.

- Eating a variety of foods can prevent high levels of exposure to a single pesticide.

It is important to use care when using pesticides in and around your home.

- Be sure to read all labels and warnings before using a pesticide. Follow the instructions carefully.

- Only use the recommended amount.

- Store and dispose of unused pesticides safely.

- Before using pesticides, remove children and pets from the area.

- Keep pesticides out of reach of children, preferably in cabinets or sheds with locks or child-proof latches.

- If someone is exposed to pesticides and still conscious, having trouble breathing, or having convulsions, contact the National Poison Control Center at 800-222-1112. In case of emergency, call 911 or your local emergency service first.

You can also reduce your pesticide use by preventing pest infestations and controlling pests with methods other than pesticides.

- Take steps to prevent infestations inside and outside. This includes removing water or food that may attract pests, destroying areas where pests may hide or breed, and sealing entry holes.

- Use biological methods to control pests, such as attracting birds and bats to eat insects.

- Use manual pest control methods, like pulling weeds or setting traps.

- Consider natural pesticides that do not contain synthetic chemicals.

If you hire a pest control company, make sure they inspect your home, let you know which chemicals they will use, and address your safety concerns before you sign a contract.

Environmental hormones

What are environmental hormones and how can I be exposed to them?

Environmental hormones are also called endocrine disruptors. These are chemicals that can act like or interfere with natural hormones in the human body.

What are the health effects from exposure to environmental hormones?

These chemicals can reduce fertility. They may also play a role in the development of cancers and reproductive disorders like endometriosis. In infants and fetuses, environmental hormones can also affect the developing reproductive and nervous systems and organs.

Some common environmental hormones known to affect human health are:

- Dichloro-diphenyl-trichloroethane (DDT), a pesticide now banned in the United States, and some other pesticides.

- Polychlorinated biphenyls (PCBs), chemicals that are banned for most uses in the United States but remain in soil and water.

- Diethylstilbestrol (DES), a drug used to prevent miscarriages until it was banned in the 1970s. Some daughters of women who took DES have developed reproductive problems and vaginal and cervical cancer.

- Phthalates (THAL-ayts) and bisphenol A (BPA), endocrine disruptors commonly used in plastics. Research suggests these chemicals may affect fetal development. Scientists are still studying these substances in order to understand their impacts on human health.

What can I do to reduce exposure to environmental hormones?

Researchers are studying the health effects of known and suspected environmental hormones. They are developing ways to prevent too much exposure to these chemicals. The following steps may reduce your exposure to environmental hormones:

- Take steps to minimize your exposure to pesticides.

- Public water systems are required to test water for PCBs and notify you if dangerous levels are present in your water. If you have a private well, have your water tested

- Boiling, microwaving, or using the dishwasher to clean hard plastic plates, bottles, or other food containers may cause BPA to be released, increasing your risk of exposure. Discard any item that has small cracks on its surface.

- Because infants are most likely to be sensitive to BPA, parents can take steps such as using:

  - BPA-free plastic bottles and training cups

  - Glass bottles

  - Bottles with BPA-free plastic liners

  - Microwave-safe glass or paper dishes covered with paper towels in the microwave

- Some plastic medical devices may expose people to phthalates. The FDA recommends that phthalate-free equipment be used in certain medical procedures, when possible. Animal studies suggest that phthalates may affect the development of the male reproductive system, so this is especially important for women who are pregnant or breastfeeding, male infants, and male children who are near the age of puberty.

• Since 1999, U.S. manufacturers have not used phthalates in toys infants put in their mouths, such as pacifiers and teethers. The State of California banned the sale of toys and baby products containing phthalates, starting in 2009.

Chapter 6

Environmental Hazards for the Elderly

Demographic Factors that Influence the Vulnerability of Older Adults

Changes in climate during this century will be superimposed on a dramatic shift in the age distribution of Americans (with significant increases among the old and the very old), their geographic distribution, socioeconomic status, and other demographic changes.

Who are older adults? Older adults in the United States are a diverse group. Distinct subpopulations can be identified by age, race/ethnicity, socioeconomic status, degree of community and family support, general health, level of disability, and other characteristics. Older adults are expected to differ by birth cohorts, with today's older adults and those of the future likely to vary in important ways. For example, the percentage of older Americans with at least a high school education is increasing even as the percentage of those living in poverty is decreasing. If these trends continue, they could lead to significant differences in relative vulnerability between the older adults of 2040 and the current elderly population.

Text in this chapter is excerpted from "Climate Change and Older Americans: State of the Science," Environmental Health Perspectives (EHP), January 2013.

America's shifting age distribution. The older adult population in the United States is increasing dramatically (Figure 6.1). In 2009, approximately 39.5 million Americans were ≥ 65 years of age (the old); the projected population of older Americans in 2050 is 88.5 million, 19 million of whom will be ≥ 85 years of age (the very old). Older adults currently account for about 13% of America's population, but are projected to account for 20% by 2040. The projected population shift is attributable in part to the aging of the baby boom generation, as well as increases in longevity and survivorship among older Americans, and is particularly apparent in the projected increase among the very old, those ≥ 85 years of age.

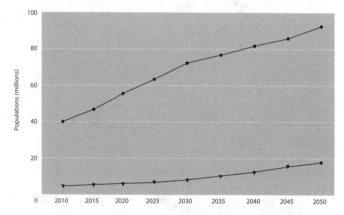

Figure 6.1. *Projected population of older adults, 2010–2050. Data from U.S. Census Bureau (2008). Projected population of older adults, 2010–2050. Data from U.S. Census Bureau (2008).*

Geographic distribution of older Americans. Some locations with growing older adult populations are likely to be increasingly affected by climate stressors, such as hurricanes, droughts, floods, infectious disease, and rising summer temperatures. Zimmerman et al. (2007) reported that more than half of the older adult population was concentrated in 170 counties (5% of all counties) in 2005. Moreover, about 20% of older Americans resided in a county where a hurricane or tropical storm was likely to make landfall over the 10-year period from 1995 through 2005. There also appeared to be a higher concentration of low-income older adults in at-risk locations.

In 2008, 51.2% of Americans ≥ 65 years of age lived in just nine states, with California, Florida, New York, Texas, and Pennsylvania accounting for the top five. These states could be especially hard hit by changing patterns of precipitation and storms. An increase in the severity of tropical storms and hurricanes could pose particular risks in Florida, where storms have historically resulted in significant property damage, injuries, and lives lost. In 2000, Florida had an older adult population of 16.8%, nearly 4% higher than the national average.

If current settlement patterns continue, future populations of older Americans will increase significantly in the Southwest and Southeast, along parts of the Atlantic and Gulf coasts, and in cities of the Northeast and Midwest that are expected to experience more frequent extreme heat events. To the extent that they are not physiologically or behaviorally adapted to high ambient temperatures, older Americans in northern cities may be particularly vulnerable to heat waves.

Other geographic factors influence the degree to which older adults are affected by climate change. Urban location is considered a risk factor for vulnerability to climate stressors, due in part to the exacerbation of summer heat by the urban heat island effect (a term that describes the relative warming of urban areas compared with their rural surroundings due to the replacement of open land and vegetation with buildings, roads, and other dark or impermeable surfaces). Other geographic risk factors include urban sprawl, characteristics of the built environment, and perceptions of neighborhood safety.

Physiological Factors that Influence the Sensitivity of Older Adults to Climate Stressors

Although many adults remain healthy and active long into their later years, old age is generally accompanied by an increased risk of certain diseases and disorders, along with changes in social factors such as increased social isolation and income loss. In this section we describe physical impairments that have been identified by multiple studies as risk factors affecting the sensitivity of older adults to climate stressors. "Sensitivity" refers to an individual's or subpopulation's responsiveness, primarily for biological reasons, to a given exposure. Although these risk factors are not confined to older adults, they may be more prevalent in the elderly as compared to the general population.

Some physiological limitations are functions of the normal aging process, but climate change may aggravate some impairments. For example, early-life exposure to air pollution (e.g., ground-level ozone) may increase the risk of respiratory and cardiovascular disorders with age. Similarly, early-life exposure to environmental toxicants whose concentrations may be affected by climate change (e.g., flood-related contaminants in drinking water) may leave affected individuals with compromised immune systems that increase their sensitivity to climate stressors in later life. Aging itself is frequently accompanied by medical conditions that may aggravate susceptibility to infectious diseases.

Respiratory impairments. Because climate change can lead to increases in ground-level ozone and higher atmospheric concentrations of fine particulates, such as dust and allergenic pollen, in drought-prone areas individuals with respiratory impairments may be more at risk. Declines in respiratory function frequently accompany aging. Older adults may be more sensitive than the general population to adverse health effects from air pollutants and airborne pathogens and allergens. Even in the absence of disease, the lungs of older adults undergo physiological changes with age that can impair breathing.

Sensitivity to ozone varies with age and can affect lung function even in healthy older adults. Studies have documented associations between acute exposure to ambient ozone and increased risk of death, as well as an increased number of emergency room visits and hospital admissions among older adults. Air pollution can exacerbate asthma and COPD, and exposure to ozone and other criteria pollutants can also increase risk of heart attack among people with diabetes, persons who are obese, and nonsmoking older adults (possibly because fine particles may penetrate the healthy lungs of nonsmokers more easily than those of smokers).

Impairments associated with diabetes. In 2009, 19.9% of older Americans 65–74 years of age had diabetes, up from 9.1% in 1980. Age-adjusted death rates for diabetes have increased among older Americans by 29% since 1981. One study projects that the prevalence of diabetes in America could double by 2050, due in part to the aging of the U.S. population. Individuals with diabetes are at higher risk for heat-related morbidity and mortality than the general population.

Cardiovascular and thermoregulatory impairments and heat sensitivity. In 2008, 31.9% of older Americans reported having heart disease, and 55.7% reported having hypertension. Cardiovascular impairment can make older adults more sensitive to health complications from warmer summers, heat waves, and air pollution. In addition, aging can impair the mechanisms that control body temperature. This effect may be exacerbated by certain illnesses and medications, such as some psychotropic drugs and cardiac medications, that can compromise thermoregulatory capacity.

Climate Stressors and the Vulnerability of Older Adults

Older adults are among the most vulnerable in the general population to the direct impacts of weather-related natural disasters. Below, we summarize climate stressors that may disproportionately affect older adults. Some of these impacts will also affect the general population, but, where indicated, older adults are expected to be more vulnerable (i.e., more sensitive and/or more highly exposed and/or less able to adapt).

Extreme heat. Climate models project that extreme heat events will become more frequent and intense and of longer duration in the decades ahead, especially in the higher latitudes, affecting large metropolitan areas in the Northeast and Midwest where populations are less well adapted. Extreme heat events are a major source of climate-related risk for older adults, with older Americans experiencing disproportionate risks of heat-related mortality. Other health outcomes from extreme heat events include heat exhaustion, heat stroke, dehydration, acute renal failure and nephritis, exacerbation of cardiopulmonary diseases, and potential aggravation of side effects of some medications such as beta blockers used to control blood pressure, some psychotropic medications, and certain drugs used to treat chronic obstructive pulmonary disease (COPD).

Between 1979 and 2004, 5,279 heat-related deaths were reported in the United States, occurring disproportionately among older adults. Heat stroke occurs at rates that are 12–23 times higher in persons ≥ 65 years of age compared with other age groups. Because of a lack of a clear case definition and the multiple factors that contribute to heat-related mortality, heat-related deaths may be underreported.

In the case of extreme temperature events, our focus is on extreme heat. But climate change may also decrease the frequency of extremely cold periods. Older Americans may benefit from warmer winters, both in terms of reduced heating costs as well as reductions in health and safety risks associated with cold weather.

Hurricanes, floods, droughts, and other extreme weather events. Climate change is likely to contribute to an increase in hurricane intensity and precipitation, as well as increases in the frequency of other extreme weather events in the United States that may disproportionately affect older adults. Nearly 60% of the flooding-related fatalities following Hurricane Katrina were among persons ≥ 65 years of age. A rapid needs assessment of older adults in Florida found that Hurricane Charley, a category 4 storm that struck in 2004, aggravated preexisting, physician-diagnosed medical conditions in 24–32% of elderly households.

Apart from the obvious risks of direct physical injury or death, extreme weather events may lead to a range of secondary health impacts including those that affect the availability and safety of food and water; interruptions in communications, utilities, and health care services; and increased risk of wildfires after drought. Hurricanes and other severe weather events may also lead to mental or emotional trauma before, during, and following the event. Analyses of pre- and post-disaster cognitive status showed decreases in working memory for middle-aged and older adults. Nursing home residents and staff have been found to have mental health needs even 5 months after a hurricane. Studies have found flood exposure to be related to health decrements in older adults, with the persistence and extent of adverse health effects positively related to flood intensity and duration.

The enduring impacts of extreme events can be significant. For example, flooding can result in contamination of drinking-water supplies, increased incidence of indoor mold and associated respiratory illnesses, and long-term relocation and property loss among affected populations. Extreme events can also compromise health care services and social support systems.

Finally, the need to evacuate a region ahead of approaching severe weather can also pose health and safety risks for older adults. In particular, logistical issues can hamper the safe evacuation of long-term care facilities. In addition to the challenge of securing appropriate transportation, the evacuating facility must ensure that the receiving facility can manage patients' needs. The demographics of the population to be evacuated helps determine the resources required. Successfully moving individuals from nursing and assisted-living facilities to a sheltering facility requires the transfer of essential patient information and resources, including medical records, medications, and medical equipment. This process was particularly problematic and poorly coordinated during the evacuation for Hurricane Katrina. During Hurricane Rita in 2005, a bus evacuating elderly nursing home residents from Houston to Dallas was involved in an accident that killed 24 people.

Climate impacts on air quality. Climate change can affect air quality by increasing the formation of ground-level ozone and by leading to higher atmospheric concentrations of fine particulates, allergens, and dust in drought-prone areas. These effects, though not restricted to older adults, are typically more severe due to preexisting medical conditions.

Assuming precursor emissions are held constant, ozone concentrations are expected to increase in the United States as a result of climate change. Higher levels of ground-level ozone can exacerbate cardiopulmonary illnesses, especially asthma and COPD and premature mortality from these diseases. Ozone injures lung tissue and promotes airway inflammation, and may have a stronger effect on respiratory disorders than on cardiovascular disease.

The changing climate has led to earlier onset of and increases in the seasonal production of allergenic pollen in middle and high latitudes in the Northern Hemisphere. Higher concentrations of atmospheric carbon dioxide may also increase pollen production in ragweed, prolong the pollen season, and increase some plant metabolites that affect allergenicity. Higher temperatures are associated with longer ragweed pollen seasons across a broad swath of midwestern states from Texas to the Canadian border.

Climate change may also lead to increases in the amount of airborne dust being transported across the Atlantic Ocean from the Sahara Desert to the Caribbean Sea. Older adults living in areas where drought has increased in frequency and/or severity may also be at greater risk because exposure to dust can exacerbate existing respiratory illnesses.

Impacts on infectious diseases. Through its impacts on natural systems, climate change can facilitate the spread or emergence of vector-borne, waterborne, and foodborne diseases in areas where they had been limited or had not existed previously. At the same time, climate change may create conditions that are inhospitable for a vector or pathogen, causing related diseases to moderate or to disappear altogether.

The abundance and distribution of some infectious disease vectors (e.g., fleas, mosquitoes, and ticks) may be affected by climate change. For example, in North America an increase in the abundance and range of deer ticks and a loss of biodiversity among animal hosts important in the disease transmission chain, could alter the prevalence of Lyme disease. If the public health infrastructure is maintained or improved, such diseases are unlikely to cause major epidemics in the United States. Nevertheless, to the extent that older adults are more likely to have compromised immune systems, vector-borne diseases may pose a greater risk.

The incidence of waterborne and foodborne illnesses can be affected by increased flooding (e.g., through contamination of food crops by flood waters and contamination of drinking water from combined sewer overflow and agricultural runoff) and other stressors associated with climate change (e.g., warmer temperatures, which may enhance bacterial growth). Although the outcome of many gastrointestinal diseases is mild and self-limiting, these diseases can be severe and even fatal among vulnerable populations, including young children, those with compromised immune systems, and older adults. In a 1985 study, children 1–4 years of age and adults > 60 years each made up about 25% of hospitalizations involving gastroenteritis, but older adults represented 85% of the associated deaths.

Factors Determining Exposure to Climate Stressors

Several factors affect the degree to which older Americans will be exposed to climate stressors; these include socioeconomic characteristics, housing characteristics, adequacy of neighborhood infrastructure, and availability of social services.

Variations in socioeconomic factors in relation to climate threats. Socioeconomic characteristics, such as income level, access to social and health services, and level of education, can influence the risk of exposure and the capacity to adapt. Older adults living in poverty or on fixed incomes may experience greater exposure to the effects of warmer summers and heat waves (e.g., due to lack of air conditioning or the reluctance to use it because of operating costs), along with other extreme weather events (e.g., due to substandard housing). Higher mortality from heat waves has been associated with poverty and lack of a high school education. Failing to complete high school is a proxy both for lower income and literacy rates, because the latter may predict the success of risk communication. The median income of older Americans in 2008 was $29,744, compared with $56,791 for Americans < 65 years of age. Almost 3.7 million older Americans (9.7% of the older adult population) were below the official poverty level in 2008. Another 2.4 million (6.3%) were classified as "near-poor" (income between the poverty level and 125% of poverty level). A supplemental poverty measure developed by the Census Bureau in 2011 shows a greater percentage of older Americans in poverty (12.7%) compared with the official 2010 measure. Data on long-term trends, based on this 2011 measure, are not yet available.

A larger proportion of older women, compared with older men, live below the poverty level in the United States. In 2010, 10.7% of American women ≥ 65 years of age lived in poverty, compared with 6.7% of men of that age. The disparity is even greater among Americans ≥ 75 years of age: 12.1% of women in that age group were living in poverty in 2010, compared with 7.5% of men.

Local or housing-related exposure considerations. Depending on its condition, quality of construction, and amenities, housing can increase or decrease exposure and reduce or exacerbate the occupants' risk of injury and illness from climate-related impacts. Manufactured or mobile homes are especially vulnerable to high winds and other storm damage. Lack of access to air conditioning and homes with fewer rooms are significant risk factors for heat-related mortality. Often, older adults on fixed incomes can ill afford the costs of cooling their homes. In deteriorating urban neighborhoods, where safety and crime are at issue, some older residents may live in a state of "self-imposed house arrest" that may prevent them from seeking needed help in their communities.

Adequacy of infrastructure. The condition of infrastructure, including utilities (e.g., telephone, gas, and electricity) and transportation, plays a vital role in determining exposure of older adults. Dramatic increases in electricity demand during heat waves can lead to brownouts or blackouts, as experienced during the Chicago, Illinois, heat wave in 1995. Interruptions in power can affect even those who are financially able to cool their homes. In addition, a lack of access to transportation can hinder evacuation during extreme weather events. Many older adults rely on public transportation. The existence, availability, adequacy, and resilience of public transportation systems will help to determine exposure.

Availability of social services. The availability of social services can affect older Americans' exposure to climate stressors. Social services originate from multiple sources, including local community organizations, neighborhood associations, aid distribution centers, assisted-living facilities, hospitals, home-care providers, and government agencies. A lack of community-based financial resources can affect the quality and provision of services. Without adequate support, existing social services may be overwhelmed by the needs of older adults—as in the 1995 Chicago heat wave, when too few ambulances and emergency personnel were available to meet demands.

Determinants of Older Adults' Adaptive Capacity

In this section we describe some of the key physiological and social factors, identified across multiple studies, that affect the degree to which older Americans—and the communities and services they depend on—can adapt to climate stressors. Adaptive capacity, together with sensitivity and exposure, collectively determine vulnerability.

Functional limitations and mobility impairments. Functional limitations—such as a decline in muscle strength, coordination, or cognitive function due to illness, chronic disease, or injury—may reduce older adults' ability to respond effectively to climate stressors. In 2007, 42% of people ≥ 65 years of age reported one or more functional limitations. In contrast, about 19% of the general population in 2005 reported a functional limitation. The prevalence of functional limitations varies by sex and age. Older women experience a higher rate of functional limitation (47%) than do older men (35%). The disparity in rates has been attributed to the fact that women tend to live longer than men, have higher rates of co-morbidity, and have higher rates of chronic health conditions such as arthritis, depression, and Alzheimer's disease. Dementia in the United States increases from an estimated 5% of the population at 71–79 years of age to 37% at ≥ 90 years. Other cognitive impairments increase from 16% at 71–79 years of age to 39% at ≥ 90 years.

Many older adults suffer from impaired balance and decreased motor strength. Osteoporosis, a condition of compromised bone strength that increases the risk of fracture in affected individuals, is highly associated with aging. In an extreme weather event, wildfire, or flood, it may be more difficult for victims with mobility impairments to respond, to evacuate (if necessary), and to recover. The risk of injury or death during or after evacuation is highest among older adults.

Economic status. Another determinant of adaptive capacity is the older adult's ability to financially support the implementation of response measures. Poverty is a primary contributor to social vulnerability. Older adults can also be more vulnerable to property damage or loss due to lack of insurance, limited personal finances, and poor credit-worthiness. Older adults may lack the financial resources to prepare for or respond to climate-related risks. Similarly, the economic vitality of a community may determine its ability to support effective hazard mitigation and disaster recovery. In sum, economically disadvantaged seniors living in disadvantaged communities have fewer resources available to support adaptation.

Racial and ethnic disparities contribute to the susceptibility of older Americans to climate change. A disproportionate percentage of some minorities live in poverty. A study of heat-related vulnerability in 50 U.S. cities identified several subpopulations as especially vulnerable to extreme heat, including African Americans, people with diabetes, and economically disadvantaged individuals. Older adults in these subpopulations have been linked to poorer health status in general, limited access to health care, and poorer housing conditions.

Because many older adults live on fixed incomes, they may be especially affected by increases in costs for energy, food, and out-of-pocket medical expenses—all of which may be aggravated by climate change. Food accounts for about 12–13% of older Americans' annual household expenditures. Since 1985, about one-third of older Americans reported expenditures on housing and utilities that exceeded 30% of household income. Out-of-pocket expenses for medical care among older Americans increased by 61% from 1999 to 2009; health care accounted for 12.9% of total expenditures among older Americans in 2009, compared with 6.4% for all consumers.

Living situation. A person's living situation has an impact on his or her adaptive capacity. With the rise of managed care, many older Americans with impairments, who previously might have been institutionalized, are now cared for at home. During or following a disaster, it may be difficult for first responders to identify, locate, and reach these dispersed populations.

Social isolation may affect the adaptive capacity of older adults to certain climate stressors. Isolation has been identified as a key risk factor for death during extreme heat events. Older adults living in isolation, especially those with cognitive impairments or mental illnesses, may not receive emergency information or may underestimate the severity or urgency of warnings. One post–Hurricane Katrina study of older adults found that although > 75% of the study group listened to news and evacuation advisories before the landfall of Hurricane Katrina, one-third of them said they might not or definitely would not evacuate.

Older Americans living alone may also be at higher risk for abuse from frauds or scams relating to home improvements or repairs before or after extreme weather events. They are also more likely to be disadvantaged in terms of their ability to evacuate because of a disability, limited income, or lack of transportation. About 30.5% of all noninstitutionalized older Americans in 2008 lived alone; 50% of women ≥ 75 years of age lived alone. In contrast, about 26% of the general U.S. population lives alone. Although 93.5% of older Americans live in the community, only 4.5% live in nursing homes and 2% live in assisted living facilities.

Technology. Communication tools and technologies, especially access to the Internet and social media, are important for transmitting key information before, during, and after extreme weather events. The availability and effectiveness of these technologies, as well as technologies and systems for rapid identification of at-risk older adults, can contribute to adaptive capacity. In situations where climate-induced pollution or climate-exacerbated diseases could affect older adults, the status, availability, and cost of preventive technologies may influence adaptive capacity.

Infrastructure. The nature and age of housing stock can affect adaptive capacity, as can other characteristics of the built environment such as urbanization, economic vitality, and development. Decaying commercial infrastructure and overall community decline were positively correlated with higher levels of heat-related mortality in the 1995 Chicago heat wave. For frail members of the older adult population who depend on life support systems, such as oxygen generators, ventilators, or electric wheelchairs, reliable electricity generation and transmission systems are crucial. In multistory residential buildings, loss of electricity disrupts the operation of elevators, which makes it more difficult, if not impossible, for older adults to obtain food, medications, and other supportive services. Power outages can also affect the availability of telephone service, pumped water in high-rise buildings, and public transit.

Human and social capital and adaptive behaviors. An active and diverse community contributes to its members' well-being. During the Chicago heat wave, older residents may have felt more at ease accessing services in neighborhoods that were more socially and commercially vibrant. Areas with larger concentrations of older adults in the population tend to have lower mortality rates, possibly due to the benefits of a shared social support network. Race and ethnicity may determine social vulnerability through the lack of access to economic and social support resources, cultural differences, and marginalization of minority communities. In their Social Vulnerability Index, Cutter et al. (2003) specifically identify African-American race, in addition to old age, as indicators of reduced adaptive capacity.

Interacting effects. Factors affecting adaptive capacity rarely act alone. Multiple factors interact to determine the adaptive capacity of older adults to climate stressors. For example, low socioeconomic status and lack of knowledge of or access to supportive institutions can combine to effectively prevent older Americans from navigating complex procedures required to obtain assistance (e.g., financial aid and social services) following a natural disaster. This situation may be more common among widows or widowers who live alone and have limited experience in obtaining assistance because such tasks had previously been managed by their spouse. Adaptive capacity depends not only on available resources, but also on effective risk communication.

Reducing Vulnerability through Effective Adaptation

In this section we identify some of the adaptation measures that can be put in place to decrease older Americans' vulnerability to climate extremes. These measures are based partly on prior experiences in responding to extreme weather events and disease outbreaks. More research is needed to document the relative effectiveness of adaptation measures and to identify and disseminate best practices.

Information and education. To successfully direct resources toward vulnerable individuals, registries of older adults and technological tools (such as geographic information systems) for quickly identifying them may be useful. Key indicators of vulnerability and preparedness may also be combined with surveillance data on older adult populations to inform prevention and preparedness strategies. While authorities and supporting organizations need to know the location and condition of older adults, individuals need access to the knowledge and tools necessary to protect and support themselves during and after extreme weather events. Television, Internet, radio, and newspaper alerts can be used to inform the population about heat waves and other impending events, explain the dangers, identify at-risk groups, and discuss prevention or response measures (e.g., emergency hotlines).

Community capabilities. Adaptations that strengthen communities' response to climate stressors can be accomplished in a number of ways. Some impacts can be ameliorated through physical design changes in neighborhoods or through early warning systems. Policy makers and planners should focus on tailoring specific local responses to optimize the use of available community resources. For instance, to reduce heat-related illness and mortality, communities can develop early warning and response or other surveillance systems. Community nurses and home health workers could reduce the risk of heat illness by educating patients about their vulnerability to heat. Local government agencies could distribute air conditioners or subsidize air conditioner use among vulnerable populations, although the distribution of electric fans is contraindicated, because the circulation of warm air in enclosed indoor spaces may actually increase heat stress. Persons with special medical needs could be encouraged to register with their local emergency management agency to ensure that they will receive necessary services or evacuation assistance. The effectiveness of communications can be strengthened by applying knowledge gained from similar efforts in other communities and by coordinating service providers. The principles of communication, effective emergency response planning and coordination, and targeted services are common themes across all effective adaptations to climate-related stressors.

Tools and measures to improve adaptation and lessen vulnerability. To understand and characterize vulnerability, Cutter et al. (2003) developed a Social Vulnerability Index that assesses the level of resilience to hazard events for U.S. communities, using county-level socioeconomic and demographic data. Similarly, Wilson et al. (2010) and Vescovi et al. (2005) proposed map-based climate change vulnerability indices. Vulnerability mapping can help planners, emergency managers, and first responders locate vulnerable individuals. To further aid prioritization and response, authorities can use rapid assessment tools to identify who needs help, how urgently, and the best course of action. For example, to reduce the urban heat island effect, planners and developers could implement preemptive strategies (e.g., planting trees and other vegetation, installing green roofs, and utilizing light-colored pavements). These measures may provide multiple benefits, because reducing urban temperatures will reduce energy costs and improve air quality.

A wide range of tools and resources exist to help public health and emergency management officials to protect older Americans from hazards related to climate change. Educational materials and disaster checklists can be developed for distribution to older Americans, their families, and caregivers through social networks, community-based services, faith-based organizations, and health care providers.

Key Findings

There is strong evidence that older Americans will be more vulnerable than the general population to climate stressors. In light of the projected increase in the population of older Americans and the fact that much of that population is concentrated in regions likely to experience significant impacts from climate change, research to identify vulnerabilities and develop strategies to improve the resilience of older adults and their communities should be a priority. Key findings of this review include the following:

Demographics. Older Americans are a diverse and rapidly growing population. The number of older adults in the United States is expected to nearly double over the next 25 years. The physiological and social characteristics of older adults vary widely by age group, living situation, income, and other demographic features. Location matters—many older Americans live in regions that could be hard hit by extreme events associated with climate change.

Primary climate stressors. In the absence of effective adaptation, climate change is likely to disproportionately affect older adults. Projected climate stressors to which older adults are particularly sensitive due to biologic traits include extreme heat and other extreme weather events, degraded air quality, and increases in the risk of infectious diseases. Some of these impacts are projected to occur in places where older adults are heavily concentrated and likely to be most exposed. This confluence of sensitivity, exposure, and adaptive capacity determines older adults' overall vulnerability to climate change.

Factors affecting exposure. Exposure is determined by local and individual factors. The quality and adequacy of buildings and infrastructure, as well as the availability of social services and community support networks, affect the degree to which older adults are likely to be exposed.

Determinants of adaptive capacity. Socioeconomic status and community resources strongly influence adaptive capacity and resilience. Financial resources allow communities to invest in effective technologies and infrastructure, provide social services, build strong institutions, and support vibrant and safe neighborhoods.

Measures to reduce vulnerability. Building capacity at both the community and individual levels is essential. Developing early warning, response, and surveillance systems, coupled with planning and development to enhance community resilience, can reduce the vulnerability of older adults and help them avoid or mitigate the impacts of climate stressors.

Research gaps. A rich store of demographic data is available on older Americans. The vulnerability of older adults to two climate stressors—extreme heat events and hurricanes—has been widely reported. Less information is available on the vulnerability of older adults to other health-related climate impacts, such as river flooding, coastal flooding from sea level rise, droughts, wildfires, changes in air quality, and contaminated food and water supplies. More research is needed to identify and develop strategies for reducing the vulnerability of older adults to climate change, and for helping them prepare for and respond to emerging threats. Assessments of health impacts from climate change have not always included age-specific analyses. Improved consistency in this regard would draw attention to vulnerable subpopulations.

In addition, it would be useful to develop indicators (at local and regional scales) of older Americans' overall vulnerability to the effects of climate change. Such indicators might include income, sex, rural or urban residence, owner-occupied home, infrastructure, education, population change, family structure/living alone, available health and social services, and special-needs populations. These indicators could help to identify locations and populations that could be targeted for capacity-building and communication strategies to reduce vulnerability. Indicators can also be used to document changes across place and time, monitor vulnerable areas, and evaluate the effectiveness of adaptation strategies.

Conclusions

Climate change will increase the exposure of a growing population of older Americans to a range of climate-related hazards. This increased exposure is of concern because older Americans are more sensitive than the general population to certain health impacts and generally have less capacity to adapt to climate stressors. The combination of these factors—exposure, sensitivity, and adaptive capacity—determines vulnerability.

More work is needed to understand the risks posed by climate change on older adults, and to communicate those risks to decision makers, public health and safety officials, and caregivers and advocates of aging populations. Public agencies can partner with nongovernmental organizations that work with older Americans to leverage communication efforts. More work is needed to develop adaptation strategies that reduce the vulnerability of older Americans to climate stressors. Given the projected growth of the older adult population, the U.S. health care system and other community services will be challenged to meet the growing demands by older adults caused by more frequent and more intense climate-related weather extremes. In the near term, it may be possible to build on and adapt some of the response strategies and communication approaches developed for heat waves and hurricanes to the broader set of climate change impacts.

Chapter 7

Environmental Justice

Environmental Justice Analysis

Environmental justice (EJ) is the fair treatment and meaningful involvement of all people regardless of race, color, national origin, or income with respect to the development, implementation, and enforcement of environmental laws, regulations, and policies. Recognizing that some populations experience higher levels of risk, Executive Order 12898, "Federal Actions to Address Environmental Justice in Minority Populations and Low-Income Populations," directs federal agencies to identify and address disproportionately high adverse human health or environmental effects on minority and low-income populations that may result from their programs, policies, and activities. The development of the environmental justice movement has precipitated a great deal of research on the racial and socioeconomic disparities in exposure to environmental health risks. These studies, often referred to as EJ analyses, evaluate risks and may also attempt to address them using other sustainability tools, such as collaborative problem-solving, and design charrettes, among others.

This chapter includes excerpts from "Environmental Justice Analysis," United States Environmental Protection Agency (EPA), June 25, 2014; and text from "CDC Health Disparities and Inequalities Report—United States, 2011," Centers for Disease Control and Prevention (CDC), January 14, 2011.

How can Environmental Justice Analyses contribute to sustainability?

Many factors may contribute to disproportionately high and adverse human health or environmental impacts, including social, psychosocial, economic, physical, chemical, and biological determinants. EJ analysis attempts to take into consideration the relationships between economic, social, and environmental systems in order to produce more equitable policy decisions. EJ analysis uses an interdisciplinary approach to analyzing and addressing environmental justice issues, and places particular emphasis on community involvement in regulatory processes. EJ analysis can be used to identify communities with high priority environmental justice concerns; improve environmental conditions and public health in minority, low-income and indigenous communities and tribes; and, provide the distributional or equity dimension to benefits and costs associated with any regulation, action, or policy.

What are the main steps in an Environmental Justice Analysis?

EJ analysis generally considers a number of factors, including proximity and exposure to environmental hazards, presence of susceptible populations, unique exposure pathways (e.g., cultural practices, subsistence diets), multiple and cumulative effects from environmental and health hazards, ability to participate in the decision-making process, and physical infrastructure (e.g., schools, access to health care). While there is no standard formula for how EJ analysis should be conducted, there are general principles and steps that most analyses follow:

- **Step 1**—identify the affected subpopulations, including low-income populations, minority populations, or tribal communities;

- **Step 2**—engage in a public and transparent dialogue with potentially affected subpopulations;

- **Step 3**—determine the affected environment, including the geographic scale of potential impact and the demographic composition within that geographic bound;

- **Step 4**—analyze how environmental and health effects are distributed and assess potential exposure and risk vectors;

- **Step 5**—develop and select alternatives in close collaboration with the subpopulations that may be disproportionally affected. The magnitude of disproportionate impact should be a factor in the environmentally preferable alternative; and,

- **Step 6**—evaluate immediate and long-term impacts on the affected environment and communities.

EJ analyses incorporate principles and methodologies from a number of different tools. Segmentation analysis may be used as part of an EJ analysis to help identify vulnerable populations, as well as trends within those specific subpopulations. Cumulative risk assessment may be used to help analyze the distribution of environmental and health effects across different subpopulations and communities. Other tools that support EJ analysis are health impact assessment and benefit-cost analysis.

What are the strengths and limits of Environmental Justice Analysis in a sustainability context?

Incorporating EJ analysis into the decision-making process promotes sustainability by highlighting the relationships between economy, society, and the environment. However, while scientific and quantitative advancements in EJ analyses have enabled researchers and stakeholders to better grasp disproportionate impacts of environmental stressors and socio-demographic conditions, the complex nature of interactions between these factors is not fully understood. For example, EJ analyses are often required to be performed without the benefit of full-scale epidemiological studies and, hence, while correlations between health impacts and populations may be apparent, analysts should be mindful that the cause and effect may not have been demonstrated.

Analysis of environmental justice issues often involves a combination of socio-demographic analyses in addition to exposure and health risk modeling over a spatial framework in order to determine how the impacts of an action are distributed across the affected population. This is often accomplished through visual mapping of one or more factors that contribute to cumulative impacts. Therefore, data for these visual maps need to include information on proximity of populations to various hazards (e.g., industrial facilities and other sources of exposure to chemicals), estimated or measured pollutant exposure concentrations, and social and health vulnerability indicators for populations (e.g., race, income, age, educational attainment, and health status). Care should be taken to ensure that the data used adequately captures the full range of activities within and conditions endemic to environmental justice areas.

The use of mapping tools provides an important spatial element to EJ analyses, allowing analysts to pinpoint areas of disproportionate impacts or areas with high concentrations of vulnerable populations, often on localized levels. However, the degree of spatial definition varies both among mapping tools and locations and the usefulness of visual tools depends on the context of the problem. When only spatial information is used, analysts must be aware of potential misinterpretations of data that demonstrate correlation between effects and population, rather than cause and effect.

How are Environmental Justice Analyses used to support EPA decision-making?

EPA is working to integrate environmental justice broadly across a wide-range of activities, including policy development, rule writing, permitting, and enforcement. In accordance with Executive Order 12898 EPA has developed plans to incorporate environmental justice and civil rights into Agency programs, policies and daily work. EPA's Plan EJ 2014, guided by former Administrator Lisa P. Jackson's Agency-wide priority for environmental justice, sets forth the following goals:

- Improve the scientific basis for regulatory and policy decisions in order to ensure that everyone enjoys the same degree of protection from environmental and health hazards and equal access to the decision-making process to have a healthy environment in which to live, learn, and work.

- Increase the relevance of science to policy making by transforming how EPA formulates, designs, prioritizes, conducts, and fosters more citizen participatory, inclusive, and collaborative processes within the scientific research enterprise.

The plan calls for additional focus on analyzing the incidence, demography and spatial distribution of environmental justice communities, as well as development of tools for assessing the disproportionate impacts that affect these communities. Consistent with Plan EJ 2014, EPA is developing a screening tool that may allow for consideration of exposure and health risk modeling based on socio-demographic characteristics (e.g., race, income, age, education attainment, and health status); distribution of environmental and public health burdens; proximity of populations to various hazards (e.g., industrial facilities and other sources of exposure to chemicals); and, stakeholder and community concerns and priorities.

EPA is developing a variety of user-friendly platforms to help decision-makers conduct EJ analyses: Geoplatform—a geospatial data platform using cloud infrastructure; Urban Atlas—a web-based mapping tool for assessing the status of local natural resources and their benefits; Community-Focused Exposure and Risk Screening Tool—a web-based tool for understanding environmental pollutant exposures and human health risk; as well as an Environmental Quality Index tool to measure county level environmental quality. In addition, EPA's Council for Regulatory Environmental Modeling (CREM) sponsors a searchable Models Knowledge Base that contains a variety of tools for environmental modeling, including a number of spatial exposure modeling tools that are helpful to EJ analysis.

Inadequate and Unhealthy Housing

Healthy homes are essential to a healthy community and population. They contribute to meeting physical needs (e.g., air, water, food, and shelter) and to the occupants' psychological and social health. Housing is typically the greatest single expenditure for a family. Safe housing protects family members from exposure to environmental hazards, such as chemicals and allergens, and helps prevent unintentional injuries. Healthy housing can support occupants throughout their life stages, promote health and safety, and support mental and emotional health. In contrast, inadequate housing contributes to infectious and chronic diseases and injuries and can affect child development adversely.

To assess the percentage of persons in the United States living in inadequate or unhealthy homes, CDC analyzed data from the American Housing Survey (AHS) for 2007 and 2009. The U.S. Census Bureau conducts AHS to assess the quality of housing in the United States and to provide up-to-date statistics to the U.S. Department of Housing and Urban Development (HUD). AHS is a national representative survey that collects data on an average of 55,000 U.S. housing units, including apartments, single-family homes, mobile homes, and vacant housing units. The same housing units are visited every 2 years during odd-numbered years, with census bureau interviewers conducting home visits or telephone interviews during April through mid-September of each survey year. Information for unoccupied units is obtained from landlords, rental agents, or neighbors.

The definition of inadequate housing is related to the basic structure and systems of a housing unit, whereas the definition of unhealthy housing is related to exposure to toxins and other environmental factors. Inadequate housing is defined as an occupied housing unit that has moderate or severe physical problems (e.g., deficiencies in plumbing, heating, electricity, hallways, and upkeep). Examples of moderate physical problems in a unit include two or more break-downs of the toilets that lasted >6 months, unvented primary heating equipment, or lack of a complete kitchen facility in the unit. Severe physical problems include lack of running hot or cold water, lack of a working toilet, and exposed wiring. (The specific algorithm used to categorize a unit as inadequate has been published elsewhere). For the purposes of this report, CDC has defined unhealthy housing as the presence of any additional characteristics that might negatively affect the health of its occupants, including evidence of rodents, water leaks, peeling paint in homes built before 1978, and absence of a working smoke detector. Other indicators of unhealthy housing, such as poor air quality from mold or radon, are not measured by AHS and therefore are not included in the analysis.

In AHS, housing unit is a house, an apartment, a flat, a manufactured (mobile) home, or one or more rooms occupied or intended for occupancy as separate living quarters. Separate living quarters have direct access to the unit from the outside or from a public hall. A household consists of all persons who occupy a housing unit. The householder is the first member contacted by the interviewer who is aged ≥18 years and is an owner or a renter of the housing unit. Household members might be a family or a nonfamily group of friends or unmarried partners. In AHS, each respondent belongs to a household, might be a householder, lives in a housing unit, or might be part of a family.

This report includes estimates of the percentage of occupied housing units that are classified as inadequate or unhealthy by selected demographic characteristics of the householder. Estimates of the relative disparity in the percentage of householders who live in inadequate housing by sex, race/ethnicity, annual income, highest level of completed education, geographic region, and disability status are reported as unadjusted odds ratios with 95% confidence intervals (CIs). Because the replicate weights are not made public, unadjusted odds ratios are the best estimates available, and CIs were calculated by using the probability weights included in the data set. This calculation method is the best available, but its use cannot determine sampling error associated with the sample design, and the method might overestimate the variance, making the CI narrower. To determine statistical significance between years or within a category, the CIs for the particular variables were compared. If the odds ratio (OR) did not fall within the confidence interval for the next year or other variable, the difference was considered statistically significant.

The proportion of housing units classified as inadequate in the United States in 2009 was 5.2%, a percentage that is unchanged from

2007. Female householders were 1.1 times more likely to occupy inadequate housing units than male householders.

In 2009, by race/ethnicity, non-Hispanic blacks had the highest odds of householders living in inadequate housing, followed by Hispanics, American Indians/Alaskan Natives, and Asians/Pacific Islanders when compared with non-Hispanic whites. In the 2009 survey, Hispanic female householders (7.4%) were significantly less likely than Hispanic male householders (8.1%) to live in inadequate housing. Non-Hispanic black female householders were significantly more likely than non-Hispanic white female householders to live in unhealthy housing during both 2007 and 2009 (OR = 1.3 and 1.4, respectively). Although the odds of a Hispanic female living in inadequate housing decreased from 2007 to 2009, the odds were still elevated (OR = 1.9 and 1.8, respectively). In 2009, householders earning an annual salary of ≤$24,999 were almost five times more likely to live in inadequate housing than those earning ≥$75,000 (8.5% versus 2.4%, respectively); however, the odds of householders earning ≤$24,999 and living in inadequate housing decreased significantly from 2007 to 2009 (Table 1). Householders without a high school diploma were more than twice as likely as those with some college education to live in inadequate housing. In 2009, for households with at least one person living with a disability, the odds of living in inadequate housing was 1.2 times higher compared with households without a person living with a disability.

The proportion of unhealthy housing units did not change significantly from 2007 to 2009. Among housing units classified as unhealthy, the magnitude of disparities varied, especially across racial/ethnic, income, and education level categories. For example, a householder earning <$25,000/year was approximately 4 times more likely to live in an inadequate housing unit as a householder making ≥$75,000 a year but was only 1.3 times more likely to live in an unhealthy, as opposed to an inadequate, home. The decrease likely can be attributed to more common characteristics associated with unhealthy homes (e.g., presence of rodents and interior water leaks), compared with inadequate homes. For example, in 2009, approximately 36.9% of surveyed respondents in housing units indicated observing rodents recently, and 10% reported having had a water leak during the previous 12 months.

The 2007–2009 AHS data indicate that the percentage of inadequate housing units in the United States is relatively stable and that the proportion of families living in inadequate housing declined among demographic groups with the highest percentages. However, the disparity by race/ethnicity, socioeconomic status, and education level is still substantial. Interventions to reduce this disparity even further are available.

Specific housing interventions that increase the health and safety of housing have been demonstrated to reduce disease among residents. For example, mitigation of active radon (which is not measured by AHS) in areas at high risk for contamination has been reported to reduce radon to acceptable levels (i.e., <4 picocuries per liter [pCi/L]), in 95% of reme-diated homes, with 69% of such homes reduced to levels <2 pCi/L. In addition, integrated pest management to reduce exposure to pesticide residue has resulted in significant decreases in both cockroach infesta-tions and levels of pyrethroid insecticides in indoor air samples (p = 0.02).

Vigorous efforts to decrease disparities in access to healthy hous-ing will have the immediate effect of decreasing disparities in health status. Among the approximately 110 million housing units in the United States, approximately 5.8 million are classified as inadequate and 23.4 million are considered unhealthy. Inadequate and unhealthy housing disproportionately affects the populations that have the few-est resources (e.g., persons with lower income and limited education). Substantial actions are needed to reduce the overall proportion of inadequate and unhealthy housing among these persons. Results pre-sented in this report can assist organizations in focusing prevention programs and interventions for these populations.

The findings in this report are subject to at least five limitations. First, data were collected through a home visit or a telephone survey. Because data are self-reported, certain demographic characteristics (e.g., income level) might have been reported incorrectly, resulting in possible misclassification. In addition, the results might overestimate or underestimate the actual number of persons living in inadequate or unhealthy homes. AHS has attempted to survey the same, or nearly the same, sample of houses for each cycle since the survey began. Therefore, the survey administrators are persistent in their efforts to contact residents, substantially reducing typical nonresponse problems associated with phone surveys. Second, certain types of living quarters were excluded from the sample, including transient accommodations, barracks for workers or members of the armed forces, and institutional accommodations (e.g., dormitories, wards, and rooming houses). Third, the replicate weights are not made public; therefore, CIs calculated by using the probability weights included in the data set are likely narrower than they would be if the replicate weights could be used. Fourth, only 2 years of data were analyzed, which makes interpreta-tion of trends difficult. Last, AHS does not link questions regarding housing to any other surveys containing health status information. CDC is working with HUD to include health status questions in the 2011 survey.

Although AHS does not link questions regarding housing to any other surveys containing health status information, the connection between health and both inadequate and unhealthy housing has been well-documented. Persons living in inadequate or unhealthy housing as defined in this analysis might be more likely to be exposed to pests and mold that exacerbate asthma as well as to lead paint hazards that limit the intellectual development of children. They might also be more likely to die in house fires as a result of faulty or missing smoke detectors. However, whether healthy, safe, and affordable housing benefits the well-being of its inhabitants beyond reducing exposures to toxins and offering protection from the risk for death by fire is unclear. The effect of housing on mental health, obesity, and healthy aging is also an area in need of additional research.

Part Two

Health Concerns and Their Environmental Triggers

Chapter 8

Cancer and Environmental Concerns

Chapter Contents

Section 8.1

Environmental Causes of Cancer

Text in this section is excerpted from "Environmental and
Occupational Interventions for Primary Prevention of Cancer:
A Cross-Sectorial Policy Framework," Environmental Health
Perspectives (EHP), April 2013.

Cancer is the second leading cause of death worldwide. In 2008,
there were 7.6 million deaths from cancer, and 12.7 million new cancer
cases. More than half of all cancers and 63% of cancer deaths occur in
low- and middle-income countries.

Estimations show that at least one-third of all cancer cases could
be prevented based on current knowledge. Although preventable
risk factors such as tobacco use, alcohol consumption, unhealthy
diet, and physical inactivity play a major role in the development
of cancer, a range of environmental factors and occupational exposures also contribute significantly to the global cancer burden.
Exposures to environmental and occupational carcinogens are often
preventable.

"Environment" is defined by the World Health Organization (WHO)
for the purpose of environmental attribution as "all the physical, chemical and biological factors external to the human host, and all related
behaviors, but excluding those natural environments that cannot reasonably be modified." This definition is limited to those parts of the
environment that can, in principle, be modified so as to reduce the
impact of the environment on health. It also excludes those behaviors
and lifestyles not strictly related to environmental exposures such as
alcohol consumption and tobacco use as well as behaviors related to
the social and cultural environment, genetics, and parts of the "unmod-
ifiable" natural environment.

Humans are exposed to numerous carcinogenic agents through
inhalation, eating, drinking, and skin contact. Since most people work
for nearly two-thirds of their lifetime, they have many, and often
prolonged, opportunities for contacts with occupational carcinogens,
resulting in the accumulation of exposure over a lifetime. WHO has
estimated that a substantial proportion of all cancers are attributable

to the environment, including work settings. For 2004, it was estimated that occupational lung carcinogens (such as arsenic, asbestos, beryllium, cadmium, and chromium) caused 111,000 lung-cancer deaths, and asbestos alone was estimated to cause 59,000 deaths from mesothelioma. Moreover, it was estimated that outdoor air pollution caused 108,000 lung-cancer deaths globally. Environmental factors that increase risks for developing cancer typically affect the general population through involuntary exposures, over which individuals have little control. Exposure to most carcinogens tends to be greatest in the most disadvantaged segments of the population.

Exposures to environmental and occupational carcinogens can be reduced or eliminated, and the cancers that result from them can be prevented through policies promoting healthy working and living environments. Primary prevention encompasses the reduction or elimination of exposure to established risk factors to prevent the occurrence of disease. Some examples of disease reduction by primary prevention include a reduction of bladder cancers among dye workers after elimination of exposure to aromatic amines; a diminution in nasal cancers among furniture workers first employed after 1940, when exposure to wood dust was reduced; and a stabilization of the incidence of pleural mesothelioma in Sweden in the 1990s, after Sweden became one of the first countries to restrict exposure to asbestos in the mid-1970s. Primary prevention that controls a common source of exposure to proven and probable carcinogens is far more effectual, and cost effective, than persuading thousands of persons to each change their individual behaviors.

Cancer and other noncommunicable diseases (NCDs) such as cardiovascular disease, chronic lung disease, and diabetes have many shared risk factors. Thus, reducing exposure to environmental and occupational carcinogens can produce important co-benefits for health. For instance, a reduction in acute coronary events has been observed after the institution of smoke-free policies in public places. Control measures to reduce outdoor air pollution from motor vehicle traffic decrease exposure to diesel exhaust gases and contribute to a reduction in cardiovascular and nonmalignant respiratory morbidity as well as a reduction of lung cancer. Banning the use of asbestos will prevent cases of lung cancer and mesothelioma as well as asbestosis, a nonmalignant fibrotic condition of the lungs. Improved urban traffic policies often reduce traffic accidents and injuries; they may also lead to the promotion of physical exercise, which is protective against a number of cancers. Environmental and occupational policies that prevent cancer also have social and economic benefits. The implementation by the

U.S. Environmental Protection Agency (EPA) of national air quality control measures mandated by the Clean Air Act (initially in 1970, and strengthened in 1977 and 1990) generated substantial economic, environmental, and health benefits: air pollution was reduced, decreasing the burden of cancer and other diseases. California is currently setting out the Safe Consumer Products regulations, one example of a U.S. regulation initiative at the subnational level on safer use of chemical products, which is a further step designed to counter chemical exposure-related diseases such as cancer.

Primary prevention offers the most cost-effective approach to reducing cancer and other NCDs; however, primary prevention has been often neglected while secondary prevention and treatment have been given priority, partly because the results of primary prevention are difficult to recognize in individuals and because its impact may take several decades to emerge. In 2012, the new cases of cancer were estimated globally to cost US$ 154 billion in medical expenses (53% of the total costs). NCDs pose a substantial human and economic burden worldwide. It is estimated that NCDs will cost US$ 47 trillion over the next 20 years, nevertheless, cancer and other NCD prevention has been a low priority for development agencies, governments, and other organizations. In June 2012, the outcome document of the Rio+20 Conference on Sustainable Development acknowledged that "the global burden and threat of NCDs constitutes one of the major challenges for sustainable development in the 21st century" and "health is a precondition for, an outcome of, and an indicator of all three dimensions [economic, social, and environmental] of sustainable development" Arguably, governments should make a strategic focus for development and sustainability by securing and promoting the health and well-being of current generations without compromising the ability of future generations to meet their own needs.

The main objective of this review was to present an evidence-based global strategy for the primary prevention of environmental and occupational cancer. Here we highlight the need for, and the feasibility of, a common global vision for primary prevention.

Conclusions

Cancer is a major problem worldwide. It causes severe and long-term human suffering for individuals and families. It has enormous economic impacts on society. It creates high costs for health-care systems and, in fact, causes the highest economic loss of all the 15 leading causes of death worldwide. The global economic impact of premature death and disability from cancer in 2008 was US$ 895 billion, not including direct costs of treatment.

A substantial proportion of all cancers is attributable to carcinogenic exposures in the environment and the workplace, and is influenced by activities in all economic and social sectors. Many of these exposures are involuntary but can be controlled or eliminated through enacting and enforcing proactive strategies for primary prevention.

The primary prevention of cancers of environmental and occupational origin reduces cancer incidence and mortality and is highly cost effective; in fact, it is not just socially beneficial because it reduces medical and other costs, but because it averts the suffering of many human beings. It requires establishing a multisectorial approach and multiple partnerships. Commitment is essential from health and non-health sectors (such as the environment, labor, housing, transport, industry, and trade sectors), community organizations, private enterprises, health and workers' compensation and insurance organizations, and other key actors at the national and international levels. All stakeholders should be involved in developing strategies to combat the environmental and occupational causes of cancer and to secure commitment to policy change at governmental levels.

Currently, in most countries the almost exclusive focus of cancer policies is on secondary prevention (i.e., early detection), diagnosis, and treatment. As shown in Table 8.1. regarding the existence and implementation of legislation or the level of advocacy, insufficient resources are devoted to primary prevention, which aims to eliminate or control exposures to environmental and occupational carcinogens. The prevailing approach is socially unfair and often unsustainable, especially in low- and middle-income countries. Opportunities should be taken to focus the global policy agenda for cancer and other NCDs in the direction of primary prevention through environmental and occupational interventions. It is crucial therefore to *a*) lay the political foundations by raising awareness that cancer control is not only about treatment, and *b*) identify innovative ways to invest in prevention through cross-sectorial collaboration.

There is sufficient evidence that primary prevention is feasible and highly effective in reducing cancer incidence. To create a blueprint for the inclusion of strategies for primary prevention of cancer of environmental and occupational origin in national cancer policies in countries around the world, we organized the WHO international conference where the "Asturias Declaration: A Call to Action" was developed. The declaration aims to introduce the mitigation of environmental and

Table 8.1. Summary of nine environmental and occupational risk factors for cancer: areas to be strengthened.

Risk	Scientific evidence in support of causation[a]	Awareness-raising measures[b]	Existence of policies/Recommendations[c]	Existence of legislation[d]	Level of advocacy for primary prevention[e]	Implementation of policies and legislation[f]	Public perception of risk[g]
Asbestos	High	High	High	High	High	Intermediate	Intermediate
POPs	Intermediate	Low	High	Intermediate	Intermediate	High	Low
Indoor radon	High	Intermediate	High	Intermediate	Intermediate	Intermediate	Low
Outdoor air pollution/ diesel exhaust	High	High	High	Intermediate	Intermediate	Intermediate	Intermediate
Indoor emissions from household combustion	Intermediate	High	High	Intermediate	Low	Intermediate	Low
Secondhand smoke	High	High	High	Intermediate	Intermediate	Intermediate	Intermediate
Ionizing radiation (medical exposure)	High	Low	Intermediate	Low	Low	Intermediate	Low
UV and tanning beds	High	High	High	Intermediate	Intermediate	Intermediate	Intermediate
Electromagnetic fields	Low	Intermediate	Low	Low	Low	Low	High

POPs, persistent organic pollutants. The methodology followed to classify the risk factors combined a review of relevant literature, consultation with scientists and public health experts, and consensus reached among participants in the WHO International Conference on "Environmental and Occupational Determinants of Cancer. Interventions for Primary Prevention."

a Amount of scientific evidence in support of causation.
b Number of awareness-raising measures (e.g., campaigns) at national and/or international level.
c Extent of governmental or nongovernmental policies, understood as principles or rules, and/or recommendations at the national and/or international level.
d Existence of legislation at national and/or international level.
e Level of advocacy (governmental and nongovernmental) for primary prevention of cancer at national and/or international level.
f Level of implementation of policies and/or legislation at national and/or international level.
g Level of the perception of risk held by the general population versus the actual amount of scientific evidence in support of causation.

occupational exposures into the global agenda for cancer and other NCDs. The declaration of Asturias states that:

Actions for primary prevention of cancer of environmental and occupational origin are still uncoordinated and do not make full use of existing knowledge about primary prevention.

There is a need to create a global strategic framework for control of environmental and occupational carcinogens that enables and promotes primary prevention more broadly.

Global strategic framework should make use of existing tools and knowledge, and would require *a*) developing and implementing screening tools to identify the main risks of cancer and other NCDs in specific settings; *b*) capacity building of the actors involved in implementation; *c*) using existing opportunities such as legislation and regulations that need to be adopted and enforced by all countries to protect their populations; *d*) tailoring risk communication about primary prevention to local circumstances and educating populations about the respective prevention strategies available; and *e*) monitoring, evaluating, and reporting on the progress made.

Section 8.2

Carcinogens

Text in this section begins with excerpts from "Environmental Carcinogens and Cancer Risk," National Cancer Institute (NCI), March 20, 2015.

Text in this section beginning with "Carcinogen List" is excerpted from "Occupational Cancer" The National Institute for Occupational Safety and Health (NIOSH), May 2, 2012.

Does any Exposure to a Known Carcinogen Always Result in Cancer?

Any substance that causes cancer is known as a carcinogen. But simply because a substance has been designated as a carcinogen does not mean that the substance will necessarily cause cancer. Many factors influence whether a person exposed to a carcinogen will develop cancer, including the amount and duration of the exposure and the individual's genetic background. Cancers caused by involuntary exposures to environmental carcinogens are most likely to occur in subgroups of the population, such as workers in certain industries who may be exposed to carcinogens on the job.

How Can Exposures to Carcinogens Be Limited?

In the United States, regulations have been put in place to reduce exposures to known carcinogens in the workplace. Outside of the workplace, people can also take steps to limit their exposure to known carcinogens, such as testing their basement for radon, quitting smoking, limiting sun exposure, or maintaining a healthy weight.

How Many Cancers Are Caused by Involuntary Exposure to Carcinogens in the Environment?

This question cannot be answered with certainty because the precise causes of most cancers are not known. Some researchers have suggested that, in most populations, environmental exposures are responsible for a relatively small proportion of total cancers (less than 4 percent), whereas other researchers attribute a higher proportion (19 percent) to environmental exposures.

Who Decides Which Environmental Exposures Cause Cancer in Humans?

Two organizations—the National Toxicology Program (NTP), an interagency program of the U.S. Department of Health and Human Services (HHS), and the International Agency for Research on Cancer (IARC), the cancer agency of the World Health Organization—have developed lists of substances that, based on the available scientific evidence, are known or are reasonably anticipated to be human carcinogens.

Specifically, the NTP publishes the Report on Carcinogens every few years. This congressionally mandated publication identifies agents, substances, mixtures, or exposures (collectively called "substances") in the environment that may cause cancer in humans. The 2014 edition lists 56 known human carcinogens and includes descriptions of the process for preparing the science-based report and the criteria used to list a substance as a carcinogen.

IARC also produces science-based reports on substances that can increase the risk of cancer in humans. Since 1971, the agency has evaluated more than 900 agents, including chemicals, complex mixtures, occupational exposures, physical agents, biological agents, and lifestyle factors. Of these, more than 400 have been identified as carcinogenic, probably carcinogenic, or possibly carcinogenic to humans.

IARC convenes expert scientists to evaluate the evidence that an agent can increase the risk of cancer. The agency describes the principles, procedures, and scientific criteria that guide the evaluations. For instance, agents are selected for review based on two main criteria: (a) there is evidence of human exposure and (b) there is some evidence or suspicion of carcinogenicity.

How Does the NTP Decide Whether to Include a Substance on Its List of Known Human Carcinogens?

As new potential carcinogens are identified, they are evaluated scientifically by the NTP's Board of Scientific Counselors and the NTP Director. Next, a draft Report on Carcinogens monograph is prepared, which is reviewed by other scientific experts as needed, the public, and other federal agencies. The draft monograph is then revised as necessary and released for additional public comment and peer review by a dedicated panel of experts. Lastly, a finalized monograph and recommendation for listing is sent to the HHS Secretary for approval.

Carcinogen List

The following is a list of substances NIOSH considers to be potential occupational carcinogens.

A number of the carcinogen classifications deal with groups of substances: aniline and homologs, chromates, dintrotoluenes, arsenic and inorganic arsenic compounds, beryllium and beryllium compounds, cadmium compounds, nickel compounds, and crystalline forms of silica. There are also substances of variable or unclear chemical makeup that are considered carcinogens, coal tar pitch volatiles, coke oven emissions, diesel exhaust and environmental tobacco smoke.

Some of the potential carcinogens listed in this index may be re-evaluated by NIOSH as new data become available and the NIOSH recommendations on these carcinogens either as to their status as a potential occupational carcinogen or as to the appropriate recommended exposure limit may change.

A
Acetaldehyde
2-Acetylaminofluorene
Acrylamide

Acrylonitrile
Aldrin
4-Aminodiphenyl
Amitrole
Aniline and homologs
o-Anisidine
p-Anisidine
Arsenic and inorganic arsenic compounds
Arsine
Asbestos
Asphalt fumes

B
Benzene
Benzidine
Benzidine-based dyes
Beryllium
Butadiene
tert-Butyl chromate; class, chromium hexavalent

C
Cadmium dust and fume
Captafol
Captan
Carbon black (exceeding 0.1% PAHs)
Carbon tetrachloride
Chlordane
Chlorinated camphene
Chlorodiphenyl (42% chlorine); class polychlorinated biphenyls
Chlorodiphenyl (54% chlorine); class polychlorinated biphenyls
Chloroform
Chloromethyl methyl ether
bis(Chloromethyl) ether
B-Chloroprene
Chromium, hexavalent [Cr(VI)]
Chromyl chloride; class, chromium hexavalent
Chrysene
Coal tar pitch volatiles; class, coal tar products
Coke oven emissions

D
DDT (dichlorodiphenyltrichloroethane)
Di-2-ethylhexyl phthalate (DEHP)

2,4-Diaminoanisoleo
o-Dianisidine-based dyes
1,2-Dibromo-3-chloropropane (DBCP)
Dichloroacetylene
p-Dichlorobenzene
3,3'-Dichlorobenzidine
Dichloroethyl ether
1,3-Dichloropropene
Dieldrin
Diesel exhaust
Diglycidyl ether (DGE); class, glycidyl ethers
4-Dimethylaminoazobenzene
Dimethyl carbomoyl chloride
1,1-Dimethylhydrazine; class, hydrazines
Dimethyl sulfate
Dinitrotoluene
Dioxane

E–G
Environmental tobacco smoke
Epichlorohydrin
Ethyl acrylate
Ethylene dibromide
Ehtylene dichloride
Ethylene oxide
Ethyleneimine
Ethylene thiourea
Formaldehyde
Gallium arsenide
Gasoline

H–K
Heptachlor
Hexachlorobutadiene
Hexachloroethane
Hexamethyl phosphoric triamide (HMPA)
Hydrazine
Kepone

M
Malonaldehyde
Methoxychlor
Methyl bromide; class, monohalomethanes

Methyl chloride
Methyl iodide; class, monohalomethanes
Methyl hydrazine; class, hydrazines
4,4'-Methylenebis(2-chloroaniline) (MBOCA)
Methylene chloride
4,4-Methylenedianiline (MDA)

N

a-Naphylamine
B-Naphylamine
Nickel, metal, soluble, insoluble, and inorganic; class, nickel, inorganic
Nickel carbonyl
Nickel sulfide roasting
4-Nitrobiphenyl
p-Nitrochlorobenzene
2-Nitronaphthalene
2-Nitropropane
N-Nitrosodimethylamine

P

Pentachloroethane; class, chloroethanes
N-Phenyl-*b*-naphthylamine; class, *b*-naphthalene
Phenyl glycidyl ether; class, glycidyl ethers
Phenylhydrazine; class, hydrazines
Propane Sultone
B-Propiolactone
Propylene dichloride
Proplyene imine
Propylene oxide

R–S

Radon
Rosin core solder, pyrolysis products (containing formaldehyde)
Silica, crystalline cristobalite
Silica, crystalline quartz
Silica, crystalline tripoli
Silica, crystalline tridymite
silica, fused
Soapstone, total dust silicates

T

Tremolite silicates
2,3,7,8-Tetrachlorodibenzo-*p*-dioxin (TCDD) (dioxin)
1,1,2,2-Tetrachloroethane

Tetrachloroethylene
Titanium dioxide
o-Tolidine-based dyes
o-Tolidine
Toluene diisocyanate (TDI)
Toluene diamine (TDA)
o-Toluidine
p-Toluidine
1,1,2-Trichloroethane; class, chloroethanes
Trichloroethylene
1,2,3-Trichloropropane

U–Z
Uranium, insoluble compounds Uranium, soluble compounds
Vinyl bromide; class, vinyl halides
Vinyl chloride
Vinyl cyclohexene dioxide
Vinylidene chloride (1,1-dichloroethylene); class, vinyl halides)
Welding fumes, total particulates
Wood dust
Zinc chromate; class, chromium hexavalent

Section 8.3

Cancer Clusters

Text in this section is excerpted from "Cancer Clusters," National
Cancer Institute (NCI), March 18, 2014.

What Is a Cancer Cluster?

A cancer cluster is the occurrence of a greater than expected number of cancer cases among a group of people in a defined geographic area over a specific time period. A cancer cluster may be suspected when people report that several family members, friends, neighbors, or coworkers have been diagnosed with the same or related types of cancer.

Cancer clusters can help scientists identify cancer-causing substances in the environment. For example, in the early 1970s, a cluster of cases of angiosarcoma of the liver, a rare cancer, was detected among workers in a chemical plant. Further investigation showed that the workers were all exposed to vinyl chloride and that workers in other plants that used vinyl chloride also had an increased rate of angiosarcoma of the liver. Exposure to vinyl chloride is now known to be a major risk factor for angiosarcoma of the liver.

However, most suspected cancer clusters turn out, on detailed investigation, not to be true cancer clusters. That is, no cause can be identified, and the clustering of cases turns out to be a random occurrence.

Where Can Someone Report a Suspected Cancer Cluster or Find Out if One Is Being Investigated?

Concerned individuals can contact their local or state health department to report a suspected cancer cluster or to find out if one is being investigated. Health departments provide the first response to questions about cancer clusters because they, together with state cancer registries, will have the most up-to-date data on cancer incidence in the area. If additional resources are needed to investigate a suspected cancer cluster, the state health department may request assistance from federal agencies, including the Centers for Disease Control and Prevention (CDC) and the Agency for Toxic Substances and Disease Registry (ATSDR), which is part of the CDC.

The CDC website provides links to state and local health departments. These agencies may also be listed in the blue pages of government listings in telephone books.

Although NCI does not lead investigations of individual cancer clusters, NCI researchers and staff may provide assistance to other investigative agencies as needed. In addition, scientists at NCI and researchers who are funded by NCI analyze variations in cancer trends, including the frequency, distribution, and patterns of cancer in groups of people. These analyses can detect patterns of cancer in specific populations. For example, NCI's Cancer Mortality Maps website uses data on deaths from the National Center for Health Statistics, which is part of the CDC, and population estimates from the U.S. Census Bureau to provide dynamically generated maps that show geographic patterns of cancer death rates throughout the United States.

How Are Suspected Cancer Clusters Investigated?

Health departments use established criteria to investigate reports of cancer clusters. The Centers for Disease Control and the Council of State and Territorial Epidemiologists have released updated guidelines for investigating suspected cancer clusters and responding to community concerns.

As a first step, the investigating agency gathers information from the person who reported the suspected cancer cluster. The investigators ask for details about the suspected cluster, such as the types of cancer and number of cases of each type, the age of the people with cancer, and the area and time period over which the cancers were diagnosed. They also ask about specific environmental hazards or concerns in the affected area.

If the review of the findings from this initial investigation suggests the need for further evaluation, investigators then compare information about cases in the suspected cluster with records in the state cancer registry and census data.

If the second step reveals a statistically significant excess of cancer cases, the third step is to determine whether an epidemiologic study can be carried out to investigate whether the cluster is associated with risk factors in the local environment. Sometimes, even if there is a clear excess of cancer cases, it is not feasible to carry out further study—for example, if the total number of cases is very small.

Finally, if an epidemiologic study is feasible, the fourth step is to determine whether the cluster of cancer cases is associated with a suspect contaminant in the environment. Even if a possible association with an environmental contaminant is found, however, further studies would be needed to confirm that the environmental contaminant did cause the cluster.

What Are the Challenges in Investigating Suspected Cancer Clusters?

Investigators face several challenges when determining whether a greater than expected number of cancer cases represents a cancer cluster.

Understanding the Kind of Cancers Involved

To assess a suspected cancer cluster accurately, investigators must determine whether the type of cancer involved is a primary cancer (a cancer that is located in the original organ or tissue where the cancer started) or a cancer that has metastasized (spread) to another site in the body from the original tissue or organ where the cancer began (also called a secondary cancer). Investigators consider only the primary cancer when they investigate a suspected cancer cluster. A confirmed cancer cluster is more likely if it involves one type of cancer than if it involves multiple different cancer types. This is because most carcinogens in the environment cause only a specific cancer type rather than causing cancer in general.

Ascertaining the Number of Cancer Cases in the Suspected Cluster

Many reported clusters include too few cancer cases for investigators to determine whether the number of cancer cases is statistically significantly greater than the expected number.

Determining Statistical Significance

To confirm the existence of a cluster, investigators must show that the number of cancer cases in the cluster is statistically significantly greater than the number of cancer cases expected given the age, sex, and racial distribution of the group of people who developed the disease. If the difference between the actual and expected number of cancer cases is statistically significant, the finding is unlikely to be the result of chance alone. However, it is important to keep in mind that even a statistically significant difference between actual and expected numbers of cases can arise by chance.

Determining the Relevant Population and Geographic Area

An important challenge in confirming a cancer cluster is accurately defining the group of people who should be considered potentially at risk of developing the specific cancer (typically the total number of people who live in a specific geographic area). When defining a cancer cluster, there can be a tendency to expand the geographic borders as additional cases of the suspected disease are discovered. However, if investigators define the borders of a cluster based on where they find cancer cases, they may alarm people about cancers that are not related to the suspected cluster. Instead, investigators first define the population and geographic area that is "at risk" and then identify cancer cases within those parameters.

Identifying a Cause for a Cluster

A confirmed cancer cluster—that is, a finding of a statistically significant excess of cancers—may not be the result of any single external cause or hazard (also called an exposure). A cancer cluster could be the result of chance, an error in the calculation of the expected number of cancer cases, differences in how cancer cases were classified, or a known cause of cancer, such as smoking. Even if a cluster is confirmed, it can be very difficult to identify the cause. People move in and out of a geographic area over time, which can make it difficult for investigators to identify hazards or potential carcinogens to which they may have been exposed and to obtain medical records to confirm the diagnosis of cancer. Also, it typically takes a long time for cancer to develop, and any relevant exposure may have occurred in the past or in a different geographic area from where the cancer was diagnosed.

Chapter 9

Respiratory Problems with Environmental Triggers

Chapter Contents

Section 9.1

Asthma and Air Pollution

This section includes excerpts from "Asthma," National Institute of Environmental and Health Sciences (NIEHS), June 3, 2015; text from "Allergens & Irritants," National Institute of Environmental and Health Sciences (NIEHS), April 23, 2015; and text from "Asthma and Its Environmental Triggers," National Institute of Environmental and Health Sciences (NIEHS), February 2012.

Description

Asthma is an inflammatory disease of the lung. This inflammatory process can occur along the entire airway from the nose to the lung. Once the airway becomes swollen and inflamed it becomes narrower, allowing less air through to the lung tissue and causing symptoms such as wheezing, coughing, chest tightness, and trouble breathing. Once considered a minor ailment affecting only a small portion of the population, asthma is now the most common chronic disorder of childhood, and affects an estimated 6.2 million children under the age of 18. The fact that asthma runs in families suggests that genetic factors play an important role in the development of the disease, however, environmental factors also contribute to the disease process. Asthma can be triggered by a wide range of substances called allergens.

Allergens and Irritants

Asthma is one of our nation's most common chronic health conditions. Many substances can aggravate allergies or increase the severity of asthma symptoms in individuals who are sensitive to these allergens or irritants.

Cigarette Smoke

Cigarette smoke contains a number of toxic chemicals and irritants. People with allergies may be more sensitive to cigarette smoke than others and research studies indicate that smoking may aggravate allergies.

Smoking does not just harm smokers but also those around them. Research has shown that children and spouses of smokers tend to have more respiratory infections and asthma than those of non-smokers. In addition, exposure to secondhand smoke can increase the risk of allergic complications such as sinusitis and bronchitis.

Common symptoms of smoke irritation are burning or watery eyes, nasal congestion, coughing, hoarseness and shortness of breath presenting as a wheeze.

Preventive Strategies

- Don't smoke and if you do, seek support to quit smoking.

- Seek smoke-free environments in restaurants, theaters, and hotel rooms.

- Avoid smoking in closed areas like homes or cars where others may be exposed to second-hand smoke.

Cockroaches

Cockroaches are one of the most common and allergenic of indoor pests.

Recent studies have found a strong association between the presence of cockroaches and increases in the severity of asthma symptoms in individuals who are sensitive to cockroach allergens.

These pests are common even in the cleanest of crowded urban areas and older dwellings. They are found in all types of neighborhoods.

The proteins found in cockroach saliva are particularly allergenic but the body and droppings of cockroaches also contain allergenic proteins.

Preventive Strategies

- Keep food and garbage in closed, tight-lidded containers. Never leave food out in the kitchen.

- Do not leave out pet food or dirty food bowls.

- Eliminate water sources that attract these pests, such as leaky faucets and drain pipes.

- Mop the kitchen floor and wash countertops at least once a week.

- Plug up crevices around the house through which cockroaches can enter.

- Limit the spread of food around the house and especially keep food out of bedrooms.

- Use bait stations and other environmentally safe pesticides to reduce cockroach infestation.

Dust Mites

Dust mites are tiny microscopic relatives of the spider and live on mattresses, bedding, upholstered furniture, carpets, and curtains.

These tiny creatures feed on the flakes of skin that people and pets shed daily and they thrive in warm and humid environments.

No matter how clean a home is, dust mites cannot be totally eliminated. However, the number of mites can be reduced by following the suggestions below.

Preventive Strategies

- Use a dehumidifier or air conditioner to maintain relative humidity at about 50% or below.

- Encase your mattress and pillows in dust-proof or allergen impermeable covers (available from specialty supply mail order companies, bedding and some department stores).

- Wash all bedding and blankets once a week in hot water (at least 130 – 140°F) to kill dust mites. Non-washable bedding can be frozen overnight to kill dust mites.

- Replace wool or feathered bedding with synthetic materials and traditional stuffed animals with washable ones.

- If possible, replace wall-to-wall carpets in bedrooms with bare floors (linoleum, tile, or wood) and remove fabric curtains and upholstered furniture.

- Use a damp mop or rag to remove dust. Never use a dry cloth since this just stirs up mite allergensDictionary of Environmental Health.

- Use a vacuum cleaner with either a double-layered microfilter bag or a HEPA filter to trap allergens that pass through a vacuum's exhaust.

- Wear a mask while vacuuming to avoid inhaling allergens, and stay out of the vacuumed area for 20 minutes to allow any dust and allergens to settle after vacuuming.

Pets and Animals

Many people think animal allergies are caused by the fur or feathers of their pet. In fact, allergies are actually aggravated by:

- proteins secreted by oil glands and shed as dander

- proteins in saliva (which stick to fur when animals lick themselves)

- aerosolized urine from rodents and guinea pigs

Keep in mind that you can sneeze with and without your pet being present. Although an animal may be out of sight, their allergens are not. This is because pet allergens are carried on very small particles. As a result pet allergens can remain circulating in the air and remain on carpets and furniture for weeks and months after a pet is gone. Allergens may also be present in public buildings, schools, etc. where there are no pets.

Preventive Strategies

- Remove pets from your home if possible.
- If pet removal is not possible, keep them out of bedrooms and confined to areas without carpets or upholstered furniture.
- If possible, bathe pets weekly to reduce the amount of allergens.
- Wear a dust mask and gloves when near rodents.
- After playing with your pet, wash your hands and clean your clothes to remove pet allergens.
- Avoid contact with soiled litter cages.
- Dust often with a damp cloth.

Pollen

Ragweed Pollen

Ragweed and other weeds such as curly dock, lambs quarters, pigweed, plantain, sheep sorrel and sagebrush are some of the most prolific producers of pollen allergens.

Although the ragweed pollen season runs from August to November, ragweed pollen levels usually peak in mid-September in many areas in the country.

In addition, pollen counts are highest between 5:00 a.m. – 10:00 a.m. and on dry, hot and windy days.

Preventive Strategies

- Avoid the outdoors between 5:00 a.m. – 10:00 a.m. Save outside activities for late afternoon or after a heavy rain, when pollen levels are lower.

- Keep windows in your home and car closed to lower exposure to pollen. To keep cool, use air conditioners and avoid using window and attic fans.

- Be aware that pollen can also be transported indoors on people and pets.

- Dry your clothes in an automatic dryer rather than hanging them outside. Otherwise pollen can collect on clothing and be carried indoors.

Grass Pollen

As with tree pollen, grass pollen is regional as well as seasonal. In addition, grass pollen levels can be affected by temperature, time of day and rain.

Of the 1,200 species of grass that grow in North America, only a small percentage of these cause allergies. The most common grasses that can cause allergies are:

- Bermuda grass
- Johnson grass
- Kentucky bluegrass
- Orchard grass
- Sweet vernal grass
- Timothy grass

Preventive Strategies

- If you have a grass lawn, have someone else do the mowing. If you must mow the lawn yourself, wear a mask.

- Keep grass cut short.

- Choose ground covers that don't produce much pollen, such as Irish moss, bunch, and dichondra.

- Avoid the outdoors between 5:00 a.m. – 10:00 a.m. Save outside activities for late afternoon or after a heavy rain, when pollen levels are lower.

- Keep windows in your home and car closed to lower exposure to pollen. To keep cool, use air conditioners and avoid using window and attic fans.

- Be aware that pollen can also be transported indoors on people and pets.

- Dry your clothes in an automatic dryer rather than hanging them outside. Otherwise pollen can collect on clothing and be carried indoors.

Tree Pollen

Trees can aggravate your allergy whether or not they are on your property, since trees release large amounts of pollen that can be distributed miles away from the original source.

Trees are the earliest pollen producers, releasing their pollen as early as January in the Southern states and as late as May or June in the Northern states.

Most allergies are specific to one type of tree such as:

- catalpa
- elm
- hickory
- olive
- pecan
- sycamore
- walnut

or to the male cultivar of certain trees. The female of these species are totally pollen-free:

- ash
- box elder
- cottonwood
- date palm
- maple (red)

- maple (silver)

- Phoenix palm

- poplar

- willow

Some people, though, do show cross-reactivity among trees in the alder, beech, birch and oak family, and the juniper and cedar family.

Preventive Strategies

- If you buy trees for your yard, look for species that do not aggravate allergies such as crape myrtle, dogwood, fig, fir, palm, pear, plum, redbud and redwood trees or the female cultivars of ash, box elder, cottonwood, maple, palm, poplar or willow trees.

- Avoid the outdoors between 5:00 a.m. – 10:00 a.m. Save outside activities for late afternoon or after a heavy rain, when pollen levels are lower.

- Keep windows in your home and car closed to lower exposure to pollen. To keep cool, use air conditioners and avoid using window and attic fans.

- Be aware that pollen can also be transported indoors on people and pets.

- Dry your clothes in an automatic dryer rather than hanging them outside. Otherwise pollen can collect on clothing and be carried indoors.

Asthma and Its Environmental Triggers

What Is Asthma?

Asthma is an inflammatory disease of the lung. This inflammatory process can occur along the entire airway from the nose to the lung. Once the airway becomes swollen and inflamed, it becomes narrower, and less air gets through to the lung tissue. This causes symptoms like wheezing, coughing, chest tightness, and trouble breathing. During an asthma attack, the muscles around the airways tighten up and the asthma symptoms become even worse than usual.

Once considered a minor ailment, asthma is now the most common chronic disorder in childhood. The prevalence of asthma has progressively increased over the past 15 years. In the United States alone, nearly 40 million people—13.3 percent of adults and 13.8 percent of children—have been diagnosed with asthma.

Does Asthma Run in Families?

Asthma does run in families, which suggests that genetics play an important role in the development of the disease. If one or both parents have asthma, the child is much more likely to develop the condition—this is known as genetic susceptibility. An NIEHS study of 615 Mexico City families showed that variations in two genes, ORMDL3 and GSDML, were associated with an increased risk of childhood asthma. These results confirm a similar study conducted among European populations.

Simple steps for decreasing indoor allergens:

- Vacuum carpets and upholstered furniture every week
- Wash sheets and blankets in hot water every week
- Encase mattresses, pillows, and box springs in allergen-impermeable covers
- Steam clean carpets and floor mats every 8 weeks
- Replace carpeting with smooth surfaces such as hardwood or vinyl

Are Allergies Related to Asthma?

Asthma can be triggered by substances in the environment called allergens. Indoor allergens from dust mites, cockroaches, dogs, cats, rodents, molds, and fungi are among the most important environmental triggers for asthma.

NIEHS scientists, along with researchers from the U.S. Department of Housing and Urban Development, conducted an extensive survey known as the National Survey of Lead Hazards and Allergens in Housing, which showed that 46 percent of the homes had dust mite allergens high enough to produce allergic reactions, while nearly 25 percent of the homes had allergen levels high enough to trigger asthma symptoms in genetically susceptible individuals. The survey also showed that nearly two-thirds of American homes have cockroach allergens.

What Can I Do to Reduce Allergens and Asthma Attacks?

NIEHS scientists identified several strategies that reduce indoor allergens and asthma symptoms—cockroach extermination, thorough professional cleaning, and in-home visits to educate the occupants about asthma management. Using these strategies, cockroach allergens were reduced by 84 percent, well below the threshold for producing asthma symptoms.

Other research showed that some simple steps—washing bedding in hot water; putting allergen-impermeable covers on pillows, box springs, and mattresses; and vacuuming and steam cleaning carpets and upholstered furniture—can significantly reduce dust mite allergen levels.

NIEHS has also collaborated with the National Institute of Allergy and Infectious Diseases to conduct the National Cooperative Inner-City Asthma Study aimed at reducing asthma among children in the inner-city.

The program targeted six allergens that trigger asthma symptoms— dust mites, cockroaches, pet dander, rodents, secondhand smoke, and mold. Allergen-impermeable covers were placed on the mattress and box spring of the child's bed, and families were given vacuum cleaners equipped with high-efficiency particulate air (HEPA) filters. A HEPA air purifier was set up in the child's bedroom to remove tobacco smoke, dog and cat allergens, and mold. Children who received the help had 19 percent fewer clinic visits, a 13 percent reduction in the use of albuterol inhalers, and 38 more symptom-free days than those in the control group.

What about Mold?

After Hurricane Katrina and the subsequent flooding in New Orleans, NIEHS partnered with the National Institute on Minority Health and Health Disparities to establish the Head-off Environmental Asthma in Louisiana (HEAL) Project. Preliminary data from the HEAL project indicates there may be an association between mold sensitivity and asthma symptoms, but more research is needed.

> Children living within 150 meters of a freeway were more likely to be diagnosed with asthma than children who lived further away.

What about the Air Pollution Outside?

While much of the asthma research has focused on indoor allergens, scientists know that outdoor pollution also plays a major role. NIEHS-funded researchers at the Keck School of Medicine of the University of Southern California studied air pollution in 10 Southern California cities and found that children living within 150 meters of a freeway were more likely to be diagnosed with asthma than children who lived further away. The researchers also found that children who had higher levels of nitrogen dioxide in the air around their homes were more likely to develop asthma symptoms. Nitrogen dioxide is one of many pollutants emitted from motor vehicles.

Scientists with the Columbia Center for Children's Environmental Health found that New York City mothers who were exposed during pregnancy to both polycyclic aromatic hydrocarbons, air pollutants from gasoline and other fossil fuels, and secondhand tobacco smoke had children who were more likely to have asthma.

Research conducted by NIEHS-funded scientists at Yale University also suggests that asthmatic children who use medication to control asthma symptoms are particularly vulnerable to the effects of ground-level ozone, a highly reactive form of oxygen that is a primary ingredient of urban smog.

Section 9.2

Chronic Obstructive Pulmonary Disease (COPD) and Bronchitis

Text in this section begins with excerpts from "Chronic Obstructive Pulmonary Disease (COPD)," Centers for Disease Control and Prevention (CDC), March 12, 2015.

Text in this section beginning with "What Is Bronchitis?" is excerpted from "What is Bronchitis?" National Heart, Lung, and Blood Institute (NHLBI), August 4, 2011.

Chronic Obstructive Pulmonary Disease (COPD)

What Is COPD?

Chronic Obstructive Pulmonary Disease, or COPD, refers to a group of diseases that cause airflow blockage and breathing-related problems. It includes emphysema, chronic bronchitis, and in some cases asthma.

What Causes COPD?

In the United States, tobacco smoke is a key factor in the development and progression of COPD, although exposure to air pollutants in the home and workplace, genetic factors, and respiratory infections also play a role. In the developing world, indoor air quality is thought to play a larger role in the development and progression of COPD than it does in the United States.

Who Has COPD?

Chronic lower respiratory disease, primarily COPD, was the third leading cause of death in the United States in 2011. Fifteen million Americans report that they have been diagnosed with COPD. More than 50% of adults with low pulmonary function were not aware that they had COPD; therefore, the actual number may be higher. The following groups were more likely to report COPD:

- People aged 65–74 years.
- Non-Hispanic Whites.

- Women.

- Individuals who were unemployed, retired, or unable to work.

- Individuals with less than a high school education.

- People with lower incomes.

- Individuals who were divorced, widowed, or separated.

- Current or former smokers.

- Those with a history of asthma.

How Can COPD Be Prevented?

Avoid inhaling tobacco smoke, home and workplace air pollutants, and respiratory infections to prevent developing COPD. Early detection of COPD might change its course and progress. A simple test, called spirometry can be used to measure pulmonary—or lung—function and detect COPD in anyone with breathing problems.

How Is COPD Treated?

Treatment of COPD requires a careful and thorough evaluation by a physician.COPD treatment can alleviate symptoms, decrease the frequency and severity of exacerbations, and increase exercise tolerance. For those who smoke, the most important aspect of treatment

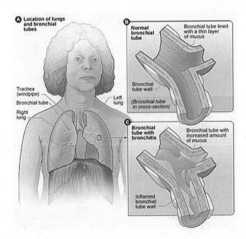

Figure 9.1. *Figure A shows the location of the lungs and bronchial tubes in the body. Figure B is an enlarged, detailed view of a normal bronchial tube. Figure C is an enlarged, detailed view of a bronchial tube with bronchitis. The tube is inflamed and contains more mucus than usual.*

is smoking cessation. Avoiding tobacco smoke and removing other air pollutants from the patient's home or workplace are also important. Symptoms such as coughing or wheezing can be treated with medication. Pulmonary rehabilitation is an individualized treatment program that teaches COPD management strategies to increase quality of life. Plans may include breathing strategies, energy-conserving techniques, and nutritional counseling. The flu can cause serious problems in people with COPD. Vaccination during flu season is recommended and respiratory infections should be treated with antibiotics, if appropriate. Patients who have low blood oxygen levels are often given supplemental oxygen.

What Is Bronchitis?

Bronchitis (bron-KI-tis) is a condition in which the bronchial tubes become inflamed. These tubes carry air to your lungs.

People who have bronchitis often have a cough that brings up mucus. Mucus is a slimy substance made by the lining of the bronchial tubes. Bronchitis also may cause wheezing (a whistling or squeaky sound when you breathe), chest pain or discomfort, a low fever, and shortness of breath.

Overview

The two main types of bronchitis are acute (short term) and chronic (ongoing).

Acute Bronchitis

Infections or lung irritants cause acute bronchitis. The same viruses that cause colds and the flu are the most common cause of acute bronchitis. These viruses are spread through the air when people cough. They also are spread through physical contact (for example, on hands that have not been washed).

Sometimes bacteria cause acute bronchitis.

Acute bronchitis lasts from a few days to 10 days. However, coughing may last for several weeks after the infection is gone.

Several factors increase your risk for acute bronchitis. Examples include exposure to tobacco smoke (including secondhand smoke), dust, fumes, vapors, and air pollution. Avoiding these lung irritants as much as possible can help lower your risk for acute bronchitis.

Most cases of acute bronchitis go away within a few days. If you think you have acute bronchitis, see your doctor. He or she will want to rule out other, more serious health conditions that require medical care.

Chronic Bronchitis

Chronic bronchitis is an ongoing, serious condition. It occurs if the lining of the bronchial tubes is constantly irritated and inflamed, causing a long-term cough with mucus. Smoking is the main cause of chronic bronchitis.

Viruses or bacteria can easily infect the irritated bronchial tubes. If this happens, the condition worsens and lasts longer. As a result, people who have chronic bronchitis have periods when symptoms get much worse than usual.

Chronic bronchitis is a serious, long-term medical condition. Early diagnosis and treatment, combined with quitting smoking and avoiding secondhand smoke, can improve quality of life. The chance of complete recovery is low for people who have severe chronic bronchitis.

What Causes Bronchitis?

Acute Bronchitis

Infections or lung irritants cause acute bronchitis. The same viruses that cause colds and the flu are the most common cause of acute bronchitis. Sometimes bacteria can cause the condition.

Certain substances can irritate your lungs and airways and raise your risk for acute bronchitis. For example, inhaling or being exposed to tobacco smoke, dust, fumes, vapors, or air pollution raises your risk for the condition. These lung irritants also can make symptoms worse.

Being exposed to a high level of dust or fumes, such as from an explosion or a big fire, also may lead to acute bronchitis.

Chronic Bronchitis

Repeatedly breathing in fumes that irritate and damage lung and airway tissues causes chronic bronchitis. Smoking is the major cause of the condition.

Breathing in air pollution and dust or fumes from the environment or workplace also can lead to chronic bronchitis.

People who have chronic bronchitis go through periods when symptoms become much worse than usual. During these times, they also may have acute viral or bacterial bronchitis.

Who Is at Risk for Bronchitis?

Bronchitis is a very common condition. Millions of cases occur every year.

Elderly people, infants, and young children are at higher risk for acute bronchitis than people in other age groups.

People of all ages can develop chronic bronchitis, but it occurs more often in people who are older than 45. Also, many adults who develop chronic bronchitis are smokers. Women are more than twice as likely as men to be diagnosed with chronic bronchitis.

Smoking and having an existing lung disease greatly increase your risk for bronchitis. Contact with dust, chemical fumes, and vapors from certain jobs also increases your risk for the condition. Examples include jobs in coal mining, textile manufacturing, grain handling, and livestock farming.

Air pollution, infections, and allergies can worsen the symptoms of chronic bronchitis, especially if you smoke.

What Are the Signs and Symptoms of Bronchitis?

Acute Bronchitis

Acute bronchitis caused by an infection usually develops after you already have a cold or the flu. Symptoms of a cold or the flu include sore throat, fatigue (tiredness), fever, body aches, stuffy or runny nose, vomiting, and diarrhea.

The main symptom of acute bronchitis is a persistent cough, which may last 10 to 20 days. The cough may produce clear mucus (a slimy substance). If the mucus is yellow or green, you may have a bacterial infection as well. Even after the infection clears up, you may still have a dry cough for days or weeks.

Other symptoms of acute bronchitis include wheezing (a whistling or squeaky sound when you breathe), low fever, and chest tightness or pain.

If your acute bronchitis is severe, you also may have shortness of breath, especially with physical activity.

Chronic Bronchitis

The signs and symptoms of chronic bronchitis include coughing, wheezing, and chest discomfort. The coughing may produce large amounts of mucus. This type of cough often is called a smoker's cough.

How Is Bronchitis Diagnosed?

Your doctor usually will diagnose bronchitis based on your signs and symptoms. He or she may ask questions about your cough, such as how long you've had it, what you're coughing up, and how much you cough.

Your doctor also will likely ask:

- About your medical history
- Whether you've recently had a cold or the flu
- Whether you smoke or spend time around others who smoke
- Whether you've been exposed to dust, fumes, vapors, or air pollution

Your doctor will use a stethoscope to listen for wheezing (a whistling or squeaky sound when you breathe) or other abnormal sounds in your lungs. He or she also may:

- Look at your mucus to see whether you have a bacterial infection
- Test the oxygen levels in your blood using a sensor attached to your fingertip or toe
- Recommend a chest x ray, lung function tests, or blood tests

How Is Bronchitis Treated?

The main goals of treating acute and chronic bronchitis are to relieve symptoms and make breathing easier.

If you have acute bronchitis, your doctor may recommend rest, plenty of fluids, and aspirin (for adults) or acetaminophen to treat fever.

Antibiotics usually aren't prescribed for acute bronchitis. This is because they don't work against viruses—the most common cause of acute bronchitis. However, if your doctor thinks you have a bacterial infection, he or she may prescribe antibiotics.

A humidifier or steam can help loosen mucus and relieve wheezing and limited air flow. If your bronchitis causes wheezing, you may need an inhaled medicine to open your airways. You take this medicine using an inhaler. This device allows the medicine to go straight to your lungs.

Your doctor also may prescribe medicines to relieve or reduce your cough and treat your inflamed airways (especially if your cough persists).

If you have chronic bronchitis and also have been diagnosed with COPD (chronic obstructive pulmonary disease), you may need medicines to open your airways and help clear away mucus. These medicines include bronchodilators (inhaled) and steroids (inhaled or pill form).

If you have chronic bronchitis, your doctor may prescribe oxygen therapy. This treatment can help you breathe easier, and it provides your body with needed oxygen.

One of the best ways to treat acute and chronic bronchitis is to remove the source of irritation and damage to your lungs. If you smoke, it's very important to quit.

Talk with your doctor about programs and products that can help you quit smoking. Try to avoid secondhand smoke and other lung irritants, such as dust, fumes, vapors, and air pollution.

How Can Bronchitis Be Prevented?

You can't always prevent acute or chronic bronchitis. However, you can take steps to lower your risk for both conditions. The most important step is to quit smoking or not start smoking.

For more information about how to quit smoking, go to the Diseases and Conditions Index Smoking and Your Heart article and the National Heart, Lung, and Blood Institute's "Your Guide to a Healthy Heart." Although these resources focus on heart health, they include general information about how to quit smoking.

Also, try to avoid other lung irritants, such as secondhand smoke, dust, fumes, vapors, and air pollution. For example, wear a mask over your mouth and nose when you use paint, paint remover, varnish, or other substances with strong fumes. This will help protect your lungs.

Wash your hands often to limit your exposure to germs and bacteria. Your doctor also may advise you to get a yearly flu shot and a pneumonia vaccine.

Chapter 10

Viruses Spread through Hazards in the Environment

Chapter Contents

Section 10.1

Avian Influenza (Bird Flu)

Text in this section is excerpted from "Influenza (Flu)," Centers for
Disease Control and Prevention (CDC), June 11, 2015.

Avian Influenza A Virus Infections in Humans

Although avian influenza A viruses usually do not infect humans,
rare cases of human infection with these viruses have been reported.
Most human infections with avian influenza A viruses have occurred
following direct or close contact with infected poultry. Illness in
humans has ranged from mild to severe.

> The spread of avian influenza A viruses from one ill person to
> another has been reported very rarely, and has been limited,
> inefficient and not sustained. However, because of the possi-
> bility that avian influenza A viruses could change and gain the
> ability to spread easily between people, monitoring for human
> infection and person-to-person transmission is extremely im-
> portant for public health.

Signs and Symptoms of Avian Influenza A Virus Infections in Humans

The reported signs and symptoms of low pathogenic avian influenza
(Avian influenza A viruses are designated as highly pathogenic avian
influenza (HPAI) or low pathogenicity avian influenza (LPAI) based
on molecular characteristics of the virus and the ability of the virus to
cause disease and mortality in chickens in a laboratory setting). (LPAI)
A virus infections in humans have ranged from conjunctivitis to influenza-like illness (e.g., fever, cough, sore throat, muscle aches) to lower
respiratory disease (pneumonia) requiring hospitalization. Highly
pathogenic avian influenza (HPAI) A virus infections in people have
been associated with a wide range of illness from conjunctivitis only,
to influenza-like illness, to severe respiratory illness (e.g. shortness

of breath, difficulty breathing, pneumonia, acute respiratory distress, viral pneumonia, respiratory failure) with multi-organ disease, sometimes accompanied by nausea, abdominal pain, diarrhea, vomiting and sometimes neurologic changes (altered mental status, seizures). LPAI H7N9 and HPAI Asian H5N1 have been responsible for most human illness worldwide to date, including the most serious illnesses and deaths.

Detecting Avian Influenza A Virus Infection in Humans

Avian influenza A virus infection in humans cannot be diagnosed by clinical signs and symptoms alone; laboratory testing is required. Avian influenza A virus infection is usually diagnosed by collecting a swab from the nose or throat of the sick person during the first few days of illness. This specimen is sent to a lab; the laboratory looks for avian influenza A virus either by using a molecular test, by trying to grow the virus, or both. (Growing avian influenza A viruses should only be done in laboratories with high levels of protection).

For critically ill patients, collection and testing of lower respiratory tract specimens may lead to diagnosis of avian influenza virus infection. For some patients who are no longer very sick or who have fully recovered, it may be difficult to find the avian influenza A virus in the specimen, using these methods. Sometimes it may still be possible to diagnose avian influenza A virus infection by looking for evidence of the body's immune response to the virus infection by detecting specific antibodies the body has produced in response to the virus. This is not always an option because it requires two blood specimens (one taken during the first week of illness and another taken 3–4 weeks later). Also, it can take several weeks to verify the results, and testing must be performed in a special laboratory, such as at CDC.

Treating Avian Influenza A Virus Infections in Humans

CDC currently recommends oseltamivir, peramivir, or zanamivir for treatment of human infection with avian influenza A viruses. Analyses of available avian influenza viruses circulating worldwide suggest that most viruses are susceptible to oseltamivir, peramivir, and zanamivir. However, some evidence of antiviral resistance has been reported in HPAI Asian H5N1 viruses and influenza A H7N9 viruses isolated from some human cases. Monitoring for antiviral resistance among avian influenza A viruses is crucial and ongoing.

Preventing Human Infection with Avian Influenza A Viruses

The best way to prevent infection with avian influenza A viruses is to avoid sources of exposure. Most human infections with avian influenza A viruses have occurred following direct or close contact with infected poultry.

People who have had contact with infected birds may be given influenza antiviral drugs preventatively. While antiviral drugs are most often used to treat flu, they also can be used to prevent infection in someone who has been exposed to influenza viruses. When used to prevent seasonal influenza, antiviral drugs are 70% to 90% effective.

Seasonal influenza vaccination will not prevent infection with avian influenza A viruses, but can reduce the risk of co-infection with human and avian influenza A viruses.

Section 10.2

Severe Acute Respiratory Syndrome (SARS)

Text in this section is excerpted from "Severe Acute Respiratory
Syndrome (SARS)," Centers for Disease Control and Prevention
(CDC), July 2, 2012.

The Disease

What Is SARS?

Severe acute respiratory syndrome (SARS) is a viral respiratory illness that was recognized as a global threat in March 2003, after first appearing in Southern China in November 2002.

What Are the Symptoms and Signs of SARS?

The illness usually begins with a high fever (measured temperature greater than 100.4°F [>38.0°C]). The fever is sometimes associated with chills or other symptoms, including headache, general feeling of discomfort, and body aches. Some people also experience mild respiratory symptoms at the outset. Diarrhea is seen in approximately

10 percent to 20 percent of patients. After 2 to 7 days, SARS patients may develop a dry, nonproductive cough that might be accompanied by or progress to a condition in which the oxygen levels in the blood are low (hypoxia). In 10 percent to 20 percent of cases, patients require mechanical ventilation. Most patients develop pneumonia.

What Is the Cause of SARS?

SARS is caused by a previously unrecognized coronavirus, called SARS-associated coronavirus (SARS-CoV). It is possible that other infectious agents might have a role in some cases of SARS.

How Is SARS Spread?

The primary way that SARS appears to spread is by close person-to-person contact. SARS-CoV is thought to be transmitted most readily by respiratory droplets (droplet spread) produced when an infected person coughs or sneezes. Droplet spread can happen when droplets from the cough or sneeze of an infected person are propelled a short distance (generally up to 3 feet) through the air and deposited on the mucous membranes of the mouth, nose, or eyes of persons who are nearby. The virus also can spread when a person touches a surface or object contaminated with infectious droplets and then touches his or her mouth, nose, or eye(s). In addition, it is possible that SARS-CoV might be spread more broadly through the air (airborne spread) or by other ways that are not now known.

What Does "Close Contact" Mean?

Close contact is defined as having cared for or lived with a person known to have SARS or having a high likelihood of direct contact with respiratory secretions and/or body fluids of a patient known to have SARS. Examples include kissing or embracing, sharing eating or drinking utensils, close conversation (within 3 feet), physical examination, and any other direct physical contact between people. Close contact does not include activities such as walking by a person or briefly sitting across a waiting room or office.

If I Were Exposed to SARS-CoV, How Long Would It Take for me to Become Sick?

The time between exposure to SARS-CoV and the onset of symptoms is called the "incubation period." The incubation period for SARS is typically 2 to 7 days, although in some cases it may be as long as 10 days. In a very small proportion of cases, incubation periods of up to 14 days have been reported.

How Long Is a Person with SARS Infectious to Others?

Available information suggests that persons with SARS are most likely to be contagious only when they have symptoms, such as fever or cough. Patients are most contagious during the second week of illness. However, as a precaution against spreading the disease, CDC recommends that persons with SARS limit their interactions outside the home (for example, by not going to work or to school) until 10 days after their fever has gone away and their respiratory (breathing) symptoms have gotten better.

Is a Person with SARS Contagious before Symptoms Appear?

To date, no cases of SARS have been reported among persons who were exposed to a SARS patient before the onset of the patient's symptoms.

What Medical Treatment Is Recommended for Patients with SARS?

CDC recommends that patients with SARS receive the same treatment that would be used for a patient with any serious community-acquired atypical pneumonia. SARS-CoV is being tested against various antiviral drugs to see if an effective treatment can be found.

If There Is Another Outbreak of SARS, How Can I Protect Myself?

If transmission of SARS-CoV recurs, there are some common-sense precautions that you can take that apply to many infectious diseases. The most important is frequent hand washing with soap and water or use of an alcohol-based hand rub. You should also avoid touching your eyes, nose, and mouth with unclean hands and encourage people around you to cover their nose and mouth with a tissue when coughing or sneezing.

Laboratory Testing

Is There a Laboratory Test for SARS?

Yes, several laboratory tests can be used to detect SARS-CoV. A reverse transcription polymerase chain reaction (RT-PCR) test can detect SARS-CoV in clinical specimens such as blood, stool, and nasal secretions. Serologic testing also can be performed to detect SARS-CoV antibodies produced after infection. Finally, viral culture has been used to detect SARS-CoV.

What Is a PCR Test?

PCR (or polymerase chain reaction) is a laboratory method for detecting the genetic material of an infectious disease agent in specimens from patients. This type of testing has become an essential tool for detecting infectious disease agents.

What Does Serologic Testing Involve?

A serologic test is a laboratory method for detecting the presence and/or level of antibodies to an infectious agent in serum from a person. Antibodies are substances made by the body's immune system to fight a specific infection.

What Does Viral Culture and Isolation Involve?

For a viral culture, a small sample of tissue or fluid that may be infected is placed in a container along with cells in which the virus can grow. If the virus grows in the culture, it will cause changes in the cells that can be seen under a microscope.

Questions about Travel and Quarantine

What Are the Different Types of Travel Notices that CDC Issues about Disease Occurrences in the World?

CDC has changed the categories of travel notices about disease occurrences abroad. The new levels of travel notices are: In the News, Outbreak Notice, Travel Health Precaution, and Travel Health Warning. These new travel levels replace Travel Alerts and Travel Advisories. The categories of travel notices were refined to be more easily understood by international travelers, Americans living abroad, healthcare providers, and the general public, and to clarify the need for recommended preventive measures. From the public health perspective, the refined levels of travel notifications will enhance the usefulness of the travel notices, enabling them to be tailored readily in response to changing events and circumstances.

151

What if I Must Travel to a Country Where SARS Cases Have Been Reported? What Precautions can I Take?

Before you leave:

- Assemble a travel health kit containing basic first aid and medical supplies. Be sure to include alcohol-based hand rub for hand hygiene.

- Inform yourself and others who may be traveling with you about SARS.

- Be sure you are up to date with all of your shots, and see your healthcare provider at least 4 to 6 weeks before travel to get any additional shots or information you may need.

- You may wish to check your health insurance plan or get additional insurance that covers medical evacuation in the event of illness.

- Identify in-country healthcare resources in advance of your trip.

While you are in an area where SARS cases have been reported:

- As with other infectious illnesses, one of the most important and appropriate preventive practices is careful and frequent hand washing. Cleaning your hands often using either soap and water or a waterless, alcohol-based hand rub removes potentially infectious materials from your skin and helps prevent disease transmission.

- To minimize the possibility of infection, observe precautions to safeguard your health. This includes avoiding settings where SARS is most likely to be transmitted, such as healthcare facilities caring for SARS patients.

- On the basis of limited available data, it would be prudent for travelers to China to avoid visiting live food markets and to avoid direct contact with civets and other wildlife from these markets. Although there is no evidence that direct contact with civets or other wild animals from live food markets has led to cases of SARS, viruses very similar to SARS-CoV—the virus that causes SARS—have been found in these animals. In addition, some persons working with these animals have evidence of infection with SARS-CoV or a very similar virus.

- CDC does not recommend the routine use of masks or other personal protective equipment while in public areas.

After your return:

- Persons returning from an area where SARS cases have been reported should monitor their health for 10 days.

- Anyone who becomes ill with fever or respiratory symptoms during this 10-day period should consult a healthcare provider. **Before your visit to a healthcare setting, tell the provider about your symptoms and recent travel so that arrangements can be made to prevent potential transmission to others in the healthcare setting.**

- Close contacts of a person with known or possible SARS should follow the recommendations for SARS patients and their close contact.

What Is the Risk to Persons Who May Have Shared a Plane or Boat Trip with a Possible SARS Patient?

Most cases of SARS have involved persons who cared for or lived with someone with SARS or who had direct contact with infectious material (e.g., respiratory secretions) from a person with SARS. Transmission of SARS on airplanes and boats can occur, but the overall risk appears to be low. If a person with possible SARS flies on an airplane while ill, CDC will request locating information from other travelers on the flight. With the help of state and local health authorities, CDC will attempt to monitor these travelers for 10 days for the development of SARS-like symptoms.

Who Notifies Quarantine Officials about Potential SARS Cases on an Airplane or Ship?

Under foreign quarantine regulations, the master of a ship or captain of an airplane coming into the United States from a foreign port is required by law to report certain illnesses among passengers. The illness must be reported to the nearest quarantine official. If possible, the crew of the airplane or ship will try to relocate the ill passenger or crew member away from others. If the passenger is only passing through a port of entry on the way to another destination, port health authorities may refer the passenger to a local health authority for assessment and care.

If I am on an Airplane or Ship with Someone Suspected of having SARS, Will I be Allowed to Continue to my Destination?

CDC does not currently recommend restricting the onward travel of healthy passengers in the event that a passenger or crew member suspected of having SARS is removed from the ship or airplane by port health authorities. All passengers and crew members exposed to SARS are requested to provide locating information and are advised to seek medical attention if they develop SARS-like symptoms.

What Does a Quarantine Official Do if a Passenger Is Identified as Having Possible SARS?

Quarantine officials arrange for appropriate medical assistance, including medical isolation, to be available when the airplane lands or the ship docks. Isolation is important not only for the sick passenger's comfort and care but also for the protection of members of the public. Isolation is recommended for travelers with possible cases of SARS until SARS can be ruled out or until they are no longer infectious. Quarantine officials will request locating information from the other passengers. CDC, with the help of state and local health authorities, will follow up with any close contacts of the ill passenger for 10 days to ensure that persons who develop symptoms during this period are identified promptly and managed appropriately.

What Does a Quarantine Official Do if a Passenger with Possible SARS Refuses to be Isolated?

Many levels of government (federal, state, and local) have the authority to compel the isolation of sick persons to protect the public. CDC will work with appropriate state and local officials if it is necessary to compel the isolation of a sick passenger.

Section 10.3

West Nile Virus

Text in this section is excerpted from "West Nile Virus," Centers for Disease Control and Prevention (CDC), March 30, 2015.

General Questions About West Nile Virus

What is West Nile virus?

West Nile virus is an arthropod-borne virus (arbovirus) most commonly spread by infected mosquitoes. West Nile virus can cause febrile illness, encephalitis (inflammation of the brain) or meningitis (inflammation of the lining of the brain and spinal cord).

West Nile virus transmission has been documented in Europe and the Middle East, Africa, India, parts of Asia, and Australia. It was first detected in North America in 1999, and has since spread across the continental United States and Canada.

How do people get infected with West Nile virus?

Most people get infected with West Nile virus by the bite of an infected mosquito. Mosquitoes become infected when they feed on infected birds. Infected mosquitoes can then spread the virus to humans and other animals.

In a very small number of cases, West Nile virus has been spread through blood transfusions, organ transplants, and from mother to baby during pregnancy, delivery, or breastfeeding.

Who is at risk for infection with West Nile virus?

Anyone living in an area where West Nile virus is present in mosquitoes can get infected. West Nile virus has been detected in all lower 48 states (not in Hawaii or Alaska). Outbreaks have been occurring every summer since 1999. The risk of infection is highest for people who work outside or participate in outdoor activities because of greater exposure to mosquitoes.

155

Is there a vaccine available to protect people from West Nile virus?

No. Currently there is no West Nile virus vaccine available for people. Many scientists are working on this issue, and there is hope that a vaccine will become available in the future.

How soon do people get sick after getting bitten by an infected mosquito?

The incubation period is usually 2 to 6 days but ranges from 2 to 14 days. This period can be longer in people with certain medical conditions that affect the immune system.

What are the symptoms of West Nile virus disease?

No symptoms in most people. Most people (70–80%) who become infected with West Nile virus do not develop any symptoms.

Febrile illness in some people. About 1 in 5 people who are infected will develop a fever with other symptoms such as headache, body aches, joint pains, vomiting, diarrhea, or rash. Most people with this type of West Nile virus disease recover completely, but fatigue and weakness can last for weeks or months.

Severe symptoms in a few people. Less than 1% of people who are infected will develop a serious neurologic illness such as encephalitis or meningitis (inflammation of the brain or surrounding tissues). The symptoms of neurologic illness can include headache, high fever, neck stiffness, disorientation, coma, tremors, seizures, or paralysis.

Recovery from severe disease may take several weeks or months. Some of the neurologic effects may be permanent. About 10 percent of people who develop neurologic infection due to West Nile virus will die.

Who is at risk for serious illness if infected with West Nile virus?

Serious illness can occur in people of any age. However, people over 60 years of age are at greatest risk for severe disease. People with certain medical conditions, such as cancer, diabetes, hypertension and kidney disease are also at greater risk for serious illness.

What should I do if I think a family member might have West Nile virus disease?

Consult a healthcare provider for evaluation and diagnosis.

How is West Nile virus disease diagnosed?

Diagnosis is based on a combination of clinical signs and symptoms and specialized laboratory tests of blood or spinal fluid. These tests typically detect antibodies that the immune system makes against the viral infection.

What is the treatment for West Nile virus disease?

There are no medications to treat or vaccines to prevent West Nile virus infection. Over-the-counter pain relievers can be used to reduce fever and relieve some symptoms.

People with milder symptoms typically recover on their own, although some symptoms may last for several weeks.

In more severe cases, patients often need to be hospitalized to receive supportive treatment, such as intravenous fluids, pain medication, and nursing care.

When do most cases of West Nile virus disease occur?

Most people are infected from June through September.

Where do most cases of West Nile virus disease occur?

West Nile virus disease cases have been reported from all 48 lower states. The only states that have not reported cases are Alaska and Hawaii. Seasonal outbreaks often occur in local areas that can vary from year to year. The weather, numbers of birds that maintain the virus, numbers of mosquitoes that spread the virus, and human behavior are all factors that can influence when and where outbreaks occur.

How can people reduce the chance of getting infected?

The most effective way to avoid West Nile virus disease is to prevent mosquito bites:

- Use insect repellents when you go outdoors. Repellents containing DEET, picaridin, IR3535, and some oil of lemon eucalyptus and para-menthane-diol products provide longer-lasting protection.

- Wear long sleeves and pants from dusk through dawn when many mosquitoes are most active.

- Install or repair screens on windows and doors. If you have it, use your air conditioning.

- Help reduce the number of mosquitoes around your home. Empty standing water from containers such as flowerpots, gutters, buckets, pool covers, pet water dishes, discarded tires, and birdbaths.

Why do my state health department and CDC sometimes report different numbers of West Nile virus cases?

The CDC case count is based on the number of cases that have been reported by each state health department to CDC. The CDC case count is updated once a week during the transmission season. State health departments might update their counts more often.

Prevention and Control

The most effective way to avoid West Nile virus disease is to prevent mosquito bites. Be aware of the West Nile virus activity in your area and take action to protect yourself and your family.

Avoid Mosquito Bites

- **Use insect repellents when you go outdoors.** Repellents containing DEET, picaridin, IR3535, and some oil of lemon eucalyptus and para-menthane-diol products provide longer-lasting protection. To optimize safety and effectiveness, repellents should be used according to the label instructions.

- **When weather permits, wear long sleeves, long pants, and socks when outdoors.** Mosquitoes may bite through thin clothing, so spraying clothes with repellent containing permethrin or another EPA-registered repellent will give extra protection. Don't apply repellents containing permethrin directly to skin. Do not spray repellent on the skin under your clothing.

- **Take extra care during peak mosquito biting hours.** Take extra care to use repellent and protective clothing from dusk to dawn or consider avoiding outdoor activities during these times.

Mosquito-Proof Your Home

- Install or repair screens on windows and doors to keep mosquitoes outside. Use your air conditioning, if you have it.

- Help reduce the number of mosquitoes around your home by emptying standing water from flowerpots, gutters, buckets, pool covers, pet water dishes, discarded tires, and birdbaths on a regular basis.

Help Your Community West Nile Virus Surveillance and Control Programs

- **Support your local community mosquito control programs.** Mosquito control activities are most often handled at the local level, such as through county or city government. The type of mosquito control methods used by a program depends on the time of year, the type of mosquitoes to be controlled, and the habitat structure. Methods can include elimination of mosquito larval habitats, application of insecticides to kill mosquito larvae, or spraying insecticides from trucks or aircraft to kill adult mosquitoes. Your local mosquito control program can provide information about the type of products being used in your area. Check with your local health department for more information. Contact information may be found in the blue (government) pages of the phone book.

- **Report dead birds to local authorities.** Dead birds may be a sign that West Nile virus is circulating between birds and the mosquitoes in an area. By reporting dead birds to state and local health departments, you can play an important role in monitoring West Nile virus. State and local agencies have different policies for collecting and testing birds, so check with your state health department to find information about reporting dead birds in your area.

Symptoms and Treatment

No symptoms in most people. Most people (70–80%) who become infected with West Nile virus do not develop any symptoms.

Febrile illness in some people. About 1 in 5 people who are infected will develop a fever with other symptoms such as headache, body aches, joint pains, vomiting, diarrhea, or rash. Most people with this type of West Nile virus disease recover completely, but fatigue and weakness can last for weeks or months.

Severe symptoms in a few people. Less than 1% of people who are infected will develop a serious neurologic illness such as encephalitis or meningitis (inflammation of the brain or surrounding tissues).

- The symptoms of neurologic illness can include headache, high fever, neck stiffness, disorientation, coma, tremors, seizures, or paralysis.
- People with certain medical conditions, such as cancer, diabetes, hypertension and kidney disease are also at greater risk for serious illness.
- Recovery from severe disease may take several weeks or months. Some of the neurologic effects may be permanent.
- About 10 percent of people who develop neurologic infection due to West Nile virus will die.

Treatment

- No vaccine or specific antiviral treatments for West Nile virus infection are available.
- Over-the-counter pain relievers can be used to reduce fever and relieve some symptoms
- In severe cases, patients often need to be hospitalized to receive supportive treatment, such as intravenous fluids, pain medication, and nursing care.

Transmission

West Nile virus is most commonly transmitted to humans by mosquitoes.

Additional routes of human infection have also been documented. It is important to note that these methods of transmission represent a very small proportion of cases:

- Blood transfusions
- Organ transplants
- Exposure in a laboratory setting
- From mother to baby during pregnancy, delivery, or breastfeeding

West Nile virus is not transmitted:

- From person-to-person or from animal-to-person through casual contact. Normal veterinary infection control precautions should be followed when caring for a horse suspected to have this or any viral infection.

- From handling live or dead infected birds. You should avoid bare-handed contact when handling any dead animal. If you are disposing of a dead bird, use gloves or double plastic bags to place the carcass in a garbage can.

- Through consuming infected birds or animals. In keeping with overall public health practice, and due to the risk of known foodborne pathogens, always follow procedures for fully cooking meat from either birds or mammals.

Transmission cycle

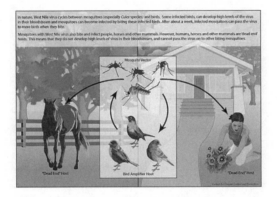

Figure 10.1. West Nile Virus Transmission Cycle

Chapter 11

Reproductive Issues and the Environment

Chapter Contents

Section 11.1

Fertility

Text in this section is excerpted from "Reproductive and Birth
Outcomes," Centers for Disease Control and Prevention (CDC),
June 6, 2014.

According to data from the National Survey of Family Growth, 11%
of U.S. couples had impaired fertility from 2006–2010. Waiting to have
a child until later in life and existing medical conditions are not the
only causes of male and female infertility. It is believed that environmental contaminants may cause infertility by creating other health
conditions. For example, some research suggests that environmental
contaminants can affect a woman's menstruation and ovulation. Low-
level exposures to compounds such as phthalates, polychlorinated
biphenyls (PCBs), dioxin, and pesticides are suspected risk factors.
Much more research needs to be done to find out how environmental
contaminants may be affecting human fertility.

Exposure and Risk

For many people who want to start a family, the dream of having
a child is not easily realized. About 6% of women in the United States
ages 15–44 years have difficulty getting pregnant or staying pregnant.
Infertility is a problem that can affect both men and women. It can be
caused by many factors which may include the following:

- Age

- Stress

- Poor diet

- Genetics

- Nutrition

- Behavior

- Some medicines

- Athletic training

- Being overweight or underweight
- Tobacco use
- Alcohol consumption
- Sexually transmitted diseases (STDs)
- Health problems that cause hormonal changes

The amount and quality of a man's sperm can be affected by:

- Alcohol
- Illegal drugs
- Environmental toxins
- Tobacco use
- Some medicines
- Radiation treatment or chemotherapy for cancer
- Age

Prevention

Most healthy women younger than 30 years of age should not worry about infertility unless they have been trying to conceive for at least a year. At this point, women and their partners should talk with their doctors about a fertility evaluation. A woman's chances of conceiving decreases quickly every year after the age of 30. Women in this age group who have been trying to conceive for six months should also talk with their doctors about having a complete and timely fertility evaluation.

Some health issues increase a woman's chances of having fertility problems. Women with the following issues should consult their doctors:

- Irregular or no menstrual periods
- Very painful periods
- Endometriosis
- Pelvic inflammatory disease
- More than one miscarriage

No matter what age, a woman should always talk to her doctor before trying to get pregnant. Doctors can help women prepare their body for a healthy baby. They can also answer questions on fertility and give advice on conceiving.

Section 11.2

Fetal Exposures Can Lead to Adult Diseases

This section includes excerpts from "Predicting Later-Life Outcomes of Early-Life Exposures," Environmental Health Perspectives (EHP), October, 2014; and text from "Environmental Health and Medicine Education," Agency for Toxic Substances and Disease Registry (ATSDR), February 15, 2014.

There are now well-described instances of human *in utero* exposures that have produced significant increases in later-life susceptibility to disease. Best known are the studies of the Dutch famine. During the winter of 1944–1945, toward the end of World War II, the population in German-occupied western Holland had only very limited food available, with an average daily intake of < 1, 000 calories for several months. Children born to women who were pregnant during this famine were small for gestational age (SGA). Later in life, this *in utero*-deprived cohort developed an increased incidence of various adult-onset diseases, including obesity, diabetes, cardiovascular disease, and renal dysfunction. In addition, the children born to members of this *in utero*-deprived cohort were also SGA, indicating a passage of this predilection through generations. Another example of the later-life consequences of an early-life chemical exposure is *in utero* and early childhood exposure to arsenic-contaminated drinking water in Chile. Beginning in 1958, with the development of a new water supply, the population of a large town in the Antofagasta region of northern Chile was exposed to very high levels of arsenic [~ 800 ppb in drinking water; the U.S. Environmental Protection Agency (EPA) maximum contaminant level is 10 ppb], an exposure that abruptly ended with the institution of water filtration in 1970. The cohort of individuals exposed to arsenic early in life was later found to have significant deficiencies in lung function and increases in cardiovascular mortality compared with a nonexposed control group.

The potential scope of the problem is illustrated by an example from the recent economics literature, where evidence of effects of the 1918 Spanish flu pandemic was seen in the economic performance and achievements of its victims. Men born to U.S. mothers who contracted the flu while pregnant had reduced educational attainment, increased rates of physical disabilities, lower socioeconomic status, 5–9% overall lower income, and approximately 30% greater welfare payments. In a Brazilian cohort born during and soon after this same flu pandemic, children of flu-exposed mothers were less likely to be literate, to have graduated college, to be employed, or to ever have had formal employment. Although not every association seen in the U.S. cohort was observed in the Brazilian counterpart—and despite the fact that no aggregate economic impact number has been estimated—the results between the two studies were impressively concordant. The end result of this body of work is the powerful indication that early-life exposures have a strong, significant, and long-lasting effect on later-life function and disease in this circumstance.

Here we discuss examples of human exposures to adverse intrauterine environments that underscore the dramatic biological consequences of interference with normal development. Human data provide strong biological plausibility connecting early-life exposures to later-life disease and raise the important question of the underlying molecular mechanisms responsible for these long-lasting effects. Because alterations in DNA sequence per se do not explain the later-life effects of these exposures, epigenetic mechanisms have been invoked. To study these epigenetic mechanisms in detail has required the development of appropriate animal models such as the agouti mouse. To date, this emerging knowledge has not been incorporated into risk assessment processes or regulatory practice. Indeed, significant scientific and conceptual barriers must still be overcome as health protective measures are developed for early-life exposures that induce molecular effects resulting in later-life disease. In this review, we explore the scientific basis for these latent effects and discuss the risk assessment context, forming the basis for the development of a research agenda designed to generate the knowledge base necessary for understanding and appropriately regulating early-life exposures.

Early-life exposures, later-life effects, and epigenetic mechanisms. In humans, early insults are associated with later-life liabilities, including prematurity, low birth weight, maternal infection during pregnancy, toxic exposures, and malnutrition. Premature birth (< 37 completed weeks gestation) is an important early-life event of increasing incidence. Decreasing age at birth has been associated with increased odds of high systolic blood pressure in a population-based cohort study of young adult men, and premature birth before 35 weeks gestational age predicted the development of diabetes in both adult men and women.

Maternal infection during pregnancy has been associated with neuropsychiatric disorders such as autism and schizophrenia. Both human and animal studies support this association, with suggested mechanisms ranging from altered hippocampal neurotransmitter signaling to persistent chronic inflammation.

Numerous early-life toxic exposures have been linked to later-life health effects, with particularly strong evidence regarding maternal smoking during pregnancy being predictive of impaired fertility, obesity, hypertension, and neurobehavioral deficits. Animal studies suggest that nicotine alone may be enough to elicit the long-term consequences of maternal smoking on progeny and that prenatal and perinatal toxicant exposures can result in latent effects, including elevated blood pressure, insulin resistance, and obesity.

Malnutrition is an example of an environmental stressor that invokes a predictive adaptive response in the developing organism). The fetus appears to use the *in utero* environment to predict and prepare for the postnatal environment. That is, an organism alters its developmental path to produce a phenotype that gives it a survival or reproductive advantage in postnatal life (Figure 11.1).

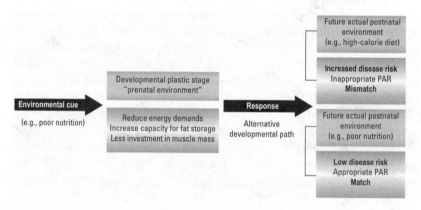

Figure 11.1. *Predictive Adaptive Response (PAR) The combination of maternal nutrition (i.e., in utero nutrition) and postnatal nutrition can be adaptive or maladaptive, leading to increased or decreased disease risk later in life. During development, an organism responds to an environmental stimulus by shifting its developmental path to a phenotype that confers a survival or reproductive advantage in postnatal life; this process of programmed adaptation is called predictive adaptive response (PAR).*

Fetal malnutrition can be defined as either overnutrition or under-nutrition, or as a deficiency of specific nutrients. Studies of the Dutch famine of 1944–1945 have implicated maternal undernutrition in the pathogenesis of multiple diseases, including coronary heart disease, hypertension, obesity, insulin resistance, and schizophrenia. Fetal nutrition is also affected by placental dysfunction and uteroplacental insufficiency. In developed countries, the diseases associated with placental insufficiency, such as maternal smoking and pregnancy-induced hypertension (e.g., preeclampsia), are the most common causes of fetal undernutrition. Preeclampsia, for example, affects up to 3 million people in the United Kingdom and 15 million people in the United States. Moreover, the incidence of diseases such as preeclampsia is increasing in developing countries. Fetal undernutrition leads to intrauterine growth restriction (IUGR; the failure of the fetus to reach its genetic growth potential due to a pathological event). IUGR in humans predicts adult disease, including hypertension, diabetes, obesity, cardiovascular disease, respiratory dysfunction, and neurocognitive disease. The relationship between IUGR and adult disease is often studied using measures such as the ponderal index (birth weight × 100/crown-heel length³). The ponderal index reflects fetal undernutrition because, when presented with limited nutrition, the fetus will maintain body length but not body weight (asymmetric growth restriction or brain sparing). A reduced ponderal index has been associated with multiple diseases, including insulin resistance, obesity, behavioral symptoms of attention deficit hyperactivity disorder, coronary heart disease, and hypertension. Other measures of fetal malnutrition in the newborn that have been predictive of adult disease include placental efficiency (fetal weight/placental weight), placental morphometry, and combinations of maternal and placental size.

IUGR in animals similarly predicts adult morbidities such as hypertension, obesity, and insulin resistance. Common animal models of fetal malnutrition include placental insufficiency, food restriction, protein restriction, micronutrient deficiency, and glucocorticoid exposure. Although the molecular pathogenesis may differ, these models give rise to a similar profile of adult diseases. Both offspring sex and the timing of exposure influence the later-life consequences of exposure.

Timing and intergenerational effects of exposures. The Dutch famine cohort illustrates the critical effect of timing of exposures in humans (Figure 11.2). Individuals who were *in utero* early in gestation during the famine suffer from an increased incidence of coronary heart disease, hypertension, dyslipidemia, and obesity, whereas those who were *in utero* midgestation suffer from an increased incidence of obstructive airway disease and impaired glucose tolerance.

In an examination of the impact of exposures across generations using the Dutch famine cohort, found evidence that progeny (F2) of women (F1) born during the famine suffered from increased neonatal adiposity and poor adult health, including neurological disorders, and respiratory and autoimmune conditions. Animal studies also provide support for the occurrence of intergenerational consequences of exposure. F1 female rats, hypertensive as a result of prenatal malnutrition, transmit the predisposition toward hypertension and endothelial dysfunction to their F2 progeny. F1 male rats exposed to the endocrine disruptor vinclozolin *in utero* may also pass on a number of disease states involving prostate, kidney, immune system, and metabolism (hypercholesterolemia) to the F4 generation.

Epigenetic mechanisms. The underlying mechanism responsible for these myriad effects of exposures is, at least in part, epigenetic (Figure 11.3). Epigenetics forms the basis of how eukaryotes regulate gene expression. Epigenetic modifications direct access of the transcriptional machinery and cofactors to regulatory regions of the gene, modulating transcriptional initiation, elongation, and termination. Studies in multiple model systems demonstrate that epigenetic modifications are important along the entire gene, including untranslated regions.

Epigenetic modifications operate as an "on/off switch" to regulate gene expression, as with imprinting, or as a rheostat control to increase or decrease expression. Epigenetic modifications that function as a rheostat are often driven by environmental conditions, particularly those that are extreme, and are thought to function as a cellular memory of previous environmental conditions, so that future environments can be physiologically anticipated. In this context, epigenetic

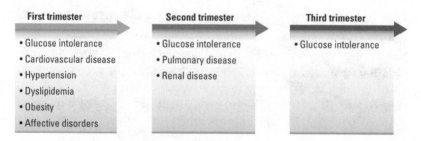

Figure 11.2. *DF Studies of the Dutch famine birth cohort underscore the importance of timing in developmental processes. The timing of in utero nutritional deprivation is associated with different later-life disease outcomes*

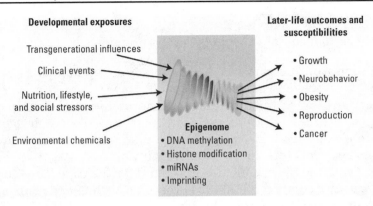

Figure 11.3. *Developmental exposures (DE) are focused through the lens of epigenetic mechanisms to influence later-life disease outcomes and susceptibilities.*

modifications may represent accessible molecular markers of early-life events that may be more stable than direct measures of gene expression. The epigenetic modifications most often studied include the histone code, DNA CpG methylation, and microRNA (miRNA) expression levels.

The histone code contains the most capacity for epigenetic modification. Each cell contains approximately 3 × 108 nucleosomes, each consisting of histone core proteins that can be differentially acetylated, methylated, or phosphorylated. Presumably, cells and tissues adjust their histone codes during development in response to ambient conditions to fine tune the regulation of gene expression in anticipation of the future extrauterine environment.

DNA methylation occurs on cytosines in CpG sequences and is associated with specific early-life events, including maternal malnutrition, *in vitro* fertilization, transplacental exposures, and IUGR. Although many different early-life events lead to similar adult phenotypes, the epigenetic modifications that occur in these exposures may be different; in other words, the end result may be the same, but the pathways giving rise to that result may be different.

miRNAs are a class of small RNAs 21–25 nucleotides in length that act as posttranscriptional regulators of gene expression. These small RNAs bind to the 3′-untranslated regions of target mRNA transcripts and disrupt the translational machinery or lead to transcript degradation, depending on the level of sequence complimentarity. Humans have approximately 1, 000 miRNAs, each of which can interact with a family of target RNAs, creating a regulatory mechanism with the potential to modulate about 60% of the protein-coding genes.

Placenta. The placenta, a readily accessible human tissue that may reflect the fetal environment, could prove to be a very useful tool for understanding the mechanisms underpinning the developmental origins of disease; it could also serve as a tissue source for biomarkers to predict later disease risk. The placenta grows and develops throughout gestation in a dynamic, highly orchestrated manner. Placental vascular development is important for the transfer of flow-limited substrates and for fetal cardiovascular loading and heart fitness. Placental growth is under the control of imprinted genes that may up- or down-regulate growth depending on the parent of origin. Placental 11-β-hydroxysteroid dehydrogenase-2 (*11βHSD2*) activity is developmentally regulated, responds to nutrients and oxygen levels, and regulates fetal exposure to maternal cortisol. Oxidative stress is increasingly seen as a regulator of placental and fetal growth and development. Pregnancies complicated by obesity, preeclampsia, and IUGR are associated with increased placental oxidative and nitrative stress, leading to covalent modifications of placental proteins based on observational studies in humans.

The placenta has a distinct DNA methylation profile that changes throughout gestation in response to environmental cues. Placental epigenetic biomarkers have emerged as an active and informative area for the identification of early-life indicators of later-life disease. Infant growth restriction has been associated with distinct patterns of placental DNA methylation. Placentas from large-for-gestational-age newborns had differential methylation of the glucocorticoid receptor (*GR*) gene. Maternal smoking has been associated with down-regulation of the placental miRNAs *miR-16*, *miR-21*, and *miR-126a*, and reduced expression of *miR-16* and *miR-21* has been associated with SGA newborns. Therefore, the placenta is a source of integrated molecular information about the developmental life history of the fetus and its environmental interactions.

In utero *and postnatal epigenetic modifications that predict end points such as obesity, insulin resistance, and hypertension.* In mice, differences in micronutrient intake during pregnancy induced differences in the coat color of offspring due to hypomethylation of the 5′ end of the agouti gene, whereas a protein-restricted diet during pregnancy led to hypomethylation of promoter regions of metabolically important regulators—the *GR* and peroxisome proliferator-activated receptor (*PPAR*) α genes. In this rodent model, hypomethylation of*GR* and *PPARα* was accompanied by an increase in their expression and that of their target genes, *PEPCK*(phosphoenolpyruvate carboxykinase) and *AOX* (acyl CoA oxidase), and the metabolic processes that they control, namely, glucogeneogenesis and β-oxidation. Altered methylation status of the liver *PPARα* promoter in juvenile offspring was due to hypomethylation of four specific CpG dinucleotides, two of which predicted the level of the mRNA transcript and persisted into adulthood. The differentially methylated CpGs corresponded to transcription factor binding sites, which suggests that changes in the epigenetic regulation of genes established during development will induce altered transcription in response to specific stimuli and modify the capacity of the tissue to respond to metabolic challenge. Other animal studies have shown that folic acid supplementation, neonatal overfeeding, constrained intrauterine blood supply, and maternal behavior alter the epigenetic regulation of genes in the offspring and that these changes are associated with an altered phenotype.

Hypomethylation of the imprinted *IGF2* (insulin-like growth factor 2) gene has been observed in genomic DNA isolated from whole blood from 60 individuals who were exposed periconceptually to famine *in utero* during the Dutch famine compared with their unexposed same-sex siblings. In two independent cohorts, the methylation status of a single CpG site in the promoter region of the retinoid X receptor α (*RXRα*) in the umbilical cord was positively associated with childhood adiposity in both boys and girls, such that *RXRα* promoter methylation explained more than one-fifth of the variance in childhood fat mass. These human studies indicate that epigenetic marks may allow identification of individuals at increased risk of chronic disease in later life before the onset of clinical disease, thus facilitating targeted intervention strategies.

PPARγ and obesity. Rates of obesity have increased in infants, young children, and adolescents, suggesting that obesity is being programmed prenatally or in early childhood. Growing evidence supports a contribution of endocrine-disrupting chemicals (EDCs) in the obesity epidemic, and mechanisms are being revealed for at least a few EDCs. Obesogens are chemicals that promote obesity by increasing the number of fat cells (and fat storage into existing fat cells), by changing the amount of calories burned at rest, by altering energy balance to favor storage of calories, and by altering the mechanisms through which the body regulates appetite and satiety. PPARγ plays an important role in nearly all aspects of adipocyte biology and is thought to be the master regulator of adipogenesis. Activation of PPARγ2 in preadipocytes increases their differentiation into adipocytes, and PPARγ is required for adipocyte differentiation *in vitro* and *in vivo*. The ligand-binding pocket of PPARγ is large and considered to be promiscuous. A number of chemicals act as PPARγ ligands, many of which are obesogenic.

One obesogen for which a mechanism of action is known is the organotin tribuytltin (TBT). In mice, a single prenatal exposure to TBT during gestation resulted in premature accumulation of fat in adipose tissues and increased size of the fat depot relative to overall body mass. In mouse pups born to TBT-treated mothers, the liver, testis, mammary gland, and inguinal adipose tissue, which normally do not store lipids before feeding commences, all had stored fat at birth. TBT has a nanomolar affinity for both RXR and PPARγ, activates PPARγ–RXR heterodimer binding to DNA, and directly regulates transcription of its target genes.

Mature adipocytes are generated from multipotent stromal cells (MSCs) found in almost all fetal and adult tissues. MSCs can differentiate into bone or adipose tissue, a balance mediated by PPARγ. Intriguingly, exposure to the environmental obesogen TBT or the pharmaceutical obesogen rosiglitazone have been reported to induce the differentiation of MSCs into adipocytes at the expense of bone via PPARγ activation. Moreover, pregnant dams treated with a single dose of TBT or rosiglitazone produced pups with MSCs that *in vitro* differentiated into adipocytes about twice as frequently as did MSCs from controls. Thiazolidinedione antidiabetic drugs such as rosiglitazone are potent activators of PPARγ and are known to increase weight and fat cell number in humans.

MSCs derived from mice exposed to TBT *in utero* have exhibited alterations in the methylation status of the CpG islands of adipogenic genes such as *AP2* and *PPARγ*. This altered methylation was associated with an increased number of preadipocytes in the MSC compartment and an increased frequency with which MSCs differentiate into adipocytes upon adipogenic stimulation. Understanding how adipocyte number is programmed at the genomic level will be of critical importance in understanding how the set point for adipocyte number is modified by chemicals, dietary factors, or the intrauterine environment.

In utero and postnatal indicators that predict diseases caused by arsenic exposure. Early-life exposure to inorganic arsenic produces a wide range of malignant and nonmalignant diseases in humans. Exposure to arsenic from naturally contaminated drinking water affects roughly 140 million people worldwide. For example, in Bangladesh, where exposure began in the early 1970s, there is a generation of women and men who have been exposed to arsenic for their entire lives. The placenta is not a barrier to arsenic; thus, children are born with blood concentrations of arsenic and its toxic metabolites similar to those present in their mothers. Increased lung cancer and bronchiectasis have been reported in young Chilean men and women who were exposed to arsenic only during prenatal and early postnatal life. Long-term follow-up of a cohort of thousands of infants exposed to arsenic-contaminated milk powder in 1955 in Japan suggests increased rates of leukemia and skin, liver, and pancreatic cancers. In Thailand, among babies of mothers who experienced varying degrees of arsenic exposure, gene expression profiles were indicative of the activation of molecular networks associated with inflammation, apoptosis, stress, and metal exposure. In arsenic-exposed adults, DNA hypomethylation has been associated with the subsequent risk of developing arsenic-induced skin lesions. Collectively, this body of work in human populations strongly suggests that developmental exposure to arsenic may induce alterations in fetal cellular functioning that may have major public health consequences, including cancer, in later life.

Introduction

Parental exposures before a child is conceived can result in adverse reproductive effects, including:

- infertility;

- spontaneous abortion; and

- genetic damage to the fetus, possibly resulting in birth defects.

Reproductive hazards can affect fertility, conception, pregnancy, delivery, or a combination of any or all of these. Studies in humans that have assessed the causal relationship between specific exposures and these outcomes have frequently faced limitations and challenges, including:

- lack of accurate assessment of the dose of the exposure to mother or fetus or both;

- a need for proper control groups to take into account the other genetic, physical and socioeconomic factors affecting reproductive toxicity;

- inadequate assessment of the background prevalence of events;

- difficulties with reliable ascertainment of outcomes; and

- multiplicity of exposures.

Exposures to hazardous substances during pregnancy can potentially affect the development of fetal organ systems. Such exposures can further lead to either gross structural changes or more subtle functional changes. During critical periods of organogenesis (i.e., the 6-week period that follows the establishment of the placental circulation). Exposures can cause profound systemic damage out of proportion with the dose response seen in adults.

Preconception-Maternal Effects

Exposure of ova to toxicants

Exposures to developing ova can have lifelong effects. The ovum from which the fetus is formed develops during the early fetal life of the mother. The ovum's development arrests in the prophase of the cell cycle until ovulation—this can occur many decades hence. Ova forming within a female fetus may be affected by exposures experienced by her mother during the mother's lifetime. Fetal ova may also be affected by the exposures of her grandmother. This is because the grandmother's exposures may have affected the mother's developing ova during the mother's fetal life.

After birth, ova rest dormant and are vulnerable to environmental insults until the time of ovulation.

Effects on fertility

Agents that interfere with the menstrual cycle and ovulation, such as hormonally active agents, may affect fertility. Mothers who smoke cigarettes may have decreased fertility.

Effects on sex ratio

A recent retrospective study showed a 33% relative decrease in male births in women who had suffered high environmental exposures to polychlorinated biphenyls (PCBs) in the 1960s (i.e., those with levels in the 90th percentile). But the data from the Yusho and Yucheng episodes (i.e., excess PCBs and furan exposure in cooking oil) showed no effect on the sex ratio, even with very high maternal exposures. Few studies have been conducted of altered sex ratio with maternal exposure to persistent pollutants. More work on this area needs to occur.

Preconception-Paternal Effects

Effects on fertility

Agents that interfere with male hormones or with hormonal feedback (e.g., testosterone, luteinizing hormone [LH]) may also affect production of healthy sperm, thus affecting fertility. Injury to spermatogonia can occur at any time and lead to infertility. Repeated, narrow windows of vulnerability occur in parallel with the continual postpubertal production of semen and regeneration of spermatozoa. Adverse reproductive outcomes may also result from transmission of toxicants in seminal fluid.

Effects on sex ratio

One study noted that children fathered by men exposed to dioxin after the Seveso, Italy accident showed a decrease in the expected male:female ratio. This same pattern was seen in a study of male workers at a 2,4,5-trichlorophenol plant in Ufa, Russia. More recent work has suggested that this effect occurs only when the exposure occurs in men before age 20. But more research is needed on how male reproduction is affected by persistent organic pollutants such as dioxin.

Preconceptual Factors Affecting Either Parent

Preconception exposures to hazardous substances are one possible reason for a change in the normal male:female sex ratio at birth. Since 1970, a distinct and unexplained trend in reduced male-to-female birth ratio has been noted in Japan and in the United States. The difference, while very small, is significant on a population level. A decline of 37 males per 100,000 births occurred in Japan and a drop of 17 males per 100,000 per live births in the United States. The reasons for these population-wide declines are unknown, but one explanation may be parental exposures to low levels of environmental contaminants.

Preconception Counseling About Known Reproductive Hazards

Preconception counseling proactively addresses issues that can significantly affect the unborn child's health or development. Methylmercury in fish and lead are examples of toxicants which, through maternal preconception exposures, can affect the developing fetus *in utero*. Anticipatory guidance includes encouraging prospective parents to protect their health and that of their unborn infant by reducing known dietary exposures to methylmercury in certain fish species. Prospective mothers who smoke should be encouraged to quit because of the effects of smoking on fertility and because of numerous effects on a pregnancy.

In utero Effects from Past Maternal Exposures

Past and current exposures can affect a developing fetus in several ways. Contaminants in a pregnant woman's past and current diet can potentially harm the fetus. Physiologic changes during pregnancy can mobilize stored toxicants, such as lead from bone or PCBs from fat cells, resulting in fetal exposure. Maternal alcohol ingestion during pregnancy can lead to fetal alcohol syndrome.

Mobilization of toxicants stored in maternal tissues

Exposures experienced by the mother before pregnancy may affect her developing fetus. Exposure to some persistent or slowly excreted chemicals can lead to body burdens stored in such places as body fat or bone. For example, a woman who experienced a pre-pregnancy exposure to lead and who was inadequately treated for lead poisoning during childhood might give birth to an infant with congenital lead poisoning. The most logical explanation for this would be storage of the lead in the mother's bones with subsequent mobilization during pregnancy.

A mother's intake before and during pregnancy of mercury-containing fish may affect her child's neurological development. According to the National Health and Nutrition Examination Survey (NHANES), exposures of concern to methylmercury in blood—a neurological toxicant found in certain fish—occurs among 6% of 16- to 49-year old women. Subgroups with high fish consumption include wives of sport-fishers, coastal dwellers, and others who could have methylmercury exposures substantially higher than the U.S. norm.

Maternal smoking during pregnancy has been associated with:

- stillbirth,
- placental abruption,
- prematurity,
- lower mean birth weight,
- birth defects such as cleft lip and palate,
- increased risk of infant mortality,

- decrements in lung function later in the life of the exposed child, and

- sudden infant death syndrome (SIDS).

A child healthcare provider's anticipatory guidance can help stop maternal consumption of tobacco and alcohol. But other chemicals are known to have an adverse effect on pregnancies. A child healthcare provider can offer guidance on these chemicals as well.

Placental Dependent Exposures

A fact of fetal life is that the fetus cannot escape transplacental transport of toxicants to which the mother is exposed. During gestation, past and current maternal exposures can affect the fetus. The placenta, whose circulation is established approximately 17 days after fertilization, acts as the most important route of exposure for genotoxins and carcinogens.

The placenta is a semipermeable membrane that permits easy transport of low-molecular-weight (i.e., carbon monoxide (CO)) and fat-soluble compounds (i.e., polycyclic aromatic hydrocarbons and ethanol), as well as compounds such as lead. Some water-soluble and high-molecular-weight compounds may also cross the placenta, albeit more slowly. The placenta has limited detoxification ability. Placental

Table 11.1. Examples of chemicals and their known adverse effects on pregnancy and neonatal outcomes.

Chemical	Adverse effect
Antineoplastic drugs	Miscarriage, low birth weight, birth defects
Certain ethylene glycol ethers such as 2-ethoxyethanol (2EE) and 2-methoxyethanol (2ME)	Miscarriage
Lead	Miscarriage, low birth weight, neuro-developmental delays
Ionizing radiation	Miscarriage, low birth weight, birth defects, childhood cancers

Adapted from [NIOSH 1999]. This partial list of chemicals is from studies that found evidence of specific chemicals' adverse human health effects. For the most current and complete list of drugs and chemicals affecting pregnancy, please refer to the US Food and Drug Administration classifications.

degradative enzymes include inducible catalase, superoxide dismutase, and mixed function oxidases. But these enzymes help to mitigate only very low toxicant concentrations.

For example, young infants and children have an increased susceptibility to CO toxicity because of their higher metabolic rates. The fetus is at especially high risk of acute toxicity from carbon monoxide. Maternal CO diffuses across the placenta and increases the levels of CO in the fetus. Fetal hemoglobin has a higher affinity for CO compared with adult hemoglobin. The elimination half-life of carboxy-hemoglobin is longer in the fetus than in the adult. Exposure to CO results in a substantial decrease in oxygen delivery to the placenta and ultimately to fetal tissues.

Healthcare professionals such as anesthetists, dental assistants, and hospital personnel, are often exposed to potentially embryotoxic hazards such as:

- anesthetic gases,
- antineoplastic agents,
- ethylene oxide,
- mercury, and
- solvents.

Studies involving these professionals have revealed significant risks for spontaneous abortions and congenital malformations. In a study of nurses and pharmacists with occupational exposure to antineoplastic agents, maternal exposure to antineoplastic agents during pregnancy resulted in a statistically significant increased risk of spontaneous abortions and stillbirths.

Several occupations and industries have been associated with adverse outcomes in pregnancy, including an increased risk of spontaneous abortion and birth defects. Some of these occupations or industries include:

- solderers and welders,
- bridge repainters,
- radiator repairers,
- battery makers,
- electronics and semi-conductor industries, and
- health care workers involved in cancer chemotherapy.

Placental Independent Exposures

Fetal exposures that can occur independently of the placenta include:

- heat,

- ionizing radiation, and

- noise.

A mother's exposure to ionizing radiation can increase the likelihood of childhood leukemia and neurologic delays.

Section 11.3

Endocrine Disruptor and Reproductive Disorders

This section includes excerpts from "Endocrine Disruptors," National Institute of Environmental Health Sciences (NIEHS), August 11, 2015; and text from "What Are Endocrine Disruptors," United States Environmental Protection Agency (EPA), August 12, 2011.

What Are Endocrine Disruptors?

The Endocrine System

Endocrine systems, also referred to as hormone systems, are found in all mammals, birds, fish, and many other types of living organisms.

They are made up of:

- Glands located throughout the body.

- Hormones that are made by the glands and released into the bloodstream or the fluid surrounding cells.

- Receptors in various organs and tissues that recognize and respond to the hormones.

Hormones are released by glands and travel throughout the body, acting as chemical messengers. Hormones interface with cells that contain matching receptors in or on their surfaces. The hormone binds with the receptor, much like a key would fit into a lock. The hormones, or keys, need to find compatible receptors, or locks, to work properly. Although hormones reach all parts of the body, only target cells with compatible receptors are equipped to respond. Once a receptor and a hormone bind, the receptor carries out the hormone's instructions by either altering the cell's existing proteins or turning on genes that will build a new protein. Both of these actions create reactions throughout the body. Researchers have identified more than 50 hormones in humans and other vertebrates.

The endocrine system regulates all biological processes in the body from conception through adulthood and into old age, including the development of the brain and nervous system, the growth and function of the reproductive system, as well as the metabolism and blood sugar levels. The female ovaries, male testes, and pituitary, thyroid, and adrenal glands are major constituents of the endocrine system.

The Endocrine Disruptor Screening Program (EDSP) focuses on the estrogen, androgen, and thyroid hormones. Estrogens are the group of hormones responsible for female sexual development. They are produced primarily by the ovaries and in small amounts by the adrenal glands. Androgens are responsible for male sex characteristics. Testosterone, the sex hormone produced by the testicles, is an androgen. The thyroid gland secretes two main hormones, thyroxine and triiodothyronine, into the bloodstream. These thyroid hormones stimulate all the cells in the body and control biological processes such as growth, reproduction, development, and metabolism. For additional information on the endocrine system and endocrine disruptors, visit the Endocrine Primer.

Endocrine Disruptors

Disruption of the endocrine system can occur in various ways. Some chemicals mimic a natural hormone, fooling the body into over-responding to the stimulus (e.g., a growth hormone that results in increased muscle mass), or responding at inappropriate times (e.g., producing insulin when it is not needed). Other endocrine disrupting chemicals block the effects of a hormone from certain receptors (e.g., growth hormones required for normal development). Still others directly stimulate or inhibit the endocrine system and cause overproduction or underproduction of hormones (e.g., an over or underactive thyroid).

Certain drugs are used to intentionally cause some of these effects, such as birth control pills. In many situations involving environmental chemicals, however, an endocrine effect is not desirable.

In recent years, some scientists have proposed that chemicals might inadvertently be disrupting the endocrine system of humans and wildlife. A variety of chemicals have been found to disrupt the endocrine systems of animals in laboratory studies, and there is strong evidence that chemical exposure has been associated with adverse developmental and reproductive effects on fish and wildlife in particular locations. The relationship of human diseases of the endocrine system and exposure to environmental contaminants, however, is poorly understood and scientifically controversial.

One example of the devastating consequences of the exposure of developing animals, including humans, to endocrine disruptors is the case of the potent drug diethylstilbestrol (DES), a synthetic estrogen. Prior to its ban in the early 1970's, doctors mistakenly prescribed DES to as many as five million pregnant women to block spontaneous abortion and promote fetal growth. It was discovered after the children went through puberty that DES affected the development of the reproductive system and caused vaginal cancer. Since then, Congress has improved the evaluation and regulation process of drugs and other chemicals. The recent requirement of the establishment of an endocrine disruptor screening program is a highly significant step.

Exposures at low levels count

The body's own normal endocrine signaling involves very small changes in hormone levels, yet we know these changes can have significant biological effects. This leads scientists to think that chemical exposures, even at low doses, can disrupt the body's delicate endocrine system and lead to disease.

In 2000, an independent panel of experts convened by NIEHS and NTP found that there was "credible evidence" that some hormone-like chemicals can affect test animals' bodily functions at very low levels — well below the "no effect" levels determined by traditional testing.

Endocrine disrupting chemicals may impact a broad range of health effects.

Although there is limited evidence to prove that low-dose exposures are causing adverse human health effects, there is a large body of research in experimental animals and wildlife suggesting that endocrine disruptors may cause:

- Reductions in male fertility and declines in the numbers of males born.

- Abnormalities in male reproductive organs.

- Female reproductive health issues, including fertility problems, early puberty, and early reproductive senescence.

- Increases in mammary, ovarian, and prostate cancers.

- Increases in immune and autoimmune diseases, and some neurodegenerative diseases.

There are data showing that exposure to BPA, as well as other endocrine disrupting chemicals with estrogenic activity, may have effects on obesity and diabetes. These data, while preliminary and only in animals, indicate the potential for endocrine disrupting agents to have effects on other endocrine systems not yet fully examined.

Effects of endocrine disruptors may begin early and be persistent

Research shows that endocrine disruptors may pose the greatest risk during prenatal and early postnatal development when organ and neural systems are developing. In animals, adverse consequences, such as subfertility, premature reproductive senescence, and cancer, are linked to early exposure, but they may not be apparent until much later in life.

Research from NIEHS investigators have shown that the adverse effects of DES in mice can be passed to subsequent generations even though they were not directly exposed. The increased susceptibility for tumors was seen in both the granddaughters and grandsons of mice who were developmentally exposed to DES. Mechanisms involved in the transmission of disease were shown to involve epigenetic events — that is altering gene function without altering DNA sequence.

New research funded by NIEHS also found that endocrine disruptors may affect not just the offspring of mothers exposed during pregnancy, but future offspring as well. The researchers found that several endocrine disrupting chemicals caused fertility defects in male rats that were passed down to nearly every male in subsequent generations. This study suggests that the compounds may have caused changes in the developing male germ cells, and that endocrine disruptors may be able to reprogram or change the expression of genes without mutating

DNA. The role of environmental endocrine disrupting chemicals in the transmission of disease from one generation to another is of great research interest to NIEHS.

What are some current areas of Research NIEHS is pursuing?

Researchers are playing a lead role in uncovering the mechanisms of action of endocrine disruptors. Today, scientists are:

- Developing new models and tools to better understand how endocrine disruptors work.

- Developing high throughput assays to determine which chemicals have endocrine disrupting activity.

- Examining the long-term effects of exposure to various endocrine disrupting compounds during development and on diseases later in life.

- Conducting epidemiological studies in human populations.

- Developing new assessments and biomarkers to determine exposure and toxicity levels—especially how mixtures of chemicals impact individuals.

- Developing intervention and prevention strategies.

How do endocrine disruptors work?

From animal studies, researchers have learned much about the mechanisms through which endocrine disruptors influence the endocrine system and alter hormonal functions.

Endocrine disruptors can:

- Mimic or partly mimic naturally occurring hormones in the body like estrogens (the female sex hormone), androgens (the male sex hormone), and thyroid hormones, potentially producing over-stimulation.

- Bind to a receptor within a cell and block the endogenous hormone from binding.

- The normal signal then fails to occur and the body fails to respond properly. Examples of chemicals that block or antagonize hormones are anti-estrogens and anti-androgens.

- Interfere or block the way natural hormones or their receptors are made or controlled, for example, by altering their metabolism in the liver.

What are some examples of endocrine disruptors?

A wide and varied range of substances are thought to cause endocrine disruption. Chemicals that are known endocrine disruptors include diethylstilbestrol (the synthetic estrogen DES), dioxin and dioxin-like compounds, polychlorinated biphenyls (PCBs), DDT, and some other pesticides.

Bisphenol A (BPA) is a chemical produced in large quantities for use primarily in the production of polycarbonate plastics and epoxy resins. The NTP Center for the Evaluation of Risks to Human Reproduction completed a review of BPA in September 2008. The NTP expressed some concern for effects on the brain, behavior, and prostate gland in fetuses, infants, and children at current human exposures to bisphenol A.

Di(2-ethylhexyl) phthalate (DEHP) is a high production volume chemical used in the manufacture of a wide variety of consumer food packaging, some children's products, and some polyvinyl chloride (PVC) medical devices. In 2006, the NTP found that DEHP may pose a risk to human development, especially critically ill male infants.

Phytoestrogens are naturally occurring substances in plants that have hormone-like activity. Examples of phytoestrogens are genistein and daidzein, which can be found in soy-derived products.

Chapter 12

Environment and Autism

Chapter Contents

Section 12.1

Relationship Between Autism and the Environment

This section includes excerpts from "Autism," National Institute of Environmental Health Sciences (NIEHS), November 28, 2014; text from "Autism and the Environment," National Institute of Environmental Health Sciences (NIEHS), July 2014; and text from "A Research Strategy to Discover the Environmental Causes of Autism and Neurodevelopmental Disabilities," Environmental health Perspectives (EHP), April 25, 2012.

Research has shown that environmental factors likely play a role in autism. Studies also indicate that genetics contribute to the disorder. The National Institute of Environmental Health Sciences (NIEHS) supports research to discover how the environment may influence autism. This important environmental research offers real promise for prevention—because you can't change your genes, but you can change your environment.

What Is Autism?

Autism, also known as ASD, is a spectrum of disorders that causes impairment in social interaction, as well as the presence of repetitive, restricted behaviors and interests. It is usually first diagnosed in early childhood.

The term spectrum refers to the wide range of symptoms, skills, and levels of impairment that those with ASD can have. Some are mildly impaired by their symptoms, while others are severely disabled.

What Are the Symptoms?

Although people with autism have a variety of symptoms that vary in severity, they all have difficulties communicating and interacting with others, and show restricted and repetitive patterns of behavior and interests. Most symptoms are noticeable by the time a child is 2–3 years old, but many children are not diagnosed until later. Early intensive behavioral intervention can improve communication, learning, and social skills in children with autism.

Autism affects people for their entire lives, and often comes with other conditions, such as epilepsy, sleep disturbances, and gastrointestinal problems. Currently, no drugs have proven effective for treating core autism symptoms.

How Is NIEHS Contributing to Autism Research?

NIEHS has steadily increased funding of autism research over the last decade, and this investment is producing important new discoveries that may help prevent autism. For example, NIEHS-funded researchers have shown that taking folic acid and avoiding infections during pregnancy can help lower autism risk. Researchers have also shown that problems with the immune system are involved in autism, and that early-life exposure to high levels of air pollution may increase risk, especially for children whose genetic makeup causes them to be more susceptible.

The NIEHS Autism Research Program has attracted talented scientists from toxicology, epidemiology, and other areas. These researchers are using new ways to measure prenatal exposures, screen for contaminants that affect brain development, and understand how environmental factors interact with genes to lead to autism.

The impact of autism

- Autism affects about one in 68 children.
- The number of children with autism more than doubled from 2000 to 2010.
- Autism is nearly five times more common in boys, one in 42, than girls, one in 189.
- People with autism had average medical expenses of $4,110 to $6,200 more per year than people without autism.
- Nearly half of children with autism, 46 percent, have average or above-average intellectual ability.

Environmental Factors Play a Role in Autism

Air pollution

Work supported by NIEHS indicates that early-life exposure to air pollution is a risk factor for autism.

- A 2011 study reported that children living within 1,014 feet, or a little less than 3.5 football fields, of a freeway, at birth, were twice as likely to develop autism.

- Building on those findings, in 2013, researchers reported an association between exposure to traffic-related air pollution, as well as components of regional air pollution, and an increased risk of autism.

- A 2014 study pointed to a likely gene-environment interaction. Children whose genetic makeup causes them to be more susceptible to the health effects of high levels of air pollution showed the highest risk for autism.

Prenatal conditions

Researchers funded by NIEHS discovered that problems with the immune system, as well as maternal conditions during pregnancy, are linked with higher autism risk.

- Research showed that some children are born to mothers with antibodies that interfere with fetal brain development in ways that could lead to autism.

- Maternal diabetes and obesity, which are associated with inflammation, both have strong links to the likelihood of having a child with autism or another developmental disability.

- During pregnancy, elevated levels of inflammation, which can come from an infection, were linked with an increased risk of having a child with autism. This finding may help to identify preventive strategies.

Nutrition

According to NIEHS-funded research, prenatal vitamins may help lower autism risk.

- Women who took a daily prenatal vitamin during the three months before and during the first month of pregnancy, were less likely to have a child with autism than women not taking the supplements. This was more evident in genetically susceptible women or children, suggesting that a gene-environment interaction could be responsible.

- A later study identified folic acid as the source of the protective effects of prenatal vitamins. Women who consumed the daily recommended dosage during the first month of pregnancy had a reduced risk of having a child with autism.

Mercury and other contaminants

There continues to be concern about autism and mercury exposure. NIEHS funds research examining this and exposures to other contaminants.

- Eating fish is the primary way that we are exposed to organic mercury. A 2013 study examined people in the Republic of Seychelles, where fish consumption is high. The study found no association between prenatal organic mercury exposure and autism behaviors.

- Scientists can test for recent exposure to organic mercury with blood tests. Researchers found that after adjusting for dietary and other mercury sources, children with autism had blood mercury levels that were similar to those found in children without autism.

- Researchers are also studying other contaminants, such as bisphenol A (BPA), phthalates, heavy metals, flame retardants, polychlorinated biphenyls (PCBs), and pesticides, to see if they affect early brain development and play a role in autism.

Collaborations

Much of the research funded by NIEHS addresses priorities identified by the Interagency Autism Coordinating Committee, which coordinates all autism efforts within the U.S. Department of Health and Human Services. NIEHS also collaborates with the U.S. Environmental Protection Agency, other NIH institutes, and various autism research and advocacy groups.

Population-Based Research

Studies that look at large numbers of people can reveal patterns that may indicate the involvement of environmental factors in autism. NIEHS funds studies with participants in various parts of the United States, as well as in Australia, Denmark, Finland, Israel, Norway, Sweden, and South Korea. Key projects include the following:

CHARGE – The Childhood Autism Risks from Genetics and the Environment study seeks to identify causes and contributing factors for autism, by conducting medical exams and collecting biological samples from children, and obtaining information on environmental exposures, health, lifestyle, sociodemographics, and behavior from their parents. Launched in 2003, this study is enrolling children with autism, children with developmental delay but not autism, and children with typical or expected development.

MARBLES and EARLI—The Markers of Autism Risk in Babies-Learning Early Signs (MARBLES), and Early Autism Risk Longitudinal Investigation (EARLI) studies are following women at high risk of giving birth to a child with autism. Women are enrolled during early pregnancy and their children followed to age 3. By collecting data from mothers and their babies throughout critical periods, these studies can better identify and measure environmental exposures that may impact the very early stages of brain development.

What's Next?

In addition to identifying environmental factors that may influence autism risk, NIEHS-funded researchers are investigating how these factors may interact with a person's genes. This information could identify new targets for prevention and therapies, and also point to areas that need to be examined in human studies.

- Researchers are studying early-life exposures, using blood samples from participants in the MARBLES study. The investigators want to understand whether these exposures cause DNA to change in a way that influences brain development and affects risk of autism.

- Stem cells from people with fragile X syndrome are being studied for gene-environment interactions. By using these stem cells to create sets of neurons that are identical, except for a gene known to be involved in autism, researchers can better understand how different forms of this gene influence susceptibility to environmental factors.

- Using data on genes known to be involved with autism, investigators are screening chemicals that interact with those genes, to identify which chemicals may increase autism risk. This research will help reveal environmental factors that increase autism risk and provide information about specific gene-environment interactions.

A Research Strategy to Discover the Environmental Causes of Autism and Neurodevelopmental Disabilities

Autism, attention deficit/hyperactivity disorder (ADHD), mental retardation, dyslexia, and other biologically based disorders of brain development affect between 400,000 and 600,000 of the 4 million children born in the United States each year. The Centers for Disease Control and Prevention (CDC) has reported that autism spectrum disorder (ASD) now affects 1.13% (1 of 88) of American children and ADHD affects 14%. Treatment of these disorders is difficult; the disabilities they cause can last lifelong, and they are devastating to families. In addition, these disorders place enormous economic burdens on society.

Although discovery research to identify the potentially preventable causes of neurodevelopmental disorders (NDDs) has increased in recent years, more research is urgently needed. This research encompasses both genetic and environmental studies.

Genetic research has received particular investment and attention and has demonstrated that ASD and certain other NDDs have a strong hereditary component. Linkage studies have identified candidate autism susceptibility genes at multiple loci, most consistently on chromosomes 7q, 15q, and 16p. Exome sequencing in sporadic cases of autism has detected new mutations, and copy number variant studies have identified several hundred copy number variants putatively linked to autism. The candidate genes most strongly implicated in NDD causation encode for proteins involved in synaptic architecture, neurotransmitter synthesis (e.g., γ-aminobutyric acid serotonin), oxytocin receptors, and cation trafficking. No single anomaly predominates. Instead, autism appears to be a family of diseases with common phenotypes linked to a series of genetic anomalies, each of which is responsible for no more than 2–3% of cases. The total fraction of ASD attributable to genetic inheritance may be about 30–40%.

Exploration of the environmental causes of autism and other NDDs has been catalyzed by growing recognition of the exquisite sensitivity of the developing human brain to toxic chemicals. This susceptibility is greatest during unique "windows of vulnerability" that open only in embryonic and fetal life and have no later counterpart. "Proof of the principle" that early exposures can cause autism comes from studies linking ASD to medications taken in the first trimester of pregnancy—thalidomide, misoprostol, and valproic acid—and to first-trimester rubella infection.

This "proof-of-principle" evidence for environmental causation is supported further by findings from prospective birth cohort epidemiological studies, many of them supported by the National Institute of Environmental Health Sciences (NIEHS). These studies enroll women during pregnancy, measure prenatal exposures in real time as they occur, and then follow children longitudinally with periodic direct examinations to assess growth, development, and the presence of disease. Prospective studies are powerful engines for the discovery of etiologic associations between prenatal exposures and NDDs. They have linked autistic behaviors with prenatal exposures to the organophosphate insecticide chlorpyrifos and also with prenatal exposures to phthalates. Additional prospective studies have linked loss of cognition (IQ), dyslexia, and ADHD to lead, methylmercury, organophosphate insecticides, organochlorine insecticides, polychlorinated biphenyls, arsenic, manganese, polycyclic aromatic hydrocarbons, bisphenol A, brominated flame retardants, and perfluorinated compounds.

Toxic chemicals likely cause injury to the developing human brain either through direct toxicity or interactions with the genome. An expert committee convened by the U.S. National Academy of Sciences (NAS) estimated that 3% of neurobehavioral disorders are caused directly by toxic environmental exposures and that another 25% are caused by interactions between environmental factors, defined broadly, and inherited susceptibilities. Epigenetic modification of gene expression by toxic chemicals that results in DNA methylation, histone modification, or changes in activity levels of non-protein-coding RNA (ncRNAs) may be a mechanism of such gene-environment interaction. Epigenetic "marks" have been shown to be able to influence gene expression and alter high-order DNA structure.

A major unanswered question is whether there are still undiscovered environmental causes of autism or other NDDs among the thousands of chemicals currently in wide use in the United States. In the past 50 years, > 80,000 new synthetic chemicals have been developed. The U.S. Environmental Protection Agency has identified 3,000 "high production volume" (HPV) chemicals that are in widest use and thus pose greatest potential for human exposure. These HPV chemicals are used today in millions of consumer products. Children and pregnant women are exposed extensively to them, and CDC surveys detect quantifiable levels of nearly 200 HPV chemicals in the bodies of virtually all Americans, including pregnant women.

The significance of early chemical exposures for children's health is not yet fully understood. A great concern is that a large number of the chemicals in widest use have not undergone even minimal assessment of potential toxicity, and only about 20% have been screened for potential toxicity during early development. Unless studies specifically examine develop-mental consequences of early exposures to untested chemicals, subclinical dysfunction caused by these exposures can go unrecognized for years. One example is the "silent epidemic" of childhood lead poisoning: From the 1940s to the 1980s, millions of American children were exposed to excessive levels of lead from paint and gasoline, resulting in reduced average intelligence by 2–5 IQ points. The late David Rall, former director of NIEHS, once observed that "If thalidomide had caused a 10-point loss of IQ instead of birth defects of the limbs, it would likely still be on the market."

To begin formulation of a systematic strategy for discovery of potentially preventable environmental causes of autism and other NDDs, the Mount Sinai Children's Environmental Health Center, with the support of the NIEHS and Autism Speaks, convened a workshop on "Exploring the Environmental Causes of Autism and Learning Disabilities." It generated a list of 10 chemicals and mixtures widely distributed in the environment that are already suspected of causing developmental neurotoxicity:

1. Lead

2. Methylmercury

3. Polychlorinated biphenyls

4. Organophosphate pesticides

5. Organochlorine pesticides

6. Endocrine disruptors

7. Automotive exhaust

8. Polycyclic aromatic hydrocarbons

9. Brominated flame retardants

10. Perfluorinated compounds

This list is not exhaustive and will almost certainly expand in the years ahead as new science emerges. It is intended to focus research in environmental causation of NDDs on a short list of chemicals where concentrated study has high potential to generate actionable findings in the near future. Its ultimate purpose is to catalyze new evidence-based programs for prevention of disease in America's children.

Section 12.2

Vaccinations, Thimerosal, and Autism

This section includes excerpts from "Vaccine Safety - Addressing Common Concerns," Centers for Disease Control and Prevention (CDC), March 17, 2015; and text from "Frequently Asked Questions About Thimerosal," Centers for Disease Control and Prevention (CDC), February 17, 2015.

Vaccines Do Not Cause Autism

Autism spectrum disorder (ASD) is a developmental disability that is caused by differences in how the brain functions. People with ASD may communicate, interact, behave, and learn in different ways. Recent estimates from CDC's Autism and Developmental Disabilities Monitoring Network found that about 1 in 68 children have been identified with ASD in communities across the United States. CDC is committed to providing essential data on ASD, searching for causes of and factors that increase the risk for ASD, and developing resources that help identify children with ASD as early as possible.

There is no link between vaccines and autism.

Some people have had concerns that ASD might be linked to the vaccines children receive, but studies have shown that there is no link between receiving vaccines and developing ASD. In 2011, an Institute of Medicine (IOM) report on eight vaccines given to children and adults found that with rare exceptions, these vaccines are very safe.

A 2013 CDC study added to the research showing that vaccines do not cause ASD. The study looked at the number of antigens (substances in vaccines that cause the body's immune system to produce disease-fighting antibodies) from vaccines during the first two years of life. The results showed that the total amount of antigen from vaccines received was the same between children with ASD and those that did not have ASD.

Vaccine ingredients do not cause autism.

One vaccine ingredient that has been studied specifically is thimerosal, a mercury-based preservative used to prevent contamination of multidose vials of vaccines. Research shows that thimerosal does not cause ASD. In fact, a 2004 scientific review by the IOM concluded that "the evidence favors rejection of a causal relationship between thimerosal-containing vaccines and autism." Since 2003, there have been nine CDC-funded or conducted studies that have found no link between thimerosal-containing vaccines and ASD, as well as no link between the measles, mumps, and rubella (MMR) vaccine and ASD in children.

Between 1999 and 2001, thimerosal was removed or reduced to trace amounts in all childhood vaccines except for some flu vaccines. This was done as part of a broader national effort to reduce all types of mercury exposure in children before studies were conducted that determined that thimerosal was not harmful. It was done as a precaution. Currently, the only childhood vaccines that contain thimerosal are flu vaccines packaged in multidose vials. Thimerosal-free alternatives are also available for flu vaccine.

Frequently Asked Questions About Thimerosal (Ethylmercury)

What is thimerosal? Is it the same as mercury?

- Thimerosal is a mercury-containing organic compound and has been used for decades in the United States and other countries. It's use as a preservative in a number of biological and drug products, including many vaccines, to help prevent potentially life threatening contamination with harmful microbes.

- Mercury is a metal found naturally in the environment and affects the human body differently than thimerosal.

What is the difference between ethylmercury and methylmercury? How are they different?

- When learning about thimerosal and mercury it is important to **understand the difference** between two different compounds that contain mercury: ethylmercury and methylmercury. They are totally different materials.

- **Methylmercury** is formed in the environment when mercury metal is present. If this material is found in the body, it is usually the result of eating some types of fish or other food. High amounts of methylmercury can harm the nervous system. This has been found in studies of some populations that have long-term exposure to methylmercury in foods at levels that are far higher than the U.S. population. In the United States, federal guidelines keep as much methylmercury as possible out of the environment and food, but over a lifetime, everyone is exposed to some methylmercury.

- **Ethylmercury** is formed when the body breaks down thimerosal. The body uses ethylmercury differently than methylmercury; ethylmercury is broken down and clears out of the blood more quickly. Low-level ethylmercury exposures from vaccines are very different from long-term methylmercury exposures, since the ethylmercury does not stay in the body.

Does thimerosal cause autism?

- No. Research does not show any link between thimerosal and autism.

Is thimerosal safe for people?

- Yes. Thimerosal has been used safely in vaccines for a long time (since the 1930s) and has a proven track record of being safe. A variety of scientists have been studying the use of vaccines that have thimerosal in them for many years. They haven't found any actual evidence that thimerosal causes harm.

Why was thimerosal removed from vaccines given to children?

- Although no evidence suggests that there are safety concerns with thimerosal, vaccine manufacturers have stopped using it as a precautionary measure.The only vaccine that still includes thimerosal as a preservative is the multi-dose inactivated influenza vaccine. There are other formulations of flu vaccine that do not include thimerosal.

- In 1999, the Food and Drug Administration (FDA) was required by law to assess the amount of mercury in all the products the agency oversees, not just vaccines. The U.S. Public Health Service decided that as much mercury as possible should be removed from vaccines, and thimerosal was the only source of mercury in vaccines.

- The decision to remove it was a made as a precautionary measure to decrease overall exposure to mercury among young infants.

- Thimerosal was removed from all childhood vaccines in 2001 with the exception of inactivated flu vaccine in multi-dose vials. However, thimerosal has been removed from all single-dose preparations of flu vaccine for children and adults. There has never been thimerosal in live attenuated flu vaccine or recombinant flu vaccine. No acceptable alternative preservative has yet been identified for multi-dose flu vaccine vials.

Why is thimerosal used in some vaccines?

- Because it prevents the growth of dangerous microbes, thimerosal is used as a preservative in multi-dose vials of flu vaccines, about a third of flu vaccine doses that are available.

  - Each time a new needle is inserted into the multi-dose vial, it is possible for microbes to get into the vial.

  - The preservative, thimerosal, prevents contamination in the multi-dose vial when individual doses are drawn from it. Receiving a vaccine contaminated with bacteria can be very dangerous.

- For two, non-flu childhood vaccines, thimerosal is used to prevent the growth of microbes (bacteria and other environmental contaminants) during the manufacturing process.

  - When thimerosal is used this way, it is removed later in the process.

  - Only trace (very tiny) amounts remain.

  - Today, the only childhood vaccines that have trace amounts of thimerosal are: one DTaP vaccine and one DTaP-Hib combination vaccine.

- Among flu vaccines that might be given to children, one manufacturer's single-dose formulation (tradename Fluvirin), which is approved for use among children 4 years and older, has trace amounts of thimerosal. All other single-dose formulations of flu vaccine have no thimerosal.

Do all flu vaccines contain thimerosal?

- No. Influenza (flu) vaccines are currently available in both thimerosal-containing and thimerosal-free versions. The total amount of flu vaccine without thimerosal as a preservative has increased over time. This year, about 2/3 of flu vaccine that is manufactured for the U.S. will be thimerosal-free.

Why is thimerosal still in some flu vaccines that children may receive?

- To produce enough flu vaccine for the entire country, some of it must be put into multi-dose vials. These vials have very tiny amounts of thimerosal as a preservative. This is necessary because each time an individual dose is drawn from a multi-dose vial with a new needle and syringe, there is the potential to contaminate the vial with harmful microbes (toxins). So, this preservative is needed to prevent contamination of the vial (as a safeguard) when individual doses are drawn from it, and keep children safe who are receiving the flu shot from the multi-dose vial. Children can safely receive flu vaccine that contains thimerosal.

- Flu vaccine that does not contain thimerosal is available in single-dose vials or single-dose syringes. One formulation of single-dose inactivated flu vaccine, Fluvirin, contains trace amounts of thimerosal.

What keeps today's childhood vaccines from becoming contaminated if they do not contain thimerosal as a preservative?

- The childhood vaccines that used to contain thimerosal as a preservative are now put into single-dose vials or syringes, so no preservative is needed. In the past, these vaccines were put into multi-dose vials, which could become contaminated when new needles were used to get vaccine out of the vial for each dose.

Was thimerosal used in all childhood vaccines?

- No. Some other vaccines, including the measles, mumps, and rubella vaccine (MMR), do not and did not ever contain thimerosal or any preservative. Varicella (chickenpox), inactivated polio (IPV), and pneumococcal conjugate vaccines have also never contained thimerosal.

- There is no thimerosal used in the vaccines on the childhood immunization schedule.

How can I find out if thimerosal is in a vaccine?

- For a complete list of vaccines and their thimerosal content level, you may visit http://www.fda.gov/BiologicsBloodVaccines/ SafetyAvailability/VaccineSafety/UCM096228. Additionally, you may ask your health care provider or pharmacist for a copy of the vaccine package insert. It lists ingredients in the vaccine and discusses any known adverse reactions.

How does thimerosal work in the body?

- Thimerosal contains "ethylmercury," which is a completely different form of mercury than elemental mercury or methylmercury, which are found in the environment and some kinds of fish. Elemental mercury and methylmercury stay in the human body and at high levels can make people sick. But ethylmercury (that is found in thimerosal) does not stay in the body a long time and clears out of the blood quickly, so it does not build up and reach harmful levels. In fact, when thimerosal enters the human body, it breaks down to ethylmercury and thiosalicylate, which are easily eliminated.

What are the possible side-effects of thimerosal?

- Most people don't have any side effects from thimerosal, but some people will have mild reactions like redness and swelling at the place where the shot was given, which only last 1 to 2 days. It's very unlikely you will have an allergic reaction to thimerosal. Research shows that most people who are allergic to thimerosal will not have a reaction when thimerosal is injected under the skin.

- Anyone who believes they have been injured by a vaccine should contact the National Vaccine Injury Compensation Program.

Does thimerosal use in vaccines interfere with brain activity?

- The study, "Thimerosal Exposure in Early Life and Neuropsychological Outcomes 7–10 Years Later," which was published on July 15, 2011, in the *Journal of Pediatric Psychology,* looked for a possible association between exposure to thimerosal-containing vaccines before birth or in the first seven months of life and neuropsychological function at ages 7–10 years old.

- This study used the same data from the study by Thompson et al published in the September 27, 2007 *New England Journal of Medicine.* The original study evaluated 1,047 children ages 7–10 and their biological mothers and concluded that ethyl mercury exposure from thimerosal-containing vaccines and immunoglobulins does not affect neuropsychological functioning at ages 7–10 years.

- The authors concluded that the weight of the evidence in this study does not support a causal association between early exposure to mercury from thimerosal-containing vaccines and immune globulins administered prenatally or during infancy and neuropsychological functioning at the age of 7–10 years for any of the other neuropsychological outcomes assessed.

Part Three

Outdoor Environmental Hazards

Chapter 13

Air Pollution

Chapter Contents

Section 13.1

Introduction

Text in this section begins with excerpts from "Air Pollution," National Institute of Environmental Health Sciences (NIEHS), May 26, 2015.

Text in this section beginning with "Acid Rain" is excerpted from "Air and Radiation," United States Environmental Protection Agency (EPA), January 22, 2015.

Basic Information

The air we breathe in many U.S. cities is being polluted by activities such as driving cars and trucks; burning coal, oil, and other fossil fuels; and manufacturing chemicals. Air pollution can even come from smaller, everyday activities such as dry cleaning, filling your car with gas, and degreasing and painting operations. These activities add gases and particles to the air we breathe. When these gases and particles accumulate in the air in high enough concentrations, they can harm us and our environment. More people in cities and surrounding counties means more cars, trucks, industrial and commercial operations, and generally means more pollution.

Air pollution is a problem for all of us. The average adult breathes over 3,000 gallons of air every day. Children breathe even more air per pound of body weight and are more susceptible to air pollution. Many air pollutants, such as those that form urban smog and toxic compounds, remain in the environment for long periods of time and are carried by the winds hundreds of miles from their origin. Millions of people live in areas where urban smog, very small particles, and toxic pollutants pose serious health concerns. People exposed to high enough levels of certain air pollutants may experience burning in their eyes, an irritated throat, or breathing difficulties. Long-term exposure to air pollution can cause cancer and long-term damage to the immune, neurological, reproductive, and respiratory systems. In extreme cases, it can even cause death.

Air pollution is a mixture of natural and man-made substances in the air we breathe. It is typically separated into two categories: outdoor air pollution and indoor air pollution.

Outdoor air pollution involves exposures that take place outside of the built environment. Examples include:

- Fine particles produced by the burning of fossil fuels (i.e. the coal and petroleum used in traffic and energy production)
- Noxious gases (sulfur dioxide, nitrogen oxides, carbon monoxide, chemical vapors, etc.)
- Ground-level ozone (a reactive form of oxygen and a primary component of urban smog)
- Tobacco smoke

Indoor air pollution involves exposures to particulates, carbon oxides, and other pollutants carried by indoor air or dust. Examples include:

- Gases (carbon monoxide, radon, etc.)
- Household products and chemicals
- Building materials (asbestos, formaldehyde, lead, etc.)
- Outdoor indoor allergens (cockroach and mouse dropping, etc.)
- Tobacco smoke
- Mold and pollen

Please note: In some instances, outdoor air pollution can make its way indoors by way of open windows, doors, ventilation, etc.

Acid Rain

"Acid rain" is a broad term describing acid rain, snow, fog, and particles. It is caused by sulfur dioxide and nitrogen oxides released by power plants, vehicles, and other sources. Acid rain harms plants, animals, and fish, and erodes bulding surfaces and national monuments. In addition, acidic particles can hurt people's lungs and reduce how far we can see through the air.

Air Quality Index (AQI)

The AQI is an index for reporting daily air quality. It tells you how clean or polluted your air is, and what associated health effects might be a concern for you. The AQI focuses on health effects you may experience within a few hours or days after breathing polluted air. EPA calculates the AQI for five major air pollutants regulated by the Clean Air Act: ground-level ozone, particle pollution (also known as particulate matter), carbon monoxide, sulfur dioxide, and nitrogen dioxide. For each of these pollutants, EPA has established national air quality standards to protect public health.Ground-level ozone and airborne particles are the two pollutants that pose the greatest threat to human health in this country.

Climate Change

Climate change refers to any significant change in measures of climate (such as temperature, precipitation, or wind) lasting for an extended period (decades or longer).

Haze and Visibility

Haze is caused when sunlight encounters tiny pollution particles in the air. It degrades visibility in many American cities and affects some of our nation's most treasured areas, including Grand Canyon, Yellowstone, Acadia, and Shenandoah.

Indoor Air Quality

Indoor air levels of many pollutants may be 2–5 times, and occasionally, more than 100 times higher than outdoor levels. Indoor air pollutants are of particular concern because most people spend as much as 90% of their time indoors. Common sources can include burning kerosene, wood or oil, smoking tobacco products, releases from household cleaners, pesticides, building materials, and radon.

Ozone Depletion

A protective ozone layer is located in the stratosphere about 22 miles above the Earth's surface. This layer protects us from the sun's harmful ultraviolet radiation. This protective shield is being damaged by chemicals such as CFCs, halons, and methyl chloroform, and can lead to harmful health effects such as skin cancer and cataracts.

Radiation

Radiation occurs naturally (e.g., radon) but we also use radioactive materials to generate electricity and to diagnose and treat medical problems. Frequent exposures to radiation can cause cancer and other adverse health effects.

Smog, Particles, and Other Common Pollutants

Breathing air pollution such as ozone (a primary ingredient in urban smog), particulate matter, carbon monoxide, nitrogen oxides, sulfur dioxide, and lead can have numerous effects on human health, including respiratory problems, hospitalization for heart or lung disease, and even premature death. Some can also have effects on aquatic life, vegetation, and animals.

Toxic Air Pollutants

Includes 188 hazardous air pollutants, such as benzene, methylene chloride, mercury, and dioxins. Some are known or suspected to cause cancer. Others may cause respiratory effects, birth defects, and reproductive and other serious health effects. Some can even cause death or serious injury if accidentally released in large amounts.

Vehicles and Engines

Cars, buses, trucks, planes, trains, boats, and other sources contribute to air pollution.

Section 13.2

Acid Rain

Text in this section is excerpted from "Acid Rain," United States Environmental Protection Agency (EPA), September 11, 2014.

Acid rain is a serious environmental problem that affects large parts of the United States and Canada. Acid rain is particularly damaging to lakes, streams, and forests and the plants and animals that live in these ecosystems.

What Is Acid Rain?

"Acid rain" is a broad term referring to a mixture of wet and dry deposition (deposited material) from the atmosphere containing higher than normal amounts of nitric and sulfuric acids. The precursors, or chemical forerunners, of acid rain formation result from both natural sources, such as volcanoes and decaying vegetation, and man-made sources, primarily emissions of sulfur dioxide (SO_2) and nitrogen oxides (NO_x) resulting from fossil fuel combustion. In the United States, roughly 2/3 of all SO_2 and 1/4 of all NO_x come from electric power generation that relies on burning fossil fuels, like coal. Acid rain occurs when these gases react in the atmosphere with water, oxygen, and other chemicals to form various acidic compounds. The result is a mild solution of sulfuric acid and nitric acid. When sulfur dioxide and nitrogen oxides are released from power plants and other sources, prevailing winds blow these compounds across state and national borders, sometimes over hundreds of miles.

Wet Deposition

Wet deposition refers to acidic rain, fog, and snow. If the acid chemicals in the air are blown into areas where the weather is wet, the acids can fall to the ground in the form of rain, snow, fog, or mist. As this acidic water flows over and through the ground, it affects a variety of plants and animals. The strength of the effects depends on several

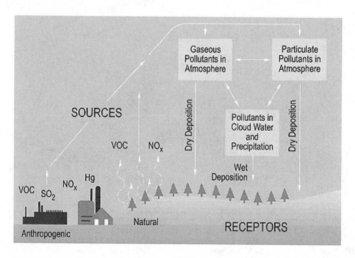

Figure 13.1. Acid Rain

factors, including how acidic the water is; the chemistry and buffering capacity of the soils involved; and the types of fish, trees, and other living things that rely on the water.

Dry Deposition

In areas where the weather is dry, the acid chemicals may become incorporated into dust or smoke and fall to the ground through dry deposition, sticking to the ground, buildings, homes, cars, and trees. Dry deposited gases and particles can be washed from these surfaces by rainstorms, leading to increased runoff. This runoff water makes the resulting mixture more acidic. About half of the acidity in the atmosphere falls back to earth through dry deposition.

Effects of Acid Rain

Acid rain causes acidification of lakes and streams and contributes to the damage of trees at high elevations (for example, red spruce trees above 2,000 feet) and many sensitive forest soils. In addition, acid rain accelerates the decay of building materials and paints, including irreplaceable buildings, statues, and sculptures that are part of our nation's cultural heritage. Prior to falling to the earth, sulfur dioxide (SO_2) and nitrogen oxide (NO_x) gases and their particulate matter derivatives—sulfates and nitrates—contribute to visibility degradation and harm public health.

Reducing Acid Rain

There are several ways to reduce acid rain—more properly called acid deposition—ranging from societal changes to individual action. It is critical that acid deposition be reduced, not only in the United States and Canada, but also throughout the world to preserve the integrity of natural habitats, as well as to reduce damage to man-made structures.

EPA has taken steps to limit the amount of NO_x and SO_2 emitted into the atmosphere because they are the main contributors to acid deposition.

Understand acid deposition's causes and effects

To understand acid deposition's causes and effects, and to track changes in the environment, scientists from EPA, state governments, and academia study acidification processes. They collect air and water samples and measure them for various characteristics such as pH and chemical composition, and research the effects of acid deposition on human-made materials such as marble and bronze. Finally, scientists work to understand the effects of sulfur dioxide (SO_2) and nitrogen oxides (NO_x)—the pollutants that cause acid deposition and contribute to particulate matter—on human health.

To solve the acid rain problem, people need to understand how acid rain damages the environment. They also need to understand what changes could be made to the air pollution sources that cause the problem. The answers to these questions help leaders make better decisions about how to control air pollution and therefore, how to reduce—or even eliminate—acid rain. Because there are many solutions to the acid rain problem, leaders have a choice of which options or combination of options are best. The next section describes some of the steps that can be taken to tackle the acid deposition problem.

Clean up smokestacks and exhaust pipes

Almost all of the electricity that powers modern life comes from burning fossil fuels such as coal, natural gas, and oil. Acid deposition is caused by two pollutants that are released into the atmosphere when fossil fuels are burned: sulfur dioxide (SO_2) and nitrogen oxides (NO_x). Coal accounts for most U.S. SO_2 emissions and a large portion of NO_x emissions. Sulfur is present in coal as an impurity, and it reacts with air when the coal is burned to form SO_2. In contrast, NO_x is formed when any fossil fuel is burned.

There are several options for reducing SO_2 emissions, including using coal containing less sulfur, washing the coal, and using devices called "scrubbers" to chemically remove the SO_2 from the gases leaving the smokestack. Power plants can also switch fuels—for example, burning natural gas creates much less SO_2 than burning coal. Certain approaches will also have the additional benefit of reducing other pollutants such as mercury and carbon dioxide (CO_2). Understanding these "co-benefits" has become important in seeking cost-effective air pollution reduction strategies. Finally, power plants can use technologies that do not burn fossil fuels. Each of these options, however, has its own costs and benefits; there is no single universal solution.

Similar to scrubbers on power plants, catalytic converters reduce NO_x emissions from cars. These devices have been required for over 20 years in the United States, and it is important to keep them working properly. Recently, tailpipe restrictions were tightened to help curb

NO$_x$ emissions. EPA also continues to make, changes to gasoline that allow it to burn cleaner.

Use alternative energy sources

There are other sources of electricity besides fossil fuels. They include nuclear power, hydropower, wind energy, geothermal energy, and solar energy. Nuclear and hydropower are used most widely in the United States, while wind, solar, and geothermal energy have not yet been harnessed on a large enough scale to make them economically-feasible alternatives.

There are also alternative energies, such as natural gas, batteries, and fuel cells, available to power automobiles.

All sources of energy have environmental costs as well as benefits. Some types of energy are more expensive to produce than others, which means that not all Americans can afford all of them. Nuclear power, hydropower, and coal are the cheapest form sof energy today, but advancements in technologies and regulatory developments may change this in the future. All of these factors must be weighed when deciding which energy source to use today and which to invest in for tomorrow.

Restore a Damaged Environment

Acid deposition penetrates deeply into the fabric of an ecosystem, changing the chemistry of the soil and streams and narrowing—sometimes to nothing—the space where certain plants and animals can survive. Because there are so many changes, it takes many years for ecosystems to recover from acid deposition, even after emissions are reduced and the rain pH is restored to normal. For example, while visibility might improve within days, and small or episodic chemical changes in streams improve within months, chronically acidified lakes, streams, forests, and soils can take years to decades, or even centuries (in the case of soils) to heal.

However, there are some things that people can do to bring back lakes and streams more quickly. Limestone or lime (a naturally occurring basic compound) can be added to acidic lakes to "cancel out" the acidity. This process, called liming, has been used extensively in Norway and Sweden but is not used very often in the United States Liming tends to be expensive, has to be done repeatedly to keep the water from returning to its acidic condition, and is considered a short-term remedy in only specific areas, rather than an effort to reduce or prevent pollution. Furthermore, it does not solve the broader problems of changes in soil chemistry and forest health in the watershed, and it does nothing to address visibility reductions, materials damage, and risk to human health. However, liming does often permit fish to remain in a lake, allowing the native population to survive in place until emissions reductions reduce the amount of acid deposition in the area.

Look to the future

As emissions from the largest known sources of acid deposition—power plants and automobiles—are reduced, EPA scientists and their colleagues must assess the reductions to make sure they are achieving the results that Congress anticipated when it created the Acid Rain Program in 1990. If these assessments show that acid deposition is still harming the environment, Congress may begin to consider additional ways to reduce emissions that cause acid deposition. It may consider additional emission reductions from sources that have already been controlled, or methods to reduce emissions from other sources. Congress may also focus on energy efficiency and alternative energy. Implementation of cost-effective mechanisms to reduce emissions and their impact on the environment will continue to evolve.

Take action as individuals

It may seem like there is not much that one individual can do to stop acid deposition. However, like many environmental problems, acid deposition is caused by the cumulative actions of millions of individual people. Therefore, each individual can also reduce their contribution to the problem and become part of the solution. Individuals can contribute directly by conserving energy, since energy production causes the largest portion of the acid deposition problem. For example, you can:

- Turn off lights, computers, and other appliances when you're not using them.

- Use energy-efficient appliances: lighting, air conditioners, heaters, refrigerators, washing machines, etc.

- Only use electric appliances when you need them.

- Keep your thermostat at 68°F in the winter and 72°F in the summer. You can turn it even lower in the winter and higher in the summer when you are away from home.

- Insulate your home as best you can.

- Carpool, use public transportation, or better yet, walk or bicycle whenever possible.

- Buy vehicles with low NO_x emissions, and properly maintain your vehicle.

- Be well informed.

Section 13.3

Haze and Visibility

This section includes excerpts from "Visibility," United States Environmental Protection Agency (EPA), July 10, 2015.

One of the most basic forms of air pollution—haze—degrades visibility in many American cities and scenic areas. Haze is caused when sunlight encounters tiny pollution particles in the air, which reduce the clarity and color of what we see, and particularly during humid conditions. Since 1988, the federal government has been monitoring visibility in national parks and wilderness areas, for example, in the Great Smoky Mountains National Park. In 1999, EPA announced a major effort to improve air quality in national parks and wilderness areas.

Basic Information

How far can you see?

Every year there are over 280 million visitors to our nation's most treasured parks and wilderness areas. Unfortunately, many visitors aren't able to see the spectacular vistas they expect. During much of the year a veil of white or brown haze hangs in the air blurring the view. Most of this haze is not natural. It is air pollution, carried by the wind often many hundreds of miles from where it originated.

In our nation's scenic areas, the visual range has been substantially reduced by air pollution. In eastern parks, average visual range has decreased from 90 miles to 15–25 miles. In the West, visual range has decreased from 140 miles to 35–90 miles.

What is haze?

Haze is caused when sunlight encounters tiny pollution particles in the air. Some light is absorbed by particles. Other light is scattered away before it reaches an observer. More pollutants mean more absorption and scattering of light, which reduce the clarity and color of what we see. Some types of particles such as sulfates, scatter more light, particularly during humid conditions.

Where does haze-forming pollution come from?

Air pollutants come from a variety of natural and manmade sources. Natural sources can include windblown dust, and soot from wildfires. Manmade sources can include motor vehicles, electric utility and industrial fuel burning, and manufacturing operations. Particulate matter pollution is the major cause of reduced visibility (haze) in parts of the United States, including many of our national parks.

Some haze-causing particles are directly emitted to the air. Others are formed when gases emitted to the air form particles as they are carried many miles from the source of the pollutants.

What else can these pollutants do to you and the environment?

Some of the pollutants which form haze have also been linked to serious health problems and environmental damage. Exposure to very small particles in the air have been linked with increased respiratory illness, decreased lung function, and even premature death. In addition, particles such as nitrates and sulfates contribute to acid rain formation which makes lakes, rivers, and streams unsuitable for many fish, and erodes buildings, historical monuments, and paint on cars.

EPA's Regional Haze Program

EPA and other agencies have been monitoring visibility in national parks and wilderness areas since 1988. In 1999, the U.S. Environmental

Protection Agency announced a major effort to improve air quality in national parks and wilderness areas. The Regional Haze Rule calls for state and federal agencies to work together to improve visibility in 156 national parks and wilderness areas such as the Grand Canyon, Yosemite, the Great Smokies, and Shenandoah.

The rule requires the states, in coordination with the Environmental Protection Agency, the National Park Service, U.S. Fish and Wildlife Service, the U.S. Forest Service, and other interested parties, to develop and implement air quality protection plans to reduce the pollution that causes visibility impairment. The first State plans for regional haze are due in the 2003–2008 timeframe. Five multi-state regional planning organizations are working together now to develop the technical basis for these plans.

Section 13.4

Ozone (Smog)

Text in this section begins with excerpts from "Ozone," National Institute of Environmental Health Sciences (NIEHS), May 22, 2014.

Text in this section beginning with "Frequently Asked Questions" is excerpted from "Ground-level Ozone—Health Effects and Frequently Asked Questions," United States Environmental Protection Agency (EPA), November 26, 2014.

Ozone is a highly reactive form of oxygen. In the upper atmosphere, ozone forms a protective layer that shields us from the sun's ultraviolet rays. At ground level, ozone is a harmful air pollutant and a primary constituent of urban smog. Ozone is produced when air pollutants from automobile emissions and manufacturing operations interact with sunlight. Long-term exposure to high concentrations of ozone can cause a significant reduction in lung function, inflammation of the airways, and respiratory distress. People with lung diseases are particularly vulnerable to the respiratory effects of ozone. Results from an NIEHS-funded study show that children who played three or more outdoor sports in areas with high ozone concentrations were more than three times as likely to develop asthma as children who did not engage in sports activities.

Health Effects

Ozone in the air we breathe can harm our health—typically on hot, sunny days when ozone can reach unhealthy levels. Even relatively low levels of ozone can cause health effects. Children, people with lung disease, older adults, and people who are active outdoors, including outdoor workers, may be particularly sensitive to ozone.

Children are at greatest risk from exposure to ozone because their lungs are still developing and they are more likely to be active outdoors when ozone levels are high, which increases their exposure. Children are also more likely than adults to have asthma.

Breathing ozone can trigger a variety of health problems including chest pain, coughing, throat irritation, and congestion. It can worsen bronchitis, emphysema, and asthma. Ground level ozone also can reduce lung function and inflame the linings of the lungs. Repeated exposure may permanently scar lung tissue.

Ozone can:

- Make it more difficult to breathe deeply and vigorously.
- Cause shortness of breath and pain when taking a deep breath.
- Cause coughing and sore or scratchy throat.
- Inflame and damage the airways.
- Aggravate lung diseases such as asthma, emphysema, and chronic bronchitis.
- Increase the frequency of asthma attacks.
- Make the lungs more susceptible to infection.
- Continue to damage the lungs even when the symptoms have disappeared.

These effects may lead to increased school absences, medication use, visits to doctors and emergency rooms, and hospital admissions. Research also indicates that ozone exposure may increase the risk of premature death from heart or lung disease.

Ozone is particularly likely to reach unhealthy levels on hot sunny days in urban environments. It is a major part of urban smog. Ozone can also be transported long distances by wind. For this reason, even rural areas can experience high ozone levels. And, in some cases, ozone can occur throughout the year in some southern and mountain regions.

Frequently Asked Questions

General

What is ozone?

Ozone is a gas composed of three atoms of oxygen. Ozone occurs both in the Earth's upper atmosphere and at ground level. Ozone can be good or bad, depending on where it is found.

Good Ozone

Good ozone occurs naturally in the upper atmosphere, 6 to 30 miles above the Earth's surface, where it forms a protective layer that shields us from the sun's harmful ultraviolet rays. This beneficial ozone is gradually being destroyed by manmade chemicals. When the protective ozone "layer" has been significantly depleted; for example, over the North or South Pole; it is sometimes called a "hole in the ozone."

Bad Ozone

Troposheric, or ground level ozone, is not emitted directly into the air, but is created by chemical reactions between oxides of nitrogen (NO_x) and volatile organic compounds (VOC). Ozone is likely to reach unhealthy levels on hot sunny days in urban environments. Ozone can also be transported long distances by wind. For this reason, even rural areas can experience high ozone levels.

High ozone concentrations have also been observed in cold months, where a few high elevation areas in the Western U.S. with high levels of local VOC and NOx emissions have formed ozone when snow is on the ground and temperatures are near or below freezing. Ozone contributes to what we typically experience as "smog" or haze, which still occurs most frequently in the summertime, but can occur throughout the year in some southern and mountain regions.

Where does ground level ozone come from?

In the Earth's lower atmosphere, near ground level, ozone is formed when pollutants emitted by cars, power plants, industrial boilers, refineries, chemical plants, and other sources chemically react in the presence of sunlight. Ozone at ground level is a harmful air pollutant.

Are ozone and smog the same thing?

While the two terms are often used interchangeably for general use, smog is more complex. Smog is primarily made up of ground level ozone combined with other gases and particle pollution.

What are the ozone levels in my community?

Air quality forecasts are often given with weather forecasts on handheld devices, online or in the paper or television. You can check ozone levels and other daily air quality information by visiting www.airnow.gov and in many areas you can receive air quality notifications through www.enviroflash.info.

What can I do to reduce ozone?

Air pollution can affect your health and the environment. There are actions every one of us can take to reduce air pollution and keep the air cleaner and precautionary measures you can take to protect your health.

Health and Ecosystems

What are the health effects of ozone?

Ozone in the air we breathe can harm our health. Even relatively low levels of ozone can cause health effects. Children, people with lung disease, older adults, and people who are active outdoors, including outdoor workers, may be particularly sensitive to ozone.

Breathing ozone can trigger a variety of health problems including chest pain, coughing, throat irritation, and congestion. It can worsen bronchitis, emphysema, and asthma. Ground level ozone also can reduce lung function and inflame the linings of the lungs. Repeated exposure may permanently scar lung tissue.

Who is most at risk?

Children are at greatest risk from exposure to ozone because their lungs are still developing and they are more likely to be active outdoors when ozone levels are high, which increases their exposure. Children are also more likely than adults to have asthma.

What are the ecological effects of ozone?

Ozone also affects sensitive vegetation and ecosystems, including forests, parks, wildlife refuges and wilderness areas. In particular, ozone harms sensitive vegetation, including forest trees and plants during the growing season.

Designations Process

What does designation mean?

After working with the states and tribes and considering the information from air quality monitors, EPA "designates" an area as attainment or nonattainment with national ambient air quality standards. If an area is designated as nonattainment states must develop and implement control plans to reduce ozone-forming pollution.

What does nonattainment mean?

The Clean Air Act identifies six common air pollutants that are found all over the United States. These pollutants can injure health, harm the environment and cause property damage. EPA calls these pollutants criteria air pollutants because the agency has developed health-based criteria (science-based guidelines) as the basis for setting permissible levels in the outdoor air.

Ozone is a criteria pollutant. There are national ambient air quality standards (NAAQS) for each of the criteria pollutants. These standards apply to the concentration of a pollutant in outdoor air. If the air quality in a geographic area meets or does better than the national standard, it is called an attainment area; areas that don't meet the national standard are called nonattainment areas.

In order to improve air quality, states must draft a plan known as a state implementation plan (SIP) to improve the air quality in nonattainment areas. The plan outlines the measures that the state will take in order to improve air quality. Once a nonattainment area meets the standards, EPA will designate the area to attainment as a "maintenance area."

How long has ozone been a problem in my area?

Ozone levels can vary from one area to the next and they can also vary over time or from one season to the next. Ozone is typically a summertime problem, but can be a year-round issue for some areas. Some areas have experienced problems with ozone for years, while other areas have not. To learn how long ozone has been a problem where you live, visit EPA's Air Trends web site.

Section 13.5

Particle Pollution

This section includes excerpts from "Particulate Matter," United
States Environmental Protection Agency (EPA), March 18, 2013;
and text from "Particulate Matter—Health," United States
Environmental Protection Agency (EPA), May 6, 2014.

"Particulate matter," also known as particle pollution or PM, is
a complex mixture of extremely small particles and liquid droplets.
Particle pollution is made up of a number of components, including
acids (such as nitrates and sulfates), organic chemicals, metals, and
soil or dust particles.

The size of particles is directly linked to their potential for causing
health problems. EPA is concerned about particles that are 10 micrometers in diameter or smaller because those are the particles that generally pass through the throat and nose and enter the lungs. Once
inhaled, these particles can affect the heart and lungs and cause serious health effects. EPA groups particle pollution into two categories:

- "Inhalable coarse particles," such as those found near roadways and dusty industries, are larger than 2.5 micrometers and
  smaller than 10 micrometers in diameter.

- "Fine particles," such as those found in smoke and haze, are 2.5
  micrometers in diameter and smaller. These particles can be
  directly emitted from sources such as forest fires, or they can
  form when gases emitted from power plants, industries and
  automobiles react in the air.

Basic Information

Particle pollution (also called particulate matter or PM) is the term
for a mixture of solid particles and liquid droplets found in the air.
Some particles, such as dust, dirt, soot, or smoke, are large or dark
enough to be seen with the naked eye. Others are so small they can
only be detected using an electron microscope.

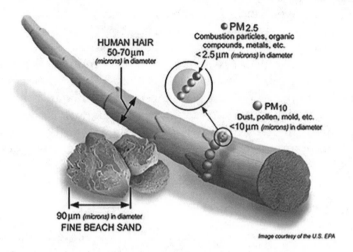

Figure 13.2. How Big Is Particle Pollution?

Particle pollution includes "inhalable coarse particles," with diameters larger than 2.5 micrometers and smaller than 10 micrometers and "fine particles," with diameters that are 2.5 micrometers and smaller. How small is 2.5 micrometers? Think about a single hair from your head. The average human hair is about 70 micrometers in diameter—making it 30 times larger than the largest fine particle.

These particles come in many sizes and shapes and can be made up of hundreds of different chemicals. Some particles, known as *primary particles* are emitted directly from a source, such as construction sites, unpaved roads, fields, smokestacks or fires. Others form in complicated reactions in the atmosphere of chemicals such as sulfur dioxides and nitrogen oxides that are emitted from power plants, industries and automobiles. These particles, known as *secondary particles*, make up most of the fine particle pollution in the country.

EPA regulates inhalable particles (fine and coarse). Particles larger than 10 micrometers (sand and large dust) are not regulated by EPA.

Health

The size of particles is directly linked to their potential for causing health problems. Small particles less than 10 micrometers in diameter pose the greatest problems, because they can get deep into your lungs, and some may even get into your bloodstream.

Exposure to such particles can affect both your lungs and your heart. Small particles of concern include "inhalable coarse particles" (such as those found near roadways and dusty industries), which are larger than 2.5 micrometers and smaller than 10 micrometers in diameter; and "fine particles" (such as those found in smoke and haze), which are 2.5 micrometers in diameter and smaller.

The Clean Air Act requires EPA to set air quality standards to protect both public health and the public welfare (e.g., visibility, crops and vegetation). Particle pollution affects both.

Health Effects

Particle pollution—especially fine particles—contains microscopic solids or liquid droplets that are so small that they can get deep into the lungs and cause serious health problems. Numerous scientific studies have linked particle pollution exposure to a variety of problems, including:

- premature death in people with heart or lung disease,

- nonfatal heart attacks,

- irregular heartbeat,

- aggravated asthma,

- decreased lung function, and

- increased respiratory symptoms, such as irritation of the airways, coughing or difficulty breathing.

People with heart or lung diseases, children and older adults are the most likely to be affected by particle pollution exposure. However, even if you are healthy, you may experience temporary symptoms from exposure to elevated levels of particle pollution.

Environmental Effects

Visibility impairment

Fine particles ($PM_{2.5}$) are the main cause of reduced visibility (haze) in parts of the United States, including many of our treasured national parks and wilderness areas.

Environmental damage

Particles can be carried over long distances by wind and then settle on ground or water. The effects of this settling include: making lakes and streams acidic; changing the nutrient balance in coastal waters and large river basins; depleting the nutrients in soil; damaging sensitive forests and farm crops; and affecting the diversity of ecosystems.

Aesthetic damage

Particle pollution can stain and damage stone and other materials, including culturally important objects such as statues and monuments.

Fast Facts

- Particles that are less than 2.5 micrometers in diameter are known as "fine" particles; those larger than 2.5 micrometers, but less than 10 micrometers, are known as "coarse" particles.

- Fine particles are easily inhaled deep into the lungs where they may accumulate, react, be cleared or absorbed.

- Scientific studies have linked particle pollution, especially fine particles, with a series of significant health problems, including:

  - premature death in people with heart or lung disease,

  - nonfatal heart attacks,

  - irregular heartbeat,

  - aggravated asthma,

  - decreased lung function, and

  - increased respiratory symptoms, such as irritation of the airways, coughing or difficulty breathing.

- Particle pollution can cause coughing, wheezing, and decreased lung function even in otherwise healthy children and adults.

- Studies estimate that thousands of elderly people die prematurely each year from exposure to fine particles.

- The average adult breathes 3,000 gallons of air per day.

- According to the American Academy of Pediatrics, children and infants are among the most susceptible to many air pollutants. Children have increased exposure compared with adults because of higher minute ventilation and higher levels of physical activity.

- Fine particles can remain suspended in the air and travel long distances. For example, a puff of exhaust from a diesel truck in Los Angeles can end up over the Grand Canyon.

- Some of the pollutants which form haze have also been linked to serious health problems and environmental damage.

- Particle pollution settles on soil and water and harms the environment by changing the nutrient and chemical balance.

- Particle pollution, unlike ozone, can occur year-round.

Chapter 14

Climate Change and Extreme Heat

Chapter Contents

227

Section 14.1

Climate Change: Overview

Text in this section is excerpted from "Climate Change Science
Overview," United States Environmental Protection Agency (EPA),
March 19, 2014.

Earth's climate is changing in ways that affect our weather, oceans, snow, ice, ecosystems, and society.

Natural causes alone cannot explain all of these changes. Human activities are contributing to climate change, primarily by releasing billions of tons of carbon dioxide (CO_2) and other heat-trapping gases, known as greenhouse gases, into the atmosphere every year.

Climate changes will continue into the future. The more greenhouse gases we emit, the larger future climate changes will be.

Changes in the climate system affect our health, environment, and economy. We can prepare for some of the impacts of climate change to reduce their effects on our well-being.

Earth's climate is changing

The global average temperature increased by more than 1.3°F over the last century. The average temperature in the Arctic rose by almost twice as much. The buildup of greenhouse gases in our atmosphere and the warming of the planet are responsible for other changes, such as:

- Changing precipitation patterns

- Increases in ocean temperatures, sea level, and acidity

- Melting of glaciers and sea ice

Natural causes alone cannot explain recent changes

Natural processes such as changes in the sun's energy, shifts in ocean currents, and others affect Earth's climate. However, they do not explain the warming that we have observed over the last half-century.

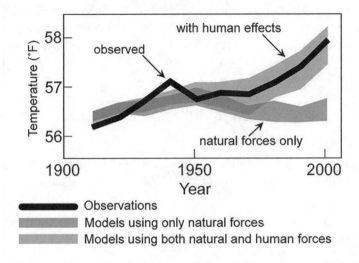

Figure 14.1. *Models that account only for the effects of natural processes are not able to explain the warming over the past century. Models that also account for the greenhouse gases emitted by humans are able to explain this warming.*

Human causes can explain these changes

Most of the warming of the past half century has been caused by human emissions of greenhouse gases. Greenhouse gases come from a variety of human activities, including: burning fossil fuels for heat and energy, clearing forests, fertilizing crops, storing waste in landfills, raising livestock, and producing some kinds of industrial products.

Greenhouse gas emissions are not the only way that people can change the climate. Activities such as agriculture or road construction can change the reflectivity of Earth's surface, leading to local warming or cooling. This effect is observed in urban centers, which are often warmer than surrounding, less populated areas. Emissions of small particles, known as aerosols, into the air can also lead to reflection or absorption of the sun's energy.

Climate will continue to change unless we reduce our emissions

During the 21st century, global warming is projected to continue and climate changes are likely to intensify. Scientists have used climate models to project different aspects of future climate, including temperature, precipitation, snow and ice, ocean level, and ocean acidity. Depending on future emissions of greenhouse gases and how the climate responds, average global temperatures are projected to increase worldwide by 2°F to 11.5°F by 2100.

Climate change impacts our health, environment, and economy

Climate change affects our environment and natural resources, and impacts our way of life in many ways. For example:

- Warmer temperatures increase the frequency, intensity, and duration of heat waves, which can pose health risks, particularly for young children and the elderly.

- Rising sea levels threaten coastal communities and ecosystems.

- Changes in the patterns and amount of rainfall, as well as changes in the timing and amount of stream flow, can affect water supplies and water quality and the production of hydroelectricity.

- Changing ecosystems influence geographic ranges of many plant and animal species and the timing of their lifecycle events, such as migration and reproduction.

- Increases in the frequency and intensity of extreme weather events, such as heat waves, droughts, and floods, can increase losses to property, cause costly disruptions to society, and reduce the availability and affordability of insurance.

We can prepare for some of the likely climate change impacts to reduce their effect on ecosystem and human well-being. Making such preparations is known as adaptation. Examples of adaptation include strengthening water conservation programs, upgrading stormwater systems, developing early warning systems for extreme heat events, and preparing for stronger storms through better emergency preparation and response strategies.

Section 14.2

Heat and Climate Change

Text in this section begins with excerpts from "Global Environmental Health," National Institute of Environmental Health Sciences (NIEHS), March 28, 2013.

Text in this section beginning with "Extreme Heat" is excerpted from "Climate Change," Centers for Disease Control and Prevention (CDC), July 1, 2014.

Prolonged exposure to extreme heat can cause heat exhaustion, heat cramps, heat stroke, and death, as well as exacerbate preexisting chronic conditions, such as various respiratory, cerebral, and cardiovascular diseases. These serious health consequences usually affect more vulnerable populations such as the elderly, children, and those with existing cardiovascular and respiratory diseases. Socioeconomic factors, such as economically disadvantaged and socially isolated individuals, are also at risk from heat-related burdens. As global temperatures rise and extreme heat events increase in frequency due to climate change we can expect to see more heat-related illnesses and mortality. Public health systems need to be prepared for extreme events and responses will demand a concerted effort among the public health community, the medical establishment, emergency responses teams, the housing authority, and law enforcement in order to quickly identify and serve the populations vulnerable to extreme heat events.

Health Impacts

- Increased temperatures and increase in extreme heat events cause heat exhausting, heat stroke, and death, especially in vulnerable populations.
- High concentrations of buildings in urban areas cause urban heat island effect, generation and absorbing heat, making the urban center several degrees warmer than surrounding areas.

Mitigation and Adaptation

- Heat early warning systems and proactive heat wave response plans

231

- Increased air conditioning use
- Decreased time spent outdoors during extreme heat events
- Increased use of sun-shielding clothing

Research Needs

- Developing and implementing a standard definition of heat-related health outcomes, as well as standard methodologies for surveillance of outcomes and evaluation of adaptations
- Understanding risk factors for illness and death associated with both acute exposure to extreme heat events and long-term, chronic exposure to increased average temperatures
- Quantifying the combined effects of exposure to heat waves and ambient air pollution on excessive illness and death
- Determining attributes of communities, including regional and seasonal differences, that are more resilient or vulnerable to adverse health impacts from heat waves
- Assessing the health benefits of the use of environmental design principles to reduce high thermal mass of urban areas
- Enhancing the ability of current climate models to capture the observed frequency and intensity of heat waves across various timescales to support weather-climate predictions and use of heat early warning systems in decision making
- Evaluating heat response plans, focusing on environmental risk factors, identification of high-risk populations, effective communications strategies, and rigorous methods for evaluating effectiveness on the local level

Extreme Heat

The Tracking Network collects data on heat-related deaths and illnesses throughout the United States and provides information so people can protect themselves.

Heat-related Deaths

Extreme heat events, or heat waves, are a leading cause of extreme weather-related deaths in the United States. The number of heat-related deaths is rising. For example, in 1995, 465 heat-related deaths occurred in Chicago. From 1999 to 2010, a total of 7,415 people died of heat-related deaths, an average of about 618 deaths a year.

Heat Stress

Heat stress is heat-related illness caused by your body's inability to cool down properly. The body normally cools itself by sweating. But under some conditions, sweating just isn't enough. In such cases, a person's body temperature rises rapidly. Very high body temperatures may damage the brain or other vital organs.

Several factors affect the body's ability to cool itself during extremely hot weather. When the humidity is high, sweat will not evaporate as quickly, preventing the body from releasing heat quickly. Other conditions related to risk include age, obesity, fever, dehydration, heart disease, mental illness, poor circulation, sunburn, and prescription drug and alcohol use.

Heat stress ranges from milder conditions like heat rash and heat cramps, to the most common type, heat exhaustion. The most serious heat-related illness is heat stroke. Heat stroke can cause death or permanent disability if emergency treatment is not provided.

Risk Factors

Anyone can develop heat stress. However, the following groups of people have higher risks for experiencing heat stress or heat-related death:

- Infants and children up to four years of age,
- People 65 years of age and older,
- People who are overweight, and
- People who are ill or on certain medications

Prevention

Heat-related death or illnesses are preventable if you follow a few simple steps.

- Stay in an air-conditioned area during the hottest hours of the day. If you don't have air conditioning in your home, go to a public place such as a shopping mall or a library to stay cool. Cooling stations and senior centers are also available in many large cities for people of all ages.

- Wear light, loose-fitting clothing.

- Drink water often. Don't wait until you are thirsty.

- Avoid unnecessary hard work or activities if you are outside or in a building without air-conditioning.

- Avoid unnecessary sun exposure. When in the sun, wear a hat, preferably with a wide brim.

Air conditioning is the strongest protective factor against heat-related illness. Exposure to air conditioning for even a few hours a day will reduce the risk for heat-related illness.

Chapter 15

Noise Pollution and UV Radiation

Noise pollution

What Is Noise Pollution?

The traditional definition of noise is "unwanted or disturbing sound." Sound becomes unwanted when it either interferes with normal activities such as sleeping, conversation, or disrupts or diminishes one's quality of life. The fact that you can't see, taste or smell it may help explain why it has not received as much attention as other types of pollution, such as air pollution, or water pollution. The air around us is constantly filled with sounds, yet most of us would probably not say we are surrounded by noise. Though for some, the persistent and escalating sources of sound can often be considered an annoyance. This "annoyance" can have major consequences, primarily to one's overall health.

Health Effects

Noise pollution adversely affects the lives of millions of people. Studies have shown that there are direct links between noise and health.

This chapter includes excerpts from "Noise Pollution," United States Environmental Protection Agency (EPA) July 16, 2012; and text from "Radiation-Emitting Products," U.S. Food and Drug Administration (FDA), September 26, 2013.

Problems related to noise include stress related illnesses, high blood pressure, speech interference, hearing loss, sleep disruption, and lost productivity. Noise Induced Hearing Loss (NIHL) is the most common and often discussed health effect, but research has shown that exposure to constant or high levels of noise can cause countless adverse health affects.

Protection from Noise

Individuals can take many steps to protect themselves from the harmful effects of noise pollution. If people must be around loud sounds, they can protect their ears with hearing protection (e.g., ear plugs or ear muffs). There are various strategies for combating noise in your home, school, workplace, and the community.

The Role of EPA

Under the Clean Air Act, the EPA administrator established the Office of Noise Abatement and Control (ONAC) to carry out investigations and studies on noise and its effect on the public health and welfare. Through ONAC, the EPA coordinated all Federal noise control activities, but in 1981 the Administration concluded that noise issues were best handled at the State and local level. As a result, ONAC was closed and primary responsibility of addressing noise issues was transferred to State and local governments. However, EPA retains authority to investigate and study noise and its effect, disseminate information to the public regarding noise pollution and its adverse health effects, respond to inquiries on matters related to noise, and evaluate the effectiveness of existing regulations for protecting the public health and welfare, pursuant to the Noise Control Act of 1972 and the Quiet Communities Act of 1978.

Ultraviolet (UV) Radiation

What is UV Radiation?

All radiation is a form of energy, most of which is invisible to the human eye. UV radiation is only one form of radiation and it is measured on a scientific scale called the electromagnetic (EM) spectrum.

UV radiation is only one type of EM energy you may be familiar with. Radio waves that transmit sound from a radio station's tower to your stereo, or between cell phones; microwaves, like those that heat your food in a microwave oven; visible light that is emitted from the lights in your home; and X-rays like those used in hospital X-ray machines to capture images of the bones inside your body, are all forms of EM energy.

UV radiation is the portion of the EM spectrum between X-rays and visible light.

How is radiation classified on the electromagnetic spectrum?

Electromagnetic radiation is all around us, though we can only see some of it. All EM radiation (also called EM energy) is made up of minute packets of energy or 'particles,' called photons, which travel in a wave-like pattern and move at the speed of light. The EM spectrum is divided into categories defined by a range of numbers. These ranges describe the activity level, or how energetic the photons are, and the size of the wavelength in each category.

For example, at the bottom of the spectrum radio waves have photons with low energies, so their wavelengths are long with peaks that are far apart. The photons of microwaves have higher energies, followed by infrared waves, UV rays, and X-rays. At the top of the spectrum, gamma rays have photons with very high energies and short wavelengths with peaks that are close together.

What are the different types of UV radiation?

The most common form of UV radiation is sunlight, which produces three main types of UV rays:

- UVA

- UVB

- UVC

UVA rays have the longest wavelengths, followed by UVB, and UVC rays which have the shortest wavelengths. While UVA and UVB rays are transmitted through the atmosphere, all UVC and some UVB rays are absorbed by the Earth's ozone layer. So, most of the UV rays you come in contact with are UVA with a small amount of UVB.

Like all forms of light on the EM spectrum, UV radiation is classified by wavelength. Wavelength describes the distance between the peaks in a series of waves.

- UVB rays have a short wavelength that reaches the outer layer of your skin (the epidermis)

- UVA rays have a longer wavelength that can penetrate the middle layer of your skin (the dermis)

What effect does UV radiation have on my body?

Both UVA and UVB rays can cause damage to your skin. Sunburn is a sign of short-term overexposure, while premature aging and skin cancer are side effects of prolonged UV exposure.

Certain oral and topical medicines, such as antibiotics, birth control pills, and benzoyl peroxide products, as well as some cosmetics, may increase skin and eye sensitivity to UV in all skin types. Check the label and ask your doctor for more information.

Sunlight is not the only source of UV radiation you may encounter.

Other sources include:

- Tanning booths
- Mercury vapor lighting (often found in stadiums and school gyms)
- Some halogen, fluorescent, and incandescent lights
- Some types of lasers

Are there health benefits of exposure to UV radiation?

Exposure to UVB radiation helps the skin produce a type of vitamin D (vitamin D3), which plays an important role—along with calcium—in bone and muscle health. However, the amount of UVB exposure needed to obtain a benefit depends on several factors, such as: the amount of vitamin D in your diet, skin color, sunscreen use, clothing, where you live (latitude and altitude), time of day, and time of year. Also, the FDA has not cleared or approved any indoor tanning device for producing vitamin D.

UV radiation, in the form of lasers, lamps, or a combination of these devices and topical medications that increase UV sensitivity, are sometimes used to treat patients with certain diseases who have not responded to other methods of therapy. Also known as phototherapy, this method of UV exposure is performed by a trained healthcare professional under the supervision of a dermatologist. Studies suggest that phototherapy can help treat unresponsive and severe cases of several diseases, including:

- Rickets
- Psoriasis
- Eczema
- Vitiligo
- Lupus

Phototherapy involves exposing a patient to a carefully monitored dose of UV radiation on a regular schedule. In some cases, effective therapy requires that a patient's skin is first treated with a prescription drug, ointment, or bath that increases its UV sensitivity. While this type of therapy does not eliminate the negative side effects of UV exposure, treatment is carefully supervised by a doctor to ensure that the benefits outweigh the risks.

Does where I live affect the amount of UV radiation I am exposed to?

Many factors determine how much UV you are exposed to, including:

- Geography
- Altitude
- Time of year
- Time of day
- Weather conditions
- Reflection

Geography

UV rays are strongest in areas close to the equator. Because the sun is directly over the equator, UV rays only travel a short distance through the atmosphere to reach these areas. UV radiation is also the strongest near the equator because ozone in these areas is naturally thinner, so there is less to absorb the UV radiation.

UV exposure is lower in areas further from the equator because the sun is farther away. Exposure is also decreased because UV rays must travel a greater distance through ozone-rich portions of the atmosphere to reach the earth's surface.

UV exposure is also greater in areas of snow, sand, pavement, and water due to the reflective properties of these surfaces.

Altitude

Altitude is another contributing factor to the amount of UV. Higher altitudes have greater UV exposure because there is less atmosphere to absorb UV rays.

Time of Year

The sun's angle in relation to the Earth varies according to season. During the summer months the sun is in a more direct angle, resulting in a greater amount of UV radiation.

Time of Day

UV is most intense at noon when the sun is at its highest point in the sky, and UV rays have the least distance to travel through the atmosphere. Especially in the hot summer months, it is a good idea to remain indoors during the peak sun hours of 10am and 4pm.

Weather Conditions

Many people believe that you cannot get sunburned on a cloudy day; this is simply not the case. Even under cloud cover it is possible to damage your skin and eyes, and cause long-term damage. It is important that you protect yourself with sunscreen, even in cloudy weather.

Reflection

Some surfaces, such as snow, sand, grass, or water can reflect much of the UV radiation that reaches them. Sunglasses rated for 100% UV protection, a wide-brim hat, and broad-spectrum sunscreen can help protect your eyes and skin from reflected UV rays.

What is the UV Index (UVI)?

The Ultraviolet Index (UVI) is a rating scale, with numbers from 1 to 11, which indicate the amount of skin-damaging UV rays reaching the Earth's surface during the day.

The daily UVI forecasts the amount of UV reaching your area at noon when the sun typically reaches its highest point in the sky. The higher the UVI number, the more intense the UV rays you will be exposed to.

The Environmental Protection Agency (EPA) offers UVI forecasts by ZIP code on their UV Index page.

Many illustrations of the UVI use a system of colors to designate levels of UV exposure for a particular area on the map. The World Health Organization (WHO) has developed an internationally recognized system of colors corresponding to levels of the UVI.

Table 15.1. Categorization of UVI

Category	UVI Range	Color
Low	0–2	Green
Moderate	3–5	Yellow
High	6–7	Orange
Very High	8–10	Red
Extreme	11+	Purple

Chapter 16

Drinking Water

Chapter Contents

Section 16.1

Drinking Water Contaminants

This section includes excerpts from "Healthy Homes," Centers for Disease Control and Prevention (CDC), May 19, 2014; text from "Contaminant Candidate List (CCL) and Regulatory Determination," United States Environmental Protection Agency (EPA), November 17, 2014; and text from "Water: Drinking Water Contaminants," United States Environmental Protection Agency (EPA), October 29, 2014.

Drinking Water Safety

The United States has one of the safest drinking water supplies in the world. However, each year, outbreaks of illness related to contaminants in drinking water are reported to the Centers for Disease Control and Prevention. People should know where their drinking water (tap or bottled) comes from, how it has been treated, and whether it is safe to drink. The quality of drinking water from the tap can vary depending on whether its source is a regulated water system or an unregulated small community system or private well. Home tap water may also be filtered.

Tap water from any system can be contaminated from

- chemicals and minerals that occur naturally, such as arsenic;
- viruses, bacteria, and parasites;
- local land-use practices, such as pesticide use;
- industry;
- sewer overflow and failing septic systems.

The U.S. Environmental Protection Agency (EPA) regulates drinking (tap) water from large public water systems across the country. However, about one in seven Americans relies on private wells and small public water systems—systems that EPA does not regulate. People who rely on private wells for their drinking water are responsible for ensuring that their well water is safe.

Types of Drinking Water Contaminants

The Safe Drinking Water Act defines the term "contaminant" as meaning any physical, chemical, biological, or radiological substance or matter in water. Therefore, the law defines "contaminant" very broadly as being anything other than water molecules. Drinking water may reasonably be expected to contain at least small amounts of some contaminants. Some drinking water contaminants may be harmful if consumed at certain levels in drinking water while others may be harmless. The presence of contaminants does not necessarily indicate that the water poses a health risk.

Only a small number of the universe of contaminants as defined above are listed on the Contaminant Candidate List (CCL). The CCL serves as the first level of evaluation for unregulated drinking water contaminants that may need further investigation of potential health effects and the levels at which they are found in drinking water.

The following are general categories of drinking water contaminants and examples of each:

- **Physical** contaminants primarily impact the physical appearance or other physical properties of water. Examples of physical contaminants are sediment or organic material suspended in the water of lakes, rivers and streams from soil erosion.

- **Chemical** contaminants are elements or compounds. These contaminants may be naturally occurring or man-made. Examples of chemical contaminants include nitrogen, bleach, salts, pesticides, metals, toxins produced by bacteria, and human or animal drugs.

- **Biological** contaminants are organisms in water. They are also referred to as microbes or microbiological contaminants. Examples of biological or microbial contaminants include bacteria, viruses, protozoan, and parasites.

- **Radiological** contaminants are chemical elements with an unbalanced number of protons and neutrons resulting in unstable atoms that can emit ionizing radiation. Examples of radiological contaminants include cesium, plutonium and uranium.

List of Contaminants and Their Maximum Contaminant Levels (MCLs)

Microorganisms

Table 16.1. Microorganisms and Their Maximum Contaminant Levels

Contaminant	MCLG[1] (mg/L)[2]	MCL or TT[1] (mg/L)[2]	Potential Health Effects from Long-Term Exposure Above the MCL (unless specified as short-term)	Sources of Contaminant in Drinking Water
Cryptosporidium	zero	TT[3]	Gastrointestinal illness (such as diarrhea, vomiting, and cramps)	Human and animal fecal waste
Giardia lamblia	zero	TT[3]	Gastrointestinal illness (such as diarrhea, vomiting, and cramps)	Human and animal fecal waste
Heterotrophic plate count (HPC)	n/a	TT[3]	HPC has no health effects; it is an analytic method used to measure the variety of bacteria that are common in water. The lower the concentration of bacteria in drinking water, the better maintained the water system is.	HPC measures a range of bacteria that are naturally present in the environment
Legionella	zero	TT[3]	Legionnaire's Disease, a type of pneumonia	Found naturally in water; multiplies in heating systems
Total Coliforms (including fecal coliform and E. Coli)	zero	5.0%[4]	Not a health threat in itself; it is used to indicate whether other potentially harmful bacteria may be present[5]	Coliforms are naturally present in the environment; as well as feces; fecal coliforms and E. coli only come from human and animal fecal waste.

Turbidity	n/a	TT[3]	Turbidity is a measure of the cloudiness of water. It is used to indicate water quality and filtration effectiveness (such as whether disease-causing organisms are present). Higher turbidity levels are often associated with higher levels of disease-causing microorganisms such as viruses, parasites and some bacteria. These organisms can cause symptoms such as nausea, cramps, diarrhea, and associated headaches.	Soil runoff
Viruses (enteric)	zero	TT[3]	Gastrointestinal illness (such as diarrhea, vomiting, and cramps)	Human and animal fecal waste

Disinfection Byproducts

Table 16.2. Disinfection Byproducts and Their Maximum Contaminant Levels

Contaminant	MCLG[1] (mg/L)[2]	MCL or TT[1] (mg/L)[2]	Potential Health Effects from Long-Term Exposure Above the MCL (unless specified as short-term)	Sources of Contaminant in Drinking Water
Bromate	zero	0.01	Increased risk of cancer	By-product of drinking water disinfection
Chlorite	0.8	1	Anemia; infants and young children: nervous system effects	By-product of drinking water disinfection
Haloacetic acids (HAA5)	n/a[6]	0.060[7]	Increased risk of cancer	By-product of drinking water disinfection
Total Trihalomethanes (TTHMs)	—> n/a[6]	—> 0.080[7]	Liver, kidney, or central nervous system problems; increased risk of cancer	By-product of drinking water disinfection

Disinfectants

Table 16.3. Disinfectants and Their Maximum Contaminant Levels

Contaminant	MCLG[1] (mg/L)[2]	MCL or TT[1] (mg/L)[2]	Potential Health Effects from Long-Term Exposure Above the MCL (unless specified as short-term)	Sources of Contaminant in Drinking Water
Chloramines (as Cl_2)	MRDLG=4[1]	MRDL=4.0[1]	Eye/nose irritation; stomach discomfort, anemia	Water additive used to control microbes

Table 16.3. Continued

Contaminant	MCLG[1] (mg/L)[2]	MCL or TT[1] (mg/L)[2]	Potential Health Effects from Long-Term Exposure Above the MCL (unless specified as short-term)	Sources of Contaminant in Drinking Water
Chlorine (as Cl_2)	MRDLG=4[1]	MRDL=4.0[1]	Eye/nose irritation; stomach discomfort	Water additive used to control microbes
Chlorine dioxide (as ClO_2)	MRDLG=0.8[1]	MRDL=0.8[1]	Anemia; infants and young children: nervous system effects	Water additive used to control microbes

Inorganic Chemicals

Table 16.4. Inorganic Chemicals and Their Maximum Contaminant Levels

Contaminant	MCLG[1] (mg/L)[2]	MCL or TT[1] (mg/L)[2]	Potential Health Effects from Long-Term Exposure Above the MCL (unless specified as short-term)	Sources of Contaminant in Drinking Water
Antimony	0.006	0.006	Increase in blood cholesterol; decrease in blood sugar	Discharge from petroleum refineries; fire retardants; ceramics; electronics; solder
Arsenic	0	0.010 as of 01/23/06	Skin damage or problems with circulatory systems, and may have increased risk of getting cancer	Erosion of natural deposits; runoff from orchards, runoff from glass and electronics production wastes

Table 16.4. Continued

Contaminant	MCLG[1] (mg/L)[2]	MCL or TT[1] (mg/L)[2]	Potential Health Effects from Long-Term Exposure Above the MCL (unless specified as short-term)	Sources of Contaminant in Drinking Water
Asbestos (fiber > 10 micrometers)	7 million fibers per liter (MFL)	7 MFL	Increased risk of developing benign intestinal polyps	Decay of asbestos cement in water mains; erosion of natural deposits
Barium	2	2	Increase in blood pressure	Discharge of drilling wastes; discharge from metal refineries; erosion of natural deposits
Beryllium	0.004	0.004	Intestinal lesions	Discharge from metal refineries and coal-burning factories; discharge from electrical, aerospace, and defense industries
Cadmium	0.005	0.005	Kidney damage	Corrosion of galvanized pipes; erosion of natural deposits; discharge from metal refineries; runoff from waste batteries and paints
Chromium (total)	0.1	0.1	Allergic dermatitis	Discharge from steel and pulp mills; erosion of natural deposits

Table 16.4. Continued

Contaminant	MCLG[1] (mg/L)[2]	MCL or TT[1] (mg/L)[2]	Potential Health Effects from Long-Term Exposure Above the MCL (unless specified as short-term)	Sources of Contaminant in Drinking Water
Copper	1.3	TT[7]; Action Level=1.3	Short-term exposure: Gastrointestinal distress Long-term exposure: Liver or kidney damage People with Wilson's Disease should consult their personal doctor if the amount of copper in their water exceeds the action level	Corrosion of household plumbing systems; erosion of natural deposits
Cyanide (as free cyanide)	0.2	0.2	Nerve damage or thyroid problems	Discharge from steel/metal factories; discharge from plastic and fertilizer factories
Fluoride	4	4	Bone disease (pain and tenderness of the bones); Children may get mottled teeth	Water additive which promotes strong teeth; erosion of natural deposits; discharge from fertilizer and aluminum factories

Table 16.4. Continued

Contaminant	MCLG[1] (mg/L)[2]	MCL or TT[1] (mg/L)[2]	Potential Health Effects from Long-Term Exposure Above the MCL (unless specified as short-term)	Sources of Contaminant in Drinking Water
Lead	zero	TT[7]; Action Level=0.015	Infants and children: Delays in physical or mental development; children could show slight deficits in attention span and learning abilities Adults: Kidney problems; high blood pressure	Corrosion of household plumbing systems; erosion of natural deposits
Mercury (inorganic)	0.002	0.002	Kidney damage	Erosion of natural deposits; discharge from refineries and factories; runoff from landfills and croplands
Nitrate (measured as Nitrogen)	10	10	Infants below the age of six months who drink water containing nitrate in excess of the MCL could become seriously ill and, if untreated, may die. Symptoms include shortness of breath and blue-baby syndrome.	Runoff from fertilizer use; leaking from septic tanks, sewage; erosion of natural deposits

Table 16.4. Continued

Contaminant	MCLG[1] (mg/L)[2]	MCL or TT[1] (mg/L)[2]	Potential Health Effects from Long-Term Exposure Above the MCL (unless specified as short-term)	Sources of Contaminant in Drinking Water
Nitrite (measured as Nitrogen)	1	1	Infants below the age of six months who drink water containing nitrite in excess of the MCL could become seriously ill and, if untreated, may die. Symptoms include shortness of breath and blue-baby syndrome.	Runoff from fertilizer use; leaking from septic tanks, sewage; erosion of natural deposits
Selenium	0.05	0.05	Hair or fingernail loss; numbness in fingers or toes; circulatory problems	Discharge from petroleum refineries; erosion of natural deposits; discharge from mines
Thallium	0.0005	0.002	Hair loss; changes in blood; kidney, intestine, or liver problems	Leaching from ore-processing sites; discharge from electronics, glass, and drug factories

Organic Chemicals

Table 16.5. Organic Chemicals and Their Maximum Contaminant Levels

Contaminant	MCLG[1] (mg/L)[2]	MCL or TT[1] (mg/L)[2]	Potential Health Effects from Long-Term Exposure Above the MCL (unless specified as short-term)	Sources of Contaminant in Drinking Water
Acrylamide	zero	TT[8]	Nervous system or blood problems; increased risk of cancer	Added to water during sewage/ wastewater treatment
Alachlor	zero	0.002	Eye, liver, kidney or spleen problems; anemia; increased risk of cancer	Runoff from herbicide used on row crops
Atrazine	0.003	0.003	Cardiovascular system or reproductive problems	Runoff from herbicide used on row crops
Benzene	zero	0.005	Anemia; decrease in blood platelets; increased risk of cancer	Discharge from factories; leaching from gas storage tanks and landfills
Benzo(a)pyrene (PAHs)	zero	0.0002	Reproductive difficulties; increased risk of cancer	Leaching from linings of water storage tanks and distribution lines
Carbofuran	0.04	0.04	Problems with blood, nervous system, or reproductive system	Leaching of soil fumigant used on rice and alfalfa

Table 16.5. Continued

Contaminant	MCLG[1] (mg/L)[2]	MCL or TT[1] (mg/L)[2]	Potential Health Effects from Long-Term Exposure Above the MCL (unless specified as short-term)	Sources of Contaminant in Drinking Water
Carbon tetrachloride	zero	0.005	Liver problems; increased risk of cancer	Discharge from chemical plants and other industrial activities
Chlordane	zero	0.002	Liver or nervous system problems; increased risk of cancer	Residue of banned termiticide
Chlorobenzene	0.1	0.1	Liver or kidney problems	Discharge from chemical and agricultural chemical factories
2,4-D	0.07	0.07	Kidney, liver, or adrenal gland problems	Runoff from herbicide used on row crops
Dalapon	0.2	0.2	Minor kidney changes	Runoff from herbicide used on rights of way
1,2-Dibromo-3-chloropropane (DBCP)	zero	0.0002	Reproductive difficulties; increased risk of cancer	Runoff/leaching from soil fumigant used on soybeans, cotton, pineapples, and orchards
o-Dichlorobenzene	0.6	0.6	Liver, kidney, or circulatory system problems	Discharge from industrial chemical factories
p-Dichlorobenzene	0.075	0.075	Anemia; liver, kidney or spleen damage; changes in blood	Discharge from industrial chemical factories

Table 16.5. Continued

Contaminant	MCLG[1] (mg/L)[2]	MCL or TT[1] (mg/L)[2]	Potential Health Effects from Long-Term Exposure Above the MCL (unless specified as short-term)	Sources of Contaminant in Drinking Water
1,2-Dichloroethane	zero	0.005	Increased risk of cancer	Discharge from industrial chemical factories
1,1-Dichloroethylene	0.007	0.007	Liver problems	Discharge from industrial chemical factories
cis-1,2-Dichloroethylene	0.07	0.07	Liver problems	Discharge from industrial chemical factories
trans-1,2-Dichloroethylene	0.1	0.1	Liver problems	Discharge from industrial chemical factories
Dichloromethane	zero	0.005	Liver problems; increased risk of cancer	Discharge from drug and chemical factories
1,2-Dichloropropane	zero	0.005	Increased risk of cancer	Discharge from industrial chemical factories
Di(2-ethylhexyl) adipate	0.4	0.4	Weight loss, liver problems, or possible reproductive difficulties.	Discharge from chemical factories
Di(2-ethylhexyl) phthalate	zero	0.006	Reproductive difficulties; liver problems; increased risk of cancer	Discharge from rubber and chemical factories

Table 16.5. Continued

Contaminant	MCLG[1] (mg/L)[2]	MCL or TT[1] (mg/L)[2]	Potential Health Effects from Long-Term Exposure Above the MCL (unless specified as short-term)	Sources of Contaminant in Drinking Water
Dinoseb	0.007	0.007	Reproductive difficulties	Runoff from herbicide used on soybeans and vegetables
Dioxin (2,3,7,8-TCDD)	zero	0.00000003	Reproductive difficulties; increased risk of cancer	Emissions from waste incineration and other combustion; discharge from chemical factories
Diquat	0.02	0.02	Cataracts	Runoff from herbicide use
Endothall	0.1	0.1	Stomach and intestinal problems	Runoff from herbicide use
Endrin	0.002	0.002	Liver problems	Residue of banned insecticide
Epichlorohydrin	zero	TT[8]	Increased cancer risk, and over a long period of time, stomach problems	Discharge from industrial chemical factories; an impurity of some water treatment chemicals
Ethylbenzene	0.7	0.7	Liver or kidneys problems	Discharge from petroleum refineries
Ethylene dibromide	zero	0.00005	Problems with liver, stomach, reproductive system, or kidneys; increased risk of cancer	Discharge from petroleum refineries

Table 16.5. Continued

Contaminant	MCLG[1] (mg/L)[2]	MCL or TT[1] (mg/L)[2]	Potential Health Effects from Long-Term Exposure Above the MCL (unless specified as short-term)	Sources of Contaminant in Drinking Water
Glyphosate	0.7	0.7	Kidney problems; reproductive difficulties	Runoff from herbicide use
Heptachlor	zero	0.0004	Liver damage; increased risk of cancer	Residue of banned termiticide
Heptachlor epoxide	zero	0.0002	Liver damage; increased risk of cancer	Breakdown of heptachlor
Hexachlorobenzene	zero	0.001	Liver or kidney problems; reproductive difficulties; increased risk of cancer	Discharge from metal refineries and agricultural chemical factories
Hexachlorocyclo-pentadiene	0.05	0.05	Kidney or stomach problems	Discharge from chemical factories
Lindane	0.0002	0.0002	Liver or kidney problems	Runoff/leaching from insecticide used on cattle, lumber, gardens
Methoxychlor	0.04	0.04	Reproductive difficulties	Runoff/leaching from insecticide used on fruits, vegetables, alfalfa, livestock
Oxamyl (Vydate)	0.2	0.2	Slight nervous system effects	Runoff/leaching from insecticide used on apples, potatoes, and tomatoes

Table 16.5. Continued

Contaminant	MCLG[1] (mg/L)[2]	MCL or TT[1] (mg/L)[2]	Potential Health Effects from Long-Term Exposure Above the MCL (unless specified as short-term)	Sources of Contaminant in Drinking Water
Polychlorinated biphenyls (PCBs)	zero	0.0005	Skin changes; thymus gland problems; immune deficiencies; reproductive or nervous system difficulties; increased risk of cancer	Runoff from landfills; discharge of waste chemicals
Pentachlorophenol	zero	0.001	Liver or kidney problems; increased cancer risk	Discharge from wood preserving factories
Picloram	0.5	0.5	Liver problems	Herbicide runoff
Simazine	0.004	0.004	Problems with blood	Herbicide runoff
Styrene	0.1	0.1	Liver, kidney, or circulatory system problems	Discharge from rubber and plastic factories; leaching from landfills
Tetrachloroethylene	zero	0.005	Liver problems; increased risk of cancer	Discharge from factories and dry cleaners
Toluene	1	1	Nervous system, kidney, or liver problems	Discharge from petroleum factories
Toxaphene	zero	0.003	Kidney, liver, or thyroid problems; increased risk of cancer	Runoff/leaching from insecticide used on cotton and cattle
2,4,5-TP (**Silvex**)	0.05	0.05	Liver problems	Residue of banned herbicide

Table 16.5. Continued

Contaminant	MCLG[1] (mg/L)[2]	MCL or TT[1] (mg/L)[2]	Potential Health Effects from Long-Term Exposure Above the MCL (unless specified as short-term)	Sources of Contaminant in Drinking Water
1,2,4-Trichlorobenzene	0.07	0.07	Changes in adrenal glands	Discharge from textile finishing factories
1,1,1-Trichloroethane	0.2	0.2	Liver, nervous system, or circulatory problems	Discharge from metal degreasing sites and other factories
1,1,2-Trichloroethane	0.003	0.005	Liver, kidney, or immune system problems	Discharge from industrial chemical factories
Trichloroethylene	zero	0.005	Liver problems; increased risk of cancer	Discharge from metal degreasing sites and other factories
Vinyl chloride	zero	0.002	Increased risk of cancer	Leaching from PVC pipes; discharge from plastic factories
Xylenes (total)	10	10	Nervous system damage	Discharge from petroleum factories; discharge from chemical factories

Radionuclides

Table 16.6. Radionuclides and their Maximum Contaminant Levels

Contaminant	MCLG[1] (mg/L)[2]	MCL or TT[1] (mg/L)[2]	Potential Health Effects from Long-Term Exposure Above the MCL (unless specified as short-term)	Sources of Contaminant in Drinking Water
Alpha particles	none[7] ---------- zero	15 picocuries per Liter (pCi/L)	Increased risk of cancer	Erosion of natural deposits of certain minerals that are radioactive and may emit a form of radiation known as alpha radiation
Beta particles and photon emitters	none[7] ---------- zero	4 millirems per year	Increased risk of cancer	Decay of natural and man-made deposits of certain minerals that are radioactive and may emit forms of radiation known as photons and beta radiation
Radium 226 and Radium 228 (combined)	none[7] ---------- zero	5 pCi/L	Increased risk of cancer	Erosion of natural deposits
Uranium	zero	30 ug/L as of 12/08/03	Increased risk of cancer, kidney toxicity	Erosion of natural deposits

Notes:

[1] **Definitions:**

- Maximum Contaminant Level Goal (MCLG) - The level of a contaminant in drinking water below which there is no known or expected risk to health. MCLGs allow for a margin of safety and are non-enforceable public health goals.

- Maximum Contaminant Level (MCL) - The highest level of a contaminant that is allowed in drinking water. MCLs are set as

261

close to MCLGs as feasible using the best available treatment technology and taking cost into consideration. MCLs are enforceable standards.

- Maximum Residual Disinfectant Level Goal (MRDLG) - The level of a drinking water disinfectant below which there is no known or expected risk to health. MRDLGs do not reflect the benefits of the use of disinfectants to control microbial contaminants.)

- Treatment Technique (TT) - A required process intended to reduce the level of a contaminant in drinking water.

- Maximum Residual Disinfectant Level (MRDL) - The highest level of a disinfectant allowed in drinking water. There is convincing evidence that addition of a disinfectant is necessary for control of microbial contaminants.

[2] Units are in milligrams per liter (mg/L) unless otherwise noted. Milligrams per liter are equivalent to parts per million (PPM).

[3] EPA's surface water treatment rules require systems using surface water or ground water under the direct influence of surface water to

(1) disinfect their water, and

(2) filter their water or

meet criteria for avoiding filtration so that the following contaminants are controlled at the following levels:

- *Cryptosporidium:* Unfiltered systems are required to include *Cryptosporidium* in their existing watershed control provisions

- *Giardia lamblia*: 99.9% removal/inactivation.

- Viruses: 99.99% removal/inactivation.

- *Legionella:* No limit, but EPA believes that if *Giardia* and viruses are removed/inactivated, according to the treatment techniques in the Surface Water Treatment Rule,*Legionella* will also be controlled.

- Turbidity: For systems that use conventional or direct filtration, at no time can turbidity (cloudiness of water) go higher than 1 Nephelometric Turbidity Unit (NTU), and samples for turbidity must be less than or equal to 0.3 NTUs in at least 95 percent of the samples in any month. Systems that use filtration other than the conventional or direct filtration must follow state limits, which must include turbidity at no time exceeding 5 NTUs.

- Heterotrophic Plate Count (HPC): No more than 500 bacterial colonies per milliliter.

- Long Term 1 Enhanced Surface Water Treatment: Surface water systems or groundwater under the direct influence (GWUDI) systems serving fewer than 10,000 people must comply with the applicable Long Term 1 Enhanced Surface Water Treatment Rule provisions (such as turbidity standards, individual filter monitoring, *Cryptosporidium* removal requirements, updated watershed control requirements for unfiltered systems).

- Long Term 2 Enhanced Surface Water Treatment Rule: This rule applies to all surface water systems or ground water systems under the direct influence of surface water. The rule targets additional *Cryptosporidium* treatment requirements for higher risk systems and includes provisions to reduce risks from uncovered finished water storage facilities and to ensure that the systems maintain microbial protection as they take steps to reduce the formation of disinfection byproducts.

- Filter Backwash Recycling: The Filter Backwash Recycling Rule requires systems that recycle to return specific recycle flows through all processes of the system's existing conventional or direct filtration system or at an alternate location approved by the state.

[4]No more than 5.0% samples total coliform-positive (TC-positive) in a month. (For water systems that collect fewer than 40 routine samples per month, no more than one sample can be total coliform-positive per month.) Every sample that has total coliform must be analyzed for either fecal coliforms or *E. coli* if two consecutive TC-positive samples, and one is also positive for *E.coli* fecal coliforms, system has an acute MCL violation.

[5] Fecal coliform and *E. coli* are bacteria whose presence indicates that the water may be contaminated with human or animal wastes. Disease-causing microbes (pathogens) in these wastes can cause diarrhea, cramps, nausea, headaches, or other symptoms. These pathogens may pose a special health risk for infants, young children, and people with severely compromised immune systems.

[6] Although there is no collective MCLG for this contaminant group, there are individual MCLGs for some of the individual contaminants:

- Trihalomethanes: bromodichloromethane (zero); bromoform (zero); dibromochloromethane (0.06mg/L): chloroform (0.07 mg/L.

- Haloacetic acids: dichloroacetic acid (zero); trichloroacetic acid (0.02 mg/L); monochloroacetic acid (0.07 mg/L). Bromoacetic acid and dibromoacetic acid are regulated with this group but have no MCLGs.

[7] Lead and copper are regulated by a treatment technique that requires systems to control the corrosiveness of their water. If more than 10% of tap water samples exceed the action level, water systems must take additional steps. For copper, the action level is 1.3 mg/L, and for lead is 0.015 mg/L.

[8] Each water system must certify, in writing, to the state (using third-party or manufacturer's certification) that when acrylamide and epichlorohydrin are used to treat water, the combination (or product) of dose and monomer level does not exceed the levels specified, as follows:

- Acrylamide = 0.05% dosed at 1 mg/L (or equivalent)

- Epichlorohydrin = 0.01% dosed at 20 mg/L (or equivalent)

Section 16.2

Lead in Drinking Water

Text in this section is excerpted from "Water: Basic Information about Regulated Drinking Water Contaminants," United States Environmental Protection Agency (EPA), June 26, 2015.

Basic Information about Lead in Drinking Water

The United States Environmental Protection Agency (EPA) regulates lead in drinking water to protect public health. Lead may cause health problems if present in public or private water supplies in amounts greater than the drinking water standard set by EPA.

What is lead?

Lead is a toxic metal that was used for many years in products found in and around homes. Even at low levels, lead may cause a range of health effects including behavioral problems and learning disabilities. Children six years old and under are most at risk because this is when the brain is developing. The primary source of lead exposure for most children is lead-based paint in older homes. Lead in drinking water can add to that exposure.

Uses for lead

Lead is sometimes used in household plumbing materials or in water service lines used to bring water from the main to the home. A prohibition on lead in plumbing materials has been in effect since 1986. The lead ban, which was included in the 1986 Amendments of the Safe Drinking Water Act, states that only "lead free" pipe, solder, or flux may be used in the installation or repair of (1) public water systems, or (2) any plumbing in a residential or non-residential facility providing water for human consumption, which is connected to a public water system. But even "lead free" plumbing may contain traces of lead. The term "lead free" means that solders and flux may not contain more than 0.2 percent lead, and that pipes and pipe fittings may not contain more than 8.0 percent lead. Faucets and other end use devices must be tested and certified against the ANSI – NSF Standard 61 to be considered lead free.

What are lead's health effects?

Infants and children who drink water containing lead in excess of the action level could experience delays in their physical or mental development. Children could show slight deficits in attention span and learning abilities. Adults who drink this water over many years could develop kidney problems or high blood pressure.

This health effects language is not intended to catalog all possible health effects for lead. Rather, it is intended to inform consumers of the most significant and probable health effects, associated with lead in drinking water.

What are EPA's drinking water regulations for lead?

In 1974, Congress passed the Safe Drinking Water Act. This law requires EPA to determine the level of contaminants in drinking water at which no adverse health effects are likely to occur with an adequate margin of safety. These non-enforceable health goals, based solely on possible health risks are called maximum contaminant level goals (MCLG). The MCLG for lead is zero. EPA has set this level based on the best available science which shows there is no safe level of exposure to lead.

For most contaminants, EPA sets an enforceable regulation called a maximum contaminant level (MCL) based on the MCLG. MCLs are set as close to the MCLGs as possible, considering cost, benefits and the ability of public water systems to detect and remove contaminants using suitable treatment technologies. However, because lead contamination of drinking water often results from corrosion of the plumbing materials belonging to water system customers, EPA established a treatment technique rather than an MCL for lead. A treatment technique is an enforceable procedure or level of technological performance which water systems must follow to ensure control of a contaminant. The treatment technique regulation for lead (referred to as the Lead and Copper rule) requires water systems to control the corrosivity of the water. The regulation also requires systems to collect tap samples from sites served by the system that are more likely to have plumbing materials containing lead. If more than 10% of tap water samples exceed the lead action level of 15 parts per billion, then water systems are required to take additional actions including:

- Taking further steps optimize their corrosion control treatment (for water systems serving 50,000 people that have not fully optimized their corrosion control).

- Educating the public about lead in drinking water and actions consumers can take to reduce their exposure to lead.

- Replacing the portions of lead service lines (lines that connect distribution mains to customers) under the water system's control.

EPA promulgated the Lead and Copper Rule in 1991 and revised the regulation in 2000 and 2007. States may set more stringent drinking water regulations than EPA.

How does lead get into my drinking water?

The major sources of lead in drinking water are corrosion of household plumbing systems; and erosion of natural deposits. Lead enters the water ("leaches") through contact with the plumbing. Lead leaches into water through corrosion—a dissolving or wearing away of metal caused by a chemical reaction between water and your plumbing. Lead can leach into water from pipes, solder, fixtures and faucets (brass), and fittings. The amount of lead in your water also depends on the types and amounts of minerals in the water, how long the water stays in the pipes, the amount of wear in the pipes, the water's acidity and its temperature.

Although the main sources of exposure to lead are ingesting paint chips and inhaling dust, EPA estimates that 20 percent or more of human exposure to lead may come from lead in drinking water. Infants who consume mostly mixed formula can receive 40 to 60 percent of their exposure to lead from drinking water.

How will I know if lead is in my drinking water?

Have your water tested for lead. A list of certified laboratory of labs are available from your state or local drinking water authority. Testing costs between $20 and $100. Since you cannot see, taste, or smell lead dissolved in water, testing is the only sure way of telling whether there are harmful quantities of lead in your drinking water. You should be particularly suspicious if your home has lead pipes (lead is a dull gray metal that is soft enough to be easily scratched with a house key) or if you see signs of corrosion (frequent leaks, rust-colored water). Your water supplier may have useful information, including whether the service connector used in your home or area is made of lead. Testing is especially important in high-rise buildings where flushing might not work.

If your water comes from a household well, check with your health department or local water systems that use ground water for information on contaminants of concern in your area.

How can I reduce lead in drinking water at home?

Flush your pipes before drinking, and only use cold water for consumption. The more time water has been sitting in your home's pipes, the more lead it may contain. Anytime the water in a particular faucet has not been used for six hours or longer, "flush" your cold-water pipes by running the water until it becomes as cold as it will get. This could take as little as five to thirty seconds if there has been recent heavy water use such as showering or toilet flushing. Otherwise, it could take two minutes or longer. Your water utility will inform you if longer flushing times are needed to respond to local conditions.

Use only water from the cold-water tap for drinking, cooking, and especially for making baby formula. Hot water is likely to contain higher levels of lead. The two actions recommended above are very important to the health of your family. They will probably be effective in reducing lead levels because most of the lead in household water usually comes from the plumbing in your house, not from the local water supply.

Should I be concerned about lead in drinking water in my child's school or child care facility?

Children spend a significant part of their days at school or in a child care facility. The faucets that provide water used for consumption, including drinking, cooking lunch, and preparing juice and infant formula, should be tested.

How do I learn more about my drinking water?

EPA strongly encourages people to learn more about their drinking water, and to support local efforts to protect and upgrade the supply of safe drinking water. Your water bill or telephone book's government listings are a good starting point for local information.

Contact your water utility. EPA requires all community water systems to prepare and deliver an annual consumer confidence report (CCR) (sometimes called a water quality report) for their customers by July 1 of each year. If your water provider is not a community water system, or if you have a private water supply, request a copy from a nearby community water system.

Section 16.3

Household Wells

Text in this section begins with excerpts from "Water: Private Wells—Frequent Questions," United States Environmental Protection Agency (EPA), March 6, 2012; text in this section beginning with "What You Can Do" is excerpted from "Water: Private Wells—What You Can Do," United States Environmental Protection Agency (EPA), March 6, 2012.

Frequent Questions

How can I test the quality of my private drinking water supply?

Consider testing your well for pesticides, organic chemicals, and heavy metals before you use it for the first time. Test private water supplies annually for nitrate and coliform bacteria to detect contamination problems early. Test them more frequently if you suspect a problem. Be aware of activities in your watershed that may affect the water quality of your well, especially if you live in an unsewered area.

Reasons to Test Your Water

Table16.7. below will help you spot problems. The last five problems listed are not an immediate health concern, but they can make your water taste bad, may indicate problems, and could affect your well long term.

If you use a private laboratory to conduct the testing, nitrate and bacteria samples will typically cost between $10 and $20 to complete. Testing for other contaminants will be more expensive. For example, testing for pesticides or organic chemicals may cost from several hundred to several thousand dollars. Only use laboratories that are certified to do drinking water tests. To find a certified laboratory in your state, you can contact:

- A State Certification Officer to get a list of certified water testing labs in your state, or

- Your local health department may also test private well water for free. Phone numbers for your local, county, or state health

Table 16.7. Reasons to Test Your Water

Conditions or Nearby Activities:	Test for:
Recurring gastro-intestinal illness	Coliform bacteria
Household plumbing contains lead	pH, lead, copper
Radon in indoor air or region is radon rich	Radon
Corrosion of pipes, plumbing	Corrosion, pH, lead
Nearby areas of intensive agriculture	Nitrate, pesticides, coliform bacteria
Coal or other mining operations nearby	Metals, pH, corrosion
Gas drilling operations nearby	Gas drilling operations nearby
Dump, junkyard, landfill, factory, gas station, or dry-cleaning operation nearby	Volatile organic compounds, total dissolved solids, pH, sulfate, chloride, metals
Odor of gasoline or fuel oil, and near gas station or buried fuel tanks	Volatile organic compounds
Objectionable taste or smell	Hydrogen sulfide, corrosion, metals
Stained plumbing fixtures, laundry	Iron, copper, manganese
Salty taste and seawater, or a heavily salted roadway nearby	Chloride, total dissolved solids, sodium
Scaly residues, soaps don't lather	Hardness
Rapid wear of water treatment equipment	pH, corrosion
Water softener needed to treat hardness	Manganese, iron
Water appears cloudy, frothy, or colored	Color, detergents

department are available under the "health" or "government" listings in your phone book.

Most laboratories mail back the sample results within a week or two. If a contaminant is detected, the results will include the concentration found and an indication of whether this level exceeds a drinking water health standard.

If a standard is exceeded in your sample, retest the water supply immediately and contact your public health department for assistance. Some problems can be handled quickly. For example, high bacteria concentrations can sometimes be controlled by disinfecting a well. Filters or other on-site treatment processes may also remove some contaminants. Other problems may require a new source of water, or a new, deeper well. If serious problems persist, you may need to rely on bottled water until a new water source can be obtained.

You should test private water supplies annually for nitrates, coliform bacteria, total dissolved solids, and pH levels to detect contamination problems early. Test more frequently if a problem was found in earlier tests.

What concerns should I have after a flood if I have a private well?

Stay away from the well pump while flooded to avoid electric shock, AND . . .

- Do not drink or wash from the flooded well to avoid becoming sick.
- Get assistance from a well or pump contractor to clean and turn on the pump.
- After the pump is turned back on, pump the well until the water runs clear to rid the well of flood water.
- If the water does not run clear, get advice from the county or state health department or extension service.

How can I protect my private water supply?

Protect your water supply by carefully managing activities near the water source. For households using a domestic well, this includes keeping contaminants away from sinkholes and the well itself. Keep hazardous chemicals out of septic systems.

- Periodically inspect exposed parts of the well for problems such as:
  - cracked, corroded, or damaged well casing
  - broken or missing well cap
  - settling and cracking of surface seals.
- Slope the area around the well to drain surface runoff away from the well.
- Install a well cap or sanitary seal to prevent unauthorized use of, or entry into, the well.
- Have the well tested once a year for coliform bacteria, nitrates, and other constituents of concern.
- Keep accurate records of any well maintenance, such as disinfection or sediment removal, that may require the use of chemicals in the well.

- Hire a certified well driller for any new well construction, modification, or abandonment and closure.

- Avoid mixing or using pesticides, fertilizers, herbicides, degreasers, fuels, and other pollutants near the well.

- Do not dispose of wastes in dry wells or in abandoned wells.

- Do not cut off the well casing below the land surface.

- Pump and inspect septic systems as often as recommended by your local health department.

- Never dispose of harsh chemicals, solvents, petroleum products, or pesticides in a septic system or dry well.

What You Can Do

Private, individual wells are the responsibility of the homeowner. To help protect your well, here are some steps you can take:

Have your water tested periodically. It is recommended that water be tested every year for total coliform bacteria, nitrates, total dissolved solids, and pH levels. If you suspect other contaminants, test for those. Always use a state certified laboratory that conducts drinking water tests. Since these can be expensive, spend some time identifying potential problems.

Testing more than once a year may be warranted in special situations:

- someone in your household is pregnant or nursing
- there are unexplained illnesses in the family
- your neighbors find a dangerous contaminant in their water
- you note a change in water taste, odor, color, or clarity
- there is a spill of chemicals or fuels into or near your well
- when you replace or repair any part of your well system

Identify potential problems as the first step to safeguarding your drinking water. The best way to start is to consult a local expert, someone that knows your area, such as the local health department, agricultural extension agent, a nearby public water system, or a geologist at a local university (See more detailed information below).

Be aware of your surroundings. As you drive around your community, take note of new construction. Check the local newspaper for articles about new construction in your area.

Check the paper or call your local planning or zoning commission for announcements about hearings or zoning appeals on development or industrial projects that could possibly affect your water.

Attend these hearings, ask questions about how your water source is being protected, and don't be satisfied with general answers. Make statements like "If you build this landfill (just an example), what will you do to ensure that my water will be protected." See how quickly they answer and provide specifics about what plans have been made to specifically address that issue.

Identify Potential Problem Sources

To start your search for potential problems, begin close to home. Do a survey around your well:

- is there livestock nearby?

- are pesticides being used on nearby agricultural crops or nurseries?

- do you use lawn fertilizers near the well?

- is your well "downstream" from your own or a neighbor's septic system?

- is your well located near a road that is frequently salted or sprayed with de-icers during winter months?

- do you or your neighbors dispose of household wastes or used motor oil in the backyard, even in small amounts?

If any of these items apply, it may be best to have your water tested and talk to your local public health department or agricultural extension agent to find way to change some of the practices which can affect your private well.

In addition to the immediate area around your well, you should be aware of other possible sources of contamination that may already be part of your community or may be moving into your area. Attend any local planning or appeal hearings to find out more about the construction of facilities that may pollute your drinking water. Ask to see the environmental impact statement on the project. See if underground drinking water sources has been addressed. If not, ask why.

Common Sources of Potential Ground Water Contamination

Table 16.8. Potential Ground Water Contamination Sources

Category	Contaminant Source
Agricultural	• Animal burial areas • Drainage fields/wells • Animal feedlots • Irrigation sites • Fertilizer storage/use • Manure spreading areas/pits, lagoons • Pesticide storage/use
Commercial	• Airports • Jewelry/metal plating • Auto repair shops • Laundromats • Boatyards • Medical institutions • Car washes • Paint shops • Construction areas • Photography establishments • Cemeteries Process waste water drainage • Dry cleaners fields/wells • Gas stations • Railroad tracks and yards • Golf courses • Research laboratories • Scrap and junkyards • Storage tanks
Industrial	• Asphalt plants • Petroleum production/storage • Chemical manufacture/storage • Pipelines • Electronic manufacture • Process waste water drainage Electroplaters fields/wells • Foundries/metal fabricators • Septage lagoons and sludge • Machine/metalworking shops • Storage tanks • Mining and mine drainage • Toxic and hazardous spills • Wood preserving facilities

Table 16.8. Continued

Category	Contaminant Source
Residential	• Fuel Oil • Septic systems, cesspools • Furniture stripping/refinishing • Sewer lines • Household hazardous products • Swimming pools (chemicals) • Household lawns
Other	• Hazardous waste landfills • Recycling/reduction facilities • Municipal incinerators • Road deicing operations • Municipal landfills • Road maintenance depots • Municipal sewer lines • Storm water drains/basins/wells • Open burning sites • Transfer stations

Section 16.4

Fluoride

Text in this section is excerpted from "Water: Basic Information about Regulated Drinking Water Contaminants - Basic Information about Fluoride in Drinking Water," United States Environmental Protection Agency (EPA), July 23, 2013.

Basic Information about Fluoride in Drinking Water

EPA regulates fluoride in drinking water to protect public health. Fluoride may cause health problems if present in public or private water supplies in amounts greater than the drinking water standard set by EPA.

What is fluoride?

Fluoride compounds are salts that form when the element, fluorine, combines with minerals in soil or rocks.

Uses for fluoride.

Many communities add fluoride to their drinking water to promote dental health.

What are fluoride's health effects?

Exposure to excessive consumption of fluoride over a lifetime may lead to increased likelihood of bone fractures in adults, and may result in effects on bone leading to pain and tenderness. Children aged 8 years and younger exposed to excessive amounts of fluoride have an increased chance of developing pits in the tooth enamel, along with a range of cosmetic effects to teeth.

This health effects language is not intended to catalog all possible health effects for fluoride. Rather, it is intended to inform consumers of some of the possible health effects associated with fluoride in drinking water.

What are EPA's drinking water regulations for fluoride?

In 1974, Congress passed the Safe Drinking Water Act. This law requires EPA to determine the level of contaminants in drinking water at which no adverse health effects are likely to occur. These non-enforceable health goals, based solely on possible health risks and exposure over a lifetime with an adequate margin of safety, are called maximum contaminant level goals (MCLG). Contaminants are any physical, chemical, biological or radiological substances or matter in water.

The MCLG for fluoride is 4.0 mg/L or 4.0 ppm. EPA has set this level of protection based on the best available science to prevent potential health problems. EPA has set an enforceable regulation for fluoride, called a maximum contaminant level (MCL), at 4.0 mg/L or 4.0 ppm. MCLs are set as close to the health goals as possible, considering cost, benefits and the ability of public water systems to detect and remove contaminants using suitable treatment technologies. In this case, the MCL equals the MCLG, because analytical methods or treatment technology do not pose any limitation.

EPA has also set a secondary standard (SMCL) for fluoride at 2.0 mg/L or 2.0 ppm. Secondary standards are non-enforceable guidelines regulating contaminants that may cause cosmetic effects (such as skin or tooth discoloration) or aesthetic effects (such as taste, odor, or color) in drinking water. EPA recommends secondary standards to water systems but does not require systems to comply. However, states may choose to adopt them as enforceable standards. Tooth discoloration and/or pitting is caused by excess fluoride exposures during the formative period prior to eruption of the teeth in children. The secondary standard of 2.0 mg/L is intended as a guideline for an upper bound level in areas which have high levels of naturally occurring fluoride. The level of the SMCL was set based upon a balancing of the beneficial effects of protection from tooth decay and the undesirable effects of excessive exposures leading to discoloration.

Fluoride is voluntarily added to some drinking water systems as a public health measure for reducing the incidence of cavities among the treated population. The decision to fluoridate a water supply is made by the state or local municipality, and is not mandated by EPA or any other Federal entity. The Centers for Disease Control and Prevention (CDC) provides recommendations about the optimal levels of fluoride in drinking water in order to prevent tooth decay.

The drinking water standards are currently under review. The Safe Drinking Water Act requires EPA to periodically review the national primary drinking water regulation for each contaminant and revise the regulation, if appropriate. In 2003 and as part of the first Six Year Review, EPA reviewed the drinking water standard for fluoride and found that new health and exposure data were available on orally ingested fluoride. EPA requested that the National Research Council (NRC) of the National Academies of Science (NAS) conduct a review of this data and in 2006, the NRC published their evaluation in a report entitled, Fluoride in Drinking Water: A Scientific Review of EPA's Standards. The NRC recommended that EPA update its fluoride risk assessment to include new data on health risks and better estimates of total exposure.

In March 2010 and as part of the second Six Year Review, the Agency indicated that the Office of Water was in the process of developing its health and exposure assessments to address the NRC's recommendations. The Agency finalized the risk and exposure assessments for fluoride in January 2011 and announced its intent to review the drinking water regulations for fluoride to determine whether revisions are appropriate.

How does fluoride get into my drinking water?

Some fluoride compounds, such as sodium fluoride and fluorosilicates, dissolve easily into ground water as it moves through gaps and pore spaces between rocks. Most water supplies contain some naturally occurring fluoride. Fluoride also enters drinking water in discharge from fertilizer or aluminum factories. Also, many communities add fluoride to their drinking water to promote dental health.

A federal law called the Emergency Planning and Community Right to Know Act (EPCRA) requires facilities in certain industries, which manufacture, process, or use significant amounts of toxic chemicals, to report annually on their releases of these chemicals.

How will I know if fluoride is in my drinking water?

When routine monitoring indicates that fluoride levels are above the MCL, your water supplier must take steps to reduce the amount of fluoride so that it is below that level. Water suppliers must notify their customers as soon as practical, but no later than 30 days after the system learns of the violation. Additional actions, such as providing alternative drinking water supplies, may be required to prevent serious risks to public health.

If your water comes from a household or private well, check with your health department or local water systems that use ground water for information on contaminants of concern in your area.

How will fluoride be removed from my drinking water?

The following treatment method(s) have proven to be effective for removing fluoride to below 4.0 mg/L or 4.0 ppm: distillation or reverse osmosis.

How do I learn more about my drinking water?

EPA strongly encourages people to learn more about their drinking water, and to support local efforts to protect the supply of safe drinking water and upgrade the community water system. Your water bill or telephone book's government listings are a good starting point for local information.

Contact your water utility. EPA requires all community water systems to prepare and deliver an annual consumer confidence report (CCR) (sometimes called a water quality report) for their customers by July 1 of each year. If your water provider is not a community water system, or if you have a private water supply, request a copy from a nearby community water system.

Section 16.5

Disinfectants in Drinking Water

Text in this section is excerpted from "Water: Basic Information about Regulated Drinking Water Contaminants," United States Environmental Protection Agency (EPA), December 13, 2013.

Basic Information about Disinfectants in Drinking Water: Chloramine, Chlorine and Chlorine Dioxide

To protect drinking water from disease-causing organisms, or pathogens, water suppliers often add a disinfectant, such as chlorine, to drinking water. However, disinfection practices can be complicated because certain microbial pathogens, such as *Cryptosporidium*, are highly resistant to traditional disinfection practices. Also, disinfectants themselves can react with naturally-occurring materials in the water to form byproducts, such as trihalomethanes and haloacetic acids, which may pose health risks.

A major challenge for water suppliers is how to control and limit the risks from pathogens and disinfection byproducts. It is important to provide protection from pathogens while simultaneously minimizing health risks to the population from disinfection byproducts.

What are disinfectants, how are they used, and what are their health effects in drinking water at levels above the maximum residual disinfectant level?

Table 16.9. Disinfectants—Uses and Health Effects

Disinfectant (Chemical Abstract Service Registry Number)	Definition and uses	Health Effects
Chloramine (as Cl2) (10599-90-3)	Chloramine (as Cl2) is a water additive used to control microbes, particularly as a residual disinfectant in distribution system pipes. It is formed when ammonia is added to water containing free chlorine.	Some people who use water containing chloramine in excess of the maximum residual disinfectant level could experience irritating effects to their eyes and nose, stomach discomfort or anemia.

Table 16.9. Continued

Disinfectant (Chemical Abstract Service Registry Number)	Definition and uses	Health Effects
	Monochloramine is one form of chloramines commonly used for4 disinfection by municipal water systems. Other chloramines (di- and tri-) are not intentionally used to disinfect drinking water and are generally not formed during the drinking water disinfection process.	
Chlorine (as Cl2) (10049-04-4)	The gaseous or liquid form of chlorine (CL2) is a water additive used by municipal water systems to control microbes. It is relatively inexpensive and has the lowest production and operating costs and longest history for large continuous disinfection operations. Chlorine is a powerful oxidant.	Some people who use water containing chlorine well in excess of the maximum residual disinfectant level could experience irritating effects to their eyes and nose. Some people who drink water containing chlorine well in excess of the maximum residual disinfectant level could experience stomach discomfort.
Chlorine dioxide (as ClO2)(10049-04-4)	Chlorine dioxide is a water additive used to control microbes and can be used to control tastes and odors. It rapidly disappears from stored water.	Some infants, young children, and fetuses of pregnant women who drink water containing chlorine dioxide in excess of the maximum residual disinfectant level could experience nervous system effects. Some people who drink water containingchlorine dioxide well in excess of the MRDL for many years may experience anemia.

This health effects language is not intended to catalog all possible health effects for disinfectants. Rather, it is intended to inform consumers of some of the possible health effects associated with disinfectants in drinking water when the rule was finalized

What are EPA's drinking water regulations for disinfectants?

In 1974, Congress passed the Safe Drinking Water Act. This law requires EPA to determine the level of residual disinfectants in drinking water at which no adverse health effects are likely to occur. These non-enforceable health goals, based solely on possible health risks and exposure over a lifetime, with an adequate margin of safety, are called maximum residual disinfectant level goals (MRDLG). Contaminants are any physical, chemical, biological or radiological substances or matter in water. EPA sets MRDLGs based on the best available science to prevent potential health problems.

Based on the MRDLG, EPA has set enforceable regulations for disinfectants, called a maximum residual disinfectant level (MRDL), at the following levels:

MRDLs are set as close to the health goals as possible, considering cost, benefits and the ability of public water systems to detect and remove contaminants using suitable treatment technologies. In this case, the MRDL equals the MRDLG, because analytical methods or treatment technology do not pose any limitation. States may set more stringent drinking water MRDLGs and MRDLs for disinfectants than EPA.

The following drinking water regulations apply to disinfectants and disinfection byproducts:

- Stage 1 Disinfectants and Disinfection Byproducts Rule (Stage 1 DBP) (December 16, 1998).

  The Stage 1 Disinfectants and Disinfection Byproducts Rule reduces exposure to disinfection byproducts for customers of community water systems and non-transient non-community systems, including those serving fewer than 10,000 people, that

Table 16.10. MRDLG and MRDL levels for disinfectants

Disinfectant	MRDLG	MRDL
Chloramine	4 milligrams per liter (mg/L) or 4 parts per million (ppm)	4.0 mg/L or 4 ppm as an annual average
Chlorine	4 mg/L or 4 ppm	4.0 mg/L or 4 ppm as an annual average
Chlorine Dioxide	0.8 mg/L or 800 parts per billion (ppb)	0.8 mg/L or 800 ppb

add a disinfectant to the drinking water during any part of the treatment process.

- Stage 2 Disinfectants and Disinfection Byproducts Rule (Stage 2 DBP) (December 15, 2005).

  Stage 2 DBP rule builds upon earlier rules that addressed disinfection byproducts to improve your drinking water quality and provide additional public health protection from disinfection byproducts.

The Safe Drinking Water Act requires EPA to periodically review the national primary drinking water regulation for each contaminant and revise the regulation, if appropriate, based on new scientific data. EPA will include the Disinfectants and Disinfection Byproducts rules in future review cycles.

How will I know if disinfectants are in my drinking water?

Public water systems using surface water or ground water under the direct influence of surface water are required to maintain a detectible disinfectant residual in the distribution system. When routine monitoring indicates that disinfectant levels are above the MRDL, your water supplier must take steps to reduce the amount of disinfectant so that it is below that level. For chlorine dioxide, water suppliers must notify their customers as soon as practical, but no later than 24 hours after the system learns of the violation. For chloramine and chlorine, water suppliers must notify their customers as soon as practical, but no later than 30 days after the system learns of the violation. Additional actions, such as providing alternative drinking water supplies, may be required to prevent serious risks to public health.

How are disinfectants controlled in my drinking water?

The following treatment method(s) have proven to be effective for removing chloramines, chlorine, and chlorine dioxide to below their MRDLs: control of treatment processes to reduce disinfectant demand and control of disinfection treatment processes to reduce disinfectant levels.

How do I learn more about my drinking water?

EPA strongly encourages people to learn more about their drinking water, and to support local efforts to protect the supply of safe drinking water and upgrade the community water system. Your water bill or telephone book's government listings are a good starting point for local information.

Contact your water utility. EPA requires all community water systems to prepare and deliver an annual consumer confidence report (CCR) (sometimes called a water quality report) for their customers by July 1 of each year. If your water provider is not a community water system, or if you have a private water supply, request a copy from a nearby community water system.

Section 16.6

Bottled Water

Text in this section is excerpted from "Drinking Water," Centers for Disease Control and Prevention (CDC), April 7, 2014.

Basics

Americans spend billions of dollars every year on bottled water. People choose bottled water for a variety of reasons including aesthetics (for example, taste), health concerns, or as a substitute for other beverages.

If you have questions about bottled water, make sure you are informed about where your bottled water comes from and how it has been treated. The standards for bottled water are set by the United States Food and Drug Administration (FDA). The FDA bases its standards on the EPA standards for tap water.

- Read the label on your bottled water. While there is currently no standardized label for bottled water, this label may tell you about the way the bottled water is treated.

- Check the label for a toll-free number or Web page address of the company that bottled the water. This may be a source of further information.

Bottled Water and Immunocompromised Individuals

People with compromised immune systems may want to take special precautions with the water they drink. In healthy individuals, the parasite *Cryptosporidium* can cause illness; however, for those with weakened immune systems, it can cause severe illness and possibly death. Look for bottled water treatments that protect against *Cryptosporidium*, which include:

- Reverse osmosis

- Distillation

- Filtration with an absolute 1 micron filter

Fluoride and Bottled Water

Some bottled waters contain fluoride, and some do not. Fluoride can occur naturally in source waters used for bottling or be added. Most bottled waters contain fluoride at levels that are less than optimal for good oral health.

Safety and Regulation

The FDA regulates bottled water under the Federal Food, Drug, and Cosmetic Act and sets standards for bottled water that are based on ones developed by EPA. If these standards are met, water is considered safe for most healthy individuals. The bottled water industry must also follow FDA's Current Good Manufacturing Practices (CGMPs) for processing and bottling drinking water.

Bottled Water Outbreaks

Although bottled water outbreaks are not often reported, they do occur. It is important for bottled water manufacturers, distributors, and consumers to:

- Protect and properly treat water before bottling

- Maintain good manufacturing processes

- Protect bottled water during shipping and storage

- Prevent contamination at the point of use (after purchase by the consumer)

The presence of contaminants in water can lead to adverse health effects, including gastrointestinal illness, reproductive problems, and neurological disorders. Infants, young children, pregnant women, the elderly, and people whose immune systems are compromised because of AIDS, chemotherapy, or transplant medications, may be especially susceptible to illness from some contaminants.

Chapter 17

Swimming Water

Recreational Water Illnesses (RWIs)

Contrary to popular belief, chlorine does not kill all germs instantly. There are germs today that are very tolerant to chlorine and were not known to cause human disease until recently. Once these germs get in the pool, it can take anywhere from minutes to days for chlorine to kill them. Swallowing just a little water that contains these germs can make you sick.

Recreational water illnesses (RWIs) are caused by germs spread by swallowing, breathing in mists or aerosols of, or having contact with contaminated water in swimming pools, hot tubs, water parks, water play areas, interactive fountains, lakes, rivers, or oceans. RWIs can also be caused by chemicals in the water or chemicals that evaporate from the water and cause indoor air quality problems.

RWIs include a wide variety of infections, such as gastrointestinal, skin, ear, respiratory, eye, neurologic, and wound infections. The most commonly reported RWI is diarrhea. Diarrheal illnesses are caused by germs such as Crypto (short for *Cryptosporidium*), *Giardia*, *Shigella*, norovirus and *E. coli* O157:H7. With RWI outbreaks on the rise, swimmers need to take an active role in helping to protect themselves and prevent the spread of germs. It is important for swimmers to learn the basic facts about RWIs so they can keep themselves and their family healthy every time they swim.

Text in this chapter is excerpted from "Healthy Swimming/Recreational Water," Centers for Disease Control and Prevention (CDC), February 5, 2015.

In the past two decades, there has been a substantial increase in the number of RWI outbreaks associated with swimming. Crypto, which can stay alive for days even in well-maintained pools, has become the leading cause of swimming pool-related outbreaks of diarrheal illness. From 2004 to 2008, reported Crypto cases increased over 200% (from 3,411 cases in 2004 to 10,500 cases in 2008).

Although Crypto is tolerant to chlorine, most germs are not. Keeping chlorine at recommended levels is essential to maintain a healthy pool. However, a 2010 study found that 1 in 8 public pool inspections resulted in pools being closed immediately due to serious code violations such as improper chlorine levels.

Pools and Hot Tubs

The benefits of water-based exercise are numerous, but to truly enjoy a safe and healthy swimming experience it is important for swimmers and hot tub users to know the steps they should take to protect themselves and others from potential health risks.

Aquatics professionals have a responsibility to provide a safe and healthy swimming environment for their patrons. Maintaining good water quality requires pool operators and staff to have specific skills.

Animals and Pools

Animals can be great companions, but if allowed in or near your pool, they can sometimes contaminate the water and spread germs that cause disease. It is important to always keep your pool clean and take precautions when animals have been in or near the pool.

Finding a Dead Animal in the Pool

Most dead animals in pools do not pose a health risk to swimmers. If you find a dead animal in the pool, following the simple removal and disinfection steps below will help ensure healthy swimming in the pool.

Dead raccoons in pools, however, can pose a health risk to swimmers. This is because raccoons might be infected with a worm called *Baylisascaris,* which can be spread to humans.

What types of dead animals are found in swimming pools?

Many different types of domestic and wild animals—including skunks, birds, mice, gophers, rats, snakes, frogs, and bats—are commonly found dead in pools.

Do dead animals in pools pose a health risk to swimmers?

Most dead animals in pools do not pose a health risk to swimmers. Many germs carried by animals infect only those animals, though a few of the germs they carry can infect people.

Most germs carried by animals are killed by chlorine within minutes in a well-maintained pool. However, to help ensure healthy swimming in a pool where a dead animal has been found, it is important to follow the simple steps below to remove the animal and disinfect the water.

What should I do if I find a dead animal in the pool?*

Follow these steps to remove the animal and disinfect the water:

- Close the pool to swimmers.

- Put on disposable gloves.

- Use a net or bucket to remove the dead animal from the pool.

- Double bag the animal in plastic garbage bags.

- Clean off any debris or dirt from the item used to remove the dead animal.

- Remove gloves and place them in the garbage bags.

- Close the garbage bags and place them in a sealed trash can to help keep wild animals away from the dead animal.

- Wash your hands thoroughly with soap and water immediately.

- Raise the free chlorine concentration to, or maintain it at, 2 parts per million (ppm); maintain the pH levels at 7.5 or less; keep the temperature at 77°F (25°C) or higher. The free chlorine and pH should remain at these levels for 30 minutes.

- Confirm that the filtration system is operating properly during this time.

- Disinfect the item used to remove the dead animal by immersing it in the pool during the 30 minute disinfection time.

---

*These cleaning and disinfection steps are for animals commonly reported to be found dead in pools. Pre-weaned calves and lambs are often infected with *Cryptosporidium*, a chlorine-tolerant germ, and could pose a health risk to swimmers if found dead in a pool.

Raccoons and Pools

Raccoons can be pests and can spread germs to humans. It is important to keep raccoons out of your pool and watch for raccoon feces (poop) in and around your pool. **Raccoon feces can sometimes contain the eggs of a worm called *Baylisascaris procyonis*,** which can infect humans, particularly children, and cause severe neurologic illness.

What is Baylisascaris?

Baylisascaris is a roundworm parasite that commonly infects raccoons. Raccoons infected with *Baylisascaris* can be found in all parts of the United States. When people are exposed to *Baylisascaris* eggs they can become ill.

What illness does Baylisascaris cause?

Baylisascaris infections in people are very rarely diagnosed. Swallowing a few *Baylisascaris* eggs can result in no or few symptoms. However, swallowing a large number of eggs can result in severe disease that affects the nervous system or eyes.

How is Baylisascaris spread?

The parasite is spread by swallowing *Baylisascaris* eggs, which are found in the feces of raccoons that are infected with *Baylisascaris*. People can be exposed to *Baylisascaris* eggs in soil, water, or on objects that have been contaminated with feces from an infected raccoon.

Additional information on the disease can be found on the CDC *Baylisascaris* Website.

If I find raccoon feces or a dead raccoon in my pool, is it safe to swim?

Not if the raccoon was infected with *Baylisascaris*. Although chlorine in pools will kill most germs that a raccoon could carry into the water, it does not kill *Baylisascaris* eggs. If raccoon feces or a dead raccoon are found in the pool:
    Close the pool to swimmers.

- If you plan to test the raccoon or its feces for *Baylisascaris*, follow the directions below.

- If you do not want to test the raccoon feces, clean the pool as described in the following sections.

How should I test raccoon feces for Baylisascaris?

- Put on disposable gloves and collect the feces or retrieve the dead raccoon. Double bag the feces or animal in plastic garbage bags. Remove gloves and place them in the garbage bags. Wash your hands thoroughly with soap and water afterwards.

- Contact Animal Control (the local government agency in charge of animal issues) or your local health department about testing raccoon feces for *Baylisascaris* eggs. The only way to find out if a raccoon is infected with *Baylisascaris* is to test the feces.

- If the lab test shows evidence of *Baylisascaris* eggs, then you need to clean your pool as described below. If the lab test is negative, you do not need to clean your pool as described below.

How do I clean my pool if it has been contaminated with Baylisascaris?

Because *Baylisascaris* eggs are particularly tough, adding chlorine to the water will not kill them. If a lab test has confirmed that the raccoon was infected with *Baylisascaris* or you don't know if the raccoon was infected because the raccoon's feces were not tested, there are two options for cleaning your pool.

*Remember to close the pool to swimmers until you have finished cleaning the pool.

Option 1:

- Filter the pool for a minimum of 24 hours and then backwash the pool filter.

- Put on disposable gloves to replace the material doing the filtering (if possible). Double bag the discarded material in plastic garbage bags. Remove gloves and place them in the garbage bags. Wash your hands thoroughly with soap and water afterwards.

Option 2:

- Backwash the pool filter.

- Drain and hose down the pool.

- Put on disposable gloves to replace the material doing the filtering (if possible). Double bag the discarded material in plastic garbage bags. Remove gloves and place them in the garbage bags. Wash your hands thoroughly with soap and water afterwards.

• Refill the pool.

What can I do to keep raccoons out of my swimming pool?

Raccoons usually choose certain locations to defecate (poop) and then use those same places repeatedly. Raccoons can also be attracted to areas where humans live and play. In pools, raccoons usually defecate in the shallow areas (for example, on the steps).

Here are some tips for keeping raccoons out of your pool:

• Cover the pool area that has been visited by raccoons.

• Keep the fence around the pool closed.

• Find out if anyone in your area is feeding raccoons, leaving pet food outside, leaving uncovered trash outside, or using trash cans that are not properly secured. Discourage this behavior as it could be attracting animals, particularly raccoons, to your pool.

• Contact Animal Control (local government office in charge of animal issues) or a pest control removal service to relocate the animal.

Birds and Pools

Many types of birds are attracted to swimming pools. As a result, swimmers might come in contact with bird droppings (poop) while in the pool. If you find bird droppings in the pool, there are a few simple steps you can take to disinfect the water and keep birds away from the pool.

Can bird droppings in the pool spread germs to swimmers?

Many germs that might be found in bird droppings can infect humans. Duck and goose droppings, in particular, might contain germs such as *E. coli*, *Salmonella*, *Campylobacter*, or *Cryptosporidium*("Crypto" for short).

Most germs in bird droppings are killed by chlorine within minutes in a well-maintained pool.

The germ Crypto, however, has a tough outer shell that allows it to survive for a long time in the environment. Crypto can survive for days even in properly chlorinated pools. Currently, CDC is not aware of any evidence of Crypto being spread directly from birds to humans.

What should I do if I find bird droppings in the pool?

Pool operators and owners should respond to finding bird droppings in the pool the same way they would respond to finding formed human feces (poop) in the pool. The Healthy Swimming Program's Fecal Incident Response Recommendations provide step-by-step guidance on how to properly decontaminate the water in these situations.

Follow these steps to remove bird droppings and disinfect the water:

- Close the pool to swimmers.
- Put on disposable gloves.
- Remove the bird droppings using a net or bucket. Do not vacuum the droppings from the pool.
- Clean off any debris or dirt from the item used to remove the bird droppings.
- Disinfect the item used to remove the droppings by immersing it in the pool during the 30-minute disinfection time described below.
- Remove and dispose of gloves.
- Wash your hands thoroughly with soap and water immediately.
- Raise the free chlorine concentration to, or maintain it at, 2 parts per million (ppm); maintain the pH level at 7.5 or less; keep the temperature at 77°F (25°C) or higher. The free chlorine and pH should remain at these levels for 30 minutes.
- Confirm that the filtration system is operating properly.

How can I keep birds away from the pool area?

The following steps can help encourage birds, other than ducks and geese (more information on ducks and geese is provided below), to leave the swimming pool area:

- Remove plants that produce edible nuts, fruits, and berries.
- Remove bird feeders.

- Trim or remove trees and shrubs to limit branches hanging around or over the pool that can be used by roosting birds.

How can I keep ducks and geese away from the pool area?

Do not feed ducks or geese; providing food attracts them and encourages them to return. Many types of ducks and geese eat grass, so reducing the area of grass lawns around the swimming pool or putting up barriers that prohibit movement between swimming pools and grass lawns, such as fences and hedges, might also help. Removing domestic ducks and geese from the pool area can also help decrease the likelihood that wild ducks and geese will be attracted to the area.

The U.S. Department of Agriculture has additional information on how to manage ducks and geese (also known as waterfowl) in their document Assistance with Waterfowl Damage.

What can I do to get rid of ducks and geese already in the pool area?

In the United States, most birds, including ducks and geese, are protected by the Federal Migratory Bird Treaty Act and state laws. Local laws might also apply. Therefore, legal options for dealing with birds are limited and may require a permit. Consult the U.S. Fish and Wildlife Services and your state wildlife agency for more information.

Inflatable and Plastic Pools (Kiddie Pools)

Small Inflatable and Plastic Pools Can Spread Illness

Small inflatable pools and plastic pools (usually 3 to 5 feet diameter) or other small water play attractions (for example, slides) have been associated with the spread of recreational water illnesses (RWIs). RWIs can be spread by swallowing or having contact with contaminated recreational water. These illnesses are caused by germs such as Crypto (short for *Cryptosporidium*), *E. coli* O157:H7, and *Shigella*.

Small inflatable and plastic pools are typically filled with tap water. Some people in the United States have a disinfectant in their tap water but this is not adequate to kill germs that may get into water used for swimming. Sources of information exist about how to disinfect these pools. However, it may not be practical to kill germs by adding chlorine bleach to small pools. This is because the chlorine dose cannot be easily determined or safely monitored to ensure that the right amount of chlorine continuously stays in the water. These pools also do not have filters to remove particles that could prevent the chlorine from working well. Using these types of pools increases the risk of spreading RWIs brought into the water by swimmers with a diarrheal illness.

The use of small inflatable and plastic pools in child care programs or schools should be discouraged. This includes small child care settings in private homes. The larger number of children from different families in child care settings and schools can increase the risk for spreading RWIs.

Children from one family or household are often bathed together so they are unlikely to be at increased risk of spreading diarrheal illness to each other if allowed to use the same inflatable or plastic pool. However, allowing larger numbers of children from different families to use these pools is likely to increase the risk of spreading diarrheal illnesses. Any household deciding to use these types of small pools should follow the steps below to reduce the spread of illness:

Before Use

- Do not allow a child who is ill with diarrhea or vomiting to use the pool.

- Give children a cleansing soap shower or bath before they swim.

- Talk to parents or caregivers about their children's health before these children use the pool.

During Use

- Remind children to avoid getting pool water in their mouths.

- Respond to feces in the pool or a child with a dirty diaper.

- Clear the pool of children, empty, and then clean it. In the case of diarrheal incidents, once the pool has been cleaned and is completely dry, leave it in the sun for at least four hours.

After Use

- Drain or empty the pool. Medium and larger-sized inflatable and plastic pools that cannot be emptied daily should have filters and appropriate disinfection systems that meet the same codes and requirements as full-sized swimming pools.

- Clean the pool and allow it to dry. Once the pool is completely dry, leave it in the sun for at least four hours.

Remember that these small pools can also pose a drowning hazard if not properly supervised or enclosed. Local swimming pool codes may require fences around small inflatable and plastic pools.

Water Play Areas and Interactive Fountains

Keeping Water Play Areas / Interactive Fountains Clean

A more recent addition to the recreational water attraction scene is the water play area (may also be called an interactive fountain, wet deck, splash pad, spray pad, or spray park). People may not realize that although there is no standing water in these attractions, the spray water will rinse any contaminants (for example, diarrhea, vomit, and dirt) down into the water holding area and be sprayed again. In other words, the water is recycled through the system. As a result, it is possible for the water to become contaminated and cause outbreaks of illness.

Because water play areas / interactive fountains are relatively new, health departments may not have specific requirements for how this water is treated. It pays to be proactive by building water play areas or interactive fountains like any other water attraction is built. They should include adequate disinfection and filtration systems even if this is not currently required by the local or state pool code. The addition of secondary disinfection, like ultraviolet light or ozone, should be considered and is now required in New York State. Health departments should also ensure that pool codes are updated to include water features that do not have standing water.

Outbreaks Associated with Water Play Areas / Interactive Fountains

During the summer of 2005, an outbreak of cryptosporidiosis occurred at Seneca Lake State Park in New York. Over 1,700 people may have been infected with 425 laboratory-confirmed cases of cryptosporidiosis and 1,374 probable cases were identified. *Cryptosporidium* was traced to the water tanks that supplied the 11,000-square-foot wet deck (spraypark). In response, New York passed emergency public health regulations to govern the design and sanitation of such attractions statewide.

A 1999 outbreak of diarrheal illness affected 44% of patrons (an estimated 4,800 people) who visited a new interactive fountain in a beachside park. When officials from the health department inspected the interactive fountain, they found that the water drained from the play area into an underground reservoir for recirculation. The problem turned out to be a result of inadequate chlorination and the lack of a filtration system. The chlorine tablet erosion feeder had not been filled for weeks and the designers did not include a filtration system.

Regulation and Inspection of Pools and Hot Tubs

Pool regulations and codes are developed by government agencies to make sure that treated recreational water facilities (for example, pools, hot tubs, and water parks) provide a clean, healthy, and safe environment for the public. These regulations set minimum standards (such as the amount of chlorine that should be in the pool) to decrease the public's risk of illness and injury. To ensure that these regulations are followed, state and local officials regularly inspect treated recreational water venues.

Model Aquatic Health Code

The Model Aquatic Health Code (MAHC) is a voluntary guidance document based on science and best practices that can help local and state authorities and the aquatics sector make swimming and other water activities healthier and safer. States and localities can use the MAHC to create or update existing pool codes to reduce risk for outbreaks, drowning, and pool-chemical injuries. The MAHC guidelines address the design, construction, operation, maintenance, policies, and management of public aquatic facilities.

Chapter 18

Harmful Algae Blooms

Harmful algal blooms (HABs) are a major environmental problem in all 50 states. Known as red tides, blue-green algae or cyanobacteria, harmful algal blooms have severe impacts on human health, aquatic ecosystems and the economy.

Algal blooms can be toxic. Keep people and pets away from water that is green, scummy or smells bad.

What are harmful algal blooms?

Harmful algal blooms are overgrowths of algae in water. Some produce dangerous toxins in fresh or marine water but even nontoxic blooms hurt the environment and local economies.

What are the effects of harmful algal blooms?

Harmful algal blooms can:

- Produce extremely dangerous toxins that can sicken or kill people and animals

- Create dead zones in the water

- Raise treatment costs for drinking water

- Hurt industries that depend on clean water

Text in this chapter is excerpted from "Nutrient Pollution," United States Environmental Protection Agency (EPA), October 23, 2014.

What causes harmful algal blooms?

Harmful algal blooms need:

- Sunlight
- Slow-moving water
- Nutrients (nitrogen and phosphorus)

Nutrient pollution from human activities makes the problem worse, leading to more severe blooms that occur more often.

Algae are vitally important to marine and fresh-water ecosystems, and most species of algae are not harmful. Algal blooms occur in natural waters used for drinking and/or recreation when certain types of microscopic algae grow quickly in water, often in response to changes in levels of chemicals such as nitrogen and phosphorus from fertilizer, in the water. Algal blooms can deplete the oxygen and block the sunlight that other organisms need to live, and some can produce toxins that are harmful to the health of the environment, plants, animals, and people. Harmful algal blooms have threatened beaches, drinking water sources, and even the boating venue for the 2008 Olympic Games in Beijing, China. Cyanobacteria (blue-green algae) and red tides are examples of algae that can bloom and produce toxins that may be harmful to human and animal health. HABs can occur in marine, estuarine, and fresh waters, and HABs appear to be increasing along the coastlines and in the surface waters of the United States, according to the National Oceanic and Atmospheric Administration (NOAA). HAB epidemiologists have led a number of studies to investigate the public health impacts of blue-green algae blooms and Florida red tide. The studies have demonstrated that there is the potential for exposure to potent HAB-related toxins during recreational and occupational activities on water bodies with ongoing blooms.

Although scientists do not yet understand fully how HABs affect human health, authorities in the United States and abroad are monitoring HABs and developing guidelines for HAB-related public health action. The U.S. Environmental Protection Agency (EPA) has added certain algae associated with HABs to its Drinking Water Contaminant Candidate List. This list identifies organisms and toxins that EPA believes are priorities for investigation.

Many states regularly experience HABs, and state public health departments are often are asked to provide guidance about HAB-associated human and animal illnesses. HSB subject matter experts help states to develop their public health responses to HAB events, including providing outreach and education materials and assessing exposure and the potential for health effects.

Cyanobacteria (blue-green algae)

Cyanobacteria, also known as blue-green algae, grow in any type of water and are photosynthetic (use sunlight to create food and support life). Cyanobacteria live in terrestrial, fresh, brackish, or marine water. They usually are too small to be seen, but sometimes can form visible colonies, called an algal bloom. Cyanobacteria have been found among the oldest fossils on earth and are one of the largest groups of bacteria. Cyanobacteria have been linked to human and animal illnesses around the world, including North and South America, Africa, Australia, Europe, Scandinavia, and China.

Cyanobacterial blooms and how they form

Cyanobacterial blooms (a kind of algal bloom) occur when organisms that are normally present grow exuberantly. Within a few days, a bloom of cyanobacteria can cause clear water to become cloudy. The blooms usually float to the surface and can be many inches thick, especially near the shoreline. Cyanobacterial blooms can form in warm, slow-moving waters that are rich in nutrients such as fertilizer runoff or septic tank overflows. Blooms can occur at any time, but most often occur in late summer or early fall.

They can occur in marine, estuarine, and fresh waters, but the blooms of greatest concern are the ones that occur in fresh water, such as drinking water reservoirs or recreational waters.

What a cyanobacterial bloom looks like

Some cyanobacterial blooms can look like foam, scum, or mats on the surface of fresh water lakes and ponds. The blooms can be blue, bright green, brown, or red and may look like paint floating on the water. Some blooms may not affect the appearance of the water. As algae in a cyanobacterial bloom die, the water may smell bad.

Harmful Marine Algae

Harmful marine algae, such as those associated with red tides, occur in the ocean and can produce toxins that may harm or kill fish and marine animals. There are many kinds of marine algae that produce toxins that can accumulate in shellfish. In the US, one of the illnesses that may result from eating algal toxin-contaminated shellfish is neurotoxic shellfish poisoning (NSP). NSP is caused by eating shellfish contaminated with brevetoxins, which are produced by Karenia brevis, the marine algae associated with Florida red tides. NSP is a short-term illness with neurologic symptoms (such as tingling fingers or toes) and gastrointestinal symptoms. There are very few cases of NSP in the US because coastal states carefully monitor their shellfish beds and close the beds to harvesting if high concentrations of brevetoxins are detected in the water or the shellfish. Brevetoxins may also be in the air along the Gulf coast of Florida during Florida red tide events and may symptoms such as eye irritation and a sore throat in healthy people. People who have asthma may have symptoms, such as chest tightness, that last for several days after exposure. Ciguatera tides fish poisoning is another disease associated with toxins produced by marine algae. The toxin responsible, called ciguatoxin, accumulates through the food web, and very high levels may exist in reef fish, particularly (but not only) large carnivorous reef fish.

Red Tide

Background: Algae are vitally important to marine ecosystems, and most species of algae are not harmful. However, under certain environmental conditions, microscopic marine algae called Karenia brevis (K. brevis) grow quickly, creating blooms that can make the ocean appear red or brown. People often call these blooms "red tide."

K. brevis produces powerful toxins called brevetoxins, which have killed millions of fish and other marine organisms. Red tides have damaged the fishing industry, shoreline quality, and local economies in states such as Texas and Florida. Because K. brevis blooms move based on winds and tides, pinpointing a red tide at any given moment is difficult.

Red tides occur throughout the world, affecting marine ecosystems in Scandinavia, Japan, the Caribbean, and the South Pacific. Scientists first documented a red tide along Florida's Gulf Coast in fall 1947, when residents of Venice, Florida, reported thousands of dead fish and a "stinging gas" in the air, according to Mote Marine Laboratory. However, Florida residents have reported similar events since the mid-1800s.

Assessing the Impact on Public Health

In addition to killing fish, brevetoxins can become concentrated in the tissues of shellfish that feed on K. brevis. People who eat these shellfish may suffer from neurotoxic shellfish poisoning, a food poisoning that can cause severe gastrointestinal and neurologic symptoms, such as tingling fingers or toes.

The human health effects associated with eating brevetoxin-tainted shellfish are well documented. However, scientists know little about how other types of environmental exposures to brevetoxin—such as breathing the air near red tides or swimming in red tides—may affect humans. Anecdotal evidence suggests that people who swim among brevetoxins or inhale brevetoxins dispersed in the air may experience irritation of the eyes, nose, and throat, as well as coughing, wheezing, and shortness of breath. Additional evidence suggests that people with existing respiratory illness, such as asthma, may experience these symptoms more severely.

Ciguatera

Ciguatera fish poisoning (or ciguatera) is an illness caused by eating fish that contain toxins produced by a marine microalgae called *Gambierdiscus toxicus*. Barracuda, black grouper, blackfin snapper, cubera snapper, dog snapper, greater amberjack, hogfish, horse-eye jack, king mackerel, and yellowfin grouper have been known to carry ciguatoxins. People who have ciguatera may experience nausea, vomiting, and neurologic symptoms such as tingling fingers or toes. They also may find that cold things feel hot and hot things feel cold. Ciguatera has no cure. Symptoms usually go away in days or weeks but can last for years. People who have ciguatera can be treated for their symptoms.

Chapter 19

Ocean Contamination

Chapter Contents

Section 19.1

Marine Debris

Text in this section is excerpted from "Water: Marine Debris," United States Environmental Protection Agency (EPA), March 6, 2012.

Basic Information

Marine debris is any persistent solid material that is directly or indirectly disposed of or abandoned into the aquatic environment. Marine debris is a problem in oceans, coasts, and watersheds throughout the world. Successfully addressing marine debris depends on managing its sources, movement, and impacts. EPA works to prevent, control, and reduce sources and movement of pollution that may become marine debris.

Marine Debris Sources

Most marine debris comes from a variety of human activities on land or at sea. Sources of marine debris are not limited to the coasts. Moreover, marine debris can result from human activities anywhere in the watershed, from an overturned trash can miles away from the ocean to litter left on a beach. Objects such as detergent bottles, plastic bags, cigarette butts, hazardous medical wastes, and discarded fishing line are all materials that can become marine debris.

Overview

Marine debris is often the result of deliberate or accidental actions by people on land or at sea. Improperly covered trash bins, litter, debris left in streets and on beaches, and items thrown overboard can all become marine debris. Items can travel far before landing on shorelines or settling in the ocean. Marine debris can come from anywhere in a watershed, and be carried by rivers, streams, and other waterways into the ocean. To better understand and control marine debris we must address the actions that generate or transport marine debris.

The National Marine Debris Monitoring Program determined that 49 percent of debris on U.S. beaches is from land-based sources, 18 percent is from ocean-based sources, and 33 percent is from a general source that could be considered land or ocean-based. However, regardless of the source or type, all marine debris impacts our oceans, beaches, and waterways.

Land-Based Sources

Land-Based Sources

- Municipal landfills
- Transport of litter and waste (on land or on waterways)
- Storm water discharge
- Industrial or manufacturing
- Litter and waste generated in coastal and inland zones from improper waste management
- Natural events

Marine debris from land-based sources washes, blows, or is released into the water from coastal areas or farther inland. Sources of land-based marine debris include individuals, facilities (e.g., manufacturing), municipalities (e.g., combined sewer overflows), and natural disasters.

Individuals

Individuals can contribute to marine debris through both accidental and deliberate actions. On the beach and piers, individuals leave trash or toss it into the water. Further inland, people lose or throw trash on the streets or improperly manage their waste and garbage bins. The inland actions can lead to trash in storm drains, rivers, and other waterways. Once in these waterways, the trash can be carried to our oceans. Any items, from plastic bottles, food wrappings, and cigarette butts to larger items such as lawn care containers or even refrigerators, can become marine debris.

Facilities and Construction

Land-based marine debris can come from industrial and manufacturing facilities, as well as construction and demolition sites. Facilities can generate marine debris if their production, equipment, trash disposal, and waste streams are improperly managed. Additionally, industrial by-products, particularly plastic resin pellets, may also become marine debris during transport or disposal. Similar to industrial materials, construction and demolition materials can become marine debris if appropriate disposal practices are not followed or if equipment or supplies are left unsecured. These debris items can include scrap metal, unused parts, paint buckets, and packaging materials.

Municipalities

Trash can come from many different sources in a municipality and becomes marine debris. The amount of marine debris that enters the ocean from municipal storm sewer systems often depends on the municipal infrastructure supporting waste management. Combined sewer systems and storm water systems can carry debris into coastal and ocean waters, especially during heavy rain events. Debris can be picked up during rain flow and carried into a drain or may have been intentionally thrown into a drain. Typical debris entering these systems includes medical waste and street litter. Municipalities also maintain landfills. Collection and transport of waste to these sites may result in marine debris if materials are mishandled or accidentally lost. Finally, lack of waste management options may result in the improper dumping of wastes, which can lead to more materials entering our waterways and oceans.

Natural Events

Natural events, such as tornadoes, hurricanes, floods, and tsunamis, can all generate and carry debris into the marine environment. During the 2005 hurricane season, the Sabine National Wildlife Refuge in Louisiana had approximately nine million cubic yards of debris across 1,770 acres of marsh. Debris resulting from natural weather events can be almost anything, from roofs to plastic straws, depending on the severity and scale of the event. The most common items include containers and other unsecured outdoor items.

Ocean-Based Sources

Sources of ocean-based marine debris include vessels and other structures and natural events. Moreover, it is activities on these vessels and platforms, such as waste mishandling and improperly

---

Ocean-Based Sources

- Merchant shipping, ferries, and cruise liners
- Fishing vessels
- Public vessels
- Private vessels
- Offshore oil and gas platforms, and drilling rigs
- Aquaculture installations
- Natural events

---

securing equipment, which lead to marine debris, since the materials can be swept, blown, or thrown overboard.

Vessels and Other Structures

Recreational and commercial vessels, platforms, and other structures at sea are all potential sources of marine debris. Similar to marine debris originating from land-based sources, debris from ocean-based sources is a result of accidental or deliberate human actions. Marine debris can come from mismanagement of ship wastes and equipment, or from accidental loss of gear overboard. This debris can consist of food containers and trash from the galley, fishing gear (e.g., nets, ropes, and light sticks), cargo and equipment.

Marine debris can also come from abandoned vessels and offshore materials and equipment, like aquaculture installations and buoys. Pieces from these structures can break off due to improper securing and heavy sea conditions and settle to the ocean floor or end up onshore.

Natural Events

Inclement weather, strong seas, and natural events can also cause accidental loss of waste and cargo from vessels and other structures at sea. This debris may be lost due to inadequate securing of equipment and poor loading practices.

Marine Debris Impacts

Marine debris is a major pollution problem affecting every waterway. Impacts can be experienced locally, nationally, and internationally and threaten human health and safety, the economy, and the environment. Direct impacts of marine debris include aquatic wildlife starvation, suffocation, or death, as well as human health and safety hazards. Indirect impacts of marine debris include ecosystem alteration and tourism and fishing losses.

Overview

Marine debris impacts the environment, economy, and human health and safety. The extent of the impacts is determined by the type of marine debris and where it settles in the ocean (e.g., submerged, floating, or within a sensitive habitat). Fishing nets, plastic bags, and tires can sink to the ocean floor and break and smother coral reefs. Fishing line can float along the ocean surface and catch vessel propellers causing costly damage. A syringe can wash up on the beach and be stepped on by a beachgoer resulting in a wound and possibly an infection. Regardless of the type or the location of the marine debris, it can have serious impacts.

Environmental Impacts

Environmental impacts are wide ranging and can be both direct and indirect. Direct impacts occur when marine life is physically harmed by marine debris through ingestion or entanglement (e.g., a turtle mistakes a plastic bag for food) or marine debris physically alters a sensitive ecosystem (e.g., a fishing net is dragged along the ocean floor by strong ocean currents and breaks and smothers a coral reef). Environmental impacts can also be indirect, such as when a marine debris cleanup results in ecological changes.

Direct Environmental Impacts

Ingestion

Seabirds, sea turtles, fish, and marine mammals often ingest marine debris that they mistake for food. Ingesting marine debris can seriously harm marine life. For example, whales and sea turtles often mistake plastic bags for squid, and birds often mistake plastic pellets for fish eggs. Moreover, a study of 38 green turtles found that 61 percent had ingested some form of marine debris including plastic bags, cloth, and rope or string.

At other times, animals accidentally eat the marine debris while feeding on natural food. Ingestion can lead to starvation or malnutrition when the marine debris collects in the animal's stomach causing the animal to feel full. Starvation also occurs when ingested marine debris in the animal's system prevents vital nutrients from being absorbed. Internal injuries and infections may also result from ingestion. Some marine debris, especially some plastics, contain toxic substances that can cause death or reproductive failure in fish, shellfish, or any marine life. In fact, some plastic particles have even been determined to contain certain chemicals up to one million times the amount found in the water alone.

Entanglement

Marine life can become entangled in marine debris causing serious injury or death. Entanglement can lead to suffocation, starvation, drowning, increased vulnerability to predators, or other injury. Marine debris can constrict an entangled animal's movement which results in exhaustion or development of an infection from deep wounds caused by tightening material. For example, volunteers participating in the 2008 International Coastal Cleanup event discovered 443 animals and birds entangled or trapped by marine debris.

Ecosystem Alteration

The direct impacts of marine debris are not limited to mobile animals. Plants, other immobile living organisms, and sensitive ecosystems can all be harmed by marine debris. Coral reefs can be damaged by derelict fishing gear that breaks or suffocates coral. Plants can be smothered by plastic bags and fishing nets. The ocean floor ecosystems can be damaged and altered by the movement of an abandoned vessel or other marine debris.

Indirect Environmental Impacts

Ecosystem Alteration

Efforts to remove marine debris can harm ecosystems. Mechanical beach raking uses a tractor or other mechanical device to remove marine debris from beaches and marine shorelines and can adversely impact shoreline habitats. This removal technique can be harmful to aquatic vegetation, nesting birds, sea turtles, and other types of aquatic life. Beach raking also can contribute to beach erosion and disturbance of natural vegetation when the raking is conducted too close to a dune.

Invasive Species

Marine debris can contribute to the transfer and movement of invasive species. Floating marine debris can carry invasive species from one location to another. Invasive species use the marine debris as a type of "raft" to move from one body of water to another. In a study performed by the British Antarctic Survey in 2002, it was estimated that man-made debris found in the oceans has approximately doubled the number of different species found in the subtropics.

Economic Impacts

Marine debris can harm three important components of our economy: tourism, fishing, and navigation. Economic impacts are felt through loss in tourism dollars and catch revenue, as well as costly vessel repairs.

Tourism

Marine debris is unsightly and unwelcoming to beachgoers, which can result in lost revenue from tourism. In severe cases, marine debris can even cause beach closures. The costs to remove and dispose of the marine debris can be high and the loss of tourism dollars can be even higher. In an attempt to stop the draining of trash to the ocean, the Los Angeles County's Department of Public Works and the Flood Control District spends $18 million each year on street sweeping, catch basin cleanouts, cleanup programs, and litter prevention and education efforts.

Fishing

Fisheries experience significant economic impacts from marine debris. Commercial fisheries are impacted when commercial fish and shellfish become bycatch in lost fishing nets or other fishing gear. This type of bycatch can result in both immediate losses in the standing stock of available seafood, and decreases in the long-term sustainability of the stock due to negative impacts on its reproductive ability. For example, the Gulf States Marine Fisheries Commission has predicted blue crab ghost fishery leads to a loss of up to 4 to 10 million crabs a year in Louisiana alone. Fisheries also can be financially affected when fishing gear and vessels are entangled or damaged by marine debris. The high cost of replacing fishing gear and vessels, as well as loss of days at sea for fishing, can cause small fisheries to go out of business.

Navigation

Floating marine debris is a navigational hazard that entangles propellers and clogs cooling water intake valves. Repairing boats damaged by marine debris is both time consuming and expensive.

Human Health and Safety Impacts

Marine debris impacts humans by endangering health and safety. Beachgoers can be injured by stepping on broken glass, cans, needles or other items. Similar to marine organisms, swimmers and divers can also become entangled in abandoned netting and fishing lines. Passengers on vessels that strike or become entangled in floating or submerged marine debris may be injured or killed if the vessel is damaged or disabled.

Prevention, Control, and Reduction

EPA's marine pollution control (Themes and Priority Programs), solid wastes treatment and control, wastewater management, and pollution prevention programs all provide potential solutions for addressing sources, movement, and impacts of marine debris. Specific laws and regulations provide EPA with the statutory authority to support marine debris Prevention, Control, and Reduction.

Monitoring and Research

Successfully addressing marine debris depends on identifying and managing its sources, transport, and impacts. EPA has funded various marine debris research projects and grants along beaches, coasts, and watersheds to help determine and monitor these sources and their impacts, including the National Marine Debris Monitoring Program.

What You can Do

Individuals play an important role in preventing marine debris. Anyone can help reduce the amount of trash in our oceans by understanding and changing the behaviors that lead to marine debris. Whether you are out on the open ocean or simply walking down the street, you can help protect our oceans by disposing of trash properly and preventing it from being carried by wind or rain into a body of water.

Many different actions can make a difference. Decreasing the amount of waste generated and ensuring that it is disposed of properly can result in less marine debris. Recycling and reusing can significantly decrease the amount of litter reaching marine and coastal waters. Volunteer coastal cleanups and public education efforts also help reduce the amount of debris reaching our waterways.

Section 19.2

How Oil Harms Animals and Plants in Marine Environments

Text in this section is excerpted from "How Oil Harms Animals and Plants in Marine Environments," National Oceanic and Atmospheric Administration (NOAA), July 7, 2015.

In general, oil spills can affect animals and plants in two ways: from the oil itself and from the response or cleanup operations. Understanding both types of impacts can help spill responders minimize overall impacts to ecological communities and help them to recover much more quickly.

Spilled oil can harm living things because its chemical constituents are poisonous. This can affect organisms both from internal exposure to oil through ingestion or inhalation and from external exposure through skin and eye irritation. Oil can also smother some small species of fish or invertebrates and coat feathers and fur, reducing birds' and mammals' ability to maintain their body temperatures.

We have a series of guidance documents that describe the biology of and impacts of oil on sea turtles, mangroves, and coral reefs. Each one includes related planning and response considerations for oil spills which may affect these particularly sensitive organisms and habitats.

What Creatures Are Most Affected by Oil Spills?

Since most oils float, the creatures most affected by oil are animals like sea otters and seabirds that are found on the sea surface or on shorelines if the oil comes ashore. During most oil spills, seabirds are harmed and killed in greater numbers than other kinds of creatures. Sea otters can easily be harmed by oil, since their ability to stay warm depends on their fur remaining clean. If oil remains on a beach for a while, other creatures, such as snails, clams, and terrestrial animals may suffer.

What Measures Are Taken When an Animal Comes in Contact with Oil?

Most states have regulations about the specific procedures to follow. Untrained people should not try to capture any oiled bird or animal. At most U.S. spills, a bird and/or mammal rehabilitation center is set up to care for oiled animals.

What Type of Spilled Oil Causes the Most Harm?

The type of oil spilled matters because different types of oil behave differently in the environment, and animals and birds are affected differently by different types of oil. However, it's not so easy to say which kind is worst.

First, we should distinguish between "light" and "heavy" oils. Fuel oils, such as gasoline and diesel fuel, are very "light" oils. Light oils are very volatile (they evaporate relatively quickly), so they usually don't remain for long in the aquatic or marine environment (typically no longer than a few days). If they spread out on the water, as they do when they are accidentally spilled, they will evaporate relatively quickly.

However, while they are present, light oils present two significant hazards. First, some can ignite or explode. Second, many light oils, such as gasoline and diesel, are also considered to be toxic. They can kill animals or plants that they touch, and they also are dangerous to humans who breathe their fumes or get them on their skin.

In contrast, very "heavy" oils (like bunker oils, which are used to fuel ships) look black and may be sticky for a time until they weather sufficiently, but even then they can persist in the environment for months or even years if not removed. While these oils can be very persistent, they are generally significantly less acutely toxic than lighter oils. Instead, the short-term threat from heavy oils comes from their ability to smother organisms whereas over the long-term, some chronic health effects like tumors may result in some organisms.

Also, if heavy oils get onto the feathers of birds, the birds may die of hypothermia (they lose the ability to keep themselves warm). We

315

observe this same effect if sea otters become oiled. After days or weeks, some heavy oils will harden, becoming very similar to an asphalt road surface. In this hardened state, heavy oils will probably not harm animals or plants that come in contact with them.

In between light and heavy oils are many different kinds of medium oils, which will last for some amount of time in the environment and will have different degrees of toxicity. Ultimately, the effects of any oil depend on where it is spilled, where it goes, and what animals and plants, or people, it affects.

Section 19.3

Nonpoint Source Pollution and Its Effect on Ocean

Text in this section begins with excerpts from "Water: Polluted Runoff," United States Environmental Protection Agency (EPA), August 27, 2012.

Text in this section beginning with "The biggest source of pollution in the ocean" is excerpted from "What is the biggest source of Pollution in the ocean?" National Oceanic and Atmospheric Administration (NOAA), May 29, 2015.

Nonpoint Source Pollution

What is nonpoint source pollution?

Nonpoint source pollution generally results from land runoff, precipitation, atmospheric deposition, drainage, seepage or hydrologic modification. The term "nonpoint source" is defined to mean any source of water pollution that does not meet the legal definition of "point source" in section 502(14) of the Clean Water Act. That definition states:

The term "point source" means any discernible, confined and discrete conveyance, including but not limited to any pipe, ditch, channel, tunnel, conduit, well, discrete fissure, container, rolling stock, concentrated animal feeding operation, or vessel or other floating craft, from which pollutants are or may be discharged. This term does not include agricultural storm water discharges and return flows from irrigated agriculture.

Unlike pollution from industrial and sewage treatment plants, non-point source (NPS) pollution comes from many diffuse sources. NPS pollution is caused by rainfall or snowmelt moving over and through the ground. As the runoff moves, it picks up and carries away natural and human-made pollutants, finally depositing them into lakes, rivers, wetlands, coastal waters and ground waters.

Nonpoint source pollution can include:

- Excess fertilizers, herbicides and insecticides from agricultural lands and residential areas

- Oil, grease and toxic chemicals from urban runoff and energy production

- Sediment from improperly managed construction sites, crop and forest lands, and eroding streambanks

- Salt from irrigation practices and acid drainage from abandoned mines

- Bacteria and nutrients from livestock, pet wastes and faulty septic systems

- Atmospheric deposition and hydromodification

States report that nonpoint source pollution is the leading remaining cause of water quality problems. The effects of nonpoint source pollutants on specific waters vary and may not always be fully assessed. However, we know that these pollutants have harmful effects on drinking water supplies, recreation, fisheries and wildlife.

The biggest source of pollution in the ocean

Most ocean pollution begins on land

When large tracts of land are plowed, the exposed soil can erode during rainstorms. Much of this runoff flows to the sea, carrying with it agricultural fertilizers and pesticides.

Eighty percent of pollution to the marine environment comes from the land. One of the biggest sources is called nonpoint source pollution, which occurs as a result of runoff. Nonpoint source pollution includes many small sources, like septic tanks, cars, trucks, and boats, plus larger sources, such as farms, ranches, and forest areas. Millions of motor vehicle engines drop small amounts of oil each day onto roads and parking lots. Much of this, too, makes its way to the sea.

Some water pollution actually starts as air pollution, which settles into waterways and oceans. Dirt can be a pollutant. Top soil or silt from fields or construction sites can run off into waterways, harming fish and wildlife habitats.

Nonpoint source pollution can make river and ocean water unsafe for humans and wildlife. In some areas, this pollution is so bad that it causes beaches to be closed after rainstorms.

More than one-third of the shellfish-growing waters of the United States are adversely affected by coastal pollution.

Correcting the harmful effects of nonpoint source pollution is costly. Each year, millions of dollars are spent to restore and protect areas damaged or endangered by nonpoint source pollutants. NOAA works with the U.S. Environmental Protection Agency, Department of Agriculture, and other federal and state agencies to develop ways to control nonpoint source pollution. These agencies work together to monitor, assess, and limit nonpoint source pollution that may result naturally and by human actions.

NOAA's Coastal Zone Management Program is helping to create special nonpoint source pollution control plans for each coastal state participating in the program. When nonpoint source pollution does cause problems, NOAA scientists help track down the exact causes and find solutions.

Section 19.4

How to Protect Marine Environment

Text in this section is excerpted from "Protecting the Marine Environment," United States Environmental Protection Agency (EPA), June 29, 2015.

The world's coastal waters and oceans are deteriorating due to increasing coastal development, pollution from ships, land-based sources of pollution, habitat destruction, and other threats. EPA helps shape U.S. Government positions on international marine pollution issues, protecting U.S. environmental and economic interests throughout the world's oceans. EPA works with U.S. government agency partners, foreign nations, industry and nongovernmental organizations to ensure that international decisions and management of marine pollution issues support EPA's mission: To protect human health and to safeguard the natural environment—air, water, and land—upon which life depends.

EPA is working to reduce marine degradation in different ways. For example, EPA works with the International Maritime Organization to develop and implement legal standards that address vessel source pollution and ocean dumping. EPA also works with the United Nations Caribbean Environment Program based in Jamaica, focused on reducing land-based sources of marine pollution, including in the Gulf of Mexico and the wider Caribbean region.

Pollution from Land-Based Sources and Activities

Global Programme of Action for the Protection of the Marine Environment from Land-Based Activities

The Global Programme of Action for the Protection of the Marine Environment from Land-Based Activities (GPA) is designed to be a source of conceptual and practical guidance for national and/or regional authorities to devise and implement sustained actions to prevent, reduce, control and/or eliminate marine degradation from land-based activities. On November 5, 1995, the GPA was adopted at an intergovernmental meeting in Washington, DC. The aims of the GPA are:

preventing the degradation of the marine environment from land-based activities by facilitating the realization of the duty of States to preserve and protect the marine environment. [The GPA] is designed to assist States in taking actions individually or jointly within their respective policies priorities and resources, which will lead to the prevention, reduction, control and /or elimination of degradation of the marine environment, as well as to its recovery from the impacts of land-based activities. Achievement of the aims of the Programme of Action will contribute to maintaining and, where appropriate, ensuring the protection of human health, as well as promoting the conservation and sustainable use of marine living resources.

The recommendations and principles contained in the GPA are used to focus policy decisions, regional initiatives and international cooperation to protect human health and marine environmental resources.

Land-Based Sources Protocol for the Wider Caribbean Region

EPA led the negotiations for the Protocol Concerning Pollution from Land-Based Sources and Activities (LBS Protocol), which was signed in 1999 in Aruba, Netherlands Antilles, and entered into force in 2010 at the Cartagena Convention. The LBS Protocol is a legally binding protocol to the Convention for the Protection and Development of the Marine Environment of the Wider Caribbean (Cartagena Convention).

The Wider Caribbean Region includes those countries that border:

- eastern Florida south of 30 north latitude,

- the Straits of Florida,

- the Gulf of Mexico, or

- the Caribbean Sea.

The seaward boundary of the region is the 200-mile Exclusive Economic Zone of each country.

EPA joined the US delegation at the first meeting of the Conference of the Parties to the LBS Protocol (LBS COP 1), which took place on October 24, 2012 in Punta Cana, Dominican Republic. EPA continues to play a leadership role for the U.S. government in projects under the UNEP Caribbean Environment Programme.

The United Nations Environment Programme/Caribbean Environment Programme (UNEP/CEP) is the Secretariat for the Cartagena Convention as well as the three Protocols: Land-Based Sources (LBS) Protocol; Protocol Concerning Specially Protected Areas and Wildlife; and, Protocol Concerning Pollution from Land-Based Sources and Activities.

In addition to staff in Washington, DC, EPA staff in the Caribbean Environmental Protection Division provide expertise and coordination with countries of the Wider Caribbean Region. The Office of International and Tribal Affairs also coordinates with experts in EPA's Gulf of Mexico Program on pollution prevention issues.

The LBS Protocol incorporates the following general obligation to address land-based sources of pollution in the Wider Caribbean Region:

Each Contracting Party shall, in accordance with its laws, the provisions of this Protocol, and international law, take appropriate measures to prevent, reduce and control pollution of the Convention area from land-based sources and activities, using for this purpose the best practicable means at its disposal and in accordance with its capabilities.

EPA is the U.S. government technical focal point for the implementation of the LBS Protocol, which focuses on two key issues: domestic sewage (wastewater) and agricultural non-point source (nutrient) pollution.

Pollution from Ships

Antifouling Paints

EPA's Office of International and Tribal Affairs (OITA) led an inter-agency working group negotiating U.S. policy and then helped negotiate on behalf of the U.S. for the global antifouling treaty that was developed at the International Maritime Organization (IMO). The treaty was completed in October 2001 and legally entered into force in 2008.

Air Pollution

EPA is leading U.S. Government efforts to address air pollution from ships including discussions at the International Maritime Organization (IMO) relating to MARPOL 73/78 Annex VI and greenhouse gas emissions from ships. EPA coordinates closely with the State Department's climate office and the U.S. Coast Guard.

Ballast Water Discharges

EPA is a member of an interagency working group for the U.S. delegation to IMO's Marine Environment Protection Committee (MEPC). The committee is currently engaged in the implementation of a global treaty for the Control and Management of Ships' Ballast Water and Sediments that is intended to reduce the introduction of harmful aquatic species. Although this Convention has not yet entered into force, EPA works with others to assess proposals for IMO approval of ballast water management systems that may be employed on international shipping.

Ocean Dumping

The Convention on the Prevention of Marine Pollution by Dumping of Wastes and Other Matter (commonly refered to as the London Convention) was signed in London in 1972. Article I of the London Convention states:

Contracting Parties shall individually and collectively promote the effective control of all sources of pollution of the marine environment, and pledge themselves especially to take all practicable steps to prevent the pollution of the sea by the dumping of waste and other matter that is liable to create hazards to human health, to harm living resources and marine life, to damage amenities or to interfere with other legitimate uses of the sea.

In 1996, a Protocol was developed to amend the London Convention to ban ocean disposal of radioactive wastes and incineration at sea. Article II of the 1996 Protocol defines the objectives of this amendment as:

Contracting Parties shall individually and collectively protect and preserve the marine environment from all sources of pollution and take effective measures, according to their scientific, technical and economic capabilities, to prevent, reduce and where practicable eliminate pollution caused by dumping or incineration at sea of wastes or other matter. Where appropriate, they shall harmonize their policies in this regard.

Marine Litter

Marine trash and litter refers to man-made solid materials that have been intentionally or accidentally released by humans into inland water bodies, near or on the shore, and in the open ocean. While a wide range of materials may be released, the majority is in the form of plastics. Plastics and other aquatic trash have reached all the world's oceans and have become a global problem.

Plastics can persist in the marine environment for a considerable time period, in some cases for hundreds of years or even longer. Over time, as a result of prolonged sun exposure and other physical and chemical elements, plastics deteriorate in the marine environment into numerous tiny fragments, called microplastics. In this way, they can easily enter the food web. Since these microplastics are less visible, their potential environment and health implications are less obvious. These items pose potential threats to marine life, coral reefs, boats, coastal ecosystems, wastewater and sewage infrastructure, and human health.

EPA programs address all types of marine trash and litter, not just plastic trash, as other forms of aquatic trash also have adverse ecological and human health impacts.

Internationally, EPA works on marine trash and litter prevention through the Protocol Concerning Pollution from Land Based Sources and Activities to the Cartagena Convention. EPA serves as the national focal point for the Protocol. EPA also participates in the Global Partnership on Marine Litter, a voluntary coordination mechanism of international agencies, governments, NGOs, academia, private sector, and civil society that work together to reduce and prevent marine trash and litter.

Chapter 20

Soil Contamination

Chapter Contents

Section 20.1

An Overview

Text in this section is excerpted from "Superfund," United States
Environmental Protection Agency (EPA), August 10, 2011.

What kind of contamination is it?

Soil contamination is either solid or liquid hazardous substances
mixed with the naturally occurring soil. Usually, contaminants in the
soil are physically or chemically attached to soil particles, or, if they are
not attached, are trapped in the small spaces between soil particles.

How did it get there?

Soil contamination results when hazardous substances are either
spilled or buried directly in the soil or migrate to the soil from a spill that
has occurred elsewhere. For example, soil can become contaminated
when small particles containing hazardous substances are released
from a smokestack and are deposited on the surrounding soil as they fall
out of the air. Another source of soil contamination could be water that
washes contamination from an area containing hazardous substances
and deposits the contamination in the soil as it flows over or through it.

How does it hurt animals, plants, and humans?

Contaminants in the soil can hurt plants when they attempt to
grow in contaminated soil and take up the contamination through
their roots. Contaminants in the soil can adversely impact the health of
animals and humans when they ingest, inhale, or touch contaminated
soil, or when they eat plants or animals that have themselves been
affected by soil contamination. Animals ingest and come into contact
with contaminants when they burrow in contaminated soil. Humans
ingest and come into contact with contaminants when they play in
contaminated soil or dig in the soil as part of their work. Certain contaminants, when they contact our skin, are absorbed into our bodies.
When contaminants are attached to small surface soil particles they
can become airborne as dust and can be inhaled.

How can we clean it up?

There are three general approaches to cleaning up contaminated soil: 1) soil can be excavated from the ground and be either treated or disposed; 2) soil can be left in the ground and treated in place; or 3) soil can be left in the ground and contained to prevent the contamination from becoming more widespread and reaching plants, animals, or humans. Containment of soil in place is usually done by placing a large plastic cover over the contaminated soil to prevent direct contact and keep rain water from seeping into the soil and spreading the contamination. Treatment approaches can include: flushing contaminants out of the soil using water, chemical solvents, or air; destroying the contaminants by incineration; encouraging natural organisms in the soil to break them down; or adding material to the soil to encapsulate the contaminants and prevent them from spreading.

Section 20.2

Pesticides

Text in this section is excerpted from "About Pesticides," United States Environmental Protection Agency (EPA), August 6, 2014.

What is a pesticide?

A pesticide is any substance or mixture of substances intended for:

- preventing,
- destroying,
- repelling, or
- mitigating any pest.

Though often misunderstood to refer only to insecticides, the term pesticide also applies to herbicides, fungicides, and various other substances used to control pests.

Under United States law, a pesticide is also any substance or mixture of substances intended for use as a plant regulator, defoliant, or desiccant.

What is a pest?

Pests are living organisms that occur where they are not wanted or that cause damage to crops or humans or other animals. Examples include:

- insects,
- mice and other animals,
- unwanted plants (weeds),
- fungi,
- microorganisms such as bacteria and viruses, and
- prions.

Do household products contain pesticides?

Many household products are pesticides. All of these common products are considered pesticides:

- Cockroach sprays and baits.
- Insect repellents for personal use.
- Rat and other rodent poisons.
- Flea and tick sprays, powders, and pet collars.
- Kitchen, laundry, and bath disinfectants and sanitizers.
- Products that kill mold and mildew.
- Some lawn and garden products, such as weed killers.
- Some swimming pool chemicals.

What is the balance between the risks and benefits of pesticides?

By their very nature, most pesticides create some risk of harm—Pesticides can cause harm to humans, animals, or the environment because they are designed to kill or otherwise adversely affect living organisms.

At the same time, pesticides are useful to society—Pesticides can kill potential disease-causing organisms and control insects, weeds, and other pests.

Are some pesticides safer than others?

Biologically-based pesticides, such as pheromones and microbial pesticides, are becoming increasingly popular and often are safer than traditional chemical pesticides. In addition, EPA is registering reduced-risk conventional pesticides in increasing numbers.

What about pest control devices?

A pest control "device" is any instrument or contrivance (other than a firearm) intended for trapping, destroying, repelling, or mitigating any pest. A black light trap is an example of a device.

What substances are not regulated as pesticides?

The U.S. definition of pesticides is quite broad, but it does have some exclusions:

- Drugs used to control diseases of humans or animals (such as livestock and pets) are not considered pesticides; such drugs are regulated by the Food and Drug Administration.

- Fertilizers, nutrients, and other substances used to promote plant survival and health are not considered plant growth regulators and thus are not pesticides.

- Biological control agents, except for certain microorganisms, are exempted from regulation by EPA. (Biological control agents include beneficial predators such as birds or ladybugs that eat insect pests.)

- Products which contain certain low-risk ingredients, such as garlic and mint oil, have been exempted from Federal registration requirements, although State regulatory requirements may still apply. For a list of ingredients which may be exempt, and a discussion of allowable label claims for such products, see EPA's Pesticide Registration Notice 2000-6, "Minimum Risk Pesticides Exempted under FIFRA Section 25(b)."

Section 20.3

Pharmaceuticals and Personal Care Products (PPCPs) as Pollutants

Text in this section is excerpted from "Pharmaceuticals and Personal Care Products (PPCPs)," United States Environmental Protection Agency (EPA), February 29, 2012.

What are "PPCPs"?

Pharmaceuticals and Personal Care Products as Pollutants (PPCPs) refers, in general, to any product used by individuals for personal health or cosmetic reasons or used by agribusiness to enhance growth or health of livestock. PPCPs comprise a diverse collection of thousands of chemical substances, including prescription and over-the-counter therapeutic drugs, veterinary drugs, fragrances, lotions, and cosmetics.

What are the major sources of PPCPs in the environment?

Sources of PPCPs:

- Human activity (e.g., bathing, shaving, swimming)
- Illicit drugs
- Veterinary drug use, especially antibiotics and steroids
- Agribusiness
- Residues from pharmaceutical manufacturing (well defined and controlled)
- Residues from hospitals

The importance of individuals adding chemicals to the environment has been largely overlooked. The discovery of PPCPs in water and soil shows even simple activities like shaving, using lotion, or taking medication affect the environment in which you live.

People contribute PPCPs to the environment when:

- medication residues pass out of the body and into sewer lines,
- externally-applied drugs and personal care products they use wash down the shower drain, and
- unused or expired medications are placed in the trash.

Personal use and manufacturing of illicit drugs are a less visible source of PPCPs entering the environment.

Many of the issues pertaining to the introduction of drugs to the environment from human usage also pertain to veterinary use, especially for antibiotics and steroids.

What is the overall scientific concern?

Studies have shown that pharmaceuticals are present in our nation's waterbodies. Further research suggests that certain drugs may cause ecological harm. More research is needed to determine the extent of ecological harm and any role it may have in potential human health effects. To date, scientists have found no evidence of adverse human health effects from PPCPs in the environment.

Reasons for concern:

- Large quantities of PPCPs can enter the environment after use by individuals or domestic animals.

- Sewage systems are not equipped for PPCP removal. Currently, there are no municipal sewage treatment plants that are engineered specifically for PPCP removal or for other unregulated contaminants. Effective removal of PPCPs from treatment plants varies based on the type of chemical and on the individual sewage treatment facilities.

- The risks are uncertain. The risks posed to aquatic organisms, and to humans are unknown, largely because the concentrations are so low. While the major concerns have been the resistance to antibiotics and disruption of aquatic endocrine systems (the system of glands that produce hormones that help control the body's metabolic activity) by natural and synthetic sex steroids, many other PPCPs have unknown consequences. There are no known human health effects from such low-level exposures in drinking water, but special scenarios (one example being fetal exposure to low levels of medications that a mother would ordinarily be avoiding) require more investigation.

- The number of PPCPs are growing. In addition to antibiotics and steroids, over 100 individual PPCPs have been identified (as of 2007) in environmental samples and drinking water.

Should we be worried about ecological and / or human health?

Studies have shown that pharmaceuticals are present in some of our nation's waterbodies. Further research suggests that there may be some ecological harm when certain drugs are present. To date, no evidence has been found of human health effects from PPCPs in the environment.

Where are PPCPs found in the environment?

PPCPs are found where people or animals are treated with drugs and people use personal care products. PPCPs are found in any water body influenced by raw or treated sewage, including rivers, streams, ground water, coastal marine environments, and many drinking water sources. PPCPs have been identified in most places sampled.

The U.S. Geological Survey (USGS) implemented a national reconnaissance to provide baseline information on the environmental occurrence of PPCPs in water resources.

PPCPs in the environment are frequently found in aquatic environments because PPCPs dissolve easily and don't evaporate at normal temperature and pressures. Practices such as the use of sewage sludge ("biosolids") and reclaimed water for irrigation brings PPCPs into contact with the soil.

How is the disposal of unused pharmaceuticals regulated by the US EPA?

The Resource Conservation and Recovery Act (RCRA) is a federal law controlling the management and disposal of solid and hazardous wastes produced by a wide variety of industries and sources. The RCRA program regulates the management and disposal of hazardous pharmaceutical wastes produced by pharmaceutical manufacturers and the health care industry. Under RCRA, a waste is a hazardous waste if it is specifically listed by the EPA or if it exhibits one or more of the following four characteristics: ignitability, corrosivity, reactivity and toxicity.

How do I properly dispose of unwanted pharmaceuticals?

In February 2007, the White House Office of National Drug Control Policy issued the first consumer guidance for the Proper Disposal of Prescription Drugs . Proper disposal of drugs is a straightforward way for individuals to prevent pollution.

RCRA does not regulate any household waste, which includes medications/pharmaceutical waste generated in a household. While discarded pharmaceuticals under the control of consumers are not regulated by RCRA, EPA encourages the public:

- To take advantage of pharmaceutical take-back programs or household hazardous waste collection programs that accept pharmaceuticals,

- If there are no take-back programs near you,

  - contact your state and local waste management authorities (the disposal of household waste is primarily regulated on the state and local levels) with questions about discarding unused pharmaceuticals, whether or not these materials meet the definition of hazardous waste.

  - follow any specific disposal instructions that may be printed on the label or accompanying patient information.

Section 20.4

Effects of Industrial Agriculture

Text in this section is excerpted from "Ag 101," United States
Environmental Protection Agency (EPA), June 27, 2012.

Potential Environmental Impacts of Animal Feeding Operations

USEPA's 1998 *National Water Quality Inventory* indicates that
agricultural operations, including animal feeding operations (AFOs),
are a significant source of water pollution in the U.S. States estimate that agriculture contributes in part to the impairment of at least
170,750 river miles, 2,417,801 lake acres, and 1,827 estuary square
miles (Table 20.1.). Agriculture was reported to be the most common
pollutant of rivers and streams.

However, one should not overlook the many positive environmental
benefits of agriculture. For example, agricultural practices that conserve soil and increase productivity while improving soil quality also
increase the amount of carbon-rich organic matter in soils, thereby
providing a global depository for carbon dioxide drawn from the atmosphere by growing plants. The same farming practices that promote
soil conservation also decrease the amount of carbon dioxide accumulating in the atmosphere and threatening global warming.

Other benefits compared to urban or industrial land use include
greatly reduced storm runoff, groundwater recharge and water purifi-
cation as infiltrating surface water filters through plant residue, roots
and several feet of soil to reach groundwater.

In many watersheds, animal manures represent a significant portion of the total fertilizer nutrients added. In a few counties, with
heavy concentrations of livestock and poultry, nutrients from confined
animals exceed the uptake potential of non-legume harvested crop-
land and hayland. USDA estimates that recoverable manure nitrogen
exceeds crop system needs in 266 of 3,141 counties in the U.S. (8%)
and that recoverable manure phosphorus exceeds crop system needs
in 485 counties (15%). It should be pointed out that while legumes
are able to produce their own nitrogen, they will use applied nitrogen

instead if it is available. The USDA analysis does not consider actual manure management practices used or transport of applied nutrients outside the county; however, it is a useful indicator of excess nutrients on a broad scale. Whole-farm nutrient balance is a very useful tool to identify potential areas of excess.

Air emissions from Animal Feeding Operations (AFO) can be odorous. Furthermore, volatilized ammonia can be redeposited on the earth and contribute to eutrophication of surface waters.

Animal manures are a valuable fertilizer and soil conditioner, if applied under proper conditions at crop nutrient requirements. Potential sources of manure pollution include open feedlots, pastures, treatment lagoons, manure stockpiles or storage, and land application fields. Oxygen-demanding substances, ammonia, nutrients (particularly nitrogen and phosphorus), solids, pathogens, and odorous compounds are the pollutants most commonly associated with manure. Manure is also a potential source of salts and trace metals, and to a lesser extent, antibiotics, pesticides and hormones. This problem has been magnified as poultry and livestock production has become more concentrated. AFO pollutants can impact surface water, groundwater, air, and soil. In surface water, manure's oxygen demand and ammonia content can result in fish kills and reduced biodiversity. Solids can increase turbidity and smother benthic organisms. Nitrogen and phosphorus can contribute to eutrophication and associated algae blooms which can produce negative aesthetic impacts and increase drinking water treatment costs. Turbidity from the blooms can reduce penetration of sunlight in the water column and thereby limit growth of seagrass beds and other submerged aquatic vegetation, which serve as critical habitat for fish, crabs, and other aquatic organisms. Decay of the algae (as well as night-time algal respiration) can lead to depressed oxygen levels, which can result in fish kills and reduced biodiversity. Eutrophication is also a factor in blooms of toxic algae and other toxic estuarine microorganisms, such as *Pfiesteria piscicida*. These organisms can impact human health as well as animal health. Human and animal health can also be impacted by pathogens and nitrogen in animal manure. Nitrogen is easily transformed into the nitrate form and if transported to drinking water sources can result in potentially fatal health risks to infants. Trace elements in manure may also present human and ecological risks. Salts can contribute to salinization and disruption of the ecosystem. Antibiotics, pesticides, and hormones may have low-level, long-term ecosystem effects.

In ground water, pathogens and nitrates from manure can impact human health via drinking water. Nitrate contamination is more prevalent in ground waters than surface waters. According to the U.S. EPA, nitrate is the most widespread agricultural contaminant in drinking water wells, and nearly 2% of our population (1.5 million people) is exposed to elevated nitrate levels from drinking water wells.

Table 20.2 lists the leading pollutants impairing surface water quality in the U.S. Agricultural production is a potential source of most of these.

Table 20.1. Summary of U.S. Water Quality Impairment Survey

Total Quantity in US	Amount of Waters Surveyed	Quantity Impaired by All Sources	Quantity Impaired by Agriculture
Rivers 3,662,255 miles	23% of total 840,402 miles	36% of surveyed 248,028 miles	59% of impaired 170,750 miles
Lakes, Ponds, and Reservoirs 41,600,000 acres	42% of total 17,400,000 acres	39% of surveyed 6,541,060 acres	31% of impaired 2,417,801 acres
Estuaries 90,500 square miles	32% of total 28,889 square miles	38% of surveyed 11,025 square miles	15% of impaired 1,827 square miles

Reference: National Water Quality Inventory: 1998 Report to Congress (EPA, 2000a). AFOs are a subset of the agriculture category. Summaries of impairment by other sources are not presented here.

Table 20.2. Five Leading Pollutants Causing Water Quality Impairment in the U.S.

Rank	Rivers	Lakes	Estuaries
1	Siltation (38%)	Nutrients (44%)	Pathogens (47%)
2	Pathogens (36%)	Metals (27%)	Oxygen-Depleting Substances (42%)
3	Nutrients (29%)	Siltation (15%)	Metals (23%)
4	Oxygen-Depleting Substances (23%)	Oxygen-Depleting Substances (14%)	Nutrients (23%)
5	Metals (21%)	Suspended Solids (10%)	Thermal Modifications (18%)

Section 20.5

Solid Waste and Landfills – Effects

This section includes excerpts from "Wastes—Non-Hazardous
Waste—Municipal Solid Waste," United States Environmental
Protection Agency (EPA), June 25, 2015; text from "Landfill
Gas," United States Environmental Protection Agency (EPA),
May 29, 2015; and text from "Landfill Gas—Frequently Asked
Questions," United States Environmental Protection Agency (EPA),
April 6, 2011.

Municipal Solid Waste

Municipal Solid Waste (MSW)—more commonly known as trash
or garbage—consists of everyday items we use and then throw away,
such as product packaging, grass clippings, furniture, clothing, bottles,
food scraps, newspapers, appliances, paint, and batteries. This comes
from our homes, schools, hospitals, and businesses.

After 30 years of tracking MSW, the report has been expanded to
include additional information on source reduction (waste prevention)
of MSW, information on historical landfill tipping fees for MSW, and
information on construction and demolition debris generation, which
is outside of the scope of MSW.

The new name also emphasizes the importance of sustainable
materials management (SMM). SMM refers to the use and reuse of
materials in the most productive and sustainable ways across their
entire life cycle. SMM practices conserve resources, reduce wastes,
slow climate change and minimize the environmental impacts of the
materials we use.

In 2013, Americans generated about 254 million tons of trash and
recycled and composted about 87 million tons of this material, equivalent to a 34.3 percent recycling rate. On average, we recycled and
composted 1.51 pounds of our individual waste generation of 4.40
pounds per person per day.

EPA encourages practices that reduce the amount of waste
needing to be disposed of, such as waste prevention, recycling, and
composting.

- Source reduction, or waste prevention, is designing products to reduce the amount of waste that will later need to be thrown away and also to make the resulting waste less toxic.

- Recycling is the recovery of useful materials, such as paper, glass, plastic, and metals, from the trash to use to make new products, reducing the amount of virgin raw materials needed.

- Composting involves collecting organic waste, such as food scraps and yard trimmings, and storing it under conditions designed to help it break down naturally. This resulting compost can then be used as a natural fertilizer.

In 2013, newspapers/mechanical papers recovery was about 67 percent (5.4 million tons), and about 60 percent of yard trimmings were recovered. Organic materials continue to be the largest component of MSW. Paper and paperboard account for 27 percent and yard trimmings and food account for another 28 percent. Plastics comprise about 13 percent; metals make up 9 percent; and rubber, leather, and textiles account for 9 percent. Wood follows at around 6 percent and glass at 5 percent. Other miscellaneous wastes make up approximately 3 percent of the MSW generated in 2013.

This section describes the requirements for disposal and combustion of MSW:

- Landfills are engineered areas where waste is placed into the land. Landfills usually have liner systems and other safeguards to prevent polluting the groundwater.

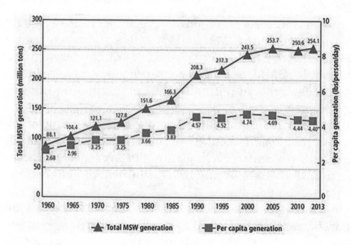

Figure 20.1. MSW Generation Rates, 1960–2013

- *Energy Recovery from Waste* is the conversion of non-recyclable waste materials into useable heat, electricity, or fuel.

- *Transfer Stations* are facilities where municipal solid waste is unloaded from collection vehicles and briefly held while it is reloaded onto larger, long-distance transport vehicles for shipment to landfills or other treatment or disposal facilities.

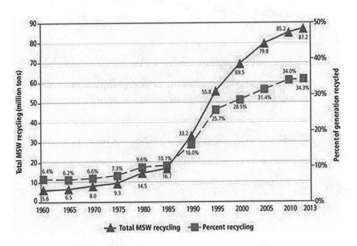

Figure 20.2. MSW Recycling Rates, 1960–2013

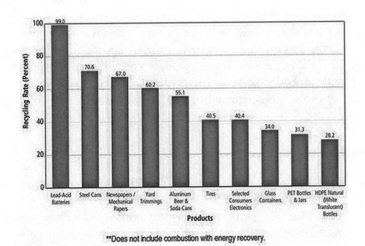

Figure 20.3. Recycling Rates of Selected Products, 2013**

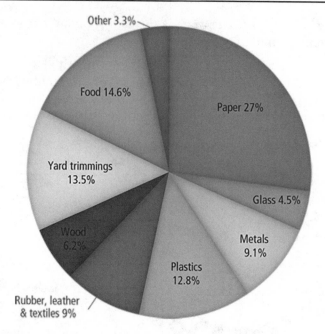

Figure 20.4. *Total MSW Generation (by Material), 2013, 254 Million Tons (before recycling)*

Resource Conservation

Recycling and composting prevented 87.2 million tons of material away from being disposed in 2013, up from 15 million tons in 1980. This prevented the release of approximately 186 million metric tons of carbon dioxide equivalent into the air in 2013—equivalent to taking over 39 million cars off the road for a year. Learn more about how common wastes and materials, including food and yard wastes, paper, metals, and electronics, contribute to MSW generation and how they can be recycled.

Landfill gas

Landfill gas (LFG) is a natural byproduct of the decomposition of organic material in landfills. LFG is comprised of roughly 50 percent methane (the primary component of natural gas), 50 percent carbon dioxide (CO_2) and a small amount of non-methane organic compounds. Methane is a potent greenhouse gas with a global warming potential that is 25 times greater than CO_2.

Methane Emissions from Landfills

Municipal solid waste (MSW) landfills are the third-largest source of human-related methane emissions in the United States, accounting for approximately 18.2 percent of these emissions in 2012. At the same time, methane emissions from landfills represent a lost opportunity to capture and use a significant energy resource.

When MSW is first deposited in a landfill, it undergoes an aerobic (with oxygen) decomposition stage when little methane is generated. Then, typically within less than 1 year, anaerobic conditions are established and methane-producing bacteria begin to decompose the waste and generate methane.

Converting Landfill Gas to Energy

Instead of escaping into the air, LFG can be captured, converted and used as an energy source. Using LFG helps to reduce odors and other hazards associated with LFG emissions, and it helps prevent methane from migrating into the atmosphere and contributing to local smog and global climate change. Learn more about the benefits of using LFG.

LFG is extracted from landfills using a series of wells and a blower/flare (or vacuum) system. This system directs the collected gas to a central point where it can be processed and treated depending upon the ultimate use for the gas. From this point, the gas can be flared, used to generate electricity, replace fossil fuels in industrial and manufacturing operations, or upgraded to pipeline—quality gas where the gas may be used directly or processed into an alternative vehicle fuel. Diagrams and photographs of the various components of an LFG collection system:

- LFG well

- LFG wellhead

- LFG wells and collection piping

- LFG system

- LFG treatment/blower/flare station

- LFG flare

Several options are available for converting LFG to energy. Below are descriptions of some of the typical project types.

Electricity Generation

About three-fourths of currently operational projects in the United States generate electricity from LFG. Electricity for on-site use or sale to the grid can be generated using a variety of technologies, including internal combustion engines, turbines, microturbines, and fuel cells. The vast majority of projects use internal combustion (reciprocating) engines or turbines, with microturbine technology being used at smaller landfills and in niche applications.

Direct Use

Directly using LFG to offset the use of another fuel (for example, natural gas, coal or fuel oil) is occurring in about one-fourth of the currently operational projects. LFG can be used directly in a boiler, dryer, kiln, greenhouse or other thermal application. LFG can also be used directly to evaporate leachate. Innovative direct uses include firing pottery and glass-blowing kilns; powering and heating greenhouses and an ice rink; and heating water for an aquaculture (fish farming) operation. Current industries using LFG include auto manufacturing, chemical production, food processing, pharmaceuticals, cement and brick manufacturing, wastewater treatment, consumer electronics and products, paper and steel production, and prisons and hospitals.

Cogeneration

Cogeneration, also known as combined heat and power or CHP, projects use LFG to generate both electricity and thermal energy, usually in the form of steam or hot water. Several cogeneration projects have been installed at industrial operations, using both engines and turbines. The efficiency gains of capturing the thermal energy in addition to electricity generation can make these projects very attractive.

Alternate Fuels

Production of alternate fuels from LFG is an emerging area. LFG has been successfully delivered to the natural gas pipeline system as both a high-Btu and medium-Btu fuel. LFG can also be used to produce the equivalent of compressed natural gas (CNG) or liquid natural gas (LNG).

How is landfill gas generated?

Landfill gas (LFG) is generated during the natural process of bacterial decomposition of organic material contained in municipal solid waste (MSW) landfills. A number of factors influence the quantity of gas that a MSW landfill generates and the components of that gas. These factors include, but are not limited to, the types and age of the waste buried in the landfill, the quantity and types of organic compounds in the waste, and the moisture content and temperature of the waste. Temperature and moisture levels are influenced by the surrounding climate.

What components make up landfill gas?

By volume, LFG is about 50 percent methane and 50 percent carbon dioxide and water vapor. It also contains small amounts of nitrogen, oxygen, and hydrogen, less than 1 percent nonmethane organic compounds (NMOCs), and trace amounts of inorganic compounds. Some of these compounds have strong, pungent odors (for example, hydrogen sulfide). NMOCs consist of certain hazardous air pollutants (HAPs) and volatile organic compounds (VOCs), which can react with sunlight to form ground-level ozone (smog) if uncontrolled. Nearly 30 organic hazardous air pollutants have been identified in uncontrolled LFG, including benzene, toluene, ethyl benzene, and vinyl chloride. Exposure to these pollutants can lead to adverse health effects. Thermal treatment of NMOCs (including HAPs and VOCs) and methane through flaring or combustion in an engine, turbine, boiler, or other device greatly reduces the emission of these compounds.

How are nonmethane organic compounds generated in landfill gas?

NMOCs are contained in discarded items such as household cleaning products, materials coated with or containing paints and adhesives, and other items. During the waste decomposition process, NMOC can be stripped from the waste by methane, carbon dioxide, and other gases and carried in LFG. Three different mechanisms are responsible for the production of NMOCs and their movement into LFG: (1) vaporization (the change of state from liquid or solid to vapor) of organic compounds until the equilibrium vapor concentration is reached, (2) chemical reaction of materials present in the landfill, and (3) biological decomposition of heavier organic compounds into lighter, more volatile constituents.

At what concentrations are nonmethane organic compounds typically found in uncontrolled landfill gas?

Concentrations of NMOCs in uncontrolled LFG can vary depending on several factors, including the type of waste discarded in the landfill, the climate surrounding the landfill, and the physical properties of the individual organic compound. EPA's *Compilation of Air Pollutant Emission Factors (AP–42)* presents the default concentration of NMOC as 595 parts per million by volume (ppmv). Of this total, 110 ppmv are considered HAP compounds, according to default concentrations in *AP–42*. Therefore, total uncontrolled concentrations of organic HAPs at MSW landfills are typically less than 0.02 percent of the total LFG. The *Standards of Performance for New Stationary Sources (NSPS) and National Emission Standards for Hazardous Air Pollutants* (NESHAP) regulations require combustion of NMOC, a surrogate for organic HAP, at a destruction efficiency of 98 percent or to an outlet concentration of 20 ppmv NMOC.

Can landfill gas combustion be used as an energy resource?

LFG can be an asset when it is used as a source of energy to create electricity or heat. It is classified as a medium-Btu gas with a heating value of 350 to 600 Btu per cubic foot, approximately half that of natural gas. LFG can often be used in place of conventional fossil fuels in certain applications. It is a reliable source of energy because it is generated 24 hours a day, 7 days a week. By using LFG to produce energy, landfills can significantly reduce their emissions of methane and avoid the need to generate energy from fossil fuels, thus reducing emissions of carbon dioxide, sulfur dioxide, nitrogen oxides, and other pollutants from fossil fuel combustion.

Chapter 21

Bioterrorism and Chemical Emergencies

Chapter Contents

Section 21.1

Bioterrorism

Text in this section is excerpted from "Anthrax—Bioterrorism,"
Centers for Disease Control and Prevention (CDC), August 29, 2013.

A biological attack, or bioterrorism, is the intentional release of viruses, bacteria, or other germs that can sicken or kill people, livestock, or crops. *Bacillus anthracis*, the bacteria that causes anthrax, is one of the most likely agents to be used in a biological attack.

The Threat

We do not know if or when another anthrax attack might occur. However, federal agencies have worked for years with health departments across the country to plan and prepare for an anthrax attack. If such an emergency were to occur in the United States, CDC and other federal agencies would work closely with local and state partners to coordinate a response.

Why Would Anthrax Be Used as a Weapon?

If a bioterrorist attack were to happen, *Bacillus anthracis*, the bacteria that causes anthrax, would be one of the biological agents most likely to be used. Biological agents are germs that can sicken or kill people, livestock, or crops. Anthrax is one of the most likely agents to be used because

- Anthrax spores are easily found in nature, can be produced in a lab, and can last for a long time in the environment.

- Anthrax makes a good weapon because it can be released quietly and without anyone knowing. The microscopic spores could be put into powders, sprays, food, and water. Because they are so small, you may not be able to see, smell, or taste them.

- Anthrax has been used as a weapon before.

Anthrax has been used as a weapon around the world for nearly a century. In 2001, powdered anthrax spores were deliberately put into letters that were mailed through the U.S. postal system. Twenty-two people, including 12 mail handlers, got anthrax, and five of these 22 people died.

How Dangerous Is Anthrax?

A subset of select agents and toxins have been designated as Tier 1 because these biological agents and toxins present the greatest risk of deliberate misuse with significant potential for mass casualties or devastating effect to the economy, critical infrastructure, or public confidence, and pose a severe threat to public health and safety. *Bacillus anthracis* is a Tier 1 agent.

What Might an Anthrax Attack Look Like?

An anthrax attack could take many forms. For example, it could be placed in letters and mailed, as was done in 2001, or it could be put into food or water. Anthrax also could be released into the air from a truck, building, or plane. This type of attack would mean the anthrax spores could easily be blown around by the wind or carried on people's clothes, shoes, and other objects. It only takes a small amount of anthrax to infect a large number of people.

If anthrax spores were released into the air, people could breathe them in and get sick with anthrax. Inhalation anthrax is the most serious form and can kill quickly if not treated immediately. If the attack were not detected by one of the monitoring systems in place in the United States, it might go unnoticed until doctors begin to see unusual patterns of illness among sick people showing up at emergency rooms.

Preparedness

Hopefully, an attack involving anthrax will never happen in the United States. However, there are steps that you and your family can take to help prepare if an anthrax emergency ever did happen. If such an emergency were to occur in the United States, CDC and other federal agencies would be ready to respond.

Detection and Response

If anthrax were used as a weapon in the United States, the attack could be detected in one of two ways. Monitoring systems set up nationwide might detect the anthrax after it was released. Or, it might go unnoticed until doctors begin to see unusual patterns of illness among patients in emergency rooms. At that point, alert doctors might suspect anthrax and order lab tests to diagnose anthrax.

It could take days for labs to confirm anthrax in those early samples. But with enough evidence, CDC and other health agencies would not need to wait for lab confirmation before they took action.

CDC and partners could respond by:

- Sending samples through the Laboratory Response Network (LRN)

- Continuing to test samples to learn more about the strain of anthrax

- Deploying field staff to talk to patients and learn more about how they were exposed

- Shipping out medicine and supplies from the Strategic National Stockpile (SNS) to local Points of Dispensing (PODs)

- Providing guidance to clinicians, health departments and other partners on how to respond

- Communicating life-saving information to the public

Section 21.2

Chemical Emergencies

Text in this section begins with excerpts from "Emergency Preparedness and Response," Centers for Disease Control and Prevention (CDC), April 17, 2013.

Text in this section beginning with "Chemical Agents" is excerpted from Emergency Preparedness and Response—Chemical Agents," Centers for Disease Control and Prevention (CDC), April 8, 2013.

Chemical Emergencies Overview

The CDC has a key role in protecting the public's health in an emergency involving the release of a chemical that could harm people's health. This section provides information to help people be prepared to protect themselves during and after such an event.

What chemical emergencies are

A chemical emergency occurs when a hazardous chemical has been released and the release has the potential for harming people's health. Chemical releases can be unintentional, as in the case of an industrial accident, or intentional, as in the case of a terrorist attack.

Where hazardous chemicals come from

Some chemicals that are hazardous have been developed by military organizations for use in warfare. Examples are nerve agents such as sarin and VX, mustards such as sulfur mustards and nitrogen mustards, and choking agents such as phosgene. It might be possible for terrorists to get these chemical warfare agents and use them to harm people.

Many hazardous chemicals are used in industry (for example, chlorine, ammonia, and benzene). Others are found in nature (for example, poisonous plants). Some could be made from everyday items such as household cleaners. These types of hazardous chemicals also could be obtained and used to harm people, or they could be accidentally released.

Types and categories of hazardous chemicals

Scientists often categorize hazardous chemicals by the type of chemical or by the effects a chemical would have on people exposed to it. The categories/types used by the Centers for Disease Control and Prevention are as follows:

- Biotoxins—poisons that come from plants or animals

- Blister agents/vesicants—chemicals that severely blister the eyes, respiratory tract, and skin on contact

- Blood agents—poisons that affect the body by being absorbed into the blood

- Caustics (acids)—chemicals that burn or corrode people's skin, eyes, and mucus membranes (lining of the nose, mouth, throat, and lungs) on contact

- Choking/lung/pulmonary agents—chemicals that cause severe irritation or swelling of the respiratory tract (lining of the nose and throat, lungs)

- Incapacitating agents—drugs that make people unable to think clearly or that cause an altered state of consciousness (possibly unconsciousness)

- Long-acting anticoagulants—poisons that prevent blood from clotting properly, which can lead to uncontrolled bleeding

- Metals—agents that consist of metallic poisons

- Nerve agents—highly poisonous chemicals that work by preventing the nervous system from working properly

- Organic solvents—agents that damage the tissues of living things by dissolving fats and oils

- Riot control agents/tear gas—highly irritating agents normally used by law enforcement for crowd control or by individuals for protection (for example, mace)

- Toxic alcohols—poisonous alcohols that can damage the heart, kidneys, and nervous system

- Vomiting agents—chemicals that cause nausea and vomiting

Hazardous chemicals by name (A–Z list)

If you know the name of a chemical but aren't sure what category it would be in, you can look for the chemical by name on the A–Z List of Chemical Agents.

A

- Abrin
- Adamsite (DM)
- Ammonia
- Arsenic
- Arsine (SA)

B

- Barium
- Benzene
- Brevetoxin

- Bromine (CA)
- Bromobenzylcyanide (CA)
- BZ

C

- Carbon Monoxide
- Chlorine (CL)
- Chloroacetophenone (CN)
- Chlorobenzylidenemalononitrile (CS)
- Chloropicrin (PS)
- Chromium
- Colchicine
- Cyanide

D

- Dibenzoxazepine (CR)
- Digitalis
- Distilled mustard (HD)

E

- Ethylene glycol

F

- Fentanyls and other opioids

H

- Hydrazine
- Hydrofluoric acid (hydrogen fluoride)
- Hydrogen chloride
- Hydrogen cyanide (AC)
- Hydrogen fluoride (hydrofluoric acid)

L

- Lewisite (L, L-1, L-2, L-3)
- Long-acting anticoagulant (super warfarin)

M

- Mercury
- Methyl bromide
- Methyl isocyanate
- Mustard gas (H) (sulfur mustard)

N

- Nicotine
- Nitrogen mustard (HN-1, HN-2, HN-3)

O

- Opioids
- Osmium tetroxide

P

- Paraquat
- Phosgene (CG)
- Phosgene oxime (CX)
- Phosphine
- Phosphorus, elemental, white or yellow
- Potassium cyanide (KCN)

R

- Ricin

S

- Sarin (GB)
- Saxitoxin

- Selenium
- Sodium azide
- Sodium cyanide (NaCN)
- Sodium monofluoroacetate (compound 1080)
- Soman (GD)
- Stibine
- Strychnine
- Sulfur mustard (H) (mustard gas)
- Sulfuryl fluoride
- Super warfarin (long-acting anticoagulant)

T

- Tabun (GA)
- Tetrodotoxin
- Thallium
- Trichothecene

V

- VX

W

- White phosphorus

Part Four

Household and Indoor Environmental Hazards

Chapter 22

Indoor Air Quality – An Introduction

About the Indoor Environments Division

The EPA's Indoor Environments Division (IED) is responsible for conducting research and educating the public about indoor environmental issues, including health risks and the means by which human exposures can be reduced. IED educates the public about health risks associated with a variety of indoor environmental pollutants and sources of pollution, including radon,mold and moisture, secondhand smoke, indoor wood smoke, and environmental asthma triggers.

The Indoor Environments Division creates partnerships with public and private sector organizations to encourage the public to take action to minimize their health risk and mitigate indoor air quality problems. In some cases, IED provides competitive grants to tribes, non-profit organizations and academic institutions.

Indoor Air Quality and Environmental Justice

EPA defines environmental justice (EJ) as "the fair treatment and meaningful involvement of all people regardless of race, color, national origin, or income with respect to the development, implementation, and enforcement of environmental laws, regulations, and policies."

Text in this chapter is excerpted from "An Introduction to Indoor Air Quality (IAQ)," United States Environmental Protection Agency (EPA), November 22, 2014.

To effectively address EJ concerns, the Agency recognizes that communities must be the driver for local solutions. However, far too many communities lack the capacity to truly affect their environmental conditions. This includes some conditions found indoors. Many reports and studies indicate that low-income, minority, tribal and indigenous communities may be disproportionately impacted by indoor asthma triggers, secondhand smoke, mold, radon and other indoor pollutants. IED provides guidance and programs to build community capacity and improve indoor air quality in buildings where people live, learn and work.

What Causes Indoor Air Problems?

Indoor pollution sources that release gases or particles into the air are the primary cause of indoor air quality problems in homes. Inadequate ventilation can increase indoor pollutant levels by not bringing in enough outdoor air to dilute emissions from indoor sources and by not carrying indoor air pollutants out of the home. High temperature and humidity levels can also increase concentrations of some pollutants.

Pollutant Sources

There are many sources of indoor air pollution in any home. These include combustion sources such as oil, gas, kerosene, coal, wood, and tobacco products; building materials and furnishings as diverse as deteriorated,asbestos-containing insulation, wet or damp carpet, and cabinetry or furniture made of certain pressed wood products; products for household cleaning and maintenance, personal care, or hobbies; central heating and cooling systems and humidification devices; and outdoor sources such asradon, pesticides, and outdoor air pollution.

The relative importance of any single source depends on how much of a given pollutant it emits and how hazardous those emissions are. In some cases, factors such as how old the source is and whether it is properly maintained are significant. For example, an improperly adjusted gas stove can emit significantly more carbon monoxidethan one that is properly adjusted.

Some sources, such as building materials, furnishings, and household products like air fresheners, release pollutants more or less continuously. Other sources, related to activities carried out in the home, release pollutants intermittently. These include smoking, the use of unvented or malfunctioning stoves, furnaces, or space heaters, the use of solvents in cleaning and hobby activities, the use of paint strippers in redecorating activities, and the use of cleaning products and pesticides in housekeeping. High pollutant concentrations can remain in the air for long periods after some of these activities.

Amount of Ventilation

If too little outdoor air enters a home, pollutants can accumulate to levels that can pose health and comfort problems. Unless they are built with special mechanical means of ventilation, homes that are designed and constructed to minimize the amount of outdoor air that can "leak" into and out of the home may have higher pollutant levels than other homes. However, because some weather conditions can drastically reduce the amount of outdoor air that enters a home, pollutants can build up even in homes that are normally considered "leaky."

How Does Outdoor Air Enter a House?

Outdoor air enters and leaves a house by: infiltration, natural ventilation, and mechanical ventilation. In a process known as infiltration, outdoor air flows into the house through openings, joints, and cracks in walls, floors, and ceilings, and around windows and doors. In natural ventilation, air moves through opened windows and doors. Air movement associated with infiltration and natural ventilation is caused by air temperature differences between indoors and outdoors and by wind. Finally, there are a number of mechanical ventilation devices, from outdoor-vented fans that intermittently remove air from a single room, such as bathrooms and kitchen, to air handling systems that use fans and duct work to continuously remove indoor air and distribute filtered and conditioned outdoor air to strategic points throughout the house. The rate at which outdoor air replaces indoor air is described as the air exchange rate. When there is little infiltration, natural ventilation, or mechanical ventilation, the air exchange rate is low and pollutant levels can increase.

Indoor Air Pollution and Health

Health effects from indoor air pollutants may be experienced soon after exposure or, possibly, years later.

Immediate effects

Immediate effects may show up after a single exposure or repeated exposures. These include irritation of the eyes, nose, and throat, headaches, dizziness, and fatigue. Such immediate effects are usually short-term and treatable. Sometimes the treatment is simply eliminating the person's exposure to the source of the pollution, if it can be identified. Symptoms of some diseases, including asthma, hypersensitivity pneumonitis, and humidifier fever, may also show up soon after exposure to some indoor air pollutants.

The likelihood of immediate reactions to indoor air pollutants depends on several factors. Age and pre-existing medical conditions are two important influences. In other cases, whether a person reacts to a pollutant depends on individual sensitivity, which varies tremendously from person to person. Some people can become sensitized to biological pollutants after repeated exposures, and it appears that some people can become sensitized to chemical pollutants as well.

Certain immediate effects are similar to those from colds or other viral diseases, so it is often difficult to determine if the symptoms are a result of exposure to indoor air pollution. For this reason, it is important to pay attention to the time and place symptoms occur. If the symptoms fade or go away when a person is away from home, for example, an effort should be made to identify indoor air sources that may be possible causes. Some effects may be made worse by an inadequate supply of outdoor air or from the heating, cooling, or humidity conditions prevalent in the home.

Long-term effects

Other health effects may show up either years after exposure has occurred or only after long or repeated periods of exposure. These effects, which include some respiratory diseases, heart disease, and cancer, can be severely debilitating or fatal. It is prudent to try to improve the indoor air quality in your home even if symptoms are not noticeable.

While pollutants commonly found in indoor air are responsible for many harmful effects, there is considerable uncertainty about what concentrations or periods of exposure are necessary to produce specific health problems. People also react very differently to exposure to indoor air pollutants. Further research is needed to better understand which health effects occur after exposure to the average pollutant concentrations found in homes and which occurs from the higher concentrations that occur for short periods of time.

Chapter 23

Harmful Agents in Indoor Air

Chapter Contents

Section 23.1

Biological Contaminants

Text in this section is excerpted from "An Introduction to Indoor Air
Quality (IAQ)—Biological Pollutants," United States Environmental
Protection Agency (EPA), June 21, 2012.

Biological contaminants include bacteria, molds, mildew, viruses,
animal dander and cat saliva, house dust, mites, cockroaches, and
pollen. There are many sources of these pollutants. Pollens originate
from plants; viruses are transmitted by people and animals; bacteria
are carried by people, animals, and soil and plant debris; and household
pets are sources of saliva and animal dander. The protein in urine from
rats and mice is a potent allergen. When it dries, it can become airborne. Contaminated central air handling systems can become breeding grounds for mold, mildew, and other sources of biological contaminants and can then distribute these contaminants through the home.

By controlling the relative humidity level in a home, the growth of
some sources of biologicals can be minimized. A relative humidity of
30–50 percent is generally recommended for homes. Standing water,
water-damaged materials, or wet surfaces also serve as a breeding
ground for molds, mildews, bacteria, and insects. House dust mites,
the source of one of the most powerful biological allergens, grow in
damp, warm environments.

Sources

Common biological contaminants include mold, dust mites, pet dander (skin flakes), droppings and body parts from cockroaches, rodents
and other pests or insects, viruses, and bacteria. Many of these biological contaminants are small enough to be inhaled.

Biological contaminants are, or are produced by, living things. Biological contaminants are often found in areas that provide food and
moisture or water. For example, damp or wet areas such as cooling
coils, humidifiers, condensate pans, or unvented bathrooms can be
moldy. Draperies, bedding, carpet, and other areas where dust collects
may accumulate biological contaminants.

Health Effects from Biological Contaminants

Some biological contaminants trigger allergic reactions, including hypersensitivity pneumonitis, allergic rhinitis, and some types of asthma. Infectious illnesses, such as influenza, measles, and chicken pox are transmitted through the air. Molds and mildews release disease-causing toxins. Symptoms of health problems caused by biological pollutants include sneezing, watery eyes, coughing, shortness of breath, dizziness, lethargy, fever, and digestive problems.

Allergic reactions occur only after repeated exposure to a specific biological allergen. However, that reaction may occur immediately upon re-exposure or after multiple exposures over time. As a result, people who have noticed only mild allergic reactions, or no reactions at all, may suddenly find themselves very sensitive to particular allergens.

Some diseases, like humidifier fever, are associated with exposure to toxins from microorganisms that can grow in large building ventilation systems. However, these diseases can also be traced to microorganisms that grow in home heating and cooling systems and humidifiers. Children, elderly people, and people with breathing problems, allergies, and lung diseases are particularly susceptible to disease-causing biological agents in the indoor air.

Mold, dust mites, pet dander, and pest droppings or body parts can trigger asthma. Biological contaminants, including molds and pollens can cause allergic reactions for a significant portion of the population. Tuberculosis, measles, *staphylococcus* infections, *Legionella* and influenza are known to be transmitted by air.

Reducing Exposure to Biological Contaminants

General good housekeeping, and maintenance of heating and air conditioning equipment, are very important. Adequate ventilation and good air distribution also help. The key to mold control is moisture control. If mold is a problem, clean up the mold and get rid of excess water or moisture. Maintaining the relative humidity between 30% and 60% will help control mold, dust mites, and cockroaches. Employ integrated pest management to control insect and animal allergens. Cooling tower treatment procedures exist to reduce levels of *Legionella* and other organisms.

- *Install and use exhaust fans that are vented to the outdoors in kitchens and bathrooms and vent clothes dryers outdoors.* These actions can eliminate much of the moisture that builds up from everyday activities. There are exhaust fans on the market that produce little noise, an important consideration for some people. Another benefit to using kitchen and bathroom exhaust fans is that they can reduce levels of organic pollutants that vaporize from hot water used in showers and dishwashers.

- *Ventilate the attic and crawl spaces to prevent moisture build-up.* Keeping humidity levels in these areas below 50 percent can prevent water condensation on building materials.

- *If using cool mist or ultrasonic humidifiers, clean appliances according to manufacturer's instructions and refill with fresh water daily.* Because these humidifiers can become breeding grounds for biological contaminants, they have the potential for causing diseases such as hypersensitivity pneumonitis and humidifier fever. Evaporation trays in air conditioners, dehumidifiers, and refrigerators should also be cleaned frequently.

- *Thoroughly clean and dry water-damaged carpets and building materials (within 24 hours if possible) or consider removal and replacement.* Water-damaged carpets and building materials can harbor mold and bacteria. It is very difficult to completely rid such materials of biological contaminants.

- *Keep the house clean. House dust mites, pollens, animal dander, and other allergy-causing agents can be reduced, although not eliminated, through regular cleaning.* People who are allergic to these pollutants should use allergen-proof mattress encasements, wash bedding in hot (130° F) water, and avoid room furnishings that accumulate dust, especially if they cannot be washed in hot water. Allergic individuals should also leave the house while it is being vacuumed because vacuuming can actually increase airborne levels of mite allergens and other biological contaminants. Using central vacuum systems that are vented to the outdoors or vacuums with high efficiency filters may also be of help.

- *Take steps to minimize biological pollutants in basements.* Clean and disinfect the basement floor drain regularly. Do not finish a basement below ground level unless all water leaks are patched and outdoor ventilation and adequate heat to prevent condensation are provided. Operate a dehumidifier in the basement if needed to keep relative humidity levels between 30% and 50%.

Section 23.2

Carbon Monoxide

Text in this section is excerpted from "An Introduction to Indoor
Air Quality (IAQ)—Carbon Monoxide (CO)," United States
Environmental Protection Agency (EPA), March 14, 2013.

Carbon monoxide is an odorless, colorless and toxic gas. Because
it is impossible to see, taste or smell the toxic fumes, CO can kill you
before you are aware it is in your home. At lower levels of exposure,
CO causes mild effects that are often mistaken for the flu. These symptoms include headaches, dizziness, disorientation, nausea and fatigue.
The effects of CO exposure can vary greatly from person to person
depending on age, overall health and the concentration and length of
exposure.

Sources of Carbon Monoxide

Unvented kerosene and gas space heaters; leaking chimneys and
furnaces; back-drafting from furnaces, gas water heaters, wood stoves,
and fireplaces; gas stoves; generators and other gasoline powered equipment; automobile exhaust from attached garages; and tobacco smoke.
Incomplete oxidation during combustion in gas ranges and unvented gas
or kerosene heaters may cause high concentrations of CO in indoor air.
Worn or poorly adjusted and maintained combustion devices (e.g., boilers, furnaces) can be significant sources, or if the flue is improperly sized,
blocked, disconnected, or is leaking. Auto, truck, or bus exhaust from
attached garages, nearby roads, or parking areas can also be a source.

Health Effects Associated with Carbon Monoxide

At low concentrations, fatigue in healthy people and chest pain in
people with heart disease. At higher concentrations, impaired vision
and coordination; headaches; dizziness; confusion; nausea. Can cause
flu-like symptoms that clear up after leaving home. Fatal at very high
concentrations. Acute effects are due to the formation of carboxyhemoglobin in the blood, which inhibits oxygen intake. At moderate

363

concentrations, angina, impaired vision, and reduced brain function may result. At higher concentrations, CO exposure can be fatal.

Levels in Homes

Average levels in homes without gas stoves vary from 0.5 to 5 parts per million (ppm). Levels near properly adjusted gas stoves are often 5 to 15 ppm and those near poorly adjusted stoves may be 30 ppm or higher.

Steps to Reduce Exposure to Carbon Monoxide

It is most important to be sure combustion equipment is maintained and properly adjusted. Vehicular use should be carefully managed adjacent to buildings and in vocational programs. Additional ventilation can be used as a temporary measure when high levels of CO are expected for short periods of time.

- Keep gas appliances properly adjusted.

- Consider purchasing a vented space heater when replacing an unvented one.

- Use proper fuel in kerosene space heaters.

- Install and use an exhaust fan vented to outdoors over gas stoves.

- Open flues when fireplaces are in use.

- Choose properly sized wood stoves that are certified to meet EPA emission standards. Make certain that doors on all wood stoves fit tightly.

- Have a trained professional inspect, clean, and tune-up central heating system (furnaces, flues, and chimneys) annually. Repair any leaks promptly.

- Do not idle the car inside garage.

> **ALERT: Put generators outside.**
>
> Never use a generator inside homes, garages, crawlspaces, sheds, or similar areas. Deadly levels of carbon monoxide can quickly build up in these areas and can linger for hours, even after the generator has shut off.

Measurement Methods

Some relatively high-cost infrared radiation adsorption and electrochemical instruments do exist. Moderately priced real-time measuring devices are also available. A passive monitor is currently under development.

Exposure Limits

[OSHA PEL] The current Occupational Safety and Health Administration (OSHA) permissible exposure limit (PEL) for carbon monoxide is 50 parts per million (ppm) parts of air (55 milligrams per cubic meter (mg/m(3))) as an 8-hour time-weighted average (TWA) concentration.

[NIOSH REL] The National Institute for Occupational Safety and Health (NIOSH) has established a recommended exposure limit (REL) for carbon monoxide of 35 ppm (40 mg/m(3)) as an 8-hour TWA and 200 ppm (229 mg/m(3)) as a ceiling [NIOSH 1992]. The NIOSH limit is based on the risk of cardiovascular effects.

[ACGIH TLV] The American Conference of Governmental Industrial Hygienists (ACGIH) has assigned carbon monoxide a threshold limit value (TLV) of 25 ppm (29 mg/m(3)) as a TWA for a normal 8-hour workday and a 40-hour workweek. The ACGIH limit is based on the risk of elevated carboxyhemoglobin levels.

Section 23.3

Combustion Pollutants

Text in this section is excerpted from "An Introduction to Indoor Air Quality (IAQ)—Sources of Combustion Products," United States Environmental Protection Agency (EPA), July 3, 2012.

Sources of Combustion Products

In addition to environmental tobacco smoke, other sources of combustion products are unvented kerosene and gas space heaters, woodstoves, fireplaces, and gas stoves. The major pollutants released are carbon monoxide, nitrogen dioxide, and particles. Unvented kerosene heaters may also generate acid aerosols.

Combustion gases and particles also come from chimneys and flues that are improperly installed or maintained and cracked furnace heat exchangers. Pollutants from fireplaces and woodstoves with no dedicated outdoor air supply can be "back-drafted" from the chimney into the living space, particularly in weatherized homes.

Health Effects of Combustion Products

Carbon monoxide is a colorless, odorless gas that interferes with the delivery of oxygen throughout the body. At high concentrations can cause a range of symptoms from headaches, dizziness, weakness, nausea, confusion, and disorientation, to fatigue in healthy people and episodes of increased chest pain in people with chronic heart disease. The symptoms of carbon monoxide poisoning are sometimes confused with the flu or food poisoning. Fetuses, infants, elderly people, and people with anemia or with a history of heart or respiratory disease can be especially sensitive to carbon monoxide exposures.

Nitrogen dioxide is a reddish brown, irritating odor gas that irritates the mucous membranes in the eye, nose, and throat and causes shortness of breath after exposure to high concentrations. There is evidence that high concentrations or continued exposure to low levels of nitrogen dioxide increases the risk of respiratory infection; there is also evidence from animals studies that repeated exposures to elevated nitrogen dioxide levels may lead, or contribute, to the development of lung disease such as emphysema. People at particular risk from exposure to nitrogen dioxide include children and individuals with asthma and other respiratory diseases.

Particles, released when fuels are incompletely burned, can lodge in the lungs and irritate or damage lung tissue. A number of pollutants, including radon and benzo(a)pyrene, both of which can cause cancer, attach to small particles that are inhaled and then carried deep into the lung.

Reducing Exposure to Combustion Products in Homes

- Take special precautions when operating fuel-burning unvented space heaters.

- Consider potential effects of indoor air pollution if you use an unvented kerosene or gas space heater. Follow the manufacturer's directions, especially instructions on the proper fuel and keeping the heater properly adjusted. A persistent yellow-tipped flame is generally an indication of maladjustment and increased pollutant emissions. While a space heater is in use, open a door from the room where the heater is located to the rest of the house and open a window slightly.

- Install and use exhaust fans over gas cooking stoves and ranges and keep the burners properly adjusted.

- Using a stove hood with a fan vented to the outdoors greatly reduces exposure to pollutants during cooking. Improper adjustment, often indicated by a persistent yellow-tipped flame, causes increased pollutant emissions. Ask your gas company to adjust the burner so that the flame tip is blue. If you purchase a new gas stove or range, consider buying one with pilot less ignition because it does not have a pilot light that burns continuously. Never use a gas stove to heat your home. Always make certain the flue in your gas fireplace is open when the fireplace is in use.

- Keep woodstove emissions to a minimum. Choose properly sized new stoves that are certified as meeting EPA emission standards.

- Make certain that doors in old woodstoves are tight-fitting. Use aged or cured (dried) wood only and follow the manufacturer's directions for starting, stoking, and putting out the fire in woodstoves. Chemicals are used to pressure-treat wood; such wood should never be burned indoors.

- Have central air handling systems, including furnaces, flues, and chimneys, inspected annually and properly repair cracks or damaged parts.

- Blocked, leaking, or damaged chimneys or flues release harmful combustion gases and particles and even fatal concentrations of carbon monoxide.

- Strictly follow all service and maintenance procedures recommended by the manufacturer, including those that tell you how frequently to change the filter. If manufacturer's instructions are not readily available. change filters once every month or two during periods of use. Proper maintenance is important even for new furnaces because they can also corrode and leak combustion gases, including carbon monoxide.

Section 23.4

Flame Retardants (Polybrominated Diphenyl Ethers, or PBDEs)

Text in this section is excerpted from "Toxic Substances Portal—
Polybrominated Diphenyl Ethers (PBDEs)," Agency for Toxic
Substances & Disease Registry (ATSDR), March 25, 2014.

Polybrominated diphenyl ethers (PBDEs) are man-made chemicals found in plastics used in a variety of consumer products to make them difficult to burn. Very little is known about the health effects of PBDEs in people, but effects have been reported in animals. PBDEs have not been found in any of the 1,647 current or former National Priority List (NPL) sites identified by the Environmental Protection Agency (EPA).

What are PBDEs?

Polybrominated diphenyl ethers (PBDEs) are flame-retardant chemicals that are added to plastics and foam products to make them difficult to burn. There are different kinds of PBDEs; some have only a few bromine atoms attached, while some have as many as ten bromine attached to the central molecule.

PBDEs exist as mixtures of similar chemicals called congeners. Because they are mixed into plastics and foams rather than bound to them, PBDEs can leave the products that contain them and enter the environment.

What happens to PBDEs when they enter the environment?

- PBDEs enter air, water, and soil during their manufacture and use in consumer products.

- In air, PBDEs can be present as particles, but eventually settle to soil or water.

- Sunlight can degrade some PBDEs.

- PBDEs do not dissolve easily in water, but stick to particles and settle to the bottom of river or lakes.

- Some PBDEs can accumulate in fish but usually at low concentrations.

How might I be exposed to PBDEs?

- The concentrations of PBDEs in human blood, breast milk, and body fat indicate that most people are exposed to low levels of PBDEs.

- You may be exposed to PBDEs from eating foods or breathing air contaminated with PBDEs.

- Workers involved in the manufacture of PBDEs or products that contain PBDEs may be exposed to higher levels than usual.

- Occupational exposure can also occur in people who work in enclosed spaces where PBDE-containing products are repaired or recycled.

How can PBDEs affect my health?

There is no definite information on health effects of PBDEs in people. Rats and mice that ate food with moderate amounts of PBDEs for a few days had effects on the thyroid gland. Those that ate smaller amounts for weeks or months had effects on the thyroid and the liver. Large differences in effects are seen between highly-brominated and less-brominated PBDEs in animal studies.

Preliminary evidence suggests that high concentrations of PBDEs may cause neurobehavioral alterations and affect the immune system in animals.

How likely are PBDEs to cause cancer?

We do not know whether PBDEs can cause cancer in humans. Rats and mice that ate food with decabromodiphenyl ether (one type of PBDE) throughout their lives, developed liver tumors. Based on this evidence, the EPA has classified decabromodiphenyl ether as a possible human carcinogen. PBDEs with fewer bromine atoms than decabromodiphenyl ether are listed by the EPA as not classifiable as to human carcinogenicity due to the lack of human and animal cancer studies.

369

How can PBDEs affect children?

Children are exposed to PBDEs in generally the same way as adults, mainly by eating contaminated food. Because PBDEs dissolve readily in fat, they can accumulate in breast milk and may be transferred to babies and young children.

Exposure to PBDEs in the womb and through nursing has caused thyroid effects and neurobehavioral alterations in newborn animals, but not birth defects. It is not known if PBDEs can cause birth defect in children.

How can families reduce the risk of exposure to PBDEs?

- Children living near hazardous waste sites should be discouraged from playing in the dirt near these sites. Children should also be discouraged from eating dirt and should wash their hands frequently.

- People who are exposed to PBDEs at work should shower and change clothes before going home each day. Work clothes should be stored and laundered separately from the rest of your family's clothes.

Is there a medical test to show whether I've been exposed to PBDEs?

There are tests that can detect PBDEs in blood, body fat, and breast milk. These tests can tell whether you have been exposed to high levels of the chemicals, but cannot tell the exact amount or type of PBDE you were exposed to, or whether harmful effects will occur. Blood tests are the easiest and safest for detecting recent exposures to large amounts of PBDEs. These tests are not routinely available at the doctor's office, but samples can be sent to laboratories that have the appropriate equipment.

Has the federal government made recommendations to protect human health?

The EPA requires that companies that transport, store, or dispose p-bromodiphenyl ether (a particular PBDE compound) follow the rules and regulations of the federal hazardous waste management program. The EPA requires that industry tell the National Response Center each time 100 pounds or more of p-bromodiphenyl ether are released to the environment.

Section 23.5

Formaldehyde

Text in this section is excerpted from "Toxic Substances Portal—
Formaldehyde," Agency for Toxic Substances & Environment
Registry (ATSDR), May 12, 2015.

Everyone is exposed to small amounts of formaldehyde in air and
some foods and products. Formaldehyde can cause irritation of the
eyes, nose, and throat and neurological effects. Formaldehyde has been
found in at least 29 of the 1,669 National Priorities List sites identified
by the Environmental Protection Agency (EPA).

What is formaldehyde?

At room temperature, formaldehyde is a colorless, flammable gas
that has a distinct, pungent smell. Small amounts of formaldehyde
are naturally produced by plants, animals, and humans.

It is used in the production of fertilizer, paper, plywood, and
urea-formaldehyde resins. It is also used as a preservative in some
foods and in many house-hold products, such as antiseptics, medicines,
and cosmetics.

What happens to formaldehyde when it enters the environment?

- Once formaldehyde is in the air, it is quickly broken down, usually within hours.

- Formaldehyde dissolves easily but does not last a long time in
  water.

- Formaldehyde evaporates from shallow soils.

- Formaldehyde does not build up in plants and animals.

How might I be exposed to formaldehyde?

- The primary way you can be exposed to formaldehyde is by
  breathing air containing it.

- Releases of formaldehyde into the air occur from industries using or manufacturing formaldehyde, wood products (such as particle-board, plywood, and furniture), automobile exhaust, cigarette smoke, paints and varnishes, and carpets and permanent press fabrics.

- Indoor air contains higher levels of formaldehyde than outdoor air. Levels of formaldehyde measured in indoor air range from 0.02–4 parts per million (ppm). Formaldehyde levels in outdoor air range from 0.0002 to 0.006 ppm in rural and suburban areas and 0.001 to 0.02 ppm in urban areas.

- Breathing contaminated workplace air. The highest potential exposure occurs in the formaldehyde-based resins industry.

How can formaldehyde affect my health?

Nasal and eye irritation, neurological effects, and increased risk of asthma and/or allergy have been observed in humans breathing 0.1 to 0.5 ppm. Eczema and changes in lung function have been observed at 0.6 to 1.9 ppm.

Decreased body weight, gastrointestinal ulcers, liver and kidney damage were observed in animals orally exposed to 50–100 milligrams/kilogram/day (mg/kg/day) formaldehyde.

How likely is formaldehyde to cause cancer?

The Department of Health and Human Services (HHS) determined in 2011 that formaldehyde is a known human carcinogen based on sufficient human and animal inhalation studies.

How can formaldehyde affect children?

A small number of studies have looked at the health effects of formaldehyde in children. It is very likely that breathing formaldehyde will result in nose and eye irritation. We do not know if the irritation would occur at lower concentrations in children than in adults.

There is some evidence of asthma or asthma-like symptoms for children exposed to formaldehyde in homes.

Animal studies have suggested that formaldehyde will not cause birth defects in humans.

How can families reduce the risk of exposure to formaldehyde?

Formaldehyde is usually found in the air, and levels are usually higher indoors than outdoors. Opening windows and using fans to bring fresh air indoors are the easiest ways to lower levels in the house. Not smoking and not using unvented heaters indoors can lower the formaldehyde levels.

Formaldehyde is given off from a number of products used in the home. Removing formaldehyde sources in the home can reduce exposure. Providing fresh air, sealing unfinished manufactured wood surfaces, and washing new permanent press clothing before wearing can help lower exposure.

Is there a medical test to show whether I've been exposed to formaldehyde?

Formaldehyde cannot be reliably measured in blood, urine, or body tissues following exposure. Formaldehyde is produced in the body and would be present as a normal constituent in body tissues and fluids.

Has the federal government made recommendations to protect human health?

The US EPA has determined that exposure to formaldehyde in drinking water at concentrations of 10 milligrams/liter (mg/L) for 1 day or 5 mg/L for 10 days is not expected to cause any adverse effects in children.

The US EPA has also determined that a lifetime exposure to 1 mg/L of formaldehyde in drinking water is not expected to cause any adverse health effects.

The Occupational Health and Safety Administration (OSHA) has limited workers' exposure to an average of 0.75 ppm for an 8-hour workday, 40-hour workweek.

The U.S. Department of Housing and Urban Development (HUD) has set standards for formaldehyde emissions in manufactured housing of less than 0.2 ppm for plywood and 0.3 ppm for particle board. The HUD standards are designed to provide an ambient air level of 0.4 ppm or less in manufactured housing.

Section 23.6

Household Chemicals

Text in this section begins with excerpts from "Water: Best
Management Practices—Proper Disposal of Hazardous Wastes,"
United States Environmental Protection Agency (EPA), July 1, 2014.

Text in this section beginning with "Chemicals in the household"
is excerpted from "Gulf of Mexico Program—Chemicals in the
Household," United States Environmental Protection Agency (EPA),
January 30, 2014.

Description

Many products found in homes contain chemicals potentially harmful to both people and the environment. Chemical products such as
oven cleaners, paint removers, bug killers, solvents, and drain cleaners are just a few common hazardous products in the home. Over
the last 20 years, concern about the disposal of such products has
been growing. In 1976, the Resource Conservation and Recovery Act
(RCRA) was passed, regulating the procedures governing the generation, storage, transport, treatment, and disposal of hazardous materials. Although this legislation has mitigated some of the problems
associated with commercial hazardous material disposal, more needs
to be done to reduce and properly dispose of home hazardous wastes.

Hazardous products include the following:

- Cleaning products: oven cleaner, floor wax, furniture polish,
  drain cleaner, and spot remover

- Car care and maintenance: motor oil, battery acid, gasoline, car
  wax, engine cleaner, antifreeze, degreaser, radiator flush, and
  rust preventative

- Home improvement products: paints, preservatives, strippers,
  brush cleaners, and solvents

- Other products labeled toxic, flammable, or corrosive, or containing lye, phenols, petroleum distillates, or trichlorobenzene

Applicability

Municipal household hazardous waste programs are widely applicable and vary in scope. They can range from simply informing the public about the hazards of some commonly used household chemicals to establishing a household hazardous waste collection facility. More elaborate programs are best suited to larger communities that have existing facilities such as a municipal solid waste collection area. Municipalities with more limited resources can implement a limited education campaign and expand the program as resources become available.

Implementation

First, communities should inform their residents about the potential effects of hazardous household materials on water quality and inform them how to properly store, handle, and dispose of the chemicals. Citizens are frequently unaware that their bad habits lead to water pollution. Once informed of the environmental dangers posed by chemicals, they can adjust their behaviors to protect water quality.

Municipalities can also inform residents about less-toxic alternatives to household hazardous wastes. The use of alternative products can be promoted through pamphlets, inserts in utility bills, or workshops. Nontoxic products can offer the same effectiveness as hazardous products but with less impact on the environment. See the Alternatives to Toxic Substances fact sheet for some examples of these alternatives. An effective community household hazardous waste collection program instructs the public how to dispose of hazardous household items, it tells them the hours and location of collection facilities, and informs them which items are acceptable or unacceptable at the collection facility. This information can be provided through pamphlets, handbooks, posters, magnets, workshops, or other means. Local scout troops and other service organizations could also be recruited to help distribute door hangings or flyers as part of their projects.

Municipalities should try to partner with the solid waste disposal services in their communities for help with public education. If disposal services make it clear that they do not pick up hazardous materials, then residents will be alerted to the need for alternative disposal. These solid waste collection companies can also provide users with hazardous waste collection site information through their company's website, newsletter, and billing statements.

In the spring of 1998, four Pennsylvania counties (Lehigh, Northampton, Monroe, and Schuylkill) partnered with two private waste-disposal companies, Safety-Kleen Services and Curbside, Inc., and two volunteer groups, Pennsylvania's Senior Environment Corps and the Environmental Alliance for Senior Involvement (EASI), to launch the first curbside pickup service for household hazardous waste on the East Coast. Known as the Door-to-Door Collection program, this new initiative will allow residents in the four counties to properly dispose of paints, paint thinners, solvents, motor oil, and other substances that should not be disposed of with household garbage. The partnership not only provides a curbside pickup program for household hazardous waste, but it also shows citizens how to prevent the accumulation of chemicals in the home environment. A key element of this service is convenience for area residents. Customers can make a phone call, put their waste in a container, and schedule a pickup.

Public outreach documents should include information about storing household hazardous wastes. For example, municipalities can recommend that residents tightly seal paint cans before storing. Paint should be kept in dry areas that will not freeze, away from sparks or flames. Pesticides should be stored in a dry area in their original containers with the labels intact. They should be stored in a separate locked cabinet or other secure structure, away from children and pets, food, medical supplies, cleaning products, heat, flames, or sparks.

Citizens should also know how to properly apply hazardous materials, especially how much is sufficient and how to avoid releasing materials into the environment. For example, many people who change their own automobile oil think that the only time that oil might be released is during draining and refilling. Approximately 75 percent of the 420 million oil filters sold annually are disposed of in landfills. If recycled, these oil filters would yield 17.8 million gallons of oil and 161,500 tons of steel. Furthermore, approximately 850 million gallons of collected used oil could be reclaimed for use as a fuel supplement or lubricant (Arner, 1996).

To minimize the disposal of hazardous products, it is important that the citizens know that it is best to use only those products that are absolutely necessary, and to use nontoxic alternatives whenever possible. For example, it is possible to clean ovens by applying table salt to spills, then scrubbing with soda water. Also, approximately a cup of baking soda combined with a cup of white vinegar and a cup of ammonia in a gallon of warm water makes an excellent multi-purpose cleaner.

Disposal of home hazardous products also requires special attention. When use of hazardous household products is unavoidable, municipalities should emphasize to citizens that household hazardous wastes should not be flushed down the drain because these drains lead to either a home septic system or a municipal treatment plant, neither of which has adequate capability to remove hazardous chemicals from wastewater. Toxic chemicals might also disrupt microbial processes in septic tanks and treatment plants, reducing their effectiveness. Some of the toxins can be removed, but a significant portion of these chemicals passes through treatment processes and ultimately contaminates water resources. They should also be informed that home hazardous products should never be poured on the ground, into gutters, or down storm drains where they will eventually enter storm sewers and be transported untreated into nearby waterbodies.

Many municipalities have started hazardous waste disposal and recycling centers. In fact, many communities have established hazardous waste collection days when hazardous products are collected from homes and taken to an approved facility for disposal. The municipality must make the effort to inform its citizens of the hours and locations of such sites and what materials are accepted there. The City of Austin, Texas, provides information about their household hazardous waste disposal program (City of Austin, Texas, 2001). The site includes background information, the hours and location of the collection facility (with a map), materials accepted at the facility, details about disposing of business waste, hazardous waste recycling opportunities, and chemicals management. Similarly, the City of Fort Worth, Texas set up a regional Environmental Collection Center and developed a website that lists acceptable materials to allow the public to properly dispose of chemicals (City of Fort Worth, Texas, 2004).

The Shelby County website also provides information to citizens on alternatives to toxic household chemicals and options for paint and solvent disposal.

Some communities establish partnerships with service stations to collect hazardous waste. This way, citizens from throughout the community can go to the most convenient location. The number of collection centers will depend on population size and municipal resources. A general guideline is one collection center for 3,500 to 25,000 residents, two for 25,000 to 100,000 residents, and three for populations of more than 100,000 (Arner, 1996). Hazardous waste collection days should be well publicized to ensure the message is received. Setting a schedule for collection days, such as the first Monday of every month, will help citizens know when they can drop off household hazardous wastes.

When collected, materials must be managed as hazardous wastes. Time and resources must be allocated to obtain the services of a registered hazardous waste management firm to safely remove and dispose of chemicals. In many cases, these firms can take over the operation of the collection event to maximize safety and ensure that no spills occur.

The Pennsylvania Department of Environmental Protection (DEP) has published an excellent guidance manual for municipalities and other groups to start a household hazardous waste program. The manual includes information about budgeting and funding, restrictions, materials to collect and exclude, estimating collection amounts, suggested timelines, and operational tips.

Benefits

Properly disposing of household hazardous wastes ensures that contamination through leaks and spills does not occur. If toxic wastes are disposed of with regular garbage, they could destroy landfill liners and compromise other disposal areas.

Limitations

Municipalities with limited resources can form partnerships with private sanitary services, or environmental or service groups, to help collect hazardous wastes and advertise the program. Municipalities must make an effort to establish these partnerships at the outset of the program so that the groups can take over a portion of the administrative planning and implementation.

Effectiveness

No matter the scope of the household hazardous waste program, whether it is an educational campaign or a full-fledged collection program, citizens will have an increased awareness of the problems caused by mishandling and improper disposal of hazardous chemicals. Municipalities can gauge the effectiveness of their household hazardous waste program by surveying residents about their perceptions and behavior after educational materials have been distributed. The effectiveness of an established program can be measured by the amount of materials collected on amnesty days or on a monthly or yearly basis at full-time collection facilities.

Cost

Costs for household hazardous waste programs can be high, especially if a collection program is selected. In some states, municipalities can apply for grants to help pay for household hazardous waste collection. Pennsylvania's 1994 Household Hazardous Waste Funding Act (HHW) reimburses municipalities for 50 percent of the developmental and operational costs associated with HHW collection programs, up to a total of $100,000 per county per year (Pennsylvania DEP, 1999). Any municipality that registers a HHW collection program with DEP is eligible to apply for a grant. Grants are provided on a first-registered, first-conducted basis, and prioritized according to criteria laid out in the Act. (Priority is given to existing programs and those operated by counties, multi-county groups, and first and second-class cities.) Additionally, the Small Business and Household Pollution Prevention Act provides 80 percent grants to counties to develop and implement pollution prevention education programs for households and small businesses, even if conducted in the absence of a collection program. Municipalities should check with their state environmental agencies to identify grant programs they can use for household hazardous waste programs.

To lessen hazardous waste disposal costs, recycling programs can reuse some chemicals. Austin, Texas, offers a hazardous waste recycling program that allows residents to select from new or used chemicals dropped-off by other residents (City of Austin, Texas, 2001). Instead of incinerating these products at great expense, the facility will give them to anyone who wants them on a first-come, first-served basis. Products may include paint, solvents, automotive fluids, pesticides, fertilizers, cleaning products, or other chemicals. In its first four months of operation, the public reuse center saved $3,207 in disposal costs. There were 300 participants, and 14,562 pounds of hazardous waste were reused.

Chemicals in the Household

Table 23.1. Hazardous Ingredients in Household Products

CHEMICAL PRODUCTS	HAZARDOUS INGREDIENTS	POSSIBLE ALTERNATIVES AND HINTS
Toilet Cleaners	Muriatic (hydrochloric) acid Oxalic acid Paradichlorobenzene Calcium hypochlorite	Toilet brush and baking soda; mild detergent; vinegar soak for tub and sink fixtures; avoid skin contact and breathing fumes.

Table 23.1. Continued

CHEMICAL PRODUCTS	HAZARDOUS INGREDIENTS	POSSIBLE ALTERNATIVES AND HINTS
Drain Cleaners	Sodium or potassium hydroxide Sodium hypochloride	Plunger; flush drain with 1/4 cup baking soda and vinegar; avoid skin contact and breathing fumes.
Bleach Cleaners	Sodium or potassium hydroxide Hydrogen peroxide Sodium or calcium hypochlorite	½ cup white vinegar or baking soda for laundry; avoid skin contact and breathing fumes.
Dishwashing detergent	Chlorine Surfactants	1 part borax to 1 part baking soda; handle all cleaning solutions with care.
Ammonia-based cleaners (all purpose Ethanol cleaners)	Ammonia	Vinegar and salt water mix for surfaces; baking soda and water.
Glass cleaners	Ammonia Naphthalene	Wash windows with ¼ to ½ cup white vinegar to 1 quart warm water, rub dry with newspaper.
Fabric softener	Ammonia	1 cup white vinegar or 1/4 cup baking soda in final rinse water.
Air fresheners	Cresol Phenol Formaldehyde	Open box of baking soda or dish of vanilla; simmer cloves; open windows or use exhaust fans.
Laundry detergent	Surfactants	Avoid breathing powder.
Mothballs	Naphthalene Paradichlorobenzene	Cedar chips; newspapers; lavender, flowers, or other aromatic herbs and spices.
Rug and upholstery cleaners	Naphthalene Paradichlorobenzene Oxalic acid Diethylene glycol	Baking soda on rug, then vacuum.
Floor and furniture polish	Diethylene glycol Petroleum distillates Nitrobenzene Mineral Spirits	1 part lemon oil, 2 parts olive/ vegetable oil; vegetable oil soap.

Table 23.1. Continued

CHEMICAL PRODUCTS	HAZARDOUS INGREDIENTS	POSSIBLE ALTERNATIVES AND HINTS
Furniture strippers	Acetone Methyl ethyl Ketone Alcohols Xylene Toluene Methylene chloride	Equal portions of boiled linseed oil, turpentine, and vinegar with steel wool; sandpaper or heatgun; use in well-ventilated areas or outdoors; handle all solvents with care.
Stains/finishes	Mineral spirits Glycol ethers Ketones Halogenated hydrocarbons Naphtha Xylene Toluene	Natural earth pigment finishes; use in well ventilated areas or outdoors; handle all dyes and paints with care.
Enamel or oil-based paints	Pigments Aliphatic hydrocarbons	Water-based paints if appropriate; always use in well-ventilated areas.
Latex paint	Mercury	Handle all paints with care.
Antifreeze	Ethylene glycol	Clean up all spills.
Automobile batteries	Sulfuric acid Lead	Bring old batteries to recycling center; avoid skin contact; wash spills with plenty of water.
Automobile lubricants (transmission and brake fluids, used oils)	Hydrocarbons (benzene) Mineral Oils Glycol ethers Heavy metals	Seal used oil in plastic container and bring to recycling

Notes

- The listed alternatives are offered as options and are not represented as recommended courses of action.

- Several listed alternatives are also potentially hazardous and can cause harm if handled improperly.

- Various commercial products which fall into the product categories listed here may not contain all of the listed chemical constituents.

Section 23.7

Pesticides

Text in this section is excerpted from "An Introduction to Indoor Air Quality (IAQ)—Pesticides," United States Environmental Protection Agency (EPA), June 21, 2012.

According to a recent survey, 75 percent of U.S. households used at least one pesticide product indoors during the past year. Products used most often are insecticides and disinfectants. Another study suggests that 80 percent of most people's exposure to pesticides occurs indoors and that measurable levels of up to a dozen pesticides have been found in the air inside homes. The amount of pesticides found in homes appears to be greater than can be explained by recent pesticide use in those households; other possible sources include contaminated soil or dust that floats or is tracked in from outside, stored pesticide containers, and household surfaces that collect and then release the pesticides. Pesticides used in and around the home include products to control insects (insecticides), termites (termiticides), rodents (rodenticides), fungi (fungicides), and microbes (disinfectants). They are sold as sprays, liquids, sticks, powders, crystals, balls, and foggers.

In 1990, the American Association of Poison Control Centers reported that some 79,000 children were involved in common household pesticide poisonings or exposures. In households with children under five years old, almost one-half stored at least one pesticide product within reach of children.

EPA registers pesticides for use and requires manufacturers to put information on the label about when and how to use the pesticide. It is important to remember that the "-cide" in pesticides means "to kill." These products can be dangerous if not used properly.

In addition to the active ingredient, pesticides are also made up of ingredients that are used to carry the active agent. These carrier agents are called "inerts" in pesticides because they are not toxic to the targeted pest; nevertheless, some inerts are capable of causing health problems.

Sources of Pesticides

Products used to kill household pests (insecticides, termiticides, and disinfectants). Also, products used on lawns and gardens that drift or are tracked inside the house.

Pesticides are classed as semi-volatile organic compounds and include a variety of chemicals in various forms. Pesticides are chemicals that are used to kill or control pests which include bacteria, fungi, and other organisms, in addition to insects and rodents. Pesticides are inherently toxic.

Health Effects

Irritation to eye, nose, and throat; damage to central nervous system and kidney; increased risk of cancer. Symptoms may include headache, dizziness, muscular weakness, and nausea. Chronic exposure to some pesticides can result in damage to the liver, kidneys, endocrine and nervous systems.

Both the active and inert ingredients in pesticides can be organic compounds; therefore, both could add to the levels of airborne organics inside homes. However, as with other household products, there is insufficient understanding at present about what pesticide concentrations are necessary to produce these effects.

Exposure to high levels of cyclodiene pesticides, commonly associated with misapplication, has produced various symptoms, including headaches, dizziness, muscle twitching, weakness, tingling sensations, and nausea. In addition, EPA is concerned that cyclodienes might cause long-term damage to the liver and the central nervous system, as well as an increased risk of cancer.

There is no further sale or commercial use permitted for the following cyclodiene or related pesticides: chlordane, aldrin, dieldrin, and heptachlor. The only exception is the use of heptachlor by utility companies to control fire ants in underground cable boxes.

Levels in Homes

Preliminary research shows widespread presence of pesticide residues in homes.

Steps to Reduce Exposure

- Use strictly according to manufacturer's directions.

- Mix or dilute outdoors.

- Apply only in recommended quantities.

- Increase ventilation when using indoors. Take plants or pets outdoors when applying pesticides/flea and tick treatments.

- Use non-chemical methods of pest control where possible.

- If you use a pest control company, select it carefully.

- Do not store unneeded pesticides inside home; dispose of unwanted containers safely.

- Store clothes with moth repellents in separately ventilated areas, if possible.

- Keep indoor spaces clean, dry, and well ventilated to avoid pest and odor problems.

Read the label and follow the directions. It is illegal to use any pesticide in any manner inconsistent with the directions on its label.

Unless you have had special training and are certified, never use a pesticide that is restricted to use by state-certified pest control operators. Such pesticides are simply too dangerous for application by a non-certified person. Use only the pesticides approved for use by the general public and then only in recommended amounts; increasing the amount does not offer more protection against pests and can be harmful to you and your plants and pets.

Ventilate the area well after pesticide use.

Mix or dilute pesticides outdoors or in a well-ventilated area and only in the amounts that will be immediately needed. If possible, take plants and pets outside when applying pesticides/flea and tick treatments.

Use non-chemical methods of pest control when possible.

Since pesticides can be found far from the site of their original application, it is prudent to reduce the use of chemical pesticides outdoors as well as indoors. Depending on the site and pest to be controlled, one or more of the following steps can be effective: use of biological pesticides, such as Bacillus thuringiensis, for the control of gypsy moths; selection of disease-resistant plants; and frequent washing of indoor plants and pets. Termite damage can be reduced or prevented by making certain that wooden building materials do not come into direct contact with the soil and by storing firewood away from the home. By appropriately fertilizing, watering, and aerating lawns, the need for chemical pesticide treatments of lawns can be dramatically reduced.

If you decide to use a pest control company, choose one carefully.

Ask for an inspection of your home and get a written control program for evaluation before you sign a contract. The control program should list specific names of pests to be controlled and chemicals to be used; it should also reflect any of your safety concerns. Insist on a proven record of competence and customer satisfaction.

Dispose of unwanted pesticides safely.

If you have unused or partially used pesticide containers you want to get rid of, dispose of them according to the directions on the label or on special household hazardous waste collection days. If there are no such collection days in your community, work with others to organize them.

Keep exposure to moth repellents to a minimum.

One pesticide often found in the home is paradichlorobenzene, a commonly used active ingredient in moth repellents. This chemical is known to cause cancer in animals, but substantial scientific uncertainty exists over the effects, if any, of long-term human exposure to paradichlorobenzene. EPA requires that products containing paradichlorobenzene bear warnings such as "avoid breathing vapors" to warn users of potential short-term toxic effects. Where possible, paradichlorobenzene, and items to be protected against moths, should be placed in trunks or other containers that can be stored in areas that are separately ventilated from the home, such as attics and detached garages. Paradichlorobenzene is also the key active ingredient in many air fresheners (in fact, some labels for moth repellents recommend that these same products be used as air fresheners or deodorants). Proper ventilation and basic household cleanliness will go a long way toward preventing unpleasant odors.

Integrated Pest Management

If chemicals must be used, use only the recommended amounts, mix or dilute pesticides outdoors or in an isolated well ventilated area, apply to unoccupied areas, and dispose of unwanted pesticides safely to minimize exposure.

Section 23.8

Radon

Text in this section is excerpted from "Radon—A Citizen's Guide
to Radon," United States Environmental Protection Agency (EPA),
January 10, 2013.

EPA Recommends

- Test your home for radon — it's easy and inexpensive.

- Fix your home if your radon level is 4 picocuries per liter, or
  pCi/L, or higher.

- Radon levels less than 4 pCi/L still pose a risk, and in many
  cases may be reduced.

Radon is estimated to cause thousands of lung cancer deaths in
the U.S. each year.

Overview

Radon is a cancer-causing, radioactive gas.

You can't see radon. And you can't smell it or taste it. But it may
be a problem in your home.

Radon is estimated to cause many thousands of deaths each year.
That's because when you breathe air containing radon, you can get
lung cancer. In fact, the Surgeon General has warned that radon is
the second leading cause of lung cancer in the United States today.
Only smoking causes more lung cancer deaths. **If you smoke and
your home has high radon levels, your risk of lung cancer is
especially high.**

Radon can be found all over the U.S.

Radon comes from the natural (radioactive) breakdown of uranium
in soil, rock and water and gets into the air you breathe. Radon can be
found all over the U.S. It can get into any type of building — homes,

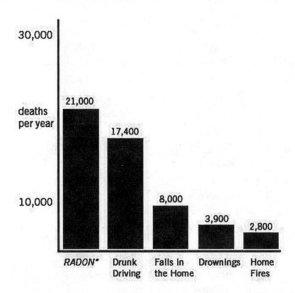

Figure 23.1. * Radon is estimated to cause about 21,000 lung cancer deaths per year, according to EPA's 2003 Assessment of Risks from Radon in Homes (EPA 402-R-03-003). The numbers of deaths from other causes are taken from the Centers for Disease Control and Prevention's 2005-2006 National Center for Injury Prevention and Control Report and 2006 National Safety Council Reports.

offices, and schools — and result in a high indoor radon level. But you and your family are most likely to get your greatest exposure at home, where you spend most of your time.

You should test for radon.

Testing is the only way to know if you and your family are at risk from radon. EPA and the Surgeon General recommend testing all homes below the third floor for radon. EPA also recommends testing in schools.

Testing is inexpensive and easy — it should only take a few minutes of your time. Millions of Americans have already tested their homes for radon.

You can fix a radon problem.

Radon reduction systems work and they are not too costly. Some radon reduction systems can reduce radon levels in your home by up to 99%. Even very high levels can be reduced to acceptable levels.

New homes can be built with radon-resistant features.

Radon-resistant construction techniques can be effective in preventing radon entry. When installed properly and completely, these simple and inexpensive techniques can help reduce indoor radon levels in homes. In addition, installing them at the time of construction makes it easier and less expensive to reduce radon levels further if these passive techniques don't reduce radon levels to below 4 pCi/L. **Every new home should be tested after occupancy, even if it was built radon-resistant.** If radon levels are still in excess of 4 pCi/L, the passive system should be activated by having a qualified mitigator install a vent fan.

How Does Radon Get Into Your Home?

Radon is a radioactive gas. It comes from the natural decay of uranium that is found in nearly all soils. It typically moves up through the ground to the air above and into your home through cracks and other holes in the foundation. Your home traps radon inside, where it can build up. Any home may have a radon problem. This means new and old homes, well-sealed and drafty homes, and homes with or without basements.

Radon from soil gas is the main cause of radon problems. Sometimes radon enters the home through well water (see "Radon in Water" below). In a small number of homes, the building materials can give off radon, too. However, building materials rarely cause radon problems by themselves.

Any home may have a radon problem.

Radon Gets In Through:

1. Cracks in solid floors
2. Construction joints
3. Cracks in walls
4. Gaps in suspended floors
5. Gaps around service pipes
6. Cavities inside walls
7. The water supply

Nearly 1 out of every 15 homes in the U.S. is estimated to have elevated radon levels. Elevated levels of radon gas have been found in homes in your state. Contact your state radon office for general information about radon in your area. While radon problems may be more common in some areas, any home may have a problem. The only way to know about your home is to test.

Radon can also be a problem in schools and workplaces. Ask your state radon office about radon problems in schools, daycare and child-care facilities, and workplaces in your area.

How to Test Your Home

You can't see radon, but it's not hard to find out if you have a radon problem in your home. All you need to do is test for radon. Testing is easy and should only take a few minutes of your time.

The amount of radon in the air is measured in "picocuries per liter of air," or "pCi/L." There are many kinds of low-cost "do-it-yourself" radon test kits you can get through the mail and in some hardware stores and other retail outlets. If you prefer, or if you are buying or selling a home, you can hire a qualified tester to do the testing for you. You should first contact your state radon office about obtaining a list of qualified testers. You can also contact a private radon proficiency program for lists of privately certified radon professionals serving your area.

There are Two General Ways to Test for Radon:

Short-Term Testing:

The quickest way to test is with short-term tests. Short-term tests remain in your home for two days to 90 days, depending on the device. "Charcoal canisters," "alpha track," "electret ion chamber," "continuous monitors," and "charcoal liquid scintillation" detectors are most commonly used for short-term testing. Because radon levels tend to vary from day to day and season to season, a short-term test is less likely than a long-term test to tell you your year-round average radon level. If you need results quickly, however, a short-term test followed by a second short-term test may be used to decide whether to fix your home.

> Testing is easy and should only take a few minutes of your time.

Long-Term Testing:

Long-term tests remain in your home for more than 90 days. "Alpha track" and "electret" detectors are commonly used for this type of testing. A long-term test will give you a reading that is more likely to tell you your home's year-round average radon level than a short-term test.

How To Use a Test Kit:

Follow the instructions that come with your test kit. If you are doing a short-term test, close your windows and outside doors and keep them closed as much as possible during the test. Heating and air-conditioning system fans that re-circulate air may be operated. Do not operate fans or other machines which bring in air from outside. Fans that are part of a radon-reduction system or small exhaust fans operating only for short periods of time may run during the test. If you are doing a short-term test lasting just 2 or 3 days, be sure to close your windows and outside doors at least 12 hours **before** beginning the test too. You should not conduct short-term tests lasting just 2 or 3 days during unusually severe storms or periods of unusually high winds. The test kit should be placed in the lowest lived-in level of the home (for example, the basement if it is frequently used, otherwise the first floor). It should be put in a room that is used regularly (like a living room, playroom, den or bedroom) but **not** your kitchen or bathroom. Place the kit at least 20 inches above the floor in a location where it won't be disturbed - away from drafts, high heat, high humidity, and exterior walls. Leave the kit in place for as long as the package says. Once you've finished the test, reseal the package and send it to the lab specified on the package right away for analysis. You should receive your test results within a few weeks.

EPA Recommends the Following Testing Steps:

Step 1. Take a short-term test. If your result is 4 pCi/L or higher, take a follow-up test (Step 2) to be sure.

Step 2. Follow up with either a long-term test or a second short-term test:

- For a better understanding of your year-round average radon level, take a long-term test.

- If you need results quickly, take a second short-term test.

The higher your initial short-term test result, the more certain you can be that you should take a short-term rather than a long-term follow up test. If your first short-term test result is more than twice EPA's 4 pCi/L action level, you should take a second short-term test immediately.

Step 3. If you followed up with a long-term test: Fix your home if your long-term test result is 4 pCi/L or more. If you followed up with a second short-term test: The higher your short-term results, the more certain you can be that you should fix your home. Consider fixing your home if the average of your first and second test is 4 pCi/L or higher.

What Your Test Results Mean

The average indoor radon level is estimated to be about 1.3 pCi/L, and about 0.4 pCi/L of radon is normally found in the outside air. The U.S. Congress has set a long-term goal that indoor radon levels be no more than outdoor levels. While this goal is not yet technologically achievable in all cases, most homes today *can* be reduced to 2 pCi/L or below.

Sometimes short-term tests are less definitive about whether or not your home is above 4 pCi/L. This can happen when your results are close to 4 pCi/L. For example, if the average of your two short-term test results is 4.1 pCi/L, there is about a 50% chance that your year-round average is somewhat below 4 pCi/L. However, EPA believes that any radon exposure carries some risk – no level of radon is safe. Even radon levels below 4 pCi/L pose some risk, and you can reduce your risk of lung cancer by lowering your radon level.

If your living patterns change and you begin occupying a lower level of your home (such as a basement) you should retest your home on that level.

Even if your test result is below 4 pCi/L, you may want to test again sometime in the future.

> Test your home now and save your results. If you find high radon levels, fix your home before you decide to sell it.

Radon and Home Sales

More and more home buyers and renters are asking about radon levels before they buy or rent a home. Because real estate sales happen quickly, there is often little time to deal with radon and other issues. The best thing to do is to test for radon NOW and save the results in case the buyer is interested in them. Fix a problem if it exists so it won't complicate your home sale. If you are planning to move, read EPA's pamphlet "Home Buyer's and Seller's Guide to Radon," which addresses some common questions. You can also use the results of two short-term tests done side-by-side (four inches apart) to decide whether to fix your home.

During home sales:

- Buyers often ask if a home has been tested, and if elevated levels were reduced.

- Buyers frequently want tests made by someone who is not involved in the home sale. Your state radon office can assist you in identifying a qualified tester.

- Buyers might want to know the radon levels in areas of the home (like a basement they plan to finish) that the seller might not otherwise test.

Today many homes are built to prevent radon from coming in. Building codes in your state or local area may require these radon-resistant construction features. If you are buying or renting a new home, ask the owner or builder if it has radon-resistant features. The EPA recommends building new homes with radon-resistant features in high radon potential (Zone 1) areas. Even if built radon-resistant, every new home should be tested for radon after occupancy. If you have a test result of 4 pCi/L or more, consult a qualified mitigator to estimate the cost of upgrading to an active system by adding a vent fan to reduce the radon level. In an **existing home**, the cost to install a radon mitigation system is about the same as for other common home repairs.

Radon in Water

There are two main sources for the radon in your home's indoor air, the soil and the water supply. Compared to radon entering the home through water, radon entering your home through the soil is usually a much larger risk.

The radon in your water supply poses an inhalation risk and an ingestion risk. Research has shown that your risk of lung cancer from breathing radon in air is much larger than your risk of stomach cancer from swallowing water with radon in it. Most of your risk from radon in water comes from radon released into the air when water is used for showering and other household purposes.

Radon in your home's water is not usually a problem when its source is surface water. A radon in water problem is more likely when its source is ground water, e.g., a private well or a public water supply system that uses ground water. If you are concerned that radon may be entering your home through the water and your water comes from a public water supply, contact your water supplier.

If you've tested your private well and have a radon in water problem, it can be fixed. Your home's water supply can be treated in two ways. Point-of-entry treatment can effectively remove radon from the water before it enters your home. Point-of-use treatment devices remove radon from your water at the tap, but only treat a small portion of the water you use and are not effective in reducing the risk from breathing radon released into the air from all water used in the home.

> If you've tested the air in your home and found a radon problem, and your water comes from a well, have your water tested.

How to Lower the Radon Levels in Your Home

Since there is no known safe level of radon, there can always be some risk. But the risk can be reduced by lowering the radon level in your home.

There are several proven methods to reduce radon in your home, but the one primarily used is a vent pipe system and fan, which pulls radon from beneath the house and vents it to the outside. This system, known as a soil suction radon reduction system, does not require major changes to your home. Sealing foundation cracks and other openings makes this kind of system more effective and cost-efficient. Similar systems can also be installed in houses with crawl spaces. Radon contractors can use other methods that may also work in your home. The right system depends on the design of your home and other factors.

The cost of reducing radon in your home depends on how your home was built and the extent of the radon problem. Most homes can be fixed for about the same cost as other common home repairs. The cost to fix can vary widely; consult with your state radon office or get one or more estimates from qualified mitigators. The cost is much less if a passive system was installed during construction.

Radon and Home Renovations

If you are planning any major structural renovation, such as converting an unfinished basement area into living space, it is especially important to test the area for radon before you begin the renovation. If your test results indicate a radon problem, radon-resistant techniques can be inexpensively included as part of the renovation. Because major renovations can change the level of radon in any home, always test again after work is completed.

Lowering high radon levels requires technical knowledge and special skills. You should use a contractor who is trained to fix radon problems. A qualified contractor can study the radon problem in your home and help you pick the right treatment method.

Check with your state radon office for names of qualified or state certified radon contractors in your area. You can also contact private radon proficiency programs for lists of privately certified radon professionals in your area. For more information on private radon proficiency programs, visit www.epa.gov/radon/radontest.html. Picking someone to fix your radon problem is much like choosing a contractor for other home repairs—you may want to get references and more than one estimate.

If you are considering fixing your home's radon problem yourself, you should first contact your state radon office for guidance and assistance (see www.epa.gov/radon/whereyoulive.html).

Most homes can be fixed for about the same cost as other common home repairs.

You should also test your home again after it is fixed to be sure that radon levels have been reduced. Most soil suction radon reduction systems include a monitor that will indicate whether the system is operating properly. In addition, it's a good idea to retest your home every two years to be sure radon levels remain low.

The Risk of Living with Radon

Radon gas decays into radioactive particles that can get trapped in your lungs when you breathe. As they break down further, these particles release small bursts of energy. This can damage lung tissue and lead to lung cancer over the course of your lifetime. Not everyone exposed to elevated levels of radon will develop lung cancer. And the amount of time between exposure and the onset of the disease may be many years.

Like other environmental pollutants, there is some uncertainty about the magnitude of radon health risks. However, we know more about radon risks than risks from most other cancer-causing substances. This is because estimates of radon risks are based on studies of cancer in humans (underground miners).

Smoking combined with radon is an especially serious health risk. Stop smoking and lower your radon level to reduce your lung cancer risk.

Children have been reported to have greater risk than adults of certain types of cancer from radiation, but there are currently no conclusive data on whether children are at greater risk than adults from radon.

Your chances of getting lung cancer from radon depend mostly on:

- **How much radon is in your home**

- **The amount of time you spend in your home**

- **Whether you are a smoker or have ever smoked**

> Scientists are more certain about radon risks than from most other cancer-causing substances.

Table 23.2. Radon Risk If You Smoke

Radon Level	If 1,000 people who smoked were exposed to this level over a lifetime*...	The risk of cancer from radon exposure compares to**...	WHAT TO DO: Stop smoking and...
20 pCi/L	About 260 people could get lung cancer	250 times the risk of drowning	Fix your home
10 pCi/L	About 150 people could get lung cancer	200 times the risk of dying in a home fire	Fix your home

Table 23.2. Continued

Radon Level	If 1,000 people who smoked were exposed to this level over a lifetime*...	The risk of cancer from radon exposure compares to**...	WHAT TO DO: Stop smoking and...
8 pCi/L	About 120 people could get lung cancer	30 times the risk of dying in a fall	Fix your home
4 pCi/L	About 62 people could get lung cancer	5 times the risk of dying in a car crash	Fix your home
2 pCi/L	About 32 people could get lung cancer	6 times the risk of dying from poison	Consider fixing between 2 and 4 pCi/L
1.3 pCi/L	About 20 people could get lung cancer	(Average indoor radon level)	(Reducing radon levels below 2 pCi/L is difficult.)
0.4 pCi/L	About 3 people could get lung cancer	(Average outdoor radon level)	

Note: If you are a former smoker, your risk may be lower.

* *Lifetime risk of lung cancer deaths from EPA Assessment of Risks from Radon in Homes (EPA 402-R-03-003).*

** *Comparison data calculated using the Centers for Disease Control and Prevention's 1999-2001 National Center for Injury Prevention and Control Reports.*

Table 23.3. Radon Risk If You've Never Smoked

Radon Level	If 1,000 people who never smoked were exposed to this level over a lifetime*...	The risk of cancer from radon exposure compares to**...	WHAT TO DO:
20 pCi/L	About 36 people could get lung cancer	35 times the risk of drowning	Fix your home
10 pCi/L	About 18 people could get lung cancer	20 times the risk of dying in a home fire	Fix your home

Table 23.3. Continued

Radon Level	If 1,000 people who never smoked were exposed to this level over a lifetime*...	The risk of cancer from radon exposure compares to**...	WHAT TO DO:
8 pCi/L	About 15 people could get lung cancer	4 times the risk of dying in a fall	Fix your home
4 pCi/L	About 7 people could get lung cancer	The risk of dying in a car crash	Fix your home
2 pCi/L	About 4 person could get lung cancer	The risk of dying from poison	Consider fixing between 2 and 4 pCi/L
1.3 pCi/L	About 2 people could get lung cancer	(Average indoor radon level)	(Reducing radon levels below 2 pCi/L is difficult.)
0.4 pCi/L		(Average outdoor radon level)	

Note: If you are a former smoker, your risk may be higher.
 * Lifetime risk of lung cancer deaths from EPA Assessment of Risks from Radon in Homes (EPA 402-R-03-003).
 ** Comparison data calculated using the Centers for Disease Control and Prevention's 1999-2001 National Center for Injury Prevention and Control Reports.

Radon Myths

MYTH: Scientists aren't sure radon really is a problem.

FACT: Although some scientists dispute the precise number of deaths due to radon, all the major health organizations (like the Centers for Disease Control and Prevention, the American Lung Association, and the American Medical Association) agree with estimates that radon causes thousands of preventable lung cancer deaths every year. This is especially true among smokers, since the risk to smokers is much greater than to non-smokers.

MYTH: Radon testing is difficult, time consuming and expensive.

FACT: Radon testing is easy. You can test your home yourself or hire a qualified radon test company. Either approach takes only a small amount of time and effort.

MYTH: Homes with radon problems can't be fixed.

FACT: There are simple solutions to radon problems in homes. Hundreds of thousands of homeowners have already fixed radon problems in their homes. Most homes can be fixed for about the same cost as other common home repairs; check with one or more qualified mitigators. Call your state radon office for help in identifying qualified mitigation contractors.

MYTH: Radon affects only certain kinds of homes.

FACT: House construction can affect radon levels. However, radon can be a problem in homes of all types: old homes, new homes, drafty homes, insulated homes, homes with basements, homes without basements. Local geology, construction materials, and how the home was built are among the factors that can affect radon levels in homes.

MYTH: Radon is only a problem in certain parts of the country.

FACT: High radon levels have been found in every state. Radon problems do vary from area to area, but the only way to know your radon level is to test.

MYTH: A neighbor's test result is a good indication of whether your home has a problem.

FACT: It's not. Radon levels can vary greatly from home to home. The only way to know if your home has a radon problem is to test it.

MYTH: Everyone should test their water for radon.

FACT: Although radon gets into some homes through water, it is important to first test the air in the home for radon. If your water comes from a public water supply that uses ground water, call your water supplier. If high radon levels are found and the home has a private well, call the Safe Drinking Water Hotline at 1 800-426-4791 for information on testing your water.

MYTH: It's difficult to sell homes where radon problems have been discovered.

FACT: Where radon problems have been fixed, home sales have not been blocked or frustrated. The added protection is some times a good selling point.

MYTH: I've lived in my home for so long, it doesn't make sense to take action now.

FACT: You will reduce your risk of lung cancer when you reduce radon levels, even if you've lived with a radon problem for a long time.

MYTH: Short-term tests can't be used for making a decision about whether to fix your home.

FACT: A short-term test, followed by a second short-term test* can be used to decide whether to fix your home. However, the closer the average of your two short-term tests is to 4 pCi/L, the less certain you can be about whether your year-round average is above or below that level. Keep in mind that radon levels below 4 pCi/L still pose some risk. Radon levels can be reduced in most homes to 2 pCi/L or below.

* If the radon test is part of a real estate transaction, the result of two short-term tests can be used in deciding whether to mitigate.

Section 23.9

Secondhand Smoke

Text in this section is excerpted from "Smoke-free Homes—
Health Effects of Exposure to Secondhand Smoke," United States
Environmental Protection Agency (EPA), November 30, 2011.

What is Secondhand Smoke?

Secondhand smoke is a mixture of the smoke given off by the burning end of a cigarette, pipe, or cigar, and the smoke exhaled by smokers. Secondhand smoke is also called environmental tobacco smoke (ETS) and exposure to secondhand smoke is sometimes called involuntary or passive smoking. Secondhand smoke contains more that 4,000 substances, several of which are known to cause cancer in humans or animals.

- EPA has concluded that exposure to secondhand smoke can cause **lung cancer** in adults who do not smoke. EPA estimates that exposure to secondhand smoke causes approximately 3,000 lung cancer deaths per year in nonsmokers.

- Exposure to secondhand smoke has also been shown in a number of studies to increase the risk of heart disease.

Did You Know?

11% of children aged 6 years and under are exposed to ETS in their homes on a regular basis (4 or more days per week).

The National Survey on Environmental Management of Asthma and Children's Exposure to Environmental Tobacco Smoke

---

Serious Health Risks to Children

Children are particularly vulnerable to the effects of secondhand smoke because they are still developing physically, have higher breathing rates than adults, and have little control over their indoor environments. Children exposed to high doses of secondhand smoke, such as those whose mothers smoke, run the greatest relative risk of experiencing damaging health effects.

- Exposure to secondhand smoke can **cause asthma** in children who have not previously exhibited symptoms.

- Exposure to secondhand smoke increases the risk for **Sudden Infant Death Syndrome**.

- Infants and children younger than 6 who are regularly exposed to secondhand smoke are at increased risk of lower respiratory track infections, such as **pneumonia and bronchitis**.

- Children who regularly breathe secondhand smoke are at increased risk for **middle ear infections**.

Health Risks to Children with Asthma

- Asthma is the most common chronic childhood disease affecting 1 in 13 school aged children on average.

- Exposure to secondhand smoke can cause new cases of asthma in children who have not previously shown symptoms.

- Exposure to secondhand smoke can trigger asthma attacks and make asthma symptoms more severe.

The Science Behind the Risks

1. **Surgeon General Warning: Secondhand Smoke Puts Children At Risk**

On June 27th, 2006, the Surgeon General released a major new report on involuntary exposure to secondhand smoke, concluding that secondhand smoke causes disease and death in children and non-smoking adults. The report finds a causal relationship between secondhand smoke exposure and Sudden Infant Death Syndrome (SIDS), and declares that the home is becoming the predominant location for exposure of children and adults to secondhand smoke.

2. **The National Survey on Environmental Management of Asthma and Children's Exposure to Environmental Tobacco Smoke (NSEMA/CEE)** (U.S. Environmental Protection Agency, 2004)

Key findings:

- 11% of children aged 6 years and under are exposed to ETS in their homes on a regular basis (4 or more days per week) compared to 20% in the 1998 National Health Interview Survey (NHIS).

- Parents are responsible for 90% of children's exposure to ETS.

- Exposure to ETS is higher and asthma prevalence is more likely in households with low income and low education levels.

- Children with asthma have as much exposure to ETS as children without asthma.

- Read the Report: Fact Sheet: National Survey on Environmental Management of Asthma and Children's Exposure to Environmental Tobacco Smoke

3. **Respiratory Health Effects of Passive Smoking (Also Known as Exposure to Secondhand Smoke or Environmental Tobacco Smoke - ETS)** (U.S. Environmental Protection Agency, 1992)

Key findings:

In adults:

- ETS is a human lung carcinogen, responsible for approximately 3,000 lung cancer deaths annually in U.S. non-smokers. ETS has been classified as a Group A carcinogen under EPA's carcinogen assessment guidelines. This classification is reserved for those compounds or mixtures which have been shown to cause cancer in humans, based on studies in human populations.

In children:

- ETS exposure increases the risk of lower respiratory tract infections such as bronchitis and pneumonia. EPA estimates that between 150,000 and 300,000 of these cases annually in infants and young children up to 18 months of age are attributable to exposure to ETS. Of these, between 7,500 and 15,000 will result in hospitalization.

- ETS exposure increases the prevalence of fluid in the middle ear, a sign of chronic middle ear disease.

- ETS exposure in children irritates the upper respiratory tract and is associated with a small but significant reduction in lung function.

- ETS exposure increases the frequency of episodes and severity of symptoms in asthmatic children. The report estimates that 200,000 to 1,000,000 asthmatic children have their condition worsened by exposure to environmental tobacco smoke.

- ETS exposure is a risk factor for new cases of asthma in children who have not previously displayed symptoms.

- Read the Report: U.S. Environmental Protection Agency, Office of Research and Development, Office of Health and Environmental Assessment, Washington, DC, EPA/600/6-90/006F, December, 1992

Chapter 24

Mold and Moisture

Introduction to Molds

Molds in the Environment

Molds live in the soil, on plants, and on dead or decaying matter. Outdoors, molds play a key role in the breakdown of leaves, wood, and other plant debris. Molds belong to the kingdom Fungi, and unlike plants, they lack chlorophyll and must survive by digesting plant materials, using plant and other organic materials for food. Without molds, our environment would be overwhelmed with large amounts of dead plant matter.

Molds produce tiny spores to reproduce, just as some plants produce seeds. These mold spores can be found in both indoor and outdoor air, and settled on indoor and outdoor surfaces. When mold spores land on a damp spot, they may begin growing and digesting whatever they are growing on in order to survive. Since molds gradually destroy the things they grow on, you can prevent damage to building materials and furnishings and save money by eliminating mold growth.

Moisture control is the key to mold control. Molds need both food and water to survive; since molds can digest most things, water is the factor that limits mold growth. Molds will often grow in damp or wet

This chapter includes excerpts from "Mold Remediation in Schools and Commercial Buildings," United States Environmental Protection Agency (EPA), March 5, 2012; and text from "A Brief Guide to Mold, Moisture, and Your Home," United States Environmental Protection Agency (EPA), April 4, 2015.

areas indoors. Common sites for indoor mold growth include bathroom tile, basement walls, areas around windows where moisture condenses, and near leaky water fountains or sinks. Common sources or causes of water or moisture problems include roof leaks, deferred maintenance, condensation associated with high humidity or cold spots in the building, localized flooding due to plumbing failures or heavy rains, slow leaks in plumbing fixtures, and malfunction or poor design of humidification systems. Uncontrolled humidity can also be a source of moisture leading to mold growth, particularly in hot, humid climates.

Health Effects and Symptoms Associated with Mold Exposure

When moisture problems occur and mold growth results, building occupants may begin to report odors and a variety of health problems, such as headaches, breathing difficulties, skin irritation, allergic reactions, and aggravation of asthma symptoms; all of these symptoms could potentially be associated with mold exposure.

All molds have the potential to cause health effects. Molds produce allergens, irritants, and in some cases, toxins that may cause reactions in humans. The types and severity of symptoms depend, in part, on the types of mold present, the extent of an individual's exposure, the ages of the individuals, and their existing sensitivities or allergies.

Potential Health Effects Associated with Inhalation Exposure to Molds and Mycotoxins

Allergic Reactions (e.g., rhinitis and dermatitis or skin rash); Asthma; Hypersensitivity Pneumonitis; Other Immunologic Effects

Research on mold and health effects is ongoing. This list is not intended to be all-inclusive.

The health effects listed above are well documented in humans. Evidence for other health effects in humans is less substantial and is primarily based on case reports or occupational studies.

Specific reactions to mold growth can include the following:

- **Allergic Reactions** Inhaling or touching mold or mold spores may cause allergic reactions in sensitive individuals. Allergic reactions to mold are common – these reactions can be immediate or delayed. Allergic responses include hay fever-type symptoms, such as sneezing, runny nose, red eyes, and skin rash (dermatitis). Mold spores and fragments can produce allergic reactions in sensitive individuals regardless of whether the mold is dead or alive. Repeated or single exposure to mold or mold spores may cause previously non-sensitive individuals to become sensitive. Repeated exposure has the potential to increase sensitivity.

- **Asthma** Molds can trigger asthma attacks in persons who are allergic (sensitized) to molds. The irritants produced by molds may also worsen asthma in non-allergic (non-sensitized) people.

- **Hypersensitivity Pneumonitis** Hypersensitivity pneumonitis may develop following either short-term (acute) or long-term (chronic) exposure to molds. The disease resembles bacterial pneumonia and is uncommon.

- **Irritant Effects** Mold exposure can cause irritation of the eyes, skin, nose, throat, and lungs, and sometimes can create a burning sensation in these areas.

- **Opportunistic Infections** People with weakened immune systems (i.e., immune-compromised or immune-suppressed individuals) may be more vulnerable to infections by molds (as well as more vulnerable than healthy persons to mold toxins). *Aspergillus fumigatus*, for example, has been known to infect the lungs of immune-compromised individuals. These individuals inhale the mold spores which then start growing in their lungs. *Trichoderma* has also been known to infect immune-compromised children.

Healthy individuals are usually not vulnerable to opportunistic infections from airborne mold exposure. However, molds can cause common skin diseases, such as athlete's foot, as well as other infections such as yeast infections.

Mold Toxins (Mycotoxins)

Molds can produce toxic substances called mycotoxins. Some mycotoxins cling to the surface of mold spores; others may be found within spores. More than 200 mycotoxins have been identified from common molds, and many more remain to be identified. Some of the molds that are known to produce mycotoxins are commonly found in moisture-damaged buildings. Exposure pathways for mycotoxins can include inhalation, ingestion, or skin contact. Although some mycotoxins are well known to affect humans and have been shown to be responsible for human health effects, for many mycotoxins, little information is available.

Aflatoxin B1 is perhaps the most well known and studied mycotoxin. It can be produced by the molds *Aspergillus flavus* and *Aspergillus parasiticus* and is one of the most potent carcinogens known. Ingestion of aflatoxin B1 can cause liver cancer. There is also some evidence that inhalation of aflatoxin B1 can cause lung cancer. Aflatoxin B1 has been found on contaminated grains, peanuts, and other human and animal foodstuffs. However, *Aspergillus flavus* and *Aspergillus parasiticus* are *not* commonly found on building materials or in indoor environments.

Much of the information on the human health effects of inhalation exposure to mycotoxins comes from studies done in the workplace and some case studies or case reports.

Toxic Molds

Some molds, such as *Aspergillus versicolor* and *Stachybotrys atra (chartarum)*, are known to produce potent toxins under certain circumstances. Although some mycotoxins are well known to affect humans and have been shown to be responsible for human health effects, for many mycotoxins, little information is available, and in some cases research is ongoing. For example, some strains of *Stachybotrys atra* can produce one or more potent toxins. In addition, preliminary reports from an investigation of an outbreak of pulmonary hemorrhage in infants suggested an association between pulmonary hemorrhage and exposure to *Stachybotrys chartarum*. Review of the evidence of this association at CDC resulted in an a published clarification stating that such an association was not established. Research on the possible causes of pulmonary hemorrhage in infants continues. Consult the Centers for Disease Control and Prevention (CDC) for more information on pulmonary hemorrhage in infants.

*Many symptoms and human health effects attributed to inhalation of mycotoxins have been reported including: mucous membrane irritation, skin rash, nausea, immune system suppression, acute or chronic liver damage, acute or chronic central nervous system damage, endocrine effects, and cancer. More studies are needed to get a clear picture of the health effects related to most mycotoxins. However, it is clearly prudent to avoid exposure to molds and mycotoxins.

Some molds can produce several toxins, and some molds produce mycotoxins only under certain environmental conditions. The presence of mold in a building does not necessarily mean that mycotoxins are present or that they are present in large quantities.

Note: Information on ingestion exposure, for both humans and animals, is more abundant—wide range of health effects has been reported following ingestion of moldy foods including liver damage, nervous system damage, and immunological effects.

Microbial Volatile Organic Compounds (mVOCs)

Some compounds produced by molds are volatile and are released directly into the air. These are known as microbial volatile organic compounds (mVOCs). Because these compounds often have strong and/ or unpleasant odors, they can be the source of odors associated with molds. Exposure to mVOCs from molds has been linked to symptoms such as headaches, nasal irritation, dizziness, fatigue, and nausea. Research on mVOCs is still in the early phase.

Glucans or Fungal Cell Wall Components (also known as β-(1->)-D-Glucans)

Glucans are small pieces of the cell walls of molds which may cause inflammatory lung and airway reactions. These glucans can affect the immune system when inhaled. Exposure to very high levels of glucans or dust mixtures including glucans may cause a flu-like illness known as Organic Dust Toxic Syndrome (ODTS). This illness has been primarily noted in agricultural and manufacturing settings.

Spores

Mold spores are microscopic (2–10 $u\mu$) and are naturally present in both indoor and outdoor air. Molds reproduce by means of spores. Some molds have spores that are easily disturbed and waft into the air and settle repeatedly with each disturbance. Other molds have sticky spores that will cling to surfaces and are dislodged by brushing against them or by other direct contact. Spores may remain able to grow for years after they are produced. In addition, whether or not the spores are alive, the allergens in and on them may remain allergenic for years.

A Brief Guide to Mold, Moisture, and Your Home

Mold Basics

- The **key** to **mold control** is **moisture control**.

- If mold is a problem in your home, you should **clean up the mold promptly** *and* **fix the water problem.**

- It is important to **dry** water-damaged areas and items **within 24–48 hours** to prevent mold growth.

Why is mold growing in my home?

Molds are part of the natural environment. Outdoors, molds play a part in nature by breaking down dead organic matter such as fallen leaves and dead trees, but indoors, mold growth should be avoided. Molds reproduce by means of tiny spores; the spores are invisible to the naked eye and float through outdoor and indoor air. Mold may begin growing indoors when mold spores land on surfaces that are wet. There are many types of mold, and none of them will grow without water or moisture.

Can mold cause health problems?

Molds are usually not a problem indoors, unless mold spores land on a wet or damp spot and begin growing. Molds have the potential to cause health problems. Molds produce allergens (substances that can cause allergic reactions), irritants, and in some cases, potentially toxic substances (mycotoxins). Inhaling or touching mold or mold spores may cause allergic reactions in sensitive individuals. Allergic responses include hay fever-type symptoms, such as sneezing, runny nose, red eyes, and skin rash (dermatitis). Allergic reactions to mold are common. They can be immediate or delayed. Molds can also cause asthma attacks in people with asthma who are allergic to mold. In addition, mold exposure can irritate the eyes, skin, nose, throat, and lungs of both mold-allergic and non-allergic people. Symptoms other than the allergic and irritant types are not commonly reported as a result of inhaling mold. Research on mold and health effects is ongoing.

This guidance provides a brief overview; it does not describe all potential health effects related to mold exposure.

How do I get rid of mold?

It is impossible to get rid of all mold and mold spores indoors; some mold spores will be found floating through the air and in house dust.

The mold spores will not grow if moisture is not present. Indoor mold growth can and should be prevented or controlled by controlling moisture indoors. If there is mold growth in your home, you must clean up the mold **and** fix the water problem. If you clean up the mold, but don't fix the water problem, then most likely, the mold problem will come back.

Mold Cleanup

Who should do the cleanup depends on a number of factors. One consideration is the size of the mold problem. If the moldy area is less than about 10 square feet (less than roughly a 3 ft. by 3 ft. patch), in most cases, you can handle the job yourself,follow the guidelines. However:

- If there has been a lot of water damage, and/or mold growth covers more than 10 square feet, consult EPA's *Mold Remediation in Schools and Commercial Buildings*. Although focused on schools and commercial buildings, this document is applicable to other building types.

- If you choose to hire a contractor (or other professional service provider) to do the cleanup, make sure the contractor has experience cleaning up mold. Check references and ask the contractor to follow the recommendations in EPA's *Mold Remediation in Schools and Commercial Buildings*, the guidelines of the American Conference of Governmental Industrial Hygenists (ACGIH), or other guidelines from professional or government organizations.

- If you suspect that the heating/ventilation/air conditioning (HVAC) system may be contaminated with mold (it is part of an identified moisture problem, for instance, or there is mold near the intake to the system), consult EPA's guide *Should You Have the Air Ducts in Your Home Cleaned?* before taking further action. Do not run the HVAC system if you know or suspect that it is contaminated with mold – it could spread mold throughout the building.

- If the water and/or mold damage was caused by sewage or other contaminated water, then call in a professional who has experience cleaning and fixing buildings damaged by contaminated water.

- If you have health concerns, consult a health professional before starting cleanup.

Mold Cleanup Guidelines

Tips and techniques

The tips and techniques presented in this section will help you clean up your mold problem. Professional cleaners or remediators may use methods not covered in this publication. Please note that mold may cause staining and cosmetic damage. It may not be possible to clean an item so that its original appearance is restored.

- **Fix plumbing leaks and other water problems as soon as possible. Dry all items completely.**

- **Scrub mold off hard surfaces with detergent and water, and dry completely.**

- Absorbent or porous materials, such as ceiling tiles and carpet, may have to be thrown away if they become moldy. Mold can grow on or fill in the empty spaces and crevices of porous materials, so the mold may be difficult or impossible to remove completely.

- Avoid exposing yourself or others to mold (see discussions: What to Wear When Cleaning Moldy Areas and Hidden Mold).

- Do not paint or caulk moldy surfaces. Clean up the mold and dry the surfaces before painting. Paint applied over moldy surfaces is likely to peel.

- If you are unsure about how to clean an item, or if the item is expensive or of sentimental value, you may wish to consult a specialist. Specialists in furniture repair, restoration, painting, art restoration and conservation, carpet and rug cleaning, water damage, and fire or water restoration are commonly listed in phone books. Be sure to ask for and check references. Look for specialists who are affiliated with professional organizations.

Bathroom Tip

Places that are often or always damp can be hard to maintain completely free of mold. If there's some mold in the shower or elsewhere in the bathroom that seems to reappear, **increasing ventilation** (running a fan or opening a window) and **cleaning more frequently** will usually prevent mold from recurring, or at least keep the mold to a minimum.

What to Wear When Cleaning Moldy Areas

It is important to take precautions to **LIMIT YOUR EXPOSURE** to mold and mold spores.

- **Avoid breathing in mold or mold spores.** In order to limit your exposure to airborne mold, you may want to wear an N-95 respirator, available at many hardware stores and from companies that advertise on the Internet. (They cost about $12 to $25.) Some N-95 respirators resemble a paper dust mask with a nozzle on the front, others are made primarily of plastic or rubber and have removable cartridges that trap most of the mold spores from entering. In order to be effective, the respirator or mask must fit properly, so carefully follow the instructions supplied with the respirator. Please note that the Occupational Safety and Health Administration (OSHA) requires that respirators fit properly (fit testing) when used in an occupational setting; consult OSHA for more information (800–321-OSHA or www.osha.gov).

- **Wear gloves.** Long gloves that extend to the middle of the forearm are recommended. When working with water and a mild detergent, ordinary household rubber gloves may be used. If you are using a disinfectant, a biocide such as chlorine bleach, or a strong cleaning solution, you should select gloves made from natural rubber, neoprene, nitrile, polyurethane, or PVC (see Cleanup and Biocides). Avoid touching mold or moldy items with your bare hands.

- **Wear goggles.** Goggles that do not have ventilation holes are recommended. Avoid getting mold or mold spores in your eyes.

How Do I Know When the Remediation or Cleanup Is Finished?

You must have completely fixed the water or moisture problem before the cleanup or remediation can be considered finished.

- You should have completed mold removal. Visible mold and moldy odors should not be present. Please note that mold may cause staining and cosmetic damage.

- You should have revisited the site(s) shortly after cleanup and it should show no signs of water damage or mold growth.

- People should have been able to occupy or re-occupy the area without health complaints or physical symptoms.

- Ultimately, this is a judgment call; there is no easy answer.

Moisture and Mold Prevention and Control Tips

- When water leaks or spills occur indoors – **ACT QUICKLY**. If wet or damp materials or areas are dried 24-48 hours after a leak or spill happens, in most cases mold will not grow.

- Clean and repair roof gutters regularly.

- Make sure the ground slopes away from the building foundation, so that water does not enter or collect around the foundation.

- Keep air conditioning drip pans clean and the drain lines unobstructed and flowing properly.

- Keep indoor humidity low. If possible, keep indoor humidity below 60 percent (ideally between 30 and 50 percent) relative humidity. Relative humidity can be measured with a moisture or humidity meter, a small, inexpensive ($10–$50) instrument available at many hardware stores.

- If you see condensation or moisture collecting on windows, walls or pipes ACT QUICKLY to dry the wet surface and reduce the moisture/water source. Condensation can be a sign of high humidity.

Actions that will help to reduce humidity

- Vent appliances that produce moisture, such as clothes dryers, stoves, and kerosene heaters to the outside where possible. (Combustion appliances such as stoves and kerosene heaters produce water vapor and will increase the humidity unless vented to the outside.)

- Use air conditioners and/or de-humidifiers when needed.

- Run the bathroom fan or open the window when showering. Use exhaust fans or open windows whenever cooking, running the dishwasher or dishwashing, etc.

Actions that will help prevent condensation

- Reduce the humidity.

- Increase ventilation or air movement by opening doors and/or windows, when practical. Use fans as needed.

- Cover cold surfaces, such as cold water pipes, with insulation.

- Increase air temperature.

Testing or Sampling for Mold

Is sampling for mold needed? **In most cases, if visible mold growth is present, sampling is unnecessary.** Since no EPA or other federal limits have been set for mold or mold spores, sampling cannot be used to check a building's compliance with federal mold standards. Surface sampling may be useful to determine if an area has been adequately cleaned or remediated. Sampling for mold should be conducted by professionals who have specific experience in designing mold sampling protocols, sampling methods, and interpreting results. Sample analysis should follow analytical methods recommended by the American Industrial Hygiene Association (AIHA), the American Conference of Governmental Industrial Hygienists (ACGIH), or other professional organizations.

Hidden Mold

Suspicion of hidden mold

You may suspect hidden mold if a building smells moldy, but you cannot see the source, or if you know there has been water damage and residents are reporting health problems. Mold may be hidden in places such as the back side of dry wall, wallpaper, or paneling, the top side of ceiling tiles, the underside of carpets and pads, etc. Other possible locations of hidden mold include areas inside walls around pipes (with leaking or condensing pipes), the surface of walls behind furniture (where condensation forms), inside ductwork, and in roof materials above ceiling tiles (due to roof leaks or insufficient insulation).

Investigating hidden mold problems

Investigating hidden mold problems may be difficult and will require caution when the investigation involves disturbing potential sites of mold growth. For example, removal of wallpaper can lead to a massive release of spores if there is mold growing on the underside of the paper. If you believe that you may have a hidden mold problem, consider hiring an experienced professional.

Cleanup and Biocides

Biocides are substances that can destroy living organisms. The use of a chemical or biocide that kills organisms such as mold (chlorine bleach, for example) is not recommended as a routine practice during

413

mold cleanup. There may be instances, however, when professional judgment may indicate its use (for example, when immune-compromised individuals are present). In most cases, it is not possible or desirable to sterilize an area; a background level of mold spores will remain—these spores will not grow if the moisture problem has been resolved. If you choose to use disinfectants or biocides, always ventilate the area and exhaust the air to the outdoors. Never mix chlorine bleach solution with other cleaning solutions or detergents that contain ammonia because toxic fumes could be produced.

Please note: Dead mold may still cause allergic reactions in some people, so it is not enough to simply kill the mold, it must also be removed.

Chapter 25

Asbestos

Highlights

Exposure to asbestos usually occurs by breathing contaminated air in workplaces that make or use asbestos. Asbestos is also found in the air of buildings containing asbestos that are being torn down or renovated. Asbestos exposure can cause serious lung problems and cancer. This substance has been found in at least 83 of the 1,585 National Priorities List sites identified by the Environmental Protection Agency (EPA).

What is asbestos?

Asbestos is the name given to a group of six different fibrous minerals (amosite, chrysotile, crocidolite, and the fibrous varieties of tremolite, actinolite, and anthophyllite) that occur naturally in the environment. Asbestos minerals have separable long fibers that are strong and flexible enough to be spun and woven and are heat resistant. Because of these characteristics, asbestos has been used for a wide range of manufactured goods, mostly in building materials (roofing shingles, ceiling and floor tiles, paper products, and asbestos cement products), friction products (automobile clutch, brake, and transmission parts), heat-resistant fabrics, packaging, gaskets, and coatings. Some vermiculite or talc products may contain asbestos.

Text in this chapter is excerpted from "Toxic Substances Portal—Asbestos," Agency for Toxic Substances and Disease Registry (ATSDR), October 26, 2011.

What happens to asbestos when it enters the environment?

Asbestos fibers can enter the air or water from the breakdown of natural deposits and manufactured asbestos products. Asbestos fibers do not evaporate into air or dissolve in water. Small diameter fibers and particles may remain suspended in the air for a long time and be carried long distances by wind or water before settling down. Larger diameter fibers and particles tend to settle more quickly.

Asbestos fibers are not able to move through soil. Asbestos fibers are generally not broken down to other compounds and will remain virtually unchanged over long periods.

How might I be exposed to asbestos?

We are all exposed to low levels of asbestos in the air we breathe. These levels range from 0.00001 to 0.0001 fibers per milliliter of air and generally are highest in cities and industrial areas.

People working in industries that make or use asbestos products or who are involved in asbestos mining may be exposed to high levels of asbestos. People living near these industries may also be exposed to high levels of asbestos in air.

Asbestos fibers may be released into the air by the disturbance of asbestos-containing material during product use, demolition work, building or home maintenance, repair, and remodeling. In general, exposure may occur only when the asbestos-containing material is disturbed in some way to release particles and fibers into the air.

Drinking water may contain asbestos from natural sources or from asbestos-containing cement pipes.

How can asbestos affect my health?

Asbestos mainly affects the lungs and the membrane that surrounds the lungs. Breathing high levels of asbestos fibers for a long time may result in scar-like tissue in the lungs and in the pleural membrane (lining) that surrounds the lung. This disease is called asbestosis and is usually found in workers exposed to asbestos, but not in the general public. People with asbestosis have difficulty breathing, often a cough, and in severe cases heart enlargement. Asbestosis is a serious disease and can eventually lead to disability and death.

Breathing lower levels of asbestos may result in changes called plaques in the pleural membranes. Pleural plaques can occur in workers and sometimes in people living in areas with high environmental levels of asbestos. Effects on breathing from pleural plaques alone are not usually serious, but higher exposure can lead to a thickening of the pleural membrane that may restrict breathing.

How likely is asbestos to cause cancer?

The Department of Health and Human Services (DHHS), the World Health Organization (WHO), and the EPA have determined that asbestos is a human carcinogen.

It is known that breathing asbestos can increase the risk of cancer in people. There are two types of cancer caused by exposure to asbestos: lung cancer and mesothelioma. Mesothelioma is a cancer of the thin lining surrounding the lung (pleural membrane) or abdominal cavity (the peritoneum). Cancer from asbestos does not develop immediately, but shows up after a number of years. Studies of workers also suggest that breathing asbestos can increase chances of getting cancer in other parts of the body (stomach, intestines, esophagus, pancreas, and kidneys), but this is less certain. Early identification and treatment of any cancer can increase an individual's quality of life and survival.

Cigarette smoke and asbestos together significantly increase your chances of getting lung cancer. Therefore, if you have been exposed to asbestos you should stop smoking. This may be the most important action that you can take to improve your health and decrease your risk of cancer.

How can asbestos affect children?

We do not know if exposure to asbestos will result in birth defects or other developmental effects in people. Birth defects have not been observed in animals exposed to asbestos.

It is likely that health effects seen in children exposed to high levels of asbestos will be similar to the effects seen in adults.

How can families reduce the risk of exposure to asbestos?

Materials containing asbestos that are not disturbed or deteriorated do not, in general, pose a health risk and can be left alone. If you suspect that you may be exposed to asbestos in your home, contact your state or local health department or the regional offices of EPA to find out how to test your home and how to locate a company that is trained to remove or contain the fibers.

Is there a medical test to show whether I've been exposed to asbestos?

Low levels of asbestos fibers can be measured in urine, feces, mucus, or lung washings of the general public. Higher than average levels of asbestos fibers in tissue can confirm exposure but not determine whether you will experience any health effects.

A thorough history, physical exam, and diagnostic tests are needed to evaluate asbestos-related disease. Chest x-rays are the best screening tool to identify lung changes resulting from asbestos exposure. Lung function tests and computerized axial tomography (CAT) scans also assist in the diagnosis of asbestos-related disease.

Has the federal government made recommendations to protect human health?

In 1989, EPA banned all new uses of asbestos; uses established before this date are still allowed. EPA established regulations that require school systems to inspect for damaged asbestos and to eliminate or reduce the exposure by removing the asbestos or by covering it up. EPA regulates the release of asbestos from factories and during building demolition or renovation to prevent asbestos from getting into the environment.

EPA has proposed a concentration limit of 7 million fibers per liter of drinking water for long fibers (lengths greater than or equal to 5 μm).

The Occupational Safety and Health Administration has set limits of 100,000 fibers with lengths greater than or equal to 5 μm per cubic meter of workplace air for 8-hour shifts and 40-hour work weeks.

Chapter 26

Lead at Home

Sources of Lead at Home

Older Homes and Buildings

If your home was built before 1978, there is a good chance it has lead-based paint. In 1978, the federal government banned consumer uses of lead-containing paint, but some states banned it even earlier. Lead from paint, including lead-contaminated dust, is one of the most common causes of lead poisoning.

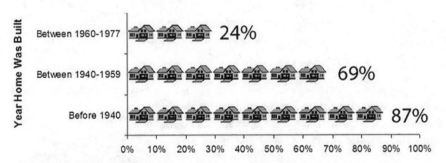

Figure 26.1. *Older Homes are More Likely to Contain Lead-Based Paint*

Text in this chapter is excerpted from "Lead—Protect Your Family," United States Environmental Protection Agency (EPA), June 9, 2015.

- Lead paint is still present in millions of homes, sometimes under layers of newer paint. If the paint is in good shape, the lead paint is usually not a problem. Deteriorating lead-based paint (peeling, chipping, chalking, cracking, damaged, or damp) is a hazard and needs immediate attention.

- It may also be a hazard when found on surfaces that children can chew or that get a lot of wear-and-tear, such as:

  - Windows and window sills

  - Doors and door frames

  - Stairs, railings, banisters, and porches

- Be sure to keep all paint in excellent shape and clean up dust frequently.

- Lead in household dust results from indoor sources such as deteriorating lead-based paint.

- Lead dust can also be tracked into the home from soil outside that is contaminated by deteriorated exterior lead-based paint and other lead sources, such as industrial pollution and past use of leaded gasoline.

- Renovation, repair or painting activities can create toxic lead dust when painted surfaces are disturbed or demolished.

- Pipes and solder—Lead is used in some water service lines and household plumbing materials. Lead can leach, or enter the water, as water flows through the plumbing. Lead pipes and lead solder were commonly used until 1986.

Soil, Yards, and Playgrounds

Lead is naturally-occurring, and it can be found in high concentrations in some areas. In addition, soil, yards and playgrounds can become contaminated when exterior lead-based paint from houses or buildings flakes or peels and gets into the soil. Soil may also be contaminated from past use of leaded gasoline in cars, from industrial sources, or even from contaminated sites, including former lead smelters.

Lead in soil can be ingested as a result of hand-to-mouth activity that is common for young children and from eating vegetables that may have taken up lead from soil in the garden. Lead in soil may also be inhaled if resuspended in the air, or tracked into your house thereby spreading the contamination.

Check the exterior of your home, including porches and fences, for flaking or deteriorating lead-based paint that may contaminate soil in your yard or be tracked into your house. To avoid tracking contaminated soil into your house, put doormats outside and inside all entryways, and remove your shoes before entering.

To reduce exposure to lead, after playing or working outdoors, EPA recommends that children and adults leave their shoes at the door or use door mats, and wash their hands. To keep children from playing in soil near your home, plant bushes close to the house.

Also, older playground equipment can still contain old lead-based paint, and artificial turf and playground surfaces made from shredded rubber can contain lead. Take precautions to ensure young children do not eat shredded rubber, or put their hands in their mouth before washing them.

Dust

Lead in household dust results from indoor sources such as old lead paint on surfaces that are frequently in motion or bump or rub together (such as window frames), deteriorating old lead paint on any surface, home repair activities, tracking lead contaminated soil from the outdoors into the indoor environment, or even from lead dust on clothing worn at a job site.

Even in well-maintained homes, lead dust can form when lead-based paint is scraped, sanded or heated during home repair activities. Lead paint chips and dust can get on surfaces and objects that people touch. Settled lead dust can re-enter the air when the home is vacuumed or swept, or people walk through it. To reduce exposure to lead dust, it is especially important to maintain all painted surfaces in good condition, and to clean frequently, to reduce the likelihood of chips and dust forming. Using a lead-safe certified renovator to perform renovation, repair and painting jobs is a good way to reduce the likelihood of contaminating your home with lead-based paint dust.

Products

Lead can be found in many products:

- **Painted toys, furniture and toy jewelry**— That favorite dump truck or rocking chair handed down in the family, antique doll furniture, or toy jewelry could contain lead-based paint or contain lead in the material it is made from. Biting or swallowing toys or toy jewelry that contain lead can cause a child to suffer from lead poisoning.

421

Cosmetics

- **Food or liquid containers** — Food and liquids stored or served in lead crystal or lead-glazed pottery or porcelain can become contaminated because lead can leach from these containers into the food or liquid.

- **Plumbing products** — Materials like pipes and fixtures that contain lead can corrode over time.

Drinking Water

Lead can enter drinking water through corrosion of plumbing materials, especially where the water has high acidity or low mineral content that corrodes pipes and fixtures. Homes built before 1986 are more likely to have lead pipes, fixtures and solder. However, new homes are also at risk: even legally "lead-free" plumbing may contain up to eight percent lead. Beginning January 2014, changes to the Safe Drinking Water Act will further reduce the maximum allowable lead content of pipes, pipe fittings, plumbing fittings, and fixtures to 0.25 percent. The most common problem is with brass or chrome-plated brass faucets and fixtures with lead solder, from which significant amounts of lead can enter into the water, especially hot water.

Corrosion is a dissolving or wearing away of metal caused by a chemical reaction between water and your plumbing. A number of factors are involved in the extent to which lead enters the water including the chemistry of the water (acidity and alkalinity), the amount of lead it comes into contact with, how long the water stays in the plumbing materials, and the presence of protective scales or coatings inside the plumbing materials.

To address corrosion of lead and copper into drinking water, EPA issued the Lead and Copper Rule (LCR) under the authority of the Safe Drinking Water Act. The LCR requires corrosion control treatment to prevent lead and copper from contaminating drinking water. Corrosion control treatment means systems must make drinking water less corrosive to the materials it comes into contact with on its way to consumers' taps.

Jobs and Hobbies

You could bring lead home on your hands or clothes, or contaminate your home directly if you:

- Work with lead and/or lead-based paint (for example, renovation and painting, mining, smelting, battery recycling, refinishing old furniture, autobody, shooting ranges).

- Have a hobby that uses lead (for example, hunting, fishing, stained glass, stock cars, making pottery).

- Lead can be found in shot, fishing sinkers and jigs, came and solder used in stained glass, weights used in stock cars, dyes and glazes used in pottery, and many other places.

If you have a job or hobby where you may come into contact with lead:

- never put leaded materials (for example, fishing sinkers, lead came or solder for stained glass or leaded pottery clay or glaze) in your mouth,

- avoid handling food or touching your mouth or face while engaged in working with lead materials and wash hands before eating or drinking following such activities,

- shower and change clothes before entering your vehicle or coming home,

- launder your work and hobby clothes separately from the rest of your family's clothes, and

- keep all work and hobby materials away from living areas.

Folk Remedies

Some folk remedies that contain lead, such as "greta" and "azarcon," are used to treat an upset stomach. Some folk remedies for morning sickness, including "nzu," "poto" and "calabash chalk," contain dangerous levels of lead and other chemicals. Consuming even small amounts of lead can be harmful. Lead poisoning from folk remedies can cause serious and irreversible illness.

How to make your home lead-safe

Check Your Home

If your home was built before 1978, have your home tested for lead and learn about potential lead hazards. Fix any hazards that you may have. You can get your home checked in one or both of the following ways:

- A paint inspection—Tells you the lead content of every different type of painted surface in your home, but does not tell you if the paint is a hazard or how to deal with it. This is most appropriate when you are buying a home or signing a lease, before you renovate, and to help you determine how to maintain your home for lead safety.

- A risk assessment—Tells you if there are any sources of serious lead exposure such as peeling paint and lead dust, and tells you what actions to take to address these hazards. This is most helpful if you want to know if lead is causing exposure to your family now.

Have qualified professionals do the work. There are standards in place for certifying lead-based paint professionals to ensure the work is done safely, reliably, and effectively. You can have a combined risk assessment and inspection.

Maintain Your Home's Condition

It is very important to care for the lead-painted surfaces in your home. Lead-based paint in good condition is usually not harmful. If your home was built before 1978:

- Regularly check your home for chipping, peeling, or deteriorating paint, and address issues promptly without excessive sanding. If you must sand, sand the minimum area needed, wet the area first, and clean up thoroughly.

- Regularly check all painted areas that rub together or get lots of wear, like windows, doors, and stairways, for any signs of deterioration.

- Regularly check for paint chips or dust – if you see some, remove carefully with a damp paper towel and discard in the trash, then wipe the surface clean with a wet paper towel.

- Wipe down flat surfaces, like window sills, at least weekly with a damp paper towel and throw away the paper towel.

- Mop smooth floors (using a damp mop) weekly to control dust.

- Remember to test for the presence of lead and lead hazards by a lead professional – this will tell you where you must be especially careful.

Here are more tips to help you reduce or prevent your family's exposure to lead dust. It's best to follow these steps weekly.

Cleaning Uncarpeted Floors

Do use:

- Damp mopping, with standard sponge or string type mops and an all-purpose cleaner.
- Standard vacuum cleaners if no visible dust or debris from chipping or flaking paint is present.

Don't use:

- Mops with a scrubber strip attached.
- Powered buffing or polishing machines, or vacuums with beater bars that may wear away the painted surface.

Cleaning Carpets and Rugs

Do use:

- Wet scrubbing or steam cleaning methods to remove stains.
- Standard vacuum cleaners if no visible dust or debris from chipping or flaking paint is present. Use only vacuums with HEPA filters otherwise.

Don't use:

- Dry sweeping of surface dust and debris.
- Shaking or beating of carpets and rugs.

Cleaning or Dusting Walls and other Painted Surfaces

Do use:

- Soft, dampened, disposable cloths with an all-purpose cleaner.

Don't use:

- Steel wool, scouring pads, and abrasive cleaners.
- Solvent cleaners that may dissolve paint.
- Excessive rubbing of spots to remove them.

Before you renovate

- Find a lead-safe certified renovation firm in your area. Renovations, repair jobs and paint jobs in pre-1978 homes and buildings can create significant amounts of lead-based paint dust. If your contractor will disturb lead-based paint while renovating, repairing or painting your home, he or she must be trained in lead-safe work practices.

- Read EPA's fact sheet on using a lead-safe certified contractor.

- If you are a do-it yourselfer, learn how to protect yourself and your family from exposure to lead-based paint.

- If you are a renter, learn your rights.

Test your home's drinking water

Testing your home's drinking water is the only way to confirm if lead is present. Most water systems test for lead at a certain number of homes as a regular part of water monitoring. These tests give a system-wide picture of whether or not corrosion is being controlled but do not reflect conditions at each home served by that water system. Since each home has different plumbing pipes and materials, test results are likely to be different for each home.

You may want to test your water if:

- your home has lead pipes (lead is a dull gray metal that is soft enough to be easily scratched with a house key), or

- your non-plastic plumbing was installed before 1986.

You can buy lead testing kits in home improvement stores to collect samples to then send to a laboratory for analysis. EPA recommends sending samples to a certified laboratory for analysis; lists are available from state or local drinking water authority. Your water supplier may also have useful information, including whether the service line connecting your home to the water main is made of lead.

If your home tests positive for lead:

- **Flush your pipes before drinking, and only use cold water for cooking and drinking.** Anytime the water in a particular faucet has not been used for six hours or longer, flush your cold-water pipes by running the water until it becomes cold. Contact your water utility to verify flushing times for your area.

- **Consider replacing lead-containing plumbing fixtures.** If you are considering this, keep in mind that the Safe Drinking Water Act (SDWA) requires that only lead-free pipe, solder, or flux may be used in the installation or repair of a public water system, or any plumbing in residential or non-residential facility providing water for human consumption. "Lead-free" under the SDWA means that solders and flux may not contain more than 0.2 percent lead, and pipe, pipe fittings, and well pumps may not contain more than 8.0 percent lead. Beginning January 2014, changes to the Safe Drinking Water Act will further reduce the maximum allowable lead content of pipes, pipe fittings, plumbing fittings, and fixtures to 0.25 percent.

SDWA also requires plumbing fittings and fixtures intended to dispense water for human consumption (e.g., kitchen and bathroom faucets) meet a lead leaching standard. Those fittings and fixtures should be certified according to NSF/ANSI Standard 61 for lead reduction.

- **Consider alternative sources or treatment of water.** If you discover that you have high levels of lead in your home, you should consider using bottled water or a water filter. There are many home water filters that are certified for effective lead reduction, but devices that are not designed to remove lead will not work. Verify the claims of manufacturers by checking with independent certifying organizations. NSF International and the Water Quality Association provide lists of treatment devices they have certified. Underwriters Laboratoriesis also a good resource for certified devices. Be sure to maintain and replace a filter device in accordance with the manufacturer's instructions to protect water quality.

Refer to the manufacturer's instructions for maintenance procedures. If not maintained properly, some treatment devices may increase lead and other contaminant levels.

Protect your children where they learn and play

Lead poisoning is entirely preventable. Learn what you can do to stop children from coming into contact with lead before they are harmed.

Test your child

Find out if your child has elevated levels of lead in his or her blood. Because lead poisoning often occurs with no obvious symptoms, it

427

frequently goes unrecognized. You can test your child for lead poisoning by asking your pediatrician to do a simple blood test. Children with elevated blood lead levels can have serious health effects. If you know your child has lead poisoning, talk to your pediatrician and local health agency about what you can do.

Check the condition of schools and childcare facilities

Although your home may be free of lead-based paint hazards, your child could still be exposed elsewhere, particularly if they spend time in a building built before 1978. Ask your child's school board or facilities manager if they regularly inspect for lead hazards. Here is a list of places to look:

- Interior painted areas—Examine walls and interior surfaces to see if the paint is cracking, chipping, or peeling, and check areas on doors or windows where painted surfaces may rub together.

- Exterior painted areas—Check exterior paint as well; it can flake off and contaminate nearby soil where children may play.

- Surrounding areas—Be sure there are no large structures nearby with peeling or flaking paint that could contaminate the soil around play areas.

- Cleaning practices—Make sure the staff washes any pacifiers, toys, or bottles that fall on the floor. Also, make sure the staff has the children wash their hands thoroughly after playing outside and before eating or sleeping.

- Play areas—Look to see if areas where children play are dust-free and clean. Outside, check for bare soil and test for lead.

- Playground equipment—Older equipment can contain lead-based paint.

- Painted toys and furniture—Make sure the paint is not cracking, chipping, or peeling. Inquire about whether a childcare center's toys comply with the requirements of the Consumer Product Safety Commission (CPSC).

- Also, ask about testing all of the drinking water outlets in the facility and on the playground, especially those that provide water for drinking, cooking, and preparing juice and infant formula.

Chapter 27

Volatile Organic Compounds (VOCs)

Volatile organic compounds (VOCs) are emitted as gases from certain solids or liquids. VOCs include a variety of chemicals, some of which may have short- and long-term adverse health effects. Concentrations of many VOCs are consistently higher indoors (up to ten times higher) than outdoors. VOCs are emitted by a wide array of products numbering in the thousands. Examples include: paints and lacquers, paint strippers, cleaning supplies, pesticides, building materials and furnishings, office equipment such as copiers and printers, correction fluids and carbonless copy paper, graphics and craft materials including glues and adhesives, permanent markers, and photographic solutions.

Organic chemicals are widely used as ingredients in household products. Paints, varnishes, and wax all contain organic solvents, as do many cleaning, disinfecting, cosmetic, degreasing, and hobby products. Fuels are made up of organic chemicals. All of these products can release organic compounds while you are using them, and to some degree, when they are stored.

EPA's Office of Research and Development's "Total Exposure Assessment Methodology (TEAM) Study" (Volumes I through IV, completed in 1985) found levels of about a dozen common organic

Text in this chapter is excerpted from "Indoor Air—An Introduction to Indoor Air Quality (IAQ)," United States Environmental Protection Agency (EPA), July 10, 2012.

pollutants to be 2 to 5 times higher inside homes than outside, regardless of whether the homes were located in rural or highly industrial areas. TEAM studies indicated that while people are using products containing organic chemicals, they can expose themselves and others to very high pollutant levels, and elevated concentrations can persist in the air long after the activity is completed.

Sources

Household products including: paints, paint strippers, and other solvents; wood preservatives; aerosol sprays; cleansers and disinfectants; moth repellents and air fresheners; stored fuels and automotive products; hobby supplies; dry-cleaned clothing.

Health Effects

Eye, nose, and throat irritation; headaches, loss of coordination, nausea; damage to liver, kidney, and central nervous system. Some organics can cause cancer in animals; some are suspected or known to cause cancer in humans. Key signs or symptoms associated with exposure to VOCs include conjunctival irritation, nose and throat discomfort, headache, allergic skin reaction, dyspnea, declines in serum cholinesterase levels, nausea, emesis, epistaxis, fatigue, and dizziness.

The ability of organic chemicals to cause health effects varies greatly from those that are highly toxic, to those with no known health effect. As with other pollutants, the extent and nature of the health effect will depend on many factors including level of exposure and length of time exposed. Eye and respiratory tract irritation, headaches, dizziness, visual disorders, and memory impairment are among the immediate symptoms that some people have experienced soon after exposure to some organics. At present, not much is known about what health effects occur from the levels of organics usually found in homes. Many organic compounds are known to cause cancer in animals; some are suspected of causing, or are known to cause cancer in humans.

Levels in Homes

Studies have found that levels of several organics average 2 to 5 times higher indoors than outdoors. During and for several hours immediately after certain activities, such as paint stripping, levels may be 1,000 times background outdoor levels.

Steps to Reduce Exposure

Increase ventilation when using products that emit VOCs. Meet or exceed any label precautions. Do not store opened containers of unused paints and similar materials within the school. Formaldehyde, one of the best known VOCs, is one of the few indoor air pollutants that can be readily measured. Identify, and if possible, remove the source. If not possible to remove, reduce exposure by using a sealant on all exposed surfaces of paneling and other furnishings. Use integrated pest management techniques to reduce the need for pesticides.

- Use household products according to manufacturer's directions.

- Make sure you provide plenty of fresh air when using these products.

- Throw away unused or little-used containers safely; buy in quantities that you will use soon.

- Keep out of reach of children and pets.

- Never mix household care products unless directed on the label.

Follow label instructions carefully.

Potentially hazardous products often have warnings aimed at reducing exposure of the user. For example, if a label says to use the product in a well-ventilated area, go outdoors or in areas equipped with an exhaust fan to use it. Otherwise, open up windows to provide the maximum amount of outdoor air possible.

Throw away partially full containers of old or unneeded chemicals safely.

Because gases can leak even from closed containers, this single step could help lower concentrations of organic chemicals in your home. (Be sure that materials you decide to keep are stored not only in a well-ventilated area but are also safely out of reach of children.) Do not simply toss these unwanted products in the garbage can. Find out if your local government or any organization in your community sponsors special days for the collection of toxic household wastes. If such days are available, use them to dispose of the unwanted containers safely. If no such collection days are available, think about organizing one.

Buy limited quantities.

If you use products only occasionally or seasonally, such as paints, paint strippers, and kerosene for space heaters or gasoline for lawn mowers, buy only as much as you will use right away.

Keep exposure to emissions from products containing methylene chloride to a minimum.

Consumer products that contain methylene chloride include paint strippers, adhesive removers, and aerosol spray paints. Methylene chloride is known to cause cancer in animals. Also, methylene chloride is converted to carbon monoxide in the body and can cause symptoms associated with exposure to carbon monoxide. Carefully read the labels containing health hazard information and cautions on the proper use of these products. Use products that contain methylene chloride outdoors when possible; use indoors only if the area is well ventilated.

Keep exposure to benzene to a minimum.

Benzene is a known human carcinogen. The main indoor sources of this chemical are environmental tobacco smoke, stored fuels and paint supplies, and automobile emissions in attached garages. Actions that will reduce benzene exposure include eliminating smoking within the home, providing for maximum ventilation during painting, and discarding paint supplies and special fuels that will not be used immediately.

Keep exposure to perchloroethylene emissions from newly dry-cleaned materials to a minimum.

Perchloroethylene is the chemical most widely used in dry cleaning. In laboratory studies, it has been shown to cause cancer in animals. Recent studies indicate that people breathe low levels of this chemical both in homes where dry-cleaned goods are stored and as they wear dry-cleaned clothing. Dry cleaners recapture the perchloroethylene during the dry-cleaning process so they can save money by re-using it, and they remove more of the chemical during the pressing and finishing processes. Some dry cleaners, however, do not remove as much perchloroethylene as possible all of the time. Taking steps to minimize your exposure to this chemical is prudent. If dry-cleaned goods have a strong chemical odor when you pick them up, do not accept them until they have been properly dried. If goods with a chemical odor are returned to you on subsequent visits, try a different dry cleaner.

Chapter 28

Radiation Exposure Risks

Chapter Contents

Section 28.1

Microwave and Radiation Risks

Text in this section is excerpted from "Radiation-Emitting Products—
Microwave Oven Radiation," U.S. Food and Drug Administration
(FDA), October 8, 2014.

About Microwaves

Microwaves are used to detect speeding cars, to send telephone and
television communications, and to treat muscle soreness. Industry
uses microwaves to dry and cure plywood, to cure rubber and resins,
to raise bread and doughnuts, and to cook potato chips. But the most
common consumer use of microwave energy is in microwave ovens.

The Food and Drug Administration (FDA) has regulated the manufacture of microwave ovens since 1971. On the basis of current knowledge about microwave radiation, the Agency believes that ovens that
meet the FDA standard and are used according to the manufacturer's
instructions are safe for use.

What is Microwave Radiation?

Microwaves are a form of "electromagnetic" radiation; that is, they
are waves of electrical and magnetic energy moving together through
space. Electromagnetic radiation ranges from the energetic x-rays to
the less energetic radio frequency waves used in broadcasting. Microwaves fall into the radio frequency band of electromagnetic radiation. Microwaves should not be confused with x-rays, which are more
powerful.

Microwaves have three characteristics that allow them to be used
in cooking: they are reflected by metal; they pass through glass, paper,
plastic, and similar materials; and they are absorbed by foods.

Cooking with Microwaves

Microwaves are produced inside the oven by an electron tube called
a magnetron. The microwaves are reflected within the metal interior

of the oven where they are absorbed by food. Microwaves cause water molecules in food to vibrate, producing heat that cooks the food. That's why foods high in water content, like fresh vegetables, can be cooked more quickly than other foods. The microwave energy is changed to heat as it is absorbed by food, and does not make food "radioactive" or "contaminated."

Although heat is produced directly in the food, microwave ovens do not cook food from the "inside out." When thick foods are cooked, the outer layers are heated and cooked primarily by microwaves while the inside is cooked mainly by the conduction of heat from the hot outer layers.

Microwave cooking can be more energy efficient than conventional cooking because foods cook faster and the energy heats only the food, not the whole oven compartment. Microwave cooking does not reduce the nutritional value of foods any more than conventional cooking. In fact, foods cooked in a microwave oven may keep more of their vitamins and minerals, because microwave ovens can cook more quickly and without adding water.

Glass, paper, ceramic, or plastic containers are used in microwave cooking because microwaves pass through these materials. Although such containers can not be heated by microwaves, they can become hot from the heat of the food cooking inside. Some plastic containers should not be used in a microwave oven because they can be melted by the heat of the food inside. Generally, metal pans or aluminum foil should also not be used in a microwave oven, as the microwaves are reflected off these materials causing the food to cook unevenly and possibly damaging the oven. The instructions that come with each microwave oven indicate the kinds of containers to use. They also cover how to test containers to see whether or not they can be used in microwave ovens.

FDA recommends that microwave ovens not be used in home canning. It is believed that neither microwave ovens nor conventional ovens produce or maintain temperatures high enough to kill the harmful bacteria that occur in some foods while canning.

Microwave Oven Safety Standard

The Food and Drug Administration (FDA) has the responsibility for carrying out an electronic product radiation control program mandated by the Electronic Product Radiation Control provisions of the Food Drug and Cosmetic Act. Through its Center for Devices and Radiological Health, FDA sets and enforces standards of performance for electronic products to assure that radiation emissions do not pose a hazard to public health.

435

A Federal standard limits the amount of microwaves that can leak from an oven throughout its lifetime to 5 milliwatts (mW) of microwave radiation per square centimeter at approximately 2 inches from the oven surface. This limit is far below the level known to harm people. Microwave energy also decreases dramatically as you move away from the source of radiation. A measurement made 20 inches from an oven would be approximately one-hundredth of the value measured at 2 inches.

The standard also requires all ovens to have two independent interlock systems that stop the production of microwaves the moment the latch is released or the door opened. In addition, a monitoring system stops oven operation in case one or both of the interlock systems fail. The noise that many ovens continue to make after the door is open is usually the fan. The noise does not mean that microwaves are being produced. There is no residual radiation remaining after microwave production has stopped. In this regard a microwave oven is much like an electric light that stops glowing when it is turned off.

All ovens must have a label stating that they meet the safety standard. In addition, FDA requires that all ovens have a label explaining precautions for use. This requirement may be dropped if the manufacturer has proven that the oven will not exceed the allowable leakage limit even if used under the conditions cautioned against on the label.

To make sure the standard is met, FDA tests microwave ovens in its own laboratory. FDA also evaluates manufacturers' radiation testing and quality control programs at their factories.

Although FDA believes the standard assures that microwave ovens do not present any radiation hazard, the Agency continues to reassess its adequacy as new information becomes available.

Microwave Ovens and Health

Much research is under way on microwaves and how they might affect the human body. It is known that microwave radiation can heat body tissue the same way it heats food. Exposure to **high levels of microwaves** can cause a painful burn. The lens of the eye is particularly sensitive to intense heat, and exposure to high levels of microwaves can cause cataracts. Likewise, the testes are very sensitive to changes in temperature. Accidental exposure to high levels of microwave energy can alter or kill sperm, producing temporary sterility. But these types of injuries—burns, cataracts, temporary sterility—can only be caused by exposure to large amounts of microwave radiation, much more than the 5mW limit for microwave oven leakage.

Less is known about what happens to people exposed to **low lev-els of microwaves**. Controlled, long-term studies involving large numbers of people have not been conducted to assess the impact of low level microwave energy on humans. Much research has been done with experimental animals, but it is difficult to translate the effects of microwaves on animals to possible effects on humans. For one thing, there are differences in the way animals and humans absorb micro-waves. For another, experimental conditions can't exactly simulate the conditions under which people use microwave ovens. However, these studies do help us better understand the possible effects of radiation.

The fact that many scientific questions about exposure to low-lev-els of microwaves are not yet answered require FDA to continue to enforcement of radiation protection requirements. Consumers should take certain common sense precautions.

Have Radiation Injuries Resulted from Microwave Ovens?

There have been allegations of radiation injury from microwave ovens, but none as a direct result of microwave exposure. The injuries known to FDA have been injuries that could have happened with any oven or cooking surface. For example, many people have been burned by the hot food, splattering grease, or steam from food cooked in a microwave oven.

Ovens and Pacemakers

At one time there was concern that leakage from microwave ovens could interfere with certain electronic cardiac pacemakers. Similar concerns were raised about pacemaker interference from electric shav-ers, auto ignition systems, and other electronic products. FDA does not specifically require microwave ovens to carry warnings for peo-ple with pacemakers. The problem has been largely resolved because pacemakers are now designed to be shielded against such electrical interference. However, patients with pacemakers may wish to consult their physicians if they have concerns.

Checking Ovens For Leakage

There is little cause for concern about excess microwaves leak-ing from ovens unless the door hinges, latch, or seals are damaged. In FDA's experience, most ovens tested show little or no detectable microwave leakage. If there is some problem and you believe your oven might be leaking excessive microwaves, contact the oven manufacturer, a microwave oven service organization, your state health department, or the nearest FDA office.

A word of caution about the microwave testing devices being sold to consumers: FDA has tested a number of these devices and found them generally inaccurate and unreliable. If used, they should be relied on only for a very approximate reading. The sophisticated testing devices used by public health authorities to measure oven leakage are far more accurate and are periodically tested and calibrated.

Tips on Safe Microwave Oven Operation

- Follow the manufacturer's instruction manual for recommended operating procedures and safety precautions for your oven model.

- Don't operate an oven if the door does not close firmly or is bent, warped, or otherwise damaged.

- Never operate an oven if you have reason to believe it will continue to operate with the door open.

- As an added safety precaution, don't stand directly against an oven (and don't allow children to do this) for long periods of time while it is operating.

- Users should not heat water or liquids in the microwave oven for excessive amounts of time.

Section 28.2

Cell Phones and Radiation Risks

Text in this section is excerpted from "Radiation-Emitting Products—Cell Phones," U.S. Food and Drug Administration (FDA), October 1, 2014.

Health Issues

Do cell phones pose a health hazard?

Many people are concerned that cell phone radiation will cause cancer or other serious health hazards. The weight of scientific evidence has not linked cell phones with any health problems.

Cell phones emit low levels of radiofrequency energy (RF). Over the past 15 years, scientists have conducted hundreds of studies looking at the biological effects of the radiofrequency energy emitted by cell phones. While some researchers have reported biological changes associated with RF energy, these studies have failed to be replicated. The majority of studies published have failed to show an association between exposure to radiofrequency from a cell phone and health problems.

The low levels of RF cell phones emit while in use are in the microwave frequency range. They also emit RF at substantially reduced time intervals when in the stand-by mode. Whereas high levels of RF can produce health effects (by heating tissue), exposure to low level RF that does not produce heating effects causes no known adverse health effects.

The biological effects of radiofrequency energy should not be confused with the effects from other types of electromagnetic energy.

Very high levels of electromagnetic energy, such as is found in x-rays and gamma rays can ionize biological tissues. Ionization is a process where electrons are stripped away from their normal locations in atoms and molecules. It can permanently damage biological tissues including DNA, the genetic material.

The energy levels associated with radiofrequency energy, including both radio waves and microwaves, are not great enough to cause the ionization of atoms and molecules. Therefore, RF energy is a type of non-ionizing radiation. Other types of non-ionizing radiation include visible light, infrared radiation (heat) and other forms of electromagnetic radiation with relatively low frequencies.

While RF energy doesn't ionize particles, large amounts can increase body temperatures and cause tissue damage. Two areas of the body, the eyes and the testes, are particularly vulnerable to RF heating because there is relatively little blood flow in them to carry away excess heat.

Reducing Exposure: Hands-free Kits and Other Accessories

Steps to reduce exposure to radiofrequency energy

If there is a risk from being exposed to radiofrequency energy (RF) from cell phones—and at this point we do not know that there is—it is probably very small. But if you are concerned about avoiding even potential risks, you can take a few simple steps to minimize your RF exposure.

• Reduce the amount of time spent using your cell phone

• Use speaker mode or a headset to place more distance between your head and the cell phone.

Hands-free kits

Hand-free kits may include audio or Bluetooth headsets and various types of body-worn accessories such as belt-clips and holsters. Combinations of these can be used to reduce RF energy absorption from cell phone.

Headsets can substantially reduce exposure since the phone is held away from the head in the user's hand or in approved body-worn accessories. Cell phones marketed in the U.S. are required to meet RF exposure compliance requirements when used against the head and against the body.

Since there are no known risks from exposure to RF emissions from cell phones, there is no reason to believe that hands-free kits reduce risks. Hands-free kits can be used for convenience and comfort. They are also required by law in many states if you want to use your phone while driving.

Cell phone accessories that claim to shield the head from RF radiation

Since there are no known risks from exposure to RF emissions from cell phones, there is no reason to believe that accessories that claim to shield the head from those emissions reduce risks. Some products that claim to shield the user from RF absorption use special phone cases, while others involve nothing more than a metallic accessory attached to the phone. Studies have shown that these products generally do not work as advertised. Unlike "hand-free" kits, these so-called "shields" may interfere with proper operation of the phone. The phone may be forced to boost its power to compensate, leading to an increase in RF absorption.

Interference with Pacemakers and Other Medical Devices

Potential interference

Radiofrequency energy (RF) from cell phones can interact with some electronic devices. This type of interference is called electromagnetic interference (EMI). For this reason, FDA helped develop a detailed test method to measure EMI of implanted cardiac pacemakers and defibrillators from cell phones. This test method is now part of a standard sponsored by the Association for the Advancement of Medical Instrumentation (AAMI). This standard will allow manufacturers to ensure that cardiac pacemakers and defibrillators are safe from cell phone EMI.

FDA continues to monitor the use of cell phones for possible interactions with other medical devices. Should harmful interference be found to occur, FDA will conduct testing to assess the interference and work to resolve the problem.

Precautions for pacemaker wearers

If EMI were to occur, it could affect a pacemaker in one of three ways:

- Stopping the pacemaker from delivering the stimulating pulses that regulate the heart's rhythm

- Causing the pacemaker to deliver the pulses irregularly

- Causing the pacemaker to ignore the heart's own rhythm and deliver pulses at a fixed rate

But based on current research, cell phones would not seem to pose a significant health problem for the vast majority of pacemaker wearers. Still, people with pacemakers may want to take some simple precautions to be sure that their cell phones don't cause a problem.

- Hold the phone to the ear opposite the side of the body where the pacemaker is implanted to add some extra distance between the pacemaker and the phone

- Avoid placing a turned-on phone next to the pacemaker implant (e.g., don't carry the phone in a shirt or jacket pocket directly over the pacemaker)

Hearing Aids and Cell Phones

People who wear hearing aids or have implanted hearing devices may experience some difficulties when trying to use cell phones. Some cell phones can cause radiofrequency interference with hearing aids, so the user hears high-pitched whistling sounds, buzzes, or static.

Fortunately, the compatibility of cell phones and hearing aids is improving. Some phones have lower radiofrequency emissions or use different technologies that can reduce the unwanted effects on hearing aids. The FCC now requires cell phone manufacturers to test and rate their wireless handsets' hearing aid compatibility using the American National Standards Institute (ANSI) C63.19 standard. These ratings give an indication of the likelihood a cell phone may interfere with hearing aids; the higher the rating, the less likely the cell phone-hearing aid combination will experience undesired interference. Hearing aid users should read and understand these ratings when choosing a cell phone.

Children and Cell Phones

The scientific evidence does not show a danger to any users of cell phones from RF exposure, including children and teenagers. The steps adults can take to reduce RF exposure apply to children and teenagers as well.

- Reduce the amount of time spent on the cell phone

- Use speaker mode or a headset to place more distance between the head and the cell phone.

Some groups sponsored by other national governments have advised that children be discouraged from using cell phones at all. For example, The Stewart Report from the United Kingdom made such a recommendation in December 2000. In this report a group of independent experts noted that no evidence exists that using a cell phone causes brain tumors or other ill effects. Their recommendation to limit cell phone use by children was strictly precautionary; it was not based on scientific evidence that any health hazard exists.

Current Research Results

Is there a connection between certain health problems and exposure to radiofrequency fields via cell phone use?

The results of most studies conducted to date indicate that there is not. In addition, attempts to replicate and confirm the few studies that did show a connection have failed.

According to current data, the FDA believes that the weight of scientific evidence does not show an association between exposure to radiofrequency from cell phones and adverse health outcomes. Still, there is consensus that additional research is warranted to address gaps in knowledge, such as the effects of cell phone use over the long-term and on pediatric populations.

The World Health Organization's International Agency for Research on Cancer Classified Radiofrequency Fields as Possibly Carcinogenic to Humans on May 31, 2011.

The International Agency for Research on Cancer (IARC), through the *Monographs* program, seeks to identify environmental factors that can increase the risk of cancer in humans. IARC uses the following categories to classify environmental agents:

Group 1: Carcinogenic to humans.
Group 2A: Probably carcinogenic to humans.
Group 2B: Possibly carcinogenic to humans.
Group 3: Not classifiable as to its carcinogenicity to humans.
Group 4: Probably not carcinogenic to humans.

IARC has classified radiofrequency fields in Group 2B, possibly carcinogenic to humans.

IARC interprets the 2B classification as meaning there is limited evidence showing radiofrequency carcinogenicity in humans and less than sufficient evidence of carcinogenicity in experimental animals.

For perspective, IARC has classified the following other agents as "possibly carcinogenic to humans":

- Coffee

- Extremely low frequency electromagnetic fields (power line frequency)

- Talc-based body powder

Significant Ongoing Studies

International Cohort Study on Mobile Phone Users (COSMOS)

The COSMOS study aims to conduct long-term health monitoring of a large group of people to determine if there are any health issues linked with long-term exposure to radiofrequency energy from cell phone use. The COSMOS study will follow approximately 300,000 adult cell phone users in Europe for 20 to 30 years.

Risk of brain cancer from exposure to radiofrequency fields in childhood and adolescence (MOBI-KIDS)

MOBI-KIDS is an international study investigating the relationship between exposure to radiofrequency energy from communication technologies, including cell phones, and brain cancer in young people. This is an international, multi-center study involving 14 European and non-European countries.

Surveillance, Epidemiology and End Results (SEER) program of the National Cancer Institute

The SEER Program of the National Cancer Institute (NCI) actively follows cancer statistics in the United States. If cell phones play a role in increasing the risk of brain cancer, rates would be expected to increase. However, between 1987 and 2008, SEER data shows that despite the sharp increase in heavy cell phone use in the U.S., the overall age-adjusted incidence of brain cancer did not increase.

Cell Phone Industry Actions

Although the existing scientific data do not support a change in FDA regulation of cell phones, the FDA has urged the cell phone industry to take a number of steps, including:

- Support additional research on possible biological effects of radiofrequency fields for the type of signal emitted by cell phones;

- Improve cell phone design by minimizing radiofrequency exposure to the user; and

- Cooperate in providing cell phone users with the latest scientific information on health concerns caused by radiofrequency exposure.

Safety Standards

The FDA also is working with voluntary standard setting bodies such as the Institute of Electrical and Electronics Engineers (IEEE), the International Commission on Non-Ionizing Radiation Protection (ICNIRP) and others to assure that safety standards continue to adequately protect the public.

Radiofrequency Background

What is radiofrequency energy (RF)?

Radiofrequency (RF) energy is another name for radio waves. It is one form of electromagnetic energy which consists of waves of electric and magnetic energy moving together (radiating) through space. The area where these waves are found is called an electromagnetic field.

Other forms of electromagnetic energy:

* gamma rays

* x-rays

* light.

Radio waves are created due to the movement of electrical charges in antennas. As they are created, these waves radiate away from the antenna at the speed of light.

Waves are measured by:

* the distances covered by one cycle of the wave (wavelength)

* the number of waves that pass a certain point in one second (frequency).

The frequency of an RF signal is usually expressed in units called hertz (Hz).

* One Hz equals one wave per second.

* One kilohertz (kHz) equals one thousand waves per second

* One megahertz (MHz) equals one million waves per second

* One gigahertz (GHz) equals one billion waves per second.

RF energy includes waves with frequencies ranging from about 3000 waves per second (3 kHz) to 300 billion waves per second (300 GHz).

Microwaves are a subset of radio waves that have frequencies ranging from around 300 million waves per second (300 MHz) to three billion waves per second (3 GHz).

How is radiofrequency energy used?

- Telecommunications
- Radio and TV broadcasting
- Cell phones
- Pagers
- Cordless phones
- Police and fire-department radios
- Point-to-point links (microwave communication links)
- Satellite communications
- Microwave ovens
- Radar
- Industrial heaters and sealers
- Mold plastic
- Glue wood
- Seal leather
- Process food
- Medical uses
- Pacemaker monitoring and programming

Section 28.3

Electric and Magnetic Field (EMF) Exposure

Text in this section is excerpted from "Electric and Magnetic Fields,"
National Institute of Environmental Health Sciences (NIEHS),
September 18, 2014.

Electric and Magnetic Fields

Description

Electric and magnetic fields (EMFs) are invisible areas of energy, often referred to as radiation, that are associated with the use of electrical power and various forms of natural and man-made lighting. EMFs are typically characterized by wavelength or frequency into one of two radioactive categories:

- Non-ionizing: low-level radiation which is generally perceived as harmless to humans

- Ionizing: high-level radiation which has the potential for cellular and DNA damage

Table 28.1. Radiation—Facts

Radiation Type	Definition	Forms of Radiation	Source Examples
Non-Ionizing	Low to mid-frequency radiation which is generally perceived as harmless due to its lack of potency.	• Extremely Low Frequency (ELF) • Radiofrequency (RF) • Microwaves • Visual Light	• Microwave ovens • Computers • House energy smart meters • Wireless (wifi) networks • Cell Phones • Bluetooth devices • Power lines • MRIs

Table 28.1. Continued

Radiation Type	Definition	Forms of Radiation	Source Examples
Ionizing	Mid to high-frequency radiation which can, under certain circumstances, lead to cellular and or DNA damage with prolonged exposure.	• Ultraviolet (UV) • X-Rays • Gamma	• Ultraviolet light • X-Rays ranging from $30 * 10^{16}$ Hz to $30 * 10^{19}$ Hz • Some gamma rays

Electromagnetic Spectrum

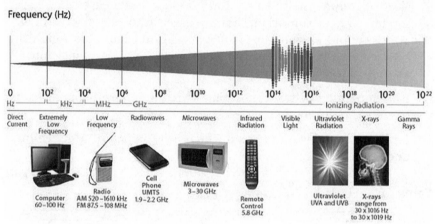

Figure 28.1. Range of Frequency

Can EMFs be harmful to my health?

During the 1990s, most EMF research focused on extremely low frequency exposures stemming from conventional power sources, such as power lines, electrical substations, or home appliances. While some of these studies showed a possible link between EMF field strength and an increased risk for childhood leukemia, their findings indicated that such an association was weak. Now, in the age of cellular telephones, wireless routers, and portable GPS devices (all known sources of EMF radiation), concerns regarding a possible connection between EMFs and adverse health effects still persists, though current research continues to point to the same weak association.

Additionally, the few studies that have been conducted on adults show no evidence of a link between EMF exposure and adult cancers, such as leukemia, brain cancer, and breast cancer. Nevertheless, NIEHS recommends continued education on practical ways of reducing exposures to EMFs.

Does my cell phone emit EMF radiation?

Measured in units called hertz, cell phone emissions, a form of radiofrequency radiation, exist at the lower end of the non-ionizing radiation spectrum at the 900–1900 megahertz range. At present, the weight of the current scientific evidence has not conclusively linked cell phone use with any adverse health problems, though scientists admit that more research is needed. To that end, the National Toxicology Program (NTP), headquartered at NIEHS, is leading the largest laboratory rodent study, to date, on cell phone radiofrequency exposure, the findings of which are expected sometime in 2015.

What if I live near a power line?

It is important to remember that the strength of a magnetic field decreases dramatically with increasing distance from the source. This means that the strength of the field reaching a house or structure will be significantly weaker than it was at its point of origin, a concept which is illustrated on page 37 of the NIEHS educational booklet, "EMF: Electric and Magnetic Fields Associated with the Use of Electric Power." For example, a magnetic field measuring 57.5 milligauss immediately beside a 230 kilovolt transmission line measures just 7.1 milligauss at a distance of 100 feet, and 1.8 milligauss at a distance of 200 feet.

How can I find out if I'm being exposed to EMFs?

If you are concerned about EMFs emitted by a power line or substation in your area, you can contact your local power company to schedule an on-site reading. You can also measure EMFs yourself with the use of a gaussmeter, which is available for purchase online through a number of retailers.

Part Five

Foodborne Hazards

Chapter 29

Food Safety

Chapter Contents

Section 29.1

Food Safety at Home

Text in this section is excerpted from "Charts: Food Safety at a Glance," FoodSafety.gov, U.S. Department of Health & Human Services (DHHS), July 16, 2015.

Preparing and Cooking Food

One of the basics of food safety is cooking food to its proper temperature. Foods are properly cooked when they are heated for a long enough time and at a high enough temperature to kill the harmful bacteria that cause foodborne illness.

Safe Minimum Cooking Temperatures

Use this chart and a food thermometer to ensure that meat, poultry, seafood, and other cooked foods reach a safe minimum internal temperature.

Remember, you can't tell whether meat is safely cooked by looking at it. Any cooked, uncured red meats – including pork – can be pink, even when the meat has reached a safe internal temperature.

Why the Rest Time is Important

After you remove meat from a grill, oven, or other heat source, allow it to rest for the specified amount of time. During the rest time, its temperature remains constant or continues to rise, which destroys harmful germs.

Table 29.1. *Safe Minimum Cooking Temperatures*

Category	Food	Temperature (°F)	Rest Time
Ground Meat & Meat Mixtures	Beef, Pork, Veal, Lamb	160	None
	Turkey, Chicken	165	None
Fresh Beef, Veal, Lamb	Steaks, roasts, chops	145	3 minutes
Poultry	Chicken & Turkey, whole	165	None
	Poultry breasts, roasts	165	None
	Poultry thighs, legs, wings	165	None
	Duck & Goose	165	None
	Stuffing (cooked alone or in bird)	165	None
Pork and Ham	Fresh pork	145	3 minutes
	Fresh ham (raw)	145	3 minutes
	Precooked ham (to reheat)	140	None
Eggs & Egg Dishes	Eggs	Cook until yolk and white are firm	None
	Egg dishes	160	None
Leftovers & Casseroles	Leftovers	165	None
	Casseroles	165	None
Seafood	Fin Fish	145 or cook until flesh is opaque and separates easily with a fork.	None
	Shrimp, lobster, and crabs	Cook until flesh is pearly and opaque.	None
	Clams, oysters, and mussels	Cook until shells open during cooking.	None
	Scallops	Cook until flesh is milky white or opaque and firm.	None

Meat and Poultry Roasting Chart

If you prefer, you may choose to cook these meats and poultry to higher temperatures.

Table 29.2. *Meat and Poultry Roasting Charts*

Red Meat, Type	Oven °F	Timing	Minimum Internal Temperature & Rest Time
BEEF, FRESH			
Beef, rib roast, bone-in; 4 to 8 pounds	325	23 to 30 min/lb	145 °F and allow to rest for at least 3 minutes
Beef, rib roast, boneless; 4 pounds	325	39 to 43 min/lb	
Beef, eye round roast; 2 to 3 pounds	325	20 to 22 min/lb	
Beef, tenderloin roast, whole; 4 to 6 lbs	425	45 to 60 minutes total	
Beef, tenderloin roast, half; 2 to 3 lbs	425	35 to 45 minutes total	
POULTRY: Times are for unstuffed poultry. Add 15 to 30 minutes for stuffed birds. The internal temperature should reach 165°F in the center of the stuffing.			
Turkey, whole;	325	30 min/lb	165 °F and check the internal temperature in the innermost part of the thigh, innermost part of the wing and the thickest part of the breast.
Chicken, whole; 4 to 8 pounds	375	20 to 30 min/lb	
CAPON, whole; 4 to 8 pounds	375	20 to 30 min/lb	
CORNISH HENS, whole; 18 to 24 oz.	350	50 to 60 minutes total	
DUCK, domestic, whole	375	20 min/lb	
DUCK, wild, whole	350	18 to 20 min/lb	
GOOSE, domestic or wild, whole	325	20 to 25 min/lb	
PHEASANT, young, whole, 2 pounds	350	30 min/lb	
QUAIL, whole	425	20 minutes total	
LAMB			
Lamb, leg, bone-in; 5 to 9 pounds	325	20-26 min/lb	145 °F and allow to rest for at least 3 minutes
Lamb, leg, boneless; 4 to 7 pounds			

Table 29.2. *Continued*

Red Meat, Type	Oven °F	Timing	Minimum Internal Temperature & Rest Time
PORK, FRESH			
Pork, loin roast, bone-in; 3 to 5 pounds	325	20-25 min/lb	145 °F and allow to rest for at least 3 minutes
Pork, loin roast boneless; 2 to 4 pounds	325	23-33 min/lb	
Pork, crown roast; 6 to 10 lbs	325	20-25 min/lb	
Pork, tenderloin; ½ to 1½ lbs	425	20-30 minutes total	
PORK, CURED			
Ham, cook-before-eating, bone-in; Whole, 14 to 16 pounds	325	18-20 min/lb	145 °F and allow to rest for at least 3 minutes
Ham, cook-before-eating, bone-in; Half, 7 to 8 pounds	325	22-25 min/lb	
Ham, fully cooked, bone-in; Whole, 14 to 16 pound	325	15-18 min/lb	140 °F
Ham, fully cooked, bone-in; Half, 7 to 8 pounds	325	18-25 min/lb	140 °F
Ham, fully cooked, boneless; 3 to 4 lbs	325	27-33 min/lb	140 °F
Ham, country, dried	(see label directions)		
VEAL			
Veal, boneless roast, rump or shoulder; 2 to 3 pounds	325	25-30 min/lb	145 °F and allow to rest for at least 3 minutes
Veal, bone-in roast, loin; 3 to 4 pounds	325	30-34 min/lb	

Ham Cooking Chart

Table 29.3. *Ham cooking Chart*

Category	Cut	Weight in Pounds	Minutes Per Pound
Smoked ham, cook-before-eating	Whole, bone in	10 to 14	18 to 20
	Half, bone in	5 to 7	22 to 25
	Shank or butt portion, bone in	3 to 4	3 to 4

Table 29.3. *Continued*

Category	Cut	Weight in Pounds	Minutes Per Pound
	Arm picnic shoulder, boneless	5 to 8	30 to 35
	Shoulder roll (butt), boneless	2 to 4	35 to 40
Smoked ham, cooked	Whole, bone in	10 to 14	15 to 18
	Half, bone in	5 to 7	18 to 24
	Arm picnic shoulder, boneless	5 to 8	25 to 30
	Canned ham, boneless	3 to 10	15 to 20
	Vacuum packed, boneless	6 to 12	10 to 15
	Spiral cut, whole or half	7 to 9	10 to 18
Fresh ham, uncooked	Whole leg, bone in	12 to 16	22 to 26
	Whole leg, boneless	10 to 14	24 to 28
	Half, bone in	5 to 8	35 to 40

For country ham (dried, whole or half):

1. Soak 4 to 12 hours in refrigerator.

2. Cover with water, then boil 20 to 25 minutes per pound.

3. Drain, glaze, and brown at 400°F for 15 minutes.

Turkey Thawing Chart

Table 29.4. *Turkey Thawing Chart*

Turkey Size	In the Refrigerator (Approximately 24 hours for every 4-5 lbs.)	In Cold Water (Approximately 30 minutes per lb.)
4 to 12 pounds	1 to 3 days	2 to 6 hours
12 to 16 pounds	3 to 4 days	6 to 8 hours
16 to 20 pounds	4 to 5 days	8 to 10 hours
20 to 24 pounds	5 to 6 days	10 to 12 hours

Turkey Roasting Chart

For a fresh or thawed turkey:
1. Set the oven to 325 °F.
2. Cook to 165 °F.

Table 29.5. *Turkey Roasting Chart*

Size of Turkey	Unstuffed	Stuffed
4 to 6 pounds (breast)	1 1/2 to 2 1/4 hours	Not usually applicable
6 to 8 pounds (breast)	2 1/4 to 3 1/4 hours	2 1/2 to 3 1/2 hours
8 to 12 pounds	2 3/4 to 3 hours	3 to 3 1/2 hours
12 to 14 pounds	3 to 3 3/4 hours	3 1/2 to 4 hours
14 to 18 pounds	3 3/4 to 4 1/4 hours	4 to 4 1/4 hours
18 to 20 pounds	4 1/4 to 4 1/2 hours	4 1/4 to 4 3/4 hours
20 to 24 pounds	4 1/2 to 5 hours	4 3/4 to 5 1/4 hours

Alternative Ways to Cook Turkey

Always make sure whole turkeys reach a safe minimum internal temperature of 165 °F. Use a meat thermometer to measure the temperature in the innermost part of the thigh and wing and the thickest part of the breast.

Table 29.6. *Alternate Ways to Cook Turkey*

Method	Size	Estimated Cooking Time	Notes
Electric Roaster Oven	8 to 24 lbs.	Generally same times as for oven roasting.	Minimum oven temperature 325 °F. Check appliance manual.
Grilling: Covered Charcoal Grill or Covered Gas Grill	8 to 16 lbs.	15 to 18 minutes per pound. DO NOT STUFF.	Air in the grill must maintain 225 to 300 °F; use drip pan.
Smoking	8 to 12 lbs.	20 to 30 minutes per pound. DO NOT STUFF.	Air in the smoker must maintain 225 to 300 °F; use drip pan with liquid.
Deep Fat Frying	8 to 12 lbs.	3 to 5 minutes per pound. DO NOT STUFF.	Oil must maintain 350 °F. Follow manufacturer's instructions.
Microwaving	8 to 14 lbs.	9 to 10 minutes per pound on medium (50%) power. DO NOT STUFF.	Use oven cooking bag. Rotate during cooking.

Section 29.2

Food Safety Regulations

Text in this section is excerpted from "Guidance and Regulation,"
U.S. Food and Drug Administration (FDA), May 12, 2015.

Guidance and Regulation

Guidance Documents and Regulatory Information by Topic

- **Guidance Documents:** Guidance documents represent FDA's current thinking on a topic. They do not create or confer any rights for or on any person and do not operate to bind FDA or the public. You can use an alternative approach if the approach satisfies the requirements of the applicable statutes and regulations.

- **Regulatory Information:** FDA issues regulations to implement its statutory authority. The regulations can create binding obligations and have the force of law.

FDA Food Safety Modernization Act (FSMA)

FSMA is the most sweeping reform of FDA's food safety authority in more than 70 years. This act gives FDA new and enhanced mandates and authorities to protect consumers and promote public health.

Food Facility Registration

Information on the requirement that owners, operators, or agents in charge of domestic or foreign facilities that manufacture, process, pack, or hold food for consumption in the United States must register with FDA.

Current Good Manufacturing Practices (CGMPs)

Descriptions of the methods, equipment, facilities, and controls for producing processed food and dietary supplements. Following CGMPs ensures the quality of processed foods and dietary supplements. It also ensures that processed food or dietary supplements are packaged and labeled as specified in the master manufacturing record.

Hazard Analysis and Critical Control Points (HACCP)

HACCP is a management system in which food safety is addressed through the analysis and control of biological, chemical, and physical hazards. This includes raw material production, procurement and handling, manufacturing, distribution, and consumption of the finished product.

Retail Food Protection

More than 3,000 state, local, and tribal agencies have primary responsibility to regulate the retail food and food service industries in the United States. FDA assists regulatory agencies and the industries they regulate by providing a model Food Code, guidance, training, program evaluation, and technical assistance.

Imports and Exports

Information on:

- Importing food products into the United States, including Prior Notice of Imported Food

- Exporting food products from the United States, including export certificates

Federal/State Food Programs

Information about milk and seafood safety cooperative programs with FDA and state and local health and regulatory agencies.

- Interstate Milk Shippers List
- Interstate Shellfish Shippers List

Food Protection Plan, 2007

FDA developed the Food Protection Plan to address the changes in food sources, production, and consumption. The plan presents a robust strategy to protect the nation's food supply from both unintentional contamination and deliberate attack.

Section 29.3

Irradiated Foods

Text in this section begins with excerpts from "Food Irradiation:
What you need to know," U.S. Food and Drug Administration
(FDA), May 7, 2015; text in this section beginning with "What is the
radiation dose to the food?" is excerpted from "Food Irradiation,"
United States Environmental Protection Agency (EPA), June 29,
2015.

Food Irradiation: What You Need to Know

*Food irradiation (the application of ionizing radiation to food) is a
technology that improves the safety and extends the shelf life of foods
by reducing or eliminating microorganisms and insects. Like pasteur-
izing milk and canning fruits and vegetables, irradiation can make
food safer for the consumer.*

The Food and Drug Administration (FDA) is responsible for
regulating the sources of radiation that are used to irradiate food.
FDA approves a source of radiation for use on foods only after it has
determined that irradiating the food is safe.

Why Irradiate Food?

Irradiation can serve many purposes.

- **Prevention of Foodborne Illness** – irradiation can be used
  to effectively eliminate organisms that cause foodborne illness,
  such as *Salmonella* and *Escherichia coli* (*E. coli*).

- **Preservation** – irradiation can be used to destroy or inactivate
  organisms that cause spoilage and decomposition and extend the
  shelf life of foods.

- **Control of Insects** – irradiation can be used to destroy insects
  in or on tropical fruits imported into the United States. Irradiation also decreases the need for other pest-control practices that
  may harm the fruit.

- **Delay of Sprouting and Ripening** – irradiation can be used to inhibit sprouting (e.g., potatoes) and delay ripening of fruit to increase longevity.

- **Sterilization** – irradiation can be used to sterilize foods, which can then be stored for years without refrigeration. Sterilized foods are useful in hospitals for patients with severely impaired immune systems, such as patients with AIDS or undergoing chemotherapy. Foods that are sterilized by irradiation are exposed to substantially higher levels of treatment than those approved for general use.

Debunking Irradiation Myths

Irradiation does not make foods radioactive, compromise nutritional quality, or noticeably change the taste, texture, or appearance of food. In fact, any changes made by irradiation are so minimal that it is not easy to tell if a food has been irradiated.

How Is Food Irradiated?

There are three sources of radiation approved for use on foods.

- **Gamma rays** are emitted from radioactive forms of the element cobalt (Cobalt 60) or of the element cesium (Cesium 137). Gamma radiation is used routinely to sterilize medical, dental and household products and is also used for the radiation treatment of cancer.

- **X-rays** are produced by reflecting a high-energy stream of electrons off a target substance (usually one of the heavy metals) into food. X-rays are also widely used in medicine and industry to produce images of internal structures.

- **Electron beam** (or e-beam) is similar to X-rays and is a stream of high-energy electrons propelled from an electron accelerator into food.

Is Irradiated Food Safe to Eat?

FDA has evaluated the safety of irradiated food for more than thirty years and has found the process to be safe. The World Health Organization (WHO), the Centers for Disease Control and Prevention (CDC) and the U.S. Department of Agriculture (USDA) have also endorsed the safety of irradiated food.

What Foods Have Been Approved for Irradiation?

FDA has approved a variety of foods for irradiation in the United States including:

- Beef and Pork
- Crustaceans (e.g., lobster, shrimp, and crab)
- Fresh Fruits and Vegetables
- Lettuce and Spinach
- Molluscan Shellfish (e.g., oysters, clams, mussels, and scallops)
- Poultry
- Seeds for Sprouting (e.g., for alfalfa sprouts)
- Shell Eggs
- Spices and Seasonings

How Will I Know if My Food Has Been Irradiated?

FDA requires that irradiated foods bear the international symbol for irradiation. Look for the Radura symbol along with the statement "Treated with radiation" or "Treated by irradiation" on the food label. Bulk foods, such as fruits and vegetables, are required to be individually labeled or to have a label next to the sale container. FDA does not require that individual ingredients in multi-ingredient foods (e.g., spices) be labeled.

Figure 29.1. Four Steps for Safe Food Handling

It is important to remember that irradiation is not a replacement for proper food-handling practices by producers, processors and consumers. Irradiated foods need to be stored, handled and cooked in the same way as non-irradiated foods, because they could still become contaminated with disease-causing organisms after irradiation if the rules of basic food safety are not followed.

What is the radiation dose to the food?

Radiation doses vary for different foodstuffs. For the vast majority of foods, the limit is less than 10 kilo Gray. The U.S. Food and Drug Administration (FDA) sets radiation dose limits for specific food types:

The dose limit for spices and seasons is higher, because they are consumed in very small quantities.

Table 29.7. *Radiation Dose to the Food*

Food Type	Dose (kilo Grays)
Fruit	1
Poultry	3
Spices, Seasonings	30

Chapter 30

Food Allergies and Intolerance

Food Allergies: What You Need to Know

Each year, millions of Americans have allergic reactions to food. Although most food allergies cause relatively mild and minor symptoms, some food allergies can cause severe reactions, and may even be life-threatening.

There is no cure for food allergies. Strict avoidance of food allergens—and early recognition and management of allergic reactions to food—are important measures to prevent serious health consequences.

FDA's Role:

Labeling

To help Americans avoid the health risks posed by food allergens, Congress passed the **Food Allergen Labeling and Consumer Protection Act of 2004 (FALCPA).** The law applies to all foods whose labeling is regulated by FDA, both domestic and imported. (FDA regulates the labeling of all foods, except for poultry, most meats, certain egg products, and most alcoholic beverages.)

Text in this chapter is excerpted from "Food Allergies: What You Need to know," U.S. Food and Drug Administration (FDA), May 12, 2015.

- Before FALCPA, the labels of foods made from two or more ingredients were required to list all **ingredients** by their common or usual names. The names of some ingredients, however, do not clearly identify their food source.

- Now, the law requires that labels must clearly identify the **food source names** of all ingredients that are—or contain any protein derived from—the **eight most common food allergens**, which FALCPA defines as "**major food allergens**."

As a result, food labels help allergic consumers to identify offending foods or ingredients so they can more easily avoid them.

About Foods Labeled *Before* **January 1, 2006**

FALCPA did not require relabeling of food products labeled before January 1, 2006, which were made with a major food allergen that did not identify its food source name in the ingredient list. Although it is unlikely that any of these foods are still on store shelves, always use special care to read the complete ingredient list on food labels when you go shopping.

Food Allergies

What to Do If Symptoms Occur

The appearance of symptoms after eating food may be a sign of a food allergy. The food(s) that caused these symptoms should be avoided, and the affected person, should contact a doctor or health care provider for appropriate testing and evaluation.

- Persons found to have a food allergy should be taught to **read labels** and **avoid the offending foods**. They should also be taught, in case of accidental ingestion, to **recognize the early symptoms** of an allergic reaction, and be properly educated on—and armed with—appropriate treatment measures.

- Persons with a known food allergy who begin experiencing symptoms while, or after eating a food should **initiate treatment immediately**, and go to a **nearby emergency room** if symptoms progress.

The Hard Facts: Severe Food Allergies Can Be Life-Threatening

Following ingestion of a food allergen(s), a person with food allergies can experience a severe, life-threatening allergic reaction called **anaphylaxis.**

This can lead to:

- constricted airways in the lungs
- severe lowering of blood pressure and shock (**"anaphylactic shock"**)
- suffocation by swelling of the throat

Each year in the U.S., it is estimated that anaphylaxis to food results in:

- 30,000 emergency room visits
- 2,000 hospitalizations
- 150 deaths

Prompt administration of epinephrine by autoinjector (e.g., Epipen) during early symptoms of anaphylaxis may help prevent these serious consequences.

What Are Major Food Allergens?

While more than 160 foods can cause allergic reactions in people with food allergies, the law identifies the eight most common allergenic foods. These foods account for 90 percent of food allergic reactions, and are the food sources from which many other ingredients are derived.

The eight foods identified by the law are:

1. **Milk**
2. **Eggs**
3. **Fish** (e.g., bass, flounder, cod)
4. **Crustacean shellfish** (e.g., crab, lobster, shrimp)
5. **Tree nuts** (e.g., almonds, walnuts, pecans)
6. **Peanuts**
7. **Wheat**
8. **Soybeans**

These eight foods, and any ingredient that contains protein derived from one or more of them, are designated as "major food allergens" by FALCPA.

How Major Food Allergens Are Listed

The law requires that food labels identify the food source names of all major food allergens used to make the food. This requirement is met if the common or usual name of an ingredient (e.g., buttermilk) that is a major food allergen already identifies that allergen's food source name (i.e., milk). Otherwise, the allergen's food source name must be declared at least once on the food label in one of two ways.

The name of the food source of a major food allergen must appear:

1. In parentheses following the name of the ingredient.

   Examples: "lecithin (soy)," "flour (wheat)," and "whey (milk)"

– OR –

2. Immediately after or next to the list of ingredients in a "contains" statement.

   Example: "Contains Wheat, Milk, and Soy."

Know the Symptoms

Symptoms of food allergies typically appear from within a few minutes to two hours after a person has eaten the food to which he or she is allergic.

Allergic reactions can include:

- Hives
- Flushed skin or rash
- Tingling or itchy sensation in the mouth
- Face, tongue, or lip swelling
- Vomiting and/or diarrhea
- Abdominal cramps
- Coughing or wheezing
- Dizziness and/or lightheadedness
- Swelling of the throat and vocal cords
- Difficulty breathing
- Loss of consciousness

About Other Allergens:

Persons may still be allergic to—and have serious reactions to—foods *other* than the eight foods identified by the law. So, always be sure to read the food label's ingredient list carefully to avoid the food allergens in question.

Food Allergen "Advisory" Labeling

FALCPA's labeling requirements do not apply to the potential or unintentional presence of major food allergens in foods resulting from "cross-contact" situations during manufacturing, e.g., because of shared equipment or processing lines. In the context of food allergens, "cross-contact" occurs when a residue or trace amount of an allergenic food becomes incorporated into another food not intended to contain it. FDA guidance for the food industry states that food allergen advisory statements, e.g., "may contain [allergen]" or "produced in a facility that also uses [allergen]" should not be used as a substitute for adhering to current good manufacturing practices and must be truthful and not misleading. FDA is considering ways to best manage the use of these types of statements by manufacturers to better inform consumers.

Chapter 31

Common Chemical Contaminants in the Food Supply

Chapter Contents

Section 31.1

Persistent Organic Pollutants (POPs)

Text in this section is excerpted from "Persistent Organic Pollutants:
A Global Issue, A Global Response," United States Environmental
Protection Agency (EPA), June 29, 2015.

A Global Issue

Persistent organic pollutants (POPs) are toxic chemicals that adversely affect human health and the environment around the world. Because they can be transported by wind and water, most POPs generated in one country can and do affect people and wildlife far from where they are used and released. They persist for long periods of time in the environment and can accumulate and pass from one species to the next through the food chain. To address this global concern, the United States joined forces with 90 other countries and the European Community to sign a groundbreaking United Nations treaty in Stockholm, Sweden, in May 2001. Under the treaty, known as the Stockholm Convention, countries agreed to reduce or eliminate the production, use, and/or release of 12 key POPs (see box), and specified under the Convention a scientific review process that has led to the addition of other POPs chemicals of global concern.

Many of the POPs included in the Stockholm Convention are no longer produced in this country. However, U.S. citizens and habitats can still be at risk from POPs that have persisted in the environment from unintentionally produced POPs that are released in the United States, from POPs that are released elsewhere and then transported here (by wind or water, for example), or from both. Although most developed nations have taken strong action to control POPs, a great number of developing nations have only fairly recently begun to restrict their production, use, and release.

The Stockholm Convention adds an important global dimension to our national and regional efforts to control POPs. Though the United States is not yet a Party to the Stockholm Convention, the Convention has played a prominent role in the control of harmful chemicals on both a national and global level. For example, EPA and the states have significantly reduced the release of dioxins and furans to land, air, and water from U.S. sources. In addition to assessing dioxins, EPA has also been working diligently on the reduction of DDT from global sources. The United States and Canada signed an agreement for the Virtual Elimination of Persistent Toxic Substances in the Great Lakes to reduce emissions from toxic substances. The United States has also signed the regional protocol of the United Nations Economic Commission for Europe on POPs under the Convention on Long-Range Trans boundary Air Pollution which addresses the Stockholm Convention POPs and other chemicals.

In addition to the POPs-related agreements the United States has taken part in signing, the United States has also provided ample

The "Dirty Dozen"

aldrin [1]

chlordane [1]

dichlorodiphenyl trichloroethane (DDT)[1]

dieldrin[1]

endrin[1]

heptachlor[1]

hexachlorobenzene [1,2]

mirex[1]

toxaphene[1]

polychlorinated biphenyls (PCBs) [1,2]

polychlorinated dibenzo-p-dioxins[2](dioxins)

polychlorinated dibenzofurans[2] (furans)

   1 Intentionally Produced.
   2 Unintentionally Produced - Result from some industrial
     processes and combustion.

(For more information about the dirty dozen, see Table 31.1. below.)

NOTE: These are the chemicals initially addressed by the Stockholm Convention when negotiated. Since that time, other chemicals have been added to the Convention. See www.pops. int for the complete list.

Many of the POPs included in the Stockholm Convention are no longer produced in this country. However, U.S. citizens and habitats can still be at risk from POPs that have persisted in the environment.

financial and technical support to countries across the globe supporting POPs reduction. A few of these initiatives include dioxin and furan release inventories in Asia and Russia, and the reduction of PCB sources in Russia.

What are POPs?

Many POPs were widely used during the boom in industrial production after World War II, when thousands of synthetic chemicals were introduced into commercial use. Many of these chemicals proved beneficial in pest and disease control, crop production, and industry. These same chemicals, however, have had unforeseen effects on human health and the environment.

Many people are familiar with some of the most well-known POPs, such as PCBs, DDT, and dioxins. POPs include a range of substances that include:

1. Intentionally produced chemicals currently or once used in agriculture, disease control, manufacturing, or industrial processes. Examples include PCBs, which have been useful in a variety of industrial applications (e.g., in electrical transformers and large capacitors, as hydraulic and heat exchange fluids, and as additives to paints and lubricants) and DDT, which is still used to control mosquitoes that carry malaria in some parts of the world.

2. Unintentionally produced chemicals, such as dioxins, that result from some industrial processes and from combustion (for example, municipal and medical waste incineration and backyard burning of trash).

The DDT Dilemma

DDT is likely one of the most famous and controversial pesticides ever made. An estimated 4 billion pounds of this inexpensive and historically effective chemical have been produced and applied worldwide since 1940. In the United States, DDT was used extensively on agricultural crops, particularly cotton, from 1945 to 1972. DDT was also used to protect soldiers from insect-borne diseases such as malaria and typhus during World War II, and it remains a valuable public health tool in parts of the tropics. The heavy use of this highly persistent chemical, however, led to widespread environmental contamination and the accumulation of DDT in humans and wildlife - a phenomenon brought to public attention by Rachel Carson in her 1962 book, *Silent Spring*. A wealth of scientific laboratory and field data have now confirmed research from the 1960s that suggested, among other effects, that high levels of DDE (a metabolite of DDT) in certain birds of prey caused their eggshells to thin so dramatically they could not produce live offspring.

One bird species especially sensitive to DDE was the bald eagle. Public concern about the eagles' decline and the possibility of other long-term harmful effects of DDT exposure to both humans and wildlife prompted the Environmental Protection Agency (EPA) to cancel the registration of DDT in 1972. The bald eagle has since experienced one of the most dramatic species recoveries in our history.

Transboundary Travelers

A major impetus for the Stockholm Convention was the finding of POPs contamination in relatively pristine Arctic regions—thousands of miles from any known source. Much of the evidence for long-range transport of airborne gaseous and particulate substances to the United States focuses on dust or smoke because they are visible in satellite images. Tracing the movement of most POPs in the environment is complex because these compounds can exist in different phases (e.g., as a gas or attached to airborne particles) and can be exchanged among environmental media. For example, some POPs can be carried for many miles when they evaporate from water or land surfaces into the air, or when they adsorb to airborne particles. Then, they can return to Earth on particles or in snow, rain, or mist. POPs also travel through oceans, rivers, lakes, and to a lesser extent, with the help of animal carriers, such as migratory species.

What Domestic Actions Have Been Taken to Control POPs?

The United States has taken strong domestic action to reduce emissions of POPs. For example, none of the original POPs pesticides listed in the Stockholm Convention is registered for sale and distribution in the United States today and in 1978, Congress prohibited the manufacture of PCBs and severely restricted the use of remaining PCB stocks. In addition, since 1987, EPA and the states have effectively reduced environmental releases of dioxins and furans to land, air, and water from U.S. sources. These regulatory actions, along with voluntary efforts by U.S. industry, resulted in a greater than 85 percent decline in total dioxin and furan releases after 1987 from known industrial sources. To better understand the risks associated with dioxin releases, EPA has been conducting a comprehensive reassessment of dioxin science and will be evaluating additional actions that might further protect human health and the environment.

Stopping DDT Use

Over the years, the United States has taken a number of steps to restrict the use of DDT:

1969: After studying the persistence of DDT residues in the environment, the U.S. Department of Agriculture (USDA) cancels the registration of certain uses of DDT (on shade trees, on tobacco, in the home, and in aquatic environments).

1970: USDA cancels DDT applications on crops, commercial plants, and wood products, as well as for building purposes.

1972: Under the authority of EPA, the registrations of the remaining DDT products are canceled.

1989: The remaining exempted uses (public health use for controlling vector-borne diseases, military use for quarantine, and prescription drug use for controlling body lice) are voluntarily stopped.

Today: There is no U.S. registration for DDT, meaning that it cannot legally be sold or distributed in the United States.

Controlling Dioxins

EPA has pursued regulatory control and management of dioxins and furans releases to air, water, and soil. The Clean Air Act requires the application of maximum achievable control technology for hazardous air pollutants, including dioxins and furans. Major sources regulated under this authority include municipal, medical, and hazardous waste incineration; pulp and paper manufacturing; and certain metals production and refining processes. Dioxin releases to water are managed through a combination of risk-based and technology-based tools established under the Clean Water Act. The cleanup of dioxin-contaminated land is an important part of the EPA Superfund and Resource Conservation and Recovery Act Corrective Action programs. Voluntary

478

actions to control dioxins and furans include EPA's Persistent, Bioaccumulative, and Toxics Program and the Dioxin Exposure Initiative, both of which gather information to inform future actions and further reduce risks associated with dioxin exposure.

How Do POPs Affect People and Wildlife?

Studies have linked POPs exposures to declines, diseases, or abnormalities in a number of wildlife species, including certain kinds of fish, birds, and mammals. Wildlife also can act as sentinels for human health: abnormalities or declines detected in wildlife populations can sound an early warning bell for people. Behavioral abnormalities and birth defects in fish, birds, and mammals in and around the Great Lakes, for example, led scientists to investigate POPs exposures in human populations.

In people, reproductive, developmental, behavioral, neurologic, endocrine, and immunologic adverse health effects have been linked to POPs. People are mainly exposed to POPs through contaminated foods. Less common exposure routes include drinking contaminated water and direct contact with the chemicals. In people and other mammals alike, POPs can be transferred through the placenta and breast milk to developing offspring. It should be noted, however, that despite this potential exposure, the known benefits of breast-feeding far outweigh the suspected risks.

A number of populations are at particular risk of POPs exposure, including people whose diets include large amounts of fish, shellfish, or wild foods that are high in fat and locally obtained. For example, indigenous peoples may be particularly at risk because they observe cultural and spiritual traditions related to their diet. To them, fishing and hunting are not sport or recreation, but are part of a traditional, subsistence way of life, in which no useful part of the catch is wasted. In remote areas of Alaska and elsewhere, locally obtained subsistence food may be the only readily available option for nutrition.

In addition, sensitive populations such as children, the elderly, and those with suppressed immune systems, are typically more susceptible to many kinds of pollutants, including POPs. Because POPs have been linked to reproductive impairments, men and women of child-bearing age may also be at risk.

POPS and the Food Chain

POPs work their way through the food chain by accumulating in the body fat of living organisms and becoming more concentrated as they move from one creature to another. This process is known as biomagnification. When contaminants found in small amounts at the bottom of the food chain biomagnify, they can pose a significant hazard to predators that feed at the top of the food chain. This means that even small releases of POPs can have significant impacts.

Biomagnification in Action: A 1997 study by the Arctic Monitoring and Assessment Programme, called *Arctic Pollution Issues: A State of the Arctic Environment Report*, found that caribou in Canada's Northwest Territories had as much as 10 times the levels of PCBs as the lichen on which they grazed; PCB levels in the wolves that fed on the caribou were magnified nearly 60 times as much as the lichen.

The Role of Science

Although scientists have more to learn about POPs chemicals, decades of scientific research have greatly increased our knowledge of POPs' impacts on people and wildlife. For example, laboratory studies have shown that low doses of certain POPs adversely affect some organ systems and aspects of development. Studies also have shown that chronic exposure to low doses of certain POPs can result in reproductive and immune system deficits. Exposure to high levels of certain POPs chemicals—higher than normally encountered by humans and wildlife—can cause serious damage or death. Epidemiological studies of exposed human populations and studies of wildlife might provide more information on health impacts. However, because such studies are less controlled than laboratory studies, other stresses cannot be ruled out as the cause of adverse effects.

As we continue to study POPs, we will learn more about the risk of POPs exposure to the general public, how much certain species (including people) are exposed, and what effects POPs have on these species and their ecosystems. EPA developed a report summarizing the science on POPs.

Reservoirs of POPs

POPs can be deposited in marine and freshwater ecosystems through effluent releases, atmospheric deposition, runoff, and other means. Because POPs have low water solubility, they bond strongly to particulate matter in aquatic sediments. As a result, sediments can serve as reservoirs or "sinks" for POPs. When sequestered in these sediments, POPs can be taken out of circulation for long periods of time. If disturbed, however, they can be reintroduced into the ecosystem and food chain, potentially becoming a source of local, and even global contamination.

Table 31.1. *The "Dirty Dozen"*

POP	Global Historical Use/ Source	Overview of U.S. Status
aldrin and dieldrin	Insecticides used on crops such as corn and cotton; also used for termite control.	Under FIFRA: No U.S. registrations; most uses canceled in 1969; all uses by 1987. All tolerances on food crops revoked in 1986. No production, import, or export.
chlordane	Insecticide used on crops, including vegetables, small grains, potatoes, sugarcane, sugar beets, fruits, nuts, citrus, and cotton. Used on home lawn and garden pests. Also used extensively to control termites.	Under FIFRA: No U.S. registrations; most uses canceled in 1978; all uses by 1988. All tolerances on food crops revoked in 1986. No production (stopped in 1997), import, or export. Regulated as a hazardous air pollutant (CAA).
DDT	Insecticide used on agricultural crops, primarily cotton, and insects that carry diseases such as malaria and typhus.	Under FIFRA: No U.S. registrations; most uses canceled in 1972; all uses by 1989. Tolerances on food crops revoked in 1986. No U.S. production, import, or export. DDE (a metabolite of DDT) regulated as a hazardous air pollutant (CAA). Priority toxic pollutant (CWA).
endrin	Insecticide used on crops such as cotton and grains; also used to control rodents.	Under FIFRA, no U.S. registrations; most uses canceled in 1979; all uses by 1984. No production, import, or export. Priority toxic pollutant (CWA).
mirex	Insecticide used to combat fire ants, termites, and mealybugs. Also used as a fire retardant in plastics, rubber, and electrical products.	Under FIFRA, no U.S. registrations; all uses canceled in 1977. No production, import, or export.

Table 31.1. *(Continued)*

POP	Global Historical Use/ Source	Overview of U.S. Status
heptachlor	Insecticide used primarily against soil insects and termites. Also used against some crop pests and to combat malaria.	Under FIFRA: Most uses canceled by 1978; registrant voluntarily canceled use to control fire ants in underground cable boxes in early 2000. All pesticide tolerances on food crops revoked in 1989. No production, import, or export.
hexachlorobenzene	Fungicide used for seed treatment. Also an industrial chemical used to make fireworks, ammunition, synthetic rubber, and other substances. Also unintentionally produced during combustion and the manufacture of certain chemicals. Also an impurity in certain pesticides.	Under FIFRA, no U.S. registrations; all uses canceled by 1985. No production, import, or export as a pesticide. Manufacture and use for chemical intermediate (as allowed under the Convention). Regulated as a hazardous air pollutant (CAA). Priority toxic pollutant (CWA).
PCBs	Used for a variety of industrial processes and purposes, including in electrical transformers and capacitors, as heat exchange fluids, as paint additives, in carbonless copy paper, and in plastics. Also unintentionally produced during combustion.	Manufacture and new use prohibited in 1978 (TSCA). Regulated as a hazardous air pollutant (CAA). Priority toxic pollutant (CWA).
toxaphene	Insecticide used to control pests on crops and livestock, and to kill unwanted fish in lakes.	Under FIFRA: No U.S. registrations; most uses canceled in 1982; all uses by 1990. All tolerances on food crops revoked in 1993. No production, import, or export. Regulated as a hazardous air pollutant (CAA).

Table 31.1. *(Continued)*

POP	Global Historical Use/ Source	Overview of U.S. Status
dioxins and furans	Unintentionally produced during most forms of combustion, including burning of municipal and medical wastes, backyard burning of trash, and industrial processes. Also can be found as trace contaminants in certain herbicides, wood preservatives, and in PCB mixtures.	Regulated as hazardous air pollutants (CAA). Dioxin in the form of 2,3,7,8-TCDD is a priority toxic pollutant (CWA).

Acronyms:
FIFRA: *Federal Insecticide, Fungicide and Rodenticide Act*
TSCA: *Toxic Substances Control Act*
CAA: *Clean Air Act*
CWA: *Clean Water Act*

Section 31.2

Polychlorinated Biphenyls (PCBs)

This section includes excerpts from "Polychlorinated Biphenyls (PCBs)—Basic Information," United States Environmental Protection Agency (EPA), April 8, 2013; text from "Polychlorinated Biphenyls (PCBs)—Health Effects," Environmental Protection Agency (EPA), June 14, 2013; and text from "CFR – Code of Federal Regulations Title 21—Unavoidable Contaminants in Food for Human Consumption and Food-Packaging Material ," U.S. Food and Drug Administration (FDA), September 1, 2014

Basic Information

PCBs belong to a broad family of man-made organic chemicals known as chlorinated hydrocarbons. PCBs were domestically manufactured from 1929 until their manufacture was banned in 1979. They have a range of toxicity and vary in consistency from thin, light-colored liquids to yellow or black waxy solids. Due to their non-flammability, chemical stability, high boiling point, and electrical insulating properties, PCBs were used in hundreds of industrial and commercial applications including electrical, heat transfer, and hydraulic equipment; as plasticizers in paints, plastics, and rubber products; in pigments, dyes, and carbonless copy paper; and many other industrial applications.

Commercial Use of PCBs

Although no longer commercially produced in the United States, PCBs may be present in products and materials produced before the 1979 PCB ban. Products that may contain PCBs include:

- Transformers and capacitors
- Other electrical equipment including voltage regulators, switches, reclosers, bushings, and electromagnets
- Oil used in motors and hydraulic systems
- Old electrical devices or appliances containing PCB capacitors
- Fluorescent light ballasts
- Cable insulation
- Thermal insulation material including fiberglass, felt, foam, and cork
- Adhesives and tapes
- Oil-based paint
- Caulking
- Plastics
- Carbonless copy paper
- Floor finish

The PCBs used in these products were chemical mixtures made up of a variety of individual chlorinated biphenyl components, known as congeners. Most commercial PCB mixtures are known in the United States by their industrial trade names. The most common trade name is Aroclor.

Release and Exposure of PCBs

Prior to the 1979 ban, PCBs entered the environment during their manufacture and use in the United States. Today PCBs can still be released into the environment from poorly maintained hazardous waste sites that contain PCBs; illegal or improper dumping of PCB wastes; leaks or releases from electrical transformers containing PCBs; and disposal of PCB-containing consumer products into municipal or other landfills not designed to handle hazardous waste. PCBs may also be released into the environment by the burning of some wastes in municipal and industrial incinerators.

Once in the environment, PCBs do not readily break down and therefore may remain for long periods of time cycling between air, water, and soil. PCBs can be carried long distances and have been found in snow and sea water in areas far away from where they were released into the environment. As a consequence, PCBs are found all over the world. In general, the lighter the form of PCB, the further it can be transported from the source of contamination.

PCBs can accumulate in the leaves and above-ground parts of plants and food crops. They are also taken up into the bodies of small organisms and fish. As a result, people who ingest fish may be exposed to PCBs that have bioaccumulated in the fish they are ingesting.

Health Effects of PCBs

PCBs have been demonstrated to cause a variety of adverse health effects. PCBs have been shown to cause cancer in animals. PCBs have also been shown to cause a number of serious non-cancer health effects in animals, including effects on the immune system, reproductive system, nervous system, endocrine system and other health effects. Studies in humans provide supportive evidence for potential carcinogenic and non-carcinogenic effects of PCBs. The different health effects of PCBs may be interrelated, as alterations in one system may have significant implications for the other systems of the body. The potential health effects of PCB exposure are discussed in greater detail below.

Cancer

EPA uses a weight-of-evidence approach in evaluating the potential carcinogenicity of environmental contaminants. EPA's approach permits evaluation of the complete carcinogenicity database, and allows the results of individual studies to be viewed in the context of all of the other available studies. Studies in animals provide conclusive evidence that PCBs cause cancer. Studies in humans raise further concerns regarding the potential carcinogenicity of PCBs. Taken together, the data strongly suggest that PCBs are probable human carcinogens.

PCBs are one of the most widely studied environmental contaminants, and many studies in animals and human populations have been performed to assess the potential carcinogenicity of PCBs. EPA's first assessment of PCB carcinogenicity was completed in 1987. At that time, data were limited to Aroclor 1260. In 1996, at the direction of Congress, EPA completed a reassessment of PCB carcinogenicity, titled "PCBs: Cancer Dose-Response Assessment and Application to Environmental Mixtures." In addition to Aroclor 1260, new studies provided data on Aroclors 1016, 1242, and 1254. EPA's cancer reassessment reflected the Agency's commitment to the use of the best science in evaluating health effects of PCBs. EPA's cancer reassessment was peer reviewed by 15 experts on PCBs, including scientists from government, academia and industry. The peer reviewers agreed with EPA's conclusion that PCBs are probable human carcinogens.

The cancer reassessment determined that PCBs are probable human carcinogens, based on the following information:

There is clear evidence that PCBs cause cancer in animals. EPA reviewed all of the available literature on the carcinogenicity of PCBs in animals as an important first step in the cancer reassessment. An industry scientist commented that "all significant studies have been reviewed and are fairly represented in the document." The literature presents overwhelming evidence that PCBs cause cancer in animals. An industry-sponsored peer-reviewed rat study, characterized as the "gold standard study" by one peer reviewer, demonstrated that every commercial PCB mixture tested caused cancer. The new studies reviewed in the PCB reassessment allowed EPA to develop more accurate potency estimates than previously available for PCBs. The reassessment provided EPA with sufficient information to develop a range of potency estimates for different PCB mixtures, based on the incidence of liver cancer and in consideration of the mobility of PCBs in the environment.

The reassessment resulted in a slightly decreased cancer potency estimate for Aroclor 1260 relative to the 1987 estimate due to the use of additional dose-response information for PCB mixtures and refinements in risk assessment techniques (e.g., use of a different animal-to-human scaling factor for dose). The reassessment concluded that the types of PCBs likely to be bioaccumulated in fish and bound to sediments are the most carcinogenic PCB mixtures.

In addition to the animal studies, a number of epidemiological studies of workers exposed to PCBs have been performed. Results of human studies raise concerns for the potential carcinogenicity of PCBs. Studies of PCB workers found increases in rare liver cancers and malignant melanoma. The presence of cancer in the same target organ (liver) following exposures to PCBs both in animals and in humans and the finding of liver cancers and malignant melanomas across multiple human studies adds weight to the conclusion that PCBs are probable human carcinogens.

Some of the studies in humans have not demonstrated an association between exposures to PCBs and disease. However, epidemiological studies share common methodological limitations that can affect their ability to discern important health effects (or define them as statistically significant) even when they are present. Often, the number of individuals in a study is too small for an effect to be revealed, or there are difficulties in determining actual exposure levels, or there are multiple confounding factors (factors that tend to co-occur with PCB exposure, including smoking, drinking of alcohol, and exposure to other chemicals in the workplace). Epidemiological studies may not be able to detect small increases in cancer over background unless the cancer rate following contaminant exposure is very high or the exposure produces a very unusual type of cancer. However, studies that do not demonstrate an association between exposure to PCBs and disease should not be characterized as negative studies. These studies are most appropriately viewed as inconclusive. Limited studies that produce inconclusive findings for cancer in humans do not mean that PCBs are safe.

It is very important to note that the composition of PCB mixtures changes following their release into the environment. The types of PCBs that tend to bioaccumulate in fish and other animals and bind to sediments happen to be the most carcinogenic components of PCB mixtures. As a result, people who ingest PCB-contaminated fish or other animal products and contact PCB-contaminated sediment may be exposed to PCB mixtures that are even more toxic than the PCB mixtures contacted by workers and released into the environment.

EPA's peer reviewed cancer reassessment concluded that PCBs are probable human carcinogens. EPA is not alone in its conclusions regarding PCBs. The International Agency for Research on Cancer has declared PCBs to be probably carcinogenic to humans. The National Toxicology Program has stated that it is reasonable to conclude that PCBs are carcinogenic in humans. The National Institute for Occupational Safety and Health has determined that PCBs are a potential occupational carcinogen.

Non-Cancer Effects

EPA evaluates all of the available data in determining the potential noncarcinogenic toxicity of environmental contaminants, including PCBs. Extensive study has been conducted in animals, including non-human primates using environmentally relevant doses. EPA has found clear evidence that PCBs have significant toxic effects in animals, including effects on the immune system, the reproductive system, the nervous system and the endocrine system. The body's regulation of all of these systems is complex and interrelated. As a result, it is not surprising that PCBs can exert a multitude of serious adverse health effects. A discussion of the potential non-cancer health effects of PCBs is presented below.

Immune Effects

The immune system is critical for fighting infections, and diseases of the immune system have very serious potential implications for the health of humans and animals. The immune effects of PCB exposure have been studied in Rhesus monkeys and other animals. It is important to note that the immune systems of Rhesus monkeys and humans are very similar. Studies in monkeys and other animals have revealed a number of serious effects on the immune system following exposures to PCBs, including a significant decrease in size of the thymus gland (which is critical to the immune system) in infant monkeys, reductions in the response of the immune system following a challenge with sheep red blood cells (a standard laboratory test that determines the ability of an animal to mount a primary antibody response and develop protective immunity), and decreased resistance to Epstein-Barr virus and other infections in PCB-exposed animals. Individuals with diseases of the immune system may be more susceptible to pneumonia and viral infections. The animal studies were not able to identify a level of PCB exposure that did not cause effects on the immune system.

In humans, a recent study found that individuals infected with Epstein-Barr virus had a greater association of increased exposures to PCBs with increasing risk of non-Hodgkins lymphoma than those who had no Epstein-Barr infection. This finding is consistent with increases in infection with Epstein Barr virus in animals exposed to

PCBs. Since PCBs suppress the immune system and immune system suppression has been demonstrated as a risk factor for non-Hodgkin's lymphoma, suppression of the immune system is a possible mechanism for PCB-induced cancer. Immune effects were also noted in humans who experienced exposure to rice oil contaminated with PCBs, dibenzofurans and dioxins.

Taken together, the studies in animals and humans suggest that PCBs may have serious potential effects on the immune systems of exposed individuals.

Reproductive Effects

Reproductive effects of PCBs have been studied in a variety of animal species, including Rhesus monkeys, rats, mice and mink. Rhesus monkeys are generally regarded as the best laboratory species for predicting adverse reproductive effects in humans. Potentially serious effects on the reproductive system were seen in monkeys and a number of other animal species following exposures to PCB mixtures. Most significantly, PCB exposures were found to reduce the birth weight, conception rates and live birth rates of monkeys and other species and PCB exposure reduced sperm counts in rats. Effects in monkeys were long-lasting and were observed long after the dosing with PCBs occurred.

Studies of reproductive effects have also been carried out in human populations exposed to PCBs. Children born to women who worked with PCBs in factories showed decreased birth weight and a significant decrease in gestational age with increasing exposures to PCBs. Studies in fishing populations believed to have high exposures to PCBs also suggest similar decreases. This same effect was seen in multiple species of animals exposed to PCBs, and suggests that reproductive effects may be important in humans following exposures to PCBs.

Neurological Effects

Proper development of the nervous system is critical for early learning and can have potentially significant implications for the health of individuals throughout their lifetimes. Effects of PCBs on nervous system development have been studied in monkeys and a variety of other animal species. Newborn monkeys exposed to PCBs showed persistent and significant deficits in neurological development, including visual recognition, short-term memory and learning. Some of these studies were conducted using the types of PCBs most commonly found in human breast milk.

Studies in humans have suggested effects similar to those observed in monkeys exposed to PCBs, including learning deficits and changes in activity associated with exposures to PCBs. The similarity in effects observed in humans and animals provide additional support for the potential neurobehavioral effects of PCBs.

Endocrine Effects

There has been significant discussion and research on the effects of environmental contaminants on the endocrine system ("endocrine disruption"). While the significance of endocrine disruption as a widespread issue in humans and animals is a subject of ongoing study, PCBs have been demonstrated to exert effects on thyroid hormone levels in animals and humans. Thyroid hormone levels are critical for normal growth and development, and alterations in thyroid hormone levels may have significant implications.

It has been shown that PCBs decrease thyroid hormone levels in rodents, and that these decreases have resulted in developmental deficits in the animals, including deficits in hearing. PCB exposures have also been associated with changes in thyroid hormone levels in infants in studies conducted in the Netherlands and Japan. Additional research will be required to determine the significance of these effects in the human population.

Other Non-Cancer Effects

A variety of other non-cancer effects of PCBs have been reported in animals and humans, including dermal and ocular effects in monkeys and humans, and liver toxicity in rodents. Elevations in blood pressure, serum triglyceride, and serum cholesterol have also been reported with increasing serum levels of PCBs in humans.

In summary, PCBs have been demonstrated to cause a variety of serious health effects. PCBs have been shown to cause cancer and a number of serious non-cancer health effects in animals, including effects on the immune system, reproductive system, nervous system, and endocrine system. Studies in humans provide supportive evidence for the potential carcinogenicity and non-carcinogenic effects of PCBs. The different health effects of PCBs may be interrelated, as alterations in one system may have significant implications for the other regulatory systems of the body.

PCBs in Food

Tolerances for polychlorinated biphenyls (PCBs).

Polychlorinated biphenyls (PCBs) are toxic, industrial chemicals. Because of their widespread, uncontrolled industrial applications, PCBs have become a persistent and ubiquitous contaminant in the environment. As a result, certain foods and animal feeds, principally those of animal and marine origin, contain PCBs as unavoidable, environmental contaminants. PCBs are transmitted to the food portion (meat, milk, and eggs) of food-producing animals ingesting PCB-contaminated animal feed. In addition, a significant percentage of paper food-packaging materials contain PCBs which may migrate to the packaged food. The source of PCBs in paper food-packaging materials is primarily of certain types of carbonless copy paper (containing 3 to 5 percent PCBs) in waste paper stocks used for manufacturing recycled paper. Therefore, temporary tolerances for residues of PCBs as unavoidable environmental or industrial contaminants are established for a sufficient period of time following the effective date of this paragraph to permit the elimination of such contaminants at the earliest practicable time. For the purposes of this paragraph, the term polychlorinated biphenyls (PCBs) is applicable to mixtures of chlorinated biphenyl compounds, irrespective of which mixture of PCBs is present as the residue. The temporary tolerances for residues of PCBs are as follows:

1. 1.5 parts per million in milk (fat basis).

2. 1.5 parts per million in manufactured dairy products (fat basis).

3. 3 parts per million in poultry (fat basis).

4. 0.3 parts per million in eggs.

5. 0.2 parts per million in finished animal feed for food-producing animals (except the following finished animal feeds: feed concentrates, feed supplements, and feed premixes).

6. 2 parts per million in animal feed components of animal origin, including fishmeal and other by-products of marine origin and in finished animal feed concentrates, supplements, and premixes intended for food producing animals.

7. 2 parts per million in fish and shellfish (edible portion). The edible portion of fish excludes head, scales, viscera, and inedible bones.

8. 0.2 parts per million in infant and junior foods.

9. 10 parts per million in paper food-packaging material intended for or used with human food, finished animal feed and any components intended for animal feeds. The tolerance shall not apply to paper food-packaging material separated from the food therein by a functional barrier which is impermeable to migration of PCB's.

Section 31.3

Dioxins and Furan

Text in this section begins with excerpts from "Persistent Bioaccumulative and Toxic (PBT) Chemical Program," United States Environmental Protection Agency (EPA), April 18, 2011. Text in this section beginning with "What is Furan?" is excerpted from "Questions and Answers on the Occurrence of Furan in Food," U.S. Food and Drug Administration (FDA), July 2, 2015.

What is Dioxin (2,3,7,8-TCDD)?

The term Dioxin is commonly used to refer to a family of toxic chemicals that all share a similar chemical structure and a common mechanism of toxic action. This family includes seven of the polychlorinated dibenzo dioxins (PCDDs), ten of the polychlorinated dibenzo furans (PCDFs) and twelve of the polychlorinated biphenyls (PCBs). PCDDs and PCDFs are not commercial chemical products but are trace level unintentional by-products of most forms of combustion and several industrial chemical processes. PCBs were produced commercially in large quantities until production was stopped in 1977. Dioxin levels in the environment have been declining since the early seventies and have been the subject of a number of federal and state regulations and clean-up actions; however, current exposures levels still remain a concern.

Why are we concerned?

Because dioxins are widely distributed throughout the environment in low concentrations, are persistent and bioaccumulated, most people have detectable levels of dioxins in their tissues. These levels, in the low parts per trillion, have accumulated over a lifetime and will persist for years, even if no additional exposure were to occur. This background exposure is likely to result in an increased risk of cancer and is uncomfortably close to levels that can cause subtle adverse non-cancer effects in animals and humans.

What harmful effects can dioxin produce?

Dioxins have been characterized by EPA as likely to be human carcinogens and are anticipated to increase the risk of cancer at background levels of exposure.

In 1997, the International Agency for Research on Cancer classified 2,3,7,8 TCDD, the best studied member of the dioxin family, a known human carcinogen. 2,3,7,8 TCDD accounts for about 10% of our background dioxin risk.

At body burden levels 10 times or less above those attributed to average background exposure, adverse non-cancer health effects have been observed both in animals and to a more limited extent, in humans. In animals these effects include changes in hormone systems, alterations in fetal development, reduced reproductive capacity, and immunosuppression. Effects specifically observed in humans include changes in markers of early development and hormone levels. At much higher doses, dioxins can cause a serious skin disease in humans called chloracne.

What is furan?

Furan is a colorless, volatile liquid used in some chemical manufacturing industries. Furan has occasionally been reported to be found in foods. Now scientists at FDA have discovered that furan forms in some foods more commonly than previously thought. This discovery is likely a result of our ability to detect compounds at exceedingly low levels with the latest analytical instruments rather than a change in the presence of furan. The scientists think the furan forms in the food during traditional heat treatment techniques, such as cooking, jarring, and canning.

The term "furans" is sometimes used interchangeably with "dioxins." Does this mean that furan is a dioxin-like compound?

No, furan is not a dioxin-like compound. The term "furans" is sometimes used as shorthand for a group of environmental contaminants called the dibenzofurans, which have dioxin-like activity. In addition "furans" refers to a large class of compounds of widely varying structures including, for example, nitrofurans. These chemicals have different effects than the furan that is now being studied.

What foods has FDA tested? What foods has furan been found in?

So far, FDA has focused on testing canned or jarred foods, because these foods are heated in sealed containers. Furan has been found in such canned or jarred foods as soups, sauces, beans, pasta meals, and baby foods. Data on furan in foods can be found on FDA's website.

How much of a risk is furan in foods?

Furan causes cancer in animals in studies where animals are exposed to furan at high doses. Because furan levels have been measured in only a few foods to date, it is difficult for FDA scientists to accurately calculate levels of furan exposure in food and to estimate a risk to consumers. However, FDA's preliminary estimate of consumer exposure is well below what FDA expects would cause harmful effects. FDA will continue to thoroughly evaluate these preliminary data and conduct additional studies to better determine the potential risk to human health.

The new data show furan in baby foods. Is furan in baby foods of special concern?

No. These data are exploratory and provide only a very limited and incomplete picture of the levels of furan in foods. These data alone do not indicate exposure or risk. FDA's preliminary estimate of consumer exposure is well below what FDA expects would cause harmful effects. FDA has no evidence that consumers should alter their infants' and children's diets and eating habits to avoid exposure to furan.

How did FDA make these findings?

In the course of investigations to confirm the accuracy of a report that furan may be formed in food under certain circumstances, FDA scientists discovered that a wider variety of foods that were heat treated than previously thought contained varying levels of furan.

Why is furan a concern?

Furan is listed in the Department of Health and Human Services list of carcinogens, and considered as possibly carcinogenic by the International Agency for Research on Cancer, based on studies in laboratory animals at high exposures. The concern is whether furan may also cause cancer in humans through long-term exposure to very low levels of furan in foods.

Did furan suddenly appear in food?

No, furan did not suddenly appear in food and has likely been present in food for many years. Furan appears to result from heat treatment techniques, such as canning and jarring, which have long been essential methods of safe food preparation and preservation. Scientists have previously reported finding furan in a small number of foods. What's new now is that FDA scientists have developed a new method that can measure exceedingly low levels of furan and applied that method to a wide variety of foods.

What is FDA doing about furan in foods?

Since first investigating furan in foods with a semi-quantitative method, FDA has refined its method to give quantitative furan measurements, applied that method to a limited number of foods, and begun planning for a larger survey of foods. FDA has also published in the *Federal Register* a call for data on furan from the scientific community. In addition, FDA is holding a public Food Advisory Committee meeting on June 8, 2004, to seek input on what data are needed to fully assess the risk, if any, posed by furan to consumers. FDA will evaluate the available data and will develop an action plan that will outline the agency's goals and planned activities on the issue of furan in food. The action plan will consider such items as an expanded food survey, studies to identify mechanisms of formation in foods and potential strategies to reduce furan levels, and toxicology studies to address mechanisms of furan toxicity and dose-response.

How does furan form in foods?

Exactly how furan forms in food is unknown. Early indications are that there are probably multiple mechanisms of furan formation. Heating is probably an important contributing factor to furan formation in foods, but heat may not be the only pathway to furan formation.

How do the levels of furan in canned foods relate to foods as eaten?

It is possible that canned or jarred foods that have measurable furan levels right after opening may contain lower levels of furan after they are heated in open containers, as they typically would be prior to consumption. Furan is volatile, and a portion may evaporate when foods are heated in an open container, such as a pot. To test this hypothesis, FDA will compare furan levels in foods directly from a can or jar and after heating them as a consumer ordinarily would before consumption.

Chapter 32

Contaminants in Fish and Shellfish

Chapter Contents

Section 32.1

Mercury in Seafood

Text in this section begins with excerpts from "Food—What You Need to Know About Mercury in Fish and Shellfish (Brochure)," U.S. Food and Drug Administration (FDA), June 10, 2014.

Text in this section beginning with "Mercury Levels in Commercial Fish and Shellfish" is excerpted from "Food—Mercury Levels in Commercial Fish and Shellfish (1990-2010)," U.S. Food and Drug Administration (FDA), October 8, 2014.

The Facts

Fish and shellfish are an important part of a healthy diet. Fish and shellfish contain high-quality protein and other essential nutrients, are low in saturated fat, and contain omega-3 fatty acids. A well-balanced diet that includes a variety of fish and shellfish can contribute to heart health and children's proper growth and development. So, women and young children in particular should include fish or shellfish in their diets due to the many nutritional benefits.

However, nearly all fish and shellfish contain traces of mercury. For most people, the risk from mercury by eating fish and shellfish is not a health concern. Yet, some fish and shellfish contain higher levels of mercury that may harm an unborn baby or young child's developing nervous system. The risks from mercury in fish and shellfish depend on the amount of fish and shellfish eaten and the levels of mercury in the fish and shellfish. Therefore, the Food and Drug Administration (FDA) and the Environmental Protection Agency (EPA) are advising women who may become pregnant, pregnant women, nursing mothers, and young children to avoid some types of fish and eat fish and shellfish that are lower in mercury.

3 Safety Tips

By following these 3 recommendations for selecting and eating fish or shellfish, women and young children will receive the benefits of eating fish and shellfish and be confident that they have reduced their exposure to the harmful effects of mercury.

1. Do not eat

They contain high levels of mercury.

- **Shark**
- **Swordfish**
- **King Mackerel**
- **Tilefish**

2. Eat up to 12 ounces (2 average meals) a week of a variety of fish and shellfish that are lower in mercury.

- Five of the most commonly eaten fish that are low in mercury are shrimp, canned light tuna, salmon, pollock, and catfish.

- Another commonly eaten fish, albacore ("white") tuna has more mercury than canned light tuna. So, when choosing your two meals of fish and shellfish, you may eat up to 6 ounces (one average meal) of albacore tuna per week.

3. Check local advisories about the safety of fish caught by family and friends in your local lakes, rivers, and coastal areas.

If no advice is available, eat up to 6 ounces (one average meal) per week of fish you catch from local waters, but don't consume any other fish during that week.

Follow these same recommendations when feeding fish and shellfish to your young child, but serve smaller portions.

Frequently Asked Questions about Mercury in Fish and Shellfish

What is mercury and methylmercury?

Mercury occurs naturally in the environment and can also be released into the air through industrial pollution. Mercury falls from the air and can accumulate in streams and oceans and is turned into methylmercury in the water. It is this type of mercury that can be harmful to your unborn baby and young child. Fish absorb the methylmercury as they feed in these waters and so it builds up in them. It builds up more in some types of fish and shellfish than others, depending on what the fish eat, which is why the levels vary.

I'm a woman who could have children but I'm not pregnant - so why should I be concerned about methylmercury?

If you regularly eat types of fish that are high in methylmercury, it can accumulate in your blood stream over time. Methylmercury is removed from the body naturally, but it may take over a year for the levels to drop significantly. Thus, it may be present in a woman even before she becomes pregnant. This is the reason why women who are trying to become pregnant should also avoid eating certain types of fish.

Is there methylmercury in all fish and shellfish?

Nearly all fish and shellfish contain traces of methylmercury. However, larger fish that have lived longer have the highest levels of methylmercury because they've had more time to accumulate it. These large fish (swordfish, shark, king mackerel and tilefish) pose the greatest risk. Other types of fish and shellfish may be eaten in the amounts recommended by FDA and EPA.

I don't see the fish I eat in the advisory. What should I do?

If you want more information about the levels in the various types of fish you eat, see the FDA food safety website or the EPA website at www.epa.gov/ost/fish.

What about fish sticks and fast food sandwiches?

Fish sticks and "fast-food" sandwiches are commonly made from fish that are low in mercury.

The advice about canned tuna is in the advisory, but what's the advice about tuna steaks?

Because tuna steak generally contains higher levels of mercury than canned light tuna, when choosing your two meals of fish and shellfish, you may eat up to 6 ounces (one average meal) of tuna steak per week.

What if I eat more than the recommended amount of fish and shellfish in a week?

One week's consumption of fish does not change the level of methylmercury in the body much at all. If you eat a lot of fish one week, you can cut back for the next week or two. Just make sure you average the recommended amount per week.

Where do I get information about the safety of fish caught recreationally by family or friends?

Before you go fishing, check your Fishing Regulations Booklet for information about recreationally caught fish. You can also contact your local health department for information about local advisories. You need to check local advisories because some kinds of fish and shellfish caught in your local waters may have higher or much lower than average levels of mercury. This depends on the levels of mercury in the water in which the fish are caught. Those fish with much lower levels may be eaten more frequently and in larger amounts.

Mercury Levels in Commercial Fish and Shellfish (1990-2010)

The Table 32.1 is sorted by MERCURY CONCENTRATION MEAN (PPM) from fish with lowest levels of mercury to highest levels of mercury.

Table 32.1. Mercury Levels in Commercial Fish and Shellfish (1990-2010)

SPECIES	MERCURY CONCENTRATION MEAN (PPM)	MERCURY CONCENTRATION MEDIAN (PPM)	MERCURY CONCENTRATION STDEV (PPM)	MERCURY CONCENTRATION MIN (PPM)	MERCURY CONCENTRATION MAX (PPM)	NO. OF SAMPLES	SOURCE OF DATA
SCALLOP	0.003	ND	0.007	ND	0.033	39	FDA 1991-2009
SALMON (CANNED)*	0.008	ND	0.017	ND	0.086	34	FDA 1992-2009
CLAM*	0.009	0.002	0.011	ND	0.028	15	FDA 1991-2010
SHRIMP*	0.009	0.001	0.013	ND	0.05	40	FDA 1991-2009
OYSTER	0.012	ND	0.035	ND	0.25	61	FDA 1991-2009
SARDINE	0.013	0.01	0.015	ND	0.083	90	FDA 2002-2010
TILAPIA*	0.013	0.004	0.023	ND	0.084	32	FDA 1991-2008
ANCHOVIES	0.017	0.014	0.015	ND	0.049	14	FDA 2007-2010
SALMON (FRESH/FROZEN)*	0.022	0.015	0.034	ND	0.19	94	FDA 1991-2009
SQUID	0.023	0.016	0.022	ND	0.07	42	FDA 2005-2010
CATFISH	0.025	0.005	0.057	ND	0.314	57	FDA 1991-2010
POLLOCK	0.031	0.003	0.089	ND	0.78	95	FDA 1991-2008
CRAWFISH	0.033	0.035	0.012	ND	0.051	46	FDA 1991 -2007
SHAD AMERICAN	0.045	0.039	0.045	0.013	0.186	13	FDA 2007-2010
MACKEREL ATLANTIC (N.Atlantic)	0.05	N/A	N/A	0.02	0.16	80	NMFS REPORT 1978
MULLET	0.05	0.014	0.078	ND	0.27	20	FDA 1991-2008
WHITING	0.051	0.052	0.03	ND	0.096	13	FDA 1991-2008
HADDOCK (Atlantic)	0.055	0.049	0.033	ND	0.197	50	FDA 1991-2009
FLATFISH [2*]	0.056	0.05	0.045	ND	0.218	71	FDA 1991-2009
BUTTERFISH	0.058	N/A	N/A	ND	0.36	89	NMFS REPORT 1978

Table 32.1. *Continued*

SPECIES	MERCURY CONCENTRATION MEAN (PPM)	MERCURY CONCENTRATION MEDIAN (PPM)	MERCURY CONCENTRATION STDEV (PPM)	MERCURY CONCENTRATION MIN (PPM)	MERCURY CONCENTRATION MAX (PPM)	NO. OF SAMPLES	SOURCE OF DATA
CROAKER ATLANTIC (Atlantic)	0.065	0.061	0.05	ND	0.193	57	FDA 2002 - 2009
CRAB [1]	0.065	0.05	0.096	ND	0.61	93	FDA 1991-2009
TROUT (FRESHWATER)	0.071	0.025	0.141	ND	0.678	35	FDA 1991 -2008
HAKE	0.079	0.067	0.064	ND	0.378	49	FDA 1994-2009
JACKSMELT	0.081	0.05	0.103	0.011	0.5	23	FDA 1997-2007
HERRING	0.084	0.048	0.128	ND	0.56	26	FDA 2006-2009
MACKEREL CHUB (Pacific)	0.088	N/A	N/A	0.03	0.19	30	NMFS REPORT 1978
WHITEFISH	0.089	0.067	0.084	ND	0.317	37	FDA 1991-2008
SHEEPSHEAD	0.093	0.088	0.059	ND	0.17	6	FDA 2007 - 2009
LOBSTER (Spiny)	0.093	0.062	0.097	ND	0.27	13	FDA 1991-2005
LOBSTER (NORTHERN / AMERICAN)	0.107	0.086	0.076	ND	0.23	9	FDA 2005-2007
CARP	0.11	0.134	0.099	ND	0.271	14	FDA 1992 - 2007
COD	0.111	0.066	0.152	ND	0.989	115	FDA 1991-2010
PERCH OCEAN*	0.121	0.102	0.125	ND	0.578	31	FDA 1991-2010
TUNA (CANNED, LIGHT)	0.128	0.078	0.135	ND	0.889	551	FDA 1991-2010
SKATE	0.137	N/A	N/A	0.04	0.36	56	NMFS REPORT 1978

503

Table 32.1. Continued

SPECIES	MERCURY CONCENTRATION MEAN (PPM)	MERCURY CONCENTRATION MEDIAN (PPM)	MERCURY CONCENTRATION STDEV (PPM)	MERCURY CONCENTRATION MIN (PPM)	MERCURY CONCENTRATION MAX (PPM)	NO.OF SAMPLES	SOURCE OF DATA
BUFFALOFISH	0.137	0.12	0.094	0.032	0.43	17	FDA 1992-2008
TUNA (FRESH/ FROZEN, SKIPJACK)	0.144	0.15	0.119	0.022	0.26	3	FDA 1993 - 2007
TILEFISH (Atlantic)	0.144	0.099	0.122	0.042	0.533	32	FDA 2002-04
PERCH (Freshwater)	0.15	0.146	0.112	ND	0.325	19	FDA 1991-2007
BASS (SALTWATER, BLACK, STRIPED) [3]	0.152	0.084	0.201	ND	0.96	82	FDA 1991-2010
LOBSTER (Species Unknown)	0.166	0.143	0.099	ND	0.451	71	FDA 1991-2008
SNAPPER	0.166	0.113	0.244	ND	1.366	67	FDA 1991-2007
MONKFISH	0.181	0.139	0.075	0.106	0.289	9	FDA 2006-2008
MACKEREL SPANISH (S. Atlantic)	0.182	N/A	N/A	0.05	0.73	43	NMFS REPORT 1978
SCORPIONFISH	0.233	0.181	0.139	0.098	0.456	6	FDA 2007 - 2008
WEAKFISH (SEA TROUT)	0.235	0.157	0.216	0	0.744	46	FDA 1991-2005
HALIBUT	0.241	0.188	0.225	ND	1.52	101	FDA 1992-2009
CROAKER WHITE (Pacific)	0.287	0.28	0.069	0.18	0.41	15	FDA 1997
TUNA (CANNED, ALBACORE)	0.35	0.338	0.128	ND	0.853	451	FDA 1991-2010
TUNA (FRESH/ FROZEN, YELLOWFIN)	0.354	0.311	0.231	0	1.478	231	FDA 1991-2010

504

Table 32.1. Continued

SPECIES	MERCURY CONCENTRATION MEAN (PPM)	MERCURY CONCENTRATION MEDIAN (PPM)	MERCURY CONCENTRATION STDEV (PPM)	MERCURY CONCENTRATION MIN (PPM)	MERCURY CONCENTRATION MAX (PPM)	NO. OF SAMPLES	SOURCE OF DATA
BASS CHILEAN	0.354	0.303	0.299	ND	2.18	74	FDA 1994-2010
TUNA (FRESH/ FROZEN, ALBACORE)	0.358	0.36	0.138	ND	0.82	43	FDA 1992-2008
SABLEFISH	0.361	0.265	0.241	0.09	1.052	26	FDA 2004 - 2009
BLUEFISH	0.368	0.305	0.221	0.089	1.452	94	FDA 1991-2009
TUNA (FRESH/ FROZEN, ALL)	0.391	0.34	0.266	0	1.816	420	FDA 1991 - 2010
TUNA (FRESH/ FROZEN, Species Unknown)	0.415	0.339	0.308	0	1.3	120	FDA 1991-2010
GROUPER (ALL SPECIES)	0.448	0.399	0.278	0.006	1.205	53	FDA 1991-2005
MACKEREL SPANISH (Gulf of Mexico)	0.454	N/A	N/A	0.07	1.56	66	NMFS REPORT 1978
MARLIN*	0.485	0.39	0.237	0.1	0.92	16	FDA 1992-1996
ORANGE ROUGHY	0.571	0.562	0.183	0.265	1.12	81	FDA 1991-2009
TUNA (FRESH/ FROZEN, BIGEYE)	0.689	0.56	0.341	0.128	1.816	21	FDA 1991 - 2005
MACKEREL KING	0.73	N/A	N/A	0.23	1.67	213	GULF OF MEXICO REPORT 2000
SHARK	0.979	0.811	0.626	ND	4.54	356	FDA 1990-2007
SWORDFISH	0.995	0.87	0.539	ND	3.22	636	FDA 1990-2010
TILEFISH (Gulf of Mexico)	1.45	N/A	N/A	0.65	3.73	60	NMFS REPORT 1978

505

Source of data: FDA 1990-2010, "National Marine Fisheries Service Survey of Trace Elements in the Fishery Resource" Report 1978, "The Occurrence of Mercury in the Fishery Resources of the Gulf of Mexico" Report 2000

Mercury was measured as Total Mercury except for species (*) when only Methylmercury was analyzed.

ND-mercury concentration below detection level (Level of Detection (LOD)=0.01ppm)

N/A-data not available

†The following species have been removed from the tables:

- Bass (freshwater) – not commercial

- Pickerel – not commercial

‡Standard deviation data generated from data 1990 to 2010.
¹Includes: Blue, King, Snow
²Includes: Flounder, Plaice, Sole
³Includes: Sea bass/ Striped Bass/ Rockfish

NOTE: On February 8, 2006, technical changes were made to the data that was posted on January 19, 2006. The changes corrected data or more properly characterized the species of fish or shellfish sampled. On October 6, 2014, technical changes were made to allow viewers to review the list in order of mercury levels and in alphabetical order by fish species.

Section 32.2

Shellfish Poisoning

Text in this section begins with excerpts from "Food—BBB – Various Shellfish-Associated Toxins," U.S. Food and Drug Administration (FDA), October 7, 2014; text in this section beginning with "Paralytic shellfish poisoning" is excerpted from "Travelers' Health—Food Poisoning from Marine Toxins," Centers for Disease Control and Prevention (CDC), July 10, 2015.

Name of the Organism:

Various Shellfish-Associated

Shellfish poisoning is caused by a group of toxins elaborated by planktonic algae (dinoflagellates, in most cases) upon which the shellfish feed. The toxins are accumulated and sometimes metabolized by the shellfish. The 20 toxins responsible for paralytic shellfish poisonings (PSP) are all derivatives of saxitoxin. Diarrheic shellfish poisoning (DSP) is presumably caused by a group of high molecular weight polyethers, including okadaic acid, the dinophysis toxins, the pectenotoxins, and yessotoxin. Neurotoxic shellfish poisoning (NSP) is the result of exposure to a group of polyethers called brevetoxins. Amnesic shellfish poisoning (ASP) is caused by the unusual amino acid, domoic acid, as the contaminant of shellfish.

Nature of Acute Disease:

Paralytic Shellfish Poisoning (PSP)
Diarrheic Shellfish Poisoning (DSP)
Neurotoxic Shellfish Poisoning (NSP)
Amnesic Shellfish Poisoning (ASP)

Nature of Disease:

Ingestion of contaminated shellfish results in a wide variety of symptoms, depending upon the toxins(s) present, their concentrations in the shellfish and the amount of contaminated shellfish consumed. In the case of PSP, the effects are predominantly neurological and include tingling, burning, numbness, drowsiness, incoherent speech, and respiratory paralysis. Less well characterized are the symptoms associated with DSP, NSP, and ASP. DSP is primarily observed as a generally mild gastrointestinal disorder, i.e., nausea, vomiting, diarrhea, and abdominal pain accompanied by chills, headache, and fever. Both gastrointestinal and neurological symptoms characterize NSP, including tingling and numbness of lips, tongue, and throat, muscular aches, dizziness, reversal of the sensations of hot and cold, diarrhea, and vomiting. ASP is characterized by gastrointestinal disorders (vomiting, diarrhea, abdominal pain) and neurological problems (confusion, memory loss, disorientation, seizure, coma).

Diagnosis of Human Illness:

Diagnosis of shellfish poisoning is based entirely on observed symptomatology and recent dietary history.

Associated Foods:

All shellfish (filter-feeding molluscs) are potentially toxic. However, PSP is generally associated with mussels, clams, cockles, and scallops; NSP with shellfish harvested along the Florida coast and the Gulf of Mexico; DSP with mussels, oysters, and scallops, and ASP with mussels.

Relative Frequency of Disease:

Good statistical data on the occurrence and severity of shellfish poisoning are largely unavailable, which undoubtedly reflects the inability to measure the true incidence of the disease. Cases are frequently misdiagnosed and in general, infrequently reported. Of these toxicoses, the most serious from a public health perspective appears to be PSP. The extreme potency of the PSP toxins has, in the past, resulted in an unusually high mortality rate.

Course of Disease and Complications:

PSP: Symptoms of the disease develop fairly rapidly, within 0.5 to 2 hours after ingestion of the shellfish, depending on the amount of toxin consumed. In severe cases respiratory paralysis is common, and death may occur if respiratory support is not provided. When such support is applied within 12 hours of exposure, recovery usually is complete, with no lasting side effects. In unusual cases, because of the weak hypotensive action of the toxin, death may occur from cardiovascular collapse despite respiratory support.

NSP: Onset of this disease occurs within a few minutes to a few hours; duration is fairly short, from a few hours to several days. Recovery is complete with few after effects; no fatalities have been reported.

DSP: Onset of the disease, depending on the dose of toxin ingested, may be as little as 30 minutes, to 2 to 3 hours, with symptoms of the illness lasting as long as 2 to 3 days. Recovery is complete with no after effects; the disease is generally not life-threatening.

ASP: The toxicosis is characterized by the onset of gastrointestinal symptoms within 24 hours; neurological symptoms occur within 48 hours. The toxicosis is particularly serious in elderly patients, and includes symptoms reminiscent of Alzheimer's disease. All fatalities to date have involved elderly patients.

Target Populations:

All humans are susceptible to shellfish poisoning. Elderly people are apparently predisposed to the severe neurological effects of the ASP toxin. A disproportionate number of PSP cases occur among tourists or others who are not native to the location where the toxic shellfish are harvested. This may be due to disregard for either official quarantines or traditions of safe consumption, both of which tend to protect the local population.

Food Analysis:

The mouse bioassay has historically been the most universally applied technique for examining shellfish (especially for PSP); other bioassay procedures have been developed but not generally applied. Unfortunately, the dose-survival times for the DSP toxins in the mouse assay fluctuate considerably and fatty acids interfere with the assay, giving false-positive results; consequently, a suckling mouse assay that has been developed and used for control of DSP measures fluid accumulation after injection of the shellfish extract. In recent years considerable effort has been applied to development of chemical assays to replace these bioassays. As a result, a good high performance liquid chromatography (HPLC) procedure has been developed to identify individual PSP toxins (detection limit for saxitoxin = 20 fg/100 g of meats; 0.2 ppm), an excellent HPLC procedure (detection limit for okadaic acid = 400 ng/g; 0.4 ppm), a commercially available immunoassay (detection limit for okadaic acid = 1 fg/100 g of meats; 0.01 ppm) for DSP and a totally satisfactory HPLC procedure for ASP (detection limit for domoic acid = 750 ng/g; 0.75 ppm).

Health Effects of Shellfish Poisoning

Paralytic Shellfish Poisoning

Paralytic shellfish poisoning (PSP) is the most common and most severe form of shellfish poisoning. PSP is caused by eating shellfish contaminated with saxitoxins produced by dinoflagellates from *Aelxandrium, Pyrodinium,* and *Gymnodinium* genera. Symptoms usually appear 30–60 minutes after eating toxic shellfish and include numbness and tingling of the face, lips, tongue, arms, and legs. There may be headache, nausea, vomiting, and diarrhea. Severe cases are associated with ingestion of large doses of toxin and clinical features such as ataxia, dysphagia, mental status changes, flaccid paralysis, and respiratory failure. The case-fatality ratio is dependent on the availability of modern medical care, including mechanical ventilation. The death rate may be particularly high in children.

Neurotoxic Shellfish Poisoning

Neurotoxin shellfish poisoning is caused by eating shellfish contaminated with brevetoxins produced by the dinoflagellate *K. brevis.* Neurotoxic shellfish poisoning usually presents as gastroenteritis accompanied by minor neurologic symptoms resembling mild ciguatera poisoning or mild paralytic shellfish poisoning. Inhalation of aerosolized toxin in the sea spray associated with a Florida red tide (*K. brevis* bloom) can induce bronchoconstriction and may cause acute, temporary respiratory discomfort in healthy people. People with asthma may experience more severe and prolonged respiratory effects.

Diarrheic Shellfish Poisoning

Diarrheic shellfish poisoning (DSP) is caused by eating shellfish contaminated with a group of toxins that include polyether molecules (such as okadaic acid) produced by dinoflagellates from the genera *Dinophysis* and *Prorocentrum lima.* DSP produces chills, nausea, vomiting, abdominal cramps, and diarrhea. No deaths have been reported.

Amnesic Shellfish Poisoning

Amnesic shellfish poisoning (ASP) is a rare form of shellfish poisoning caused by eating shellfish, particularly blue mussels, contaminated with domoic acid produced by the diatom *Nitzchia pungens.* The first cases of ASP were reported after an outbreak associated with eating contaminated cultivated mussels. These cases were reported to have severe gastroenteric and neurologic symptoms. More recently, domoic acid exposure via the food web was implicated in die-off of marine mammals along the US Pacific Coast.

Section 32.3

How the U.S. Food and Drug Administration Regulates Imported Seafood

Text in this section begins with excerpts from "Food—imported seafood Safety Program," U.S. Food and Drug Administration (FDA), March 24, 2015; text in this section beginning with "How do drug residues end up in food?" is excerpted from "How FDA Regulates Seafood: FDA Detains Imports of Farm-Raised Chinese Seafood," U.S. Food and Drug Administration (FDA), October 14, 2014.

The Imported Seafood Safety Program

FDA is responsible for the safety of all fish and fishery products entering the United States. The agency uses every available tool to identify immediate or potential threats as well as the best course of action to protect public health and safety. As part of the FDA's import safety effort, the agency provides as much available information and guidance as possible to consumers, industry, and government about seafood safety.

Hazard Analysis and Critical Control Points

FDA's multifaceted and risk-informed seafood safety program relies on various measures of compliance with its seafood Hazard Analysis and Critical Control Points (HACCP) regulations, which describe a management system in which food safety is addressed through the analysis and control of biological, chemical, and physical hazards from raw material production, procurement and handling, to manufacturing, distribution and consumption of the finished product.

For imported seafood, these measures include:

- inspections of foreign processing facilities,

- sampling of seafood offered for import into the United States,

- domestic surveillance sampling of imported products,

- inspections of seafood importers,

- evaluations of filers of seafood products,

- foreign country program assessments, and

- relevant information from our foreign partners and FDA overseas offices.

Foreign Inspections and Global Presence

FDA has increased the number of foreign site inspections in recent years, and is working globally to better accomplish its domestic mission to promote and protect the public health of the United States. FDA has strengthened and better coordinated its international engagements by establishing permanent FDA posts abroad in strategic locations. The posting of FDA staff in certain overseas regions is a key part of the agency's strategy for expanding oversight of imported food.

PREDICT

FDA is also implementing a new screening system for imports, the Predictive Risk-based Evaluation for Dynamic Import Compliance Targeting (PREDICT), which will improve the current electronic screening system by targeting higher risk products for exam and sampling and minimizing the delays of shipments of lower risk products. PREDICT will improve the agency's ability to detect trends and investigate patterns. This in turn, will help to make more efficient use of FDA's import resources and allow FDA to adjust import sampling levels for seafood products over time and as appropriate.

Foreign Country Assessments

Foreign country assessments are systems reviews that offer FDA a broad view of the ability of the country's industry and regulatory infrastructure to control aquaculture drugs. These assessments allow FDA to become familiar with the controls that a country's competent authority is implementing for the distribution, availability, and use of animal drugs. FDA uses country assessments to evaluate the country's laws for, and implementation of, control of animal drug residues in the aquaculture products it ships to the United States.

The country assessment program helps FDA direct its foreign inspection and border surveillance resources more effectively and efficiently and allows FDA to work directly with countries to resolve drug residue problems.

FDA uses information from country assessments to:

- better target (i.e., increase or decrease) surveillance sampling of imported aquaculture products;

- inform its decisions on what new analytical methods it needs to develop and what drugs or chemicals it should target for surveillance sampling;

- inform its planning of foreign seafood HACCP inspections;

- provide additional evidence for potential regulatory actions, such as an import alert;

- improve collaboration with foreign government and industry contacts to achieve better compliance with FDA's regulatory requirements; and

- better understand the causes for significant changes in a country's drug residue problems, such as a sudden spike in noncompliant samples.

Results of Country Assessments

The assessment trip to China in 2006 was a key consideration in issuance of the China country-wide import alert for specific aquaculture products from China in 2007.

The country assessments for China in 2006, Chile in 2008, and India in 2010 were considered and resulted in increased sampling and testing under the compliance program and special assignments for aquaculture products from these countries (e.g., eel from China, salmon from Chile, and shrimp from India).

Food Safety Modernization Act of 2011

FDA conducts its seafood safety oversight activities in conformance with its statutory authorities, which have recently been expanded by the Food Safety Modernization Act (FSMA). FSMA represents the first major overhaul of FDA's food safety law in more than 70 years and will transform FDA's food safety program. FSMA closes significant and longstanding gaps in FDA's food safety authority, with new safeguards to prevent, rather than react, to food safety problems, and gives FDA important new tools to ensure that imported seafood is as safe as domestic seafood.

Integrated Food Safety System

FDA collaborates with the President's Food Safety Working Group to modernize food safety by building collaborative partnerships with consumers, industry and regulatory partners.

For example, FDA and the National Marine Fisheries Service's (NMFS) Seafood Inspection Program have certain common and related objectives in carrying out their respective regulatory and service activities that lend themselves to cooperation under a Memorandum of Understanding (MOU) that sets forth the working arrangements between the agencies that facilitate each agency's efforts to discharge its responsibilities related to the inspection of fish and fishery products.

National Residue Monitoring Program

In addition to implementing the new FSMA authorities, FDA will continue the national residue monitoring program and recognizes the benefit of such a program to ensure that foods are not contaminated with illegal animal drug residues. FSMA directs FDA to establish a program for testing of food by accredited laboratories and will require that food be tested by accredited laboratories in some circumstances, such as in support of admission of imported food. FDA is developing the laboratory accreditation program as part of its FSMA implementation efforts.

How do drug residues end up in fish?

Some fish are given drugs to treat bacterial and parasitic diseases that cause major mortalities in fish. FDA's Center for Veterinary Medicine (CVM) regulates drugs given to animals. CVM conducts research to improve the drug approval process and expand the number of safe drugs available for fish production. CVM also develops methods to detect unapproved chemicals in fish tissues so that harmful drug residues don't wind up in the fish on your plate.

Is imported seafood required to meet the same standards as domestic seafood?

Yes. Imported foods must be pure, wholesome, safe to eat, and produced under sanitary conditions. FDA requires imported seafood to be free of harmful residues. Importers must comply with regulations under the Federal Food, Drug and Cosmetic Act and the Fair Packaging and Labeling Act. In addition, seafood must be processed in accordance with FDA's Hazard Analysis and Critical Control Point (HACCP) regulations. A 1997 regulation, "Procedures for the Safe and Sanitary Processing and Importing of Fish and Fishery Products," requires seafood processors to identify food safety hazards and apply preventive measures to control hazards that could cause foodborne illness.

What other specific FDA regulatory programs focus on seafood?

National Shellfish Sanitation Program: Administered by FDA, this program provides for the sanitary harvest and production of fresh and frozen molluscan shellfish (oysters, clams, and mussels). FDA conducts reviews of foreign and domestic molluscan shellfish safety programs.

Salmon Control Plan: This is a voluntary, cooperative program among industry, FDA, and the Grocery Manufacturers Association/Food Products Association. It's designed to provide control over processing and plant sanitation, and to address concerns in the salmon canning industry.

Low-Acid Canned Food (LACF) Program: To ensure safety from harmful bacteria or their toxins, especially the deadly *Clostridium botulinum (C botulinum)* in canned foods, regulations were established to ensure that commercial canning establishments apply proper processing, controls, such as heating the canned food at the proper temperature for a sufficient time to destroy the toxin-forming bacteria. Products such as canned tuna and salmon are examples of LACF seafood products.

How does FDA know when there is a safety concern associated with seafood?

FDA, in collaboration with state regulatory counterparts, conducts in-plant inspections that focus on product safety, plant/food hygiene, economic fraud, and other compliance concerns. FDA also receives notice of every seafood entry coming from a foreign country and selects entries from which to collect and analyze samples. FDA laboratories analyze samples for the presence of various safety hazards and contaminants, such as pathogens, chemical contaminants, unapproved food additives and drugs, pesticides, and toxins. Through close collaboration with the Centers for Disease Control (CDC) and state and foreign regulatory partners, FDA also learns of seafood safety concerns that arise through reports of illness potentially associated with seafood products.

What steps does FDA take when problems with seafood are detected?

For imported seafood, FDA has the authority to detain the food at the border to keep it from entering the country. This happens when FDA's analysis of such products indicate that they are not in compliance with the laws and regulations enforced by FDA. FDA can subsequently refuse entries of detained products if evidence of compliance is not provided by the importer or the importer does not correct the problem.

FDA has developed a number of import alerts that address problems found in seafood products in the past. An import alert identifies products that are suspected of violating the law so that FDA field personnel and U.S. Customs and Border Protection staff can stop these entries at the border prior to distribution in the United States. Usually, these import alerts will describe the products or firms that are subject to detention without physical examination. When products are detained without physical examination, the burden for demonstrating compliance of the product falls on the importer. Such compliance must be demonstrated before the product can enter U.S. commerce.

FDA can recommend criminal prosecution or injunction of responsible domestic firms and individuals, as well as seizure of contaminated products in commercial distribution within the U.S. FDA also works with domestic seafood processors to initiate voluntary recalls of contaminated products that may pose a safety concern to consumers.

What kind of research on seafood safety does FDA do?

FDA conducts research to better understand the nature and severity posed by various safety hazards, and other defects which may affect quality and economic integrity and to develop methods to minimize these risks. There are FDA laboratories specializing in seafood research on the Atlantic, Gulf, and Pacific coasts to address regional problems related to toxins and contaminants. FDA also has a facility in Laurel, MD for conducting state-of-the-art research on drugs used in aquaculture.

What is the consumer's role in seafood safety?

As with any food, consumers should take precautions to reduce the risk of foodborne illness associated with seafood. This includes properly selecting, preparing, and storing seafood. For example, consumers should only buy food from reputable sources and buy fresh seafood that is refrigerated or properly iced. Also, most seafood should be cooked to an internal temperature of 145°F. Some people are at greater risk for foodborne illness and should not eat raw or partially cooked fish or shellfish. This includes pregnant women, young children, older adults, and people with compromised immune systems.

Chapter 33

Effects of Growth Promoters in Dairy and Meat

Chapter Contents

Section 33.1

Antibiotics Resistance and Food Safety

This section includes excerpts from "National Antimicrobial
Resistance Monitoring System," Centers for Disease Control and
Prevention (CDC), September 15, 2014.

Antimicrobial resistance is one of our most serious health threats.
Infections from resistant bacteria are now too common, and some
pathogens have even become resistant to multiple types or classes of
antibiotics (antimicrobials used to treat bacterial infections). Antibiotic-resistant infections can also come from the food we eat.

The germs that contaminate food can be resistant because of the
use of antibiotics in people, and in food animals. We can prevent many
of these infections by:

- Using antibiotics carefully,

- Keeping *Salmonella* and other bacteria out of the food we eat, and

- Following food safety guidelines.

Recent outbreaks in 2011, 2011-2012, and 2013 of multi-drug resistant *Salmonella* traced to ground beef and poultry show how animal
and human health are linked.

Frequently Asked Questions

Antibiotics and resistance

What is an antibiotic?

An antibiotic is a type of drug that kills or stops the growth of
bacteria. Examples include penicillin and ciprofloxacin, and there are
many others.

What does "susceptible" mean when it comes to antibiotics?

The term "susceptible" means that the antibiotic can kill the bacteria or stop its growth. For example, when we say that a type of bacteria

is susceptible to the antibiotic penicillin, it means that penicillin kills or stops the growth of that bacteria.

What is antibiotic resistance?

Antibiotic resistance is the ability of bacteria to resist the effects of an antibiotic—that is, the bacteria are not killed, and their growth is not stopped.

Resistant bacteria survive exposure to the antibiotic and continue to multiply in the body, potentially causing more harm and spreading to other animals or people.

Antibiotics and food safety

How do resistant bacteria in food animals end up in our food?

All animals carry bacteria in their intestines. Giving antibiotics to animals will kill most bacteria, but resistant bacteria can survive and multiply.

- When food animals are slaughtered and processed, these bacteria can contaminate the meat or other animal products.

- These bacteria can also get into the environment when an animal poops and may spread to produce that is irrigated with contaminated water.

Food can get contaminated whether the bacteria are resistant to antibiotics or not.

How do people get infections with resistant bacteria from animals?

People can get exposed to resistant bacteria from animals when they:

- Handle or eat meat or produce contaminated with resistant bacteria; or

- Come into contact with the animals' poop (either directly or when it's on a surface).

What effects do resistant infections have on people?

Some resistant infections cause severe illness. People with these infections:

- May require increased recovery time;

- Tend to incur increased medical expenses; and/or

- May die from infection.

What are some other consequences of antibiotic resistance?

Sometimes the bacteria that cause infections are resistant to the drug of choice and this drug doesn't work. Physicians must then recommend second- or third-choice drugs for treatment, but these drugs might be less effective, more toxic, and more expensive. Preserving the effectiveness of antibiotics is vital to protecting human and animal health.

Antibiotics and food-producing animals

Is antibiotic resistance in food animals an important problem for human health?

Yes, antibiotic resistance is an important problem for human health. Antibiotic use in any setting may lead to development of resistance. There is strong evidence that some antibiotic resistance in bacteria is caused by antibiotic use in food animals.

What causes antibiotic resistance in food animals?

Any use of antibiotics can lead to resistance. However, when animals are given antibiotics for growth promotion or increased feed efficiency, bacteria are exposed to low doses of these drugs over a long period of time. This long-term, low-level exposure to antibiotics may lead to the survival and growth of resistant bacteria.

- Antibiotics used in high concentrations for a short time for treating infections in individual animals is less risky.

- Resistant bacteria can pass on resistance to their offspring and can also pass some resistance traits to other kinds of bacteria.

What uses are antibiotics approved for in food animals?

In food animals, FDA has approved the use of antibiotics for:

- *Disease treatment* for animals that are sick;

- *Disease control* for a group of animals when some of the animals are sick;

- *Disease prevention* for a group of healthy animals that are at risk of becoming sick; and

- *Growth promotion* or *increased feed efficiency* in a herd or flock of animals to promote weight gain.

How commonly are antibiotics used in food animals?

Antibiotics are used quite commonly in food animals. This use may contribute to the development of antibiotic-resistant bacteria. However, there is currently no system to track the precise amount of antibiotics used in food animals in the United States.

How do we know that antibiotic use in food animals is linked to resistant infections in humans?

Scientists around the world have provided strong evidence that antibiotic use in food animals can lead to resistant infections in humans. Studies have shown that:

- Antibiotic use in food animals allows antibiotic-resistant bacteria to thrive while susceptible bacteria die;

- Resistant bacteria can be transmitted from food animals to humans through contaminated food;

- Resistant bacteria in food can cause infections in humans; and

- Infections with resistant bacteria can cause illnesses that are more severe and more likely to result in death as well as higher health care costs.

Can we stop using antibiotics in food animals?

No, we cannot stop all antibiotic use in food animals. Antibiotics are valuable tools for reducing animal disease and suffering. But decisions about what antibiotics to use and how to use them must be made with consideration of their potential impact on human health.

Section 33.2

Recombinant Bovine Growth Hormone (rBGH)

This section includes excerpts from "Report on the Food and
Drug Administration's Review of the Safety of Recombinant
Bovine Somatotropin," U.S. and Drug Administration (FDA),
July 28, 2014.

Report on the Food and Drug Administration's Review of the Safety of Recombinant Bovine Somatotropin

Introduction

On November 5, 1993, following extensive review of the data to
support the safety and effectiveness of the product, the Food and Drug
Administration (FDA or Agency) approved the Monsanto Companys
New Animal Drug Application for Posilac containing a recombinant
bovine growth hormone (rbGH) (also known as recombinant bovine
somatotropin, rbST, or Sometribove).

Growth hormone (GH) is a protein hormone produced in the pituitary gland of animals including humans and is essential for normal
growth, development, and health maintenance. Approximately 60
years ago, it was discovered that injecting cows with GH extracted
from cattle pituitary glands increased milk production. In the 1980s, it
became technically possible and economically feasible to produce large
quantities of bovine GH (bGH) using recombinant DNA processes. The
Posilac product contains a recombinant bGH (rbGH) which is essentially the same as (pituitary derived) bGH.

In order to grant approval of Posilac, FDA determined, among other
things, that food products from cows treated with rbGH are safe for
consumption by humans. Vermont Public Interest Research Group
and Rural Vermont have questioned the validity of this finding based
on an analysis by reviewers at Health Canada (the Canadian counterpart of the FDA). This analysis, based in large part on a 90-day rat
study, challenges the Agency's human health findings and argues that
possible adverse health effects of Posilac were not addressed because
long term toxicology studies to ascertain human health safety were
not required by FDA or conducted by Monsanto.

FDA has completed a comprehensive, page by page audit of the human food safety sections of the investigational new animal drug file and master file supporting the rbGH approval. This audit examined all the studies used in determining the human food safety of rbGH, including the 90-day rat oral toxicity study and the report of the antibody response to oral rbGH upon which the Canadian reviewers relied. Upon determining that a review had not been performed of the antibody data during the course of the original review of the Monsanto application, these data were reviewed in their entirety. As set forth in detail below, FDA believes that the Canadian reviewers did not interpret the study results correctly and that there are no new scientific concerns regarding the safety of milk from cows treated with rbGH. The determination that long term studies were not necessary for assessing the safety of rbGH was based on studies which show that: bGH is biologically inactive in humans even if injected, rbGH is orally inactive, and bGH and rbGH are biologically indistinguishable.

Absorption

When taken orally, proteins typically are broken down in the digestive process and are not absorbed into the body. To determine whether an rbGH product had biologically significant oral activity, the Agency required the drugs sponsor to perform short-term toxicology studies to assess whether biologically active rbGH was being absorbed into the body. Absorption of biologically active rbGH into the body could indicate a need for longer term studies to assess the possible impact on various body organs, particularly the liver. The study was conducted by orally administering rbGH to rats for 28 days at 100 times the daily dose administered to dairy cattle. FDA determined that there was no evidence for the absorption of biologically active rbGH following oral administration because there were no dose-related trends associated with oral administration of rbGH to rats for 28 days.

The Canadian analysis takes issue with the Agency's findings regarding a 90-day rat oral toxicity study performed by Monsanto to fulfill a requirement of the European Union (EU) for rbGH approval. The study was conducted by a Searle laboratory of Monsanto and submitted to FDA pursuant to FDA's requirement that all relevant safety information for an investigational new animal drug be included in the sponsor's application. The FDA reviewed the study in 1989, except as noted below, and it was determined that there were no observed effects from oral administration at any dose. In this study, there was evidence that oral administration of rbGH produced an antibody response; however, such response was consistent with that produced by a number of food proteins and is not necessarily an indication of absorption of intact rbGH.

As rbGH produces significant biological effects when injected into rats, this study supported the inability of rbGH to cause significant biological effects following oral administration even at doses 50 times greater than the injected dose.

The report of the 90-day rat oral toxicity study included discussion of a satellite study group of rats. This satellite study was conducted to investigate the antibody response to rbGH as an indirect measure of the possible absorption of rbGH from the rat gastrointestinal tract. This satellite study was not reviewed when originally submitted. Once this oversight was detected, the Agency immediately undertook the review of the data.

FDA's review of the antibody response study "Determination of Sometribove immunoglobulin in rat serum" was completed on November 30, 1998. The study showed:

1. Six out of 30 rats receiving 5 mg ($10-3$ grams)/kg/day oral rbGH, and 9 out of 30 rats receiving 50 mg/kg/day produced antibodies, while there was no measurable response at 0.5 mg/kg/day (500 μg ($10-6$grams)/kg/day). Thus, at high doses these data appear to show some systemic anti-rbGH response to the oral administration of rbGH to rats.

2. The methodology used in this study, however, was inadequate to determine the systemic bioavailability of oral rbGH. Immune cells throughout the body, including cells in the gastrointestinal tract and in the systemic circulation, produce antibodies. Antibodies produced in the gastrointestinal tract, however, can travel from the gastrointestinal tract to the systemic circulation. Thus the presence of antibodies in the systemic circulation is not proof of systemic absorption of rbGH from the gastrointestinal tract.

3. The level of antibodies present in rat plasma is relatively low and would not be expected to have any adverse effect on the host.

4. It may be calculated, based upon consumption of 1.5 liter of milk per day, by a 10 kg child, with a concentration of approximately 5 micrograms (μg: $10-6$) rbST per liter of

milk, that children are exposed to 7.5 μg/kg/day. This concentration is several hundred fold below the lowest dose that elicited antibody production in the submitted study (0.5 mg/kg/day). Thus, the daily amount of rbGH needed to result in systemic antibody levels is orders of magnitude above that which could reasonably be expected to be consumed on a daily basis.

It is noted that there were no dose-related effects on body weight or organ weight found in either the 90-day oral exposure study or the pivotal 28-day oral exposure study in rats, demonstrating a lack of biological activity.

In addition, a study published in 1988 by Seaman et al. demonstrated that orally administered doses of up to 40 mg/kg/day of bovine somatotropin had no effect on weight gain (while such effects were observed following injection of the drug). This study demonstrated a dose-dependent increased weight gain in hypophysectomized rats administered bovine somatotropin at doses of 0.15, 0.30, and 0.60 mg/kg/day for up to 9 days by subcutaneous injection. Oral administration of bovine somatotropin at doses up to 40 mg/kg/day had no effect on body weight gain in this sensitive bioassay. Subcutaneous administration of bovine somatotropin to hypophysectomized rats resulted in a modest increase in serum antibodies to rbGH by the end of the study (day 9) coupled with measurable plasma levels of bovine somatotropin by radioimmunoassay. Oral administration resulted in no detectable levels of bovine somatotropin in the blood while there was a detectable production of antibodies. Seaman et al. conclude that this study does not provide evidence for the absorption of intact somatotropin following oral administration as there was no effect on weight gain nor could somatotropin be measured by the analytical method. The authors conclude that the antibody response was most likely directed toward recognizable fragments of the parent protein molecule rather than intact bovine somatotropin. As to the question of whether the antibody response itself might be considered an adverse effect, the authors cite several reports showing that the vast majority of healthy infants and 15 – 30% of adults have antibodies to various dietary proteins, especially milk-derived proteins. The FDA reviewed the study published by Seaman et al. and generally agreed with the reported conclusions.

FDA believes that the available data confirm that biologically significant amounts of rbGH are not absorbed in humans following the consumption of milk from cows treated with rbGH. Oral toxicity studies of longer duration are not necessary because rbGH at dietary levels found in the milk of rbGH-treated cows is not significantly biologically available.

Thyroid cysts and Prostate Infiltration

In addition to the antibody results, concern has been raised that the 90-day rat study suggested that rbGH caused the rats to develop thyroid cysts and an infiltration of cells into the prostate. It is argued that such results, if true, would be evidence of absorption of rbGH and possible harmful effects.

An examination of the individual animal reports for gross and histopathological findings revealed thyroid cysts in all treatment groups, including the positive and negative controls. Neither frequency nor severity of these cysts appeared to be related to rbGH administration by either the oral or subcutaneous routes, at any dose, in either gender. Thyroid cysts are enlarged thyroid follicles, and are not related to cancer formation.

A similar examination also was made for the prostate observations. The mononuclear cell infiltration observed is an indication of mild inflammation, and again, is not related to cancer formation. The prostate and accessory sex glands are frequent sites of inflammatory changes in male rats. These changes are common in older rats, but they also occur in young adult rats. Although there appears to be a dose-related increase in the number of rats showing mononuclear cell infiltration following oral administration, there was no difference between the negative and positive control groups. If the prostatic changes were induced by rbGH, it would be expected that the frequency and severity of changes would be significantly greater in the positive versus the negative control group. Therefore, as with the thyroid cysts, these observations do not appear to be related to treatment of the rats with rbGH. Neither the thyroid nor prostate changes provide any evidence of an observable effect of rbGH in the rat and do not provide evidence of absorption.

IGF-I

The Canadian report indicates that milk from rbGH-treated cows contains significantly elevated levels of insulin-like growth factor I (IGF-I) in milk, and presents human health safety concerns. IGF-I is a protein normally found in all humans, and is not intrinsically harmful. IGF-I is necessary for normal growth, development, and health maintenance. Circulating plasma levels of the hormone increase from birth to late puberty and subsequently decline in adults to approximately 100 ng (10-9 grams)/ml (range = 42 – 308 ng/ml for men and women >23 yrs). IGF-1 is structurally similar to insulin and, like insulin, is not biological effective following oral administration.

The safety of IGF-I in milk was thoroughly considered by FDA in its review of the Posilac application. Some early studies suggested that treatment of dairy cows with rbGH produced a slight, but statistically significant, increase in the average milk IGF-I concentration. FDA determined that this modest increase in milk IGF-I concentration was not a human food safety concern because it was less than the natural variation in milk IGF-I levels observed during lactation and was less than the fluctuation observed in milk from treated and control cows prior to rbGH administration.

Since making that analysis, however, FDA has received and reviewed several more comprehensive studies designed to ascertain the effect of rbGH treatment on milk IGF-I levels. These studies have demonstrated that the levels of IGF-I found in milk from treated cows are within the range of those normally found in milk from untreated cows. In 1993, the JECFA Committee concluded, "the most definitive and comprehensive studies demonstrate that IGF-I concentrations [in milk] are not altered after rbGH treatment." The 1998 JECFA Committee report summarized a study showing no significant difference in commercially available milk labeled as coming from non-rbGH treated cows and milk from cows presumed to be treated with rbGH but not labeled as to treatment.

A recent study has been published on the association between prostate cancer and IGF-I. This study showed a positive correlation between the level of IGF-I in plasma and the increased risk of prostate cancer. Although the mechanism responsible for induction of cancer has not been characterized fully, it is clear that IGF-I is not the causative agent.

FDA has examined the literature and finds no definitive evidence of any direct link between IGF-I and breast cancer. Some authors have hypothesized a link, whereas others have expressed that while IGF-I is one of several growth factors and hormones that can contribute to an increase in cell numbers of many cell types invitro, no one factor is responsible for changing normal cells into cancerous cells. Furthermore, FDA has been advised that there is no substantive evidence that IGF-I causes normal breast cells to become cancerous.

In evaluating the potential for human health risk from a natural component of the body, one can examine the effect of an increased exposure to IGF-I by employing several assumptions (i.e., IGF-I levels in milk from rbGH-treated cows are increased from 4 ng/ml to 6 ng/ml, all of the IGF-I in milk is absorbed into the body, and absorbed IGF-I is confined to the vascular compartment). Assuming 5000 ml blood plasma volume in a 60 kg person and assuming this person consumes 1.5 liters of milk containing 9000 ng IGF-I from rbGH-treated cows (as opposed to 6000 ng IGF-I in milk from untreated cows), the maximum increase in blood IGF-I would be less than 2 ng/ml of which only one-third could be attributed to the use of rbGH. This minute increase would dilute into the endogenous pool of circulating IGF-I. IGF-I entering the circulation is rapidly bound to serum binding proteins which attenuate the biological activity.

It bears repeating that the assumptions that milk levels of IGF-I are increased following treatment with rbGH and that biologically active IGF-I is absorbed into the body are not supported by the main body of science. Careful analysis of the published literature fails to provide compelling evidence that milk from rbGH-treated cows contains increased levels of IGF-I compared to milk from untreated cows. Despite recent studies that demonstrate that milk proteins protect IGF-I from digestion, the vast majority of the published work indicates that very little IGF-I is absorbed following ingestion. The most recent 1998 review by the JECFA concluded that, "the concentration of IGF-I in milk from rbGH-treated cows is orders of magnitude lower than the physiological amounts produced in the gastrointestinal tract and other parts of the body. Thus, the concentration of IGF-I would not increase either locally in the gastrointestinal tract or systemically, and the potential for IGF-I to promote tumor growth would not increase when milk from rbGH-treated cows was consumed; there is thus no appreciable risk for consumers."

Effect of rbGH on Infants and Children

Strong concerns over the potential risk to infants and children of milk containing rbGH were expressed by Vermont Public Interest Group and Rural Vermont but no specific issues were raised to substantiate this concern. The FDA considers the impact on high-risk populations in assessing the safety of new animal drugs. For rbGH in particular, issues related to levels of IGF-I in infant formula were carefully examined by FDA. Other concerns, including the hypothetical development of insulin-dependent diabetes mellitus following the consumption of milk from rbGH-treated cows, have been reviewed by the Agency as well as other national and international scientists. To date, all of these reviews have concluded that consumption by infants and children of milk and edible products from rbGH-treated cows is safe.

Mastitis

An August 6, 1992 General Accounting Office (GAO) report found that FDA's review of rbGH had met all established guidelines and that bovine growth hormone did not appear to represent a direct human health risk. However, because rbGH-treated cows tended to have a small but significantly greater incidence of mastitis, GAO recommended that the degree to which antibiotics must be used to treat mastitis should be evaluated in rbGH-treated cows with respect to human food safety. In response to GAO's recommendation, FDA's Center for Veterinary Medicine convened its Veterinary Medicine Advisory Committee and other expert consultants for an open public hearing on March 31, 1993. The Committee concluded that, while rbGH treatment might cause a statistically significant increase in mastitis, the human health risk posed by the possible increased use of antibiotics to treat the mastitis was insignificant. Again, the recent JECFA report addressed the issue of antibiotic use associated with rbGH use. The Committee concluded "The use of rbGH would not result in a higher risk to human health due to the use of antibiotics to treat mastitis and that the increased potential for drug residues in milk could be managed by practices currently in use within the dairy industry and by following directions for use."

External Reviews have confirmed validity of FDA Review

The FDA's review of rbGH has been scrutinized by both the Department of Health and Human Services' Office of Inspector General (OIG) and by GAO, as well as by JECFA. On February 21, 1992, the OIG announced that an audit of issues related to FDA's review of rbGH found no evidence to question FDA's process for determining the human food safety of rbGH. The OIG found that sufficient research had been conducted to substantiate the safety of the milk and meat of rbGH-treated cows for human consumption. In addition, the OIG found no evidence that indicated that FDA or Monsanto engaged in manipulation or suppression of animal health test data. As noted above, the

August 6, 1992 GAO report found that FDA's review of rbGH had met all established guidelines and concluded that bovine growth hormone did not pose a risk for human consumption. In its reviews, JECFA also came to the conclusion that rbGH can be used without any appreciable risk to the health of consumers.

Chapter 34

Food Additives

Overview of Food Ingredients, Additives and Colors

For centuries, ingredients have served useful functions in a variety of foods. Our ancestors used salt to preserve meats and fish, added herbs and spices to improve the flavor of foods, preserved fruit with sugar, and pickled cucumbers in a vinegar solution. Today, consumers demand and enjoy a food supply that is flavorful, nutritious, safe, convenient, colorful and affordable. Food additives and advances in technology help make that possible.

There are thousands of ingredients used to make foods. The Food and Drug Administration (FDA) maintains a list of over 3000 ingredients in its database "Everything Added to Food in the United States," many of which we use at home every day (e.g., sugar, baking soda, salt, vanilla, yeast, spices, and colors).

Still, some consumers have concerns about additives because they may see the long, unfamiliar names and think of them as complex chemical compounds. In fact, every food we eat—whether a just-picked strawberry or a homemade cookie—is made up of chemical compounds that determine flavor, color, texture, and nutrient value. All food additives are carefully regulated by federal authorities and various international organizations to ensure that foods are safe to eat and are accurately labeled.

Text in this chapter is excerpted from "Overview of Food Ingredients, Additives & Colors," U.S. Food and Drug Administration (FDA), December 2, 2014.

The purpose of this section is to provide helpful background information about food and color additives: what they are, why they are used in foods and how they are regulated for safe use.

Questions and Answers about Food and Color Additives

How are ingredients listed on a product label?

Food manufacturers are required to list all ingredients in the food on the label. On a product label, the ingredients are listed in order of predominance, with the ingredients used in the greatest amount first, followed in descending order by those in smaller amounts. The label must list the names of any FDA-certified color additives (e.g., FD&C Blue No. 1 or the abbreviated name, Blue 1). But some ingredients can be listed collectively as "flavors," "spices," "artificial flavoring," or in the case of color additives exempt from certification, "artificial colors," without naming each one. Declaration of an allergenic ingredient in a collective or single color, flavor, or spice could be accomplished by simply naming the allergenic ingredient in the ingredient list.

What are dyes and lakes in color additives?

Certified color additives are categorized as either dyes or lakes. **Dyes** dissolve in water and are manufactured as powders, granules, liquids or other special-purpose forms. They can be used in beverages, dry mixes, baked goods, confections, dairy products, pet foods and a variety of other products.

Lakes are the water insoluble form of the dye. Lakes are more stable than dyes and are ideal for coloring products containing fats and oils, or items lacking sufficient moisture to dissolve dyes. Typical uses include coated tablets, cake and donut mixes, hard candies and chewing gums.

Do additives cause childhood hyperactivity?

Although this hypothesis was popularized in the 1970's, results from studies on this issue either have been inconclusive, inconsistent, or difficult to interpret due to inadequacies in study design. A Consensus Development Panel of the National Institutes of Health concluded in 1982 that for some children with attention deficit hyperactivity disorder (ADHD) and confirmed food allergy, dietary modification has produced some improvement in behavior. Although the panel said that elimination diets should not be used universally to treat childhood hyperactivity, since there is no scientific evidence to predict which children may benefit, the panel recognized that initiation of a trial of dietary treatment or continuation of a diet in patients whose families and physicians perceive benefits may be warranted. However, a 1997 review published in the *Journal of the American Academy of Child & Adolescent Psychiatry* noted there is minimal evidence of efficacy and extreme difficulty inducing children and adolescents to comply with restricted diets. Thus, dietary treatment should not be recommended, except possibly with a small number of preschool children who may be sensitive to tartrazine, known commonly as FD&C Yellow No.5 (*See* question below). In 2007, synthetic certified color additives again came under scrutiny following publication of a study commissioned by the UK Food Standards Agency to investigate whether certain color additives cause hyperactivity in children. Both the FDA and the European Food Safety Authority independently reviewed the results from this study and each has concluded that the study does not substantiate a link between the color additives that were tested and behavioral effects.

What is the difference between natural and artificial ingredients? Is a naturally produced ingredient safer than an artificially manufactured ingredient?

Natural ingredients are derived from natural sources (e.g., soybeans and corn provide lecithin to maintain product consistency; beets provide beet powder used as food coloring). Other ingredients are not found in nature and therefore must be synthetically produced as artificial ingredients. Also, some ingredients found in nature can be manufactured artificially and produced more economically, with greater purity and more consistent quality, than their natural counterparts. For example, vitamin C or ascorbic acid may be derived from an orange or produced in a laboratory. Food ingredients are subject to the same strict safety standards regardless of whether they are naturally or artificially derived.

Are certain people sensitive to FD&C Yellow No. 5 in foods?

FD&C Yellow No. 5, is used to color beverages, dessert powders, candy, ice cream, custards and other foods. FDA's Committee on Hypersensitivity to Food Constituents concluded in 1986 that FD&C

Yellow No. 5 might cause hives in fewer than one out of 10,000 people. It also concluded that there was no evidence the color additive in food provokes asthma attacks. The law now requires Yellow No. 5 to be identified on the ingredient line. This allows the few who may be sensitive to the color to avoid it.

Do low-calorie sweeteners cause adverse reactions?

No. Food safety experts generally agree there is no convincing evidence of a cause and effect relationship between these sweeteners and negative health effects in humans. The FDA has monitored consumer complaints of possible adverse reactions for more than 15 years.

For example, in carefully controlled clinical studies, aspartame has not been shown to cause adverse or allergic reactions. However, persons with a rare hereditary disease known as phenylketonuria (PKU) must control their intake of phenylalanine from all sources, including aspartame. Although aspartame contains only a small amount of phenylalanine, labels of aspartame-containing foods and beverages must include a statement advising phenylketonurics of the presence of phenylalanine.

Individuals who have concerns about possible adverse effects from food additives or other substances should contact their physicians.

How do they add vitamins and minerals to fortified cereals?

Adding nutrients to a cereal can cause taste and color changes in the product. This is especially true with added minerals. Since no one wants cereal that tastes like a vitamin supplement, a variety of techniques are employed in the fortification process. In general, those nutrients that are heat stable (such as vitamins A and E and various minerals) are incorporated into the cereal itself (they're baked right in). Nutrients that are not stable to heat (such as B-vitamins) are applied directly to the cereal after all heating steps are completed. Each cereal is unique—some can handle more nutrients than others can. This is one reason why fortification levels are different across all cereals.

What is the role of modern technology in producing food additives?

Many new techniques are being researched that will allow the production of additives in ways not previously possible. One approach is the use of biotechnology, which can use simple organisms to produce food additives. These additives are the same as food components found in nature. In 1990, FDA approved the first bioengineered enzyme rennin, which traditionally had been extracted from calves' stomachs for use in making cheese.

Types of Food Ingredients

The following summary lists the types of common food ingredients, why they are used, and some examples of the names that can be found on product labels. Some additives are used for more than one purpose.

Table 34.1. *Types of Food Ingredients*

Types of Ingredients	What They Do	Examples of Uses	Names Found on Product Labels
Preservatives	Prevent food spoilage from bacteria, molds, fungi, or yeast (antimicrobials); slow or prevent changes in color, flavor, or texture and delay rancidity (antioxidants); maintain freshness	Fruit sauces and jellies, beverages, baked goods, cured meats, oils and margarines, cereals, dressings, snack foods, fruits and vegetables	Ascorbic acid, citric acid, sodium benzoate, calcium propionate, sodium erythorbate, sodium nitrite, calcium sorbate, potassium sorbate, BHA, BHT, EDTA, tocopherols (Vitamin E)
Sweeteners	Add sweetness with or without the extra calories	Beverages, baked goods, confections, table-top sugar, substitutes, many processed foods	Sucrose (sugar), glucose, fructose, sorbitol, mannitol, corn syrup, high fructose corn syrup, saccharin, aspartame, sucralose, acesulfame potassium (acesulfame-K), neotame

Table 34.1. *Continued*

Types of Ingredients	What They Do	Examples of Uses	Names Found on Product Labels
Color Additives	Offset color loss due to exposure to light, air, temperature extremes, moisture and storage conditions; correct natural variations in color; enhance colors that occur naturally; provide color to colorless and "fun" foods	Many processed foods, (candies, snack foods margarine, cheese, soft drinks, jams/jellies, gelatins, pudding and pie fillings)	FD&C Blue Nos. 1 and 2, FD&C Green No. 3, FD&C Red Nos. 3 and 40, FD&C Yellow Nos. 5 and 6, Orange B, Citrus Red No. 2, annatto extract, beta-carotene, grape skin extract, cochineal extract or carmine, paprika oleoresin, caramel color, fruit and vegetable juices, saffron (Note: Exempt color additives are not required to be declared by name on labels but may be declared simply as colorings or color added)
Flavors and Spices	Add specific flavors (natural and synthetic)	Pudding and pie fillings, gelatin dessert mixes, cake mixes, salad dressings, candies, soft drinks, ice cream, BBQ sauce	Natural flavoring, artificial flavor, and spices
Flavor Enhancers	Enhance flavors already present in foods (without providing their own separate flavor)	Many processed foods	Monosodium glutamate (MSG), hydrolyzed soy protein, autolyzed yeast extract, disodium guanylate or inosinate

Table 34.1. *Continued*

Types of Ingredients	What They Do	Examples of Uses	Names Found on Product Labels
Fat Replacers (and components of formulations used to replace fats)	Provide expected texture and a creamy "mouth-feel" in reduced-fat foods	Baked goods, dressings, frozen desserts, confections, cake and dessert mixes, dairy products	Olestra, cellulose gel, carrageenan, polydextrose, modified food starch, microparticulated egg white protein, guar gum, xanthan gum, whey protein concentrate
Nutrients	Replace vitamins and minerals lost in processing (enrichment), add nutrients that may be lacking in the diet (fortification)	Flour, breads, cereals, rice, macaroni, margarine, salt, milk, fruit beverages, energy bars, instant breakfast drinks	Thiamine hydrochloride, riboflavin (Vitamin B2), niacin, niacinamide, folate or folic acid, beta carotene, potassium iodide, iron or ferrous sulfate, alpha tocopherols, ascorbic acid, Vitamin D, amino acids (L-tryptophan, L-lysine, L-leucine, L-methionine)
Emulsifiers	Allow smooth mixing of ingredients, prevent separation Keep emulsified products stable, reduce stickiness, control crystallization, keep ingredients dispersed, and to help products dissolve more easily	Salad dressings, peanut butter, chocolate, margarine, frozen desserts	Soy lecithin, mono- and diglycerides, egg yolks, polysorbates, sorbitan monostearate

Table 34.1. *Continued*

Types of Ingredients	What They Do	Examples of Uses	Names Found on Product Labels
Stabilizers and Thickeners, Binders, Texturizers	Produce uniform texture, improve "mouth-feel"	Frozen desserts, dairy products, cakes, pudding and gelatin mixes, dressings, jams and jellies, sauces	Gelatin, pectin, guar gum, carrageenan, xanthan gum, whey
pH Control Agents and acidulants	Control acidity and alkalinity, prevent spoilage	Beverages, frozen desserts, chocolate, low acid canned foods, baking powder	Lactic acid, citric acid, ammonium hydroxide, sodium carbonate
Leavening Agents	Promote rising of baked goods	Breads and other baked goods	Baking soda, monocalcium phosphate, calcium carbonate
Anti-caking agents	Keep powdered foods free-flowing, prevent moisture absorption	Salt, baking powder, confectioner's sugar	Calcium silicate, iron ammonium citrate, silicon dioxide
Humectants	Retain moisture	Shredded coconut, marshmallows, soft candies, confections	Glycerin, sorbitol
Yeast Nutrients	Promote growth of yeast	Breads and other baked goods	Calcium sulfate, ammonium phosphate
Dough Strengtheners and Conditioners	Produce more stable dough	Breads and other baked goods	Ammonium sulfate, azodicarbonamide, L-cysteine
Firming Agents	Maintain crispness and firmness	Processed fruits and vegetables	Calcium chloride, calcium lactate
Enzyme Preparations	Modify proteins, polysaccharides and fats	Cheese, dairy products, meat	Enzymes, lactase, papain, rennet, chymosin
Gases	Serve as propellant, aerate, or create carbonation	Oil cooking spray, whipped cream, carbonated beverages	Carbon dioxide, nitrous oxide

Chapter 35

Foodborne Bacterial Illnesses

Chapter Contents

Section 35.1

Introduction to Foodborne Illnesses

Text in this section is excerpted from "Foodborne Illnesses," National
Institute of Diabetes and Digestive and Kidney Diseases (NIDDK),
June 25, 2014.

What are foodborne illnesses?

Foodborne illnesses are infections or irritations of the gastrointestinal (GI) tract caused by food or beverages that contain harmful bacteria, parasites, viruses, or chemicals. The GI tract is a series of hollow organs joined in a long, twisting tube from the mouth to the anus. Common symptoms of foodborne illnesses include vomiting, diarrhea, abdominal pain, fever, and chills.

Most foodborne illnesses are acute, meaning they happen suddenly and last a short time, and most people recover on their own without treatment. Rarely, foodborne illnesses may lead to more serious complications. Each year, an estimated 48 million people in the United States experience a foodborne illness. Foodborne illnesses cause about 3,000 deaths in the United States annually.

What causes foodborne illnesses?

Bacteria

Bacteria are tiny organisms that can cause infections of the GI tract. Not all bacteria are harmful to humans.

Some harmful bacteria may already be present in foods when they are purchased. Raw foods including meat, poultry, fish and shellfish, eggs, unpasteurized milk and dairy products, and fresh produce often contain bacteria that cause foodborne illnesses. Bacteria can contaminate food—making it harmful to eat—at any time during growth, harvesting or slaughter, processing, storage, and shipping.

Foods may also be contaminated with bacteria during food preparation in a restaurant or home kitchen. If food preparers do not thoroughly wash their hands, kitchen utensils, cutting boards, and other kitchen surfaces that come into contact with raw foods, cross-contamination—the spread of bacteria from contaminated food to uncontaminated food—may occur.

If hot food is not kept hot enough or cold food is not kept cold enough, bacteria may multiply. Bacteria multiply quickly when the temperature of food is between 40 and 140 degrees. Cold food should be kept below 40 degrees and hot food should be kept above 140 degrees. Bacteria multiply more slowly when food is refrigerated, and freezing food can further slow or even stop the spread of bacteria. However, bacteria in refrigerated or frozen foods become active again when food is brought to room temperature. Thoroughly cooking food kills bacteria.

Many types of bacteria cause foodborne illnesses. Examples include

- *Salmonella*, a bacterium found in many foods, including raw and undercooked meat, poultry, dairy products, and seafood. *Salmonella* may also be present on egg shells and inside eggs.

- *Campylobacter jejuni (C. jejuni),* found in raw or undercooked chicken and unpasteurized milk.

- *Shigella,* a bacterium spread from person to person. These bacteria are present in the stools of people who are infected. If people who are infected do not wash their hands thoroughly after using the bathroom, they can contaminate food that they handle or prepare. Water contaminated with infected stools can also contaminate produce in the field.

- *Escherichia coli (E. coli),* which includes several different strains, only a few of which cause illness in humans. *E. coli* O157:H7 is the strain that causes the most severe illness. Common sources of *E. coli* include raw or undercooked hamburger, unpasteurized fruit juices and milk, and fresh produce.

- *Listeria monocytogenes (L. monocytogenes),* which has been found in raw and undercooked meats, unpasteurized milk, soft cheeses, and ready-to-eat deli meats and hot dogs.

- *Vibrio,* a bacterium that may contaminate fish or shellfish.

- *Clostridium botulinum (C. botulinum),* a bacterium that may contaminate improperly canned foods and smoked and salted fish.

Viruses

Viruses are tiny capsules, much smaller than bacteria, that contain genetic material. Viruses cause infections that can lead to sickness.

People can pass viruses to each other. Viruses are present in the stool or vomit of people who are infected. People who are infected with a virus may contaminate food and drinks, especially if they do not wash their hands thoroughly after using the bathroom.

Common sources of foodborne viruses include

- food prepared by a person infected with a virus
- shellfish from contaminated water
- produce irrigated with contaminated water

Common foodborne viruses include

- norovirus, which causes inflammation of the stomach and intestines
- hepatitis A, which causes inflammation of the liver

Parasites

Parasites are tiny organisms that live inside another organism. In developed countries such as the United States, parasitic infections are relatively rare.

Cryptosporidium parvum and *Giardia intestinalis* are parasites that are spread through water contaminated with the stools of people or animals who are infected. Foods that come into contact with contaminated water during growth or preparation can become contaminated with these parasites. Food preparers who are infected with these parasites can also contaminate foods if they do not thoroughly wash their hands after using the bathroom and before handling food.

Trichinella spiralis is a type of roundworm parasite. People may be infected with this parasite by consuming raw or undercooked pork or wild game.

Chemicals

Harmful chemicals that cause illness may contaminate foods such as

- fish or shellfish, which may feed on algae that produce toxins, leading to high concentrations of toxins in their bodies. Some types of fish, including tuna and mahi mahi, may be contaminated with bacteria that produce toxins if the fish are not properly refrigerated before they are cooked or served.
- certain types of wild mushrooms.

- unwashed fruits and vegetables that contain high concentrations of pesticides.

Who gets foodborne illnesses?

Anyone can get a foodborne illness. However, some people are more likely to develop foodborne illnesses than others, including

- infants and children
- pregnant women and their fetuses
- older adults
- people with weak immune systems

These groups also have a greater risk of developing severe symptoms or complications of foodborne illnesses.

What are the symptoms of foodborne illnesses?

Symptoms of foodborne illnesses depend on the cause. Common symptoms of many foodborne illnesses include

- vomiting
- diarrhea or bloody diarrhea
- abdominal pain
- fever
- chills

Symptoms can range from mild to serious and can last from a few hours to several days.

C. botulinum and some chemicals affect the nervous system, causing symptoms such as

- headache
- tingling or numbness of the skin
- blurred vision
- weakness
- dizziness
- paralysis

What are the complications of foodborne illnesses?

Foodborne illnesses may lead to dehydration, hemolytic uremic syndrome (HUS), and other complications. Acute foodborne illnesses may also lead to chronic—or long lasting—health problems.

Dehydration

When someone does not drink enough fluids to replace those that are lost through vomiting and diarrhea, dehydration can result. When dehydrated, the body lacks enough fluid and electrolytes—minerals in salts, including sodium, potassium, and chloride—to function properly. Infants, children, older adults, and people with weak immune systems have the greatest risk of becoming dehydrated.

Signs of dehydration are

- excessive thirst
- infrequent urination
- dark-colored urine
- lethargy, dizziness, or faintness

Signs of dehydration in infants and young children are

- dry mouth and tongue
- lack of tears when crying
- no wet diapers for 3 hours or more
- high fever
- unusually cranky or drowsy behavior
- sunken eyes, cheeks, or soft spot in the skull

Also, when people are dehydrated, their skin does not flatten back to normal right away after being gently pinched and released.

Severe dehydration may require intravenous fluids and hospitalization. Untreated severe dehydration can cause serious health problems such as organ damage, shock, or coma—a sleeplike state in which a person is not conscious.

HUS

Hemolytic uremic syndrome is a rare disease that mostly affects children younger than 10 years of age. HUS develops when *E. coli* bacteria lodged in the digestive tract make toxins that enter the bloodstream. The toxins start to destroy red blood cells, which help the blood to clot, and the lining of the blood vessels.

In the United States, *E. coli O157:H7* infection is the most common cause of HUS, but infection with other strains of *E. coli,* other bacteria, and viruses may also cause HUS. A recent study found that about 6 percent of people with *E. coli O157:H7* infections developed HUS. Children younger than age 5 have the highest risk, but females and people age 60 and older also have increased risk.

Symptoms of *E. coli O157:H7* infection include diarrhea, which may be bloody, and abdominal pain, often accompanied by nausea, vomiting, and fever. Up to a week after *E. coli* symptoms appear, symptoms of HUS may develop, including irritability, paleness, and decreased urination. HUS may lead to acute renal failure, which is a sudden and temporary loss of kidney function. HUS may also affect other organs and the central nervous system. Most people who develop HUS recover with treatment. Research shows that in the United States between 2000 and 2006, fewer than 5 percent of people who developed HUS died of the disorder. Older adults had the highest mortality rate—about one-third of people age 60 and older who developed HUS died.

Studies have shown that some children who recover from HUS develop chronic complications, including kidney problems, high blood pressure, and diabetes.

Other Complications

Some foodborne illnesses lead to other serious complications. For example, *C. botulinum* and certain chemicals in fish and seafood can paralyze the muscles that control breathing. *L. monocytogenes* can cause spontaneous abortion or stillbirth in pregnant women.

Research suggests that acute foodborne illnesses may lead to chronic disorders, including

- **reactive arthritis,** a type of joint inflammation that usually affects the knees, ankles, or feet. Some people develop this disorder following foodborne illnesses caused by certain bacteria, including *C. jejuni* and *Salmonella.* Reactive arthritis usually lasts fewer than 6 months, but this condition may recur, or become chronic arthritis.

- **irritable bowel syndrome (IBS),** a disorder of unknown cause that is associated with abdominal pain, bloating, and diarrhea or constipation or both. Foodborne illnesses caused by bacteria increase the risk of developing IBS.

- **Guillain-Barré syndrome,** a disorder characterized by muscle weakness or paralysis that begins in the lower body and progresses to the upper body. This syndrome may occur after foodborne illnesses caused by bacteria, most commonly *C. jejuni.* Most people recover in 6 to 12 months.

A recent study found that adults who had recovered from *E. coli O157:H7* infections had increased risks of high blood pressure, kidney problems, and cardiovascular disease.

When should people with foodborne illnesses see a health care provider?

People with any of the following symptoms should see a health care provider immediately:

- signs of dehydration
- prolonged vomiting that prevents keeping liquids down
- diarrhea for more than 2 days in adults or for more than 24 hours in children
- severe pain in the abdomen or rectum
- a fever higher than 101 degrees
- stools containing blood or pus
- stools that are black and tarry
- nervous system symptoms
- signs of HUS

If a child has a foodborne illness, parents or guardians should not hesitate to call a health care provider for advice.

How are foodborne illnesses diagnosed?

To diagnose foodborne illnesses, health care providers ask about symptoms, foods and beverages recently consumed, and medical history. Health care providers will also perform a physical examination to look for signs of illness.

Diagnostic tests for foodborne illnesses may include a stool culture, in which a sample of stool is analyzed in a laboratory to check for signs of infections or diseases. A sample of vomit or a sample of the suspected food, if available, may also be tested. A health care provider may perform additional medical tests to rule out diseases and disorders that cause symptoms similar to the symptoms of foodborne illnesses.

If symptoms of foodborne illnesses are mild and last only a short time, diagnostic tests are usually not necessary.

How are foodborne illnesses treated?

The only treatment needed for most foodborne illnesses is replacing lost fluids and electrolytes to prevent dehydration.

Over-the-counter medications such as loperamide (Imodium) and bismuth subsalicylate (Pepto-Bismol and Kaopectate) may help stop diarrhea in adults. However, people with bloody diarrhea—a sign of bacterial or parasitic infection—should not use these medications. If diarrhea is caused by bacteria or parasites, over-the-counter medications may prolong the problem. Medications to treat diarrhea in adults can be dangerous for infants and children and should only be given with a health care provider's guidance.

If the specific cause of the foodborne illness is diagnosed, a health care provider may prescribe medications, such as antibiotics, to treat the illness.

Hospitalization may be required to treat life-threatening symptoms and complications, such as paralysis, severe dehydration, and HUS.

Eating, Diet, and Nutrition

The following steps may help relieve the symptoms of foodborne illnesses and prevent dehydration in adults:

- drinking plenty of liquids such as fruit juices, sports drinks, caffeine-free soft drinks, and broths to replace fluids and electrolytes

- sipping small amounts of clear liquids or sucking on ice chips if vomiting is still a problem

- gradually reintroducing food, starting with bland, easy-to-digest foods such as rice, potatoes, toast or bread, cereal, lean meat, applesauce, and bananas

- avoiding fatty foods, sugary foods, dairy products, caffeine, and alcohol until recovery is complete

Infants and children present special concerns. Infants and children are likely to become dehydrated more quickly from diarrhea and vomiting because of their smaller body size. The following steps may help relieve symptoms and prevent dehydration in infants and children:

- giving oral rehydration solutions such as Pedialyte, Naturalyte, Infalyte, and CeraLyte to prevent dehydration

- giving food as soon as the child is hungry

- giving infants breast milk or full-strength formula, as usual, along with oral rehydration solutions

Older adults and adults with weak immune systems should also drink oral rehydration solutions to prevent dehydration.

How are foodborne illnesses prevented?

Foodborne illnesses can be prevented by properly storing, cooking, cleaning, and handling foods.

- Raw and cooked perishable foods—foods that can spoil—should be refrigerated or frozen promptly. If perishable foods stand at room temperature for more than 2 hours, they may not be safe to eat. Refrigerators should be set at 40 degrees or lower and freezers should be set at 0 degrees.

- Foods should be cooked long enough and at a high enough temperature to kill the harmful bacteria that cause illnesses. A meat thermometer should be used to ensure foods are cooked to the appropriate internal temperature:

- 145 degrees for roasts, steaks, and chops of beef, veal, pork, and lamb, followed by 3 minutes of rest time after the meat is removed from the heat source

- 160 degrees for ground beef, veal, pork, and lamb

- 165 degrees for poultry

- Cold foods should be kept cold and hot foods should be kept hot.

- Fruits and vegetables should be washed under running water just before eating, cutting, or cooking. A produce brush can be used under running water to clean fruits and vegetables with firm skin.

- Raw meat, poultry, seafood, and their juices should be kept away from other foods.

- People should wash their hands for at least 20 seconds with warm, soapy water before and after handling raw meat, poultry, fish, shellfish, produce, or eggs. People should also wash their hands after using the bathroom, changing diapers, or touching animals.

- Utensils and surfaces should be washed with hot, soapy water before and after they are used to prepare food. Diluted bleach—1 teaspoon of bleach to 1 quart of hot water—can also be used to sanitize utensils and surfaces.

Traveler's Diarrhea

People who visit certain foreign countries are at risk for traveler's diarrhea, which is caused by eating food or drinking water contaminated with bacteria, viruses, or parasites. Traveler's diarrhea can be a problem for people traveling to developing countries in Africa, Asia, Latin America, and the Caribbean. Visitors to Canada, most European countries, Japan, Australia, and New Zealand do not face much risk for traveler's diarrhea.

To prevent traveler's diarrhea, people traveling from the United States to developing countries should avoid

- drinking tap water, using tap water to brush their teeth, or using ice made from tap water

- drinking unpasteurized milk or milk products

- eating raw fruits and vegetables, including lettuce and fruit salads, unless they peel the fruits or vegetables themselves

- eating raw or rare meat and fish

- eating meat or shellfish that is not hot when served

- eating food from street vendors

Travelers can drink bottled water, bottled soft drinks, and hot drinks such as coffee or tea.

People concerned about traveler's diarrhea should talk with a health care provider before traveling. The health care provider may recommend that travelers bring medication with them in case they develop diarrhea during their trip. Health care providers may advise some people—especially people with weakened immune systems—to take antibiotics before and during a trip to help prevent traveler's diarrhea. Early treatment with antibiotics can shorten a bout of traveler's diarrhea.

Points to Remember

- Foodborne illnesses are infections or irritations of the gastro-intestinal (GI) tract caused by food or beverages that contain harmful bacteria, parasites, viruses, or chemicals.

- Anyone can get a foodborne illness. However, some people are more likely to develop foodborne illnesses than others, including infants and children, pregnant women and their fetuses, older adults, and people with weakened immune systems.

- Symptoms of foodborne illnesses depend on the cause. Common symptoms of many foodborne illnesses include vomiting, diarrhea or bloody diarrhea, abdominal pain, fever, and chills.

- Foodborne illnesses may lead to dehydration, hemolytic uremic syndrome (HUS), and other complications. Acute foodborne illnesses may also lead to chronic—or long lasting—health problems.

- The only treatment needed for most foodborne illnesses is replacing lost fluids and electrolytes to prevent dehydration.

- Foodborne illnesses can be prevented by properly storing, cooking, cleaning, and handling foods.

Hope through Research

The Division of Digestive Diseases and Nutrition at the National Institute of Diabetes and Digestive and Kidney Diseases (NIDDK) supports basic and clinical research into GI diseases, including foodborne illnesses. Researchers are investigating the relationship between foodborne illnesses and digestive disorders such as IBS. Researchers are also studying ways to prevent foodborne illnesses. Clinical trials include

- The Role of Intestinal Inflammation in Irritable Bowel Syndrome, funded by the NIDDK under National Institutes of Health (NIH) clinical trial number NCT01072903

- Shigella Sonnel O-SPC/rBRU Conjugate Vaccine, funded under NIH clinical trial number NCT01369927

- Phase I Safety and Efficacy Study of CVD 1902, a Live, Attenuated Oral Vaccine to Prevent *Salmonella Enterica* Serovar Paratyphi A Infection, funded under NIH clinical trial number NCT01129453

Participants in clinical trials can play a more active role in their own health care, gain access to new research treatments before they are widely available, and help others by contributing to medical research.

Section 35.2

Bovine Spongiform Encephalopathy (Mad Cow Disease)

Text in this section is excerpted from "Bovine Spongiform
Encephalopathy (BSE), or Mad Cow Disease," Centers for Disease
Control and Prevention (CDC), February 6, 2015.

About BSE

BSE (bovine spongiform encephalopathy) is a progressive neuro-logical disorder of cattle that results from infection by an unusual transmissible agent called a prion. The nature of the transmissible agent is not well understood. Currently, the most accepted theory is that the agent is a modified form of a normal protein known as prion protein. For reasons that are not yet understood, the normal prion protein changes into a pathogenic (harmful) form that then damages the central nervous system of cattle.

Research indicates that the first probable infections of BSE in cows occurred during the 1970's with two cases of BSE being identified in 1986. BSE possibly originated as a result of feeding cattle meat-and-bone meal that contained BSE-infected products from a spontaneously occurring case of BSE or scrapie-infected sheep products. Scrapie is a prion disease of sheep. There is strong evidence and general agree-ment that the outbreak was then amplified and spread throughout the United Kingdom cattle industry by feeding rendered, prion-infected, bovine meat-and-bone meal to young calves.

The BSE epizootic in the United Kingdom peaked in January 1993 at almost 1,000 new cases per week. Over the next 17 years, the annual numbers of BSE cases has dropped sharply—

- 11 cases in 2010

- 225 cases in 200

- 1,443 cases in 2000

- 14,562 cases in 1995

Cumulatively, through the end of 2010, more than 184,500 cases of BSE had been confirmed in the United Kingdom alone in more than 35,000 herds.

There exists strong epidemiologic and laboratory evidence for a causal association between a new human prion disease called variant Creutzfeldt-Jakob disease (vCJD) that was first reported from the United Kingdom in 1996 and the BSE outbreak in cattle. The interval between the most likely period for the initial extended exposure of the population to potentially BSE-contaminated food (1984-1986) and the onset of initial variant CJD cases (1994-1996) is consistent with known incubation periods for the human forms of prion disease.

BSE in North America

Through February 2015, BSE surveillance has identified 24 cases in North America: 4 BSE cases in the United States and 20 in Canada. Of the 4 cases identified in the United States, one was born in Canada; of the 20 cases identified in Canada, one was imported from the United Kingdom.

Strong evidence indicates that BSE has been transmitted to humans primarily in the United Kingdom, causing a variant form of Creutzfeldt-Jakob disease (vCJD). In the United Kingdom, where over 1 million cattle may have been infected with BSE, a substantial species barrier appears to protect humans from widespread illness. Since variant CJD was first reported in 1996, a total of only 227 patients with this disease have been reported worldwide. The risk to human health from BSE in the United States is extremely low.

Control Measures

Public health control measures, such as surveillance, culling sick animals, or banning specified risk materials, have been instituted in many countries, particularly in those with indigenous cases of confirmed BSE, in order to prevent potentially BSE-infected tissues from entering the human food supply.

The most stringent control measures include a UK program that excludes all animals more than 30 months of age from the human food and animal feed supplies. The program appears to be highly effective.

In June 2000, the European Union Commission on Food Safety and Animal Welfare strengthened the European Union's BSE control measures by requiring all member states to remove specified risk materials from animal feed and human food chains as of October 1, 2000; such bans had already been instituted in most member states. Other control measures include banning the use of mechanically recovered meat from the vertebral column of cattle, sheep, and goats for human food and BSE testing of all cattle more than 30 months of age destined for human consumption.

Feed Bans

As of October 26, 2009, a regulation issued by FDA in April 2009 came into effect establishing an enhanced BSE-related feed ban in the United States. This enhanced ban will further harmonize BSE feed control measures in the U.S. with those in Canada (see below). In addition, FDA continues to enforce its important 1997 mammalian-to-ruminant feed ban through its BSE inspection and BSE feed testing programs.

As of July 12, 2007, an enhanced BSE-related feed ban came into effect in Canada. CFIA established this ban to more effectively prevent and quickly eliminate BSE from Canada. The enhanced ban prohibits most proteins, including potentially BSE infectious tissues known as "specified risk materials" (SRM) from all animal feeds, pet foods, and fertilizers, not just from cattle feed as required by the ban instituted in 1997. The 1997 feed ban in Canada was similar to the feed ban instituted in the United States that same year. As recently reported by CFIA, removing SRM from the entire animal feed system addresses risks associated with the potential contamination of cattle feed during production, distribution, storage, and use. Applying the same measure to pet food and fertilizer materials addresses the possible exposure of cattle and other susceptible animals to these products. CFIA expects that with this new ban, BSE should be eliminated from the Canadian cattle herd by about the year 2017.

The Canadian-born cow confirmed to be infected with BSE in 2015 illustrates the difficulty in determining the effectiveness of previously instituted feed bans to prevent BSE transmissions. The initial feed bans established in both the United States and Canada were instituted in 1997. After an assessment by USDA and its Canadian counterparts, the Canadian feed ban was judged to be fully effective as of March 1999. However, largely because of recognized limitations of this ban and the ban established in the United States, new, enhanced feed bans went into effect in Canada, July 12, 2007, and in the U.S., October 26, 2009. While USDA has confirmed no U.S.-born cattle as having a classic form of BSE, Canadian cattle born after March 1999 have been legally imported into the United States for any purpose since November 19, 2007.

Prevention

Prevention Measures against BSE Spread

To prevent BSE from entering the United States, severe restrictions were placed on the importation of live ruminants, such as cattle, sheep, and goats, and certain ruminant products from countries where BSE was known to exist. These restrictions were later extended to include importation of ruminants and certain ruminant products from all European countries.

Because the use of ruminant tissue in ruminant feed was probably a necessary factor responsible for the BSE outbreak in the United Kingdom and because of the current evidence for possible transmission of BSE to humans, the U.S. Food and Drug Administration instituted a ruminant feed ban in June 1997 that became fully effective as of October 1997. As of October 26, 2009, a regulation issued by FDA in April 2009 came into effect establishing an enhanced BSE-related feed ban in the U.S. This enhanced feed ban will further harmonize BSE feed control measures in the U.S. with those in Canada (see below). In addition, FDA continues to enforce its important 1997 mammalian-to-ruminant feed ban through its BSE inspection and BSE feed testing programs.

As of July 12, 2007, an enhanced BSE-related feed ban came into effect in Canada. CFIA established this ban to more effectively prevent and quickly eliminate BSE from Canada. The enhanced ban prohibits most proteins, including potentially BSE infectious tissues known as "specified risk materials" (SRM) from all animal feeds, pet foods, and fertilizers, not just from cattle feed as required by the ban instituted in 1997. The 1997 feed ban in Canada was similar to the feed ban instituted in the United States that same year. As recently reported by CFIA, removing SRM from the entire animal feed system addresses risks associated with the potential contamination of cattle feed during production, distribution, storage, and use. Applying the same measure to pet food and fertilizer materials addresses the possible exposure of cattle and other susceptible animals to these products. With this ban in place, CFIA expects BSE should be eliminated from the Canadian cattle herd by about the year 2017.

In late 2001, the Harvard Center for Risk Assessment study of various scenarios involving BSE in the U.S. concluded that the FDA ruminant feed rule provides a major defense against this disease.

Section 35.3

Campylobacter

Text in this section is excerpted from "National Center for Emerging and Zoonotic Infectious Diseases—Campylobacter," Centers for Disease Control and Prevention (CDC), June 3, 2014.

What is campylobacteriosis?

Campylobacteriosis is an infectious disease caused by bacteria of the genus *Campylobacter*. Most people who become ill with campylobacteriosis get diarrhea, cramping, abdominal pain, and fever within two to five days after exposure to the organism. The diarrhea may be bloody and can be accompanied by nausea and vomiting. The illness typically lasts about one week. Some infected persons do not have any symptoms. In persons with compromised immune systems, *Campylobacter* occasionally spreads to the bloodstream and causes a serious life-threatening infection.

How common is **Campylobacter?**

Campylobacter is one of the most common causes of diarrheal illness in the United States. Most cases occur as isolated, sporadic events, not as part of recognized outbreaks. Active surveillance through the Foodborne Diseases Active Surveillance Network (FoodNet) indicates that about 14 cases are diagnosed each year for each 100,000 persons in the population. Many more cases go undiagnosed or unreported, and campylobacteriosis is estimated to affect over 1.3 million persons every year. Campylobacteriosis occurs much more frequently in the summer months than in the winter. The organism is isolated from infants and young adults more frequently than from persons in other age groups and from males more frequently than females. Although *Campylobacter* infection does not commonly cause death, it has been estimated that approximately 76 persons with *Campylobacter* infections die each year.

What sort of germ is Campylobacter?

Campylobacter organisms are spiral-shaped bacteria that can cause disease in humans and animals. Most human illness is caused by one species, called *Campylobacter jejuni*, but human illness can also be caused by other species. *Campylobacter jejuni* grows best at 37°C to 42°C, the approximate body temperature of a bird (41°C to 42°C), and seems to be well adapted to birds, who carry it without becoming ill. These bacteria are fragile. They cannot tolerate drying and can be killed by oxygen. They grow only in places with less oxygen than the amount in the atmosphere. Freezing reduces the number of *Campylobacter* bacteria on raw meat.

How is the infection diagnosed?

Many different kinds of infections can cause diarrhea and bloody diarrhea. *Campylobacter* infection is diagnosed when a culture of a stool specimen yields the bacterium.

How can campylobacteriosis be treated?

Almost all persons infected with *Campylobacter* recover without any specific treatment. Patients should drink extra fluids as long as the diarrhea lasts. Antimicrobial therapy is warranted only for patients with severe disease or those at high risk for severe disease, such as those with immune systems severely weakened from medications or other illnesses. Azithromycin and fluoroquinolones (e.g., ciprofloxacin) are commonly used for treatment of these infections, but resistance to fluoroquinolones is common. Antimicrobial susceptibility testing can help guide appropriate therapy.

Are there long-term consequences?

Most people who get campylobacteriosis recover completely within two to five days, although sometimes recovery can take up to 10 days.

Rarely, *Campylobacter* infection results in long-term consequences. Some people develop arthritis. Others may develop a rare disease called Guillain-Barré syndrome that affects the nerves of the body beginning several weeks after the diarrheal illness. This occurs when a person's immune system is "triggered" to attack the body's own nerves resulting in paralysis. The paralysis usually lasts several weeks and requires intensive medical care. It is estimated that approximately one in every 1,000 reported *Campylobacter* illnesses leads to Guillain-Barré syndrome. As many as 40% of Guillain-Barré syndrome cases in this country may be triggered by campylobacteriosis.

How do people get infected with this germ?

Campylobacteriosis usually occurs in single, sporadic cases, but it can also occur in outbreaks, when two or more people become ill from the same source. Most cases of campylobacteriosis are associated with eating raw or undercooked poultry meat or from cross-contamination of other foods by these items. Outbreaks of *Campylobacter* have most often been associated with unpasteurized dairy products, contaminated water, poultry, and produce. Animals can also be infected, and some people get infected from contact with the stool of an ill dog or cat. The organism is not usually spread from one person to another, but this can happen if the infected person is producing a large volume of diarrhea.

It only takes a very few *Campylobacter* organisms (fewer than 500) to make a person sick. Even one drop of juice from raw chicken meat can have enough *Campylobacter* in it to infect a person! One way to become infected is to cut poultry meat on a cutting board, and then use the unwashed cutting board or utensil to prepare vegetables or other raw or lightly cooked foods. The *Campylobacter* organisms from the raw meat can get onto the other foods.

How does food or water get contaminated with Campylobacter?

Many chicken flocks are infected with *Campylobacter* but show no signs of illness. *Campylobacter* can be easily spread from bird to bird through a common water source or through contact with infected feces. When an infected bird is slaughtered, *Campylobacter* organisms can be transferred from the intestines to the meat. In 2011, *Campylobacter* was found on 47% of raw chicken samples bought in grocery stores and tested through the National Antimicrobial Resistance Monitoring

System (NARMS). *Campylobactercan* also be present in the giblets, especially the liver.

Unpasteurized milk can become contaminated if the cow has an infection with *Campylobacter* in her udder or if the milk is contaminated with manure. Surface water and mountain streams can become contaminated from infected feces from cows or wild birds. *Campylobacter* is common in the developing world, and travelers to foreign countries are at risk for becoming infected with *Campylobacter*. Approximately one-fifth (19%) of *Campylobacter* cases identified in FoodNet are associated with international travel.

What can be done to prevent Campylobacter infection?

Some simple food handling practices can help prevent *Campylobacter* infections.

- Cook all poultry products thoroughly. Make sure that the meat is cooked throughout (no longer pink) and any juices run clear. All poultry should be cooked to reach a minimum internal temperature of 165°F.

- If you are served undercooked poultry in a restaurant, send it back for further cooking.

- Wash hands with soap before preparing food.

- Wash hands with soap after handling raw foods of animal origin and before touching anything else.

- Prevent cross-contamination in the kitchen by using separate cutting boards for foods of animal origin and other foods and by thoroughly cleaning all cutting boards, countertops, and utensils with soap and hot water after preparing raw food of animal origin.

- Do not drink unpasteurized milk or untreated surface water.

- Make sure that persons with diarrhea, especially children, wash their hands carefully and frequently with soap to reduce the risk of spreading the infection.

- Wash hands with soap after contact with pet feces.

Physicians who diagnose campylobacteriosis and clinical laboratories that identify this organism should report their findings to the local health department. If many cases occur at the same time, it may mean that an outbreak has occurred in which many people were exposed to a common contaminated food item or water source. If this food or water is still available, more people could get infected. Public health departments investigate outbreaks to identify the source so that action can be taken to prevent more cases.

Section 35.4

Escherichia Coli

Text in this section is excerpted from "Food Poisoning: E. coli," FoodSafety.gov, United States Department of Health and Human Services (DHHS), July 16, 2015.

Escherichia Coli (E. coli) is the name of a type of bacteria that lives in your intestines and in the intestines of animals. Although most types of *E. coli* are harmless, some types can make you sick.

The worst type of *E. coli*, known as *E. coli O157:H7*, causes bloody diarrhea and can sometimes cause kidney failure and even death. *E. coli O157:H7* makes a toxin called Shiga toxin and is known as a Shiga toxin-producing *E. coli (STEC)*. There are many other types of STEC, and some can make you just as sick as *E. coli O157:H7*.

Table 35.1. *E. coli*

Sources	Contaminated food, especially undercooked ground beef, unpasteurized (raw) milk and juice, soft cheeses made from raw milk, and raw fruits and vegetables (such as sprouts)
	Contaminated water, including drinking untreated water and swimming in contaminated water
	Animals and their environment: particularly cows, sheep, and goats. If you don't wash your hands carefully after touching an animal or its environment, you could get an *E. coli* infection.
	Feces of infected people

Table 35.1. *Continued*

Incubation Period	1-10 days
Symptoms	Severe diarrhea that is often bloody, severe abdominal pain, and vomiting. Usually, little or no fever is present.
	Symptoms of HUS include decreased urine production, dark or tea-colored urine, and facial pallor.
Duration of Illness	5-10 days. Most people will be better in 6-8 days.
	If HUS develops, it usually occurs after about 1 week.
What Do I Do?	Drink plenty of fluids and get rest. If you cannot drink enough fluids to prevent dehydration or if your symptoms are severe (including blood in your stools or severe abdominal pain), call your doctor. Antibiotics should not be used to treat this infection.
How Can I Prevent It?	• Avoid eating high-risk foods, especially undercooked ground beef, unpasteurized milk or juice, soft cheeses made from unpasteurized milk, or alfalfa sprouts. • Use a food thermometer to make sure that ground beef has reached a safe internal temperature of 160° F. • Wash hands before preparing food, after diapering infants, and after contact with cows, sheep, or goats, their food or treats, or their living environment .

One severe complication associated with *E. coli* infection is hemolytic uremic syndrome (HUS). The infection produces toxic substances that destroy red blood cells, causing kidney injury. HUS can require intensive care, kidney dialysis, and transfusions.

Section 35.5

Salmonella

Text in this section is excerpted from " Salmonella," Centers for Disease Control and Prevention (CDC), March 9, 2015.

What Is Salmonellosis?

Salmonella is a bacteria that makes people sick. It was discovered by an American scientist named Dr. Salmon, and has been known to cause illness for over 125 years.

Most people infected with *Salmonella* develop diarrhea, fever, and abdominal cramps between 12 and 72 hours after infection. The illness usually lasts 4 to 7 days, and most individuals recover without treatment. In some cases, diarrhea may be so severe that the patient needs to be hospitalized. In these patients, the *Salmonella* infection may spread from the intestines to the blood stream, and then to other body sites. In these cases, *Salmonella* can cause death unless the person is treated promptly with antibiotics. The elderly, infants, and those with impaired immune systems are more likely to have a severe illness.

How Common Is **Salmonella** *Infection?*

CDC estimates that approximately 1.2 million illnesses and approximately 450 deaths occur due to non-typhoidal *Salmonella* annually in the United States. There are many different kinds of *Salmonella* bacteria. *Salmonella* serotype Typhimurium and *Salmonella* serotype Enteritidis are the most common in the United States. *Salmonella* infections are more common in the summer than winter.

Who Is at Highest Risk for **Salmonella** *Infection?*

Children are at the highest risk for *Salmonella* infection. Children under the age of 5 have higher rates of *Salmonella* infection than any other age group. Young children, older adults, and people with weakened immune systems are the most likely to have severe infections.

Are There Long-Term Consequences to a **Salmonella** *Infection?*

People with diarrhea due to a *Salmonella* infection usually recover completely, although it may be several months before their bowel habits are entirely normal.

A small number of people with *Salmonella* develop pain in their joints. This is called reactive arthritis. Reactive arthritis can last for months or years and can lead to chronic arthritis, which can be difficult to treat. Antibiotic treatment of the initial *Salmonella* infection does not make a difference in whether or not the person develops arthritis. People with reactive arthritis can also develop irritation of the eyes and painful urination.

How Can **Salmonella** *Infections Be Diagnosed?*

Diagnosing salmonellosis requires testing a clinical specimen (such as stool or blood) from an infected person to distinguish it from other illnesses that can cause diarrhea, fever, and abdominal cramps. Once *Salmonella* is identified in the specimen, additional testing can be done to further characterize the *Salmonella*.

Prevention

Quick Tips for Preventing Salmonella

- Cook poultry, ground beef, and eggs thoroughly. Do not eat or drink foods containing raw eggs, or raw (unpasteurized) milk.

- If you are served undercooked meat, poultry or eggs in a restaurant, don't hesitate to send it back to the kitchen for further cooking.

- Wash hands, kitchen work surfaces, and utensils with soap and water immediately after they have been in contact with raw meat or poultry.

- Be particularly careful with foods prepared for infants, the elderly, and the immunocompromised.

- Wash hands with soap after handling reptiles, birds, or baby chicks, and after contact with pet feces.

- Avoid direct or even indirect contact between reptiles (turtles, iguanas, other lizards, snakes) and infants or immunocompromised persons.

- Don't work with raw poultry or meat, and an infant (e.g., feed, change diaper) at the same time.

- Mother's milk is the safest food for young infants. Breastfeeding prevents salmonellosis and many other health problems.

More About Prevention

There is no vaccine to prevent salmonellosis. Because foods of animal origin may be contaminated with *Salmonella*, people should not eat raw or undercooked eggs, poultry, or meat. Raw eggs may be unrecognized in some foods, such as homemade Hollandaise sauce, Caesar and other homemade salad dressings, tiramisu, homemade ice cream, homemade mayonnaise, cookie dough, and frostings. Poultry and meat, including hamburgers, should be well-cooked, not pink in the middle. Persons also should not consume raw or unpasteurized milk or other dairy products. Produce should be thoroughly washed.

Cross-contamination of foods should be avoided. Uncooked meats should be kept separate from produce, cooked foods, and ready-to-eat foods. Hands, cutting boards, counters, knives, and other utensils should be washed thoroughly after touching uncooked foods. Hand should be washed before handling food, and between handling different food items.

People who have salmonellosis should not prepare food or pour water for others until their diarrhea has resolved. Many health departments require that restaurant workers with *Salmonella* infection have a stool test showing that they are no longer carrying the *Salmonella* bacterium before they return to work.

People should wash their hands after contact with animal feces. Because reptiles are particularly likely to have *Salmonella*, and it can contaminate their skin, everyone should immediately wash their hands after handling reptiles. Reptiles (including turtles) are not appropriate pets for small children and should not be in the same house as an infant. *Salmonella* carried in the intestines of chicks and ducklings contaminates their environment and the entire surface of the animal. Children can be exposed to the bacteria by simply holding, cuddling, or kissing the birds. Children should not handle baby chicks or other young birds. Everyone should immediately wash their hands after touching birds, including baby chicks and ducklings, or their environment.

Some prevention steps occur everyday without you thinking about it. Pasteurization of milk and treatment of municipal water supplies are highly effective prevention measures that have been in place for decades. In the 1970s, small pet turtles were a common source of salmonellosis in the United States, so in 1975, the sale of small turtles was banned in this country. However, in 2008, they were still being sold, and cases of *Salmonella* associated with pet turtles have been reported. Improvements in farm animal hygiene, in slaughter plant practices, and in vegetable and fruit harvesting and packing operations may help prevent salmonellosis caused by contaminated foods. Better education of food industry workers in basic food safety and restaurant inspection procedures may prevent cross-contamination and other food handling errors that can lead to outbreaks. Wider use of pasteurized egg in restaurants, hospitals, and nursing homes is an important prevention measure. In the future, irradiation or other treatments may greatly reduce contamination of raw meat.

Section 35.6

Listeria

Text in this section is excerpted from "Listeria," FoodSafety.gov, United States Department of Health & Human Services (DHHS), July 16, 2015.

Listeria is the name of a bacteria found in soil and water and some animals, including poultry and cattle. It can be present in raw milk and foods made from raw milk. It can also live in food processing plants and contaminate a variety of processed meats.

Listeria is unlike many other germs because it can grow even in the cold temperature of the refrigerator. *Listeria* is killed by cooking and pasteurization.

Table 35.2. Listeria

Sources	• Ready-to-eat deli meats and hot dogs • Refrigerated pâtés or meat spreads • Unpasteurized (raw) milk and dairy products • Soft cheese made with unpasteurized milk, such as queso fresco, Feta, Brie, Camembert • Refrigerated smoked seafood • Raw sprouts
Incubation Period	3-70 days
Symptoms	Fever, stiff neck, confusion, weakness, vomiting, sometimes preceded by diarrhea
Duration of Illness	Days to weeks

Who's at Risk?	• Older adults
	• Pregnant women
	• People with weakened immune systems
	• Organ transplant patients who are receiving drugs to prevent the body from rejecting the organ
	• People with certain diseases, such as:
	  • HIV/AIDS or other autoimmune diseases
	  • Cancer
	  • End-stage renal disease

Table 35.2. *Continued*

	• Liver disease • Alcoholism • Diabetes
What Do I Do?	If you are very ill with fever or stiff neck, consult your doctor immediately. Antibiotics given promptly can cure the infection and, in pregnant women, can prevent infection of the fetus.
How Do I Prevent It?	• Do not drink raw (unpasteurized) milk, and do not eat foods that have unpasteurized milk in them. • Wash hands, knives, countertops, and cutting boards after handling and preparing uncooked foods. • Rinse raw produce thoroughly under running tap water before eating. • Keep uncooked meats, poultry, and seafood separate from vegetables, fruits, cooked foods, and ready-to-eat foods. • Thoroughly cook raw food from animal sources, such as meat, poultry, or seafood to a safe internal temperature. • Wash hands, knives, countertops, and cutting boards after handling and preparing uncooked foods. • Consume perishable and ready-to-eat foods as soon as possible. • Persons in higher risk groups should heat hot dogs, cold cuts, and deli meats before eating them.

At Risk Populations

Listeriosis, an infection caused by *Listeria,* can pose major risks for certain populations. Pregnant women, older adults, and individuals with weakened immune systems are at greater risk.

Pregnant Women

Pregnant women are approximately 20 times more likely than other healthy adults to get listeriosis. In pregnant women, it is typically a mild, flu-like illness. In the child, listeriosis can lead to miscarriage, stillbirth, or life-long health problems.

Older Adults

As adults age, it is normal for their bodies not to work as well as they did when they were younger. Changes in their organs and body systems are expected as they grow older. These changes often make them more susceptible to contracting a foodborne illness such as Listeriosis.

Other at Risk Populations

A properly functioning immune system works to clear infection and other foreign agents from the body. However, certain conditions including cancer and its treatments, diabetes, HIV/AIDS, and organ or bone marrow transplants can weaken the immune system – making the body more susceptible to many types of infections, including foodborne illness such as Listeriosis.

Section 35.7

Shigella

Text in this section is excerpted from "Shigella," FoodSafety.gov, United States Department of Health & Human Services (DHHS), July 16, 2015.

Shigellosis is an infectious disease caused by *Shigella*. The *Shigella* germ is a family of bacteria that can cause diarrhea in humans. People with shigellosis shed the bacteria in their feces. The bacteria can spread from an infected person to contaminate water or food, or directly to another person. Getting just a little bit of the *Shigella* bacteria into your mouth is enough to cause symptoms.

Table 35.3. *Shigella*

Sources	Contaminated food or water, or contact with an infected person. Foods most often associated with Shigellaoutbreaks are salads and sandwiches that involve a lot of hand contact in their preparation, and raw vegetables contaminated in the field.
Incubation Period	1-7 days (usually 1-3 days)
Symptoms	Sudden abdominal cramping, fever, diarrhea that may be bloody or contains mucus, nausea and vomiting

Table 35.3. *Continued*

Duration of Illness	2-7 days
Who's at Risk?	Children, especially toddlers aged 2-4
What Do I Do?	Drink plenty of fluids and get rest. Stay home from school or work to avoid spreading the bacteria to others. If you cannot drink enough fluids to prevent dehydration, call your doctor.
How Do I Prevent It?	• Wash hands with soap carefully and frequently, especially after going to the bathroom, after changing diapers, and before preparing foods or beverages. • Dispose of soiled diapers properly • Disinfect diaper changing areas after using them. • Keep children with diarrhea out of child care settings while they are ill. • Supervise handwashing of toddlers and small children after they use the toilet. • Do not prepare food for others while ill with diarrhea • Avoid swallowing water from ponds, lakes, or untreated pools. • When traveling in developing countries, drink only treated or boiled water, and eat only cooked hot foods or fruits you peel yourself.

The illness is most commonly seen in child-care settings and schools. Shigellosis is a cause of traveler's diarrhea, from contaminated food and water in developing countries.

Section 35.8

Botulism

Text in this section is excerpted from "National Center for Emerging
and Zoonotic Infectious Diseases—Botulism," Centers for Disease
Control and Prevention (CDC), April 25, 2014.

What is botulism?

Botulism is a rare but serious paralytic illness caused by a nerve
toxin that is produced by the bacterium *Clostridium botulinum* and
sometimes by strains of *Clostridium butyricum* and *Clostridium
baratii*. There are five main kinds of botulism. Foodborne botulism is
caused by eating foods that contain the botulinum toxin. Wound botulism is caused by toxin produced from a wound infected with *Clostridium botulinum*. Infant botulism is caused by consuming the spores of
the botulinum bacteria, which then grow in the intestines and release
toxin. Adult intestinal toxemia (adult intestinal colonization) botulism
is a very rare kind of botulism that occurs among adults by the same
route as infant botulism. Lastly, iatrogenic botulism can occur from
accidental overdose of botulinum toxin. All forms of botulism can be
fatal and are considered medical emergencies. Foodborne botulism is
a public health emergency because many people can be poisoned by
eating a contaminated food.

What kind of germ is **Clostridium botulinum?**

Clostridium botulinum is the name of a group of bacteria. They can
be found in soil. These rod-shaped organisms grow best in low oxygen
conditions. The bacteria form spores which allow them to survive in
a dormant state until exposed to conditions that can support their
growth. There are seven types of botulism toxin designated by the
letters A through G; only types A, B, E and F cause illness in humans.

How common is botulism?

In the United States, an average of 145 cases are reported each year.
Of these, approximately 15% are foodborne, 65% are infant botulism,

and 20% are wound. Adult intestinal colonization and iatrogenic botulism also occur, but rarely. Outbreaks of foodborne botulism involving two or more persons occur most years and are usually caused by home-canned foods. Most wound botulism cases are associated with black-tar heroin injection, especially in California.

What are the symptoms of botulism?

The classic symptoms of botulism include double vision, blurred vision, drooping eyelids, slurred speech, difficulty swallowing, dry mouth, and muscle weakness. Infants with botulism appear lethargic, feed poorly, are constipated, and have a weak cry and poor muscle tone. These are all symptoms of the muscle paralysis caused by the bacterial toxin. If untreated, these symptoms may progress to cause paralysis of the respiratory muscles, arms, legs, and trunk. In foodborne botulism, symptoms generally begin 18 to 36 hours after eating a contaminated food, but they can occur as early as 6 hours or as late as 10 days.

How is botulism diagnosed?

Physicians may consider the diagnosis if the patient's history and physical examination suggest botulism. However, these clues are usually not enough to allow a diagnosis of botulism. Other diseases such as Guillain-Barré syndrome, stroke, and myasthenia gravis can appear similar to botulism, and special tests may be needed to exclude these other conditions. These tests may include a brain scan, spinal fluid examination, nerve conduction test (electromyography, or EMG), and a tensilon test for myasthenia gravis. Tests for botulinum toxin and for bacteria that cause botulism can be performed at some state health department laboratories and at CDC.

How can botulism be treated?

The respiratory failure and paralysis that occur with severe botulism may require a patient to be on a breathing machine (ventilator) for weeks or months, plus intensive medical and nursing care. The paralysis slowly improves. Botulism can be treated with an antitoxin which blocks the action of toxin circulating in the blood. Antitoxin for infants is available from the California Department of Public Health, and antitoxin for older children and adults is available through CDC. If given before paralysis is complete, antitoxin can prevent worsening and shorten recovery time. Physicians may try to remove contaminated food still in the gut by inducing vomiting or by using enemas.

Wounds should be treated, usually surgically, to remove the source of the toxin-producing bacteria followed by administration of appropriate antibiotics. Good supportive care in a hospital is the mainstay of therapy for all forms of botulism.

Are there complications from botulism?

Botulism can result in death due to respiratory failure. However, in the past 50 years the proportion of patients with botulism who die has fallen from about 50% to 3-5%. A patient with severe botulism may require a breathing machine as well as intensive medical and nursing care for several months, and some patients die from infections or other problems related to remaining paralyzed for weeks or months. Patients who survive an episode of botulism poisoning may have fatigue and shortness of breath for years and long-term therapy may be needed to aid recovery.

How can botulism be prevented?

Many cases of botulism are preventable. Foodborne botulism has often been from home-canned foods with low acid content, such as asparagus, green beans, beets and corn and is caused by failure to follow proper canning methods. However, seemingly unlikely or unusual sources are found every decade, with the common problem of improper handling during manufacture, at retail, or by consumers; some examples are chopped garlic in oil, canned cheese sauce, chile peppers, tomatoes, carrot juice, and baked potatoes wrapped in foil. In Alaska, foodborne botulism is caused by fermented fish and other aquatic game foods. Persons who do home canning should follow strict hygienic procedures to reduce contamination of foods, and carefully follow instructions on safe home canning including the use of pressure canners/cookers as recommended through county extension services or from the US Department of Agriculture. Oils infused with garlic or herbs should be refrigerated. Potatoes which have been baked while wrapped in aluminum foil should be kept hot until served or refrigerated. Because the botulinum toxin is destroyed by high temperatures, persons who eat home-canned foods should consider boiling the food for 10 minutes before eating it to ensure safety. Wound botulism can be prevented by promptly seeking medical care for infected wounds and by not using injectable street drugs. Most infant botulism cases cannot be prevented because the bacteria that causes this disease is in soil and dust. The bacteria can be found inside homes on floors, carpet, and countertops even after cleaning. Honey can contain the bacteria that causes infant botulism so, children less than 12 months old should not be fed honey. Honey is safe for persons 1 year of age and older.

What are public health agencies doing to prevent or control botulism?

Public education about botulism prevention is an ongoing activity. Information about safe canning is widely available for consumers. Persons in state health departments and at CDC are knowledgeable about botulism and available to consult with physicians 24 hours a day. If antitoxin is needed to treat a patient, it can be quickly delivered to a physician anywhere in the country. Suspected outbreaks of botulism are quickly investigated, and if they involve a commercial product, the appropriate control measures are coordinated among public health and regulatory agencies. Physicians should immediately report suspected cases of botulism to their state health department.

Section 35.9

Staphylococcus

Text in this section is excerpted from "Staphylococcus," FoodSafety. gov, United States Department of Health & Human Services (DHHS), July 16, 2015.

Staphylococcus aureus (or *Staph aureus*) is a type of bacteria commonly found on the skin and hair as well as in the noses and throats of people and animals. These bacteria are present in up to 25 percent of healthy people and are even more common among those with skin, eye, nose, or throat infections.

Staphylococcus can cause food poisoning when a food handler contaminates food and then the food is not properly refrigerated. Other sources of food contamination include the equipment and surfaces on which food is prepared. These bacteria multiply quickly at room temperature to produce a toxin that causes illness. *Staphylococcus* is killed by cooking and pasteurization.

Table 35.4. Staphylococcus

Sources	Foods that are made with hand contact and require no additional cooking, such as: • Salads, such as ham, egg, tuna, chicken, potato, and macaroni • Bakery products, such as cream-filled pastries, cream pies, and chocolate éclairs • Sandwiches • Other sources include milk and dairy products, as well as meat, poultry, eggs, and related products.
Incubation Period	1-6 hours
Symptoms	Nausea, vomiting, diarrhea, loss of appetite, severe abdominal cramps, mild fever
Duration of Illness	24-48 hours
What Do I Do?	Drink plenty of fluids and get rest. If you cannot drink enough fluids to prevent dehydration, call your doctor.
How Can I Prevent Illness?	• Wash hands and under fingernails vigorously with soap and water before handling and preparing food. • Do not prepare food if you have a nose or eye infection. • Do not prepare or serve food for others if you have wounds or skin infections on your hands or wrists. • Keep kitchens and food-serving areas clean and sanitized. • If food is prepared more than two hours before serving, keep hot foods hot (over 140° F) and cold foods cold (40° F or under). • Store cooked food in a wide, shallow container and refrigerate as soon as possible.

Chapter 36

Foodborne Viral Illnesses

Chapter Contents

Section 36.1

Hepatitis A

This section includes excerpts from "Viral Hepatitis—Hepatitis A Information," Centers for Disease Control and Prevention (CDC), May 31, 2015.

Hepatitis A is a liver infection caused by the Hepatitis A virus (HAV). Hepatitis A is highly contagious. It is usually transmitted by the fecal-oral route, either through person-to-person contact or consumption of contaminated food or water. Hepatitis A is a self-limited disease that does not result in chronic infection. More than 80% of adults with Hepatitis A have symptoms but the majority of children do not have symptoms or have an unrecognized infection. Antibodies produced in response to Hepatitis A last for life and protect against reinfection. The best way to prevent Hepatitis A is by getting vaccinated.

Hepatitis A FAQs for the Public

Overview

What is hepatitis?

"Hepatitis" means inflammation of the liver. Toxins, certain drugs, some diseases, heavy alcohol use, and bacterial and viral infections can all cause hepatitis. Hepatitis is also the name of a family of viral infections that affect the liver; the most common types are Hepatitis A, Hepatitis B, and Hepatitis C.

What is the difference between Hepatitis A, Hepatitis B, and Hepatitis C?

Hepatitis A, Hepatitis B, and Hepatitis C are diseases caused by three different viruses. Although each can cause similar symptoms, they have different modes of transmission and can affect the liver differently. Hepatitis A appears only as an acute or newly occurring infection and does not become chronic. People with Hepatitis A usually improve without treatment. Hepatitis B and Hepatitis C can also begin as acute infections, but in some people, the virus remains in the body, resulting in chronic disease and long term liver problems. There are vaccines to prevent Hepatitis A and B; however, there is not one for Hepatitis C. If a person has had one type of viral hepatitis in the past, it is still possible to get the other types.

What is Hepatitis A?

Hepatitis A is a contagious liver disease that results from infection with the Hepatitis A virus. It can range in severity from a mild illness lasting a few weeks to a severe illness lasting several months. Hepatitis A is usually spread when a person ingests fecal matter—even in microscopic amounts—from contact with objects, food, or drinks contaminated by the feces, or stool, of an infected person.

Statistics

How common is Hepatitis A in the United States?

In 2013, there were an estimated 3,473 acute hepatitis A infection in the United States.

Is Hepatitis A decreasing in the United States?

Yes. Rates of Hepatitis A in the United States are the lowest they have been in 40 years. The Hepatitis A vaccine was introduced in 1995 and health professionals now routinely vaccinate all children, travelers to certain countries, and persons at risk for the disease. Many experts believe Hepatitis A vaccination has dramatically affected rates of the disease in the United States.

Transmission / Exposure

How is Hepatitis A spread?

Hepatitis A is usually spread when the Hepatitis A virus is taken in by mouth from contact with objects, food, or drinks contaminated by the feces (or stool) of an infected person. A person can get Hepatitis A through:

- Person to person contact

- when an infected person does not wash his or her hands properly after going to the bathroom and touches other objects or food

- when a parent or caregiver does not properly wash his or her hands after changing diapers or cleaning up the stool of an infected person

- when someone has sex or sexual contact with an infected person. (not limited to anal-oral contact)

- Contaminated food or water

- Hepatitis A can be spread by eating or drinking food or water contaminated with the virus. (This can include frozen or under-cooked food.) This is more likely to occur in countries where Hepatitis A is common and in areas where there are poor sanitary conditions or poor personal hygiene. The food and drinks most likely to be contaminated are fruits, vegetables, shellfish, ice, and water. In the United States, chlorination of water kills Hepatitis A virus that enters the water supply.

Who is at risk for Hepatitis A?

Although anyone can get Hepatitis A, in the United States, certain groups of people are at higher risk, such as those who:

- Travel to or live in countries where Hepatitis A is common

- Are men who have sexual contact with other men

- Use illegal drugs, whether injected or not

- Have clotting-factor disorders, such as hemophilia

- Live with someone who has Hepatitis A

- Have oral-anal sexual contact with someone who has Hepatitis A

I think I have been exposed to Hepatitis A. What should I do?

If you have any questions about potential exposure to Hepatitis A, call your health professional or your local or state health department.

If you were recently exposed to Hepatitis A virus and have not been vaccinated against Hepatitis A, you might benefit from an injection of either immune globulin or Hepatitis A vaccine. However, the vaccine or immune globulin must be given within the first 2 weeks after exposure to be effective. A health professional can decide what is best on the basis of your age and overall health.

What should I do if I ate at a restaurant that had an outbreak of Hepatitis A?

Talk to your health professional or a local health department official for guidance. Outbreaks usually result from one of two sources of contamination: an infected food handler or an infected food source. Your health department will investigate the cause of the outbreak.

Keep in mind that most people do not get sick when someone at a restaurant has Hepatitis A. However, if an infected food handler is infectious and has poor hygiene, the risk goes up for patrons of that restaurant. In such cases, health officials might try to identify patrons and provide Hepatitis A vaccine or immune globulin if they can find them within 2 weeks of exposure.

On rare occasions, the source of the infection can be traced to contaminated food. Foods can become contaminated at any point along the process: growing, harvesting, processing, handling, and even after cooking. In these cases, health officials will try to determine the source of the contamination and the best ways to minimize health threats to the public.

What is PEP or postexposure prophylaxis?

PEP or postexposure prophylaxis refers to trying to prevent or treat a disease after someone is exposed to it.

Who should get PEP after being exposed to Hepatitis A?

A health professional can decide whether or not a person needs PEP after exposure to Hepatitis A. People who might benefit from PEP include those who:

- Live with someone who has Hepatitis A

- Have recently had sexual contact with someone who has Hepatitis A

- Have recently shared injection or non-injection illegal drugs with someone who has Hepatitis A

- Have had ongoing, close personal contact with a person with Hepatitis A, such as a regular babysitter or caregiver

- Have been exposed to food or water known to be contaminated with Hepatitis A virus

If I have had Hepatitis A in the past, can I get it again?

No. Once you recover from Hepatitis A, you develop antibodies that protect you from the virus for life. An antibody is a substance found in the blood that the body produces in response to a virus. Antibodies protect the body from disease by attaching to the virus and destroying it.

Can I donate blood if I have had Hepatitis A?

If you had Hepatitis A when you were 11 years of age or older, you cannot donate blood. If you had Hepatitis A before age 11, you may be able donate blood. Check with your blood donation center.

How long does Hepatitis A virus survive outside the body?

The Hepatitis A virus is extremely hearty. It is able to survive the body's highly acidic digestive tract and can live outside the body for months. High temperatures, such as boiling or cooking food or liquids for at least 1 minute at 185°F (85°C), kill the virus, although freezing temperatures do not.

Symptoms

Does Hepatitis A cause symptoms?

Not always. Some people get Hepatitis A and have no symptoms of the disease. Adults are more likely to have symptoms than children.

What are the symptoms of Hepatitis A?

Some people with Hepatitis A do not have any symptoms. If you do have symptoms, they may include the following:

- Fever
- Fatigue
- Loss of appetite
- Nausea
- Vomiting
- Abdominal pain
- Dark urine
- Clay-colored bowel movements

- Joint pain

- Jaundice (a yellowing of the skin or eyes)

How soon after exposure to Hepatitis A will symptoms appear?

If symptoms occur, they usually appear anywhere from 2 to 6 weeks after exposure. Symptoms usually develop over a period of several days.

How long do Hepatitis A symptoms last?

Symptoms usually last less than 2 months, although some people can be ill for as long as 6 months.

Can a person spread Hepatitis A without having symptoms?

Yes. Many people, especially children, have no symptoms. In addition, a person can transmit the virus to others up to 2 weeks before symptoms appear.

How serious is Hepatitis A?

Almost all people who get Hepatitis A recover completely and do not have any lasting liver damage, although they may feel sick for months. Hepatitis A can sometimes cause liver failure and death, although this is rare and occurs more commonly in persons 50 years of age or older and persons with other liver diseases, such as Hepatitis B or C.

Diagnosis / Treatment

How will I know if I have Hepatitis A?

A doctor can determine if you have Hepatitis A by discussing your symptoms and taking a blood sample.

How is Hepatitis A treated?

There are no special treatments for Hepatitis A. Most people with Hepatitis A will feel sick for a few months before they begin to feel better. A few people will need to be hospitalized. During this time, doctors usually recommend rest, adequate nutrition, and fluids. People with Hepatitis A should check with a health professional before taking any prescription pills, supplements, or over-the-counter medications, which can potentially damage the liver. Alcohol should be avoided.

Prevention / Vaccination

Can Hepatitis A be prevented?

Yes. The best way to prevent Hepatitis A is through vaccination with the Hepatitis A vaccine. Vaccination is recommended for all children, for travelers to certain countries, and for people at high risk for infection with the virus. Frequent handwashing with soap and warm water after using the bathroom, changing a diaper, or before preparing food can help prevent the spread of Hepatitis A.

What is the Hepatitis A vaccine?

The Hepatitis A vaccine is a shot of inactive Hepatitis A virus that stimulates the body's natural immune system. After the vaccine is given, the body makes antibodies that protect a person against the virus. An antibody is a substance found in the blood that is produced in response to a virus invading the body. These antibodies are then stored in the body and will fight off the infection if a person is exposed to the virus in the future.

Who should get vaccinated against Hepatitis A?

Hepatitis A vaccination is recommended for:

- All children at age 1 year
- Travelers to countries that have high rates of Hepatitis A
- Men who have sexual contact with other men
- Users of injection and non-injection illegal drugs
- People with chronic (lifelong) liver diseases, such as Hepatitis B or Hepatitis C
- People who are treated with clotting-factor concentrates
- People who work with Hepatitis A infected animals or in a Hepatitis A research laboratory

How is the Hepatitis A vaccine given?

The Hepatitis A vaccine is given as 2 shots, 6 months apart. The Hepatitis A vaccine also comes in a combination form, containing both Hepatitis A and B vaccine, that can be given to persons 18 years of age and older. This form is given as 3 shots, over a period of 6 months.

Is the Hepatitis A vaccine effective?

Yes, the Hepatitis A vaccine is highly effective in preventing Hepatitis A virus infection. Protection begins approximately 2 to 4 weeks after the first injection. A second injection results in long-term protection.

Is the Hepatitis A vaccine safe?

Yes, the Hepatitis A vaccine is safe. No serious side effects have resulted from the Hepatitis A vaccine. Soreness at the injection site is the most common side effect reported. As with any medicine, there are very small risks that a serious problem could occur after someone gets the vaccine. However, the potential risks associated with Hepatitis A are much greater than the potential risks associated with the Hepatitis A vaccine. Before the Hepatitis A vaccine became available in the Unites States, more than 250,000 people were infected with Hepatitis A virus each year. Since the licensure of the first Hepatitis A vaccine in 1995, millions of doses of Hepatitis A vaccine have been given in the United States and worldwide.

Who should not receive the Hepatitis A vaccine?

People who have ever had a serious allergic reaction to the Hepatitis A vaccine or who are known to be allergic to any part of the Hepatitis A vaccine should not receive the vaccine. Tell your doctor if you have any severe allergies. Also, the vaccine is not licensed for use in infants under age 1 year.

Who should get the Hepatitis A vaccine before traveling?

Anyone traveling to or working in countries with high rates of Hepatitis A should talk to a health professional about getting vaccinated. He or she is likely to recommend vaccination or a shot of immune globulin before traveling to countries in Central or South America, Mexico, and certain parts of Asia, Africa, and Eastern Europe.

What is immune globulin?

Immune globulin is a substance made from human blood plasma that contains antibodies that protect against infection. It is given as a shot and provides short-term protection (approximately 3 months) against Hepatitis A. Immune globulin can be given either before exposure to the Hepatitis A virus (such as before travel to a country where Hepatitis A is common) or to prevent infection after exposure to the

Hepatitis A virus. Immune globulin must be given within 2 weeks after exposure for the best protection.

Why is the Hepatitis A vaccine recommended before traveling?

Traveling to places where Hepatitis A virus is common puts a person at high risk for Hepatitis A. The risk exists even for travelers to urban areas, those who stay in luxury hotels, and those who report that they have good hygiene and are careful about what they eat and drink. Travelers can minimize their risk by avoiding potentially contaminated water or food, such as drinking beverages (with or without ice) of unknown purity, eating uncooked shellfish, and eating uncooked fruits or vegetables that are not peeled or prepared by the traveler personally. Risk for infection increases with duration of travel and is highest for those who live in or visit rural areas, trek in back-country areas, or frequently eat or drink in settings with poor sanitation. Since a simple, safe vaccine exists, experts recommend that travelers to certain countries be vaccinated.

How soon before travel should the Hepatitis A vaccine be given?

The first dose of Hepatitis A vaccine should be given as soon as travel is planned. Two weeks or more before departure is ideal, but anytime before travel will provide some protection.

I'm leaving for my trip in a few days. Can I still get the Hepatitis A vaccine?

Experts now say that the first dose of Hepatitis A vaccine can be given at any time before departure. This will provide some protection for most healthy persons.

Will the Hepatitis A vaccine protect someone from other forms of hepatitis?

Hepatitis A vaccine will only protect someone from Hepatitis A. A separate vaccine is available for Hepatitis B. There is also a combination vaccine that protects a person from Hepatitis A and Hepatitis B. No vaccine is available for Hepatitis C at this time.

Can Hepatitis A vaccine be given to immunocompromised persons, such as hemodialysis patients or persons with AIDS?

Yes. Because Hepatitis A vaccine is inactivated (not "live"), it can be given to people with compromised immune systems.

Is it harmful to have an extra dose of Hepatitis A vaccine or to repeat the entire Hepatitis A vaccine series?

No, getting extra doses of Hepatitis A vaccine is not harmful.

What should be done if the last dose of Hepatitis A vaccine is delayed?

The second or last dose should be given by a health professional as soon as possible. The first dose does not need to be given again.

Where can I get the Hepatitis A vaccine?

Speak with your health professional or call your local public health department, may offer free or low-cost vaccines for adults. For children, check out http://www.cdc.gov/vaccines/programs/vfc/parents/default.htm.

Section 36.2

Noroviruses

This section includes excerpts from "Norovirus," Centers for Disease Control and Prevention (CDC), July 26, 2013.

Overview

Norovirus is a very contagious virus. You can get norovirus from an infected person, contaminated food or water, or by touching contaminated surfaces. The virus causes your stomach or intestines or both to get inflamed (acute gastroenteritis). This leads you to have stomach pain, nausea, and diarrhea and to throw up.

Anyone can be infected with norovirus and get sick. Also, you can have norovirus illness many times in your life. Norovirus illness can be serious, especially for young children and older adults.

Norovirus is the most common cause of acute gastroenteritis in the United States. Each year, it causes 19-21 million illnesses and contributes to 56,000-71,000 hospitalizations and 570-800 deaths. Norovirus is also the most common cause of foodborne-disease outbreaks in the United States.

The best way to help prevent norovirus is to practice proper hand washing and general cleanliness.

Symptoms

Norovirus causes inflammation of the stomach or intestines or both. This is called acute gastroenteritis.

The most common symptoms—

- diarrhea

- throwing up

- nausea

- stomach pain

Other symptoms—

- fever

- headache

- body aches

If you have norovirus illness, you can feel extremely ill and throw up or have diarrhea many times a day. This can lead to dehydration, especially in young children, older adults, and people with other illnesses.

A person usually develops symptoms 12 to 48 hours after being exposed to norovirus. Most people with norovirus illness get better within 1 to 3 days.

Symptoms of dehydration—

- decrease in urination

- dry mouth and throat

- feeling dizzy when standing up

Children who are dehydrated may cry with few or no tears and be unusually sleepy or fussy.

Transmission

Norovirus is a highly contagious virus. Anyone can get infected with norovirus and get sick. Also, you can get norovirus illness many times in your life. One reason for this is that there are many different types of noroviruses. Being infected with one type of norovirus may not protect you against other types.

Norovirus can be found in your stool (feces) even before you start feeling sick. The virus can stay in your stool for 2 weeks or more after you feel better.

You are most contagious

- when you are sick with norovirus illness, and

- during the first few days after you recover from norovirus illness.

You can become infected with norovirus by accidentally getting stool or vomit from infected people in your mouth. This usually happens by

- eating food or drinking liquids that are contaminated with norovirus,

- touching surfaces or objects contaminated with norovirus then putting your fingers in your mouth, or

- having contact with someone who is infected with norovirus (for example, caring for or sharing food or eating utensils with someone with norovirus illness).

Norovirus can spread quickly in closed places like daycare centers, nursing homes, schools, and cruise ships. Most norovirus outbreaks happen from November to April in the United States.

Preventing Norovirus Infection

Practice proper hand hygiene

Wash your hands carefully with soap and water—

- especially after using the toilet and changing diapers, and

- always before eating, preparing, or handling food.

Noroviruses can be found in your vomit or stool even before you start feeling sick. The virus can stay in your stool for 2 weeks or more after you feel better. So, it is important to continue washing your hands often during this time.

Alcohol-based hand sanitizers can be used in addition to hand washing. But, they should not be used as a substitute for washing with soap and water.

Wash fruits and vegetables and cook seafood thoroughly

Carefully wash fruits and vegetables before preparing and eating them. Cook oysters and other shellfish thoroughly before eating them.

Be aware that noroviruses are relatively resistant. They can survive temperatures as high as 140°F and quick steaming processes that are often used for cooking shellfish.

Food that might be contaminated with norovirus should be thrown out.

Keep sick infants and children out of areas where food is being handled and prepared.

When you are sick, do not prepare food or care for others who are sick

You should not prepare food for others or provide healthcare while you are sick and for at least 3 days after symptoms stop. This also applies to sick workers in settings such as schools and daycares where they may expose people to norovirus.

Many local and state health departments require that food workers and preparers with norovirus illness not work until at least 48 hours after symptoms stop. If you were recently sick, you can be given different duties in the restaurant, such as working at a cash register or hosting.

Clean and disinfect contaminated surfaces

After throwing up or having diarrhea, immediately clean and disinfect contaminated surfaces. Use a chlorine bleach solution with a concentration of 1000–5000 ppm (5–25 tablespoons of household bleach [5.25%] per gallon of water) or other disinfectant registered as effective against norovirus by the Environmental Protection Agency (EPA).

Wash laundry thoroughly

Immediately remove and wash clothes or linens that may be contaminated with vomit or stool (feces).

You should

- handle soiled items carefully without agitating them,

- wear rubber or disposable gloves while handling soiled items and wash your hands after, and

- wash the items with detergent at the maximum available cycle length then machine dry them.

Treatment

There is no specific medicine to treat people with norovirus illness. Norovirus infection cannot be treated with antibiotics because it is a viral (not a bacterial) infection.

If you have norovirus illness, you should drink plenty of liquids to replace fluid lost from throwing up and diarrhea. This will help prevent dehydration.

Sports drinks and other drinks without caffeine or alcohol can help with mild dehydration. But, these drinks may not replace important nutrients and minerals. Oral rehydration fluids that you can get over the counter are most helpful for mild dehydration.

Dehydration can lead to serious problems. Severe dehydration may require hospitalization for treatment with fluids given through your vein (intravenous or IV fluids). If you think you or someone you are caring for is severely dehydrated, call the doctor.

Chapter 37

Acrylamide from High-Temperature Cooking

What is acrylamide?

Acrylamide is a chemical widely used during the manufacturing of paper, dye, and other industrial products. It can also be formed when certain foods are cooked at high temperatures. Frying, baking, or roasting certain foods, such as potatoes or grains, can create acrylamide. French fries and potato chips, for example, may have measurable acrylamide levels. Acrylamide is also found in cigarette smoke.

How do people get exposed to acrylamide?

Food and cigarette smoke are the major sources of acrylamide exposure.

How does acrylamide get into foods?

When certain foods are cooked at high temperatures, sugars, such as glucose and fructose, can react with the free amino acid, asparagine, to form acrylamide. Acrylamide forms as part of a chemical reaction,

This chapter includes excerpts from "National Toxicology Program— Acrylamide," National Institute of Environmental Health Sciences (NIEHS), November 2013; and text from "You Can Help Cut Acrylamide in Your Diet," U.S. Food and Drug Administration (FDA), February 6, 2015.

known as the Maillard reaction, which contributes to the aroma, taste, and color of cooked foods. Acrylamide is one of the hundreds of chemicals that can form during the Maillard reaction.

Why did the NTP study acrylamide?

The nomination to study acrylamide came from the U.S. Food and Drug Administration (FDA). FDA wanted high quality data from animal studies, to help support risk assessments to understand any potential risks to humans. Acrylamide has been previously shown to cause several types of cancer in animals, but more information was needed to better understand how acrylamide causes tumors and at what doses the tumors occurred in animals. NTP also conducted studies on glycidamide, the major metabolite of acrylamide. When acrylamide is consumed through food, the body converts it to glycidamide. Since this conversion may differ among rodent species, comparing the effects of acrylamide and glycidamide in rats and mice provides meaningful support for human health risk assessments. The NTP studies on acrylamide and glycidamide were conducted at the FDA National Center for Toxicological Research (NCTR), as part of an interagency collaboration between NIEHS and FDA/NCTR.

What did the NTP studies find?

The two-year NTP studies of acrylamide, given in an animal's drinking water, found clear evidence of carcinogenic activity in male and female rats and mice, based on tumors in multiple sites.

For example, tumors were found in the mammary and thyroid glands in female rats, and the reproductive organs in male rats. Tumors of the lung were among those observed in mice.

Additionally, NTP conducted parallel studies on glycidamide, which was also found to be a multisite carcinogen in both male and female rats and mice. The types of tumors induced by glycidamide were the same as those seen in acrylamide. Findings of clear evidence of carcinogenic activity in both sexes of rats and mice, and at multiple sites, is relatively uncommon and indicative of a strong carcinogenic response.

What do the NTP studies mean for humans?

Acrylamide is already classified as reasonably anticipated to be a human carcinogen. Estimating the potential risks to humans, associated with dietary exposure to acrylamide, involves difficult analyses and judgments that are well beyond the intent of the NTP technical report. NTP studies will help FDA make better scientific assessments of the risk posed to the human population at low levels of exposure, and to identify risk management options that may be warranted for reducing food-related acrylamide exposure.

Are acrylamide levels regulated?

FDA is currently developing guidance for industry on reduction of acrylamide levels in food products. FDA also regulates the amount of acrylamide in a variety of materials that come in contact with food. The U.S. Environmental Protection Agency (EPA) regulates acrylamide levels in drinking water.

You Can Help Cut Acrylamide in Your Diet

If you're trying to lose weight, you may already be telling your waiter to hold the fries. Now there's another health benefit you can reap: Cutting down on certain fried foods can also help you cut down on the amount of acrylamide you eat. That's a good thing because high levels of acrylamide have been found to cause cancer in animals, and on that basis scientists believe it is likely to cause cancer in humans as well.

FDA chemist Lauren Robin explains that acrylamide is a chemical that can form in some foods—mainly plant-based foods—during high-temperature cooking processes like frying and baking. These include potatoes, cereals, coffee, crackers or breads, dried fruits and many other foods. According to the Grocery Manufacturers Association, acrylamide is found in 40 percent of the calories consumed in the average American diet.

While acrylamide has probably been around as long as people have been baking, roasting, toasting or frying foods, it was only in 2002 that scientists first discovered the chemical in food. Since then, the FDA has been actively investigating the effects of acrylamide as well as potential measures to reduce it. Today, the FDA posts a draft document with practical strategies to help growers, manufacturers and food service operators lower the amount of acrylamide in foods associated with higher levels of the chemical.

In addition, there are a number of steps you and your family can take to cut down on the amount of acrylamide in the foods you eat.

Acrylamide forms from sugars and an amino acid that are naturally present in food. It does not form, or forms at lower levels, in dairy, meat and fish products. The formation occurs when foods are cooked at home and in restaurants, as well as when they are made commercially.

"Generally speaking, acrylamide is more likely to accumulate when cooking is done for longer periods or at higher temperatures," Robin says. Boiling and steaming foods do not typically form acrylamide.

Tips for Cutting Down on Acrylamide

Given the widespread presence of acrylamide in foods, it isn't feasible to completely eliminate acrylamide from one's diet, Robin says. Nor is it necessary. Removing any one or two foods from your diet would not have a significant effect on overall exposure to acrylamide.

However, here are some steps you can take to help decrease the amount of acrylamide that you and your family consume:

- Frying causes acrylamide formation. If frying frozen fries, follow manufacturers' recommendations on time and temperature and avoid overcooking, heavy crisping or burning.

- Toast bread to a light brown color rather than a dark brown color. Avoid very brown areas.

- Cook cut potato products such as frozen french fries to a golden yellow color rather than a brown color. Brown areas tend to contain more acrylamide.

- Do not store potatoes in the refrigerator, which can increase acrylamide during cooking. Keep potatoes outside the refrigerator in a dark, cool place, such as a closet or a pantry.

FDA also recommends that you adopt a healthy eating plan, consistent with the Dietary Guidelines for Americans, including:

- Eat plenty of fruits, vegetables, whole grains, and fat-free or low-fat milk products.

- Include lean meats, poultry, fish, beans, eggs and nuts.

- Choose foods low in saturated fats, trans fat (which both raises your bad LDL cholesterol and lowers your good HDL cholesterol and is linked to heart attacks), cholesterol, salt and added sugars.

Chapter 38

Aflatoxins

A (FDA) flatoxin is a fungal toxin that commonly contaminates maize and other types of crops during production, harvest, storage or processing. Exposure to aflatoxin is known to cause both chronic and acute hepatocellular injury. In Kenya, acute aflatoxin poisoning results in liver failure and death in up to 40% of cases.

In developed countries, commercial crops are routinely screened for aflatoxin using detection techniques that are performed in a laboratory setting. Food supplies that test over the regulatory limit are considered unsafe for human consumption and destroyed.

In developing nations, many people are exposed to aflatoxin through food grown at home. Inadequate harvesting and storage techniques allow for the growth of aflatoxin-producing fungus and homegrown crops are not routinely tested for the presence of aflatoxin. As a result, an estimated 4.5 billion people living in developing countries may be chronically exposed to aflatoxin through their diet.

In May 2006, an outbreak of acute aflatoxicosis was reported in a region of Kenya where aflatoxin contamination of homegrown maize has been a recurrent problem. CDC teams worked with the Kenyan Ministry of Health to trial a rapid, portable aflatoxin screening tool that could be used in the field to identify contaminated maize and guide urgent maize replacement efforts during an outbreak. To do this, we used a portable lateral flow immunoassay; a test validated for use at

This chapter includes excerpts from "Health Studies Branch – Understanding Chemical Exposures," Centers for Disease Control and Prevention (CDC), January 13, 2012; and text from "Food—BBB – Aflatoxins," U.S. Food and Drug Administration (FDA), August 5, 2013.

commercial silo laboratories, and modified the methods for use in rural Kenya without electricity or refrigeration.

BBB - Aflatoxins

Name of the Organism:

Aflatoxins

Nature of Acute Disease:

Aflatoxicosis

Aflatoxicosis is poisoning that results from ingestion of aflatoxins in contaminated food or feed. The aflatoxins are a group of structurally related toxic compounds produced by certain strains of the fungi Aspergillus flavus and A. parasiticus. Under favorable conditions of temperature and humidity, these fungi grow on certain foods and feeds, resulting in the production of aflatoxins. The most pronounced contamination has been encountered in tree nuts, peanuts, and other oilseeds, including corn and cottonseed. The major aflatoxins of concern are designated B1, B2, G1, and G2. These toxins are usually found together in various foods and feeds in various proportions; however, aflatoxin B1 is usually predominant and is the most toxic. When a commodity is analyzed by thin-layer chromatography, the aflatoxins separate into the individual components in the order given above; however, the first two fluoresce blue when viewed under ultraviolet light and the second two fluoresce green. Aflatoxin M a major metabolic product of aflatoxin B1 in animals and is usually excreted in the milk and urine of dairy cattle and other mammalian species that have consumed aflatoxin-contaminated food or feed.

Nature of Disease:

Aflatoxins produce acute necrosis, cirrhosis, and carcinoma of the liver in a number of animal species; no animal species is resistant to the acute toxic effects of aflatoxins; hence it is logical to assume that humans may be similarly affected. A wide variation in LD50 values has been obtained in animal species tested with single doses of aflatoxins. For most species, the LD50 value ranges from 0.5 to 10 mg/kg body weight. Animal species respond differently in their susceptibility to the chronic and acute toxicity of aflatoxins. The toxicity can be influenced by environmental factors, exposure level, and duration of exposure, age, health, and nutritional status of diet. Aflatoxin B1 is a very potent carcinogen in many species, including nonhuman primates, birds, fish, and rodents. In each species, the liver is the primary target organ of acute injury. Metabolism plays a major role in determining the toxicity of aflatoxin B1; studies show that this aflatoxion requires metabolic activation to exert its carcinogenic effect, and these effects can be modified by induction or inhibition of the mixed function oxidase system.

Diagnosis of Human Illness:

Aflatoxicosis in humans has rarely been reported; however, such cases are not always recognized. Aflatoxicosis may be suspected when a disease outbreak exhibits the following characteristics: the cause is not readily identifiable the condition is not transmissible syndromes may be associated with certain batches of food treatment with antibiotics or other drugs has little effect the outbreak may be seasonal, i.e., weather conditions may affect mold growth.

The adverse effects of aflatoxins in animals (and presumably in humans) have been categorized in two general forms.

A. (Primary) Acute aflatoxicosis is produced when moderate to high levels of aflatoxins are consumed. Specific, acute episodes of disease ensue may include hemorrhage, acute liver damage, edema, alteration in digestion, absorption and/or metabolism of nutrients, and possibly death.

B. (Primary) Chronic aflatoxicosis results from ingestion of low to moderate levels of aflatoxins. The effects are usually subclinical and difficult to recognize. Some of the common symptoms are impaired food conversion and slower rates of growth with or without the production of an overt aflatoxin syndrome.

Associated Foods:

In the United States, aflatoxins have been identified in corn and corn products, peanuts and peanut products, cottonseed, milk, and tree nuts such as Brazil nuts, pecans, pistachio nuts, and walnuts. Other grains and nuts are susceptible but less prone to contamination.

Relative Frequency of Disease:

The relative frequency of aflatoxicosis in humans in the United States is not known. No outbreaks have been reported in humans. Sporadic cases have been reported in animals.

Course of Disease and Complications:

In well-developed countries, aflatoxin contamination rarely occurs in foods at levels that cause acute aflatoxicosis in humans. In view of this, studies on human toxicity from ingestion of aflatoxins have focused on their carcinogenic potential. The relative susceptibility of humans to aflatoxins is not known, even though epidemiological studies in Africa and Southeast Asia, where there is a high incidence of hepatoma, have revealed an association between cancer incidence and the aflatoxin content of the diet. These studies have not proved a cause-effect relationship, but the evidence suggests an association.

One of the most important accounts of aflatoxicosis in humans occurred in more than 150 villages in adjacent districts of two neighboring states in northwest India in the fall of 1974. According to one report of this outbreak, 397 persons were affected and 108 persons died. In this outbreak, contaminated corn was the major dietary constituent, and aflatoxin levels of 0.25 to 15 mg/kg were found. The daily aflatoxin B1 intake was estimated to have been at least 55 ug/kg body weight for an undetermined number of days. The patients experienced high fever, rapid progressive jaundice, edema of the limbs, pain, vomiting, and swollen livers. One investigator reported a peculiar and very notable feature of the outbreak: the appearance of signs of disease in one village population was preceded by a similar disease in domestic dogs, which was usually fatal. Histopathological examination of humans showed extensive bile duct proliferation and periportal fibrosis of the liver together with gastrointestinal hemorrhages. A 10-year follow-up of the Indian outbreak found the survivors fully recovered with no ill effects from the experience.

A second outbreak of aflatoxicosis was reported from Kenya in 1982. There were 20 hospital admissions with a 60% mortality; daily aflatoxin intake was estimated to be at least 38 ug/kg body weight for an undetermined number of days.

In a deliberate suicide attempt, a laboratory worker ingested 12 ug/kg body weight of aflatoxin B1 per day over a 2-day period and 6 months later, 11 ug/kg body weight per day over a 14-day period. Except for transient rash, nausea and headache, there were no ill effects; hence, these levels may serve as possible no-effect levels for aflatoxin B1 in humans. In a 14-year follow-up, a physical examination and blood chemistry, including tests for liver function, were normal.

Target Populations:

Although humans and animals are susceptible to the effects of acute aflatoxicosis, the chances of human exposure to acute levels of aflatoxin is remote in well-developed countries. In undeveloped countries, human susceptibility can vary with age, health, and level and duration of exposure.

Food Analysis:

Many chemical procedures have been developed to identify and measure aflatoxins in various commodities. The basic steps include extraction, lipid removal, cleanup, separation and quantification. Depending on the nature of the commodity, methods can sometimes be simplified by omitting unnecessary steps. Chemical methods have been developed for peanuts, corn, cottonseed, various tree nuts, and animal feeds. Chemical methods for aflatoxin in milk and dairy products are far more sensitive than for the above commodities because the aflatoxin M animal metabolite is usually found at much lower levels (ppb and ppt).

Chapter 39

Perchlorate

What are perchlorates?

Perchlorates are colorless salts that have no odor. There are five perchlorate salts that are manufactured in large amounts: magnesium perchlorate, potassium perchlorate, ammonium perchlorate, sodium perchlorate, and lithium perchlorate. Perchlorate salts are solids that dissolve easily in water.

One place where perchlorates occur naturally is in western Texas and in saltpeter deposits in Chile, where the saltpeter is used to make fertilizer. Perchlorates can also form naturally in the atmosphere, leading to trace levels of perchlorate in precipitation. Perchlorates can be very reactive chemicals that are used mainly in explosives, fireworks, road flares, and rocket motors. The solid booster rocket of the space shuttle is almost 70% ammonium perchlorate.

Perchlorates are also used for making other chemicals. Many years ago, perchlorates were used as a medication to treat an overactive thyroid gland.

What happens to perchlorates when they enter the environment?

- Perchlorates entered the environment where rockets were made, tested, and taken apart.

This chapter includes excerpts from "Toxic Substances Portal—Perchlorates," Agency for Toxic Substances and Disease Registry (ATSDR), March 25, 2014; and text from "Water: Unregulated—Perchlorate," United States Environmental Protection Agency (EPA), September 26, 2012.

- Perchlorates also enter the environment from fireworks, road safety flares, and through the use and disposal of consumer products such as bleach where perchlorate may be contained as an impurity. There is also evidence that there are natural sources of perchlorates in the environment.

- Factories that make or use perchlorates may also release them to soil and water.

- Perchlorates will not stay in soil and will wash away with rain water.

- Perchlorates will eventually end up in ground water.

- We do not know exactly how long perchlorates will last in water and soil, but the information available indicates that it is a very long time.

- Efforts to clean up the contamination of soil and water have been and continue to be made.

- Perchlorates have been found in many foods and in some drinking water supplies.

How might I be exposed to perchlorates?

- Eating food, milk, or drinking water contaminated with perchlorates. Recent studies have shown widespread exposure to low levels of perchlorate by the general population. Efforts are being made to determine the relative contribution of perchlorate from food and water.

- Living near factories that make fireworks, flares, or other explosive devices.

- Exposure before and after fireworks shows, or exposure during use of certain cleaning products and pool chemicals.

- Chewing tobacco may expose you to perchlorates because a variety of tobacco products contain perchlorates.

- Living near a waste site or a rocket manufacturing or testing facility that contains high levels of perchlorate in the soil or groundwater may expose you to higher levels.

How can perchlorates affect my health?

The health effects of perchlorate salts are due to the perchlorate itself and not to the other component (i.e., magnesium, ammonium, potassium, etc.). Perchlorate affects the ability of the thyroid gland to take up iodine. Iodine is needed to make hormones that regulate many body functions after they are released into the blood. Perchlorate's inhibition of iodine uptake must be great enough to affect the thyroid before it is considered harmful. Healthy volunteers who took about 35 milligrams (35 mg) of perchlorate every day for 14 days or 3 mg for 6 months showed no signs of abnormal functioning of their thyroid gland or any other health problem. Studies of workers exposed for years to approximately the same amount of perchlorates found no evidence of alterations in the worker's thyroids, livers, kidneys, or blood. However, there is concern that people exposed to higher amounts of perchlorate for a long time may develop a low level of thyroid activity; the name of this medical condition is hypothyroidism. Low levels of thyroid hormones in the blood may lead to adverse effects on the skin, cardiovascular system, pulmonary system, kidneys, gastrointestinal tract, liver, blood, neuromuscular system, nervous system, skeleton, male and female reproductive system, and numerous endocrine organs.

Studies in animals also have shown that the thyroid gland is the main target of toxicity for perchlorate. Perchlorate did not affect reproduction in a study in rats.

Other chemicals such as thiocyanate (in food and cigarette smoke) and nitrate (in some food), are known to inhibit iodide uptake.

How likely are perchlorates to cause cancer?

There are no studies of exposure to perchlorates and cancer in humans. Long-term exposure to perchlorates induced thyroid cancer in rats and mice, but there are reasons to believe that humans are less likely than rodents to develop this type of cancer. The National Academy of Sciences (NAS) concluded that it is unlikely that perchlorates pose a risk of thyroid cancer in humans. Perchlorates have not been classified for carcinogenic effects by the Department of Health and Human Services (DHHS) or the International Agency for Research on Cancer (IARC). The EPA determined that perchlorate is not likely to be carcinogenic to humans, at least at doses below those necessary to alter thyroid hormone homeostasis.

How can perchlorates affect children?

The most sensitive population is fetuses of pregnant women who might have hypothyroidism or iodide deficiency.

Infants and developing children may be more likely to be affected by perchlorates than adults because thyroid hormones are essential for normal growth and development.

Perchlorate has been found in breast milk. Studies of thyroid function of babies and young children whose mothers were exposed to perchlorate in their drinking water have not provided convincing evidence of thyroid abnormalities associated with perchlorate.

Studies in animals have shown that perchlorate can alter the thyroid gland in the newborn animals.

How can families reduce the risk of exposure to perchlorates?

- Although perchlorate is present in food, milk and drinking water, it is very unlikely that it will be present in the air of the average home or apartment.

- Use bottled water if you have concerns about the presence of perchlorates in your tap water.

- You may also contact local drinking water authorities and follow their advice.

- Prevent children from playing in dirt or eating dirt if you live near a waste site that has perchlorates.

Is there a medical test to show whether I've been exposed to perchlorates?

Perchlorate can be measured in the blood, urine, and breast milk with special tests. In a CDC study, perchlorate was found in urine of all the people who were sampled across the country. Because perchlorate leaves the body fairly rapidly, perchlorate in urine only indicates recent exposure, but as perchlorate is present in some foods and in some drinking water supplies, exposure to perchlorate may be frequent for some people.

Has the federal government made recommendations to protect human health?

EPA adopted a Reference Dose (RfD) for perchlorate in 2005, and issued guidance regarding the cleanup of perchlorate at Superfund sites in 2006. EPA is currently evaluating whether there is a meaningful opportunity to reduce health risk through national drinking water regulation for perchlorate.

604

Final Regulatory Determination for Perchlorate in Drinking Water

EPA has decided to regulate perchlorate under the Safe Drinking Water Act (SDWA). The science that has lead to this decision has been peer reviewed by independent scientists and public health experts including the National Academy of Sciences. This decision reverses a 2008 preliminary determination, and considers input from almost 39,000 public commenters on multiple public notices (May 2007, October 2008, and August 2009) related to perchlorate. This action notifies interested parties of EPA's decision to regulate perchlorate, but does not in itself impose any requirements on public water systems (PWSs). However, this action initiates a process to develop and establish a national primary drinking water regulation (NPDWR). Once the NPDWR is finalized, certain PWSs will be required to take action to comply with the regulation in accordance with the schedule specified in the regulation.

Chapter 40

Consumer Beverages

Chapter Contents

Section 40.1

Benzene in Commercial Beverages

Text in this section is excerpted from "Food—Questions and Answers
on the Occurrence of Benzene in Soft Drinks and Other Beverages,"
U.S. Food and Drug Administration (FDA), July 6, 2015.

What is benzene?

Benzene is a chemical that is released into the air from emissions
from automobiles and burning coal and oil. It is also used in the manufacture of a wide range of industrial products, including chemicals,
dyes, detergents, and some plastics.

Why is benzene a concern?

Benzene is a carcinogen that can cause cancer in humans. It has
caused cancer in workers exposed to high levels from workplace air.
Based on results from a Center for Food Safety and Applied Nutrition
(CFSAN) survey of almost 200 samples of soft drinks and other beverages tested for benzene conducted from 2005 through May 2007, a small
number of products sampled contained more than 5 parts per billion
(ppb) of benzene. The manufacturers have reformulated products, if
still manufactured, which were identified in the survey as containing
greater than 5 ppb benzene. CFSAN tested samples of these reformulated products and found that benzene levels were less than 1.5 ppb. The
US Environmental Protection Agency (EPA) has established a maximum
allowable level (MCL) for benzene in drinking water of 5 ppb. FDA has
adopted EPA's MCL for drinking water as an allowable level for bottled
water.

Do the levels of benzene in beverages pose a risk to public health?

The results of CFSAN's survey indicate that the levels of benzene
found in beverages to date do not pose a safety concern for consumers.
Almost all samples analyzed in our survey contained either no benzene
or levels below 5 ppb. Furthermore, benzene levels in hundreds of

samples tested by national and international government agencies and the beverage industry are consistent with those found in our survey.

How does benzene get into beverages?

Benzene can form at very low levels (ppb level) in some beverages that contain both benzoate salts and ascorbic acid (vitamin C) or erythorbic acid (a closely related substance (isomer) also known as d-ascorbic acid). Exposure to heat and light can stimulate the formation of benzene in some beverages that contain benzoate salts and ascorbic acid (vitamin C). Sodium or potassium benzoate may be added to beverages to inhibit the growth of bacteria, yeasts, and molds. Benzoate salts also are naturally present in some fruits and their juices, such as cranberries, for example. Vitamin C may be present naturally in beverages or added to prevent spoilage or to provide additional nutrients.

What steps are being taken to reduce or eliminate benzene in beverages?

FDA is working with the beverage industry to minimize benzene formation in products. For example, FDA has met with industry to determine the factors contributing to benzene formation. FDA has directly contacted those firms whose products were tested and found to contain more than 5 ppb benzene in our survey. Manufacturers have reformulated products to ensure benzene levels are minimized or eliminated. The International Council of Beverages Associations and the American Beverage Association have developed guidance for all beverage manufacturers on ways to minimize benzene formation. FDA will continue its testing program for benzene in soft drinks and other beverages to monitor levels and will inform the public and manufacturers as new data become available.

How was the problem identified?

FDA first became aware that benzene was present in some soft drinks in 1990. At that time, the soft drink industry informed the agency that benzene could form at low levels in some beverages that contained both benzoate salts and ascorbic acid. FDA and the beverage industry initiated research at that time to identify factors contributing to benzene formation. This research found that elevated temperature and light can stimulate benzene formation in the presence of benzoate salts and ascorbic acid. As a result of these findings, many manufacturers reformulated their products to reduce or eliminate benzene formation.

In November 2005, FDA received reports that benzene had been detected at low levels in some soft drinks containing benzoate salts and ascorbic acid. CFSAN immediately initiated a survey of benzene levels in soft drinks and other beverages. The vast majority of the beverages sampled to date (including those containing both benzoate salts and ascorbic acid) contained either no detectable benzene or levels well below the 5 ppb EPA MCL for benzene in drinking water.

How many and what products were found to have excessive levels of benzene?

To date, FDA has tested almost 200 soft drink and other beverages in the CFSAN survey. Benzene above 5 ppb was found in a total of ten products. Benzene above 5 ppb was found in nine of the beverage products that contain both added benzoate salts and ascorbic acid. FDA also found benzene above 5 ppb in one cranberry juice beverage with added ascorbic acid but no added benzoates (cranberries contain natural benzoates). The manufacturers have reformulated products, if still manufactured, which were identified in the survey as containing greater than 5 ppb benzene. CFSAN tested samples of these reformulated products and found that benzene levels were less than 1.5 ppb.

What about results for benzene in beverages reported in FDA's Total Diet Study (TDS)?

FDA's TDS is an ongoing FDA program that determines levels of various contaminants and nutrients in a broad variety of foods. As was previously reported by the press, FDA's TDS results from 1995 to 2001 included benzene levels in some beverages that were elevated compared with results from CFSAN's survey and other recent domestic and international studies. In 2006, the FDA conducted an evaluation of the reliability of the TDS benzene results. This evaluation concluded that the TDS procedure used to analyze benzene levels can generate benzene in beverages containing benzoate preservatives. There was also evidence of a source of benzene contamination in the TDS laboratory. Although the FDA evaluation focused on benzene in beverages, these findings also raise questions about the reliability of the method for benzene in solid foods. Because the TDS benzene results appeared to be unreliable, FDA scientists recommend that the benzene data be viewed with great caution while FDA considers removing TDS benzene data from the TDS website. There is no evidence of problems with other TDS data.

Section 40.2

Unpasteurized Juice

Text in this section begins with excerpts from "Food—Talking About Juice Safety: What You Need to Know," U.S. Food and Drug Administration (FDA), May 7, 2015.

Text in this section beginning with "Microbial Hazards due to Unpasteurized Juices" is excerpted from "Safe Practices for Food Processes," U.S. Food and Drug Administration (FDA), March 19, 2015.

Talking About Juice Safety: What You Need to Know

Juices provide many essential nutrients, but consuming untreated juices can pose health risks to your family. The FDA has received reports of serious outbreaks of foodborne illness that have been traced to drinking fruit and vegetable juice and cider that has not been treated to kill harmful bacteria.

While most people's immune systems can usually fight off the effects of foodborne illness, children, the elderly, and people with weakened immune systems risk serious illnesses or even death from drinking untreated juices.

Warning Labels

Since 1999, the FDA has required juice manufacturers to place **warning information** on product containers about the health risks of drinking untreated juice or cider. Only a small portion of all fruit and vegetable juices sold in supermarkets **is not** treated to kill harmful bacteria. These products are required to carry the following warning label:

> **WARNING:** This product has not been pasteurized, and therefore, may contain harmful bacteria that can cause serious illness in children, the elderly, and persons with weakened immune systems.

You should note that the FDA **does not** require warning labels for juice or cider that is fresh-squeezed and sold by the glass, such as at apple

611

orchards, at farm markets, at roadside stands, or in some juice bars. If you're unsure if a glass of juice or cider has been treated, be sure to ask.

2 Simple Steps to Juice Safety

When purchasing juice, take these two simple steps to protect your children.

1. Always Read the Label

Look for the warning label to avoid the purchase of untreated juices. You can find **pasteurized or otherwise treated** products in your grocers' refrigerated sections, frozen food cases, or in non-refrigerated containers, such as juice boxes, bottles, or cans. **Untreated juice** is most likely to be sold in the refrigerated section of a grocery store.

2. When in Doubt, Ask!

Always ask if you're unsure if a juice product is treated, especially for juices sold in refrigerated cases of grocery or health food stores, cider mills, or farm markets. Also, don't hesitate to ask if the labeling is unclear or if the juice or cider is sold by the glass.

Foodborne Illness: Be Aware of the Symptoms

Consuming dangerous foodborne bacteria will usually cause illness within one to three days of eating the contaminated food. However, sickness can also occur within 20 minutes or up to six weeks later. In addition, sometimes foodborne illness is confused with other types of illness. Symptoms of foodborne illness usually include:

- vomiting, diarrhea, and abdominal pain
- flu-like symptoms, such as fever, headache, and body ache

If you or your children experience these symptoms, see a health care professional who can properly diagnose foodborne illness, identify the specific bacteria involved, and prescribe the best treatment.

Did You Know?

When fruits and vegetables are fresh-squeezed, bacteria from the produce can end up in your juice or cider. Unless the produce or the juice has been treated to destroy any harmful bacteria, the juice could be contaminated.

Microbial Hazards due to unpasteurized juices

Approximately 2% of all juices sold in the United States are unpasteurized. Parish (1997) provides an excellent review of the safety of unpasteurized fruit juices. Unpasteurized juices are made from fruits and vegetables that are ground and/or pressed or squeezed to extract the juice. Unpasteurized juices are included here because they have not been thermally processed and an evaluation of outbreaks associated with these products might contribute to an understanding of risk factors for contamination of the raw fruits.

There have been very few surveys of retail juices for the presence of pathogens, probably because of the very low probability of finding pathogens in these products. Sado and others (1998) used rapid test kits to survey retail juices for the presence of *L. monocytogenes*, *E. coli* O157:H7, *Salmonella*, coliforms, and fecal coliforms. Only *L. monocytogenes* was isolated from two of 50 juices, an apple juice (pH 3.78) and an apple raspberry blend (pH 3.75).

Although there is a long history of juice-related outbreaks, they have been relatively infrequent and until 1995, were generally associated with very small commercial processors or home-prepared products. While the acidity of most fruit juices prevents the multiplication of pathogens, survival is much better than has been traditionally assumed. Pathogen viability decreases with increasing temperature due to the rapid growth of yeasts and other spoilage organisms at higher temperatures. This also leads to a decrease in shelf life.

While pathogen contamination routes have not been definitively confirmed in any juice outbreak, the use of dropped fruit, the use of non-potable water, and the presence of cattle, deer, or in one case, amphibians, in or near the orchards or groves does appear to be a reoccurring theme. Of five documented outbreaks associated with reconstituted orange juice, three have been the result of contamination by an infected handler preparing the juice. In another outbreak the water source used to reconstitute the juice was thought to be a factor.

Chapter 41

Technologically Altered Foods

Chapter Contents

Section 41.1

FDA Regulations on Genetically Engineered Foods

Text in this section begins with excerpts from "Food—Questions & Answers on Food from Genetically Engineered Plants," U.S. Food and Drug Administration (FDA), June 22, 2015.

Text in this section beginning with "Regulation of Genetically Engineered Animals" is excerpted from "For Consumers— Regulation of Genetically Engineered Animals," U.S. Food and Drug Administration (FDA), February 25, 2015.

Questions and Answers on Food from Genetically Engineered Plants

1. Are foods from genetically engineered plants regulated by FDA?

Yes. FDA regulates the safety of foods and food products from plant sources including food from genetically engineered plants. This includes animal feed, as under the Federal Food, Drug, and Cosmetic Act, food is defined in relevant part as food for man and other animals. FDA has set up a voluntary consultation process to engage with the developers of genetically engineered plants to help ensure the safety of food from these products.

2. Are foods from genetically engineered plants safe?

Foods from genetically engineered plants must meet the same requirements, including safety requirements, as foods from traditionally bred plants. FDA has a consultation process that encourages developers of genetically engineered plants to consult with FDA before marketing their products. This process helps developers determine the necessary steps to ensure their food products are safe and lawful. The goal of the consultation process is to ensure that any safety or other regulatory issues related to a food product are resolved before commercial distribution. Foods from genetically engineered plants intended to be grown in the United States that have been evaluated by FDA through the consultation process have not gone on the market until the FDA's questions about the safety of such products have been resolved.

3. How is the safety of food from a genetically engineered plant evaluated?

Evaluating the safety of food from a genetically engineered plant is a comprehensive process that includes several steps. Generally, the developer identifies the distinguishing attributes of new genetic traits and assesses whether any new material that a person consumed in food made from the genetically engineered plants could be toxic or allergenic. The developer also compares the levels of nutrients in the new genetically engineered plant to traditionally bred plants. This typically includes such nutrients as fiber, protein, fat, vitamins, and minerals. The developer includes this information in a safety assessment, which FDA's Biotechnology Evaluation Team then evaluates for safety and compliance with the law.

FDA teams of scientists knowledgeable in genetic engineering, toxicology, chemistry, nutrition, and other scientific areas as needed carefully evaluate the safety assessments taking into account relevant data and information.

FDA considers a consultation to be complete only when its team of scientists are satisfied with the developer's safety assessment and have no further questions regarding safety or regulatory issues.

4. Why do developers genetically engineer plants and which has FDA evaluated for safety?

Developers genetically engineer plants for many of the same reasons that traditional breeding is used, such as resistance to insect damage, hardiness or enhanced nutrition. As of December 2012, the FDA has completed 95 consultations, most of them on corn. The chart below shows the number of consultations completed as of April 1, 2013 for each of the genetically engineered plants FDA has reviewed. There were 30 submissions on corn, 15 on cotton, 12 each on canola and soybean, and 24 on all other crops including alfalfa, canteloupe, creeping bentgrass, flax, papaya, plum, potato, raddichio, squash, sugar beet, tomato, and wheat.

5. Which foods are made from genetically engineered plants?

The majority of genetically engineered plants—corn, canola, soybean, and cotton—are typically used to make ingredients that are

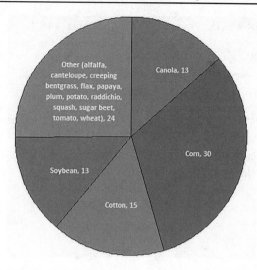

Figure 41.1. Numbers of Consultations on Genetically Engineered Crops

then used in other food products. Such ingredients include cornstarch in soups and sauces, corn syrup as a general purpose sweetener, and cottonseed oil, canola oil, and soybean oil in mayonnaise, salad dressings, cereals, breads, and snack foods.

6. Are foods from genetically engineered plants less nutritious than comparable foods?

Nutritional assessments for foods from genetically engineered plants that have been evaluated by FDA through the consultation process have shown that such foods are generally as nutritious as foods from comparable traditionally bred plants.

7. Are foods from genetically engineered plants more likely to (1) cause an allergic reaction or (2) be toxic?

The foods we have evaluated through the consultation process have not been more likely to cause an allergic or toxic reaction than foods from traditionally bred plants. When new genetic traits are introduced into plants, the developer evaluates whether any new material could be (1) allergenic or (2) toxic if consumed in foods made from the genetically engineered plants or from ingredients derived from these plants.

8. Why aren't foods from genetically engineered plants labeled?

We recognize and appreciate the strong interest that many consumers have in knowing whether a food was produced using genetic engineering. Currently, food manufacturers may indicate through voluntary labeling whether foods have or have not been developed through genetic engineering, provided that such labeling is truthful and not misleading. FDA supports voluntary labeling that provides consumers with this information and has issued draft guidance to industry regarding such labeling.

9. Are there long-term health effects of foods from genetically engineered plants?

When evaluating the safety of food from genetically engineered plants, scientists with experience in assessing the long-term safety of food and food ingredients consider several factors, such as information about the long-term safety of the food from traditionally bred crops in combination with information on the food safety of the newly introduced traits. Foods from genetically engineered plants that have been evaluated by FDA through the consultation process have not gone on the market until the FDA's questions about the safety of such products have been resolved.

Regulation of Genetically Engineered Animals

Genetic Engineering

Genetic engineering is a process in which scientists use recombinant DNA (rDNA) technology to introduce desirable traits into an organism. DNA is the chemical inside the nucleus of a cell that carries the genetic instructions for making living organisms. Scientists use rDNA techniques to manipulate DNA molecules.

Genetic engineering involves producing and introducing a piece of DNA (the rDNA construct) into an organism so new or changed traits can be given to that organism. The rDNA construct can either come from another existing organism, or be synthesized in a laboratory. Although conventional breeding methods have been used for a long time to select for desirable traits in animals, genetic engineering is a much more targeted and powerful method of actually introducing specific desirable traits into animals.

Genetic engineering is not a new technology. It has been widely used in agriculture, for example, to make crops like corn and soy resistant to pests or tolerant to herbicides. In medicine, genetic engineering is used to develop microbes that can produce pharmaceuticals. And in food, genetic engineering is used to produce enzymes that aid in baking, brewing, and cheese making.

Benefits of GE Animals

GE animals hold great promise for human and animal health, the environment, and agriculture.

- **Health protection of animals** – Animals are under development to be more resistant to very painful and harmful diseases, such as infection of the udder (mastitis) in dairy cows and bovine spongiform encephalopathy (widely referred to as "mad cow" disease) in all cattle.

- **New source of medicines** – Animals can be engineered to produce particular substances, such as human antibodies, to make infection-fighting drugs for people. These "biopharm" animals can change the way we treat chronic diseases, such as bleeding disorders, by providing large quantities of safe, health-restoring proteins that previously were available only from human cadavers.

- **Transplantation** – Pigs are being engineered so that their cells, tissues, or organs could be transplanted into humans with a reduced risk of immune rejection.

- **Less environmental impact** – Food animals are being engineered to grow more quickly, require less feed, or leave behind less environmentally damaging waste.

- **Healthier food** – Food animals, such as pigs, are under development to contain increased levels of omega-3 fatty acids, providing a more healthful product. Livestock can also be engineered to provide leaner meat or more milk.

GE Animals Regulated Under New Animal Drug Provisions

FDA regulates GE animals under the new animal drug provisions of the law, and the agency must approve them before they are allowed on the market. Food and animal feed from GE animals will undergo FDA review before the food or feed can be marketed. The Federal Food,

Drug, and Cosmetic Act defines a drug as "an article (other than food) intended to affect the structure or any function of the body of man or other animals." Therefore, the rDNA construct intended to change the structure or function of the body of the GE animal is a drug.

FDA may exercise "enforcement discretion" over some GE animals, based on their potential risk and on a case-by-case basis. This means that the agency may not require pre-market approval for a low-risk animal. For example, the agency is not requiring premarket approval for GE lab animals used for research, and did not require approval of a GE aquarium fish that glows in the dark. FDA does not expect to exercise enforcement discretion for animal species traditionally consumed as food.

Section 41.2

Cloned Meat and Dairy

This section includes excerpts from "Animal & Veterinary—A Primer on Cloning and Its Use in Livestock Operations," U.S. Food and Drug Administration (FDA), July 28, 2014.

A Primer on Cloning and Its Use in Livestock Operations

What is cloning, really?

Cloning is a complex process that lets one exactly copy the genetic, or inherited, traits of an animal (the donor). Livestock species that scientists have successfully cloned are cattle, swine, sheep, and goats. Scientists have also cloned mice, rats, rabbits, cats, mules, horses and one dog. Chickens and other poultry have not been cloned.

Most people think of livestock breeding taking place through traditional mating, in which males and females physically get together to reproduce. In fact, this is not often the case. Traditional mating is not that efficient, if the goal is to produce as many offspring as possible. For example, a male has enough sperm to produce many more offspring

621

than would be possible by traditional mating. Traditional mating also has certain risks: one or both of the animals may be injured in the process of mating. The female may be hurt by the male because he is often much larger, or an unwilling female may injure the male. There is also a risk of infection or transmission of venereal disease during traditional mating.

Because of these factors, many farmers use assisted reproductive technologies (ARTs) for breeding. These include artificial insemination, embryo transfer, and *in vitro* fertilization (a process by which egg and sperm are united outside the body). Artificial insemination was first documented in the breeding of horses in the 14th century. The first successful embryo transfer of a cow was in 1951, and the first *in vitro* fertilization (IVF)-derived animal was a rabbit born in 1959. Livestock production in the United States now uses all these methods regularly. For example, most dairy farms don't have bulls, so more than 70 percent of the Holstein cows bred in the United States are artificially inseminated. The frozen semen can come from a bull many miles, or even many states, away.

Cloning is a more advanced form of these assisted reproductive technologies. Much of the public perception of cloning likely comes from science fiction books and movies. Some people incorrectly believe that clones spring forth fully formed, or are grown in test tubes. This is just not the case.

Clones are born just like other animals. They are similar to identical twins, only born at different times. Just as twins share the same DNA, clones have the same genes as the donor animal. A clone is not a mutant, nor is it a weaker version of the original animal.

In all of the other assisted reproductive technologies, the male and female parents each contribute half of their genes to their offspring. Farmers have worked for years to choose animals with the best traits and breed them together. This increases the chance these good traits will be passed on and become more common in livestock herds. Even though farmers have been able to improve their herds over time, they still can't absolutely predict the characteristics of the offspring, not even their gender. Cloning gives the farmer complete control over the offspring's inherited traits. Thus, a farmer who clones an especially desirable but aging or injured animal knows in advance that the clone will have the genetic potential to be an especially good, younger animal. He can then use that animal to further reproduce by traditional mating or other ARTs.

Most cloning today uses a process called somatic cell nuclear transfer (SCNT). Just as with *in vitro* fertilization, scientists take an immature egg, or oocytes, from a female animal (often from ovaries obtained at the slaughterhouse). But instead of combining it with sperm, they remove the nucleus (which contains the oocytes's genes). This leaves behind the other components necessary for the initial stages of embryo development. Scientists then add the nucleus or cell from the donor animal that has the desirable traits the farmer wishes to copy. After a few other steps, the donor nucleus fuses with the ooplast (the oocytes whose nucleus has been removed), and if all goes well, starts dividing, and an embryo begins to form. The embryo is then implanted in the uterus of a surrogate dam (again the same as with *in vitro* fertilization), which carries it to term. ("Dam" is a term that livestock breeders use to refer to the female parent of an animal). The clone is delivered just like any other baby animal.

What can go wrong with cloning?

There are no complications that are unique to cloning. The problems seen in clones are also seen in animals born from natural mating or ARTs. They seem to happen more often in clones for a number of reasons that probably have to do with parts of the procedure that occur outside the body. The embryo may fail to develop properly during the *in vitro* stage or early on after transfer to the surrogate and may be flushed out of the uterus. If it does develop, the embryo may not implant properly into the uterus of the surrogate dam. Alternatively, the placenta may not form properly, and the developing animal won't get the nourishment it needs.

Large Offspring Syndrome (LOS) is seen in pregnancies of cattle and sheep that come from other ARTs and cloning. With LOS, the fetus grows too large in the uterus, making problems for the animal and its surrogate dam. LOS has not been observed in goats and swine.

Most clones that are normal at birth become as strong and healthy as any other young animals. Calf and lamb clones tend to have more health problems at birth, and may be more likely to die right after birth than conventionally bred animals. Clones born with abnormalities may continue to have health problems for the first few months of life, but by the time clones are young adults, it's not possible to tell them apart from other animals of the same age, even if you conduct a detailed examination. Scientists at FDA and research institutions have looked at extensive health records, the development of clones, and blood work for clones that's similar to what people get when they have physicals.

623

These results show that the clones are perfectly healthy, and walk, wean, grow, mature, and behave just like conventionally bred animals.

Why is there interest in cloning?

The main use of agricultural clones is to produce breeding stock, not food. Clones allow farmers to upgrade the overall quality of their herds by providing more copies of the best animals in the herd. These animals are then used for conventional breeding, and the sexually reproduced offspring become the food producing animals. These animals are not clones—they're just like other sexually reproduced animals. Just as farmers wouldn't use their best conventionally bred breeding animals as sources of food, they are equally unlikely to do so for clones.

Some examples of desirable characteristics in livestock that breeders might want in their herds include the following:

Disease resistance: Sick animals are expensive for farmers. Veterinary bills add up, and unhealthy animals don't produce as much meat or milk. A herd that is resistant to disease is extremely valuable because it doesn't lose any production time to illness, and doesn't cost the farmer extra money for veterinary treatment.

Suitability to Climate: Different types of livestock grow well in different climates. Some of this is natural and some results from selective breeding. For instance, Brahma cattle can cope with the heat and humidity of weather in the southwestern United States, but they often do not produce very high grades of meat. Cloning could allow breeders to select those cattle that can produce high quality meat or milk and thrive in extreme climates and use them to breed more cattle to be used for food production. Similarly, pork production has traditionally been centered in the eastern United States, but is moving to different regions of the United States (e.g., Utah). Cloning could allow breeders to select those swine that naturally do well in the new climate, and use those swine clones to breed more swine to be used for food production.

Quality body type: Farmers naturally want an animal whose body is well suited to its production function. For example, a dairy cow should have a large, well-attached udder so that she can produce lots of milk. She should also be able to carry and deliver calves easily. For animals that produce meat, farmers breed for strong, heavily-muscled, quick-maturing animals that will yield high quality meat in the shortest time possible. The most desirable bulls produce offspring that are relatively small at birth (so that they are easier for the female to carry and deliver) but that grow rapidly and are healthy after birth.

Fertility: Quality dairy cows should be very fertile, as a cow that doesn't get pregnant and bear calves won't produce milk. Male fertility is just as important as that of the female. The more sperm he can produce, the more females a bull can inseminate, and the more animals can be born. Beef cattle or other meat-producing animals such as swine need to have high fertility rates in order to replace animals that are sent to slaughter. Cloning allows farmers and breeders to clone those animals with high fertility rates so that they could bear offspring that would also tend to be very fertile.

Market preference: Farmers or ranchers may also want to breed livestock to meet the changing tastes of consumers. These include traits like leanness, tenderness, color, size of various cuts, etc. Preferences also vary by culture, and cloning may help tailor products to the preferences of various international markets and ethnic groups.

How does cloning help get these characteristics into the herd more quickly? As we've previously said, cloning allows the breeder to increase the number of breeding animals available to make the actual food production animals. So, if a producer wanted to introduce disease resistance into a herd rapidly, cloning could be used to produce a number of breeding animals that carry the gene for disease resistance, rather than just one. Likewise, if a breeder wants to pass on the genes of a female animal, cloning could result in multiples of that female to breed, rather than just one.

Is it safe to eat food from clones?

Yes. Food from cattle, swine, and goat clones is as safe to eat as food from any other cattle, swine, or goat. But it's important to remember that the primary purpose of clones is for breeding, not eating. Dairy, beef, or pork clones make up only a tiny fraction of the total number of food producing animals in the United States. Instead, their offspring would be the animals actually producing meat or milk for the food supply.

Dairy clones will produce milk after they give birth, and the dairy farmers will want to be able to drink that milk or put it in the food supply. Once clones used for breeding meat-producing animals can no longer reproduce, their breeders may also want to be able to put them into the food supply.

In order to determine whether there would be any risk involved in eating meat or milk from clones or their offspring, in 1999 the FDA asked the National Academy of Sciences (NAS) to identify science-based concerns associated with animal biotechnology, including cloning. The NAS gathered an independent group of top, peer-selected scientists from across the country to conduct this study. The scientists delivered their report in the fall of 2002. That report stated that theoretically there were no concerns for the safety of meat or milk from clones. On the other hand, the report expressed a low level of concern due to a lack of information on the clones at that time, and not for any specific scientific reasons. The report also stated that the meat and milk from the offspring of clones posed no unique food safety concerns.

Meanwhile, FDA itself began the most comprehensive examination of the health of livestock clones that has been conducted. The evaluation has taken over five years. This examination formed the basis of a Draft Risk Assessment to determine whether cloning posed a risk to animal health or to humans eating food from clones or their offspring. FDA conducted a thorough search of the scientific literature on clones, and identified hundreds of peer-reviewed scientific journal articles, which it then reviewed. The agency was also able to obtain health records and blood samples from almost all of the cattle clones that have been produced in the United States and data from clones produced in other countries. FDA compared these health records, and the independently analyzed blood results with similar samples from conventional animals of the same age and breed that were raised on the same farms. FDA received thousands of comments from the public in response to the Draft Risk Assessment. For the final version of the Risk Assessment, FDA conducted an up-to-date review of the literature, added additional information from hundreds of additional references, and made many changes to address some of the public comments.

After reviewing all this information, FDA found that it could not distinguish a healthy clone from a healthy conventionally bred animal. All of the blood values, overall health records, and behaviors were in the same range for clones and conventional animals of the same breed raised on the same farms. FDA also observed that milk from dairy clones does not differ significantly in composition from milk from conventionally bred animals.

In the Risk Assessment, FDA concluded that meat and milk from cattle, swine, and goat clones is as safe as food we eat from those species now. Although we don't have any particular concerns about sheep clones, we did not have enough information to make a decision on the safety of food from sheep clones.

For another study similar to the one conducted on cow clones, the agency also evaluated the health of offspring sexually derived from swine clones, as well as the composition of their meat. After reviewing this very large data set, the agency concluded that all of the blood values, overall health records, and meat composition profiles of the progeny of clones were in the same range as for very closely genetically related conventionally bred swine. Based on these results, other studies from scientific journals, and our understanding of the biological processes involved in cloning, the agency agreed with NAS that food from the sexually reproduced offspring of clones is as safe as food that we eat every day. We reiterate, however, that the sexually reproduced offspring of clones would produce almost all of the food from the overall cloning/breeding process.

Part Six

Consumer Products and Medical Hazards

Chapter 42

Perfluorooctanoic Acid (PFOA) and Fluorinated Telomers

Background

Perfluorooctanoic acid (PFOA) is a synthetic (man-made) chemical that does not occur naturally in the environment. PFOA is sometimes called "C8." Companies use PFOA to make fluoropolymers, substances with special properties that have hundreds of important manufacturing and industrial applications. Fluoropolymers impart valuable properties, including fire resistance and oil, stain, grease, and water repellency. They are used to provide non-stick surfaces on cookware and waterproof, breathable membranes for clothing, and are used in many industry segments, including the aerospace, automotive, building/construction, chemical processing, electronics, semiconductors, and textile industries.

PFOA can also be produced by the breakdown of some fluorinated telomers, substances that are used in surface treatment products to impart soil, stain, grease, and water resistance. Some telomers are

This chapter includes excerpts from "Perfluorooctanoic Acid (PFOA) and Fluorinated Telomers—Basic Information," United States Environmental Protection Agency (EPA), September 9, 2014; and text from "Perfluorooctanoic Acid (PFOA) and Fluorinated Telomers—Frequent Questions," United States Environmental Protection Agency (EPA), January 15, 2015.

also used as high performance surfactants in products that must flow evenly, such as paints, coatings, and cleaning products, fire-fighting foams for use on liquid fuel fires, or the engineering coatings used in semiconductor manufacture.

However, consumer products made with fluoropolymers and fluorinated telomers, including Teflon® and other trademark products, are not PFOA. Rather, some of them may contain trace amounts of PFOA and other related perfluorinated chemicals as impurities. The information that EPA has available, does not indicate that the routine use of consumer products poses a concern. At present, there are no steps that EPA recommends, that consumers can take to reduce exposures to PFOA.

In the late 1990's, EPA received information indicating that perfluorooctyl sulfonates (PFOS) were widespread in the blood of the general population and presented concerns for persistence, bioaccumulation and toxicity. Following discussions between EPA and the 3M, the manufacturer of PFOS, the company terminated production of these chemicals.

Findings on PFOS led EPA to review similar chemicals to determine whether they might present similar concerns. The agency began investigating PFOA in 1990s and found that it, too, is very persistent in the environment, is found at very low levels both in the environment and in the blood of the general U.S. population, and causes developmental and other adverse effects in laboratory animals.

EPA has taken steps to further investigate PFOA and related chemicals as well as to reduce their emissions and use in products. However, given the scientific uncertainties, EPA has not yet made a determination as to whether PFOA poses an unreasonable risk to the public, and there are no steps that EPA recommends that consumers take to reduce exposures to PFOA.

Frequent Questions

What is PFOA?

PFOA is an acronym for perfluorooctanoic acid, a synthetic (man-made) chemical that does not occur naturally in the environment. PFOA is sometimes called "C8."

Companies use PFOA to make fluoropolymers, substances with special properties that have thousands of important manufacturing and industrial applications. PFOA can also be produced by the breakdown of some fluorinated telomers, substances that are used in surface treatment products to impart soil, stain, grease, and water resistance.

EPA's efforts on perfluorinated chemicals (PFCs) are not limited to only PFOA. EPA is also investigating other PFCs, including perfluorooctyl sulfonate (PFOS), higher homologues of PFOA and PFOS, and other partially fluorinated chemicals that are potential precursors of these chemicals.

What are the concerns related to PFOA?

PFOA is very persistent in the environment and has been found at very low levels both in the environment and in the blood of the general U.S. population. Studies indicate that PFOA can cause developmental and other adverse effects in laboratory animals. PFOA also appears to remain in the human body for a long time. All of these factors, taken together, prompted the Agency to investigate whether PFOA might pose a risk to human health and the environment at the levels currently being found, or at levels that might be reached in the future as PFOA continues to be released into the environment.

What are fluoropolymers and telomers and how are they used?

Fluoropolymers impart valuable properties, including fire resistance and oil, stain, grease, and water repellency. They are used to provide non-stick surfaces on cookware and waterproof, breathable membranes for clothing. They are employed in hundreds of other uses in almost all industry segments, including the aerospace, automotive, building/construction, chemical processing, electrical and electronics, semiconductor, and textile industries.

Telomers are used as surfactants and as surface treatment chemicals in many products, including personal care and cleaning products; and oil, stain, grease, and water repellent coatings on carpet, textiles, leather, and paper. Some telomers are also used as high performance surfactants in products that must flow evenly, such as paints, coatings, and cleaning products, fire-fighting foams for use on liquid fuel fires, or the engineering coatings used in semiconductor manufacture.

When did the Agency begin looking into PFOA and its potential risks?

In the late 1990's, EPA received information indicating that PFOS was widespread in the blood of the general population, and presented concerns for persistence, bioaccumulation, and toxicity. Following discussions between EPA and 3M, the manufacturer of PFOS and

PFOS-related chemicals, the company terminated production of these chemicals. Findings on PFOS led EPA to review similar chemicals, including PFOA, to determine whether they might present concerns similar to those associated with PFOS.

How are people exposed to PFOA?

The Agency does not have a full understanding of how people are exposed to PFOA, which is used as an essential processing aid in the manufacture of fluoropolymers, and may also be a breakdown product of other related chemicals, called fluorinated telomers. In April 2003, EPA released a preliminary risk assessment for PFOA, and started a public process to identify and generate additional information to better understand the sources of PFOA and the pathways of human exposure. Although the public process designed to produce additional information has been completed, new information continues to be generated as a result of the process and from other activities. This new information will assist the Agency in determining if there are potential risks and what risk management steps may be appropriate.

What is the status of the Enforceable Consent Agreements (ECAs)?

An ECA is a publicly negotiated agreement among EPA, industry, and interested parties that requires certain signing parties to generate data and submit those data to EPA on a specified schedule. Test rules can take few years to complete, while typical ECAs can often be concluded in less than a year. ECAs that require new test protocols or adapted test methods can take longer to negotiate than standard ECAs. ECAs are enforceable, meaning that EPA can compel the submission of information agreed to under the ECA. Because they are negotiated in public, all parties who are interested in the data have the opportunity to participate.

PFOA is used in the manufacture of fluoropolymers. Fluoropolymers are used in a wide variety of industrial and consumer products, including non-stick cookware, chemical and fire-resistant cables and tubing, and waterproof, breathable clothing. The ECA incineration testing of fluoropolymers will help determine whether the chemicals used in these items may break down to release PFOA if they are disposed of in municipal incinerators.

PFOA may also be a breakdown product of some fluorotelomers. Fluorotelomers are used as surface application treatments on carpets, textiles, paper, leather, and construction materials to provide water, stain, grease, and soil resistance properties, and may be used as surfactants in cleaning and coating products. The ECA incineration testing of fluorotelomers will help determine whether the chemicals used in these items may break down to release PFOA if they are disposed of in municipal incinerators.

What is the status of the Agency's on-going process to reduce the scientific uncertainties and to more fully understand the pathways of human exposure and potential risks from PFOA?

EPA identified the need to improve its understanding of the sources and pathways of exposure to PFOA in 2003 and initiated a process to develop needed new data on the issue. This new information will assist the Agency in determining if there are potential risks and what risk management steps may be appropriate.

Specifically, EPA is working with industry and other stakeholders to obtain additional environmental monitoring information on PFOA, exposures resulting from incineration or loss from products as they are used over time, and telomer biodegradation as a potential source of PFOA. The Agency has finalized TSCA Section 4 ECAs and MOUs for exposure-related studies with industry in a public process involving a large number of interested parties, and is cooperating with industry and other stakeholders on additional voluntary research activities. In addition, EPA's Office of Research and Development (ORD) has collaborated with the Office of Pollution Prevention and Toxics (OPPT) and is conducting research focused on the health effects and exposures to PFOA and other perfluorinated chemicals. This research is designed to generate enhanced science knowledge and high quality data that will help the Agency address these key uncertainties in pathways of exposure and potential risks from PFOA.

Are EPA's efforts showing any results?

In August 2014, the Centers for Disease Control and Prevention reported a 41 percent reduction of PFOA in human blood from 1999 – 2010. This decline is largely attributed to EPA's efforts on perfluorinated chemicals.

Are there steps that consumers can take to reduce their exposure to PFOA?

Consumer products made with perfluorochemicals include some non-stick cookware and products such as breathable, all-weather clothing. They are also employed in hundreds of other uses in almost all industry segments, including the aerospace, automotive, building/construction, chemical processing, electrical and electronics, semiconductor, and textile industries. Telomers are used as surfactants and as surface treatment chemicals in many products, including fire fighting foams; personal care and cleaning products; and oil, stain, grease, and water repellent coatings on carpet, textiles, leather, and paper. Consumer products made with fluoropolymers and fluorinated telomers, such as Teflon and other trademark products, are not PFOA. PFOA is used as a processing aid in the manufacture of fluoropolymers and can also be produced by the breakdown of some fluorinated telomers. The information that EPA has available does not indicate that the routine use of consumer products poses a concern. At present, there are no steps that EPA recommends that consumers take to reduce exposures to PFOA.

Chapter 43

Insect Repellent

Insect Repellent Use and Safety in Children

Don't Swat Away Insect Repellent Directions

Applying insect repellent is not complicated, but before you do, be sure to read the label for any warnings and to see the active ingredients. All insect repellents, including products combined with sunscreen, should be used according to instructions on the label.

Insect repellents can be used in all ages unless the label specifically states an age limitation or precaution. As long as you read and follow label directions and take proper precautions, insect repellents with active ingredients registered by the U.S. Environmental Protection Agency (EPA) do not present health or safety concerns.

FDA recommends using products that contain active ingredients registered by EPA for use on skin and clothing. EPA registration of insect repellent active ingredients indicates the materials have been reviewed and approved for human safety and effectiveness when applied according to instructions on the label.

The active ingredients DEET and picaridin are conventional man-made, chemical repellents according to EPA. Oil of lemon eucalyptus, **oil of citronella** and IR3535 are repellents made from natural materials such as plants, bacteria, and certain minerals.

This chapter includes excerpts from "Drugs—Insect Repellent Use and Safety in Children," U.S. Food and Drug Administration (FDA), December 9, 2014; and text from "DEET," United States Environmental Protection Agency (EPA), February 20, 2015.

Insect Repellents and Children

Insect repellents containing DEET should not be used on children under 2 months of age. Oil of lemon eucalyptus products should not be used on children under 3 years of age.

When applying insect repellents to children, avoid their hands, around the eyes, and cut or irritated skin. Do not allow children to handle insect repellents. When using on children, apply to your own hands and then put it on the child. After returning indoors, wash your child's treated skin or bathe the child. Clothes exposed to insect repellants should be washed with soap and water.

Sunscreens Combined with Insect Repellents

If a sunscreen containing DEET is used, then a sunscreen-only product should be used if additional sunscreen is needed. The sunscreen that contains DEET should not be reapplied because repeated applications may increase potential toxic effects.

For sunscreen products made with natural insect repellent ingredients follow package directions. Re-application of the combination product may be all right depending upon the particular formulation. After returning indoors, wash treated skin with soap and water, especially if using repellents repeatedly in a day or on consecutive days.

How Long Does Protection Last?

Although higher concentrations of any of the active ingredients provide longer protection, concentrations above 50 percent generally do not increase protection time. Products with less than 10 percent of the active ingredient offer only limited protection, about one or two hours.

Of course, protection and duration vary considerably among products and insect species. Temperature, perspiration, exposure to water, and other factors affect duration and effectiveness.

DEET

DEET (chemical name, N, N-diethyl-meta-toluamide) is the active ingredient in many insect repellent products. It is widely used to repel biting pests such as mosquitoes and ticks. Every year, an estimated one-third of the U.S. population use DEET to protect them from mosquito-borne illnesses like West Nile Virus or malaria and tick-borne illnesses like Lyme disease and Rocky Mountain spotted fever. Products containing DEET currently are available to the public in a variety of liquids, lotions, sprays, and impregnated materials (e.g., towelettes, roll on). Formulations registered for direct application to human skin contain from 4 to 100% DEET. Except for a few veterinary uses, DEET is registered for use by consumers, and it is not used on food.

DEET is designed for direct application to people's skin to repel insects. Rather than killing them, DEET works by making it hard for these biting bugs to smell us. After it was developed by the U.S. Army in 1946, DEET was registered for use by the general public in 1957. Approximately 120 products containing DEET are currently registered with EPA by about 30 different companies.

Safety review of DEET

1998 Review

After completing a comprehensive re-assessment of DEET, EPA concluded that insect repellents containing DEET do not present a health concern. Consumers are advised to read and follow label directions when using any pesticide product, including insect repellents. Based on extensive toxicity testing, the Agency believes that the normal use of DEET does not present a health concern to the general population, including children. EPA completed this review and issued its reregistration decision (called a RED) in 1998.

2014 Review

The Agency has just completed an interim review of DEET under the Registration Review Program to ensure that it continues to meet safety standards based on current scientific knowledge. The Agency has not identified any risks of concern to human health, non-target species or the environment. We've made our proposed interim registration review decision available for public comment at www.regulations.gov under docket number EPA-HQ-OPP-2012-0162. The public comment period on this Proposed Interim Decision opened on June 4 and will close on August 4, 2014.

EPA continues to believe that the normal use of DEET does not present a health concern to the general population, including children. As always, consumers are advised to read and follow label directions in using any pesticide product, including insect repellents. Currently registered uses of DEET are also not expected to result in adverse effects for listed and non-listed endangered species, or critical habitat. As such, EPA concludes "no effect" for listed species and no adverse modification of designated critical habitat for all currently registered uses of DEET.

The Proposed Interim Decision concluded that: (1) no additional data are required at this time; and (2) no changes to the affected registrations or their labeling are needed at this time. The human health risk assessment concluded that there are no risks of concern because no toxic effects have been identified when used as a dermally applied insect repellent, and there is no dietary or occupational exposure for DEET. However, a Final Decision on the DEET registration review case will occur only after the EPA has completed an Endocrine Disruptor Screening under FFDCA section 408(p). Under the Endocrine Disruptor Screening Program, the agency has prioritized chemicals for screening and DEET is lower on the priority list than chemicals currently being tested. The agency will consider and respond to public comments on the Proposed Interim Decision for DEET, and then anticipates issuing an Interim Decision for DEET in late 2014.

Benefits of DEET Products

DEET's most significant benefit is its ability to repel potentially disease-carrying insects and ticks. The Centers for Disease Control and Prevention (CDC) receives more than 20,000 reports of Lyme disease (transmitted by deer ticks) and 100 reports of encephalitis (transmitted by mosquitoes) annually and as of June 10, 2014, eight states had reported to CDC West Nile virus infections in people, birds, or mosquitoes. Each of these diseases can cause serious health problems or even death in the case of encephalitis. Where these diseases are endemic, the CDC recommends use of insect repellents when out-of-doors. Studies in EPA's database indicate that DEET repels ticks for about two to ten hours, and mosquitoes from two to twelve hours depending on the percentage of DEET in the product.

Using DEET Products Safely

FIFRA requires that pesticides be used according to the approved label. Always follow the recommendations appearing on the product label. According to the CDC, DEET products used as directed, should not be harmful, although in rare cases using DEET products can cause skin irritation. All DEET product labels include the following directions to help reduce the chance of DEET irritating your skin or eyes:

- Read and follow all directions and precautions on this product label.

- Do not apply over cuts, wounds, or irritated skin.

- Do not apply to hands or near eyes and mouth of young children.

- Do not allow young children to apply this product.

- Use just enough repellent to cover exposed skin and/or clothing.

- Do not use under clothing.

- Avoid over-application of this product.

- After returning indoors, wash treated skin with soap and water.

- Wash treated clothing before wearing it again.

- Use of this product may cause skin reactions in rare cases.

The following additional statements will appear on the labels of all aerosol and pump spray formulation labels:

- Do not spray in enclosed areas.

- To apply to face, spray on hands first and then rub on face. Do not spray directly onto face.

Using DEET on Children

DEET is approved for use on children with no age restriction. There is no restriction on the percentage of DEET in the product for use on children, since data do not show any difference in effects between young animals and adult animals in tests done for product registration. There also are no data showing incidents that would lead EPA to believe there is a need to restrict the use of DEET.

EPA continues to believe that the normal use of DEET does not present a health concern to the general population, including children. As always, consumers are advised to read and follow label directions in using any pesticide product, including insect repellents.

What to Do in the Event of an Apparent Reaction to DEET

If you suspect that you or your child is having an adverse reaction to a DEET product, discontinue use of the product, wash treated skin, and call your local poison control center or physician for help. If you go to a doctor, take the repellent container with you.

Chapter 44

Antibacterial Soap (Triclosan)

FDA Taking Closer Look at 'Antibacterial' Soap

When you're buying soaps and body washes, do you reach for the bar or bottle labeled "antibacterial"? Are you thinking that these products, in addition to keeping you clean, will reduce your risk of getting sick or passing on germs to others?

Not necessarily, according to experts at the Food and Drug Administration (FDA).

Every day, consumers use antibacterial soaps and body washes at home, work, school, and in other public settings. Especially because so many consumers use them, FDA believes that there should be clearly demonstrated benefits to balance any potential risks.

In fact, there currently is no evidence that over-the-counter (OTC) antibacterial soap products are any more effective at preventing illness than washing with plain soap and water, says Colleen Rogers, Ph.D., a lead microbiologist at FDA.

This chapter includes excerpts from "FDA Taking Closer Look at 'Antibacterial' Soap," U.S. Food and Drug Administration (FDA), January 21, 2015; and text from "Triclosan: What Consumers Should Know," U.S. Food and Drug Administration (FDA), January 20, 2015.

Moreover, antibacterial soap products contain chemical ingredients, such as triclosan and triclocarban, which may carry unnecessary risks given that their benefits are unproven.

"New data suggest that the risks associated with long-term, daily use of antibacterial soaps may outweigh the benefits," Rogers says. There are indications that certain ingredients in these soaps may contribute to bacterial resistance to antibiotics, and may have unanticipated hormonal effects that are of concern to FDA.

In light of these data, the agency issued a proposed rule on Dec. 16, 2013 that would require manufacturers to provide more substantial data to demonstrate the safety and effectiveness of antibacterial soaps. The proposed rule covers only those consumer antibacterial soaps and body washes that are used with water. It does not apply to hand sanitizers, hand wipes or antibacterial soaps that are used in health care settings such as hospitals.

According to Rogers, the laboratory tests that have historically been used to evaluate the effectiveness of antibacterial soaps do not directly test the effect of a product on infection rates. That would change with FDA's current proposal, which would require studies that directly test the ability of an antibacterial soap to provide a clinical benefit over washing with non-antibacterial soap, Rogers says.

What Makes a Soap "Antibacterial?"

Antibacterial soaps (sometimes called antimicrobial or antiseptic soaps) contain certain chemical ingredients that plain soaps do not. These ingredients are added to many consumer products in an effort to reduce or prevent bacterial contamination.

A large number of liquid soaps labeled "antibacterial" contain triclosan, an ingredient of concern to many environmental and industry groups. Animal studies have shown that triclosan may alter the way hormones work in the body. While data showing effects in animals don't always predict effects in humans, these studies are of concern to FDA as well, and warrant further investigation to better understand how they might affect humans.

In addition, laboratory studies have raised the possibility that triclosan contributes to making bacteria resistant to antibiotics. Such resistance can have a significant impact on the effectiveness of medical treatments.

Moreover, recent data suggest that exposure to these active ingredients is higher than previously thought, raising concerns about the potential risks associated with their use regularly and over time.

A Chance to Weigh In

FDA encourages consumers, clinicians, environmental groups, scientists, industry representatives, and others to discuss and weigh in on the proposed rule and the data it discusses. The comment period extends for 180 days.

In the meantime, FDA is emphasizing that hand washing is one of the most important steps people can take to avoid getting sick and to prevent spreading germs to others. Another good source for tips and information about benefits of appropriate hand washing is the Centers for Disease Control and Prevention (CDC). Consumers can go to www.cdc.gov/handwashing.

How do you tell if a product is antibacterial? Most antibacterial products have the word "antibacterial" on the label. Also, a Drug Facts label on a soap or body wash is a sure sign a product contains antibacterial ingredients. Cosmetics must list the ingredients, but are not required to carry a Drug Facts Label.

FDA and EPA Working in Tandem on Triclosan

FDA and the Environmental Protection Agency (EPA) have been closely collaborating on science and regulatory issues related to triclosan. This joint effort will help to ensure government-wide consistency in the regulation of the chemical.

The two agencies are reviewing the effects of triclosan from two different perspectives.

EPA regulates the use of triclosan as a pesticide, and is in the process of updating its assessment of the effects of triclosan when it is used in pesticides. FDA's focus is on the effects of triclosan when it is used by consumers on a regular basis in hand soaps and body washes. By sharing information, the two agencies will be better able to measure the exposure and effects of triclosan and how these differing uses of triclosan may affect human health.

Triclosan: What Consumers Should Know

What is triclosan?

Triclosan is an ingredient added to many consumer products to reduce or prevent bacterial contamination. It may be found in products such as clothing, kitchenware, furniture, and toys. It also may be added to antibacterial soaps and body washes, toothpastes, and some cosmetics—products regulated by the U.S. Food and Drug Administration (FDA).

What is known about the safety of triclosan?

Triclosan is not currently known to be hazardous to humans. But several scientific studies have come out since the last time FDA reviewed this ingredient that merit further review.

Animal studies have shown that triclosan alters hormone regulation. However, data showing effects in animals don't always predict effects in humans. Other studies in bacteria have raised the possibility that triclosan contributes to making bacteria resistant to antibiotics.

In light of these studies, FDA is engaged in an ongoing scientific and regulatory review of this ingredient. FDA does not have sufficient safety evidence to recommend changing consumer use of products that contain triclosan at this time.

Does triclosan provide a benefit in consumer products?

For some consumer products, there is clear evidence that triclosan provides a benefit. In 1997, FDA reviewed extensive effectiveness data on triclosan in Colgate Total toothpaste. The evidence showed that triclosan in this product was effective in preventing gingivitis.

For other consumer products, FDA has not received evidence that the triclosan provides an extra benefit to health. At this time, the agency does not have evidence that triclosan in antibacterial soaps and body washes provides any benefit over washing with regular soap and water.

What consumers should know:

- Triclosan is not known to be hazardous to humans.

- FDA does not have sufficient safety evidence to recommend changing consumer use of products that contain triclosan at this time.

- At this time, FDA does not have evidence that triclosan added to antibacterial soaps and body washes provides extra health benefits over soap and water. Consumers concerned about using hand and body soaps with triclosan should wash with regular soap and water.

- Consumers can check product labels to find out whether products contain triclosan.

How can I tell if there is triclosan in a product that I am using?

Antibacterial soaps and body washes, and toothpastes are considered over-the-counter drugs. If an over-the-counter drug contains triclosan, it will be listed as an ingredient on the label, in the Drug Facts box. If a cosmetic contains triclosan, it will be included in the ingredient list on the product label.

What is FDA doing to evaluate the safety of triclosan?

We are engaged in a comprehensive scientific and regulatory review of all the available safety and effectiveness data. This includes data relevant to the emerging safety issues of bacterial resistance and endocrine disruption due to triclosan in FDA-regulated products.

We also have partnered with other Federal Agencies to study the effects of this substance on animal and environmental health.

Chapter 45

Plastics

Chapter Contents

Section 45.1

Bisphenol A

Text in this section is excerpted from "Bisphenol A (BPA)," National
Institute of Environmental Health Sciences (NIEHS), January 21, 2015.

Bisphenol A (BPA) is a chemical produced in large quantities for use
primarily in the production of polycarbonate plastics and epoxy resins.

Where is BPA found?

Polycarbonate plastics have many applications including use in
some food and drink packaging, e.g., water and infant bottles, compact
discs, impact-resistant safety equipment, and medical devices. Epoxy
resins are used as lacquers to coat metal products such as food cans,
bottle tops, and water supply pipes. Some dental sealants and com-
posites may also contribute to BPA exposure.

How does BPA get into the body?

The primary source of exposure to BPA for most people is through
the diet. While air, dust, and water are other possible sources of exposure, BPA in food and beverages accounts for the majority of daily
human exposure.

Bisphenol A can leach into food from the protective internal epoxy
resin coatings of canned foods and from consumer products such as polycarbonate tableware, food storage containers, water bottles, and baby
bottles. The degree to which BPA leaches from polycarbonate bottles
into liquid may depend more on the temperature of the liquid or bottle,
than the age of the container. BPA can also be found in breast milk.

Why are people concerned about BPA?

One reason people may be concerned about BPA is because human
exposure to BPA is widespread. The 2003-2004 National Health and
Nutrition Examination Survey (NHANES III) conducted by the Centers for Disease Control and Prevention (CDC) found detectable levels
of BPA in 93% of 2517 urine samples from people six years and older.

The CDC NHANES data are considered representative of exposures in the United States. Another reason for concern, especially for parents, may be because some animal studies report effects in fetuses and newborns exposed to BPA.

If I am concerned, what can I do to prevent exposure to BPA?

Some animal studies suggest that infants and children may be the most vulnerable to the effects of BPA. Parents and caregivers, can make the personal choice to reduce exposures of their infants and children to BPA:

- Don't microwave polycarbonate plastic food containers. Polycarbonate is strong and durable, but over time it may break down from overuse at high temperatures.

- Plastic containers have recycle codes on the bottom. Some, but not all, plastics that are marked with recycle codes 3 or 7 may be made with BPA.

- Reduce your use of canned foods.

- When possible, opt for glass, porcelain or stainless steel containers, particularly for hot food or liquids.

- Use baby bottles that are BPA free.

Section 45.2

Phthalates and Polyvinyl Chloride (PVC)

Text in this section begins with excerpts from "National Biomonitoring Program—Phthalates," Centers for Disease Control and Prevention (CDC), April 21, 2015.

Text in this section beginning with "Polyvinyl Chloride (PVC)" is excerpted from "Tox Town—Polyvinyl Chloride (PVC)," United States National Library of Medicine (NLM), May 13, 2015.

Phthalates

Phthalates are a group of chemicals used to make plastics more flexible and harder to break. They are often called plasticizers. Some phthalates are used as solvents (dissolving agents) for other materials. They are used in hundreds of products, such as vinyl flooring, adhesives, detergents, lubricating oils, automotive plastics, plastic clothes (raincoats), and personal-care products (soaps, shampoos, hair sprays, and nail polishes).

Phthalates are used widely in polyvinyl chloride plastics, which are used to make products such as plastic packaging film and sheets, garden hoses, inflatable toys, blood-storage containers, medical tubing, and some children's toys.

How People Are Exposed to Phthalates

People are exposed to phthalates by eating and drinking foods that have been in contact with containers and products containing phthalates. To a lesser extent, exposure can occur from breathing in air that contains phthalate vapors or dust contaminated with phthalate particles. Young children may have a greater risk of being exposed to phthalate particles in dust than adults because of their hand-to-mouth behaviors. Once phthalates enter a person's body, they are converted into breakdown products (metabolites) that pass out quickly in urine.

How Phthalates Affect People's Health

Human health effects from exposure to low levels of phthalates are unknown. Some types of phthalates have affected the reproductive system of laboratory animals. More research is needed to assess the human health effects of exposure to phthalates.

Levels of Phthalate Metabolites in the U.S. Population

In the *Fourth National Report on Human Exposure to Environmental Chemicals* (Fourth Report), CDC scientists measured 13 phthalate metabolites in the urine of 2,636 or more participants aged six years and older who took part in the National Health and Nutrition Examination Survey (NHANES) during 2003–2004. For several phthalate metabolites, results from the prior survey periods of 1999–2000 and 2001–2002 are also included in the Fourth Report. By measuring phthalate metabolites in urine, scientists can estimate the amount of phthalates that have entered people's bodies.

- CDC researchers found measurable levels of many phthalate metabolites in the general population. This finding indicates that phthalate exposure is widespread in the U.S. population.

- Research has found that adult women have higher levels of urinary metabolites than men for those phthalates that are used in soaps, body washes, shampoos, cosmetics, and similar personal care products.

Finding a detectable amount of phthalate metabolites in urine does not imply that the levels of one or more will cause an adverse health effect. Biomonitoring studies on levels of phthalate metabolites provide physicians and public health officials with reference values so that they can determine whether people have been exposed to higher levels of these chemicals than are found in the general population. Biomonitoring data can also help scientists plan and conduct research on exposure and health effects.

Polyvinyl Chloride (PVC)

PVC is used to make pipes and plastic medical devices.

What is polyvinyl chloride (PVC)?

Polyvinyl chloride (PVC) is an odorless and solid plastic. It is most commonly white but can also be colorless or amber. It can also come in the form of white powder or pellets. PVC is made from vinyl chloride. The chemical formula for vinyl chloride is C_2H_3Cl. PVC is made up of many vinyl chloride molecules that, linked together, form a polymer $(C_2H_3Cl)n$.

PVC is made softer and more flexible by the addition of phthalates. Bisphenol A (BPA) is also used to make PVC plastics. PVC contains high levels of chlorine.

PVC is used to make pipes, pipe fittings, pipe conduits, vinyl flooring, and vinyl siding. It is used to make wire and cable coatings, packaging materials, wrapping film, gutters, downspouts, door and window frames, gaskets, electrical insulation, hoses, sealant liners, paper and textile finishes, thin sheeting, roof membranes, swimming pool liners, weatherstripping, flashing, molding, irrigation systems, containers, and automotive parts, tops, and floor mats.

When softened with phthalates, PVC is used to make some medical devices, including intravenous (IV) bags, blood bags, blood and respiratory tubing, feeding tubes, catheters, parts of dialysis devices, and heart bypass tubing. Phthalates are used in PVC plastics such as garden hoses, inflatable recreational toys, and other toys.

Consumer products made with PVC include raincoats, toys, shoe soles, shades and blinds, upholstery and seat covers, shower curtains, furniture, carpet backing, plastic bags, videodiscs, and credit cards.

Most vinyl chloride produced in the United States is used to make PVC.

How might I be exposed to PVC?

You can be exposed to PVC by eating food or drinking water contaminated with it. At home, you can be exposed to PVC if you have PVC pipes, vinyl flooring, or other consumer products made with PVC. You can be exposed if your home has vinyl siding or if you are building or renovating your home. Exposure may occur through food packaging and containers or "shrink wrapped" packages.

You can be exposed to PVC outdoors if you have a plastic swimming pool or plastic furniture. You can be exposed if you live or work on a farm that has an irrigation system containing PVC.

You can be exposed to PVC if you are a patient in a hospital and use medical devices made with PVC.

At work, you can be exposed to PVC if you work in a facility that manufactures PVC pipes and pipe fittings, tubing, and other building and construction products. You can be exposed if you work in a facility that manufactures vinyl chloride, BPA, or phthalates. You can be exposed if you are a plumber, home builder, construction worker, health care professional, farmer, or worker in an auto manufacturing facility or repair shop.

How can PVC affect my health?

Exposure to PVC often includes exposure to phthalates, which are used to soften PVC and may have adverse health effects.

Because of PVC's heavy chlorine content, dioxins are released during the manufacturing, burning, or landfilling of PVC. Exposure to dioxins can cause reproductive, developmental, and other health problems, and at least one dioxin is classified as a carcinogen.

Dioxins, phthalates, and BPA are suspected to be endocrine disruptors, which are chemicals that may interfere with the production or activity of hormones in the human endocrine system.

Exposure to PVC dust may cause asthma and affect the lungs.

If you think your health has been affected by exposure to PVC, contact your health care professional.

For poison emergencies or questions about possible poisons, contact your local poison control center at 1-800-222-1222.

Chapter 46

Contaminants in Consumer Products

Chapter Contents

Section 46.1

Overview: Importation of Food and Cosmetics

This section includes excerpts from "Overview: Importation of Food and Cosmetics," U.S. Food and Drug Administration (FDA), June 4, 2014.

FDA's Import Program

FDA is responsible for enforcing the Federal Food, Drug, and Cosmetic Act (FD&C Act) and other laws which are designed to protect consumers' health, safety, and pocketbook. These laws apply equally to domestic and imported products.

With the exception of most meat and poultry, all food and cosmetics as defined in the FD&C Act, are subject to examination by FDA when imported or offered for import into the United States. Most meat and poultry products are regulated by the U.S. Department of Agriculture.

All color additives used in foods and cosmetics in the United States must be approved by FDA; many cannot be used unless certified in FDA's own laboratories.

Food

Food imported into the United States must meet the same laws and regulations as food produced in the United States. It must be safe and contain no prohibited ingredients, and all labeling and packaging must be informative and truthful, with the labeling information in English (or Spanish in Puerto Rico).

Imported food products are subject to FDA review when the food is offered for import at U.S. ports of entry. FDA does not certify, license, or otherwise approve individual food importers, products, labels, or shipments prior to importation. Importers can import food into the United States as long as the facilities that produce, pack, store, or otherwise handle the products are registered with FDA and meet other FDA requirements, such as sanitation.

During the entry process, firms must provide to FDA information related to the specific products and the manufacturers of the products. Based on the entry information provided and other information FDA has, FDA will decide whether the product meets U.S. requirements and can be released into U.S. commerce.

In the wake of various acts of terrorism, FDA exercises heightened vigilance in assessing food defense risk and maintaining the safety of the nation's food supply. Under provisions of the Public Health Security and Bioterrorism Preparedness and Response Act of 2002, which amended the FD&C Act, FDA established regulations requiring (1) that food facilities register with FDA and (2) the submission of prior notice of imported food.

Registration

Most facilities that manufacture, process, pack, or hold food must register with FDA biennially (every two years). This includes most foreign manufacturers and importers. There are few exceptions from the registration requirements; for example, farms and restaurants do not have to register. There is no fee to register with FDA.

Prior Notice

Under the prior notice requirements, FDA must receive notice before food is imported or offered for import into the United States. The purpose of prior notice is to enable FDA to target inspections or examinations of the imported food at U.S. ports of entry more effectively, and to determine whether there is any credible information that the imported food shipment presents a threat or serious risk to public health. Food imported or offered for import into the United States without adequate prior notice may be refused admission into the United States. Under the Food Safety and Modernization Act (FSMA) of 2010, if the imported food was refused entry in another country, the prior notice must also identify the other country (or countries) where the food was refused entry.

The prior notice requirement applies to all foods, unless excluded, for humans or animals, including:

1. Dietary supplements and dietary ingredients;

2. Infant formula;

3. Beverages (including alcoholic beverages and bottled water);

4. Fruits and vegetables;

5. Fish and Seafood;

6. Dairy products and eggs;

7. Raw agricultural commodities for use as food or as components of food;

8. Animal feed (including pet food);

9. Food and feed additives; and

10. Live food animals.

Exclusions from the prior notice requirements include:

1. Food carried by or accompanying an individual arriving in the United States for his or her personal use (i.e., for consumption by themselves, family, or friends, and not for sale or other distribution);

2. Food that is imported then exported without leaving the port of arrival until export;

3. Meat food products, poultry products, and egg products that are subject to the exclusive jurisdiction of the U.S. Department of Agriculture;

4. Food made by an individual in his or her personal residence and sent by that individual as a personal gift to an individual in the United States; and

5. Food shipped as baggage or cargo constituting the diplomatic bag (e.g., from one nation's government office to its embassy in the United States).

Cosmetics

Cosmetic products imported into the United States must meet the same laws and regulations as those produced in the United States. They must be safe for their intended uses and cannot contain prohibited ingredients. All labeling and packaging must be informative and truthful, with the labeling information in English (or Spanish in Puerto Rico). Certain cosmetic products must be labeled with warning statements.

FDA encourages cosmetic firms to register their establishments and file Cosmetic Product Ingredient Statements with FDA's Voluntary Cosmetic Registration Program (VCRP). However, firms importing products considered to be cosmetics in the United States are not required to register with FDA. The VCRP can only accept Cosmetic

Product Ingredient Statements for cosmetics that are already on the market in the United States. A registration number is not required for importing cosmetics into the United States.

Section 46.2

Importing into the U.S.

This section includes excerpts from "Importing into the U.S.," U.S. Food and Drug Administration (FDA), May 14, 2015.

Overview

Foreign firms that manufacture medical devices and/or products that emit radiation that are imported into the United States must comply with applicable U.S. regulations before, during, and after importing into the U.S. or its territories. In order to import medical devices and/or products that emit radiation into the U.S., the product must meet FDA regulatory requirements. FDA does not recognize regulatory approvals from other countries. The following is a summary of FDA requirements for medical devices and products that emit radiation.

Medical Devices

Foreign manufacturers

Foreign manufacturers must meet applicable United States (U.S.) medical device regulations in order to import devices into the U.S. even if the product is authorized for marketing in another country. These requirements include registration of establishment, listing of devices, manufacturing in accordance with the quality system regulation, medical device reporting of adverse events, and Premarket Notification 510(k) or Premarket Approval, if applicable. In addition, the foreign manufacturers must designate a United States agent. As with domestic manufacturers, foreign manufacturing sites are subject to FDA inspection. Information on U.S. regulatory requirements can be found in the Device Advice section.

Initial Importers

The initial importer of the device must register its establishment with FDA. An initial importer is any importer who furthers the marketing of a device from a foreign manufacturer to the person who makes the final delivery or sale of the device to the ultimate consumer or user, but does not repackage, or otherwise change the container, wrapper, or labeling of the device or device package. Registration information can be found under Establishment Registration.

Initial importers are also subject to Medical Device Reporting (MDR) under 21 CFR 803, Reports of Corrections and Removals under 21 CFR 806, and Medical Device Tracking under 21 CFR 821, if applicable. Under the MDR regulations importers are required to report incidents in which a device may have caused or contributed to a death or serious injury as well as report certain malfunctions. The importers must maintain an MDR event file for each adverse event. All product complaints (MDR and non-MDR events) must be forwarded to the manufacturer. Under Medical Device Tracking requirements, certain devices must be tracked through the distribution chain.

Products that emit radiation

Foreign manufacturers that export electronic products (medical device or non-medical) that emit radiation to the United States are subject to the requirements of the Federal Food, Drug, and Cosmetic Act, Subchapter C – Electronic Product Radiation Control (formerly the Radiation Control for Health and Safety Act of 1968). These requirements include performance standards, labeling, and submission of radiation safety product reports. Guidance on these requirements can be found on the Internet under Electronic Product Radiation Control. When manufacturers submit radiation safety product reports, the reports are entered into a database and assigned an accession number. Importers may submit radiation safety product reports on behalf of manufacturers.

Import Process

All medical devices that are imported into the U.S. must meet Bureau of Customs and Border Protection (CBP) requirements in addition to FDA. Product that does not meet FDA regulatory requirements may be detained upon entry.

The major responsibility of CBP is to administer the Tariff Act of 1930 as amended. Primary duties include assessment and collection of all duties, taxes, and fees on imported merchandise; administration and review of import entry forms; the enforcement of CBP and related laws; and administration of certain navigation laws and treaties. There is a working agreement between FDA and CBP for the cooperative enforcement of Section 801 of the FD& C Act.

The import process begins with the importer or filer submitting the necessary entry information to the local CBP district office. For those entries not filed electronically, a paper entry consisting of the commercial invoice, CBP entry forms CF3461/3461ALT and/or CF7501 or documentation that would need to be provided by the importer or filer.

Entry information should identify the product and include appropriate information to demonstrate that the product is in compliance with FDA regulations. Product information should include device name and product code. FDA, CDRH, issued a letter which clarifies what entry information should be provided at the time of entry. The correct information will help expedite the entry review process and increase the likelihood that your shipment may be processed based on import system screening and not held for further FDA entry review. Please note that the product code provided to CBP must include a two digit prefix identifying the medical specialty in addition to the three letter code. The medical specialty codes are as follows:

Table 46.1. Medical Specialty Codes

Number	Medical Specialty	Regulation
73	Anesthesiology	Part 868
74	Cardiovascular	Part 870
75	Chemistry	Part 862
76	Dental	Part 872
77	Ear, Nose, and Throat	Part 874
78	Gastroenterology and Urology	Part 876
79	General and Plastic Surgery	Part 878
80	General Hospital	Part 880
81	Hematology	Part 864
82	Immunology	Part 866
83	Microbiololgy	Part 866
84	Neurology	Part 882
85	Obstetrics and Gynocology	Part 884
86	Ophthalmics	Part 886
87	Orthopedics	Part 888

Table 46.1. Continued

Number	Medical Specialty	Regulation
88	Pathology	Part 864
89	Physical Medicine	Part 890
90	Radiology	Part 892
91	Toxicology	Part 862

For example, the device product code provided to CBP for sunglasses would be 86HQY. Please refer to "Classify Your Medical Device" on FDA's Device Advice website for further guidance on device classification and product codes.

Importers of radiation emitting electronic products subject to a federal performance standard are required to submit a written declaration on "Declaration of Products Subject to Radiation Control Standards," form FDA-2877, along with other import entry information, including accesssion number, if appropriate, through CBP to the appropriate FDA district office. Electronic products that fail to comply with the applicable performance standard or do not have a certification label or tag (21 CFR 1010.2) affixed to each product shall be refused entry. FDA, CDRH, has issued a letter which clarifies what entry information should be provided at the time of entry for medical and non-medical radiation emitting electronic products.

Most importers ask that domestic custom house brokers (or filers) complete these forms electronically and make the submissions on their behalf. Filers have access to the Operational and Administrative Systems for Import Support (OASIS), the FDA computerized import system. The OASIS program is an electronic interface between FDA and the CBPs Automated Commercial System (ACS). OASIS is an on-line interactive and automated system, which replaced the process of reviewing the paperwork for import entries manually.

When an entry is filed with CBP, a copy of the entry is also provided to the local FDA district office. The FDA district office then determines if the product complies with FDA requirements. The FD&C Act authorizes FDA to detain a regulated product that appears to be out of compliance with the Act. If a product appears to be out of compliance, the FDA district office will issue a "Notice of FDA Action" specifying the nature of the violation to the owner or consignee. The owner or consignee is entitled to an informal hearing in order to provide testimony regarding the admissibility of the product. If the owner fails to submit evidence that the product is in compliance or fails to submit a plan to bring the product into compliance, FDA will issue another "Notice of FDA Action" refusing admission to the product. The product then has to be exported or destroyed within 90 days. Failure to do so within 90 days may result in issuance of a Customs Redelivery Notice and an assessment for liquidated damages for up to 3 times the value of the lot.

Upon entry, FDA may examine certain devices to assure their safety and effectiveness. When this occurs, FDA will issue a notice to the importer of a record on a form titled "Notice of FDA Action." Sampling may involve examining the product at the port of entry or physical collection of a statistical portion of the lot for analysis by an FDA laboratory. If the sample is violative, or if the sample is determined to be out of compliance with required specifications, the device will be detained and the importer of record will be issued a "Notice of FDA Action" indicating that the article is being detained due to the appearance of a violation under the FD&C Act. The "Notice of FDA Action" will state the specific violations to the FD&C Act.

Under certain conditions, the importer of record of a device that has been detained, is given an opportunity to submit application for authorization to bring the device into compliance with the FD&C Act. If FDA permits reconditioning, another sample may be collected and analyzed after reconditioning. If the device is then determined to be in compliance, it will be released. Only the FDA District Office at the port of entry has the authority to authorize reconditioning and/or to release the shipment. You must provide the appropriate documentation or bring the products into compliance under the authorization from the District Office. When contacting the District Office, you should ask for the Compliance Office and provide the entry number and/or sample number as a reference.

Import for Export

A firm may import device parts, components, subassemblies, etc. for further processing or incorporation into unapproved devices which are to be subsequently exported. A firm *may not* import a *finished* unapproved device without prior marketing clearance, even if the device is to be imported solely for subsequent export. The terms "further processing" and "incorporation" as detailed in the Regulatory Procedures Manual is rather broad in its interpretation. For example, a device imported for further packaging or labeling would fall into this category; a device which is simply stored without any further action prior to export would *not* fall into this category.

The provisions for import for export under section 801 of the FD&C Act have been amended by the section 322 of Bioterrorism Act of 2002. Importers wishing to import devices (including components or an accessory of a device or other article of a device requiring further processing, which is ready or suitable for use for health-related purposes) that are intended for further processing or incorporation into another product and subsequest export must provide FDA with certain information at the time of initial importation. The information includes a statement that confirms the intent to further process such article or incorporate such article into a product to be exported and identifies entities in the chain of possession of the imported article. At the time of initial importation and before delivery to the importer, initial owner, or consignee, a bond must be executed providing for liquidated damages in the event of default, in accordance with Bureau of Customs and Border Protection (formerly called U.S. Customs) requirements. The initial owner or consignee of the article must maintain records of the use and/or destruction of such imports and must submit the records or a report to FDA upon request.

Section 46.3

Melamine

This section includes excerpts from "Food—Melamine in Tableware: Questions and Answers," U.S. Food and Drug Administration (FDA), June 20, 2014.

What is melamine?

Melamine is a chemical that has many industrial uses. In the United States, it is approved for use in the manufacturing of some cooking utensils, plates, plastic products, paper, paperboard, and industrial coatings, among other things. In addition, although it is not registered as a fertilizer in the U.S., melamine has been used as a fertilizer in some parts of the world.

Melamine may be used in the manufacturing of packaging for food products, but is not FDA-approved for direct addition to human food or animal feeds marketed in the U.S.

I recently read that plastic tableware from China contained high levels of melamine. Can the melamine from these products get into foods and drinks?

The Taiwan Consumers' Foundation recently tested plastic tableware made in China and found that it contained melamine at a level of 20,000 parts per billion. This type of tableware is manufactured with a substance called melamine-formaldehyde resin. It forms molecular structures that are molded, with heat, to form the shape of the tableware. A small amount of the melamine used to make the tableware is "left over" from this chemical reaction and remains in the plastic. This left-over melamine can migrate very slowly out of the plastic into food that comes into contact with the tableware.

If melamine from plastic tableware can get into foods and drinks, does it make the foods or drinks harmful to health?

It has been found that melamine does not migrate from melamine-formaldehyde tableware into most foods. The only measured migration, in tests, was from some samples (three out of 19 commercially available plates and cups) into acidic foods, under exaggerated conditions (that is, the food was held in the tableware at 160°F for two hours). When adjusted for actual-use conditions (cold orange juice held in the tableware for about 15 minutes), the migration would be less than 10 parts of melamine per billion parts of juice.

This is 250 times lower than the level of melamine (alone or even in combination with related compounds—analogues—known to increase its toxicity) that FDA has concluded is acceptable in foods other than infant formula (2,500 parts per billion); in other words, well below the risk level. In addition, such highly acidic foods make up only about 10% of the total diet, so the dietary level of melamine in these scenarios would be less than one part per billion.

However, when highly acidic foods are heated to extreme temperatures (e.g., 160°F or higher), the amount of melamine that migrates out of the plastic can increase. Foods and drinks should not be heated on melamine-based dinnerware in microwave ovens. Only ceramic or other cookware which specifies that the cookware is microwave-safe should be used. The food may then be served on melamine-based tableware.

Should I stop using plastic tableware?

Foods and drinks may be served on plastic tableware. Plastic tableware that does not specify that it's microwave-safe should not be used to heat foods and drinks.

How did FDA decide what level of melamine in food doesn't pose a risk to health?

A safety and risk assessment estimates the risk that specific substances have on human health, based on the best scientific data available at the time. FDA has done this type of assessment to identify the risk posed by melamine and its analogues in foods (Interim Safety and Risk Assessment of Melamine and Its Analogues in Food for Humans).

The risk assessment was conducted by scientists from FDA's Center for Food Safety and Applied Nutrition and FDA's Center for Veterinary Medicine, and included a review of the scientific literature on melamine toxicity. Animal studies also provided valuable information for this work. The assessment underwent peer review by a group of experts identified by an independent contractor.

What problems can melamine cause if people eat or drink food contaminated with it?

Products with melamine contamination above the levels noted in FDA's risk assessment may put people at risk of conditions such as kidney stones and kidney failure, and of death. Signs of melamine poisoning may include irritability, blood in urine, little or no urine, signs of kidney infection, and/or high blood pressure.

Chapter 47

Fragrance Additives

Fragrances in Cosmetics

Many products we use every day contain fragrances. Some of these products are regulated as cosmetics by FDA. Some belong to other product categories and are regulated differently, depending on how the product is intended to be used. Here is information about fragrances that people often ask about:

How to Know If a Fragrance Product Is Regulated as a Cosmetic

If a product is intended to be applied to a person's body to make the person more attractive, it's a cosmetic under the law. Here are some examples of fragrance products that are regulated as cosmetics:

- Perfume

- Cologne

- Aftershave

Fragrance ingredients are also commonly used in other products, such as shampoos, shower gels, shaving creams, and body lotions. Even some products labeled "unscented" may contain fragrance ingredients. This is because the manufacturer may add just enough fragrance to

---

Text in this chapter is excerpted from "Cosmetics—Fragrances in Cosmetics," U.S. Food and Drug Administration (FDA), September 19, 2014.

mask the unpleasant smell of other ingredients, without giving the product a noticeable scent.

Some fragrance products that are applied to the body are intended for therapeutic uses, such as treating or preventing disease, or affecting the structure or function of the body. Products intended for this type of use are treated as drugs under the law, or sometimes as both cosmetics and drugs. Here are some examples of labeling statements that will cause a product containing fragrances to be treated as a drug:

- Easing muscle aches
- Soothing headaches
- Helping people sleep
- Treating colic

Many other products that may contain fragrance ingredients, but are not applied to the body, are regulated by the Consumer Product Safety Commission. Here are some examples:

- Laundry detergents
- Fabric softeners
- Dryer sheets
- Room fresheners
- Carpet fresheners

Statements on labels, marketing claims, consumer expectations, and even some ingredients may determine a product's intended use.

"Essential Oils" and "Aromatherapy"

There is no regulatory definition for "essential oils," although people commonly use the term to refer to certain oils extracted from plants. The law treats ingredients from plants the same as those from any other source.

For example, "essential oils" are commonly used in so-called "aromatherapy" products. If an "aromatherapy" product is intended to treat or prevent disease, or to affect the structure or function of the body, it's a drug.

Similarly, a massage oil intended to lubricate the skin is a cosmetic. But if claims are made that a massage oil relieves aches or relaxes muscles, apart from the action of the massage itself, it's a drug, or possibly both a cosmetic and a drug.

Safety Requirements

Fragrance ingredients in cosmetics must meet the same requirement for safety as other cosmetic ingredients. The law does not require FDA approval before they go on the market, but they must be safe for consumers when they are used according to labeled directions, or as people customarily use them. Companies and individuals who manufacture or market cosmetics have a legal responsibility for ensuring that their products are safe and properly labeled.

Labeling of Fragrance Ingredients

If a cosmetic is marketed on a retail basis to consumers, such as in stores, on the Internet, or person-to-person, it must have a list of ingredients. In most cases, each ingredient must be listed individually. But under U.S. regulations, fragrance and flavor ingredients can be listed simply as "Fragrance" or "Flavor."

Here's why: FDA requires the list of ingredients under the Fair Packaging and Labeling Act (FPLA). This law is not allowed to be used to force a company to tell "trade secrets." Fragrance and flavor formulas are complex mixtures of many different natural and synthetic chemical ingredients, and they are the kinds of cosmetic components that are most likely to be "trade secrets."

Fragrance Allergies and Sensitivities

Some individuals may be allergic or sensitive to certain ingredients in cosmetics, food, or other products, even if those ingredients are safe for most people. Some components of fragrance formulas may have a potential to cause allergic reactions or sensitivities for some people.

FDA does not have the same legal authority to require allergen labeling for cosmetics as for food. So, if you are concerned about fragrance sensitivities, you may want to choose products that are fragrance free, and check the ingredient list carefully. If consumers have questions, they may choose to contact the manufacturer directly.

Phthalates as Fragrance Ingredients

Phthalates are a group of chemicals used in hundreds of products. The phthalate commonly used in fragrance products is diethyl phthalate, or DEP. DEP does not pose known risks for human health as it is currently used in cosmetics and fragrances.

Chapter 48

Chemicals in Beauty Products

Chapter Contents

Section 48.1

1,4-Dioxane in Cosmetics

Text in this section is excerpted from "Cosmetics—1,4-Dioxane A
Manufacturing Byproduct," U.S. Food and Drug Administration
(FDA), December 17, 2014.

What is 1,4-dioxane?

The compound 1,4-dioxane is a contaminant that may be present in
extremely small amounts in some cosmetics. It forms as a byproduct
during the manufacturing process of certain cosmetic ingredients.
These ingredients include certain detergents, foaming agents, emulsi-
fiers and solvents identifiable by the prefix, word, or syllables "PEG,"
"Polyethylene," "Polyethylene glycol," "Polyoxyethylene," "-eth-,"
or "-oxynol-." However, 1,4-dioxane itself is not used as a cosmetic
ingredient.

Is 1,4-dioxane in cosmetic products harmful?

The levels at which a chemical compound would be considered
harmful in a cosmetic depend on the conditions of use (FD&C Act,
section 601(a)). The 1,4-dioxane levels we have seen in our monitoring
of cosmetics do not present a hazard to consumers.

Concerns initially were raised in the 1970s, when studies at the
National Cancer Institute found an association between 1,4-dioxane
and cancer in animals when 1,4-dioxane was administered in high
levels in the animal feed. However, the levels in cosmetic products
are far lower than those found to be harmful in feeding studies and,
for the most part, the types of products in which it is found are only
in contact with the skin for a short time.

As a precaution, FDA followed up with skin absorption studies,
which showed that 1,4-dioxane can penetrate animal and human skin
when applied in certain preparations, such as lotions. However, further research by FDA determined that 1,4-dioxane evaporates readily, further diminishing the already small amount available for skin
absorption, even in products that remain on the skin for hours.

What is FDA doing to assure that cosmetics do not contain unsafe levels of 1,4-dioxane?

FDA has been monitoring this issue since the late 1970s. We periodically monitor the levels of 1,4-dioxane in cosmetic products, and have observed that the changes made in the manufacturing process have resulted in a significant decline in the levels of this contaminant.

FDA has not established or recommended a specific limit on the level of 1,4-dioxane in cosmetics. We have provided guidance to manufacturers alerting them to the health concerns and how to minimize 1,4-dioxane by means of a process called "vacuum stripping" at the end of the polymerization process.

If FDA were to determine that a health hazard exists, it would advise the industry and the public, and would consider its legal options for protecting the health and welfare of consumers.

Section 48.2

Lead in Cosmetics

Text in this section is excerpted from "Cosmetics—Lead in Cosmetics," U.S. Food and Drug Administration (FDA), March 26, 2014.

Cause for Concern?

Questions sometimes arise about the presence of lead in cosmetics. Lead is a mineral that occurs naturally in the earth. There are traces of lead in the food we eat and the water we drink. Usually, these traces are much too small to cause lead to be detected in our bodies. But, if exposures are too high, lead can cause serious problems. How we are exposed to lead also makes a difference. That's because our bodies handle different kinds of exposures in different ways.

The following information provides some background on what the law says about the safety of cosmetics. It also describes some cosmetic products and ingredients that FDA has looked at closely with regard to lead content.

Cosmetic Safety and U.S. Law

FDA regulates cosmetics under a law passed by Congress: the Federal Food, Drug, and Cosmetic Act. This law does not require cosmetic products or ingredients to have FDA approval before they go on the market. The only exception is for the color additives used in cosmetics.

If a cosmetic contains an ingredient or contaminant that would make the product harmful to consumers when they use it according to the labeling or in the customary or expected way, that product is considered "adulterated" under the law. Misuse of color additives also makes a cosmetic adulterated. It's against the law to market an adulterated cosmetic.

FDA can take action when we find out about a cosmetic with a safety problem. But first, we need to have reliable scientific information proving that the product is adulterated under the law.

Color Additives

The law treats color additives differently from other cosmetic ingredients. Except for coloring materials used in coal-tar hair dyes, color additives need FDA approval for their intended use before they may be used in cosmetics, food, drugs, or many medical devices.

Each color additive that FDA approves is listed in a regulation, called a "listing regulation." That regulation tells what the color additive is made of, how it is permitted to be used, and any limits on contaminants. Typically, these regulations set limits on lead at no more than 20 parts per million. When setting these limits, FDA considers factors such as how a color additive will be used and the likely exposure levels for consumers.

If a cosmetic contains a color additive that does not meet the requirements in its listing regulation, the cosmetic is adulterated under the law.

Kohl, Kahal, Al-Kahal, or Surma

This traditional eyeliner, popular in many parts of the world, is a serious health concern because it commonly contains large amounts of lead, as well as other heavy metals. These products have been linked with lead poisoning, especially among children. These products sometimes make their way into specialty markets in this country.

Lipstick

Over the years, there have been rumors and reports alleging dangerous levels of lead in lipstick. Some have questioned why FDA has not set the same limits on lead in lipstick as for lead in candy. But licking small amounts of lipstick off our lips is much different from eating candy, which people—especially children—tend to eat in much larger amounts. And even if children play with makeup, it's very unlikely that they will eat as much lipstick as they do sweet treats.

FDA analyzed hundreds of lipsticks on the market and found that levels of lead were too low to pose a health risk, especially considering the tiny amounts of lipstick that a consumer might ingest.

Progressive Hair Dyes

Under the law, coal-tar hair dyes don't need FDA approval, unlike color additives in general. But hair dyes from plant or mineral sources do. Lead acetate is a color additive that is approved for use in coloring hair. It is used in products that darken the hair gradually over time, with repeated applications. Unlike the limits on lead other color additives, lead is allowed at much higher levels in progressive hair dyes. But because of the dangers of lead exposure if these products are misused, lead acetate hair colorings must have a special warning on the label:

"Caution: Contains lead acetate. For external use only. Keep this product out of children's reach. Do not use on cut or abraded scalp. If skin irritation develops, discontinue use. Do not use to color mustaches, eyelashes, eyebrows, or hair on parts of the body other than the scalp. Do not get in eyes. Follow instructions carefully and wash hands thoroughly after use."

Section 48.3

Microbiological Safety and Cosmetics

Text in this section is excerpted from "Cosmetics—Microbiological
Safety and Cosmetics," U.S. Food and Drug Administration (FDA),
May 8, 2015.

Cosmetics can become harmful to consumers if they're contaminated with harmful microorganisms, such as certain bacteria and fungi. FDA is looking closely at the microbiological safety of cosmetics.

What the Law Says About Cosmetic Safety

Under the law, cosmetic products and ingredients, except for color additives, do not need FDA approval before they go on the market. However, they must not be "adulterated" or "misbranded."

This means they must be safe for consumers when used according to directions on the label, or in the customary or expected way, and they must be properly labeled. It also means they must not be prepared, packed, or stored in a way in which they may have become contaminated or harmful to health.

Companies and individuals who manufacture or distribute cosmetics are legally responsible for the safety of their products. This includes, for example, making sure cosmetics are free of harmful microorganisms.

While the law does not require cosmetics to have FDA approval before they go on the market, we do monitor the safety of cosmetics, including their microbiological safety, and FDA can take action against cosmetics on the market that don't comply with the law.

How Microorganisms Get into Cosmetics

Remember, cosmetic firms are legally responsible for making sure their products are safe. Some of the ways cosmetics may become contaminated with bacteria or fungi are—

- Contaminated raw materials, water or other ingredients

- Poor manufacturing conditions

- Ingredients that encourage growth of microorganisms, without an effective preservative system

- Packaging that doesn't protect a product adequately

- Poor shipping or storage conditions

- Consumer use, such as the need to dip fingers into the product

Questions FDA Is Asking, and Why

At FDA, we must base our actions on reliable information. We want to make sure our knowledge and our actions reflect the current state of science, industry practice, and products on the market.

Even if injuries from contaminated cosmetics are not common, they can be serious. For example, contaminated tattoo inks, eye-area cosmetics, and lotions and mouthwashes used in hospitals all have caused serious infections.

Here are some of the questions FDA microbiologists are exploring:

- What's the best way to test cosmetics for microbiological safety?

- What types of preservative systems are cosmetic companies using, and how effective are they?

- What kinds of microorganisms pose health risks in cosmetics?

- How are people exposed to microorganisms in cosmetics?

- What consumers are at greatest risk from certain types of contaminated cosmetics?

How Consumers Can Help Protect Against Microbial Contamination

Don't share cosmetics, with anyone. You may be sharing germs.

- Don't add water or saliva to cosmetics, such as mascara. You may be adding bacteria or other microorganisms. You'll also be watering down a preservative that's intended to keep bacteria from growing.

- Store cosmetics carefully. If cosmetics get too warm, some microorganisms may grow faster and preservatives may break down.

- Keep containers clean.

- Wash your hands before applying cosmetics, especially if you need to dip your fingers into the container.

- Pay attention to recalls and safety alerts. Microbial contamination is a common reason for recalls of cosmetics.

How to Report a Problem

If you've experienced a problem with a cosmetic, from a minor rash or headache to an illness that put you in the hospital, please tell FDA. You can even report something that didn't cause a reaction, but alerted you to a problem with the product, such as a bad smell or other sign of contamination.

You can report a problem with a cosmetic to FDA in either of these ways:

- Contact MedWatch, FDA's problem-reporting program, at 1-800-332-1088, or file a MedWatch voluntary report online,

- Contact the consumer complaint coordinator in your area.

Section 48.4

Parabens

Text in this section is excerpted from "Cosmetics—Parabens," U.S. Food and Drug Administration (FDA), December 15, 2014.

What are parabens?

Parabens are among the most commonly used preservatives in cosmetic products. Chemically, parabens are esters of p-hydroxybenzoic acid. The most common parabens used in cosmetic products are methylparaben, propylparaben, and butylparaben. Typically, more than one paraben is used in a product, and they are often used in combination with other types of preservatives to provide preservation against a broad range of microorganisms. The use of mixtures of parabens allows the use of lower levels while increasing preservative activity.

Why are preservatives used in cosmetics?

Preservatives may be used in cosmetics to protect them against microbial growth, both to protect consumers and to maintain product integrity.

What kinds of products contain parabens?

They are used in a wide variety of cosmetics, as well as foods and drugs. Cosmetics that may contain parabens include makeup, moisturizers, hair care products, and shaving products, among others. Most major brands of deodorants and antiperspirants do not currently contain parabens.

Cosmetics sold on a retail basis to consumers are required by law to declare ingredients on the label. This is important information for consumers who want to determine whether a product contains an ingredient they wish to avoid. Parabens are usually easy to identify by name, such as methylparaben, propylparaben, butylparaben, or benzylparaben.

Does FDA regulate the use of preservatives in cosmetics?

The Federal Food, Drug, and Cosmetic Act (FD&C Act) does not authorize FDA to approve cosmetic ingredients, with the exception of color additives that are not coal-tar hair dyes. In general, cosmetic manufacturers may use any ingredient they choose, except for a few ingredients that are prohibited by regulation. However, it is against the law to market a cosmetic in interstate commerce if it is adulterated. Under the FD&C Act, a cosmetic is adulterated if, among other reasons, it bears or contains any poisonous or deleterious substance which may render it injurious under the labeled conditions of use, or under customary or usual conditions of use.

Are there health risks associated with the use of parabens in cosmetics?

The Cosmetic Ingredient Review (CIR), reviewed the safety of methylparaben, propylparaben, and butylparaben in 1984 and concluded they were safe for use in cosmetic products at levels up to 25%. Typically parabens are used at levels ranging from 0.01 to 0.3%.

On November 14, 2003, the CIR began the process to reopen the safety assessments of methylparaben, ethylparaben, propylparaben, and butylparaben in order to offer interested parties an opportunity to submit new data for consideration. In September 2005, the CIR decided to re-open the safety assessment for parabens to request exposure estimates and a risk assessment for cosmetic uses. In December 2005, after considering the margins of safety for exposure to women and infants, the Panel determined that there was no need to change its original conclusion that parabens are safe as used in cosmetics. (The CIR is an industry-sponsored organization that reviews cosmetic ingredient safety and publishes its results in open, peer-reviewed literature. FDA participates in the CIR in a non-voting capacity.)

A study published in 2004 (Darbre, in the *Journal of Applied Toxicology*) detected parabens in breast tumors. The study also discussed this information in the context of the weak estrogen-like properties of parabens and the influence of estrogen on breast cancer. However, the study left several questions unanswered. For example, the study did not show that parabens cause cancer, or that they are harmful in any way, and the study did not look at possible paraben levels in normal tissue.

FDA is aware that estrogenic activity in the body is associated with certain forms of breast cancer. Although parabens can act similarly to estrogen, they have been shown to have much less estrogenic activity than the body's naturally occurring estrogen. For example, a 1998 study found that the most potent paraben tested in the study, butylparaben, showed from 10,000- to 100,000-fold less activity than naturally occurring estradiol (a form of estrogen). Further, parabens are used at very low levels in cosmetics. In a review of the estrogenic activity of parabens, the author concluded that based on maximum daily exposure estimates, it was implausible that parabens could increase the risk associated with exposure to estrogenic chemicals.

FDA believes that at the present time there is no reason for consumers to be concerned about the use of cosmetics containing parabens. However, the agency will continue to evaluate new data in this area. If FDA determines that a health hazard exists, the agency will advise the industry and the public, and will consider its legal options under the authority of the FD&C Act in protecting the health and welfare of consumers.

Section 48.5

Phthalates in Cosmetics

Text in this section is excerpted from "Cosmetics—Phthalates," U.S.
Food and Drug Administration (FDA), September 19, 2014.

What are phthalates?

Phthalates are a group of chemicals used in hundreds of products, such as toys, vinyl flooring and wall covering, detergents, lubricating oils, food packaging, pharmaceuticals, blood bags and tubing, and personal care products, such as nail polish, hair sprays, aftershave lotions, soaps, shampoos, perfumes, and other fragrance preparations.

How phthalates have been used in cosmetics

Historically, the primary phthalates used in cosmetic products have been dibutylphthalate (DBP), used as a plasticizer in products such as nail polishes (to reduce cracking by making them less brittle); dimethylphthalate (DMP), used in hair sprays (to help avoid stiffness by allowing them to form a flexible film on the hair); and diethylphthalate (DEP), used as a solvent and fixative in fragrances. According to FDA's latest survey of cosmetics, conducted in 2010, however, DBP and DMP are now used rarely. DEP is the only phthalate still commonly used in cosmetics.

Phthalates and human health

It's not clear what effect, if any, phthalates have on human health. An expert panel convened from 1998 to 2000 by the National Toxicology Program (NTP), part of the National Institute for Environmental Safety and Health, concluded that reproductive risks from exposure to phthalates were minimal to negligible in most cases.

The Centers for Disease Control and Prevention (CDC) released a report on March 21, 2001, titled "National Report on Human Exposure to Environmental Chemicals." The report described a survey of a small segment of the U.S. population for environmental chemicals

681

in urine. One group of chemicals surveyed was phthalates. However, the CDC survey was not intended to make an association between the presence of environmental chemicals in human urine and disease, but rather to learn more about the extent of human exposure to industrial chemicals.

In 2002, the Cosmetic Ingredient Review (CIR) Expert Panel reaffirmed its original conclusion (reached in 1985), finding that DBP, DMP, and DEP were safe as used in cosmetic products. Looking at maximum known concentrations of these ingredients in cosmetics, the panel evaluated phthalate exposure and toxicity data, and conducted a safety assessment for dibutylphthalate in cosmetic products. The panel found that exposures to phthalates from cosmetics were low compared to levels that would cause adverse effects in animals. (The CIR is an industry-sponsored organization that reviews cosmetic ingredient safety and publishes its results in open, peer-reviewed literature. FDA participates in CIR on a non-voting basis and may or may not accept CIR findings.)

FDA reviewed the safety and toxicity data for phthalates, including the CDC data from 2001, as well as the CIR conclusions based on reviews in 1985 and 2002. While the CDC report noted elevated levels of phthalates excreted by women of child-bearing age, neither this report nor the other data reviewed by FDA established an association between the use of phthalates in cosmetic products and a health risk. Based on this information, FDA determined that there wasn't a sound, scientific basis to support taking regulatory action against cosmetics containing phthalates.

How FDA has followed up

FDA continues to monitor levels of phthalates in cosmetic products. We have developed an analytical method for determining the levels of phthalates in cosmetic products and conducted surveys of products to determine these levels in cosmetics on the market.

What we know about infant exposure to phthalates

Infants, like all consumers, are exposed daily to phthalates from a number of sources, including air, drugs, food, plastics, water, and cosmetics.

The American Academy of Pediatrics (AAP) has published an article stating that infants exposed to infant care products, specifically baby shampoos, baby lotions, and baby powder, showed increased levels of phthalate metabolites in their urine.

Like the CDC report, this study did not establish an association between these findings and any health effects. In addition, levels of phthalates, if any, in the infant care products were not determined.

FDA included 24 children's products intended for infants and children in the survey we completed in 2006, and nearly 50 products for infants and children in the survey we completed in 2010. What we learned was that the use of phthalates in cosmetics intended for people of all ages, including infants and children, has decreased considerably since our surveys began in 2004.

How to know if there are phthalates in the cosmetics you use

Under the authority of the Fair Packaging and Labeling Act (FPLA), FDA requires an ingredient declaration on cosmetic products sold at the retail level to consumers. Consumers can tell whether some products contain phthalates by reading the ingredient declaration on the labels of such products.

However, the regulations do not require the listing of the individual fragrance ingredients; therefore, the consumer will not be able to determine from the ingredient declaration if phthalates are present in a fragrance. Also, because the FPLA does not apply to products used exclusively by professionals—for example, in salons—the requirement for an ingredient declaration does not apply to these products. Based on available safety information, DEP does not pose known risks for human health as it is currently used in cosmetics and fragrances. Consumers who nevertheless do not want to purchase cosmetics containing DEP may wish to choose products that do not include "Fragrance" in the ingredient listing.

FDA's role

Under the law, cosmetic products and ingredients, with the exception of color additives, are not subject to FDA approval before they go on the market. FDA can take action against unsafe cosmetics that are on the market, but only if we have dependable scientific evidence showing that a product or ingredient is unsafe for consumers under labeled or customary conditions of use.

At the present time, FDA does not have evidence that phthalates as used in cosmetics pose a safety risk. If we determine that a health hazard exists, we will advise the industry and the public, and will take action within the scope of our authority under the Federal Food, Drug, and Cosmetic Act in protecting the health and welfare of consumers.

Section 48.6

Talc

Text in this section is excerpted from "Cosmetics—Talc," U.S. Food and Drug Administration (FDA), March 19, 2014.

Talc is an ingredient used in many cosmetics, from baby powder to blush.

FDA's authority over cosmetic safety

Under the Federal Food, Drug and Cosmetic Act (FD&C Act), cosmetic products and ingredients, with the exception of color additives, do not have to undergo FDA review or approval before they go on the market. Cosmetics must be properly labeled, and they must be safe for use by consumers under labeled or customary conditions of use. Cosmetic companies have a legal responsibility for the safety and labeling of their products and ingredients, but the law does not require them to share their safety information with FDA.

FDA monitors for potential safety problems with cosmetic products on the market and takes action when needed to protect public health. Before we can take such action against a cosmetic, we need sound scientific data to show that it is harmful under its intended use.

Talc: What it is and how it is used in cosmetics

Talc is a naturally occurring mineral, mined from the earth, composed of magnesium, silicon, oxygen, and hydrogen. Chemically, talc is a hydrous magnesium silicate with a chemical formula of $Mg_3Si_4O_{10}(OH)_2$.

Talc has many uses in cosmetics and other personal care products; in food, such as rice and chewing gum; and in the manufacture of tablets. For example, it may be used to absorb moisture, to prevent caking, to make facial makeup opaque, or to improve the feel of a product.

Asbestos: What it is, why it's a concern, and how to prevent its occurrence in cosmetics

Asbestos is also a naturally occurring silicate mineral, but with a different crystal structure. Both talc and asbestos are naturally occurring minerals that may be found in close proximity in the earth. Unlike talc, however, asbestos is a known carcinogen. For this reason, FDA considers it unacceptable for cosmetic talc to be contaminated with asbestos.

Published scientific literature going back to the 1960s has suggested a possible association between the use of powders containing talc and the incidence of ovarian cancer. However, these studies have not conclusively demonstrated such a link, or if such a link existed, what risk factors might be involved. Nevertheless, questions about the potential contamination of talc with asbestos have been raised since the 1970s.

To prevent contamination of talc with asbestos, it is essential to select talc mining sites carefully and take steps to purify the ore sufficiently.

How FDA followed up on the latest reports

Because safety questions about the possible presence of asbestos in talc are raised periodically, FDA decided to conduct an exploratory survey of currently marketed cosmetic-grade raw material talc, as well as some cosmetic products containing talc.

Because FDA's cosmetic laboratories do not have the equipment needed to perform the analyses, we searched for a qualified outside laboratory to do the work. We contracted with AMA Analytical Services, Inc. (AMA) of Lanham, MD to conduct this laboratory survey, based on demonstrated experience with asbestos analysis in complex matrices, appropriate facilities, equipment, personnel, analytical strategy, and budget criteria. The study ran from September 28, 2009 to September 27, 2010.

How the survey was conducted

The first step was to identify cosmetic talc suppliers and talc-containing cosmetic products. We found seven talc suppliers identified in the 2008 edition of the *International Cosmetic Ingredient Dictionary and Handbook* and two more by searching online. The contract laboratory contacted each supplier to request samples of its talc. Of the nine suppliers identified, four complied with the request.

We found talc-containing cosmetic products to analyze by visiting various retail outlets in the Washington, D.C. metropolitan area. The samples identified for testing included low, medium, and high priced products, along with some from "niche" markets, in order to cover as broad a product range as possible. A total of thirty-four cosmetic products containing talc were selected, including eye shadow, blush, foundation, face powder, and body powder. All cosmetic products were purchased from retail stores in the Washington, D.C. metropolitan area.

The contract laboratory analyzed the samples using polarized light microscopy (PLM) and transmission electron microscopy (TEM) methods published by the New York State Department of Health, Environmental Laboratory Approval Program. Each sample was analyzed three times using both methods.

The results of FDA's survey and what they mean

The survey found no asbestos fibers or structures in any of the samples of cosmetic-grade raw material talc or cosmetic products containing talc. The results were limited, however, by the fact that only four talc suppliers submitted samples and by the number of products tested. For these reasons, while FDA finds these results informative, they do not prove that most or all talc or talc-containing cosmetic products currently marketed in the United States are likely to be free of asbestos contamination. As always, when potential public health concerns are raised, we will continue to monitor for new information and take appropriate actions to protect the public health.

Chapter 49

X-Rays

Medical X-Ray Imaging

Description

Medical imaging has led to improvements in the diagnosis and treatment of numerous medical conditions in children and adults.

There are many types—or modalities—of medical imaging procedures, each of which uses different technologies and techniques. Computed tomography (CT), fluoroscopy, and radiography ("conventional X-ray" including mammography) all use ionizing radiation to generate images of the body. Ionizing radiation is a form of radiation that has enough energy to potentially cause damage to DNA and may elevate a person's lifetime risk of developing cancer.

CT, radiography, and fluoroscopy all work on the same basic principle: an X-ray beam is passed through the body where a portion of the X-rays are either absorbed or scattered by the internal structures, and the remaining X-ray pattern is transmitted to a detector (e.g., film or a computer screen) for recording or further processing by a computer. These exams differ in their purpose:

- Radiography – a single image is recorded for later evaluation. Mammography is a special type of radiography to image the internal structures of breasts.

This chapter includes excerpts from "Radiation-Emitting Products—Medical X-ray Imaging," U.S. Food and Drug Administration (FDA), May 19, 2015.

- Fluoroscopy – a continuous X-ray image is displayed on a monitor, allowing for real-time monitoring of a procedure or passage of a contrast agent ("dye") through the body. Fluoroscopy can result in relatively high radiation doses, especially for complex interventional procedures (such as placing stents or other devices inside the body) which require fluoroscopy be administered for a long period of time.

- CT – many X-ray images are recorded as the detector moves around the patient's body. A computer reconstructs all the individual images into cross-sectional images or "slices" of internal organs and tissues. A CT exam involves a higher radiation dose than conventional radiography because the CT image is reconstructed from many individual X-ray projections.

Benefits/Risks

The discovery of X-rays and the invention of CT represented major advances in medicine. X-ray imaging exams are recognized as a valuable medical tool for a wide variety of examinations and procedures. They are used to:

- noninvasively and painlessly help to diagnosis disease and monitor therapy;

- support medical and surgical treatment planning; and

- guide medical personnel as they insert catheters, stents, or other devices inside the body, treat tumors, or remove blood clots or other blockages.

As in many aspects of medicine, there are risks associated with the use of X-ray imaging, which uses ionizing radiation to generate images of the body. Ionizing radiation is a form of radiation that has enough energy to potentially cause damage to DNA. Risks from exposure to ionizing radiation include:

- a small increase in the possibility that a person exposed to X-rays will develop cancer later in life. (General information for patients and health care providers on cancer detection and treatment is available from the National Cancer Institute.)

- tissue effects such as cataracts, skin reddening, and hair loss, which occur at relatively high levels of radiation exposure and are rare for many types of imaging exams. For example, the typical use of a CT scanner or conventional radiography equipment should not result in tissue effects, but the dose to the skin from some long, complex interventional fluoroscopy procedures might, in some circumstances, be high enough to result in such effects.

Another risk of X-ray imaging is possible reactions associated with an intravenously injected contrast agent, or "dye," that is sometimes used to improve visualization.

The risk of developing cancer from medical imaging radiation exposure is generally very small, and it depends on:

- radiation dose – The lifetime risk of cancer increases the larger the dose and the more X-ray exams a patient undergoes.

- patient's age – The lifetime risk of cancer is larger for a patient who receives X-rays at a younger age than for one who receives them at an older age.

- patient's sex – Women are at a somewhat higher lifetime risk than men for developing radiation-associated cancer after receiving the same exposures at the same ages.

- body region – Some organs are more radiosensitive than others.

Radiography

Description

Medical radiography is a broad term that covers several types of studies that require the visualization of the internal parts of the body using x-ray techniques. Radiography means a technique for generating and recording an x-ray pattern for the purpose of providing the user with a static image(s) after termination of the exposure. It is differentiated from *fluoroscopy, mammography*, and *computed tomography*. Radiography may also be used during the planning of radiation therapy treatment.

It is used to diagnose or treat patients by recording images of the internal structure of the body to assess the presence or absence of disease, foreign objects, and structural damage or anomaly.

During a radiographic procedure, an X-ray beam is passed through the body. A portion of the X-rays are absorbed or scattered by the internal structure and the remaining X-ray pattern is transmitted to a detector so that an image may be recorded for later evaluation. The recoding of the pattern may occur on film or through electronic means.

Uses

Radiography is used in many types of examinations and procedures where a record of a static image is desired. Some examples include:

- Dental examination
- Verification of correct placement of surgical markers prior to invasive procedures
- Mammography
- Orthopedic evaluations
- Spot film or static recording during fluoroscopy
- Chiropractic examinations

Risks / Benefits

Radiography is a type of x-ray procedure, and it carries the same types of risks as other x-ray procedures. The radiation dose the patient receives varies depending on the individual procedure, but is generally less than that received during fluoroscopy and computed tomography procedures.

The major risks associated with radiography are the small possibilities of:

- developing a radiation-induced cancer or cataracts some time later in life, and
- causing a disturbance in the growth or development of an embryo or fetus (teratogenic defect) when performed on a pregnant patient or one of childbearing age.

When an individual has a medical need, the benefit of radiography far exceeds the small cancer risk associated with the procedure. Even when radiography is medically necessary, it should use the lowest possible exposure and the minimum number of images. In most cases many of the possible risks can be reduced or eliminated with proper shielding.

Computed Tomography (CT)

Description

Computed tomography (CT), sometimes called "computerized tomography" or "computed axial tomography" (CAT), is a noninvasive medical examination or procedure that uses specialized X-ray equipment to produce cross-sectional images of the body. Each cross-sectional image represents a "slice" of the person being imaged, like the slices in a loaf of bread. These cross-sectional images are used for a variety of diagnostic and therapeutic purposes.

CT scans can be performed on every region of the body for a variety of reasons (e.g., diagnostic, treatment planning, interventional, or screening). Most CT scans are performed as outpatient procedures.

How a CT system works:

- A motorized table moves the patient through a circular opening in the CT imaging system.

- While the patient is inside the opening, an X-ray source and a detector assembly within the system rotate around the patient. A single rotation typically takes a second or less. During rotation the X-ray source produces a narrow, fan-shaped beam of X-rays that passes through a section of the patient's body.

- Detectors in rows opposite the X-ray source register the X-rays that pass through the patient's body as a snapshot in the process of creating an image. Many different "snapshots" (at many angles through the patient) are collected during one complete rotation.

- For each rotation of the X-ray source and detector assembly, the image data are sent to a computer to reconstruct all of the individual "snapshots" into one or multiple cross-sectional images (slices) of the internal organs and tissues.

CT images of internal organs, bones, soft tissue, and blood vessels provide greater clarity and more details than conventional X-ray images, such as a chest X-ray.

Uses

CT is a valuable medical tool that can help a physician:

- Diagnose disease, trauma or abnormality
- Plan and guide interventional or therapeutic procedures
- Monitor the effectiveness of therapy (e.g., cancer treatment)

Benefits / Risks

When used appropriately, the benefits of a CT scan far exceed the risks. CT scans can provide detailed information to diagnose, plan treatment for, and evaluate many conditions in adults and children. Additionally, the detailed images provided by CT scans may eliminate the need for exploratory surgery.

Concerns about CT scans include the risks from exposure to ionizing radiation and possible reactions to the intravenous contrast agent, or dye, which may be used to improve visualization. The exposure to ionizing radiation may cause a small increase in a person's lifetime risk of developing cancer. Exposure to ionizing radiation is of particular concern in pediatric patients because the cancer risk per unit dose of ionizing radiation is higher for younger patients than adults, and younger patients have a longer lifetime for the effects of radiation exposure to manifest as cancer.

However, in children and adults, the risk from a medically necessary imaging exam is quite small when compared to the benefit of accurate diagnosis or intervention. It is especially important to make sure that CT scans in children are performed with appropriate exposure factors, as use of exposure settings designed for adults can result in a larger radiation dose than necessary to produce a useful image for a pediatric patient.

Dental Cone-beam Computed Tomography

Description

Cone-beam computed tomography systems (CBCT) are a variation of traditional computed tomography (CT) systems. The CBCT systems used by dental professionals rotate around the patient, capturing data using a cone-shaped X-ray beam. These data are used to reconstruct a three-dimensional (3D) image of the following regions of the patient's anatomy: dental (teeth); oral and maxillofacial region (mouth, jaw, and neck); and ears, nose, and throat ("ENT").

Uses

Dental CBCT systems have been sold in the United States since the early 2000s and are increasingly used by radiologists and dental professionals for various clinical applications including dental implant planning, visualization of abnormal teeth, evaluation of the jaws and face, cleft palate assessment, diagnosis of dental caries (cavities), endodontic (root canal) diagnosis, and diagnosis of dental trauma.

Benefits / Risks

X-ray imaging, including dental CBCT, provides a fast, non-invasive way of answering a number of clinical questions. Dental CBCT images provide three-dimensional (3-D) information, rather than the two-dimensional (2-D) information provided by a conventional X-ray image. This may help with the diagnosis, treatment planning and evaluation of certain conditions.

Although the radiation doses from dental CBCT exams are generally lower than other CT exams, dental CBCT exams typically deliver more radiation than conventional dental X-ray exams. Concerns about radiation exposure are greater for younger patients because they are more sensitive to radiation (i.e., estimates of their lifetime risk for cancer incidence and mortality per unit dose of ionizing radiation are higher) and they have a longer lifetime for ill effects to develop.

Fluoroscopy

Description

Fluoroscopy is a type of medical imaging that shows a continuous X-ray image on a monitor, much like an X-ray movie. During a fluoroscopy procedure, an X-ray beam is passed through the body. The image is transmitted to a monitor so the movement of a body part or of an instrument or contrast agent ("X-ray dye") through the body can be seen in detail.

Benefits / Risks

Fluoroscopy is used in a wide variety of examinations and procedures to diagnose or treat patients. Some examples are:

- Barium X-rays and enemas (to view the gastrointestinal tract)
- Catheter insertion and manipulation (to direct the movement of a catheter through blood vessels, bile ducts or the urinary system)
- Placement of devices within the body, such as stents (to open narrowed or blocked blood vessels)
- Angiograms (to visualize blood vessels and organs)
- Orthopedic surgery (to guide joint replacements and treatment of fractures)

Fluoroscopy carries some risks, as do other X-ray procedures. The radiation dose the patient receives varies depending on the individual procedure. Fluoroscopy can result in relatively high radiation doses, especially for complex interventional procedures (such as placing stents or other devices inside the body) which require fluoroscopy be administered for a long period of time. Radiation-related risks associated with fluoroscopy include:

- radiation-induced injuries to the skin and underlying tissues ("burns"), which occur shortly after the exposure, and

- radiation-induced cancers, which may occur some time later in life.

The probability that a person will experience these effects from a fluoroscopic procedure is statistically very small. Therefore, if the procedure is medically needed, the radiation risks are outweighed by the benefit to the patient. In fact, the radiation risk is usually far less than other risks not associated with radiation, such as anesthesia or sedation, or risks from the treatment itself. To minimize the radiation risk, fluoroscopy should always be performed with the lowest acceptable exposure for the shortest time necessary.

Mammography

Description

Mammography is a type of medical imaging that uses x-rays to capture images (mammograms) of the internal structures of the breasts. Quality mammography can help detect breast cancer in its earliest, most treatable stages; when it is too small to be felt or detected by any other method.

Procedures

The two types of imaging currently used for mammography are

- **Screen**-film mammography where x-rays are beamed through the breast to a cassette containing a screen and film that must be developed. The image is commonly referred to as a mammogram.

- **Full** field digital mammography where x-rays are beamed through the breast to an image receptor. A scanner converts the information to a digital picture which is sent to a digital monitor and/or a printer.

Risks / Benefits

Mammography uses x-rays to produce an image of the breast, and the patient is exposed to a small dose of radiation. The Mammography

Quality Standards Act (MQSA) established baseline standards for radiation dose, personnel, equipment, and image quality.

The benefits of mammography in detecting breast cancer at an early stage outweigh the risks of radiation exposure. In some cases, early detection of a breast lump may mean that chemotherapy is unnecessary.

Part Seven

Additional Help and Information

Chapter 50

Directory of Organizations with Information About Environmental Health

Resources in this chapter were compiled from several sources deemed reliable. Inclusion does not imply endorsement. This list is not comprehensive; it is intended as a starting point for gathering of information.

Agency for Toxic Substances and Disease Registry (ATSDR)
Centers for Disease Control and Prevention
4770 Buford Hwy N.E.
Atlanta, GA 30341
800-232-4636; Fax: 888-232-6348
cdcinfo@cdc.gov
www.atsdr.cdc.gov

Asthma and Allergy Foundation of America
8201 Corporate Dr.
Ste. 1000
Landover, MD 20785
800-727-8462
info@aafa.org
www.aafa.org

Beyond Pesticides
701 E. St. S.E., Ste. 200
Washington, DC 20003
202-543-5450; Fax: 202-543-4791
info@beyondpesticides.org
www.beyondpesticides.org

Birth Defect Research for Children, Inc.
976 Lake Baldwin Ln., Ste. 104
Orlando, FL 32814
407-895-0802
staff@birthdefects.org
www.birthdefects.org

Campaign for Tobacco-Free Kids
1400 Eye St. N.W., Ste. 1200
Washington, DC 20005
202-296-5469; Fax: 202-296-5427
www.tobaccofreekids.org

Center for Environmental Health
2201 Broadway Ste. 302
Oakland, CA 94612
510-655-3900; Fax: 510-655-9100
www.ceh.org

Center for Food Safety and Applied Nutrition
5100 Paint Branch Pkwy
College Park, MD 20740
888-723-3366
www.fda.gov/Food

Center for Health, Environment, and Justice
P.O. Box 6806
Falls Church, VA 22040
703-237-2249
chej@chej.org
www.chej.org

Center for Science in the Public Interest
1220 L St. N.W.
Ste. 300
Washington, DC 20005
202-332-9110; Fax: 202-265-4954
cspi@cspinet.org
www.cspinet.org

Chemical Injury Information Network (CIIN)
P.O. Box 301
White Sulphur Springs
MT 59645
406-547-2255
chemicalinjury@ciin.org
www.ciin.org

Children's Environmental Health Network
110 Maryland Ave. N.E., Ste. 404
Washington, DC 20002
202-543-4033; Fax: 202-543-8797
cehn@cehn.org
www.cehn.org

Clean Air Task Force
18 Tremont St., Ste. 530
Boston, MA 02108
617-624-0234; Fax: 617-624-0230
info@catf.us
www.catf.us

Clean Water Fund
1444 Eye St., N.W., Ste. 400
Washington, DC 20005
202-895-0432
cwf@cleanwater.org
www.cleanwaterfund.org

The Collaborative on Health and the Environment
c/o Commonwealth
P.O. Box 316
Bolinas, CA 94924
info@healthandenvironment.org
www.healthandenvironment.org

Environment & Human Health, Inc.
1191 Ridge Rd.
North Haven, CT 06473
203-248-6582; Fax: 203-288-7571
info@ehhi.org
www.ehhi.org

Environmental Defense Fund (EDF)
257 Park Ave. S.
New York, NY 10010
212-505-2100; Fax: 212-505-2375
www.environmentaldefense.org

Environmental Health Strategy Center
565 Congress St.
Portland, ME 04101
info@preventharm.org
www.preventharm.org

Environmental Protection Agency (EPA)
1200 Pennsylvania Ave., N.W.
Washington, DC 20460
202-272-0165;
www.epa.gov

EPA National Service Center for Environmental Publications (NSCEP)
P.O. Box 42419
Cincinnati, OH 45242-0419
800-490-9198; Fax: 301-604-3408
nscep@lmsolas.com
www.epa.gov/ncepihom

Environmental Working Group (EWG)
1436 U St., N.W., Ste. 100
Washington, DC 20009
202-667-6982
www.ewg.org

Federal Emergency Management Agency (FEMA)
500 C St., S.W.
Washington, DC 20472
202-646-2500
www.fema.gov

Food and Drug Administration (FDA)
10903 New Hampshire Ave.
Silver Spring, MD 20993
888-463-6332
www.fda.gov

Food and Water Watch
1616 P St., N.W., Ste. 300
Washington, DC 20036
202-683-2500; Fax: 202-683-2501
www.foodandwaterwatch.org

Food Safety and Inspection Service
U.S. Department of Agriculture
1400 Independence Ave. S.W.
Washington, DC 20250-3700
800-877-8339
www.fsis.usda.gov

Food Safety Research Information Office (FSRIO)
USDA ARS National
Agricultural Library
10301 Baltimore Ave., Rm. 108-B
Beltsville, MD 20705-2351
301-504-5515; Fax: 301-504-7680
www.fsrio.nal.usda.gov

Friends of the Earth
1100 15th St. N.W.
11th Fl.
Washington, DC 20005
877-843-8687; Fax: 202-783-0444
www.foe.org

Greenpeace, USA
702 H St. N.W., Ste. 300
Washington, DC 20001
800-722-6995; Fax: 202-462-4507
info@wdc.greenpeace.org
www.greenpeaceusa.org

Healthy Building Network
1710 Connecticut Ave.
Washington, DC 20009
877-974-2767; Fax: 202-898-1612
info@healthybuilding.net
www.healthybuilding.net

Healthy Child Healthy World
8383 Wilshire Blvd. Ste. 800
Beverly Hills, CA 90211
424-343-0020
info@healthychild.org
www.healthychild.org

Inform, Inc.
P.O. Box 320403
Brooklyn, NY 11232
Phone: 212-361-2400
informinc.org

KidsHealth
Nemours Foundation
www.kidshealth.org

March of Dimes
1275 Mamaroneck Ave.
White Plains, NY 10605
914-997-4488 (National Office)
www.marchofdimes.com

National Cancer Institute (NCI)
NCI Public Inquiries Office
6116 Executive Blvd.
Rm. 3036A
Bethesda, MD 20892-8322
800-422-6237
www.cancer.gov

National Center for Environmental Health (NCEH)
4770 Buford Hwy N.E.
Atlanta, GA 30341-3717
800-232-4636; Fax: 888-232-6348
www.cdc.gov/nceh

National Council for Science and the Environment
1101 17th St. N.W., Ste. 250
Washington, DC 20036
202-530-5810; Fax: 202-628-4311
NCSE@NCSEonline.org
ncseonline.org

National Environmental Health Association (NEHA)
720 S. Colorado Blvd.
Ste. 1000-N
Denver, CO 80246-1926
866-956-2258; Fax: 303-691-9490
staff@neha.org
www.neha.org

National Institute for Occupational Safety and Health (NIOSH)
800-232-4636; Fax: 888-232-6348
Fax: 513-533-8347
www.cdc.gov/niosh

National Institute of Allergy and Infectious Diseases (NIAID)
Office of Communications and Government Relations
5601 Fishers Ln., MSC 9806
Bethesda, MD 20892-9806
866-284-4107; Fax: 301-402-3573
www.niaid.nih.gov

National Institute of Environmental Health Sciences (NIEHS)
Office of Communications and Public Liaison
P.O. Box 12233, MD K3-16
Research Triangle Park
North Carolina 27709-2233
919-541-3345; Fax: 301-480-2978
webcenter@niehs.nih.gov
www.niehs.nih.gov

National Institute on Aging (NIA)
Bldg. 31, Rm. 5C27
31 Center Dr., MSC 2292
Bethesda, MD 20892
800-222-4225; Fax: 301-496-1072
niaic@nia.nih.gov
www.nia.nih.gov

National Institutes of Health (NIH)
9000 Rockville Pike
Bethesda, MD 20892
301-496-4000; Fax: 301-402-9612
NIHinfo@od.nih.gov
www.nih.gov

National Library of Medicine
Reference and Web Services
8600 Rockville Pike
Bethesda, MD 20894
888-346-3656; Fax: 301-402-1384
custserv@nlm.nih.gov
www.nlm.nih.gov

National Resources Defense Council (NRDC)
40 West 20th St.
New York, NY 10011
212-727-2700; Fax: 212-727-1773
nrdcinfo@nrdc.org
www.nrdc.org

National Safety Council
1121 Spring Lake Dr.
Itasca, IL 60143-3201
800-621-7615; Fax: 630-285-1315
info@nsc.org
www.nsc.org

Office on Women's Health Department of Health and Human Services
200 Independence Ave., S.W., Rm. 712E
Washington, DC 20201
800-994-9662; Fax: 202-205-2631
www.womenshealth.gov/

Occupational Safety and Health Administration (OSHA)
200 Constitution Ave. N.W.
Washington, DC 20210
800-321-6742; Fax: 877-889-5627
www.osha.gov

Office of Children's Health Protection
1200 Pennsylvania Ave., N.W.
Mail Code 1107-T
Washington, DC 20460
202-564-2188; Fax: 202-564-2733
www2.epa.gov/children

Office of Disease Prevention and Health Promotion
1101 Wootton Pwy, LL-100
Rockville, MD 20852
Fax: 240-453-8282
healthypeople@hhs.gov
www.healthypeople.gov/

Office of Environmental Health Hazard Assessment (OEHHA)
California Environmental Protection Agency
916-323-2514
cepacomm@calepa.ca.gov
oehha.ca.gov

Organic Consumers Association
6771 South Silver Hill Dr.
Finland, MN 55603
218-226-4164; Fax: 218-353-7652
www.organicconsumers.org

Pesticide Action Network North America (PANNA)
1611 Telegraph Ave.
Ste. 1200
Oakland, CA 94612
510-788-9020
www.panna.org

Physicians for Social Responsibility
1111 14th St., N.W.
Ste. 700
Washington, DC 20005
202-667-4260; Fax: 202-667-4201
psrnatl@psr.org
www.envirohealthaction.org

Right-to-Know Network
2040 S. St., N.W., Second Fl.
Washington, DC 20009
202-234-8494; Fax: 202-234-8584
www.rtknet.org

**Science and Environmental
Health Network**
P.O Box 50733
Eugene, OR 97405
moreinfo@sehn.org
www.sehn.org

**Union of Concerned
Scientists**
National Headquarters
Two Brattle Square
Cambridge, MA 02238-3780
617-547-5552; Fax: 617-864-9405
www.ucsusa.org

United States Access Board
1331 F St. N.W., Ste. 1000
Washington, DC 20004-1111
800-872-2253; Fax: 202-272-0081
info@access-board.gov
www.access-board.gov

**U.S. Consumer Product
Safety Commission**
4330 East West Hwy
Bethesda, MD 20814
800-638-2772; Fax: 301-504-
0124 and
301-504-0025
www.cpsc.gov

**U.S. Department of
Agriculture Meat & Poultry**
Hotline
888-674-6854; Fax: 800-256-7072
MPHotline.fsis@usda.gov
www.fsis.usda.gov

**U.S. Department of Housing
and Urban Development
(HUD)**
451 7th St. S.W.
Washington, DC 20410
202-708-1112; Fax: 202-708-1455
www.hud.gov

**Washington State
Department of Health
Division of Environmental
Health**
800-525-0127
www.doh.wa.gov/ehp

Washington Toxics Coalition
4649 Sunnyside Ave. N.
Ste. 540
Seattle, WA 98103
206-632-1545
info@watoxics.org
www.watoxics.org

World Resources Institute
10 G St. N.E., Ste. 800
Washington, DC 20002
202-729-7600; Fax: 202-729-7610
www.wri.org

Chapter 51

Glossary of Terms Related to Environmental Health

absorption: The taking in of water and dissolved minerals and nutrients across cell membranes. Contrast with ingestion.

acid deposition: Acidic materials that falls from the atmoshpere to the Earth in either wet (rain, sleet, snow, fog) or dry (gases, particles) forms. More commonly referred to as acid rain, acid deposition has two components: wet and dry deposition.

acid rain: The result of sulfur dioxide ($SO2$) and nitrogen oxides (NOx) reacting in the atmosphere with water and returning to earth as rain, fog, or snow. Broadly used to include both wet and dry deposition. The acid rain page provides a great deal of information about this issue.

acute exposure: A one time exposure of relatively short duration usually less than two weeks.

adaptive capacity: The ability of a system to adjust to climate change (including climate variability and extremes) to moderate potential damages, to take advantage of opportunities, or to cope with the consequences.

adsorption: The retention of atoms, ions, or molecules onto the surface of another substance.

aerobic: Able to live, grow, or take place only when free oxygen is present.

Aerosol: A small droplet or particle suspended in the atmosphere, typically containing sulfur. Aerosols are emitted naturally (e.g., in volcanic eruptions) and as the result of human activities (e.g., by burning fossil fuels).

aflatoxins: A group of closely related toxic metabolites that are designated mycotoxins. They are produced by Aspergillus flavus and A. parasiticus. Members of the group include AFLATOXIN B1, aflatoxin B2, aflatoxin G1, aflatoxin G2, AFLATOXIN M1, and aflatoxin M2.

algal blooms: Sudden spurts of algal growth, which can affect water quality adversely and indicate potentially hazardous changes in local water chemistry.

air quality index (AQI): A numerical index used for reporting severity of air pollution levels to the public. The AQI incorporates five criteria pollutants -- ozone, particulate matter, carbon monoxide, sulfur dioxide and nitrogen dioxide -- into a single index.

allergen: A material that, as a result of coming into contact with appropriate tissues of an animal body, induces a state of allergy or hypersensitivity; generally associated with idiosyncratic hypersensitivities.

ambient air: The portion of the atmosphere external to buildings and breathed by the general public.

anaerobic: Able to live, grow, or take place where free oxygen is not present.

anaphylaxis: An immediate and severe allergic reaction to a substance (e.g. food or drugs). Symptoms include breathing difficulties, loss of consciousness, and a drop in blood pressure.

animal dander: Tiny scales of animal skin.

antimicrobial: Agent that kills microbial growth. See "disinfectant," and "sanitizer."

antitoxin: Antibodies capable of destroying toxins generated by microorganisms including viruses and bacteria.

antiviral: Literally "against-virus" -- any medicine capable of destroying or weakening a virus.

background level: Level representing the chemical, physical, and biological conditions that would result from natural geomorphological processes such as weathering or dissolution.

backwash: Flow of water through filter element(s) or media in a reverse direction to dislodge accumulated dirt, debris, and/or filter aid, and remove them from the filter tank.

benchmark Dose (BMD): A dose that produces a predetermined change in response rate of an adverse effect (called the benchmark response or BMR) compared to background.

bioaccumulation: The process in which a substance is taken up by an aquatic organism through any route, including respiration, ingestion, or direct contact with water or sediment.

bioassay: A method used to determine the toxicity of specific chemical contaminants.

biocide: A substance capable of destroying (killing) living organisms.

biodegradation: Breakdown of a chemical into smaller less complex molecules by microorganisms in environmental media (e.g., soil, water, sediment).

biological contaminants: Debris from or pieces of dead organisms.

biological pesticides: Certain microorganism, including bacteria, fungi, viruses, and protozoa, that are effective in controlling pests.

biomagnification: The increased accumulation and concentration of a contaminant at higher levels of the food chain.

body burden: The concentration of a substance which has accumulated in the body.

cancer cluster: The occurrence of a larger-than-expected number of cases of cancer within a group of people in a geographic area over a period of time.

carcinogen: Any substance that causes cancer.

carcinogenicity: The complex process whereby normal body cells are transformed to cancer cells.

chronic exposure: An exposure to a chemical or hazardous substance that occurs over a period of time usually more than 3 months.

cloning: Asexual reproduction of animals using somatic cell nuclear transfer (SCNT).

congenital: Existing at, and usually before, birth; referring to conditions that are present at birth, regardless of their causation.

conjugate vaccine: The joining together of two compounds (usually a protein and polysaccharide) to increase a vaccine's effectiveness.

coronavirus: One of a group of viruses that have a halo or crown-like (corona) appearance when viewed under a microscope.

DDT: A group of colorless chemicals, no longer made today, that was used to kill insects

detection limit: The minimum concentration of an analyte in a sample, that with a high level of confidence is not zero.

differentiation: The process whereby relatively unspecialized cells, e.g. embryonic or regenerative cells, acquire specialized structural and/ or functional features that characterize the cells, tissues, or organs of the mature organism.

disinfectant byproducts: Chemicals that may form when disinfectants (such as chlorine), react with plant matter and other naturally occurring materials in the water.

disinfectants: One of three groups of antimicrobials registered by EPA for public health uses. EPA considers an antimicrobial to be a disinfectant when it destroys or irreversibly inactivates infectious or other undesirable organisms.

dose: The amount of a substance to which a person is exposed (air, soil, dust, or water) over some time period.

dose-response assessment: The relation between dose levels and associated effects.

dry deposition: The falling of small particles and gases to the Earth without rain or snow. Dry deposition is a component of acid deposition, more commonly referred to as acid rain.

effluent: Something that flows out, especially a liquid or gaseous waste stream.

electromagnetic radiation: A traveling wave motion that results from changing electric and magnetic fields.

emulsifier: Substance added to products, such as meat spreads, to prevent separation of product components to ensure consistency.

environmental agents: Conditions other than indoor air contaminants that cause stress, comfort, and/or health problems (e.g., humidity extremes, drafts, noise, and over-crowding).

epidemiology: The study of the distribution and determinants of health-related states or events in specified populations; and the application of this study to the control of health problems.

eutrophication: A reduction in the amount of oxygen dissolved in water.

exacerbation: Any worsening of asthma. Onset can be acute and sudden, or gradual over several days.

exposure assessment: The analysis or estimation of the intensity, frequency, and duration of human exposures to an agent.

exposure pathway: A route by which a radionuclide or other toxic material can enter the body.

fecal coliforms: Coliforms that grow and ferment lactose to produce gas at 112.1°F (44.5°C) within 24 hours.

feedlot: A confined area for the controlled feeding of animals.

fibrosis: The formation of scar tissue in an organ, generally by replacement of functional organ cells by non-functional fibrous tissue.

finished water: Water that has been treated and is ready to be delivered to customers. See Source Water.

flashing: Material for allowing proper drainage around the joints and angles of the roof and penetrations through the roof and walls.

fluorinated chemical: A general, non-specific, term used synonymously with fluorochemical.

fossil fuels: Oil, natural gas, and coal. Fossil fuels were made in nature from ancient plants and animals, and today we burn them to make energy.

free chlorine: The chlorine in water not combined with other constituents; therefore, it is able to serve as an effective disinfectant.

fungicide: A substance or chemical that kills fungi.

gamma radiation: Short-wavelength electromagnetic radiation of nuclear origin, with energies between 10 keV to 9 MeV.

gene expression: The process by which a cell transcribes the information stored in its genome to carry out the functions of life.

genetic engineering: A process of inserting new genetic information into existing cells in order to modify a specific organism for the purpose of changing one of its characteristics.

genetically engineered animals: A subset of animals associated with molecular biology techniques. Includes transgenic animals, animals subjected to gene therapy and mosaic animals.

genome: The full set of genes in an individual, either haploid (the set derived from one parent) or diploid (the set derived from both parents).

germ cell: A reproductive cell such as a spermatocyte or an oöcyte, or a cell that will develop into a reproductive cell.

global warming potential: A measure of the total energy that a gas absorbs over a particular period of time (usually 100 years), compared to carbon dioxide.

greenhouse gases: Gases that occur naturally in the Earth's atmosphere and trap heat to keep the planet warm.

half-life: The time any substance takes to decay by half of its original amount. See also biological half-life, decay constant, effective half-life, radioactive half-life.

hematology: The branch of medicine that deals with the blood and blood-forming tissues.

heterotrophic: Designating or typical of organisms that derive carbon for the manufacture of cell mass from organic matter.

hib: Haemophilus influenzae type b. A bacterial infection that may result in severe respiratory infections, including pneumonia, and other diseases such as meningitis.

high-efficiency particulate air (HEPA) filter: Type of air filter that removes >99.97% of particles 0.3 um or larger at a specified flow rate of air.

histone: Chromatin protein commonly associated with the DNA of somatic cells in eukaryotes and it is involved in packaging of the DNA and the regulation of gene activity.

homologue: One of a series of compounds, each of which has a structure differing regularly by some increment (number of carbons, presence of a CH2 group) from adjacent members of the group.

house dust mite: Either of two widely distributed mites of the genus Dermatophagoides (D. farinae and D. pteronyssinus) that commonly occur in house dust and often induce allergic responses, especially in children.

humectant: Substance added to foods to help retain moisture and soft texture. An example is glycerine, which may be used in dried meat snacks.

humidifier fever: A respiratory illness caused by exposure to toxins from microorganisms found in wet or moist areas in humidifiers and air conditioners.

HVAC: Heating, ventilation, and air-conditioning system.

hypersensitivity pneumonitis: A group of respiratory diseases that cause inflammation of the lung (specifically granulomatous cells).

hypoxia: A condition where there isn't enough oxygen in the water.

immune globulin: A protein found in the blood that fights infection. Also known as gamma globulin.

imprinted genes: Those genes whose degree of expression is determined by their derivation from either the dam or the sire.

in vitro: Outside the organism, or in an artificial environment. This term applies, for example, to cells, tissues or organs cultured in glass or plastic containers.

in vivo: Literally means "in life;" a biologic or biochemical process occurring within a living organism.

incubation period: Time interval between infection (i.e., introduction of the infectious agent into the susceptible host) and the onset of the first symptom of illness known to be caused by the infectious agent.

infiltration: The downward movement of water through a soil in response to gravity and capillary suction.

ionization: The process whereby a neutral atom or molecule becomes negatively or positively charged by acquiring or losing an electron.

irradiation: Exposure to radiation.

landfills: 1) Sanitary landfills are disposal sites for nonhazardous solid wastes, 2) Secure chemical landfills are disposal sites for hazardous waste.

LD50: Lethal Dose 50%. The estimated dose at which 50% of the population is expected to die.

leachate: Water that collects contaminants as it trickles through wastes, pesticides, or fertilizers.

leaching: Process by which water removes chemicals from soil through chemical reactions and the downward movement of water.

lesions: An abnormal change in the structure of an organ, due to injury or disease.

lifetime exposure: Total amount of exposure to a substance that a human would receive in a lifetime (usually assumed to be 70 years).

lowest observed adverse effect level (LOAEL): The lowest dose in a study in which there was an observed toxic or adverse effect.

magnetron: The physical component of a microwave system that generates the microwaves.

maximum ventilation: The volume of air breathed in one minute during repetitive maximal respiratory effort. Synonymous with maximum ventilatory minute volume.

microwaves: Electromagnetic waves at frequencies 915, 2450, 5800, and 24225 MHz.

minute ventilation: Volume of air breathed in one minute. It is a product of tidal volume (VT) and breathing frequency (fB).

monosodium glutamate (MSG): Describes a climate pattern with a wind system that changes direction with the seasons; this pattern is dominant over the Arabian Sea and Southeast Asia.

mucus: The clear, viscid secretion of mucous membranes, consisting of mucin, epithelial cells, leukocytes, and various inorganic salts suspended in water.

municipal solid waste (MSW): Residential solid waste and some non-hazardous commercial, institutional, and industrial wastes. This material is generally sent to municipal landfills for disposal. See landfill.

microbial volatile organic compounds (mVOCs): A chemical made by mold that is a gas at room temperature and may have a moldy or musty odor.

neurotoxin: A toxic agent or substance that inhibits, damages or destroys the tissues of the nervous system, especially neurons, the conducting cells of your body's central nervous system.

non-ionizing radiation: Radiation that has lower energy levels and longer wavelengths than ionizing radiation. Examples include radio waves, microwaves, visible light, and infrared from a heat lamp.

non-transient non-community systems: A public water system which supplies water to 25 or more of the same people at least six months per year in places other than their residences.

oxidation: A change in a chemical characterized by the loss of electrons.

ozone: Ozone, the triatomic form of oxygen (O3), is a gaseous atmospheric constituent. In the troposphere, it is created by photochemical reactions. In high concentrations, tropospheric ozone can be harmful to a wide range of living organisms.

papain: An enzyme that can dissolve or degrade the proteins collagen and elastin to soften meat and poultry tissue. It is derived from the tropical papaya tree and is used as a meat tenderizer.

partially fluorinated chemical: A partially fluorinated chemical or fluorinated chemical is a chemical containing the element fluorine. Some of these fluorinated chemicals are potential precursors to PFOA, PFOS, PFAC, and/or PFAS.

particulates: 1) Fine liquid or solid particles such as dust, smoke, mist, fumes, or smog found in air or emissions. 2) Very small solids suspended in water; they can vary in size, shape, density, and electrical charge and can be gathered together by coagulation and flocculation.

PC (polycarbonate): A type of filter used for asbestos air sampling.

PCR (polymerase chain reaction): Laboratory method for detecting the genetic material of an infectious disease agent in specimens.

perfluoro/perfluorinated: Describes specifically a substance where all hydrogen atoms attached to carbon atoms are replaced with fluorine atoms where C-H becomes C-F.

perfluorocarbons (pfcs): A group of chemicals composed of carbon and fluorine only. These chemicals (predominantly CF4 and C2F6) were introduced as alternatives to the ozone depleting substances.

petroleum distillate: Petroleum distillates, also called hydrocarbons or petrochemicals, refer to a broad range of compounds that are extracted by distillation during the refining of crude oil.

PFCs: Perfluorinated chemicals have all carbon-hydrogen bonds in a chain replaced by carbon-fluorine bonds. Examples include perfluorooctanoic acid (PFOA) and perfluorooctane sulfonate (PFOS).

PFOA: Perfluorooctanoic acid is a fully fluorinated, eight-carbon chain carboxylic acid (C8) (CAS RN 335-67-1) sometimes used to refer to the anionic salt form.

PFOS: Perfluorooctane sulfonic acid is a fully fluorinated, eight chain sulfonic acid (CAS RN 1763-23-1) sometimes used to refer to the anionic salt form.

PFOS-related: Chemicals which may be salts of PFOS or chemicals that can degrade to PFOS. These related chemicals include, but are not limited to carboxylates, amines, ethers, iodides, alcohols, siloxanes, thioethers, urethanes, and acrylates.

pharmacology: The science that deals with the origin, nature, chemistry, effects and uses of drugs.

phenotype: The totality of the observable functional and structural characteristics of an organism as determined by its genotype and its interaction with its environment.

PM2.5: Tiny particles with an aerodynamic diameter less than or equal to 2.5 microns. This fraction of particulate matter penetrates most deeply into the lungs.

point source: Pollutant loads discharged at a specific location from pipes, outfalls, and conveyance channels from either municipal wastewater treatment plants or industrial waste treatment facilities.

polycyclic aromatic hydrocarbons (pahs): A group of organic chemicals that includes several petroleum products and their derivatives.

precursor: A chemical that can be transformed to produce another chemical. For example, some residual monomer chemicals from the telomer manufacturing process, such as telomer alcohols and telomer iodides.

radioactive contamination: The deposition of unwanted radioactive material on the surfaces of structures, areas, objects, or people. It can be airborne, external, or internal.

radionuclides: Distinct radioactive particles coming from both natural sources and human activities. Can be very long lasting as soil or water pollutants.

rancid/rancidity: Oxidation/breakdown of fat that occurs naturally causing undesirable smell and taste. BHA/BHT and tocopherols are used to keep fats from becoming rancid.

reflectivity: The ability of a surface material to reflect sunlight including the visible, infrared, and ultraviolet wavelengths.

relative humidity: Partial pressure of water vapor at the atmospheric temperature divided by the vapor pressure of water at that temperature, expressed as a percentage.

residual: Amount of a pollutant remaining in the environment after a natural or technological process has taken place; e.g., the sludge remaining after initial wastewater treatment.

resilience: A capability to anticipate, prepare for, respond to, and recover from significant multi-hazard threats with minimum damage to social well-being, the economy, and the environment.

respirator: A personal protective device that is worn over the nose and mouth to reduce the risk of inhaling hazardous airborne particles, gases, or vapors.

route of exposure: The way people come into contact with a hazardous substance. Three routes of exposure are breathing [inhalation], eating or drinking [ingestion], or contact with the skin [dermal contact].

sequester: To undergo sequestration.

shielding: The material between a radiation source and a potentially exposed person that reduces exposure.

sick building syndrome, or sbs: Term that refers to a set of symptoms that affect some number of building occupants during the time they spend in the building and diminish or go away during periods when they leave the building.

siltation: The process by which a river, lake, or other water body becomes clogged with sediment.

sink: Any process, activity or mechanism which removes a greenhouse gas, an aerosol or a precursor of a greenhouse gas or aerosol from the atmosphere.

soil gas: The gas present in soil which may contain radon.

spirometry: A medical test that measures how well the lungs exhale.

storm runoff: Storm water runoff, snowmelt runoff, and surface runoff and drainage; rainfall that does not evaporate or infiltrate the ground because of impervious land surfaces or a soil infiltration rate lower than rainfall intensity, but instead flows onto adjacent land or waterbodies or is routed into a drain or sewer system.

stressor: Any physical, chemical, or biological entity that can induce an adverse response.

substrate: Refers to bottom sediment material in a natural water system.

surface runoff: Precipitation, snowmelt, or irrigation water in excess of what can infiltrate the soil surface and be stored in small surface depressions; a major transporter of nonpoint source pollutants.

surfactant: A detergent compound that promotes lathering.

suspended solids or load: Organic and inorganic particles (sediment) suspended in and carried by a fluid (water).

tailings: Waste rock from mining operations that contains concentrations of mineral ore that are too low to make typical extraction methods economical.

telomer (or fluorotelomer): A fluorinated compound produced by a specific polymer-making process called telomerization. Most telomers are relatively small polymers, and are used in surface treatment products.

TEM (transmission electron microscopy): A microscope technology and an analytical method to identify and count the number of asbestos fibers present in a sample. Capable of achieving a magnification of 20,000x.

teratogen: A compound that causes malformations in a developing fetus.

teratogenic: Of, relating to, or causing developmental malformations.

texturizers/stabilizers/thickeners: Used in foods to help maintain uniform texture or consistency. These are substances that are commonly called binders. Examples are gelatin and carrageenan.

thimerosal: Thimerosal is a mercury-containing preservative used in some vaccines and other products since the 1930's.

toxicodynamics: The study of the cellular and molecular mechanisms of the action of a poison.

toxicity: The degree to which a substance or mixture of substances can harm humans or animals.

tremolite: A mineral in the amphibole group, that occurs as a series in which magnesium and iron can freely substitute for each other. Tremolite is the mineral when magnesium is predominant.

ultraviolet radiation (UV): The energy range just beyond the violet end of the visible spectrum. Too much ultraviolet radiation can burn the skin, cause skin cancer and cataracts, and damage vegetation.

uncertainty factors: Factors used in the adjustment of toxicity data to account for unknown variations. An uncertainty factor would adjust measured toxicity upward and downward to cover the sensitivity range of potentially more or less sensitive species.

UVA: A band of ultraviolet radiation with wavelengths from 320-400 nanometers produced by the sun: UVA is not absorbed by ozone. This band of radiation has wavelengths just shorter than visible violet light.

UVB: A band of ultraviolet radiation with wavelengths from 280-320 nanometers produced by the sun: UVB is a kind of ultraviolet light from the sun (and sun lamps) that has several harmful effects.

UVC: A band of ultraviolet radiation with wavelengths shorter than 280 nanometers: UVC is extremely dangerous, but it is completely absorbed by ozone and normal oxygen (O2).

vermiculite: A chemically inert, lightweight, fire resistant, and odorless magnesium silicate material that is generally used in construction and horticultural applications.

visibility impairment: Any humanly perceptible change in visibility (light extinction, visual range, deciview, contrast, coloration) from a previous cleaner condition.

volatile organic compound (VOC): Any organic compound that participates in atmospheric photochemical reactions except those designated by EPA as having negligible photochemical reactivity.

wet deposition: The process by which chemicals are removed from the atmosphere and deposited on the Earth's surface via rain, sleet, snow, cloudwater, and fog.

wipe sample: A wipe sample consists of using a wipe and a wetting agent that is wiped over a specified area using a template. The wipe picks up settled dust in the template area and provides an estimate of the number of fibers per area.

wood smoke: Smoke is made up of a complex mixture of gases and fine, microscopic particles produced when wood and other organic matter burn.

x-ray: Electromagnetic radiation caused by deflection of electrons from their original paths, or inner orbital electrons that change their orbital levels around the atomic nucleus.

Index

Index

X

x-ray
  defined 719
  overview 687–95

Y

"You Can Help Cut Acrylamide in
  Your Diet" (FDA) 591n
Yusho 176